for *Accounting Principles,* Fourth Canadian Edition

Check with your instructor to find out if you have access to *WileyPLUS!*

Study More Effectively with a Multimedia Text

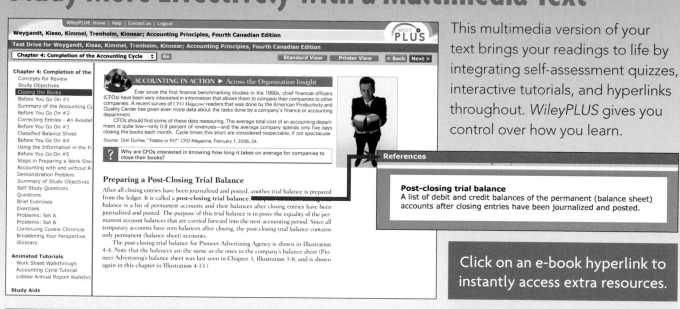

This multimedia version of your text brings your readings to life by integrating self-assessment quizzes, interactive tutorials, and hyperlinks throughout. *WileyPLUS* gives you control over how you learn.

Click on an e-book hyperlink to instantly access extra resources.

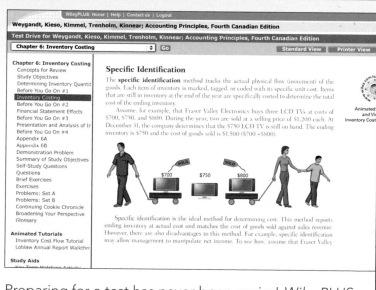

Grasp key concepts by exploring the various interactive tools in Read, Study & Practice.

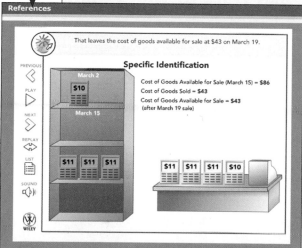

Preparing for a test has never been easier! *WileyPLUS* brings all of your course materials together and takes the stress out of organizing your study aids. A streamlined study routine saves you time and lets you focus on learning.

John Wiley & Sons Canada, Ltd.

WILEY PLUS

for *Accounting Principles,* Fourth Canadian Edition

Complete and Submit Assignments On-line Efficiently

Your homework questions contain links to the relevant section of the multimedia text, so you know exactly where to go to get help solving each problem. In addition, use the Assignment area of *WileyPLUS* to monitor all of your assignments and their due dates.

> Your instructor can assign homework online for automatic grading and you can keep up-to-date on your assignments with your assignment list.

Keep Track of Your Progress

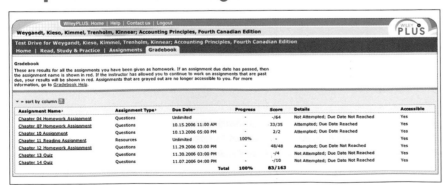

Your personal Gradebook lets you review your answers and results from past assignments as well as any feedback your instructor may have for you.

> Keep track of your progress and review your completed questions at any time.

Technical Support: http://higheredwiley.custhelp.com
Student Resource Centre: http://www.wileyplus.com

For further information regarding *WileyPLUS* and other Wiley products, please visit www.wiley.ca.

ACCOUNTING PRINCIPLES

ACCOUNTING

PRINCIPLES

FOURTH CANADIAN EDITION

▶ **Jerry J. Weygandt**   *Ph.D., C.P.A.*

Arthur Andersen Alumni Professor of Accounting
University of Wisconsin – Madison

▶ **Donald E. Kieso**   *Ph.D., C.P.A.*

KPMG Peat Marwick Emeritus Professor of Accounting
Northern Illinois University

▶ **Paul D. Kimmel**   *Ph.D., C.P.A.*

University of Wisconsin – Milwaukee

▶ **Barbara Trenholm**   *M.B.A., F.C.A.*

University of New Brunswick – Fredericton

▶ **Valerie A. Kinnear**   *M.Sc. (Bus. Admin.), C.A.*

Mount Royal College

John Wiley & Sons Canada, Ltd.

To our students — past, present, and future

Library and Archives Canada Cataloguing in Publication

Accounting principles / Jerry J. Weygandt ... [et al.].

4th Canadian ed.

Includes index.

ISBN 978-0-470-83858-7 (pt. 1)
ISBN 978-0-470-83860-0 (pt. 2)
ISBN 978-0-470-83861-7 (pt. 3)

1. Accounting--Textbooks. I. Weygandt, Jerry J.

HF5635.A3778 2006   657'.044   C2006-906471-7

Production Credits

Editorial Manager: Karen Staudinger
Publishing Services Director: Karen Bryan
Media Editor: Elsa Passera Berardi
Editorial Assistant: Sheri Coombs
Director of Marketing: Isabelle Moreau
Design & Typesetting: OrangeSprocket Communications
Cover Design: Interrobang Graphic Design
Wiley Bicentennial Logo: Richard J. Pacifico
Printing & Binding: Quebecor World Inc.

Printed and bound in the United States
1 2 3 4 5 QW 11 10 09 08 07

John Wiley & Sons Canada, Ltd.
6045 Freemont Blvd.
Mississauga, Ontario L5R 4J3
Visit our website at: www.wiley.ca

Fourth Canadian Edition

Barbara Trenholm, MBA, FCA, is a professor of accounting at the University of New Brunswick. Her teaching and educational leadership is well-known. She is a recipient of the Leaders in Management Education Award, the Global Teaching Excellence Award, and the University of New Brunswick's Merit Award and Dr. Allan P. Stuart Award for Excellence in Teaching. Several editions of the *Maclean's Guide to Canadian Universities and Colleges* have cited her as one of the University of New Brunswick's most popular professors. In 2003, she was named a Teaching Fellow of the University of New Brunswick.

Her experience and involvement in professional accounting education is widely recognized throughout Canada. She is a past-president of the New Brunswick Institute of Chartered Accountants and past-chair of the Canadian Institute of Chartered Accountants Academic Research Committee and Interprovincial Education Committee. She has served as a member of the Canadian Institute of Chartered Accountants Qualification Committee, International Qualifications Appraisal Board, Education Reeingineering Task Force, and the American Accounting Association's Globalization Initiatives Task Force. She has chaired and been a member of numerous other education committees at both the national and provincial levels of the profession.

Professor Trenholm is a member of the boards of several organizations, including Atomic Energy of Canada and Plazacorp Retail Properties. She chairs the audit committee of both of these organizations. She is a member of the Institute of Corporate Directors and has had training in best practices for corporate governance. She is a past member of the Canadian Institute of Chartered Accountants Board of Directors and the Atlantic School of Chartered Accountancy Board of Governors.

In addition to her involvement with her profession, she has an extensive record of service in leadership roles in the university and community. She has served as acting dean of the Faculty of Administration and as a member of the University Senate, in addition to chairing and serving on many university and faculty committees.

She has published widely in the field of accounting standard-setting and explored various director and auditor liability issues in journals including *Accounting Horizons*, *International Journal of Production Economics*, *CAmagazine*, *CGA Magazine*, and *CMA Magazine*. She is also the Canadian author of the Kimmel, Weygandt, Kieso, Trenholm, *Financial Accounting: Tools for Business Decision-Making*, published by John Wiley & Sons Canada, Ltd.

Valerie A. Kinnear, MSc (Bus. Admin.), CA is an accounting faculty member in the Bissett School of Business, Mount Royal College, in Calgary, Alberta. Valerie has a wide range of teaching experience, including introductory, intermediate, and advanced financial accounting as well as introductory management accounting and finance courses. She has been nominated for the Distinguished Faculty Award at Mount Royal College for her teaching expertise. Valerie has served on numerous faculty and college committees and held a variety of administrative positions at Mount Royal College, including acting dean of the School of Business, acting director of Business Education and Training in the Faculty of Continuing Education and Extension, and Program Chair of the Accounting, Financial Services, Supply Chain Management, and General Business and Insurance programs, amongst others.

She has also been active in the accounting profession. She participated in the Institute of Chartered Accountants of Alberta student education program in a variety of roles, including as an instructor, marker, author, and member of the Alberta Institute's Examinations Committee. Valerie has also served as a member of the Professional Services Policy Board of the Canadian Institute of Chartered Accountants, as a board member of the Canadian Accounting Academic Association, and as treasurer for many volunteer community organizations in Calgary.

Valerie has a Bachelor of Social Work from the University of Calgary, a Master of Science in Business Administration from the University of British Columbia, and has professional accounting experience with Price Waterhouse & Co., Farvolden and Company Chartered Accountants, and Kinnear & Smistad Chartered Accountants.

U.S. Edition

Jerry J. Weygandt, PhD, CPA, is the Arthur Andersen Alumni Professor of Accounting at the University of Wisconsin—Madison. He holds a PhD in accounting from the University of Illinois. His articles have appeared in *Accounting Review, Journal of Accounting Research, Accounting Horizons, Journal of Accountancy*, and other academic and professional journals. Professor Weygandt is the author of other accounting and financial reporting books and is a member of the American Accounting Association, the American Institute of Certified Public Accountants, and the Wisconsin Society of Certified Public Accountants. He is the recipient of the Wisconsin Institute of CPA's Outstanding Educator's Award and the Lifetime Achievement Award. In 2001 he received the American Accounting Association's Outstanding Accounting Educator Award.

Donald E. Kieso, PhD, CPA, received his bachelor's degree from Aurora University and his doctorate in accounting from the University of Illinois. He has served as chairman of the Department of Accountancy and is currently the KPMG Emeritus Professor of Accounting at Northern Illinois University. He has public accounting experience with Price Waterhouse & Co. (San Francisco and Chicago) and Arthur Andersen & Co. (Chicago) and research experience with the Research Division of the American Institute of Certified Public Accountants (New York). He has done post-doctoral work as a Visiting Scholar at the University of California at Berkeley and is a recipient of NIU's Teaching Excellence Award and four Golden Apple Teaching Awards. Professor Kieso is the author of other accounting and business books and is a member of the American Accounting Association, the American Institute of Certified Public Accountants, and the Illinois CPA Society. He is the recipient of the Outstanding Accounting Educator Award from the Illinois CPA Society, the FSA's Joseph A. Silvoso Award of Merit, the NIU Foundation's Humanitarian Award for Service to Higher Education, the Distinguished Service Award from the Illinois CPA Society, and the Community Citizen of the Year Award from Rotary International.

Paul D. Kimmel, PhD, CPA, received his bachelor's degree from the University of Minnesota and his doctorate in accounting from the University of Wisconsin. He is an Associate Professor at the University of Wisconsin—Milwaukee, and has public accounting experience with Deloitte & Touche (Minneapolis). He was the recipient of the UWM School of Business Advisory Council Teaching Award and the Reggie Taite Excellence in Teaching Award, and is a three-time winner of the Outstanding Teaching Assistant Award at the University of Wisconsin. He is also a recipient of the Elijah Watts Sells Award for Honorary Distinction for his results on the CPA exam. He is a member of the American Accounting Association and has published articles in *Accounting Review, Accounting Horizons, Advances in Management Accounting, Managerial Finance, Issues in Accounting Education*, and *Journal of Accounting Education*, as well as other journals. His research interests include accounting for financial instruments and innovation in accounting education. He has published papers and given numerous talks on incorporating critical thinking into accounting education, and helped prepare a catalogue of critical thinking resources for the Federated Schools of Accountancy.

How to Use the Study Aids in this Book

chapter|3

concepts for review >>

Before studying this chapter, you should understand or, if necessary, review:

a. The double-entry system. (Ch. 2, p. 53)
b. How to increase and decrease assets, liabilities, and owner's equity accounts using debit and credit procedures. (Ch. 2, pp. 53–55)
c. How to journalize transactions. (Ch. 2, pp. 58–60)
d. How to post transactions to the general ledger. (Ch. 2, pp. 61–62)
e. How to prepare a trial balance. (Ch. 2, pp. 69–70)

Concepts for Review, listed at the beginning of each chapter, are the accounting concepts you learned in previous chapters that you will need to know in order to understand the topics you are about to cover. Page references are provided for your review before reading the chapter.

The **Feature Story** helps you picture how the chapter topic relates to the real world of accounting and business. Throughout the chapter, references to the Feature Story will help you put new ideas in context, organize them, and remember them.

Fiscal Year Ends, but Classes Move On

Seneca College: www.senecac.on.ca

TORONTO, Ont.—In accounting, as in comedy, timing is everything. An organization's fiscal year end is like a punch line—everything leads up to it. And once it's done, you start all over again.

At Seneca College's 14 locations in the Greater Toronto Area, as at most schools, the majority of students arrive in September and leave in April or May. But the college's fiscal year ends on March 31, rather than at the end of the academic year. "The reason goes back to 1967 and the provincial act establishing community colleges in Ontario," explains Ron Currie, Seneca's Vice-President of Finance and Administration. "That's the government's year end."

If Seneca's fiscal year end were a different date, however, one thing would remain the same. Seneca must apply revenues to the fiscal period when the service is performed. This is the only way to satisfy the revenue recognition and matching principles. For example, Seneca might collect tuition for the summer term but provide teaching services in [a later] period. "Typically," says Mr. Currie, for a summer semester course, [revenue is] deferred on our balance sheet [as] activity fees."

[Most] of funding for its post-secondary [financial] grants and student tuition [and] training, however, is funded [...]. Still, the principles are the [same. Information] came along and gave us [...] in March, April, and May," Mr. [Currie] [...] defer two-thirds of it to the [...]

Expenses, too, must be recorded in the year when they are incurred. "Our utility bills and invoices for legal fees for the last month or two of the fiscal year tend to come in after our year end," Mr. Currie continues. "In order to match the expenses to the proper year, we accrue them based on an estimate."

For things like course study guides, which are usually prepared by staff in one fiscal year but sold to students the following year, it's the other way around. "In that case we take the costs associated with developing the materials and categorize them as a prepaid expense in one fiscal year and match it with the corresponding revenue in the next fiscal year."

Recording revenues and expenses in the correct period is a challenge, but one that must be met to properly reflect the school's activity in each period.

the navigator

- Understand *Concepts for Review*
- Read *Feature Story*
- Scan *Study Objectives*
- Read *Chapter Preview*
- Read text and answer *Before You Go On*
- Work *Demonstration Problem*
- Review *Summary of Study Objectives*
- Answer *Self-Study Questions*
- Complete assignments

chapter|3

chapter 3
Adjusting the Accounts

The Navigator is a learning system designed to help guide you through each chapter and help you succeed in learning the material. It consists of (1) a checklist at the beginning of each chapter, which outlines text features and study skills you will need, and (2) a series of check boxes that prompts you to use the learning aids in the chapter and set priorities as you study.

study objectives >>

After studying this chapter, you should be able to:

1. Explain the time period assumption, revenue recognition principle, matching principle, and accrual basis of accounting.
2. Prepare adjusting entries for prepayments.
3. Prepare adjusting entries for accruals.
4. Describe the nature and purpose of an adjusted trial balance, and prepare one.
5. Prepare adjusting entries for the alternative treatment of prepayments (Appendix 3A).

Study Objectives at the beginning of each chapter provide you with a framework for learning the specific concepts and procedures covered in the chapter. Each study objective reappears at the point within the chapter where the concept is discussed. You can review all the study objectives in the **Summary of Study Objectives** at the end of the chapter. End-of-chapter material is keyed to study objectives.

In Chapter 2, we examined the recording process up to and including the preparation of the trial balance. The next big step is to prepare the financial statements from the trial balance, but before this can be done, additional steps are usually needed. These steps adjust accounts for timing mismatches, like the ones Seneca College has with the tuition it receives for its summer classes and the costs it incurs to offer these classes. More specifically, adjustments make it possible to report revenues and expenses in the appropriate time period. In this chapter, we introduce the accrual accounting concepts that guide the adjustment process.

The chapter is organized as follows:

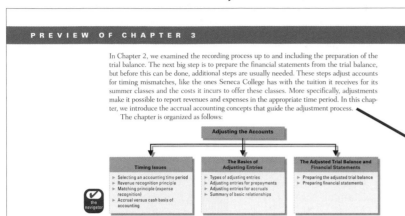

The **Preview** links the feature story with the major topics of the chapter. It also graphically outlines the major topics and subtopics that will be discussed. This narrative and visual preview gives you a mental framework upon which to arrange the new information you are about to learn.

Timing Issues

study objective 1

Explain the time period assumption, revenue recognition principle, matching principle, and accrual basis of accounting.

Accounting would be simple if we could wait until a company ended its operations to prepare its financial statements. As the following anecdote shows, if we waited until then we could easily determine the amount of lifetime income earned:

> A grocery store owner from the old country kept his accounts payable on a spindle, accounts receivable on a notepad, and cash in a shoebox. His daughter, a CGA, chided her father: "I don't understand how you can run your business this way. How do you know what you've earned?"
> "Well," her father replied, "when I arrived in Canada 40 years ago, I had nothing but the pants I was wearing. Today, your brother is a doctor, your sister is a teacher, and you are a CGA. Your mother and I have a nice car, a well-furnished house, and a home by the lake. We have a good business and everything is paid for. So, you add all that together, subtract the pants, and there's your net income."

Selecting an Accounting Time Period

Although the grocer may be correct in his evaluation, it is impr results of operations. All entities—from the corner grocery, t your college or university—find that it helps them make decis reports on the results of their activities. For example, manage financial statements. Investors want to view the results of publi quarterly. The Canada Revenue Agency requires financial sta nual income tax returns. To meet these needs, accountants ha the economic life of a business can be divided into artificial tin **time period assumption**.

Accounting time periods are generally one month, one qua ods of less than one year are called **interim periods**. Most lar report quarterly and annually.

---

116 CHAPTER 3 ► Adjusting the Accounts

Accrued Revenues

Alternative terminology
Accrued revenues are also called *accrued receivables*.

Revenues earned but not yet received in cash or recorded at the statement date are **accrued revenues**. Accrued revenues may accumulate (accrue) with the passage of time, as happens with interest revenue and rent revenue. Or they may result when services have been performed but the payment has not been billed or collected, as can happen with commissions and fees. The former are unrecorded because the earning of interest and rent does not involve daily transactions. The latter may be unrecorded because only a portion of the total service has been provided or the bill has not been prepared.

An adjusting entry is required for two purposes: (1) to show the receivable that exists at the balance sheet date, and (2) to record the revenue that has been earned during the period. Before adjustment, both assets and revenues are understated. Accordingly, as shown below, an adjusting entry for accrued revenues results in an increase (debit) to an asset account and an increase (credit) to a revenue account.

Accrued Revenues

Asset		Revenue	
Debit Adjusting Entry (+)			Credit Adjusting Entry (+)

In October, Pioneer Advertising Agency earned $200 in fees for advertising services that were not billed to clients until November. Because these services have not been billed, they have not been recorded. The following adjusting entry is made on October 31:

A	=	L	+	OE
+200				+200

Cash flows: no effect

Oct. 31	Accounts Receivable	200	
	Service Revenue		200
	To accrue revenue earned but not billed or collected.		

After the adjusting entry is posted, the accounts show the following:

Accounts Receivable				Service Revenue		
Oct. 21	10,000	Oct. 31	10,000		Oct. 21	10,000
31 Adj.	200				31 Adj.	400
Oct. 31 Bal.	200				31 Adj.	200
					Oct. 31 Adj.	10,600

The asset Accounts Receivable shows that $200 is owed by clients at the balance sheet date. The balance of $10,600 in Service Revenue represents the total revenue earned during the month. If the adjusting entry is not made, assets and owner's equity on the balance sheet, and revenues and net income on the income statement, will all be understated.

On November 10, Pioneer receives $200 cash for the services performed in October. The following entry is made:

A	=	L	+	OE
+200				OE
−200				

↑ Cash flows: +200

Nov. 10	Cash	200	
	Accounts Receivable		200
	To record cash collected on account.		

Alternative Terminology familiarizes you with other commonly used terms.

The **Accounting Equation** has been inserted in the margin next to journal entries throughout the text. This feature helps you understand the impact of each accounting transaction on the financial position and cash flows.

Colour Illustrations, such as this infographic, help you visualize and apply the information as you study. They summarize and reinforce important concepts.

Accounting in Action insight boxes give you glimpses into how companies make decisions using accounting information. These high-interest boxes are classified by four different points of view—Across the Organization, Business, Ethics, or International. Each ends with a question to show the relevance of the box. Suggested answers appear at the end of the chapter.

External Users

External users work for other organizations but have reasons to be interested in the company's financial position and performance. There are several types of external users of accounting information. Investors (owners) use accounting information to make decisions to buy, hold, or sell their ownership interest. Creditors, such as suppliers and bankers, use accounting information to evaluate the risks of granting credit or lending money. Investors and creditors are the main external users of accounting information, but there are also many other external users with a large variety of information needs and questions.

For example, labour unions want to know whether the owners can pay increased wages and benefits. Customers are interested in whether a company will continue to honour its product warranties and support its product lines. Taxing authorities, such as the Canada Revenue Agency, want to know whether the company respects the tax laws. Regulatory agencies, such as provincial securities commissions, want to know whether the company is respecting established rules. And economic planners use accounting information to forecast economic activity.

Questions that some external users may ask about a company are shown in Illustration 1-3.

Illustration 1-3 ◄
Questions asked by external users

Investors
Is the company earning enough to give me a return on my investment?

Creditors
Will the company be able to pay its debts as they come due?

Labour Unions
Can the company afford the pay raise we are asking for?

Customers
Will the company stay in business long enough to service the products I buy from it?

ACCOUNTING IN ACTION ► Across the Organization Insight

Accounting can be a useful tool in employee management, team-building, and goal setting. The junk removal company 1-800-GOT-JUNK? has an open-book policy with its employees. The staff at its Vancouver head office, nicknamed the Junktion, meets once a month to go over the financial statements line by line. One staff member is accountable (responsible) for each line item, so everyone is looking for innovative ways to cut costs. This has resulted in one staffer taking the initiative to first do a cost analysis of office expenses and then look for a new supplier. Another staffer built relationships with a local caterer and coffee shop. The "team" also meets every day for a seven-minute "huddle," where they share good news, announcements, and any hurdles they are encountering. They track the progress of their goals through company-wide games posted on a wall. And, in return, the employees share in 25 percent of the profits each year.

? How is accounting useful for non-accountants?

The Building Blocks o[...]

land, not an estimate of the asset's current worth. The going concern assumption pre[...] that the company will operate long enough to use its assets for their intended purpo[...] to complete the company's commitments.

Monetary Unit Assumption. The **monetary unit assumption** requires that only [...] action data that can be expressed as an amount of money be included in the acco[...] records. This assumption makes it possible for accounting to quantify (measure) eco[...] events. In Canada, we use the dollar to record these transactions. In Europe, the eur[...] used; in China, the yuan (CNY) is used; and so on.

This assumption does prevent some relevant information from being included in t[...] counting records. For example, the health of the owner, the quality of service, and the [...] of employees would not be included, because they cannot be quantified in money amou[...]

An important part of the monetary unit assumption is the added assumption th[...] unit of measure stays constant enough over time. In other words, inflation (a rise in prices) or deflation (a drop in prices) is ignored when adding, subtracting, or comparing dollars of different years. Assume a company purchases land in 1998 for $100,000 and that the same amount of land in a similar location costs $400,000 in 2008, 10 years later. If a second lot of land were purchased for $400,000 in 2008, the company would record a total cost of land of $500,000 ($100,000 + $400,000). The fact that these dollars had different values (or purchasing power) throughout the years is ignored. Although inflation can be a significant accounting issue in some countries, Canada's inflation policy—set out by the federal government and the Bank of Canada—is to keep inflation at between one and three percent. Consequently, inflation is considered a non-issue for accounting in Canada.

Economic Entity Assumption. An economic entity can be any organization or unit in society. It may be a company (such as Bombardier), a governmental unit (such as the Province of Alberta), a municipality (such as the Ville de Montréal), a native band council (such as the Kingsclear Indian Band), a school board (such as the Burnaby School Board), a curling championship event (such as the Tim Hortons Brier), or a club (such as the Calgary Rotary Club). The **economic entity assumption** requires the activities of the entity to be kept separate and distinct from the activities of its owner, and all other economic entities.

To illustrate, if Ellen Gélinas, owner of Ellen's Boutique, charges any of her personal living costs as expenses of the boutique, then the economic entity assumption is being violated. Similarly, the economic entity assumption assumes that the activities of Sport Chek and Sports Experts, both owned by Forzani, can be separated into two distinct economic entities for accounting purposes.

Forms of Business Organization

A business can be organized in different ways. The most common examples include a pr[...] prietorship, a partnership, and a corporation, which we will discuss here.

Proprietorship

A business owned by one person is a **proprietorship**. The owner is usually the operator of the business. Small service businesses (hair stylists, plumbers, and mechanics), farms, and small retail stores (antique shops, corner grocery stores, and bookstores) are often proprietorships.

Usually only a relatively small amount of money (capital) is needed to start in business as a proprietorship. The owner (the proprietor) receives any profits, suffers any losses, and is personally liable (responsible) for all debts of the business. There is no legal distinction between the business as an economic unit and the owner. However, the records of the business activities

Helpful hints help clarify concepts or items that are being discussed.

Helpful hint Principles and assumptions will be discussed throughout the text. The ones discussed so far are highlighted in red:

Principles
Cost
Revenue recognition
Matching
Full disclosure

Assumptions
Going concern
Monetary unit
Economic entity
Time period

Helpful Hints in the margins help clarify concepts being discussed.

Key Terms that represent essential concepts are printed in blue where they are first explained in the text. They are defined again in the end-of-chapter **Glossary**.

Before You Go On sections follow each key topic. **Review It** questions prompt you to stop and review the key points you have just studied. If you cannot answer these questions, you should go back and read the section again.

Review It questions about The Forzani Group ask you to find information in Forzani's financial statements in Appendix A at the end of the text.

Do It exercises ask you to put your newly acquired knowledge to work. They outline an **Action Plan** necessary to complete the exercise, and the accompanying **Solution** helps you see how the problem should be solved.

Related exercise material at the end of the The Before You Go On section lists similar brief exercises and exercises.

---

56 CHAPTER 2 ► The Recording Process

Illustration 2-2 ►
Expanded basic equation and debit/credit rules and effects

The normal balance of each account is on its increase side. So assets, drawings, and expense accounts have a normal debit balance, while liabilities, owner's capital, and revenue accounts have a normal credit balance.

BEFORE YOU GO ON . . .

►Review It

1. What do the terms "debit" and "credit" mean?
2. What are the effects of debits and credits on the asset, liability, and owner's equity accounts?
3. What are the effects of debits and credits on the revenue, expense, and drawings accounts?
4. What are the normal balances for these Forzani accounts: Accounts Receivable; Accounts Payable and Accrued Liabilities; Retail Revenue; and Store Operating Expense? The answer to this question is at the end of this chapter.

►Do It

Eszter Schwenke has just rented space in a shopping mall where she will open a beauty salon called Hair It Is. Long before opening day and before purchasing equipment, hiring employees, and remodelling the space, Eszter is advised to set up a double-entry set of accounting records to record all of her business transactions.

Name the balance sheet accounts that Eszter will need to record the transactions that open her business. Indicate whether the normal balance of each account is a debit or a credit.

Action Plan

• Determine the types of accounts needed. Eszter will need asset accounts for each different type of asset she invests in the business. She will need liability accounts for any debts she has.
• Understand the types of owner's equity accounts: only owner's capital will be needed when Eszter begins the business. Other owner's equity accounts will be added later.

Solution

Eszter will probably need the following accounts to record the transactions that prepare her beauty salon for opening day: Cash (debit balance); Supplies (debit balance); Equipment (debit balance); Accounts Payable (credit balance); Notes Payable (credit balance) if she borrows money; and E. Schwenke, Capital (credit balance).

Related exercise material: BE2–1, BE2–2, BE2–3, BE2–4, BE2–5, E2–2, E2–3, and E2–4.

Steps in the Recording Process

asic steps in the recording process are:

nalyze each transaction for its effects on the accounts.
nter the transaction information in a journal (book of original entry).
ansfer the journal information to the correct accounts in the ledger (book of accounts).

The Trial Balance ◄ 71

Locating Errors

The procedure for preparing a trial balance is quite simple. However, if the trial balance does not balance, locating an error in a manual accounting system can be time-consuming, tiring, and frustrating. Errors generally result from mathematical mistakes, incorrect postings, or simply recopying data incorrectly. Errors in a computerized system usually happen in the initial recording rather than because of a software error in posting or the preparation of the trial balance.

What do you do if you have a manual trial balance that does not balance? First determine the amount of the difference between the two columns of the trial balance. After you know this amount, try the following steps:

1. If the error is an amount such as $1, $100, or $1,000, re-add the trial balance columns. Recalculate the account balances.
2. If the error can be evenly divided by two, scan the trial balance to see if a balance equal to half the error has been entered in the wrong column.
3. If the error can be evenly divided by nine, retrace the account balances on the trial balance to see whether they are incorrectly copied from the ledger. For example, if a balance was $12 but was listed as $21, a $9 error has been made. Reversing the order of numbers is called a transposition error.
4. If the error cannot be evenly divided by two or nine, scan the ledger to see whether an account balance in the amount of the error has been omitted from the trial balance. Scan the journal to see whether a posting in the amount of the error has been omitted. Check your additions.

Of course, if there is more than one error, these steps may not work.

Ethics note

Auditors see errors and irregularities as two different things. An error is an unintentional mistake. So it is neither ethical nor unethical. An irregularity, on the other hand, is an intentional misstatement, which is generally viewed as unethical.

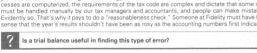

ACCOUNTING IN ACTION ► Business Insight

If you've ever made an arithmetic error, you may take some comfort from an accountant's mistake at Fidelity Investments, the world's largest mutual fund investment company. The accountant failed to include a minus sign while doing a tax calculation, which made a $1.3-billion loss look like a $1.3-billion gain. No one expects that kind of mistake at a firm like Fidelity, which has sophisticated computer systems and top investment managers.

In explaining the mistake to shareholders, Fidelity manager J. Gary Burkhead wrote: "Some people have asked how, in this age of technology, such a mistake could be made. While many of our processes are computerized, the requirements of the tax code are complex and dictate that some steps must be handled manually by our tax managers and accountants, and people can make mistakes." Evidently so. That's why it pays to do a "reasonableness check." Someone at Fidelity must have had a sense that the year's results shouldn't have been as rosy as the accounting numbers first indicated.

? Is a trial balance useful in finding this type of error?

Some Simplistic Assumptions

To keep things simple, we have made some assumptions in the material in this textbook. These include not using cents and sales taxes in the transaction data.

Use of Dollars and Cents

We have not included cents in the dollar figures we record in journal entries, general ledger

---

Ethics Notes help sensitize you to the real-world ethical dilemmas of accounting.

178 CHAPTER 4 ► Completion of the Accounting Cycle

Intangible Assets

Intangible assets are long-lived assets that do not have physical substance. They give a company rights and privileges and include such things as goodwill, patents, copyrights, trademarks, trade names, and licences. Similar to buildings and equipment, intangible assets with estimated useful lives are amortized. Similar to land, intangible assets with indefinite lives are not amortized.

Illustration 4-9 shows how Shaw Communications reported intangible assets in its balance sheet. All of Shaw Communications' intangible assets have indefinite lives, so they are not amortized.

Illustration 4-9 ►
Intangible assets section

SHAW COMMUNICATIONS INC. Balance Sheet (partial) May 31, 2006 (in thousands)		**SHAW**
Intangible assets		
Broadcast licences	$4,684,647	
Goodwill	88,111	
	4,772,758	

Current Liabilities

Current liabilities are listed first in the liabilities and equity section of the balance sheet. **Current liabilities** are obligations that are expected to be paid in the coming year from current assets or by creating other current liabilities. Current liabilities include notes payable, accounts payable, salaries payable, interest payable, sales taxes payable, unearned revenues, and current maturities of long-term liabilities (payments to be made within the next year on long-term debt). Corporations may also have income taxes payable included in the current liabilities section of the balance sheet.

Current liabilities are often listed in order of currency. That is, the liabilities that will be due first are listed first. Many companies do not use this approach, however. They simply list the items in their current liabilities section according to a company tradition. The current liabilities section from Sears Canada's balance sheet is shown in Illustration 4-10.

Illustration 4-10 ►
Current liabilities section

SEARS CANADA INC. Balance Sheet (partial) December 31, 2005 (in millions)		**Sears**
Current liabilities		
Accounts payable	$ 696.6	
Accrued liabilities	430.1	
Income and other taxes payable	322.5	
Principal payments on long-term obligations due within one year	216.1	
	1,665.3	

...ers of financial statements look closely at the relationship between current assets and ...t liabilities. This relationship is important in evaluating a company's ability to pay its ...t liabilities. We will talk more about this later in the chapter when we learn how to ...e information in the financial statements.

Financial statements appear throughout the book. Those from real companies are usually identified by a logo. Numbers or categories are frequently highlighted in coloured type to draw your attention to key information.

Practice Tools: Demonstration Problems

188 CHAPTER 4 ► Completion of the Accounting Cycle

Demonstration Problem

At the end of its first month of operations, Paquet Answering Service has the following unadjusted trial balance, with the accounts presented in alphabetical order rather than in financial statement order:

PAQUET ANSWERING SERVICE Trial Balance August 31, 2008		
	Debit	Credit
Accounts payable		$ 2,400
Accounts receivable	$ 2,800	
Accumulated amortization—building		500
Accumulated amortization—equipment		1,000
Advertising expense	400	
Amortization expense	1,500	
Building	50,000	
Cash	5,400	
Equipment	60,000	
Insurance expense	200	
Interest expense	350	
Interest payable		1,350
Land	50,000	
Long-term debt investments	15,000	
Long-term equity investments	7,000	
Mortgage payable		140,000
Prepaid insurance	2,200	
R. Paquet, capital		155,000
R. Paquet, drawings	1,000	
Salaries expense	3,200	
Service revenue		5,700
Short-term investments	4,800	
Supplies	1,000	
Supplies expense	300	
Utilities expense	800	
Totals	$305,950	$305,950

Action Plan

- Identify which accounts are balance sheet accounts and which are income statement accounts.
- If revenues are more than expenses, this results in net income; if expenses are more than revenues, this results in a net loss.
- In preparing a classified balance sheet, know the contents of each of the sections.
- In journalizing closing entries, remember that there are four entries. Revenues and expenses are closed to the Income Summary account; the Income Summary account and the drawings account are closed to owner's capital.
- Always check your work. Make sure the balance in Income Summary equals net income before closing the Income Summary account. Make sure that the balance in the owner's capital account after posting the closing entries equals the amount reported on the balance sheet.

Instructions

(a) Calculate the net income or loss for the month.
(b) Calculate owner's equity at August 31, 2008.
(c) Prepare a classified balance sheet for Paquet Answering Service at August 31, 2008. Assume that $5,000 of the mortgage payable is due over the next year.
(d) Journalize the closing entries.
(e) Create T accounts for Income Summary and R. Paquet, Capital, and post closing entries.

Solution to Demonstration Problem

(a) Net income (loss) = Revenue − expenses
= $5,700 − $400 − $1,500 − $200 − $350 − $3,200 − $300 − $800
= ($1,050)
(b) Owner's equity August 31, 2008 = Opening capital − net loss − drawings
= $155,000 − $1,050 − $1,000
= $152,950

Demonstration Problems review the chapter material. These sample problems provide you with **Action Plans** that list the strategies needed to solve the problem and **Solutions**.

A **Web icon** at various places through the book refers you to additional learning resources found on the companion website to this text.

The **Summary of Study Objectives** relates the study objectives to the key points in the chapter. It gives you another opportunity to review, as well as to see how all the key topics within the chapter are related.

The **Glossary** defines all the terms and concepts introduced in the chapter. Page references help you find any terms you need to study further. The **Web icon** tells you that there is a searchable, comprehensive glossary, as well as a Key Term Matching Activity available on the companion website.

Summary of Study Objectives

1. **Define debits and credits and illustrate how they are used to record business transactions.** The term "debit" indicates left and "credit" indicates right. Assets, drawings, and expenses are increased by debits and decreased by credits. Liabilities, owner's capital, and revenues are increased by credits and decreased by debits. The normal balance of an asset is a debit because assets are on the left side of the accounting equation. The normal balance of liabilities and owner's capital is a credit because they are on the right side of the accounting equation. Revenues are recorded as credits because credits increase owner's equity. Expenses and drawings are recorded as debits because debits decrease owner's equity.

2. **Describe the basic steps in the recording process, explain what a journal is, and journalize business transactions.** The basic steps in the recording process are as follows: (a) analyze each transaction for its effect on the accounts, (b) enter the transaction information in a journal, and (c) transfer the journal information to the correct accounts in the ledger. The first accounting record of a transaction is the entry in the journal, and the data are later transferred to the general ledger. A journal (a) discloses in one place the complete effect of a transaction, (b) provides a chronological record of transactions, (c) prevents and helps locate errors because the debit and credit amounts for each entry can be easily compared, and (d) gives an explanation of the transaction and a reference to the source document, if there is one.

3. **Explain what a ledger is, and post journal entries.** The entire group of accounts maintained by a company is called the ledger. The ledger keeps in one place all the information about changes in each of the specific account balances. Posting is the procedure of transferring journal entries to the ledger accounts. This part of the recording process brings together in each account the effects of journalized transactions.

4. **Explain the purpose of a trial balance, and prepare one.** A trial balance is a list of accounts and their balances at a specific time. Its main purpose is to prove that debits and credits are equal after posting. A trial balance also uncovers certain types of errors in journalizing and posting, and is useful in preparing financial statements.

Glossary

Study Aids: Glossary
Practice Tools: Key Term Matching Activity

Account A record of increases and decreases in a specific asset, liability, or owner's equity item. (p. 52)

Chart of accounts A list of accounts and the account numbers that identify where the accounts are in the ledger. (p. 63)

Compound entry An entry that affects three or more accounts. (p. 59)

Credit The right side of an account. (p. 52)

Debit The left side of an account. (p. 52)

Double-entry system A system that records the dual (two-... in appropriate accounts. (p. ...

... of original entry that transac-... ey are not recorded in other

General ledger A ledger that contains accounts for all assets, liabilities, equities, revenues, and expenses. (p. 60)

Journal An accounting record where transactions are recorded in chronological (date) order. (p. 58)

Journalizing The entering of transaction data in the journal. (p. 58)

Ledger A record that contains all of a company's accounts. (p. 60)

Posting The procedure of transferring journal entries to the ledger accounts. (p. 61)

T account A form of account that looks like the letter T. It has the title above the horizontal line. Debits are shown to the left of the vertical line, credits to the right. (p. 52)

Trial balance A list of accounts and their balances at a specific time, usually at the end of the accounting period. (p. 70)

Self-Study Questions

Practice Tools: Self-Assessment Quizzes

Answers are at the end of the chapter.

(SO 1) K   1. Ethics are the standards of conduct that are used to judge one's actions as:
(a) decent or indecent.
(b) successful or unsuccessful.
(c) profitable or unprofitable.
(d) right or wrong.

(SO 1) C   2. Which of the following statements about users of accounting information is incorrect?
(a) Management is an internal user.
(b) Taxing authorities are external users.
(c) Creditors are external users.
(d) Regulatory authorities are internal users.

(SO 2) K   3. The cost principle states that:
(a) assets should be recorded at cost and adjusted when their market value changes.
(b) an entity's activities should be kept separate and distinct from those of its owner.
(c) assets should be recorded at their historical (original) cost.
(d) only transaction data that can be expressed as an amount of money should be included in the accounting records.

(SO 2) C   4. Which of the following statements about basic assumptions is incorrect?
(a) The going concern assumption assumes that a company ends its operations once a year for reporting purposes.
(b) The economic entity assumption states that the activities of the entity should be kept separate from those of its owner and other entities.
(c) The monetary unit assumption makes it possible for accounting to measure economic events.
(d) An important part of the monetary unit assumption is that the monetary unit is assumed to remain stable.

5. As at December 31, after its first year of operations, Stoneland Company has assets of $3,500; revenues of $6,000; expenses of $3,500; and drawings of $500. What are the liabilities for Stoneland Company as at December 31?
(a) $1,000   (c) $2,000
(b) $1,500   (d) $2,500   (SO 3) AP

6. Net income will result during a time period when: (SO 3) C
(a) assets are greater than liabilities.
(b) assets are greater than revenues.
(c) expenses are greater than revenues.
(d) revenues are greater than expenses.

7. The effects on the accounting equation of performing services on account are: (SO 4) AP
(a) increased assets and decreased owner's equity.
(b) increased assets and increased owner's equity.
(c) increased assets and increased liabilities.
(d) increased liabilities and increased owner's equity.

8. Genesis Company buys a $10,000 machine on credit. Initially, this transaction will only affect the: (SO 4) AP
(a) income statement.
(b) balance sheet.
(c) income statement and statement of owner's equity.
(d) income statement, statement of owner's equity, and balance sheet.

9. The financial statement that reports assets, liabilities, and owner's equity is the: (SO 5) K
(a) income statement.
(b) statement of owner's equity.
(c) balance sheet.
(d) cash flow statement.

10. Which of the following items is not reported on the statement of owner's equity?   (SO 5) C
(a) Investments by the owner
(b) Drawings
(c) Net income
(d) Cash flow from operating activities

Self-Study Questions are a practice test that give you an opportunity to check your knowledge of important topics. Answers appear on the last page of the chapter.

Self-study questions are keyed to study objectives. In addition, the level of cognitive skill required to solve the question has been classified with a letter code following Bloom's Taxonomy. You will find more information about Bloom's and this coding system on page XVII of this Preface.

The **Web icon** tells you that there is a self-assessment test on the website that can further help you master this material.

Questions

(SO 1) C   1. "Accounting is ingrained in our society and it is vital to our economic system." Do you agree? Explain.

(SO 1) C   2. Why should everyone study accounting whether they are going to be an accountant or not?

(SO 1) C   3. Why are ethics important to the accounting profession? To statement users?

(SO 1) C   4. (a) Distinguish between internal and external users of accounting data. (b) How does accounting provide relevant data for these users?

(SO 1) K   5. Identify and describe the three steps in the accounting information system.

Questions allow you to explain your understanding of concepts and relationships covered in the chapter. (Keyed to Study Objectives and Bloom's Taxonomy.)

134 CHAPTER 3 ▶ Adjusting the Accounts

that was included in the trial balance for the same account." Do you agree or disagree? Why?

(SO 4) C 21. On Silver Company's trial balance, Accounts Payable is
$4,250. After the adjusting entries have been posted,
the balance in this account is still $4,250. Since there
is no change, it is not necessary to include Accounts
Payable on the adjusted trial balance. Do you agree or
disagree? Why?

(SO 4) C 22. Net income is shown on the income statement and the
statement of owner's equity. It is also indirectly included
on the balance sheet. Do you agree or disagree? Why?

*23. Some companies debit an expense account at the time (SO 5) C
the expense is prepaid instead of debiting an asset account. Will this result in a different net income or different amount of total assets on the balance sheet than
if they had instead debited an asset account when the
amount was paid? Why or why not?

*24. Jeremiah has been reading about a recent accounting (SO 5) C
scandal where the company overstated its revenue on
purpose. He then argues that it is never appropriate to
credit revenue when cash is received in advance of providing a service. Do you agree or disagree? Why?

Brief Exercises generally focus on one Study Objective at a time. They help you build confidence in your basic skills and knowledge. (Keyed to Study Objectives and Bloom's Taxonomy.)

Brief Exercises

Identify impact of transactions on cash and net income.
(SO 1) AP

BE3–1 Indicate the impact of each of the following transactions on cash and net income. The first transaction has been completed for you as an example.

Transaction	Cash	Net Income
(a) Purchased supplies for cash, $100.	–$100	$0
(b) Recorded the use of $60 of the supplies purchased in (a) in an adjusting journal entry.		
(c) Performed services on account, $1,000.		
(d) Received $800 from customers in payment of their account in (c).		
(e) Purchased office equipment for cash, $5,000.		
(f) Recorded amortization of office equipment for the period, $100.		
(g) Accrued salaries earned but not paid for the month of June, $750.		
(h) On July 3, paid $750 for salaries accrued in (g).		
(i) On May 28, received $500 cash for services to be provided in June.		

Calculate missing data for supplies.
(SO 2) AP

BE3–2 Calculate the missing information in each of the following independent situations:

	A Co.	B Co.
Supplies on hand, May 31, 2007	$ 675	$ 640
Supplies purchased during the year	1,695	2,825
Supplies on hand, May 31, 2008	225	?
Supplies used during the year	?	2,715

Prepare and post transaction **BE3–3** Spahn Cleaning Company had $945 of cleaning supplies on hand on January 1, 2008. On __, 2008, it purchased additional cleaning supplies for $3,880 on credit. On December 31, a count showed $980 of cleaning supplies on hand.

Prepare the journal entry to record the purchase of supplies during the year.
Calculate the amount of cleaning supplies used during the year.
Prepare the adjusting journal entry required at December 31, 2008.
Using T accounts, enter the January 1, 2008, balance in Cleaning Supplies and Cleaning Supplies Expense, post the two journal entries, and indicate the adjusted balance in each account.

__ On June 1, 2007, Bere Co. paid $9,900 for a one-year insurance policy. Bere Co. has a __ber 31 fiscal year end.

Prepare the June 1, 2007, journal entry.

136 CHAPTER 3 ▶ Adjusting the Accounts

Accounts payable	$ 2,570	Insurance expense	$ 1,560
Accounts receivable	7,230	Interest expense	500
Accumulated amortization—		Interest payable	125
equipment	6,200	Note payable	10,000
Amortization expense	3,100	Prepaid insurance	780
C. Winterholt, capital	15,450	Rent expense	20,965
C. Winterholt, drawings	21,000	Service revenue	48,950
Cash	1,100	Unearned service revenue	840
Equipment	27,900		

(a) Prepare the adjusted trial balance.
(b) Beside each account, identify if it should be included on the income statement (IS), statement of owner's equity (OE), or balance sheet (BS).

Prepare financial statements.
(SO 4) AP

BE3–11 Refer to BE3–10. Prepare financial statements for the year ended September 30, 2008.

Prepare and post adjusting entry for supplies.
(SO 5) AP

*BE3–12 Refer to BE3–3. Assume that instead of debiting purchases of cleaning supplies to the Cleaning Supplies account, Spahn Cleaning debits purchases of supplies to the Cleaning Supplies Expense account. Spahn's trial balance at December 31 shows Cleaning Supplies $945 and Cleaning Supplies Expense $3,880. On December 31, there is $980 of supplies on hand.

(a) Prepare the adjusting entry at December 31. Using T accounts, enter the balances in the accounts, post the adjusting entry, and indicate the adjusted balance in each account.
(b) Compare the adjusted balances in BE3–3, where an asset account was originally debited, with the adjusted balances you determined here in (a), where an expense account was originally debited. Does it matter whether an original entry is recorded to an asset account or an expense account? Explain.

Prepare and post adjusting entry for unearned revenue.
(SO 5) AP

*BE3–13 Refer to BE3–6. Assume that instead of crediting Unearned Revenue for the $1,500 one-year insurance policy, Sting Insurance Co. credits Insurance Revenue on August 1, 2007.

(a) Prepare the adjusting entry at December 31, 2007. Using T accounts, enter the balances in the accounts, post the adjusting entry, and indicate the adjusted balance in each account.
(b) Compare the adjusted balances in BE3–6, where a liability account was originally credited, with the adjusted balances you determined here in (a), where a revenue account was originally credited. Does it matter whether an original entry is recorded to a liability account or a revenue account? Explain.

Exercises

Identify point of revenue recognition.
(SO 1) AP

E3–1 The following independent situations require professional judgement to determine when to recognize revenue from the transactions:

(a) **Air Canada** sells you an advance purchase airline ticket in September for your flight home at Christmas.
(b) **Leon's Furniture** sells you a home theatre in January on a "no money down, no interest, and no payments for one year" promotional deal.
(c) The **Toronto Blue Jays** sell season tickets to games in the Rogers Centre on-line. Fans can purchase the tickets at any time, although the season does not officially begin until April. It runs from April through October.
(d) The **RBC Financial Group** loans you money at the beginning of August. The loan and the interest are repayable in full at the end of November.
(e) In August, you order a sweater from **Sears** using its on-line catalogue. Sears ships the sweater to you in September and you charge it to your Sears credit card. You receive and pay the Sears bill in October.

Exercises that gradually increase in difficulty help you to build your confidence in your ability to use the material learned in the chapter. (Keyed to Study Objectives and Bloom's Taxonomy.)

Certain exercises or problems marked with a pencil icon ▰▰▰▷ help you practise business writing skills.

Each **Problem** helps you pull together and apply several concepts of the chapter. Two sets of problems—Set A and Set B—are usually keyed to the same study objectives and cognitive level. These provide additional opportunities to apply concepts learned in the chapter.

(c) Post each of the entries in (a) and (b) to T accounts and calculate the final balance in each account. (*Note:* Posting to the Cash account is not necessary).
(d) Compare your balances in (c) above to those obtained in E3–4 part (c). Comment on your findings.

Problems: Set A

P3–1A Your examination of the 2007 records of Northland Co. shows the company collected $156,200 cash from customers and paid $107,800 cash for operating costs. If Northland followed the accrual basis of accounting, it would report the following year-end balances:

Determine income on cash and accrual bases; recommend method.
(SO 1) AP

	2007	2006
Accounts payable	$ 1,810	$ 1,640
Accounts receivable	2,900	3,200
Accumulated amortization	17,250	15,000
Prepaid insurance	1,620	1,330
Unearned revenues	1,400	1,560

Instructions

(a) Determine Northland's net income on a cash basis for 2007.
(b) Determine Northland's net income on an accrual basis for 2007.
(c) Which method do you recommend Northland use? Why?

P3–2A Burke Bros. began operations on January 1, 2008. Its fiscal year end is December 31. It prepares financial statements and adjusts its accounts annually. Selected transactions from 2008 follow:

Prepare transaction and adjusting entries for prepayments.
(SO 2) AP

1. On January 1, 2008, bought office supplies for $3,100 cash. A physical count on December 31, 2008, revealed $770 of supplies still on hand.
2. Bought a $5,040 one-year insurance policy for cash on May 1, 2008. The policy came into effect on this date.
3. On November 15, received a $1,275 advance cash payment from three clients for services to be provided in the future. As at December 31, services had been done for two of the clients ($425 each).
4. On December 15, the company paid $4,500 rent in advance for the month of January 2009.
5. On May 1, purchased equipment for $30,800 cash. The equipment has an estimated seven-year useful life.

Instructions

Prepare the journal entry for the original transaction and any adjusting journal entry required at December 31, 2008, for each of the transactions.

P3–3A Théâtre Dupuis had the following transactions during the year ended November 30, 2007:

Prepare transaction and adjusting entries.
(SO 2, 3) AP

ounted to $500 on November 30, 2006. On February 17, 2007, additional purchased for $1,750 cash. On November 30, 2007, a physical count and amounted to $300.
year that had originally been purchased on December 1, 2005, for eful life of the truck is four years.
blays each season. Season tickets sell for $176 each and 150 were sold ming 2007–2008 season, which starts in October 2007 and ends in onth). Théâtre Dupuis credited Unearned Season Ticket Revenue for
theatre is $3,500 every week for employee wages earned during a through Sunday). Wages were last paid (and recorded) on Sunday, November 30 falls on a Friday.
theatre to a local seniors' choir which uses the space for rehearsals 400 per month. The new treasurer of the choir accidentally sent a

Continuing Cookie Chronicle

(*Note:* This is a continuation of the Cookie Chronicle from Chapters 1 through 3.)

Natalie had a very busy December. At the end of the month, after Natalie has journalized and posted her December transactions and adjusting entries, her company has the following adjusted trial balance:

COOKIE CREATIONS
Adjusted Trial Balance
December 31, 2007

	Debit	Credit
Cash	$1,130	
Accounts receivable	875	
Baking supplies	350	
Prepaid insurance	1,210	
Baking equipment	1,300	
Accumulated amortization—baking equipment		$ 43
Accounts payable		75
Salaries payable		56
Unearned revenue		300
Interest payable		15
Note payable, 6%, principal and interest due November 16, 2009		2,000
N. Koebel, capital		900
N. Koebel, drawings	500	
Teaching revenue		4,315
Salaries expense	856	
Telephone expense	125	
Advertising supplies expense	165	
Baking supplies expense	1,025	
Amortization expense	43	
Insurance expense	110	
Interest expense	15	
	$7,704	$7,704

Instructions

Using the information in the adjusted trial balance, do the following:

(a) Prepare an income statement and a statement of owner's equity for the two months ended December 31, 2007, and a classified balance sheet as at December 31, 2007.
(b) Natalie has decided that her year end will be December 31, 2007. Prepare closing entries as at December 31, 2007.
(c) Prepare a post-closing trial balance.

Cumulative Coverage—Chapters 2 to 4

Lee Chan opened Lee's Window Washing on July 1, 2008. In July, the following transactions were completed:

July 1 Invested $14,000 cash in the business.
 1 Purchased a used truck for $26,400, paying $6,400 cash and signing a note payable for the balance.
 3 Purchased cleaning supplies for $850 on account.
 5 Paid $1,800 on a one-year insurance policy, effective July 1.
 12 Billed customers $3,800 for cleaning services.

The **Continuing Cookie Chronicle** is a serial problem found in each chapter. It follows the operations of a small company, Cookie Creations, throughout the text. The company is owned by a student and the purpose of the serial problem is to reinforce the application of accounting to the type of business a student could operate.

In selected chapters, a **Cumulative Coverage Problem** follows the A and B problem sets. The cumulative coverage problem pulls together, and uses, topics you have learned over several chapters.

Adjustment data consist of the following:

1. Supplies on hand cost $1,280.
2. Accrued salaries payable total $775.
3. Store equipment has an expected useful life of five years.
4. Unearned service revenue of $550 is earned.

Instructions

(a) Enter the August 31 balances in general ledger accounts.
(b) Journalize the September transactions.
(c) Post to the ledger accounts.
(d) Prepare a trial balance at September 30.
(e) Journalize and post adjusting entries.
(f) Prepare an adjusted trial balance.
(g) Prepare an income statement and a statement of owner's equity for September, and a balance sheet at September 30, 2007.

The **Broadening Your Perspective** section helps you pull together various concepts covered in the chapter and apply them to real-life business decisions.

Financial Reporting Problems familiarize you with the format, content, and uses of financial statements prepared by The Forzani Group Ltd., which are presented in Appendix A at the end of the text.

Interpreting Financial Statements asks you to apply the concepts you have learned to specific situations faced by actual companies.

BROADENING YOUR PERSPECTIVE

Financial Reporting and Analysis

Financial Reporting Problem

BYP3–1   The financial statements of **The Forzani Group** are presented in Appendix A at the end of this textbook.

Instructions

(a) What title does Forzani use for its income statement?
(b) What different types of revenues were reported by Forzani (see note 2 (h))?
(c) Does Forzani report any prepayments on its balance sheet? If yes, identify each item that is a prepaid expense or unearned (deferred) revenue. Indicate the other account title that Forzani would likely use when it prepares adjusting entries for these accounts.
(d) Does Forzani report any accruals on its balance sheet? If yes, identify each item that is an accrued revenue or accrued expense. Indicate the other account title that Forzani would likely use when it prepares adjusting entries for these accounts.

Interpreting Financial Statements

BYP3–2   Rogers Communications Inc. is a diversified Canadian communications and media company. Rogers' balance sheet included a current liability of $176,266,000 at December 31, 2005, called Unearned Revenue. The following comes from Rogers' revenue recognition policy note in its financial statements:

216   CHAPTER 4   ►   Completion of the Accounting Cycle
Instructions

(a) By what percentage did The Gap's total assets increase overall fr[...] average increase for each year?
(b) Comment on the change in The Gap's liquidity. Which measur[...] tion of The Gap's liquidity: working capital or the current ratio? [...] change in The Gap's liquidity during the period?
(c) Do you believe that The Gap's creditors should be concerned ab[...]
(d) If you were a creditor of The Gap and noted that it did not have enou[...] rent liabilities in 2001, what additional information could you ask f[...]

Critical Thinking

Collaborative Learning Activity

Note to instructor: Additional instructions and material for this group activity can be found on the Instructor Resource Site.

Study Aids:
Working in Groups

BYP4–3   In this group activity, you will classify and define accounts.

Instructions

(a) Your instructor will divide the class into groups and provide each with an envelope filled with account names. As a group, place each account in the proper financial statement classification on the handout provided.
(b) Using the second handout provided, identify each account's normal balance and whether it is permanent or temporary.
(c) You may be asked by your instructor to write a short quiz on this topic.

Communication Activity

Study Aids:
Writing Handbook

BYP4–4   Your best friend is thinking about opening a business. He has never studied accounting and has no idea about the steps that must be followed in order to produce financial statements for his business.

Instructions

Write a memo to your friend that lists and explains each of the steps in the accounting cycle in the order in which they should be completed. Include information on when each of these steps should be done and explain the purpose of the different types of journal entries and trial balances. Your memo should also discuss the optional steps in the accounting cycle.

Ethics Case

Study Aids:
Ethics in Accounting

BYP4–5   As the controller of Breathless Perfume Company, you discover a significant misstatement that overstated net income in the previous year's financial statements. The misleading financial statements are in the company's annual report, which was issued to banks and other creditors less than a month ago.
   After much thought about the consequences of telling the president, Eddy Lieman, about this misstatement, you gather your courage to inform him. Eddy says, "Hey! What they don't know won't hurt them. But, just so we set the record straight, we'll adjust this year's financial statements for last

Collaborative Learning Activities prepare you for the business world, where you will be working with many people, by giving you practice in solving problems with colleagues. They also allow you to learn from each other.

Communication Activities ask you to engage in real-life business situations using your writing, speaking, or presentation skills.

Through **Ethics Cases**, you will reflect on ethical situations an accountant typically confronts.

Answers to Chapter Questions offer suggested answers for questions that appear in the chapter's **Accounting in Action** insight boxes, **Review It** Questions based on The Forzani Group's financial statements, and **Self-Study Questions**.

After you complete your assignments, it's a good idea to go back to **The Navigator** checklist at the start of the chapter to see if you have used all the study aids of the chapter.

year's misstatement. We can absorb that misstatement better this year than last year anyway! Just don't make that kind of mistake again."

Instructions

(a) Who are the stakeholders in this situation?
(b) What are the ethical issues in this situation?
(c) As a controller, what would you do in this situation?

ANSWERS TO CHAPTER QUESTIONS

Across the Organization Insight, p. 169

Q: Why are CFOs interested in knowing how long it takes on average for companies to close their books?
A: There are two basic reasons: (1) the more time a company needs to close its books, the more it costs the company; and (2) accounting information must be timely to be useful.

Business Insight, p. 174

Q: Some of these errors happened several years ago. Why is it still important for Nortel to record entries to correct them?
A: Investors and creditors often use several years of a company's financial statements to determine if the company's performance is getting better or worse. If statements from previous years are incorrect, investors and creditors would not be able to make useful comparisons.

Answer to Forzani Review It Question 3, p. 181

Forzani's current assets include Cash, $19,266; Accounts Receivable, $68,927; Inventory, $278,002; and Prepaid Expenses, $2,647. Its current liabilities include Accounts Payable and Accrued Liabilities, $244,293; and the Current Portion of Long-Term Debt, $5,135. All amounts are listed in thousands. Forzani's current assets and current liabilities appear to be listed in order of liquidity, with the most current or liquid account listed first.

Answers to Self-Study Questions

1. b   2. c   3. a   4. d   5. c   6. b   7. a   8. c   *9. c   *10. d

 Remember to go back to the Navigator Box at the beginning of the chapter to check off your completed work.

The Use of Bloom's Taxonomy

Bloom's Taxonomy is a classification framework that you can use to develop your skills from the most basic to the most advanced competence levels: Knowledge, comprehension, application, analysis, synthesis, and evaluation. These levels are hierarchical in nature in that performance at each level requires mastery of all prior levels.

Questions, exercises, and problems at the end of each chapter of this text have been classified by the knowledge level required in answering each one. Below you will learn what your role is in each of the six skill levels and how you can demonstrate mastery at each level. Key word clues will help you recognize the skill level required for a particular question. You will also find an example from the text which will help illustrate each skill level.

(K) Knowledge (Remembering)

Student's role: "I read, listen, watch or observe, I take notes and am able to recall information, ask and respond to questions."
Student demonstrates knowledge by: stating who, what, when, why, and how in the same form in which they learned it.
Key words clues: define, identify, label, name, etc.

(C) Comprehension (Understanding)

Student's role: "I understand the information or skill. I can recognize it in other forms and I can explain it to others and make use of it."

Student demonstrates comprehension by: giving an original example of how the information would be used.

Key words clues: describe, distinguish, give example, compare, differentiate, explain, etc.

(AP) Application (Solving the Problem)

Student's role: "I can apply my prior knowledge and understanding to new situations."

Student demonstrates knowledge by: solving problems independently. Recognizing when the information or skill is needed and uses it to solve new problems or complete tasks.

Key word clues: calculate, illustrate, prepare, complete, use, produce, etc.

(AN) Analysis (Detecting)

Student's role: "I can break down the information into simpler parts and understand how these parts are related."

Student demonstrates knowledge by: recognizing patterns and hidden meanings, filling in missing information, correcting errors, identifying components and effects.

Key word clues: analyze, break down, compare, contrast, deduce, differentiate, etc.

(S) Synthesis (Creating)

Student's role: "I use all knowledge, understanding, and skills to create alternatives. I can convey this information to others effectively."

Student demonstrates knowledge by: acting as a guide to others, designing, creating.

Key word clues: relate, tell, write, categorize, devise, formulate, generalize, create, design.

(E) Evaluation (Appraisal)

Student's role: "I am open to and appreciative of the value of ideas, procedures, and methods and can make well-supported judgements, backed up by knowledge, understanding, and skills."

Student demonstrates knowledge by: formulating and presenting well-supported judgement, displaying consideration of others, examining personal options, making wise choices.

Key word clues: appraise, assess, criticize, critique, decide, evaluate, judge, justify, recommend.

How Do You Learn Best?

This questionnaire aims to find out something about your preferences for the way you work with information. You will have a preferred learning style. One part of that learning style is your preference for the intake and the output of ideas and information.

Circle the letter of the answer that best explains your preference. Circle more than one if a single answer does not match your perception. Leave blank any question that does not apply.

1. You are helping someone who wants to go to your airport, town centre, or railway station. You would:
   V) draw, or give her a map.
   A) tell her the directions.
   R) write down the directions (without a map).
   K) go with her.

2. You are not sure whether a word should be spelled "dependent" or "dependant." You would:
   V) see the words in your mind and choose by the way they look.
   A) think about how each word sounds and choose one.
   R) find it in a dictionary.
   K) write both words on paper and choose one.

3. You are planning a holiday for a group. You want some feedback from them about the plan. You would:
   V) use a map or website to show them the places.
   A) phone, text, or e-mail them.
   R) give them a copy of the printed itinerary.
   K) describe some of the highlights.

4. You are going to cook something as a special treat for your family. You would:
   V) look through the cookbook for ideas from the pictures.
   A) ask friends for suggestions.
   R) use a cookbook where you know there is a good recipe.
   K) cook something you know without the need for instructions.

5. A group of tourists wants to learn about the parks and wildlife reserves in your area. You would:
   V) show them internet pictures, photographs, or picture books.
   A) talk about, or arrange a talk for them to learn about parks or wildlife reserves.
   R) give them a book or pamphlets about the parks or wildlife reserves.
   K) take them to a park or wildlife reserve and walk with them.

6. You are about to purchase a digital camera or mobile phone. Other than price, what would most influence your decision?
   V) It is a modern design and looks good.
   A) The salesperson telling me about its features.
   R) Reading the details about its features.
   K) Trying or testing it.

7. Remember a time when you learned how to do something new. Try to avoid choosing a physical skill, e.g., riding a bike. You learned best by:
   V) diagrams and charts—visual clues.
   A) listening to somebody explaining it and asking questions.
   R) written instructions—e.g., a manual or textbook

K) watching a demonstration.

8. You have a problem with your knee. You would prefer that the doctor:
   V) showed you a diagram of what was wrong.
   A) described what was wrong.
   R) gave you a web address or something to read about it.
   K) used a plastic model of a knee to show what was wrong.

9. You want to learn a new program, skill, or game on a computer. You would:
   V) follow the diagrams in the book that came with it.
   A) talk with people who know about the program.
   R) read the written instructions that came with the program.
   K) use the controls or keyboard.

10. I like websites that have:
    V) interesting design and visual features.
    A) audio channels where I can hear music, radio programs, or interviews.
    R) interesting written descriptions, lists, and explanations.
    K) things I can click on, shift, or try.

11. Other than price, what would most influence your decision to buy a new, non-fiction book?
    V) The way it looks is appealing.
    A) A friend talks about it and recommends it.
    R) Quickly reading parts of it.
    K) It has real-life stories, experiences, and examples.

12. You are using a book, CD, or website to learn how to take photos with your new digital camera. You would like to have:
    V) diagrams showing the camera and what each part does.
    A) a chance to ask questions and talk about the camera and its features.
    R) clear written instructions with lists and bullet points about what to do.
    K) many examples of good and poor photos and how to improve them.

13. Do you prefer an instructor who likes to use
    V) diagrams, charts, or graphs?
    A) question and answer, talk, group discussions, or guest speakers?
    R) handouts, books, or readings?
    K) demonstrations, models, or practical sessions?

14. You have finished a competition or test and would like some feedback. You would like to have feedback:
    V) using graphs showing you what you had achieved.
    A) from somebody who talks it through with you.
    R) using a written description of your results.

K) using examples from what you have done.

15. You are going to choose food at a restaurant or cafe. You would:
   V) look at what others are eating or look at pictures of each dish.
   A) listen to the waiter or ask friends to recommend choices.
   R) choose from descriptions on the menu.
   K) choose something that you have had there before.

16. You have to make an important speech at a conference or special occasion. You would:
   V) make diagrams or get graphs to help explain things.
   A) write a few key words and practise saying your speech over and over.

R) write your speech and learn from reading it over several times.

K) gather many examples and stories to make the talk real and practical.

Count your choices: ☐   ☐   ☐   ☐
                  V   A   R   K

Determine whether your learning style is primarily visual (V), aural (A), reading/writing (R), or kinesthetic (K). You may have more than one learning style preference—many people do. This is known as a multimodal (MM) style. Look at the learning styles chart on the next page to determine what will help you learn the best.

Learning Styles Chart

 ## Visual

WHAT TO DO IN CLASS	WHAT TO DO WHEN STUDYING	TEXT FEATURES THAT MAY HELP YOU	WHAT TO DO PRIOR TO EXAMS
• Pay close attention to charts, drawings, and handouts your instructor uses. • Underline and highlight. • Use different colours. • Use symbols, flow charts, graphs, different arrangements on the page, white space.	• Convert your lecture notes into "page pictures." To do this: • Use the "What to do in class" strategies. • Reconstruct images in different ways. • Redraw pages from memory. • Replace words with symbols and initials. • Look at your pages.	• The Navigator • Feature Story • Preview • Infographics/Illustrations • Photos • Accounting in Action • Accounting Equation Analyses in margins • Key Terms in blue • Words in bold or italics • Demonstration Problem/Action Plan • Questions/Exercises/Problems • Financial Reporting and Analysis	• Recall your "page pictures." • Draw diagrams where appropriate. • Practise turning your visuals back into words.

Aural

WHAT TO DO IN CLASS	WHAT TO DO WHEN STUDYING	TEXT FEATURES THAT MAY HELP YOU	WHAT TO DO PRIOR TO EXAMS
• Attend lectures and tutorials. • Discuss topics with students and instructors. • Explain new ideas to other people. • Use a tape recorder. • Leave spaces in your lecture notes for later recall. • Describe overheads, pictures, and visuals to somebody who was not in class.	You may take poor notes because you prefer to listen. Therefore: • Expand your notes by talking with others and with information from your textbook. • Tape record summarized notes and listen. • Read summarized notes out loud. • Explain your notes to another "aural" person.	• Preview • Infographics/Illustrations • Accounting in Action • Review It/Do It/Action Plan • Summary of Study Objectives • Glossary • Demonstration Problem/Action Plan • Self-Study Questions • Questions/Exercises/Problems • Financial Reporting and Analysis • Critical Thinking, particularly the Collaborative Learning Activities	• Talk with the instructor. • Spend time in quiet places recalling the ideas. • Practise writing answers to old exam questions. • Say your answers out loud.

Reading/Writing

WHAT TO DO IN CLASS	WHAT TO DO WHEN STUDYING	TEXT FEATURES THAT MAY HELP YOU	WHAT TO DO PRIOR TO EXAMS
• Use lists and headings. • Use dictionaries, glossaries, and definitions. • Read handouts, textbooks, and supplemental library readings. • Use lecture notes.	• Write out words again and again. • Reread notes silently. • Rewrite ideas and principles into other words. • Turn charts, diagrams, and other illustrations into statements.	• The Navigator • Feature Story • Study Objectives • Preview • Accounting Equation Analysis in margins • Review It/Do It/Action Plan • Summary of Study Objectives • Glossary • Self-Study Questions • Questions/Exercises/Problems • Writing Problems • Financial Reporting and Analysis • Critical Thinking	• Write exam answers. • Practise with multiple choice questions. • Write paragraphs, beginnings and endings. • Write your lists in outline form. • Arrange your words into hierarchies and points.

Kinesthetic

WHAT TO DO IN CLASS	WHAT TO DO WHEN STUDYING	TEXT FEATURES THAT MAY HELP YOU	WHAT TO DO PRIOR TO EXAMS
• Use all your senses. • Go to labs, take field trips. • Listen to real-life examples. • Pay attention to applications. • Use hands-on approaches. • Use trial-and-error methods.	You may take poor notes because topics do not seem concrete or relevant. Therefore: • Put examples in your summaries. • Use case studies and applications to help with principles and abstract concepts. • Talk about your notes with another "kinesthetic" person. • Use pictures and photographs that illustrate an idea.	• The Navigator • Feature Story • Preview • Infographics/Illustrations • Review It/Do It/Action Plan • Summary of Study Objectives • Demonstration Problem/Action Plan • Self-Study Questions • Questions/Exercises/Problems • Financial Reporting and Analysis • Critical Thinking, particularly the Collaborative Learning Activities	• Write practice answers. • Role-play the exam situation

For all learning styles: Be sure to use the learning aids on the companion website to enhance your understanding of the concepts and procedures of the text. In particular, use the animated tutorials, study aids (including the searchable glossary, PowerPoint presentations, and problem-solving techniques), and practice tools (including additional demonstration problems, key term matching activities, self-assessment quizzes, and working with annual reports).

Special Student Supplements To Help You Get The Best Grade You Can

The Accounting Principles Resource Website

This site serves as a launching pad to numerous activities and resources for all students. You will find a series of study aids and practice tools: animated tutorials to help with key accounting concepts; interactive quizzes, an on-line glossary, and additional demonstration problems to help prepare for class and tests; and a comprehensive section on ethics in accounting. In addition, there are links to companies discussed in the text, downloadable resources such as a checklist of key figures and PowerPoint presentations, and much more.

www.wiley.com/canada/weygandt

WileyPLUS

Your instructor may be using *WileyPLUS*, an online suite of resources that includes a complete multi-media version of the text that will help you come to class better prepared for lectures, and allows you to track your progress throughout the course more easily. If so, you have access to a complete e-book with links to tools such as self-assessment quizzes and animated tutorials to help you study more efficiently. *WileyPLUS* is designed to provide instant feedback as you practise on your own. You can work through assignments with automatic grading or review custom-made class presentations featuring reading assignments, PowerPoint slides, and interactive simulations.

Student Study Guide

The Student Study Guide is a comprehensive review of accounting and a powerful tool for student use. Each chapter includes a preview of the chapter, study objectives, and a summary of key points in the chapter. A demonstration problem is included, in addition to other opportunities for you to practise your knowledge and skills through multiple-choice, matching questions related to key terms, and exercises linked to study objectives. Solutions to these questions, exercises, and problems explain the hows and whys so you get immediate feedback.

Working Papers

Working Papers are partially completed accounting forms for the end-of-chapter brief exercises, exercises, and problems. Journals, ledgers, T accounts, and other required working papers have been predetermined and included for each textbook assignment, so that you can redirect limited time to important accounting concepts rather than formatting.

City Cycle Practice Set

This practice set exposes you to a real-world simulation of maintaining a complete set of accounting records for a business. Business papers add a realistic dimension by enabling you to handle documents, cheques, invoices, and receipts that you would encounter in a small proprietorship. This practice set reinforces key concepts from Chapters 1 through 4 and allows you to apply the information you have learned. It is an excellent way to see how these concepts are all brought together to generate the accounting information that is essential in assessing the financial position and operating results of a company.

To The Instructor

In the previous editions of *Accounting Principles*, we sought to create a book about accounting that made the subject clear and fascinating to students. And that is still our passion: to empower students to succeed by giving them the tools and the motivation they need to excel in their accounting courses and their future careers.

Preparing for the Fourth Canadian Edition

This revision of *Accounting Principles* provided us with an opportunity to improve a textbook that had already set high standards for quality. As mentioned, our goal has always been to empower students. In order to do that, we set out to empower instructors. To acquire the understanding needed to do this, we invited instructors from across the country to join us in a discussion, not about the existing book and its accompanying resources, but about how they teach, how they would like to teach, and what materials they wanted to be able to access in order to facilitate the process. This fresh approach allowed us to see our accounting principles package in a whole new way, to build on its strengths and introduce new tools to empower all instructors, no matter their amount of teaching experience, to bring accounting to life for their students. We are really excited about the resources and new features that have been created as a result of this vision – Accounting Across the Organization, new Collaborative Learning Activities, our new Instructor Resource Site, and more.

Pedagogical Effectiveness

Our Navigator learning system continues to empower students to succeed by teaching them how to study, what to study, and why they should study. The fourth edition places increased emphasis, throughout the text, on the processes students go through as they learn.

Our Learning Styles model, incorporated in previous editions, is incorporated throughout the text to enable students with different learning approaches to help them better understand the material. We are also cognizant of the increasing diversity found within today's classrooms. The text material has been thoroughly reviewed by an instructor of English as a Second Language to ensure that Accounting Principles offers students an unprecedented level of clarity and readability.

Study objectives were combined or reorganized to facilitate learning, and stepped-out pedagogy was used to break down complex topics, making the material more manageable for students. Bloom's Taxonomy, which underlies the structure of the textbook, continues to facilitate progressive learning by categorizing material in a building block fashion. More summaries were added throughout the chapter to help

students stop and digest the material they had just learned. Before You Go On feedback sections at the end of each major study objective and Demonstration Problems were augmented in number, coverage, and level of difficulty to facilitate student understanding.

We also added new, interactive learning aids to our website, including two new animated tutorials on topics students have difficulty with—bonds and cash flow. In total, we now have seven tutorials available online to increase student understanding of difficult topics.

Relevance for Users

We heard over and over from instructors how hard it is to motivate non-accounting students to learn accounting. In order to illustrate the importance of financial accounting to non-accounting majors, we started Chapter 1 with a section about why accounting is important to everyone, not just accountants. We emphasize this point over and over throughout the text and have added a new type of Accounting in Action insight box in this edition called Across the Organization. These clearly demonstrate how accounting is used to address issues in marketing, finance, management, and other functions.

This edition continues, and expands, the inclusion of user-oriented material to demonstrate the relevance of accounting to all students, no matter their area of study. Our focus company is again The Forzani Group—the largest sporting goods retailer in Canada. Forzani was chosen because it has high name recognition with students, operates in a single industry, and has relatively simple financial statements. References to Forzani have been included throughout the chapter, including Review It questions, ratio analysis, end-of-chapter assignments, and in Forzani's financial statements in Appendix A at the end of the textbook.

This edition was also subject to a comprehensive updating to ensure that it continues to be relevant and fresh. All real-world examples were updated, or replaced, in the text as appropriate, including the chapter-opening feature stories, the Accounting in Action insight boxes, and references to real-world examples in the text and end-of-chapter material. Our textbook includes references to 205 real-world companies. In addition, 39 percent of the chapter-opening feature stories were replaced with new stories, 75 percent of the Accounting in Action insight boxes are new, and all the Review It questions relating to Forzani are new, using information from Forzani's 2006 financial statements.

We also added questions in this edition to all of our Accounting in Action insight boxes—54 boxes in total—to help students understand the application of accounting to real-life situations. Suggested answers are provided at the end of each chapter.

We continue to feature problem material that allows students to tie the concepts they are learning together and place them in context. Central to this is the Continuing Cookie

Chronicle. This serial problem allows students to apply chapter topics in an ongoing scenario where a young entrepreneur builds her small business.

Helping Instructors Teach

As mentioned, we came away from our Workshop discussions, believing that the best route to empower students is to empower instructors. Consequently, we are introducing an all-new Instructors Resource Site. Here, you will find effective teaching strategies, sample course outlines, tips and techniques on using our all-new collaborative learning activities in class, games to use in class to help students learn, information on upcoming Workshops, and much, much more. The site is designed so it is easy to find the specific tool that will help you prepare your course. The preparation of the site has been a collaborative effort and we hope that collaboration will continue. Contributions are welcome as we envision the site as a place where instructors can meet, share ideas, and learn from each other.

Instructors told us they wanted us to increase the level of difficulty in the Test Bank and add more problem-type material. We therefore added nearly 200 new exercises in this edition of the Test Bank. Each item in the Test Bank is classified by study objective and by Bloom's Taxonomy.

The Study Guide and PowerPoint presentation material were also thoroughly updated and revised in response to user comments. An additional problem was added to each chapter of the Study Guide and the number of PowerPoint slides were reduced and made more user-friendly. In addition, a student reviewed this material from their own perspective to make sure that the answers contained sufficient explanation and that no ambiguities were present. Finally, the Solutions Manual was carefully prepared and triple checked for accuracy.

Expanded Topical Coverage

Additional topical coverage was requested by instructors to help them better prepare students for the complexities of today's world of accounting. These topics had to pass a strict test to warrant their inclusion: they were added only if they represented a major concept, issue, or procedure that a beginning student should understand. Some of the more significant additions include the following:

- Chapter 1: Accounting in Action was expanded to include information about the increasing importance of accounting to both accountants and non-accountants. A description of income trusts was added as a form of business organization and the discussion of partnerships was expanded to include both limited and unlimited liability partnerships.
- Chapter 2: The Recording Process includes an explanded explanation of "normal" account balances to better relate this topic to the accounting equation.

- Chapter 7: Internal Control and Cash sees the material on "principles of internal control" changed to "control activities" and an update to the descriptions of these activities. The material related to the banking system was updated and revised.
- Chapter 8: Accounting for Receivables now has expanded material on dishonouring notes receivable that includes an example of both a situation when collection is eventually expected and one when it is not. A new section on securitization of receivables was added.
- Chapter 9: Long-lived Assets was updated to include explanations and examples of impairment of long-lived assets.
- Chapter 10: Current Liabilities was expanded to include material on contingencies to include both contingent assets and contingent liabilities.
- Chapter 11: Accounting Principles was updated for the anticipated transition to international accounting standards. The discussion of the cost principle was expanded to include the movement away from historical cost to use market values in certain situations. In addition, material was added to reflect new revenue recognition guidance in Canada and elsewhere. The discussion about the complexity and importance of revenue recognition was enhanced and examples added to clarify the various points of revenue recognition.
- Chapter 13: Corporations: Organization and Share Capital was expanded to include a section on the different types of corporations, including income trusts. Comprehensive income and its effect on shareholders' equity were introduced in this chapter.
- Chapter 14: Corporations: Dividends, Retained Earnings and Income Reporting includes an expanded discussion of cash dividends, including their effect on share prices. This chapter also has more information on comprehensive income and now includes an illustration of the statement of comprehensive income.
- Chapter 15: Long-Term Liabilities features a new discussion of the impact of debt on return on equity, in addition to earnings per share. This chapter also has more detail about how to calculate the market value of bonds and a clarified discussion of bond discounts and premiums. An explanation of how notes differ, and are similar, to bonds was added and the presentation of the current and long-term portions of liabilities in the balance sheet was expanded.
- Chapter 16: Investments was substantially rewritten to incorporate new material on trading, available-for-sale, and held-to-maturity securities.
- Chapter 17: The Cash Flow Statement now includes a general discussion about how to analyze the cash flow statement, including the impact of cash flows on a company's life cycle.

Organizational Changes

Organizational changes were made to simplify chapters or to provide instructors with greater flexibility of coverage. Some of the areas most affected are as follows:

- Chapter 3: Adjusting the Accounts reorganized and expanded the material on the revenue recognition and matching principles. In addition, amortization, previously included as a separate adjusting entry category "estimates," is now included in the discussion of the adjusting entry category "prepayments."
- Chapter 4: Completion of the Accounting Cycle repositioned the material on using a worksheet from the beginning of the chapter to an optional step in the accounting cycle.
- Chapter 5: Accounting for Merchandising Operations now integrates material on discounts for early payment into the chapter material and Appendix 5A material on purchase and sale transactions as opposed to a separate appendix on the topic.
- Chapter 6: Inventory Costing now shows calculating ending inventory first, then determining the cost of goods sold by deducting ending inventory from cost of goods available for sale, as is more common in real life. The direct calculation of cost of goods sold is now used as a proof. In addition, the adjustment of inventory to its lower of cost and market was revised to be more consistent with the methods used in intermediate accounting textbooks. Recent changes in the application of lower of cost and market were also included.
- Chapter 7: Internal Control and Cash now includes material on debit cards and bank credit cards as part of the discussion of over-the-counter receipts. This material was previously included in Chapter 8: Accounting for Receivables.
- Chapter 8: Accounting for Receivables moved the material on non-bank credit card sales to first section of chapter on recognizing accounts receivable. Material on loans secured by receivables and sale of receivables moved to the end of the chapter and included in a new section on accelerating cash receipts from receivables.
- Chapter 9: Long-lived Assets reorganized material on revision of amortization and now illustrates the relationship between capital expenditures during useful life, impairments, changes in estimates and revisions of amortization.
- Chapter 13: Corporations: Organization and Share Capital now includes material on allocating dividends between preferred and common shares. This material was previously found in Chapter 14: Corporations: Dividends, Retained Earnings and Income Reporting.
- Chapter 16: Investments changed the recording of a premium or discount on long-term bonds to be consistent with the methods used in intermediate accounting textbooks.
- Chapter 17: The Cash Flow Statement now incorporates a discussion of the indirect and direct methods within the operating activities section. In addition, the discussion of, and formula for, free cash flow was modified.

Unparalleled End-of-Chapter Material

The fourth Canadian edition continues to have a complete range of end-of-chapter material to satisfy all courses. This material guides students through the basic levels of cognitive understanding—knowledge, comprehension, application, analysis, synthesis, and evaluation—in a step-by-step process, starting first with questions, followed by brief exercises, exercises, problems, and finally, integrative cases to broaden a student's perspective.

Instructors told us they wanted more breadth and depth within each of these groupings to give them more flexibility in assigning end-of-chapter material. Using Bloom's Taxonomy of Learning, all of the end-of-chapter material was carefully reviewed. Topical gaps were identified and additional material added as required to facilitate progressive learning. Complexities were added to the Before You Go On, Self-Study Questions, and selected end-of-chapter material to increase the range and difficulty level of material available to test critical problems solving skills.

In addition, the Continuing Cookie Chronicle, a serial problem following the life of a student-owned company in each chapter, was revised and updated to make it easier for instructors to assign this problem in selected chapters only.

Instructors also told us that they needed help in using the collaborative learning activities included in previous editions. All of the collaborative learning activities were completely rewritten to reflect true group activities and not just problems that could be done in groups. In addition, extensive instructor's material was prepared with tips on how to use these activities in class, including suggestions for changing the level of difficulty depending on the current class composition. We also included quizzes in many chapters that an instructor could use to assess the students at the end of the activity.

In total, we have 1,551 different end-of-chapter items for students to test their understanding of accounting. We have added 405 new questions, brief exercises, exercises, problems, and cases to the end-of-chapter material. That means that over 26% of the end-of-chapter material is new! The remaining material was substantially updated and revised, as required.

Acknowledgements

During the course of development of *Accounting Principles, Fourth Canadian Edition*, the authors benefited from the feedback from instructors and students of accounting principles courses throughout the country, including many users of the previous editions of this text. The constructive suggestions and innovative ideas helped focus this revision on motivating students to want to learn accounting. In addition, the input and advice of the ancillary authors, contributors, and proofreaders provided valuable feedback throughout the development of this edition.

"Ensuring Student Success in Principles of Accounting" Workshop Participants

These Workshops were set up to allow instructors to meet, discuss, and share ideas. They allowed us to better understand your challenges as you endeavour to bring accounting to life for your students. They also gave us a vision, not just for the text, but for the entire package. There are plans to hold more such Workshops in the future. We hope you will join the discussion.

Past participants include:

Carole Reid Clyne, *Centennial College*
Karen Congo, *University of Western Ontario*
Cynthia Duncan, *Seneca College*
Sholeh Hosseinzadeh, *triOS College*
Shiraz Kurji, *Mount Royal College*
Bonnie Martel, *Niagara College*
Gaye Maedher, *CDI College*
Debbie Musil, *Kwantlen University College*
Vanessa Oltmann, *Malaspina College*
Michel Paquet, *SAIT Polytechnic*
Joe Pidutti, *Durham College*
Regina Plateo, *Centennial College*
David Sale, *Kwantlen University College*
Pina Salvaggio, *Dawson College*
Marie Sinnott, *College of New Caledonia*
Nancy Tait, *Fleming College*
Barrie Tober, *Niagara College*
Julie Wong, *Dawson College*
Jerry Zdril, *Grant MacEwan College*

Contributors

The following people have contributed to the supplements, the accuracy, and the overall quality of our package:

Sally Anderson, *Mount Royal College*
Joan Barlow, *Mount Royal College*
Cynthia Brown, *Bow Valley College*
Carole Reid Clyne, *Centennial College*
Shelley Coyle
Judy Cumby, *Memorial University*
Cynthia Duncan, *Seneca College*
Ian Farmer
Joanne Hinton, *University of New Brunswick*
Cécile Laurin, *Algonquin College*
Betty Mitchell, *Mount Royal College*
Debbie Musil, *Kwantlen University College*
Stella Penner, *Mount Royal College*
Marie Sinnott, *College of New Caledonia*
John Shepherd, *College of New Caledonia*
Ron Thornbury, *Seneca College*
Lori Weatherbie, *Dalhousie University*
Julie Wong, *Dawson College*
Jerry Zdril, *Grant MacEwan College*

Through their editorial contributions, the following people added to the real-world flavour of the text and its clarity:

Alison Arnot
Zofia Laubitz
David Schwinghamer

Accuracy

We have made every effort to ensure that this text is error-free. Accounting Principles has been extensively reviewed and proofed at more than five different production stages prior to publication. In addition, the end-of-chapter material has been independently solved and then checked by at least three individuals, in addition to the authors, prior to publication of the text. We would like to express our sincere gratitude to everyone who spent countless hours ensuring the accuracy of this text and the solutions to the end-of-chapter material.

Publications

We would like to thank The Forzani Group Ltd., for allowing us to reproduce its 2006 financial statements in Appendix A. We would also like to acknowledge the co-operation of the many Canadian and international companies that allowed us to include extracts from their financial statements in the text and end-of-chapter material.

A Final Note of Thanks

We appreciate the exemplary support and professional commitment given to us by the talented team in the Wiley Canada higher education division. We wish to also thank Wiley's dedicated sales representatives who work tirelessly to service your needs.

It would not have been possible to write this text without the understanding of our employers, colleagues, students, family, and friends. Together, they provided a creative and supportive environment for our work.

Suggestions and comments from all users—instructors and students alike—of this textbook and its supplements are encouraged and appreciated.

Barbara Trenholm   Valerie Kinnear
trenholm@unb.ca   vkinnear@mtroyal.ca
Fredericton, New Brunswick   Calgary, Alberta

December 2006

Part One

Chapter 1 ▶ Accounting in Action
Chapter 2 ▶ The Recording Process
Chapter 3 ▶ Adjusting the Accounts
Chapter 4 ▶ Completion of the Accounting Cycle
Chapter 5 ▶ Accounting for Merchandising Operations
Chapter 6 ▶ Inventory Costing
Chapter 7 ▶ Internal Control and Cash
Appendix A: Specimen Financial Statements: The Forzani Group Ltd.
Appendix B: Sales Taxes
Appendix C: Subsidiary Ledgers and Special Journals

Part Two

Chapter 8 ▶ Accounting for Receivables
Chapter 9 ▶ Long-Lived Assets
Chapter 10 ▶ Current Liabilities
Appendix A: Specimen Financial Statements: The Forzani Group Ltd.
Appendix B: Sales Taxes
Appendix C: Subsidiary Ledgers and Special Journals

Part Three

Chapter 11 ▶ Accounting Principles
Chapter 12 ▶ Accounting for Partnerships
Chapter 13 ▶ Corporations: Organization and Share Capital Transactions
Chapter 14 ▶ Corporations: Dividends, Retained Earnings, and Income Reporting
Chapter 15 ▶ Long-Term Liabilities
Chapter 16 ▶ Investments
Chapter 17 ▶ The Cash Flow Statement
Chapter 18 ▶ Financial Statement Analysis
Appendix A: Specimen Financial Statements: The Forzani Group Ltd.

Part Four

Chapter 19 ▶ Managerial Accounting
Chapter 20 ▶ Cost-Volume-Profit Relationships
Chapter 21 ▶ Budgetary Planning
Chapter 22 ▶ Budgetary Control and Responsibility Accounting
Chapter 23 ▶ Incremental Analysis and Capital Budgeting

Chapter 1 ▶ Accounting in Action   1
    Making the Right Moves   1

Why Is Accounting Important?   2
    Ethics in Financial Reporting   3
    Who Uses Accounting Information?   4
    Accounting as an Information System   6

The Building Blocks of Accounting   7
    Generally Accepted Accounting Principles   7
    Forms of Business Organization   9
    Accounting Equation   11

Using the Building Blocks   15
    Transaction Analysis   16
    Financial Statements   21
    Using the Information in the Financial Statements   24

Chapter 2 ▶ The Recording Process   50
    Dancing to Her Own Business Tune   50

The Account   52
    Debits and Credits   52
    Expanding the Basic Accounting Equation   55

Steps in the Recording Process   56
    The Journal   58
    The Ledger   60
    The Recording Process Illustrated   64

The Trial Balance   70
    Limitations of a Trial Balance   70
    Locating Errors   71
    Some Simplistic Assumptions   71

Chapter 3 ▶ Adjusting the Accounts   102
    Fiscal Year Ends, but Classes Move On   102

Timing Issues   104
    Selecting an Accounting Time Period   104
    Revenue Recognition Principle   105
    Matching Principle (Expense Recognition)   105
    Accrual versus Cash Basis of Accounting   106

The Basics of Adjusting Entries   108
    Types of Adjusting Entries   109
    Adjusting Entries for Prepayments   109
    Adjusting Entries for Accruals   115
    Summary of Basic Relationships   120

**The Adjusted Trial Balance and Financial
Statements**   123
    Preparing the Adjusted Trial Balance   123
    Preparing Financial Statements   124
**Appendix 3A ▶ Alternative Treatment Of Prepaid
              Expenses And Unearned Revenues**   127

Chapter 4 ▶ Completion of the
             Accounting Cycle   162
    Breezing through the Month End with Style   162

Closing the Books   164
    Preparing Closing Entries   165
    Posting Closing Entries   168
    Preparing a Post-Closing Trial Balance   169

Summary of the Accounting Cycle   171
    Work Sheets—An Optional Step   172
    Reversing Entries—An Optional Step   173
    Correcting Entries—An Avoidable Step   173

Classified Balance Sheet   175
    Standard Balance Sheet Classifications   175
    Classified Balance Sheet Illustrated   180

**Using the Information in the Financial
Statements**   181
    Working Capital   182
    Current Ratio   182
Appendix 4A ▶ Work Sheets   183
Appendix 4B ▶ Reversing Entries   186

Chapter 5 ▶ Accounting for
             Merchandising Operations   218
    Minding the Books on Campus   218

Merchandising Operations   220
    Operating Cycles   221
    Inventory Systems   221

Recording Purchases of Merchandise   224
    Subsidiary Inventory Records   225
    Sales Taxes   226
    Freight Costs   226
    Purchase Returns and Allowances   227
    Discounts   227
    Summary of Purchase Transactions   228

Recording Sales of Merchandise   229
    Sales Taxes   230
    Freight Costs   230
    Sales Returns and Allowances   231
    Discounts   232
    Summary of Sales Transactions   232

Completing the Accounting Cycle   234
    Adjusting Entries   234
    Closing Entries   235
    Post-Closing Trial Balance   236
    Summary of Merchandising Entries   236

Merchandising Financial Statements   239
    Multiple-Step Income Statement   239
    Single-Step Income Statement   242
    Classified Balance Sheet   243

Using the Information in the Financial Statements 244
Gross Profit Margin 244
Profit Margin 245
Appendix 5A ▶ Periodic Inventory System 245

Chapter 6 ▶ Inventory Costing 282

Last In, First Out 282

Determining Inventory Quantities 284
Taking a Physical Inventory 284
Determining Ownership of Goods 285

Inventory Costing 287
Specific Identification 288
Cost Flow Assumptions 289

Financial Statement Effects 295
Choice of Cost Flow Assumption 295
Inventory Errors 298

Presentation and Analysis of Inventory 302
Valuing Inventory at the Lower of Cost and
  Market (LCM) 302
Classifying and Reporting Inventory 303
Analysis 304
**Appendix 6A ▶ Inventory Cost Flow Assumptions In
        A Perpetual Inventory System** 306
Appendix 6B ▶ Estimating Inventories 310

Chapter 7 ▶ Internal Control and Cash 340

Keeping Track of the Cash 340

Internal Control 342
Control Activities 343
Limitations of Internal Control 346

Cash Controls 348
Internal Control over Cash Receipts 348
Internal Control over Cash Disbursements 353

Use of a Bank 357
Bank Deposits and Cheques 358
Bank Statements 360
Reconciling the Bank Account 363

Reporting Cash 369
Using the Information in the Financial Statements 370

Appendix A: Specimen Financial
             Statements: The Forzani
             Group Ltd.   A1
Appendix B: Sales Taxes   B1
Appendix C: Subsidiary Ledgers and
             Special Journals   C1

concepts for review >>

Concepts for Review highlight concepts from your earlier reading that you need to understand before starting the new chapter.

the navigator ✔

Before studying this chapter, you should understand or, if necessary, review:

a. How to use the study aids in this book. (*Student Owner's Manual*, pp. VII–XVI)

b. What the Bloom's Taxonomy classifications mean (K, C, AP, AN, S, and E). (*Student Owner's Manual*, p. XVII)

c. How you learn best. (*Student Owner's Manual*, pp. XVIII–XX)

d. The student supplements that come with this text. (*Student Owner's Manual*, p. XXI)

Making the Right Moves

The **Feature Story** helps you see how the chapter topic fits with the real world of accounting and business. The story will be mentioned frequently throughout the chapter.

The Forzani Group: www.forzanigroup.com

CALGARY, Alta.—When it comes to football, everyone knows you need to "keep your eye on the ball" if you want to stay in the game. In business, as in sports, an organization needs to keep a careful eye on its financial accounting information if it wants to succeed and thrive. Consider the story of Calgary-based Forzani Group Ltd., Canada's "largest and only national sporting goods retailer."

The company kicked off in 1974 when Calgary Stampeder John Forzani and three of his teammates launched Forzani's Locker Room, a small retail operation that sold athletic footwear. Gradually, the business expanded to include clothing and sports equipment. In 1988, it launched RnR, its Relaxed and Rugged banner, specializing in leisure and recreational apparel.

Five years later, in 1993, the company went public and its shares began trading on the Toronto Stock Exchange. Expansion then continued with a series of acquisitions, including the recent purchases of National Sports in 2005 and The Fitness Source in 2006.

Today, The Forzani Group operates 464 corporate and franchise stores across Canada under the names Sport Chek, Sports Experts, Coast Mountain Sports, Sport Mart, Intersport, RnR, Econosports, Atmosphere, National Sports, The Fitness Source, Tech Shop, Pegasus, Hockey Experts, and Nevada Bob's Golf. It also retails online at www.sportmart.ca and provides a sporting goods information site at www.sportchek.ca. For its fiscal year ended January 29, 2006, the company scored sales of $1 billion and net income of $14 million.

Although profits have decreased in recent years, the numbers are still rather impressive for a company that started out as a single retail outlet! In fact, this spectacular growth is the result of countless decisions made all along the way. Does a particular acquisition make sense financially? Should the company operate its stores under separate banners? Is e-commerce worth pursuing? While many factors have no doubt contributed to The Forzani Group's success, one thing is certain: to make these strategic decisions and others, the company's management relied on accounting information.

They're not the only ones. Over the years, other parties have used The Forzani Group's financial information, too. Its shareholders and potential investors have used it to make investment decisions, and its creditors have analyzed it when deciding if they should issue loans or other forms of credit.

In short, sound accounting information lets The Forzani Group and all interested parties know exactly how the business is doing at all times—an essential part of any winning strategy!

the navigator ✔

The **Navigator** learning system encourages you to use the learning aids in the chapter and set priorities as you study.

the navigator

- Understand *Concepts for Review*
- Read *Feature Story*
- Scan *Study Objectives*
- Read *Chapter Preview*
- Read text and answer *Before You Go On*
- Work *Demonstration Problem*
- Review *Summary of Study Objectives*
- Answer *Self-Study Questions*
- Complete assignments

chapter 1

Accounting in Action

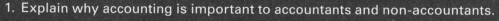

study objectives >>

Study Objectives show what you will be able to do after learning the specific concepts presented in the chapter.

the navigator

After studying this chapter, you should be able to:

1. Explain why accounting is important to accountants and non-accountants.
2. Explain generally accepted accounting principles and assumptions.
3. Use the accounting equation and explain the meaning of assets, liabilities, and owner's equity.
4. Analyze the effects of business transactions on the accounting equation.
5. Prepare financial statements.

The **Preview** outlines the major topics and subtopics you will see in the chapter.

The feature story about The Forzani Group highlights the importance of having good financial information to make good business decisions. This applies not just to companies but also to individuals. You cannot earn a living, spend money, buy on credit, make an investment, or pay taxes without receiving, using, or giving financial information. Good decision-making for companies and individuals depends on good information.

This chapter shows you that accounting is the system that produces useful financial information for decision-making. The chapter is organized as follows:

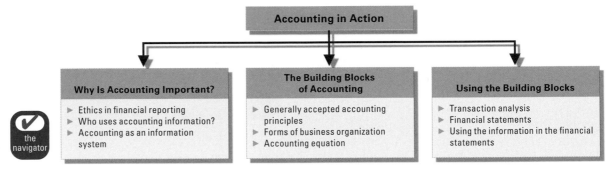

the navigator

Why Is Accounting Important?

study objective 1

Explain why accounting is important to accountants and non-accountants.

In the early 2000s, the world was shocked to learn about corporate reporting scandals in big companies like Nortel Networks and Hollinger International in Canada, Enron and WorldCom in the U.S., and Parmalat in Italy. Many schemes were uncovered that falsely increased earnings or hid a company's true financial position. As a result, there were financial restatements, company restructurings and closures, lawsuits, fines, and criminal convictions. People in general started to lose confidence in financial reporting.

One newspaper article stated that "repeated disclosures about questionable accounting practices has bruised investors' faith in the reliability of earnings reports, which in turn has sent stock prices tumbling." For example, in 2000, Nortel Networks shares traded at a high of $124.50. Over the next five years, there were stories of revenue and profit irregularities, senior executives were fired, nearly 50,000 employees were laid off, and Nortel's share price fell to a low of $3. Given the impact that this situation at Nortel Networks has had on the Canadian economy, it is obvious that our economic system depends a lot on highly transparent, reliable, and accurate financial reporting.

Because of the importance of the financial reporting system to the economy, regulators and lawmakers made a number of changes to help investors regain confidence in corporate reporting. Today, business behaviour in general, and accounting and auditing in particular, are guided by improved business practices, corporate governance, public oversight, and accountability requirements. Recent events like those at Nortel and elsewhere make it clear that it is worthwhile to study, understand, and use accounting information.

You might think this is all well and good for students who want to become accountants, but what about someone who has plans to be anything *but* an accountant?

Understanding the basics of accounting is helpful for almost every endeavour you can think of. By studying accounting, you will learn how the world of business—large and small—actually works. Whether you plan to own your own business in the future, work for someone else in their business, or invest in a business, learning how to read and interpret financial information will give you a valuable set of skills.

You will also learn a lot about management, finance, and marketing, which will give you a solid foundation for your future studies. For example, if you plan on studying marketing, you will learn how making a sale is meaningless unless it is a profitable sale and one that can eventually be collected from the customer. Marketing managers must also be able to decide pricing strategies based on costs. Accounting is what quantifies these costs and explains why a product or service costs what it does.

It doesn't matter if you plan to become a doctor, lawyer, social worker, teacher, engineer, architect, or entrepreneur—whatever you choose, a working knowledge of accounting will be relevant and useful. So think of this textbook as your introduction to accounting across the organization. Make the most of this course—it will serve you for a lifetime in ways you cannot now imagine.

On the companion website to this text, there is more information about why accounting is important and what potential career opportunities exist. In addition, there are profiles of business people who use accounting information.

> This **Web Icon** tells you about additional resources that expand on the topic being discussed.

Career Paths

Ethics in Financial Reporting

The standards of conduct that are used to judge a person's actions as right or wrong, honest or dishonest, fair or not fair are known as **ethics**. Accounting has long been called "the language of business." As we just learned from the corporate reporting scandals of the early 2000s, that language must be understandable, useful, and truthful if it is to have value. Today, more than ever before, effective financial reporting depends on sound ethical behaviour.

Fortunately, most individuals in business are ethical. Their actions are both legal and responsible. They consider the organization's interests when they make decisions. Accountants and other professionals have extensive rules of conduct to guide their behaviour with each other and the public. In addition, many companies today have codes of conduct that outline their commitment to ethical behaviour in their internal and external relationships.

> **Essential terms** are printed in blue when they first appear, and are defined in the end-of-chapter glossary.

To make you more aware of ethical situations and to give you practice at solving ethical dilemmas, we look at ethics in several ways in this book: (1) Many of the feature stories and other parts of the text discuss the great importance of ethical behaviour to financial reporting. (2) Accounting in Action insight boxes highlight ethics situations and issues in real business settings. (3) Notes in the margins give helpful hints that can make you more sensitive to ethics. (4) An Ethics Case in the end-of-chapter material simulates a business situation and asks you to put yourself in the position of a key decision-maker. (5) The companion website to this text includes a discussion of, and practice cases about, ethics and ethical issues that involve accounting and financial reporting.

Study Aids:
Ethics in Accounting

When you analyze these ethical situations, you should follow the steps outlined in Illustration 1-1.

Illustration 1-1 ▼

Steps used to analyze ethical dilemmas

1. Recognize an ethical situation and the ethical issues involved.	2. Identify and analyze the main elements in the situation.	3. Identify the alternatives, and weigh the impact of each alternative on various stakeholders.
Use your personal ethics or an organization's code of ethics to identify ethical situations and issues.	Identify the *stakeholders*—persons or groups who may be harmed or benefited. Ask the question: What are the responsibilities and obligations of the parties involved?	Select the most ethical alternative, considering all the consequences. Sometimes there will be one right answer. Other situations involve more than one possible solution. These situations require an evaluation of each alternative and the selection of the best one.

ACCOUNTING IN ACTION ▶ Ethics Insight

The recent scandals in corporate reporting have made people more and more skeptical about business ethics. Because the scandals have been frequent and have received a lot of attention, it is not surprising that the senior executives of most companies today say that they feel a lot of personal pressure to show strong ethical values in their behaviour. But are they doing so? It seems so, according to a recent global study. In this study of 365 companies in 30 countries, 90 percent of the companies specify in a formal statement of corporate values that ethical conduct is important to them. Further, these companies believe that the behaviour of management is critical for creating the appropriate "tone at the top." Chris Kelly, one of the authors of the study, explains: "Ethics-related language in formal statements not only sets corporate expectations for employee behaviour, companies are using it as a shield in an increasingly complex and global legal and regulatory environment."

Source: Chris Kelly, et al., *Deriving Value from Corporate Values*, The Aspen Institute and Booz, Allen, Hamilton Inc., 2005.

> **?** How can the "tone at the top" set by management make fraudulent financial reporting less common?

Who Uses Accounting Information?

The information that a user of financial information needs depends on the kinds of decisions that the user makes. These differences divide the users of financial information into two broad groups: internal users and external users.

Internal Users

Internal users of accounting information plan, organize, and run a business. This includes finance directors, marketing managers, human resources personnel, production supervisors, and company officers. In running a business, internal users must answer many important questions, as shown in Illustration 1-2.

Finance
Is there enough cash to pay the bills?

Marketing
What price should we sell MP3 Players for to maximize profits?

Human Resources
How many employees can we afford to hire this year?

Production
Which product line is the most profitable?

To answer these and other questions, users need detailed information on a timely basis—that is, it must be available when it is needed. Some examples of information that internal users need include forecasts of cash flows for the next year, projections of income from new sales campaigns, financial comparisons of operating alternatives, analyses of salary costs, and budgeted financial statements.

External Users

External users work for other organizations but have reasons to be interested in the company's financial position and performance. There are several types of external users of accounting information. Investors (owners) use accounting information to make decisions to buy, hold, or sell their ownership interest. Creditors, such as suppliers and bankers, use accounting information to evaluate the risks of granting credit or lending money. Investors and creditors are the main external users of accounting information, but there are also many other external users with a large variety of information needs and questions.

For example, labour unions want to know whether the owners can pay increased wages and benefits. Customers are interested in whether a company will continue to honour its product warranties and support its product lines. Taxing authorities, such as the Canada Revenue Agency, want to know whether the company respects the tax laws. Regulatory agencies, such as provincial securities commissions, want to know whether the company is respecting established rules. And economic planners use accounting information to forecast economic activity.

Questions that some external users may ask about a company are shown in Illustration 1-3.

Investors
Is the company earning enough to give me a return on my investment?

Creditors
Will the company be able to pay its debts as they come due?

Labour Unions
Can the company afford the pay raise we are asking for?

Customers
Will the company stay in business long enough to service the products I buy from it?

Illustration 1-3 ◄

Questions asked by external users

 ACCOUNTING IN ACTION ► Across the Organization Insight

Accounting can be a useful tool in employee management, team-building, and goal setting. The junk removal company 1-800-GOT-JUNK? has an open-book policy with its employees. The staff at its Vancouver head office, nicknamed the Junktion, meets once a month to go over the financial statements line by line. One staff member is accountable (responsible) for each line item, so everyone is looking for innovative ways to cut costs. This has resulted in one staffer taking the initiative to first do a cost analysis of office expenses and then look for a new supplier. Another staffer built relationships with a local caterer and coffee shop. The "team" also meets every day for a seven-minute "huddle," where they share good news, announcements, and any hurdles they are encountering. They track the progress of their goals through company-wide games posted on a wall. And, in return, the employees share in 25 percent of the profits each year.

? How is accounting useful for non-accountants?

Accounting as an Information System

Now that we understand why accounting is important to all these different internal and external users, we need understand what information accounting can give them. **Accounting** is an information system that identifies, records, and communicates the economic events of an organization to interested users. Economic events are activities related to the production and distribution of goods and services in an organization. Let's take a closer look at these activities:

1. **Identification.** Economic activities first have to be identified. This means deciding which events are evidence of economic activity by the particular organization. The sale of sporting goods by Forzani, the delivery of telephone services by Telus, and the payment of salaries by the Ottawa Senators hockey team are examples of economic events.

2. **Recording.** Once identified, economic events are recorded in order to provide a history of the organization's financial activities. Recording is done by keeping a systematic chronological diary of events and measuring them in dollars and cents. When they are recorded, economic events are also classified and summarized.

3. **Communication.** Identifying and recording activities is only useful if the information is then communicated to interested users. The information is therefore communicated in accounting reports, and the most common reports are the financial statements. To make the financial information meaningful, accountants also have to report the recorded data in a standardized way. Information from similar transactions is therefore accumulated and totalled, and kept separate from other transactions. When transactions are grouped together like this, they are being reported "in aggregate."

A vital part of communicating economic events is the accountant's ability and responsibility to analyze and interpret the reported information. In analysis, accountants use ratios, percentages, graphs, and charts to highlight significant financial trends and relationships. In interpretation, they explain the uses, meaning, and limitations of the reported data.

Appendix A of this textbook presents Forzani's financial statements in detail. You will see that The Forzani Group's transactions have been accumulated for the year ended January 29, 2006, and grouped together in categories. By presenting recorded data in aggregate, the accounting information system simplifies a large number of transactions. As a result, the company's activities are easier to understand and are more meaningful. This simplification does mean less detail, however. The Forzani Group's financial statements are highly condensed and some critics would argue that the statements are too simple. Still, Forzani is not the only organization that reports in this way. Most companies report condensed information for two reasons: it's simpler, and it also avoids revealing significant details to competitors.

We will ask you to look at Forzani's statements at different times throughout the text. At this point, they will probably look complex and confusing to you. By the end of this course, however, you'll be surprised at your ability to understand and interpret them.

Before You Go On questions at the end of major text sections are an opportunity to stop and re-examine the key points you have studied. *Related exercise material* tells you which Brief Exercises (BE) and Exercises (E) have similar study objectives.

BEFORE YOU GO ON . . .

▶Review It

1. Why is good accounting important?
2. How can the study of accounting benefit you?
3. Why are ethics important?
4. Who uses accounting information? Name some specific internal and external users of accounting information.
5. How is accounting an information system?

the navigator

Related exercise material: BE1–1, BE1–2, and E1–1.

The Building Blocks of Accounting

Every profession develops a body of theory based on principles and assumptions. Accounting is no exception. Just as a doctor follows certain standards to treat a patient's illness, an accountant follows certain standards to report financial information.

Generally Accepted Accounting Principles

The accounting profession has developed a set of standards that are generally accepted and universally practised. This common set of standards is called **generally accepted accounting principles (GAAP)**. These standards—which have evolved in response to tradition, experience, and user needs—recommend how to report economic events.

study objective 2

Explain generally accepted accounting principles and assumptions.

The Canadian Institute of Chartered Accountants (CICA)—through an Accounting Standards Board (AcSB)—has the main responsibility for developing generally accepted accounting principles in Canada. The AcSB's most important criterion for accounting principles is this: the principle should lead to external users having the most useful financial information possible when they are making business decisions. In other words, the basic objective of financial reporting is to communicate information that is useful to investors, creditors, and other users when they make decisions.

Alternative terminology
The words *standard* and *principle* mean the same thing in accounting.

To meet this objective, the AcSB creates generally accepted accounting principles after a long process of consultation with organizations and individuals that are interested in, or affected by, the principles. Its work is supervised by an independent Accounting Standards Oversight Council (AcSOC). On this council, there are representatives from business, finance, government, academe, the accounting and legal professions, and there are also regulators. The AcSOC protects the public's interests and makes sure that the AcSB also takes care of the needs of the entire business community.

Alternative Terminology notes give synonyms that you may hear or see in the workplace.

"Generally accepted" means that these principles have authoritative support through the Canadian and provincial business corporations acts and securities legislation. All companies whose shares or debt are publicly traded must follow GAAP, as published in the *CICA Handbook*. Most other companies also follow GAAP, as these principles result in the most useful information for decision-making.

It is important to understand that accounting principles are not static. They should and do change over time. Such changes ensure that their main purpose—providing information that is relevant to decision-making—continues to be met.

Internationally, accounting standards differ from country to country. One group, the International Accounting Standards Board, has been trying to reduce the differences in accounting practices by encouraging the use of one set of international standards. These are known as international financial reporting standards (IFRS). Canadian standard setters have recently decided that publicly traded companies must adopt IFRS by 2010. After that, Canadian generally accepted accounting principles will cease to exist as a separate basis of financial reporting for public companies. This will harmonize international standard setting and help investors, creditors, and others make more informed decisions about companies doing business in today's global environment.

ACCOUNTING IN ACTION ▶ International Insight

Publicly traded companies in Australia, Russia, and the European Union adopted international financial reporting standards in 2005 to harmonize their various accounting principles with one international standard. International financial reporting standards are now used as the main basis of financial reporting in more than 100 countries. China will join in 2007. Swiss pharmaceutical giant Roche, which operates in more than 150 countries, estimates that it will be able to save $100 million annually now that it can produce one set of financial statements rather than multiple sets with different accounting principles.

? How will the change to international accounting standards benefit the users of financial statements?

Cost Principle

We need to have a good understanding of generally accepted accounting principles in order to prepare and understand accounting information. Many generally accepted accounting principles will be introduced as you move forward through the text. In this chapter, we learn about the cost principle. In later chapters, we will introduce the revenue recognition principle (Chapter 3), the matching principle (Chapter 3), and the full disclosure principle (Chapter 11). Chapter 11 explores these principles in greater detail, as well as the underlying assumptions and constraints of accounting.

One of the most basic accounting principles is the **cost principle**. This principle states that assets should be recorded at their original historical cost. Cost is the value exchanged at the time something is acquired. For example, if the Gjoa Company purchased land for $100,000, the land's cost is $100,000—the amount Gjoa paid for it. But what would the company do if, by the end of the next year, the land had increased in market value to $120,000? Gjoa Company would continue to report the land at its historical cost of $100,000. At the time of acquisition, cost and market value are the same. In later periods, cost and market value vary, but the cost amount continues to be used for accounting.

Cost has an important advantage over other valuations. It is reliable. Cost is definite and verifiable. The values exchanged at the time something is acquired can be objectively measured. Users can therefore rely on the information that is supplied as they know it is based on fact. However, critics argue that cost is often not relevant. They believe market values provide more useful information.

Although there are some exceptions that we will learn about in later chapters, cost continues to be used to record most transactions because of its reliability.

Assumptions

When generally accepted accounting principles are developed, certain basic assumptions are made. These **assumptions** create a foundation for the accounting process. One assumption that underlies the cost principle is the **going concern assumption**. Two other important assumptions are the **monetary unit assumption** and the **economic entity assumption**.

Going Concern Assumption. A major factor in the decision to record a company's land at cost, rather than at market, is the **going concern assumption**. Going concern assumes the company will continue to operate in the foreseeable future. Although some businesses fail, companies generally do have a fairly high continuance rate. That is, they stay in business year after year.

Cost is the most appropriate value at which to record an asset such as the Gjoa Company's land because the land was acquired so that the business could use it, not so that it could be resold. For the company, what matters is the amount it gave up to acquire an asset such as land, not an estimate of the asset's current worth. The going concern assumption presumes that the company will operate long enough to use its assets for their intended purpose and to complete the company's commitments.

Monetary Unit Assumption. The **monetary unit assumption** requires that only transaction data that can be expressed as an amount of money be included in the accounting records. This assumption makes it possible for accounting to quantify (measure) economic events. In Canada, we use the dollar to record these transactions. In Europe, the euro (€) is used; in China, the yuan (CNY) is used; and so on.

This assumption does prevent some relevant information from being included in the accounting records. For example, the health of the owner, the quality of service, and the morale of employees would not be included, because they cannot be quantified in money amounts.

An important part of the monetary unit assumption is the added assumption that the unit of measure stays constant enough over time. In other words, inflation (a rise in prices) or deflation (a drop in prices) is ignored when adding, subtracting, or comparing dollars of different years. Assume a company purchases land in 1998 for $100,000 and that the same amount of land in a similar location costs $400,000 in 2008, 10 years later. If a second lot of land were purchased for $400,000 in 2008, the company would record a total cost of land of $500,000 ($100,000 + $400,000). The fact that these dollars had different values (or purchasing power) throughout the years is ignored. Although inflation can be a significant accounting issue in some countries, Canada's inflation policy—set out by the federal government and the Bank of Canada—is to keep inflation at between one and three percent. Consequently, inflation is considered a non-issue for accounting in Canada.

Economic Entity Assumption. An economic entity can be any organization or unit in society. It may be a company (such as Bombardier), a governmental unit (such as the Province of Alberta), a municipality (such as the Ville de Montréal), a native band council (such as the Kingsclear Indian Band), a school board (such as the Burnaby School Board), a curling championship event (such as the Tim Hortons Brier), or a club (such as the Calgary Rotary Club). The **economic entity assumption** requires the activities of the entity to be kept separate and distinct from the activities of its owner, and all other economic entities.

To illustrate, if Ellen Gélinas, owner of Ellen's Boutique, charges any of her personal living costs as expenses of the boutique, then the economic entity assumption is being violated. Similarly, the economic entity assumption assumes that the activities of Sport Chek and Sports Experts, both owned by Forzani, can be separated into two distinct economic entities for accounting purposes.

> **Helpful hints** help clarify concepts or items that are being discussed.

> **Helpful hint** Principles and assumptions will be discussed throughout the text. The ones discussed so far are highlighted in red:
>
> Principles
> **Cost**
> Revenue recognition
> Matching
> Full disclosure
>
> Assumptions
> **Going concern**
> **Monetary unit**
> **Economic entity**
> Time period

Forms of Business Organization

A business can be organized in different ways. The most common examples include a proprietorship, a partnership, and a corporation, which we will discuss here.

Proprietorship

A business owned by one person is a **proprietorship**. The owner is usually the operator of the business. Small service businesses (hair stylists, plumbers, and mechanics), farms, and small retail stores (antique shops, corner grocery stores, and bookstores) are often proprietorships.

Usually only a relatively small amount of money (capital) is needed to start in business as a proprietorship. The owner (the proprietor) receives any profits, suffers any losses, and is personally liable (responsible) for all debts of the business. There is no legal distinction between the business as an economic unit and the owner. However, the records of the business activities must be kept separate from the personal records and activities of the owner, as the economic entity assumption requires.

Many businesses in Canada are proprietorships, but they earn only a small percentage of the revenue earned by Canadian businesses as a whole.

Partnership

A business owned by two or more persons who are associated as partners is a **partnership**. In most aspects, a partnership is similar to a proprietorship, except that there is more than one owner. Partnerships are often used to organize service-type businesses, including professional practices (lawyers, doctors, architects, and accountants).

Typically, a partnership agreement (written or oral) defines the initial investments of each partner, the duties of each partner, how net income (or net loss) will be divided, and what the settlement will be if a partner dies or withdraws. As in a proprietorship, for accounting purposes the partnership activities must be kept separate from the personal activities of each partner.

Each partner generally has unlimited liability for all debts of the partnership, even if one of the other partners created the debt. This means that any of the partners can be forced to give up his or her personal assets in order to repay the partnership debt, just as can happen to an owner in a proprietorship. There are also situations where partnerships can be formed with limited liability for selected partners. We will learn more about these and other types of partnerships in Chapter 12.

Corporation

A business that is organized as a separate legal entity under federal or provincial corporation law is a **corporation**. Its ownership is divided into transferable shares. The owners of the shares (shareholders) enjoy limited liability as they risk losing only the amount that they have invested in the company's shares. They are not personally liable for the debts of the corporate entity. Shareholders may sell all or part of their shares to other investors at any time. Easy changes of ownership are part of what makes it attractive to invest in a corporation. Because ownership can be transferred without dissolving the corporation, the corporation enjoys an unlimited life.

Although there are many proprietorships and partnerships in Canada, the revenue produced by corporations is far greater. Most of the largest companies in Canada—for example, Bombardier, EnCana, Imperial Oil, Loblaw, and Magna—are corporations. Recently, more than 50 of Canada's largest corporations each reported annual revenues of more than $5 billion.

Corporations such as these are publicly traded. That is, their shares are listed on Canadian stock exchanges. More than $1.3 trillion has been invested by shareholders in the shares of the 500 largest corporations in Canada. **Public corporations** commonly distribute their financial statements to shareholders, creditors, other interested parties, and the general public upon request. Forzani is a public corporation. You can access its financial statements on its website, which is given in our feature story, as well as in Appendix A at the back of this textbook.

Other companies are **private corporations**, as they do not issue publicly traded shares. Some of the largest private companies in Canada include the Jim Pattison Group, the Irving Group, and McCain Foods. Like proprietorships and partnerships, these companies almost never distribute their financial statements publicly.

Income Trusts. A rapidly growing form of business organization in Canada is the income trust. An **income trust** is a special or limited purpose corporation that is set up specifically to invest in income-producing assets. The trust pays out most of its earnings to investors, who are called unitholders. As with proprietorships and partnerships, the trust itself does not pay any income tax. Instead, the unitholders pay income tax on the cash they receive. Accounting for income trusts is similar to accounting for corporations: the only significant difference is the accounting and reporting of equity.

Today, nearly one-quarter of the top 500 companies in Canada are income trusts. These include well-known companies such as A&W, Big Rock Brewery, the Brick Group, and Yellow Pages. Income trusts have grown rapidly over the last decade because of income tax advantages. Unitholders often pay a lower rate of income tax than the corporation would have to pay if it were not an income trust. The federal government is reviewing the tax rates of corporations in general and income trusts more specifically because it would prefer not to have so many income trusts being created for income tax reasons only. We will discuss the corporate form of organization, including income trusts, in Chapters 13 and 14.

BEFORE YOU GO ON . . .

▶Review It

1. What are generally accepted accounting principles? Give an example.
2. Explain the going concern, monetary unit, and economic entity assumptions.
3. What are the differences between a proprietorship, partnership, and corporation?
4. How is an income trust similar to, and different from, the other forms of business organization?

Related exercise material: BE1–3, BE1–4, and E1–2.

the navigator

Accounting Equation

The categories that are used for classifying economic events are also essential building blocks of accounting. The two basic elements of a business are what it owns and what it owes. Assets are the resources owned by a business. Forzani has total assets of $653 million at January 29, 2006. Liabilities and owner's equity are the rights or claims against these resources. The claims of those who are owed money or other obligations (the creditors) are called liabilities. The claims of owners are called owner's equity. Forzani has liabilities of $375 million and owner's equity of $278 million. Illustration 1-4 shows how the relationship between assets, liabilities, and owner's equity is expressed as an equation.

> **study objective 3**
>
> Use the accounting equation and explain the meaning of assets, liabilities, and owner's equity.

Assets	=	Liabilities	+	Owner's Equity
$653 million	=	$375 million	+	$278 million

Illustration 1-4 ◀

Accounting equation

This equation is called the **accounting equation**. Assets must equal the sum of liabilities and owner's equity. Because creditors' claims are paid before ownership claims if a business is liquidated, liabilities are shown before owner's equity in the accounting equation.

The accounting equation is the same for all economic entities regardless of their size, nature of business, or form of business organization. It applies to a small proprietorship such as a corner grocery store as much as it does to a large corporation such as The Forzani Group. This equation is the basis for recording and summarizing the economic events of a company.

Let's look at the categories in the accounting equation in more detail.

Assets

As noted earlier, **assets** are the resources owned by a business. They are used to carry out activities such as the production and distribution of merchandise. Every asset is capable of providing future services or benefits. In a company, that service potential or future economic benefit eventually results in cash inflows (receipts).

For example, imagine that a local pizza parlour, called Campus Pizza, owns a delivery truck. This truck provides economic benefits because it is used to deliver pizzas. Campus Pizza also owns other assets such as tables, chairs, a stereo system, a cash register, an oven, dishes, supplies, and, of course, cash. Other common examples of assets include merchandise inventory held for resale, investments, land, buildings, equipment, patents, and copyrights.

Liabilities

Liabilities are claims against assets. That is, liabilities are existing debts and obligations. For example, businesses of all sizes usually borrow money and purchase merchandise inventory and supplies on credit. Campus Pizza, for instance, purchases pizza ingredients and beverages on credit from suppliers. These obligations are called accounts payable. Campus Pizza also has a note payable to the Bank of Montreal for the money it borrowed to purchase its delivery truck. Campus Pizza may also have wages payable to employees, GST payable and PST payable to the federal and provincial governments, and property taxes payable to the municipality. All of these persons or entities that Campus Pizza owes money to are called its creditors.

A creditor who is not paid has the legal right to force the liquidation of a business. In that case, the law requires that creditor claims be paid before ownership claims are paid.

Owner's Equity

The ownership claim on total assets is known as **owner's equity**. It is equal to total assets minus total liabilities. Here is why: The assets are supplied or claimed by either creditors or owners. To find out what belongs to owners, we subtract creditors' claims (the liabilities) from assets. The remainder—owner's equity—is the owner's claim on the assets of the business. Since the claims of creditors must be paid before ownership claims, the owner's equity is often called residual equity. If the equity is negative—that is, if total liabilities are more than total assets—the term owner's deficiency (or deficit) describes the shortage.

In a proprietorship, owner's equity is increased by investments made by the owner and decreased by withdrawals made by the owner. However, the main purpose of most companies is to generate net income from business activities, and this also increases the owner's equity. Let's look at each of these equity components in more detail.

Investments. Investments by the owner are the assets the owner puts into the business in what is known as the owner's capital account. Investments may be in cash or other assets (e.g., a vehicle or computer) that are contributed by the owner. Accordingly, investments such as these result in an increase in an asset and an increase in owner's equity.

Drawings. An owner may withdraw cash (or other assets) for personal use. These withdrawals could be recorded as a direct decrease of owner's equity. However, it is generally considered better to use a separate account classification called **drawings** so that the total withdrawals for the accounting period can be determined. Drawings result in a decrease in an asset and a decrease in owner's equity.

Net Income. Revenues increase owner's equity, and expenses decrease owner's equity. **Net income** results when revenues are greater than expenses. Owner's equity then increases correspondingly. Conversely, if expenses are greater than revenues, a **net loss** results and owner's equity decreases.

Revenues. **Revenues** result from business activities that are done to earn income. Generally, revenues result from performing services, selling merchandise inventory, renting property, and lending money.

Revenues normally result in an increase in an asset (or a decrease in a liability which we will learn about in Chapter 3) and an increase in owner's equity. They come from different sources and are given different names, depending on the type of business. Campus Pizza, for instance, has two categories of revenues—pizza sales and beverage sales. Common sources of revenue include sales, fees, services, commissions, interest, and rent.

Expenses. **Expenses** are the costs of assets that are consumed and services that are used in order to earn revenue. Expenses normally result in a decrease in an asset (or an increase in a liability) and a decrease in owner's equity. Like revenues, there are many kinds of expenses and they are identified by various names, depending on the type of asset consumed or service used. For example, Campus Pizza recognizes (records) the following expenses: cost of ingredients (meat, flour, cheese, tomato paste, mushrooms, etc.), cost of beverages, wages expense, utility expense (electric, gas, and water expense), telephone expense, delivery expense (gasoline, repairs, licences, etc.), supplies expense (napkins, detergents, aprons, etc.), rent expense, insurance expense, and interest expense.

In summary, the principal sources (increases) of owner's equity are (1) investments by the owner, and (2) net income (revenues − expenses). Decreases in owner's equity result from (1) withdrawals of assets by the owner and (2) net losses. These relationships are shown in Illustration 1-5.

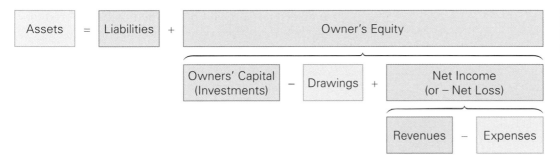

Illustration 1-5 ◄

Increases and decreases in owner's equity

Accounting Equation Distinctions by Type of Business Organization

Previously, you were introduced to different forms of business organizations—the proprietorship, partnership, and corporation. In the early chapters of this text, we focus mostly on proprietorships. Partnerships and corporations will be discussed in more detail in later chapters. Until that time, you need only a general understanding of the accounting distinctions between these types of organization. Accounting for assets, liabilities, revenues, and expenses is the same, regardless of the form of business organization. The main distinction between the forms of organizations is found in (1) the terminology that is used to name the equity section, and (2) the accounting and reporting of the owner's investments and withdrawals.

In a proprietorship, the company is owned by one person and the equity is termed owner's equity. In a partnership, because there are two or more owners, the equity is termed partners' equity. In the corporate form of business organization, the owners are the shareholders and the equity is called shareholders' equity. In Illustration 1-4, when the assets, liabilities, and equity were reported for The Forzani Group, the equity was identified as owner's equity to keep the illustration simpler. Technically, since Forzani is a corporation, this equity should have been called *shareholders'* equity. In an income trust, the owners are the unitholders and the equity is called unitholders' equity.

You have learned that, in a proprietorship, owner's equity is increased by owner's investments and net income, and decreased by owner's drawings (and a net loss, if there is one). In the same way, in a partnership, each partner's equity is increased by the investments of the partners and each partner's share of the partnership income, and decreased by the drawings of each partner (and share of a partnership loss, if there is one). In both proprietorships and partnerships, equity is summarized and reported for each owner in a one-line capital account.

It would not be practical to do such a summary of each owner's equity in a corporation, because there may be thousands of owners. A different method is therefore used. In a corporation, the investments by the owners (called shareholders) are made by purchasing shares. These investments are grouped together and called share capital, and they are the first portion of shareholders' equity. The second portion of shareholders' equity is reported as retained earnings. Retained earnings are the accumulated earnings of the company that have been retained (i.e., not paid out to shareholders). Distributions of these earnings to the shareholders are known as dividends. Dividends reduce retained earnings and ultimately shareholders' equity in the same way as drawings reduce owner's capital and ultimately owner's equity in a proprietorship or partnership.

You will recall that an income trust is a special form of corporation. We will also illustrate the equity section for an income trust here because it is slightly different from that of a general corporation. While the owners of a corporation are called shareholders and their investments are classified as share capital, the owners of an income trust are called unitholders and their investments are classified as trust unitholders' capital. Because a trust intends to also distribute any equity that it does not need for operations and, in fact, to distribute most of its earnings, the term "undistributed income" is used instead of "retained earnings" for income that the trust keeps.

Equity is reported for each different type of business organization as follows:

Proprietorship		Partnership		Corporation		Income Trust	
Owner's equity:		Partners' equity:		Shareholders' equity:		Unitholders' equity:	
V. Buré, capital	$50,000	M. Wu, capital	$ 75,000	Share capital	$500,000	Trust unitholders' capital	$500,000
		A. Scholten, capital	75,000	Retained earnings	350,000	Undistributed income	50,000
		Total partners' equity	$150,000	Total shareholders' equity	$850,000	Total unitholders' equity	$550,000

Sometimes **Review It** questions are alone; other times they are with practice exercises. The **Do It** exercises, like the one here, ask you to put your new knowledge to work. They also outline an Action Plan you need to follow to do the exercise.

BEFORE YOU GO ON . . .

▶ Review It

1. What is the accounting equation?
2. What are assets, liabilities, and owner's equity?
3. Identify some of the assets that you own personally and some of the liabilities that you owe.
4. What are the different types of equity reported by each form of business organization?

▶ Do It

Classify the following items as assets, liabilities, or owner's equity: (1) cash, (2) service revenue, (3) drawings, (4) accounts receivable, (5) accounts payable, and (6) salaries expense. For any items that affect owner's equity, please indicate whether these items increase or decrease equity.

Action Plan

- Understand that assets are resources owned by a business.
- Understand that liabilities are amounts owed by a business.
- Understand the items that affect owner's equity: Investments and revenues increase owner's equity. Drawings and expenses decrease owner's equity.

Solution

1. Cash is classified as an asset.
2. Service revenue is classified as revenue, which increases net income and ultimately owner's equity.
3. Drawings decrease owner's equity.
4. Accounts receivable are amounts that are due from customers, and are classified as an asset.
5. Accounts payable are amounts that are owed to creditors, and are classified as a liability.
6. Salaries expense is classified as an expense, which decreases net income and ultimately owner's equity.

Related exercise material: BE1–5, BE1–6, BE1–7, E1–3, E1–4, E1–5, and E1–6.

Using the Building Blocks

Transactions are the economic events of a business that are recorded. Transactions may be external or internal. External transactions are economic events between the company and some outside party. For example, the purchase of cooking equipment by Campus Pizza from a supplier, the payment of monthly rent to the landlord, and the sale of pizzas to customers are all external transactions. Internal transactions are economic events that occur entirely within one company. The use of cooking and cleaning supplies is an internal transaction for Campus Pizza.

A company may have many activities that are not by themselves business transactions. Hiring employees, answering the telephone, talking with customers, and placing an order for merchandise with a supplier are examples. Some of these activities, however, may lead to a business transaction. Employees will earn salaries, and merchandise will be delivered by the supplier. Each transaction must be analyzed for its effect on the components of the accounting equation. It must also be recorded in the accounting process. This analysis must identify the specific items that are affected and the amount of change in each item.

study objective 4

Analyze the effects of business transactions on the accounting equation.

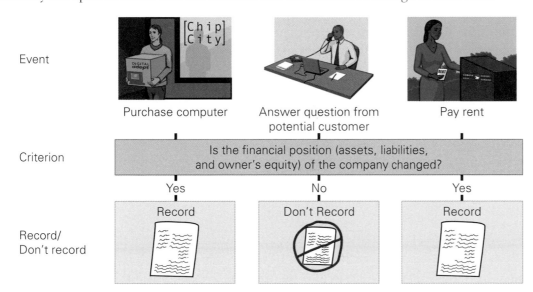

Illustration 1-6 ◀

Transaction identification process.

The two sides of the accounting equation must always be equal. Therefore, each transaction must have a dual effect on the equation. For example, if an asset is increased, there must be a corresponding

1. decrease in another asset, or
2. increase in a liability, or
3. increase in owner's equity.

Two or more items could be affected when an asset is increased. For example, as one asset is increased by $10,000, another asset could decrease by $6,000, and a liability could increase by $4,000. Any change in a liability or ownership claim also has to be analyzed like this.

Transaction Analysis

Animated Tutorials:
Accounting Cycle Tutorial

When a specific **account title** is used, the account name is capitalized.

As a general example, we will now look at transactions incurred by a computer programming business during its first month of operations. You should study these transactions until you are sure you understand them. They are not difficult, but they are important to your success in this course. Being able to analyze how transactions affect the accounting equation is essential for understanding accounting.

Transaction (1): Investment by Owner. Marc Doucet decides to open a computer programming business. On September 1, 2008, he invests $15,000 cash in the business, which he names Softbyte. This transaction results in an equal increase in assets and owner's equity. In this case, there is an increase in the asset account, Cash, $15,000, and an equal increase in the owner's equity account, M. Doucet, Capital, $15,000. The effect of this transaction on the basic equation is:

	Assets	=	Liabilities	+	Owner's Equity
					M. Doucet, Capital
	Cash	=			
(1)	+$15,000	=			+$15,000

Notice that the two sides of the basic equation remain equal. Note also that investments by an owner are not revenues. The increase therefore has to be recorded as an investment in the owner's capital account rather than as revenue from operations.

Transaction (2): Purchase of Equipment for Cash. Softbyte purchases computer equipment for $7,000 cash. This transaction results in an equal increase and decrease in total assets, though the composition of assets changes. Cash is decreased by $7,000, and the asset account Equipment is increased by $7,000. The specific effect of this transaction and the cumulative effect of the first two transactions are:

		Assets			=	Liabilities	+	Owner's Equity
								M. Doucet, Capital
	Balance	Cash	+	Equipment =				
(2)	Beginning	$15,000						$15,000
		−7,000		+$7,000				
	Ending	$ 8,000 +		$7,000	=			$15,000
			$15,000				$15,000	

Notice that total assets are still $15,000, and that Doucet's equity also remains at $15,000, the amount of his original investment.

Transaction (3): Purchase of Supplies on Credit. Softbyte purchases from the Chuah Supply Company $1,600 of computer paper and other supplies that are expected to last several months. Chuah Supply agrees to allow Softbyte to pay this bill next month (in October). This transaction is referred to as a purchase on account, or a credit purchase. Assets are increased because of the expected future benefits of using the paper and supplies. Liabilities are increased by the amount that is due to Chuah Supply Company. So, the asset Supplies is increased by $1,600, and the liability Accounts Payable is increased by the same amount. The effect on the equation is:

Balance	Assets			=	Liabilities +	Owner's Equity
	Cash +	Supplies +	Equipment =		Accounts Payable +	M. Doucet, Capital
(3) Beginning	$8,000		$7,000			$15,000
		+$1,600			+$1,600	
Ending	$8,000 +	$1,600 +	$7,000	=	$1,600 +	$15,000
		$16,600				$16,600

Total assets are now $16,600. This total is matched by a $1,600 creditor's claim and a $15,000 ownership claim.

Transaction (4): Services Provided for Cash.
Softbyte receives $1,200 cash from customers for programming services it has provided. This transaction is Softbyte's main revenue-producing activity. Remember that revenue increases net income, which then increases owner's equity. Cash is increased by $1,200, and Service Revenue is increased by $1,200. We don't have room to give details for each individual revenue and expense account in this illustration, so revenues (and expenses when we get to them) will be summarized under one column heading for Revenues and one for Expenses. However, it is important to keep track of the account titles that are affected (e.g., Service Revenue), as they will be needed when financial statements are prepared in the next section. The new balances in the equation are:

Balance	Assets			=	Liabilities +	Owner's Equity	
	Cash +	Supplies +	Equipment =		Accounts Payable +	M. Doucet, Capital +	Revenues
(4) Beginning	$8,000	$1,600	$7,000		$1,600	$15,000	
	+1,200						+$1,200
Ending	$9,200 +	$1,600 +	$7,000	=	$1,600 +	$15,000 +	$1,200
		$17,800				$17,800	

The two sides of the equation balance at $17,800.

Transaction (5): Purchase of Advertising on Credit.
Softbyte receives a bill for $250 from the local newspaper for advertising the opening of its business. It postpones payment of the bill until a later date. This transaction results in an increase in liabilities, through the Accounts Payable account, and a decrease in owner's equity, through the Advertising Expense account. The cost of advertising is an expense, and not an asset, because the benefits have already been used.

Note that owner's equity decreases because an expense is incurred, which in turn reduces net income and owner's equity. Here is the effect on the accounting equation:

Balance	Assets			=	Liabilities +	Owner's Equity		
	Cash +	Supplies +	Equipment =		Accounts Payable +	M. Doucet, Capital +	Revenues −	Expenses
(5) Beginning	$9,200	$1,600	$7,000		$1,600	$15,000	$1,200	
					+$250			−$250
Ending	$9,200 +	$1,600 +	$7,000	=	$1,850 +	$15,000 +	$1,200 −	$250
		$17,800				$17,800		

The two sides of the equation still balance at $17,800.

Expenses do not have to be paid in cash at the time they are incurred. When payment is then made on the later date, the liability Accounts Payable will be decreased and the asset Cash will also be decreased [see transaction (8)].

Transaction (6): Services Provided for Cash and Credit. Softbyte provides $3,500 of programming services for customers. Cash of $1,500 is received from customers, and the balance of $2,000 is billed to customers on account. This transaction results in an equal increase in assets and owner's equity. Three specific items are affected: Cash is increased by $1,500; Accounts Receivable is increased by $2,000; and Service Revenue is increased by $3,500. The new balances are as follows:

			Assets			= Liabilities +		Owner's Equity		
Balance	Cash	+ Accounts Receivable	+ Supplies	+ Equipment =		Accounts Payable	+ M. Doucet, Capital	+ Revenues	– Expenses
(6) Beginning	$ 9,200		$1,600	$7,000		+$1,850	$15,000	$1,200	$250
	+1,500	+$2,000						+3,500	
Ending	$10,700 +	$2,000	+ $1,600 +	$7,000	=	+$1,850 +	$15,000	+ $4,700	– $250
			$21,300					$21,300	

You might wonder why owner's equity is increased by $3,500 when only $1,500 has been collected. The reason is that the assets from earning revenues do not have to be in cash. Owner's equity is increased when revenues are earned. In Softbyte's case, revenues are earned when the service is provided. When collections on account are received at a later date, Cash will be increased and Accounts Receivable will be decreased [see transaction (9)].

Transaction (7): Payment of Expenses. The expenses paid in cash for September are store rent, $600; salaries of employees, $900; and utilities, $200. These payments result in an equal decrease in assets and owner's equity. Cash is decreased by $1,700 in total ($600 + $900 + $200) and expense accounts are increased by the same amount, which then decreases owner's equity. Here is the effect of these payments on the equation:

			Assets			= Liabilities +		Owner's Equity		
Balance	Cash	+ Accounts Receivable	+ Supplies	+ Equipment =		Accounts Payable	+ M. Doucet, Capital	+ Revenues	– Expenses
(7) Beginning	$10,700	$2,000	$1,600	$7,000		$1,850	$15,000	$4,700	$ 250
	−600								−600
	−900								−900
	−200								−200
Ending	$ 9,000 +	$2,000	+ $1,600 +	$7,000	=	$1,850 +	$15,000	+ $4,700	– $1,950
			$19,600					$19,600	

The two sides of the equation now balance at $19,600. Three lines are now needed in the analysis in order to show the different types of expenses that have been paid.

Transaction (8): Payment of Accounts Payable. Softbyte pays its $250 advertising bill in cash. Remember that the bill was previously recorded in transaction (5) as an increase in Accounts Payable and a decrease in owner's equity. This payment on account decreases the asset Cash by $250 and also decreases the liability Accounts Payable. The effect of this transaction on the equation is:

		Assets			= Liabilities +		Owner's Equity		
			Accounts			Accounts	M. Doucet,		
Balance	Cash	+ Receivable	+ Supplies	+ Equipment =	Payable	+ Capital	+ Revenues	− Expenses
(8) Beginning	$9,000	$2,000	$1,600	$7,000	$1,850	$15,000	$4,700	$1,950
	−250				−250			
Ending	$8,750 +	$2,000	+ $1,600 +	$7,000 =	$1,600 +	$15,000	+ $4,700	− $1,950
		$19,350				$19,350		

Notice that the payment of a liability for an expense that has previously been recorded does not affect owner's equity. This expense was recorded in transaction (5) and should not be recorded again.

Transaction (9): Receipt of Cash on Account. The sum of $600 in cash is received from some customers who were billed for services in transaction (6). This transaction does not change total assets, but it does change the composition of those assets. Cash is increased by $600, and Accounts Receivable is decreased by $600. The new balances are:

		Assets			= Liabilities +		Owner's Equity		
			Accounts			Accounts	M. Doucet,		
Balance	Cash	+ Receivable	+ Supplies	+ Equipment =	Payable	+ Capital	+ Revenues	− Expenses
(9) Beginning	$8,750	$2,000	$1,600	$7,000	$1,600	$15,000	$4,700	$1,950
	+600	−600						
Ending	$9,350 +	$1,400	+ $1,600 +	$7,000 =	$1,600 +	$15,000	+ $4,700	− $1,950
		$19,350				$19,350		

Note that a collection on account for services that were billed and recorded earlier does not affect owner's equity. Revenue was already recorded in transaction (6) and must not be recorded again.

Transaction (10): Withdrawal of Cash by Owner. Marc Doucet withdraws $1,300 in cash from the business for his personal use. This transaction results in an equal decrease in assets and owner's equity. The asset Cash is decreased by $1,300, and Drawings is increased by $1,300, which then decreases owner's equity, as follows:

		Assets			= Liabilities +			Owner's Equity		
			Accounts			Accounts	M. Doucet,	M. Doucet,		
Balance	Cash	+ Receivable	+ Supplies	+ Equipment =	Payable	+ Capital	− Drawings	+ Revenues	− Expenses
(10) Beginning	$9,350	$1,400	$1,600	$7,000	$1,600	$15,000		$4,700	$1,950
	−1,300						−$1,300		
Ending	$8,050 +	$1,400	+ $1,600 +	$7,000 =	$1,600 +	$15,000	− $1,300	+ $4,700	− $1,950
		$18,050				$18,050			

Note that both drawings and expenses reduce owner's equity, as shown in the accounting equation above. However, an owner's drawings are not expenses. Expenses are incurred for the purpose of earning revenue. Drawings do not generate revenue. They are a *disinvestment*; that is, the effect of an owner's cash withdrawal is the opposite of the effect of an owner's investment. Like owner's investments, drawings are not included when net income is determined.

Summary of Transactions

Illustration 1-7 ▼

Tabular summary of Softbyte transactions

Softbyte's transactions are summarized in Illustration 1-7 to show their cumulative effect on the accounting equation. The transaction number and the specific effects of each transaction are indicated.

	Cash	+ Accounts Receivable	+ Supplies	+ Equipment	= Accounts Payable	+ M. Doucet, Capital	– M. Doucet, Drawings	+ Revenues	– Expenses
(1)	+$15,000					+$15,000			
(2)	−7,000			+$7,000					
(3)			+$1,600		+$1,600				
(4)	+1,200							+$1,200	
(5)					+250				−$ 250
(6)	+1,500	+$2,000						+3,500	
(7)	−600								−600
	−900								−900
	−200								−200
(8)	−250				−250				
(9)	+600	−600							
(10)	−1,300						−$1,300		
	$ 8,050 +	$1,400 +	$1,600 +	$7,000 =	$1,600 +	$15,000 –	$1,300 +	$4,700 –	$1,950

Assets = Liabilities + Owner's Equity

$18,050 = $18,050

The illustration demonstrates some significant facts:

1. Each transaction must be analyzed for its effects on:
   (a) the three components (assets, liabilities, and owner's equity) of the accounting equation, and
   (b) specific items within each component.
2. The two sides of the equation must always be equal.

There! You made it through transaction analysis. If you feel a bit shaky on any of the transactions, it might be a good idea to get up, take a short break, and come back again to review the transactions. Make sure you understand them before moving on to the next section.

BEFORE YOU GO ON . . .

▶Review It

1. Give an example of an external transaction. Give an example of an internal transaction.
2. If an asset increases, what are the three possible effects on the accounting equation? What are the possible effects if a liability increases?

▶Do It

Transactions for the month of August by Virmari & Co., a public accounting firm, are shown below. Prepare a tabular analysis (i.e., make a table) which shows the effects of these transactions on the accounting equation, like what is shown in Illustration 1-7.

1. The owner invested $25,000 of cash in the business.
2. Office equipment was purchased on credit, $7,000.
3. Services were performed for customers for $8,000. Of this amount, $2,000 was received in cash and $6,000 is due on account.
4. Rent of $850 was paid for the month.
5. Customers on account paid $4,000 (see transaction 3).
6. The owner withdrew $1,000 of cash for personal use.

Action Plan

- Analyze the effects of each transaction on the accounting equation.
- Use appropriate account names for the account titles (not descriptions).
- Keep the accounting equation in balance.

Solution

	Assets			= Liabilities +		Owner's Equity			
		Accounts	Office	Accounts	A. Virmari,	A. Virmari,			
	Cash	+ Receivable	+ Equipment =	Payable	+ Capital	– Drawings	+ Revenues	– Expenses
1.	+$25,000				+$25,000			
2.			+$7,000	+$7,000				
3.	+2,000	+$6,000					+$8,000	
4.	–850							–$850
5.	+4,000	–4,000						
6.	–1,000					–$1,000		
	$29,150 +	$2,000 +	$7,000 =	$7,000 +	$25,000 –	$1,000 +	$8,000 –	$850

$38,150 $38,150

Related exercise material: BE1–8, BE1–9, E1–7, E1–8, E1–9, and E1–10.

the navigator

Financial Statements

After transactions are identified, recorded, and summarized, four financial statements are prepared from the summarized accounting data:

1. **Income statement.** An **income statement** presents the revenues and expenses, and the resulting net income or net loss for a specific period of time.
2. **Statement of owner's equity.** A **statement of owner's equity** summarizes the changes in owner's equity for a specific period of time.
3. **Balance sheet.** A **balance sheet** reports the assets, liabilities, and owner's equity at a specific date.
4. **Cash flow statement.** A **cash flow statement** summarizes information about the cash inflows (receipts) and outflows (payments) for a specific period of time.

Helpful hint The income statement, statement of owner's equity, and cash flow statement are all for a period of time. The balance sheet is at a point in time.

Each statement gives management, owners, and other interested parties relevant financial data.

The financial statements of Softbyte and how they relate to each other are shown in Illustration 1-8 on the following page. You will see that the statements are interrelated: (1) Net income of $2,750 shown on the income statement is added to the beginning balance of owner's capital in the statement of owner's equity. (2) Owner's capital of $16,450 at the end of the reporting period in the statement of owner's equity is also reported on the balance sheet. (3) Cash of $8,050 on the balance sheet is also reported on the cash flow statement.

To keep it simple, we did not include cents in the dollar amounts we recorded in the Softbyte example summarized in Illustration 1-7. In reality, it is important to understand that cents should be, and are, used when transactions are recorded in a company's internal accounting records. The situation is different for financial reporting purposes, however. Financial statement amounts are normally rounded to the nearest dollar, thousand dollars, or million dollars, depending on the size of the company. As mentioned earlier in the chapter, external reporting condenses and simplifies information so that it is easier for the reader to understand.

The essential features of Softbyte's four financial statements are briefly described in the following sections.

Illustration 1-8 ▶

Financial statements and their interrelationships

Helpful hint 1. Net income is calculated first and is needed to determine the ending balance in owner's equity. 2. The ending balance in owner's equity is needed for preparing the balance sheet. 3. The cash shown on the balance sheet is needed for preparing the cash flow statement.

SOFTBYTE
Income Statement
Month Ended September 30, 2008

Revenues		
Service revenue		$4,700
Expenses		
Salaries expense	$900	
Rent expense	600	
Advertising expense	250	
Utilities expense	200	
Total expenses		1,950
Net income		$2,750

SOFTBYTE
Statement of Owner's Equity
Month Ended September 30, 2008

M. Doucet, capital, September 1		$ 0
Add: Investments	$15,000	
Net income	2,750	17,750
		17,750
Less: Drawings		1,300
M. Doucet, capital, September 30		$16,450

SOFTBYTE
Balance Sheet
September 30, 2008

Assets

Cash	$ 8,050
Accounts receivable	1,400
Supplies	1,600
Equipment	7,000
Total assets	$18,050

Liabilities and Owner's Equity

Liabilities	
Accounts payable	$ 1,600
Owner's equity	
M. Doucet, capital	16,450
Total liabilities and owner's equity	$18,050

SOFTBYTE
Cash Flow Statement
Month Ended September 30, 2008

Operating activities		
Cash receipts from customers	$ 3,300	
Cash payments for operating expenses	(1,950)	
Net cash provided by operating activities		$ 1,350
Investing activities		
Purchase of equipment	$ (7,000)	
Net cash used by investing activities		(7,000)
Financing activities		
Investments by owner	$15,000	
Drawings by owner	(1,300)	
Net cash provided by financing activities		13,700
Net increase in cash		8,050
Cash, September 1		0
Cash, September 30		$ 8,050

Income Statement

Softbyte's income statement reports the revenues and expenses for a specific period of time. The income statement is prepared from the data in the owner's equity columns (specifically the Revenues and Expenses columns) of Illustration 1-7. The statement's heading names the company and type of statement, and shows the time period covered by the statement. The main purpose of the income statement is to report the profitability of the company's operations over a specified period of time (a month, quarter, or year). To indicate that it applies to a period of time, the income statement date names the time period. For Softbyte, this appears as Month Ended September 30, 2008, which means the statement is for a one-month period.

On the income statement, revenues are listed first, followed by expenses. Finally, net income (or net loss) is determined. Note that investment and withdrawal transactions between the owner and the business are not included in the measurement of net income.

Alternative terminology
The *income statement* is sometimes called the *statement of earnings* or *statement of operations*.

Statement of Owner's Equity

Softbyte's statement of owner's equity reports the changes in owner's equity for a specific period of time. Data for preparing the statement of owner's equity are taken from the owner's equity columns (specifically the Capital and Drawings columns) of the tabular summary (Illustration 1-7) and from the income statement. The heading of this statement names the company and type of statement, and shows the time period covered by the statement. The time period is the same as it is for the income statement, so it is dated Month Ended September 30, 2008. The beginning owner's equity amount is shown on the first line of the statement. Normally, zero balances are not shown. We have included one here because, unless it is the first period of operations, companies normally have a beginning balance. Then the owner's investments, the net income, and the drawings are identified. The information in this statement indicates why owner's equity has increased or decreased during the period.

What if Softbyte reported a net loss in its first month? The loss would reduce owner's capital. There would be no addition of net income, and the loss would be reported as a deduction, along with drawings.

Balance Sheet

Softbyte's balance sheet reports the assets, liabilities, and owner's equity at a specific date. The balance sheet is prepared from the Assets and Liabilities column headings and the month-end data shown in the last line of the tabular summary (Illustration 1-7). The heading of a balance sheet must identify the company, statement, and date. The balance sheet is like a snapshot of the company's financial condition at a specific moment in time (usually the end of a month, quarter, or year). To indicate that the balance sheet is at a specific point in time, the date only mentions the point in time (there is no indication of a time period). For Softbyte, this appears as September 30, 2008. Sometimes, the words "as at" precede the balance sheet date. Notice that the assets are listed at the top, followed by liabilities and owner's equity. Total assets must equal total liabilities and owner's equity. In the Softbyte balance sheet, only one liability, accounts payable, is reported. In most cases, there will be more than one liability.

Cash Flow Statement

Softbyte's cash flow statement gives information about the cash receipts and cash payments for a specific period of time. To help investors, creditors, and others analyze a company's cash, the cash flow statement reports the following: (1) the cash effects of the company's operating activities during a period, (2) the cash inflows and outflows from investing transactions (e.g., the purchase and sale of land, buildings, and equipment), (3) the cash inflows and outflows from financing transactions (e.g., borrowing and repayments of debt, and investments and withdrawals of equity), (4) the net increase or decrease in cash during the period, and (5) the cash amount at the end of the period.

Reporting the sources, uses, and change in cash is useful because investors, creditors, and others want to know what is happening to a company's most liquid resource, its money. The cash flow statement gives answers to the following simple but important questions:

1. Where did the cash come from during the period?
2. What was the cash used for during the period?
3. What was the change in the cash balance during the period?

Softbyte's cash flow statement, shown in Illustration 1-8, is for the same period of time as the income statement. Note that the positive numbers indicate cash inflows. Numbers in parentheses indicate cash outflows. Parentheses are often used in financial statements to indicate negative, or opposite, numbers. As shown in the statement, cash increased by $8,050 during the month. Cash flow from operating activities increased cash by $1,350. Cash flow from investing activities decreased cash by $7,000. Cash flow from financing activities increased cash by $13,700. At this time, you do not need to know how these amounts are determined. Chapter 17 will look at the cash flow statement in detail.

Using the Information in the Financial Statements

Practice Tools: Working with Annual Reports

Illustration 1-8 introduced the financial statements for Softbyte. Every set of financial statements also has explanatory notes and supporting schedules that are an essential part of the statements. Public corporations issue their financial statements and supplementary materials in an annual report. The **annual report** is a document that includes useful non-financial information about the company, as well as financial information.

Non-financial information may include a management discussion of the company's mission, goals and objectives, market position, and the people involved in the company. Financial information may include a review of current operations and a historical summary of key financial figures and ratios, in addition to comparative financial statements. Public company financial statements are audited and include the auditors' report. There is also a statement of management responsibility for the statements.

Now is a good time to go to Appendix A where you will find The Forzani Group Ltd.'s financial statements taken from its annual report. Carefully examine the format and content of each financial statement outlined earlier in Illustration 1-8. What similarities can you find between the financial statements in Illustration 1-8 and the more complicated financial statements for Forzani? We will continue to discuss Forzani's financial statements in later chapters.

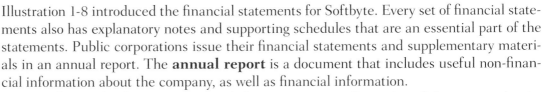

For **Review It** questions about The Forzani Group, you need to use Forzani's financial statements in Appendix A at the end of this textbook.

BEFORE YOU GO ON . . .

▶Review It

1. Describe the income statement, statement of owner's equity, balance sheet, and cash flow statement.
2. Why does it matter in which order the financial statements are prepared?
3. Explain how Forzani's financial statements are interrelated: identify specific accounts and amounts. The answer to this question is given at the end of the chapter.
4. What information is normally found in an annual report?

Related exercise material: BE1–10, BE1–11, BE1–12, E1–11, E1–12, E1–13, E1–14, and E1–15.

Demonstration Problem

Raman Balakrishnan opens his own law office on July 1, 2008. During the first month of operations, the following transactions occurred:

1. Invested $11,000 in cash in the law practice.
2. Paid $800 for July rent on office space.
3. Purchased office equipment on account, $3,000.
4. Provided legal services to clients for cash, $1,500.
5. Borrowed $700 cash from a bank on a note payable.
6. Provided legal services to a client on account, $2,000.
7. Collected $500 of the amount owed by a client on account (see transaction 6).
8. Paid monthly expenses: salaries, $500; utilities, $300; and telephone, $100.
9. Withdrew $1,000 cash for personal use.

Instructions

(a) Prepare a tabular analysis of the transactions.
(b) Prepare the income statement, statement of owner's equity, and balance sheet for Raman Balakrishnan, Barrister & Solicitor.

Practice Tools:
Demonstration Problems

The **Demonstration Problem** is a final review before you work on the assignment material. The problem-solving strategies in the margins give you tips about how to approach the problem. The solutions show both the form and the content of complete answers.

Solution to Demonstration Problem

(a)

Trans-action	Assets			=	Liabilities		+	Owner's Equity				
	Cash	+ Accounts Receivable	+ Equipment	=	Note Payable	+ Accounts Payable	+	R. Balakrishnan, Capital	− R. Balakrishnan, Drawings	+ Revenues	− Expenses
(1)	+$11,000							+$11,000			
(2)	−800										−$ 800
(3)			+$3,000			+$3,000					
(4)	+1,500									+$1,500	
(5)	+700				+$700						
(6)		+$2,000								+2,000	
(7)	+500	−500									
(8)	−500										−500
	−300										−300
	−100										−100
(9)	−1,000								−$1,000		
	$11,000 +	$1,500 +	$3,000	=	$700 +	$3,000 +		$11,000	− $1,000	+ $3,500	− $1,700

$15,500

$15,500

(b)

RAMAN BALAKRISHNAN, BARRISTER & SOLICITOR
Income Statement
Month Ended July 31, 2008

Revenues		
Fees earned		$3,500
Expenses		
Rent expense	$800	
Salaries expense	500	
Utilities expense	300	
Telephone expense	100	
Total expenses		1,700
Net income		$1,800

Action Plan

- Make sure that assets equal liabilities plus owner's equity in each transaction.
- Investments and revenues increase owner's equity. Withdrawals and expenses decrease owner's equity.
- Prepare the financial statements in the order listed.
- The income statement shows revenues and expenses for a period of time.
- The statement of owner's equity shows the changes in owner's equity for the same period of time as the income statement.
- The balance sheet reports assets, liabilities, and owner's equity at a specific date.

RAMAN BALAKRISHNAN, BARRISTER & SOLICITOR
Statement of Owner's Equity
Month Ended July 31, 2008

R. Balakrishnan, July 1		$ 0
Add: Investments	$11,000	
Net income	1,800	12,800
		12,800
Less: R. Balakrishnan, Drawings		1,000
R Balakrishnan, capital, July 31		$11,800

RAMAN BALAKRISHNAN, BARRISTER & SOLICITOR
Balance Sheet
July 31, 2008

Assets	
Cash	$11,000
Accounts receivable	1,500
Equipment	3,000
Total assets	$15,500
Liabilities and Owner's Equity	
Liabilities	
Note payable	$ 700
Accounts payable	3,000
Total liabilities	3,700
Owner's equity	
R. Balakrishnan, capital	11,800
Total liabilities and owner's equity	$15,500

the navigator

Summary of Study Objectives

1. ***Explain why accounting is important to accountants and non-accountants.*** For our economic system to function smoothly, reliable and ethical accounting and financial reporting are critical. Good accounting is important to people both inside and outside the organization. Internal users, such as management, use accounting information to plan, control, and evaluate business operations. External users include investors and creditors, among others. Accounting data are used by investors (owners) to decide whether to buy, hold, or sell their financial interests. Creditors (suppliers and bankers) evaluate the risks of granting credit or lending money based on the accounting information. Other groups that use accounting information are taxing authorities, regulatory agencies, customers, labour unions, and economic planners.

2. ***Explain generally accepted accounting principles and assumptions.*** Generally accepted accounting principles and assumptions are a common set of guidelines that are used to prepare and report accounting information. The cost principle states that assets should be recorded at their histori-

cal (original) cost. The going concern assumption presumes that a business will continue operations for enough time to use its assets for their intended purpose and to complete its commitments. The monetary unit assumption requires that only transaction data that can be expressed as an amount of money be included in the accounting records, and it assumes that the monetary unit is stable. The economic entity assumption requires the activities of each economic entity to be kept separate from the activities of its owner and other economic entities.

3. ***Use the accounting equation and explain the meaning of assets, liabilities, and owner's equity.*** The accounting equation is: Assets = Liabilities + Owner's Equity. Assets are resources owned by a business. Liabilities are creditors' claims on total assets. Owner's equity is the ownership claim on total assets.

4. ***Analyze the effects of business transactions on the accounting equation.*** Each business transaction must have a dual effect on the accounting equation. For example, if an

individual asset is increased, there must be a corresponding (1) decrease in another asset, (2) increase in a liability, and/or (3) increase in owner's equity.

5. ***Prepare financial statements.*** An income statement presents the revenues and expenses of a company for a specific period of time. A statement of owner's equity summarizes the changes in owner's equity that have occurred for a specific period of time. A balance sheet reports the assets, liabilities, and owner's equity of a business at a specific date. A cash flow statement summarizes information about the cash inflows (receipts) and outflows (payments) for a specific period of time.

Glossary

Study Aids: Glossary
Practice Tools: Key Term Matching Activity

Accounting The process of identifying, recording, and communicating the economic events of an organization to interested users of the information. (p. 6)

Accounting equation Assets = Liabilities + Owner's Equity. (p. 11)

Annual report Information that a company gives each year to its shareholders and other interested parties about its operations and financial position. It includes the financial statements and auditors' report, in addition to information and reports by management. (p. 24)

Assets Resources owned by a business. (p. 11)

Assumptions Basic assumptions (going concern, monetary unit, and economic entity) that the financial accounting structure is based on. (p. 8)

Balance sheet A financial statement that reports the assets, liabilities, and owner's equity at a specific date. (p. 21)

Cash flow statement A financial statement that provides information about the cash inflows (receipts) and cash outflows (payments) for a specific period of time. (p. 21)

Corporation A business organized as a separate legal entity under corporation law, with ownership divided into transferable shares. (p. 10)

Cost principle An accounting principle which states that assets should be recorded at their historical (original) cost. (p. 8)

Drawings Withdrawals of cash or other assets from an unincorporated business for the personal use of the owner. Drawings reduce owner's equity. (p. 12)

Economic entity assumption An assumption that requires the activities of the entity to be kept separate and distinct from the activities of its owner, and all other economic entities. (p. 9)

Ethics The standards of conduct by which one's actions are judged as right or wrong, honest or dishonest, fair or unfair. (p. 3)

Expenses The cost of assets consumed or services used in the process of earning revenue. Expenses reduce owner's equity. (p. 13)

Generally accepted accounting principles (GAAP) An accepted set of standards that indicates how to report economic events. (p. 7)

Going concern assumption An assumption which states that the entity will continue operations for enough time to use its assets for their intended purpose and to complete its obligations. (p. 8)

Income statement A financial statement that presents the revenues and expenses and resulting net income (or net loss) for a specific period of time. (p. 21)

Income trust A special or limited purpose corporation, set up specifically to invest in income-producing assets, and with its ownership divided into transferable units. (p. 10)

Investments by the owner The increase in owner's equity that results from assets put into the business by the owner. (p. 12)

Liabilities Claims of creditors on total assets. (p. 12)

Monetary unit assumption An assumption which states that only transaction data that can be expressed as an amount of money may be included in the accounting records. It is also assumed that the monetary unit is stable. (p. 9)

Net income The amount by which revenues are greater than expenses. (p. 12)

Net loss The amount by which expenses are greater than revenues. (p. 12)

Owner's equity The ownership claim on total assets. (p. 12)

Partnership An association of two or more persons to carry on as co-owners of a business for profit. (p. 10)

Proprietorship A small business owned by one person. (p. 9)

Revenues The increase in owner's equity that results from business activities that are done to earn income. (p. 13)

Statement of owner's equity A financial statement that summarizes the changes in owner's equity for a specific period of time. (p. 21)

Transactions The economic events of a business that are recorded by accountants. (p. 15)

Self-Study Questions

Practice Tools: Self-Assessment Quizzes

Answers are at the end of the chapter.

(SO 1) K 1. Ethics are the standards of conduct that are used to judge one's actions as:
(a) decent or indecent.
(b) successful or unsuccessful.
(c) profitable or unprofitable.
(d) right or wrong.

(SO 1) C 2. Which of the following statements about users of accounting information is incorrect?
(a) Management is an internal user.
(b) Taxing authorities are external users.
(c) Creditors are external users.
(d) Regulatory authorities are internal users.

(SO 2) K 3. The cost principle states that:
(a) assets should be recorded at cost and adjusted when their market value changes.
(b) an entity's activities should be kept separate and distinct from those of its owner.
(c) assets should be recorded at their historical (original) cost.
(d) only transaction data that can be expressed as an amount of money should be included in the accounting records.

(SO 2) C 4. Which of the following statements about basic assumptions is incorrect?
(a) The going concern assumption assumes that a company ends its operations once a year for reporting purposes.
(b) The economic entity assumption states that the activities of the entity should be kept separate from those of its owner and other entities.
(c) The monetary unit assumption makes it possible for accounting to measure economic events.
(d) An important part of the monetary unit assumption is that the monetary unit is assumed to remain stable.

5. As at December 31, after its first year of operations, Stone- (SO 3) land Company has assets of $3,500; revenues of $6,000; expenses of $3,500; and drawings of $500. What are the liabilities for Stoneland Company as at December 31?
(a) $1,000   (c) $2,000
(b) $1,500   (d) $2,500

6. Net income will result during a time period when: (SO 3)
(a) assets are greater than liabilities.
(b) assets are greater than revenues.
(c) expenses are greater than revenues.
(d) revenues are greater than expenses.

7. The effects on the accounting equation of performing (SO 4) services on account are:
(a) increased assets and decreased owner's equity.
(b) increased assets and increased owner's equity.
(c) increased assets and increased liabilities.
(d) increased liabilities and increased owner's equity.

8. Genesis Company buys a $10,000 machine on credit. (SO 4) Initially, this transaction will only affect the:
(a) income statement.
(b) balance sheet.
(c) income statement and statement of owner's equity.
(d) income statement, statement of owner's equity, and balance sheet.

9. The financial statement that reports assets, liabilities, (SO 5) and owner's equity is the:
(a) income statement.
(b) statement of owner's equity.
(c) balance sheet.
(d) cash flow statement.

10. Which of the following items is *not* reported on the state- (SO 5) ment of owner's equity?
(a) Investments by the owner
(b) Drawings
(c) Net income
(d) Cash flow from operating activities

Questions

(SO 1) C 1. "Accounting is ingrained in our society and it is vital to our economic system." Do you agree? Explain.

(SO 1) C 2. Why should everyone study accounting whether they are going to be an accountant or not?

(SO 1) C 3. Why are ethics important to the accounting profession? To statement users?

4. (a) Distinguish between internal and external users of (SO accounting data. (b) How does accounting provide relevant data for these users?

5. Identify and describe the three steps in the accounting (SO information system.

(SO 2) AP 6. Ouellette Travel Agency purchased land for $75,000 cash on February 1. At December 31 of the same year, the land's value had increased to $95,000. What amount should be reported for land on Ouellette's balance sheet at December 31? Would your answer differ if the land's value temporarily dropped to $65,000? Explain.

(SO 2) C 7. How does the going concern assumption support the cost principle?

(SO 2) C 8. What is the monetary unit assumption? What impact does inflation (rising prices) have on the monetary unit assumption?

(SO 2) K 9. What is the economic entity assumption?

(SO 2) C 10. Distinguish between the following forms of business organization: (1) proprietorship, (2) partnership, (3) public corporation, (4) private corporation, and (5) income trust.

(SO 3) C 11. Are the following events recorded in the accounting records? Explain your answer in each case.
(a) The owner of the company dies.
(b) Supplies are purchased on account.
(c) An employee is terminated.
(d) The company wins an award as one of the top 50 companies in Canada to work for.

(SO 3) K 12. What is the accounting equation?

(SO 3) C 13. (a) Define assets, liabilities, and owner's equity. (b) What items increase and decrease owner's equity?

(SO 3) C 14. Identify whether each of the following would be classified as an asset, liability, or owner's equity item:
(a) Cash
(f) Equipment
(b) Accounts payable
(g) Salaries payable
(c) Drawings
(h) Service revenue
(d) Accounts receivable
(i) Rent expense
(e) Supplies
(j) Note payable

(SO 4) C 15. Can a business have a transaction in which only the left (assets) side of the accounting equation is affected? If yes, give an example.

(SO 4) AP 16. Indicate how the following transactions affect the accounting equation:
(a) Paid cash for janitorial services.
(b) Purchased equipment for cash.

(c) Invested cash in the business.
(d) Paid an account payable in full.
(e) Performed services on account.

(SO 4) AP 17. Paul Dumas withdrew $10,000 from his business, Dumas's Pharmacy, which is organized as a proprietorship. Dumas's accountant recorded this withdrawal as an increase in an expense and a decrease in cash. Is this treatment correct? Why or why not?

(SO 5) C 18. A company's net income appears directly on the income statement and the statement of owner's equity. It is also included indirectly in the company's balance sheet. Do you agree? Explain.

(SO 5) C 19. Explain how the following pairs of financial statements are interrelated: (a) income statement and statement of owner's equity; (b) statement of owner's equity and balance sheet; and (c) balance sheet and cash flow statement.

(SO 5) C 20. Below are some items found in the financial statements of Kaustev Sen, M.D. Indicate in which financial statement(s) the items would appear.
(a) Service revenue
(b) Equipment
(c) Advertising expense
(d) Accounts receivable
(e) K. Sen, Capital (opening balance)
(f) K. Sen, Capital (ending balance)
(g) Wages payable
(h) Wages expense
(i) Cash
(j) Cash provided by operating activities
(k) Drawings
(l) Note payable

(SO 5) C 21. André is puzzled as he reads **Forzani's** financial statements. He notices that the numbers have all been rounded to the nearest thousand. He thought financial statements were supposed to be accurate and he is now wondering what happened to the rest of the money. Respond to André's concern.

(SO 5) C 22. **Forzani's** year end is not a fixed date; rather, it can vary slightly from one year to the next. What possible problems does this create for financial statement users?

When the financial results of **real companies** are used in the end-of-chapter material, the company's name is shown in red.

Brief Exercises

Discuss ethical issues.
(SO 1) an

BE1–1   Imagine and describe an ethical dilemma that each of the following individuals might encounter:

1. A student in an introductory accounting course
2. A production supervisor
3. A salesperson
4. A banker
5. The prime minister of Canada

Identify users of accounting information.
(SO 1) K

BE1–2   A list of decisions made by different users of accounting information follows:

1. Decide whether the company pays fair wages.
2. Decide whether the company can pay its obligations.
3. Decide whether a marketing proposal will be cost-effective.
4. Decide whether the company's net income will permit an increase in drawings.
5. Decide how the company should finance its operations.

The different users are identified in the table that follows. (a) Insert the number (1–5) of the kind of decision described above that each user would likely make. (b) Indicate whether the user is internal or external.

User	(a) Kind of Decision	(b) Internal or External User
Owner		
Marketing manager		
Creditor		
Chief financial officer		
Labour union		

Identify forms of business organization.
(SO 2) C

BE1–3   Match each of the following forms of business organization with the correct set of characteristics: proprietorship (PP), partnership (P), corporation (C), income trust (T).

(a) ___ Shared control; combined skills and resources
(b) ___ Easier to transfer ownership and raise funds; no personal liability; entity pays income tax
(c) ___ Simple to set up; founder keeps control
(d) ___ Easier to transfer ownership and raise funds; no personal liability; unitholders pay income tax

Identify principles and assumptions.
(SO 2) C

BE1–4   Match each of the following terms with the best description below:

1. Cost principle
2. Going concern assumption
3. Economic entity assumption
4. Monetary unit assumption

(a) ___ Transactions are recorded in terms of units of money.
(b) ___ Transactions are recorded based on the actual amount received or paid.
(c) ___ Accounting for a business excludes any personal transactions of the owner and the transactions of any other entity.
(d) ___ Businesses are expected to continue operating indefinitely.

Solve accounting equation.
(SO 3) AP

BE1–5   Presented below is the accounting equation. Determine the missing amounts:

Assets	=	Liabilities	+	Owner's Equity
$80,000		$48,000		(a)
(b)		$75,000		$50,000
$94,000		(c)		$38,000

BE1–6 Use the accounting equation to answer each of the following questions:

(a) Cai Company has liabilities of $200,000. The balance in Meiyu Cai's capital account is $100,000; in drawings, $40,000; revenues, $450,000; and expenses, $320,000. What is the amount of Cai Company's total assets?

(b) Pereira Company has total assets of $80,000. The balance in Karen Pereira's capital account is $25,000; in drawings, $7,000; revenues, $50,000; and expenses, $35,000. What is the amount of the company's total liabilities?

(c) Yap Co. has total assets of $600,000 and its liabilities are equal to two-thirds of its total assets. What is the amount of Yap Co.'s owner's equity?

BE1–7 At the beginning of the year, Lam Company had total assets of $700,000 and total liabilities of $500,000. Answer each of the following independent questions:

(a) If total assets increased by $150,000 during the year and total liabilities decreased by $80,000, what is the amount of owner's equity at the end of the year?

(b) During the year, total liabilities decreased by $100,000. The company incurred a net loss of $50,000. Lifei Lam made an additional investment of $100,000 and made no withdrawals. What is the amount of total assets at the end of the year?

(c) Total assets increased by $90,000 during the year. Net income was $170,000. There were no additional owner's investments, but Lifei Lam withdrew $50,000. What is the amount of total liabilities at the end of the year?

BE1–8 Presented below are six business transactions. Indicate whether the transactions increased (+), decreased (–), or had no effect (NE) on each element of the accounting equation.

1. Purchased $250 of supplies on account.
2. Performed $500 of services on account.
3. Paid $300 of operating expenses.
4. Invested $1,000 in the business.
5. Owner withdrew $400.
6. Received $500 from a customer who had been billed previously for services provided.

Use the following format, in which the first one has been done for you as an example:

				Owner's Equity		
Transaction	Assets	Liabilities	Capital	Drawings	Revenues	Expenses
1.	+$250	+$250	NE	NE	NE	NE

BE1–9 Classify each of the following items as owner's investments (I), drawings (D), revenue (R), expenses (E), or as having no effect on owner's equity (NE):

(a) ___ Costs incurred for advertising
(b) ___ Commission earnings
(c) ___ Costs incurred for insurance
(d) ___ Amounts paid to employees
(e) ___ Cash paid to purchase equipment
(f) ___ Services performed
(g) ___ Rent received
(h) ___ Utilities incurred
(i) ___ Cash distributed to owner
(j) ___ Collection of an account receivable

BE1–10 Indicate (a) whether each of the following items is an asset (A), liability (L), or part of owner's equity (OE); and (b) which financial statement—income statement (IS), statement of owner's equity (OE), or balance sheet (BS)—it would be reported on. The first one has been done for you as an example.

	(a)	(b)
1. Accounts receivable	A	BS
2. Salaries payable		
3. Office supplies		
4. Supplies expense		
5. Service revenue		
6. Note payable		
7. Cash		
8. Drawings		

Identify elements of financial statements.
(SO 5) C

BE1–11   The **Calgary Exhibition and Stampede Limited** has the following selected accounts in its corporate financial statements. In each case, identify whether the item would appear on the balance sheet (BS) or income statement (IS).

(a) ___ Accounts receivable   (g) ___ Horse racing revenue
(b) ___ Inventories   (h) ___ Accounts payable and accrued liabilities
(c) ___ Amortization expense   (i) ___ Cash and short-term deposits
(d) ___ Share capital   (j) ___ Administration, marketing, and
(e) ___ Building   park services expenses
(f) ___ Stampede revenue   (k) ___ Food and beverage revenue

Calculate net income.
(SO 5) AP

BE1–12   Schwinghamer Enterprises had a capital balance of $168,000 at the beginning of the period. At the end of the accounting period, the capital balance was $198,000.

(a) If there were no additional investments or withdrawals, what is the net income for the period?
(b) Assuming there was an additional investment of $8,000 but no withdrawals, what is the net income for the period?
(c) Assuming there was an additional investment of $10,000 and a withdrawal of $5,000, what is the net income for the period?

Exercises

Identify users and uses of accounting information.
(SO 1) C

E1–1   **Roots Canada Ltd.** is known around the world for its clothing and accessories. It has more than 125 stores in Canada and the United States, and another 20 locations in Asia.

Instructions

(a) Identify two internal users of Roots' accounting information. Write a question that each user might try to answer by using accounting information.
(b) Identify two external users of Roots' accounting information. Write a question that each user might try to answer by using accounting information.

Identify violated assumption or principle.
(SO 2) C

E1–2   Marietta Company had three major business transactions during the year:

(a) Land with a cost of $208,000 was reported at its market value of $260,000.
(b) Marietta paid the rent for an apartment for the owner's personal use and charged it to Rent Expense.
(c) Marietta wanted to make its net income look worse than it really was, so it adjusted its expenses upward to include the effects of inflation.

Instructions

In each situation, identify the assumption or principle that has been violated, if any, and state what should have been done.

E1–3 Here are some terms from the chapter:

1. Accounts payable
2. Creditor
3. Balance sheet
4. Proprietorship
5. Corporation
6. Ethics
7. Accounts receivable
8. Unitholders' equity

Instructions

Match each term with the best description that follows:

(a) ___ A company that raises money by issuing shares
(b) ___ Standards of conduct that are used to judge one's actions as right or wrong
(c) ___ Obligations to suppliers of goods
(d) ___ Amounts due from customers
(e) ___ The ownership claim on total assets in an income trust organization
(f) ___ A party that a company owes money to
(g) ___ A financial statement that reports assets, liabilities, and owner's equity at a specific date
(h) ___ A business in which the owner is personally liable for all debts of the business

E1–4 The following items (in U.S. millions) were taken from a recent balance sheet of **NIKE, Inc.** NIKE is the largest seller of athletic apparel and footwear in the world.

Accounts payable	$ 843.9	Notes payable	$ 763.3
Accounts receivable	2,262.1	Other assets	1,289.9
Cash	1,388.1	Other liabilities	1,542.2
Inventories	1,811.1	Retained earnings	4,396.5
Investments	436.6	Share capital	1,247.7
Land, buildings, and equipment	1,605.8		

Instructions

(a) Classify each of the above items as an asset (A), liability (L), or shareholders' (owner's) equity (SE) item.
(b) Show the amounts in NIKE's accounting equation by calculating the value of NIKE's total assets, total liabilities, and total shareholders' equity.

E1–5 The summaries of balance sheet and income statement data for three proprietorships follow. Two items are missing from each summary.

	Wyatt Company	Maxim Enterprises	Distasi Services
Beginning of year:			
Total assets	$ 97,000	$129,000	$60,000
Total liabilities	58,000	(c)	25,000
Total owner's equity	(a)	50,000	35,000
End of year:			
Total assets	170,000	180,000	(e)
Total liabilities	100,000	105,000	65,000
Total owner's equity	70,000	75,000	95,000
Changes during year in owner's equity:			
Investments	(b)	0	25,000
Drawings	14,000	(d)	10,000
Total revenues	215,000	100,000	(f)
Total expenses	175,000	55,000	40,000

Instructions

Determine the missing amounts.

Calculate net income (or loss).
(SO 3) AP

E1–6   The Depeau Company had the following assets and liabilities on the dates indicated:

December 31	Total Assets	Total Liabilities
2006	$400,000	$150,000
2007	560,000	175,000
2008	690,000	250,000

Don Depeau began business on January 1, 2006, with an investment of $100,000.

Instructions

Use the accounting equation and the change in owner's equity during the year to calculate the net income (or loss) for:
(a) 2006, assuming D. Depeau's drawings were $25,000 for the year.
(b) 2007, assuming D. Depeau made an additional investment of $50,000 and had no drawings in 2007.
(c) 2008, assuming D. Depeau's drawings were $20,000 for the year.

Describe effects of transactions on accounting equation.
(SO 4) C

E1–7   A list of effects on the accounting equation follows. For each effect, give an example of a transaction that would cause it.

1. Increases an asset and increases a liability.
2. Increases an asset and increases owner's equity.
3. Decreases an asset and decreases a liability.
4. Decreases an asset and decreases owner's equity.
5. Increases a liability and decreases owner's equity.
6. Increases one asset and decreases another asset.

Analyze effects of transactions.
(SO 4) AP

E1–8   Here are some transactions for the Lush Lawn Care Company:

1. Made $50,000 cash investment to start business.
2. Paid monthly rent, $600.
3. Purchased equipment on account, $5,000.
4. Billed customers for services performed, $2,500.
5. Withdrew cash for owner's personal use, $1,000.
6. Received $1,700 from customers billed in transaction 4.
7. Incurred advertising expense on account, $300.
8. Purchased additional equipment for cash, $4,000.
9. Received $1,000 from customers for services performed.
10. Paid $5,000 on account for equipment purchased in transaction 3.

Instructions

Prepare a tabular analysis of the above transactions, as shown in Illustration 1-7 in the text.

Analyze effects of transactions.
(SO 4) AP

E1–9   Lau Computer Company had the following transactions during the month of May:

1. Purchased computer terminals for $19,000 from Digital Equipment, on account.
2. Paid $4,000 for May rent of storage space.
3. Received $15,000 from customers for contracts billed in April.
4. Provided computer services to Brieske Construction Company for $3,000 cash.
5. Paid NB Power $1,000 for energy used in May.
6. Ms. Lau invested an additional $32,000 in the business.
7. Paid Digital Equipment for the terminals purchased in transaction 1.
8. Incurred advertising expense on account for May, $1,000.

Instructions

Prepare a tabular analysis of the above transactions, as shown in Illustration 1-7 in the text.

Analyze transactions and calculate net income and owner's equity.
(SO 4) AP

E1–10   An analysis of the transactions for Bourque & Co., a public accounting firm, for it's first month of operations, August 2008, follows:

	Cash	+ Accounts Receivable	+ Supplies	+ Office Equipment	= Accounts Payable	+ B. Bourque, Capital	− B. Bourque, Drawings	+ Revenues	− Expenses
1.	+$10,000					+$10,000			
2.	−2,000			+$5,000	+$3,000				
3.	−750		+$750						
4.	+2,700	+$3,400						+$6,100	
5.	−1,500				−1,500				
6.	−2,000						−$2,000		
7.	−750								−$750 Rent
8.	+450	−450							
9.	−2,900								−2,900 Salaries
10.					+550				−550 Utilities

Instructions

(a) Describe each transaction that occurred in the month.
(b) Calculate the increase in owner's equity for the month.
(c) Calculate the amount of net income for the month.

E1–11 Indicate (a) whether each of the following items is an asset (A), liability (L), or part of owner's equity (OE); and (b) which financial statement—income statement (IS), statement of owner's equity (OE), or balance sheet (BS)—it would be reported on. The first one has been done for you as an example. *Classify accounts. (SO 3, 5) C*

		(a)	(b)
1.	Accounts payable	L	BS
2.	Accounts receivable		
3.	Cash		
4.	Equipment		
5.	Interest payable		
6.	Interest revenue		
7.	Interest expense		
8.	Investment by the owner		
9.	Owner's drawings		
10.	Salaries expense		

E1–12 An analysis of transactions for Bourque & Co. for August 2008 was presented in E1–10. *Prepare financial statements. (SO 5) AP*

Instructions

Prepare an income statement and statement of owner's equity for the month and a balance sheet at August 31.

E1–13 The following information is for Serg Co. for the year ended December 31, 2008: *Prepare income statement and statement of owner's equity. (SO 5) AP*

A. Serg, capital, January 1	$48,000	A. Serg, drawings	$ 5,000
Service revenue	55,000	Salaries expense	28,000
Rent expense	7,200	Utilities expense	2,100
Interest expense	700	Advertising expense	500
Investments by owner	3,000	Other expenses	800

Instructions

Prepare an income statement and a statement of owner's equity for the year.

E1–14 Financial information for the operations of Atlantic Cruise Company for July 2008 follows: *Prepare income statement. (SO 5) AP*

Maintenance expense	$ 80,000	Food, fuel, and other operating expenses	$ 60,500
Ticket revenue	350,000	Salaries expense	132,000
Advertising expense	3,500	I. Sail, drawings	29,000

Instructions

Prepare the income statement for the month.

Calculate net income and
owner's equity and prepare
balance sheet.
(SO 5) AP

E1–15   Judy Cumby is the sole owner of Deer Park, a public camping ground near Gros Morne National Park. Judy has gathered the following financial information for the year ended December 31, 2008:

Revenues—camping fees	$160,000	Revenues—general store	$ 40,000
Operating expenses	150,000	Cash on hand	10,000
Supplies on hand	2,500	Original cost of equipment	110,000
Market value of equipment	125,000	Notes payable	70,000
Accounts payable	11,500	J. Cumby, capital, January 1	17,000
Accounts receivable	21,000	J. Cumby, drawings	5,000

Instructions

(a) Calculate Deer Park's net income for the year.
(b) Calculate Judy's owner's equity at December 31.
(c) Prepare a balance sheet at December 31.

Problems: Set A

Identify financial statements
for decision-making.
(SO 1) S

P1–1A   Financial decisions often depend more on one type of financial statement than on others. Consider the following independent, hypothetical situations:

(a) The owner of Private Label Company wants to know if there is enough cash to expand operations and at the same time keep drawing the amounts that he usually does for his personal use.
(b) An Ontario lottery winner is thinking about using her winnings to purchase the Total Fitness Company, which operates 13 fitness centres in the Toronto area.
(c) The Comeau Company is considering extending credit to a new customer. The company would require the customer to pay within 30 days of receiving the goods.

Instructions

In each situation, state whether the individual making the decision would depend mostly on information in the income statement, balance sheet, or cash flow statement. Briefly justify your choice.

Identify assumption or
principle violated.
(SO 2) C

P1–2A   Three independent situations follow:

1. In preparing its financial statements, Karim Company tried to estimate and record the impact of the recent death of its president.
2. Paradis Company recently purchased a power boat. It plans on inviting clients for outings occasionally, so the boat was paid for with company funds and recorded in the company's records. Marc Paradis's family will use the boat whenever it is not being used to entertain clients. It is estimated that the boat will be used by the family about 75 percent of the time.
3. Because of a "flood sale," equipment worth $300,000 was purchased by Montigny Company for only $200,000. The equipment was recorded at $300,000 on the company's books.

Instructions

For each of the above situations, list any assumption or principle that has been violated and explain the violation.

Determine forms of business
organization.
(SO 2) AP

P1–3A   Four independent situations follow:

(a) Three physics professors have formed a business to improve the speed of information transfers over the Internet for stock exchange transactions. Each has contributed an equal amount of cash and knowledge to the venture. While their approach looks promising, they are concerned about the legal liabilities that their business might confront.
(b) Joseph LeBlanc, a student looking for summer employment, opened a bait shop in a small shed on a local fishing dock.

(c) Tom Cheng owns an oil well. He is looking for several investors who can provide capital that will be used to develop more income-producing assets like the oil well. He can guarantee a consistent and stable cash distribution back to the investors.

(d) Darcy Becker, Ellen Sweet, and Meg Dwyer recently graduated with marketing degrees. Friends since childhood, they have decided to start a consulting business that focuses on marketing sporting goods over the Internet.

Instructions

In each case, explain what form of organization the business is likely to take: proprietorship, partnership, corporation, or income trust. Give reasons for your choice.

P1–4A   The following selected data is for Siksika Trading Company:

Liabilities at the end of the year	$510,000
Investments by the owner during the year	5,000
Assets at the beginning of the year	665,000
Drawings by the owner during the year	26,000
Net income for the year	84,000
Capital at the beginning of the year	285,000
Total revenue for the year	387,000

Determine missing amounts.
(SO 3, 4) AP

Instructions

Determine the amount of each of the following items:

(a) Liabilities at the beginning of the year   (c) Capital at the end of the year
(b) Total expenses for the year   (d) Assets at the end of the year

P1–5A   Verma's Repair Shop was started on May 1 by A. Verma. A summary of the May transactions follows:

Analyze transactions and calculate owner's equity.
(SO 3, 4) AP

May   1 Invested $14,000 to start the repair shop.
2 Purchased equipment for $8,000, paying $2,000 cash and signing a note payable for the balance.
5 Paid rent for the month, $640.
7 Purchased $350 of supplies on account.
9 Received $2,100 in cash from customers for repair services.
15 Withdrew $500 for personal use.
16 Provided repair services on account to customers, $1,800.
26 Collected $500 on account for services billed on May 16.
27 Paid for supplies purchased on May 7.
28 Paid $220 for advertising.
31 Received May telephone bill, $100.
31 Paid part-time employee salaries, $1,000.
31 Billed a customer $350 for repair services.

Instructions

(a) Prepare a tabular analysis of the effects of the above transactions on the accounting equation.
(b) From an analysis of the owner's equity, calculate the account balance in A. Verma, Capital at May 31.

P1–6A   GG Company was formed on January 1, 2008. On December 31, Guy Gélinas, the owner, prepared a balance sheet:

Prepare corrected balance sheet.
(SO 2, 5) AP

```
                              GG COMPANY
                              Balance Sheet
                            December 31, 2008
```

Assets		Liabilities and Owner's Equity	
Cash	$ 20,000	Accounts payable	$ 30,000
Accounts receivable	55,000	Notes payable	15,000
Supplies	30,000	Boat loan payable	13,000
Boat	18,000	G. Gélinas, capital	65,000
	$123,000		$123,000

Guy willingly admits that he is not an accountant by training. He is concerned that his balance sheet might not be correct. He gives you the following additional information:

1. The boat actually belongs to Guy Gélinas, not to GG Company. However, because he thinks he might take customers out on the boat occasionally, he decided to list it as an asset of the company. To be consistent, he also listed as a liability of the company the personal bank loan that he took out to buy the boat.
2. Guy spent $15,000 to purchase more supplies than he usually does, because he heard that the price of the supplies was expected to increase. It did, and the supplies are now worth $30,000. He thought it best to record the supplies at $30,000, as that is what it would have cost him to buy them today.

Instructions

(a) Identify any corrections that should be made to the balance sheet, and explain why by referring to the appropriate accounting assumption or principle.
(b) Prepare a corrected balance sheet for GG Company. (*Hint:* To get the balance sheet to balance, adjust owner's equity.)

Classify accounts and prepare accounting equation.
(SO 3, 5) AP

P1–7A   Listed in alphabetical order, the following selected items (in thousands) were taken from the Happy Valley Hotel & Resorts' December 31 financial statements:

1.	___ Accounts payable	$ 159		9.	___ Operating expenses	$661
2.	___ Accounts receivable	90		10.	___ Other assets	501
3.	___ Cash	99		11.	___ Other liabilities	256
4.	___ Hotel real estate and equipment	1,436		12.	___ Other revenue	37
5.	___ Interest expense	33		13.	___ Revenues from hotel operations	831
6.	___ Investments	161		14.	___ Salaries payable	35
7.	___ Non-hotel real estate	100		15.	___ T. Waye, capital, January 1	966
8.	___ Notes payable	802		16.	___ T. Waye, drawings	5

Instructions

(a) In each case, identify on the blank line whether the item is an asset (A), liability (L), capital (C), drawings (D), revenue (R), or expense (E) item.
(b) Indicate which financial statement—income statement (IS), statement of owner's equity (OE), or balance sheet (BS)—each item would be reported on.
(c) Show the amounts in Happy Valley's accounting equation by calculating the value of total assets, total liabilities, and total owner's equity at December 31.

Analyze transactions and prepare balance sheet.
(SO 4, 5) AP

P1–8A   Lynn Barry started her own consulting firm, Barry Consulting, on June 1, 2008. The following transactions occurred during the month of June:

June   1   Barry sold her shares in Big Country Airlines for $5,000, which she deposited in her personal bank account.
      1   Barry transferred $4,000 from her personal account to a business account in the name of Barry Consulting.
      2   Paid $600 for office rent for the month.
      3   Purchased $425 of supplies on account.

June 5 Paid $75 to advertise in the *County News*.
    9 Received $2,175 for services provided.
   12 Withdrew $800 for personal use.
   15 Performed $3,000 of services on account.
   17 Paid $1,500 for employee salaries.
   20 Paid for the supplies purchased on account on June 3.
   23 Received $2,000 for services provided on account on June 15.
   25 Signed a contract to provide consulting services to a client for $5,500. Services will be performed and paid for in July.
   26 Borrowed $5,000 from the bank on a note payable.
   29 Purchased office equipment for $1,900.
   30 Paid $150 for utilities for the month.

Instructions

(a) Prepare a tabular analysis of the effects of the above transactions on the accounting equation.
(b) Calculate net income and owner's equity for the month ended June 30.
(c) Prepare a balance sheet at June 30.

P1–9A Brian Fraser opened the Fraser Veterinary Clinic in Regina on August 1, 2008. On August 31, the balance sheet showed Cash $4,500; Accounts Receivable $1,800; Supplies $400; Office Equipment $6,500; Accounts Payable $3,200; and B. Fraser, Capital $10,000. During September, the following transactions occurred:

Analyze transactions and prepare financial statements. (SO 4, 5) AP

Sept. 1 Paid $2,800 of the accounts payable.
    1 Paid $800 rent for September.
    4 Collected $1,450 of the accounts receivable.
    5 Hired a part-time office assistant at $50 per day to start work the following week.
    8 Purchased additional office equipment for $2,000, paying $700 cash and leaving the balance on account.
   14 Performed $500 of veterinary services on account.
   15 Paid $200 for advertising.
   18 Collected $500 from customers who received services on September 14.
   20 Paid $200 for Brian's daughter and friends to go horseback riding on her birthday.
   25 Borrowed $7,500 from the Western Bank on a note payable.
   26 Sent a statement reminding a customer that he still owed the company money from August.
   28 Earned revenue of $4,300, of which $2,900 was paid in cash and the balance is due in October.
   29 Paid the part-time office assistant $675 for working nine days in September.
   30 Received the utility bill for the month, $175.
   30 Withdrew $500 for personal expenses.

Instructions

(a) Beginning with the August 31 balances, prepare a tabular analysis of the effects of the September transactions on the accounting equation.
(b) Prepare an income statement and statement of owner's equity for September, and a balance sheet at September 30.

P1–10A Judy Johansen operates an interior design business, Johansen Designs. Listed below, in alphabetical order, are the assets and liabilities of the company as at December 31, 2008, and the revenues, expenses, and drawings for the year ended December 31, 2008:

Prepare financial statements. (SO 5) AP

Accounts payable	$ 4,170	J. Johansen, drawings	$25,000
Accounts receivable	5,460	Note payable	4,250
Cash	7,420	Office supplies	375
Computer equipment	5,750	Office supplies expense	1,875
Design fee revenue	87,425	Rent expense	12,000
Furniture	8,380	Salaries expense	47,400
Interest expense	225	Utilities expense	3,800

Judy's capital at the beginning of 2008 was $21,840. She made no investments during the year.

Instructions

Prepare an income statement and statement of owner's equity for the year, and a balance sheet at December 31.

Determine missing amounts, and comment.

(SO 5) AN

> The **pencil icon** means that you have to write a detailed answer.

P1–11A Here are incomplete financial statements for Baxter Company:

BAXTER COMPANY
Balance Sheet
November 30, 2008

Assets		Liabilities and Owner's Equity	
Cash	$ 5,000	Liabilities	
Accounts receivable	10,000	Notes payable	$ 59,600
Land	(i)	Accounts payable	(iii)
Building and equipment	45,000	Total liabilities	66,500
Total assets	$ (ii)	Owner's equity	
		B. Baxter, capital	(iv)
		Total liabilities and owner's equity	$110,000

BAXTER COMPANY
Income Statement
Year Ended November 30, 2008

Revenues		
Fees earned		$80,000
Expenses		
Salaries expense	$ (v)	
Other expenses	18,000	
Supplies expense	7,000	
Total expenses		60,000
Net income		$ (vi)

BAXTER COMPANY
Statement of Owner's Equity
Year Ended November 30, 2008

B. Baxter, capital, December 1, 2007	$35,000
Add: Investments	(vii)
Net income	(viii)
	57,500
Less: B. Baxter, drawings	(ix)
B. Baxter, capital, November 30, 2008	$ (x)

Instructions

(a) Calculate the missing amounts (i) to (x).

(b) Write a memo explaining (1) the sequence for preparing the financial statements, and (2) the inter-relationships between the income statement, statement of owner's equity, and balance sheet.

Problems: Set B

P1–1B Financial decisions often depend more on one type of financial statement than others. Consider the following independent, hypothetical situations:

Identify financial statements for decision-making.
(SO 1) S

1. The Backroads Company is considering changing to a new supplier for its hiking boots.
2. A labour union is preparing for contract negotiations and wonders if it should ask the company for improved employee benefits.
3. The Caisse d'Économie Base Montréal is thinking about extending a loan to a small company. The company would be required to make interest payments at the end of each year for five years, and to repay the loan at the end of the fifth year.

Instructions

In each situation, state whether the individual making the decision would depend mostly on information in the income statement, balance sheet, or cash flow statement. Briefly justify your choice.

P1–2B Three independent situations follow:

Identify assumption or principle violated.
(SO 2) C

1. The Dot.com Company believes its people are its most significant asset. It estimates and records their value on its balance sheet.
2. Barton Co. is carrying equipment at its current market value of $100,000. The equipment had an original cost of $75,000.
3. Steph Wolfson, president of the Sound Effects Company, bought a computer for her personal use. She paid for the computer with company funds and debited the Computers account.

Instructions

For each of the above situations, list any assumption or principle that has been violated and explain the violation.

P1–3B Four independent situations follow:

Determine forms of business organization.
(SO 2) ap

(a) Dawn Addington, a student looking for summer employment, opened a vegetable stand along a busy local highway. She buys produce from local farmers each morning and then sells it in the afternoon as people return home from work.
(b) Sabra Surkis is looking for investors to expand her real estate business, which includes several shopping malls and office buildings. She expects to generate a growing cash flow that she will distribute among the investors.
(c) Three chemistry professors have formed a business which uses bacteria to clean up toxic waste sites. Each has contributed an equal amount of cash and knowledge to the venture. The use of bacteria in this situation is experimental, and legal obligations could result.
(d) Mary Emery and Richard Goedde recently graduated with graduate degrees in economics. They have decided to start a consulting business that teaches the basics of international economics to small business owners who are interested in international trade.

Instructions

In each case, explain what form of organization the business is likely to take: proprietorship, partnership, corporation, or income trust. Give reasons for your choice.

P1–4B The following selected data is for Jaroslawsky Trading Company:

Determine missing amounts.
(SO 3, 4) AP

Liabilities at the end of the year	$470,000	Drawings by the owner	
Investments by the owner		during the year	$ 34,000
during the year	11,000	Net income for the year	72,000
Assets at the beginning		Capital at the beginning	
of the year	617,000	of the year	250,000
		Total revenue for the year	348,000

Instructions

Determine the amount of each of the following items:

(a) Liabilities at the beginning of the year
(b) Total expenses for the year
(c) Capital at the end of the year
(d) Assets at the end of the year

Analyze transactions and calculate owner's equity.
(SO 3, 4) AP

P1–5B   On April 1, Angela Loken established the Loken Travel Agency. The following transactions are for her first month of operations:

Apr. 1 Deposited $12,000 in the agency's account at the Canadian Imperial Bank of Commerce.
   2 Paid rent for the month, $600.
   2 Purchased office equipment for $5,500, paying $2,000 cash and signing a note payable for the balance.
   7 Incurred $300 of advertising costs, on account.
   8 Paid $725 for office supplies.
  11 Earned $9,000 for services provided, with $1,000 paid in cash and the remainder on account.
  15 Withdrew $500 for personal use.
  25 Paid the amount due in the April 7 transaction.
  30 Paid employee salaries, $3,200.
  30 Received a bill for utilities for the month, $1,000.
  30 Received $6,000 from customers who were billed in the April 11 transaction.

Instructions

(a) Prepare a tabular analysis of the effects of the above transactions on the accounting equation.
(b) From an analysis of the owner's equity, calculate the account balance in A. Loken, Capital at April 30.

Prepare corrected balance sheet.
(SO 2, 5) AP

P1–6B   The balance sheet of Plato's Book Shop at April 30, 2008, is as follows:

PLATO'S BOOK SHOP
Balance Sheet
April 30, 2008

Assets		Liabilities and Owner's Equity	
Accounts payable	$ (12,000)	Land	$ 50,000
Accounts receivable	37,000	Notes payable	(119,000)
Building	110,000	Supplies	4,000
C. Cai, capital	(91,000)	Plug	174,000
Cash	8,000		$109,000
Equipment and furnishings	57,000		
	$109,000		

Wenhai Cai, the owner of the book shop, willingly admits that he is not an accountant. In fact, he couldn't get the balance sheet to balance without "plugging" the numbers. He gives you the following additional information:

1. A professional real estate appraiser estimated the value of the land at $50,000. The actual cost of the land was $36,000.
2. Accounts receivable includes amounts due from customers in China for 35,000 Yuan, which is about $5,000 Canadian. Wenhai didn't know how to convert the currency for reporting purposes so he added the 35,000 Yuan to the $2,000 due from Canadian customers. He thought it more important to know how much he was owed by each customer in the currency they would likely pay him with anyway.

Instructions

(a) Identify any corrections that should be made to the balance sheet, and explain why by referring to the appropriate accounting assumption or principle.
(b) Prepare a corrected balance sheet for Plato's Book Shop at April 30.

P1–7B Listed in alphabetical order, the following selected items (in thousands) were taken from Capital Aviation's June 30 financial statements:

Classify accounts and prepare accounting equation.
(SO 3, 5) AP

1. ___	Accounts payable	$1,197	11. ___	Notes payable	$2,546
2. ___	Accounts receivable	547	12. ___	Other assets	1,274
3. ___	Aircraft fuel expense	432	13. ___	Other expenses	650
4. ___	Airport fee expense	309	14. ___	Other liabilities	1,440
5. ___	Cargo revenues	151	15. ___	Other revenue	230
6. ___	Cash	632	16. ___	Passenger revenues	1,681
7. ___	C. Chung, capital, January 1	1,150	17. ___	Property and equipment	3,696
8. ___	C. Chung, drawings	4	18. ___	Salaries expense	596
9. ___	Interest revenue	60	19. ___	Spare parts, materials, and supplies	237
10. ___	Maintenance expense	78			

Instructions

(a) In each case, identify on the blank line whether the item is an asset (A), liability (L), capital (C), drawings (D), revenue (R), or expense (E) item.

(b) Indicate which financial statement—income statement (IS), statement of owner's equity (OE), or balance sheet (BS)—each item would be reported on.

(c) Show the amounts in Capital Aviation's accounting equation by calculating the value of total assets, total liabilities, and total owner's equity at December 31.

P1–8B The following events concern Anita LeTourneau, a Manitoba law school graduate, for March 2008:

Analyze transactions and prepare balance sheet.
(SO 4, 5) AP

1. On March 4, she spent $10 on a lottery ticket.
2. On March 7, she won $240,000 in the lottery and immediately quit her job as a legal assistant.
3. On March 10, she decided to open her own law practice, and deposited $40,000 of her winnings in a business chequing account.
4. On March 14, she purchased a new condominium with a down payment of $100,000 from her personal funds plus a home mortgage of $200,000.
5. On March 15, Ms. LeTourneau signed a rental agreement for her law office space for $1,000 a month, starting March 15. She paid the first month's rent as it is due on the 15th of each month.
6. On March 20, she hired a receptionist. He will be paid $500 a week and will begin working on March 24.
7. On March 21, she purchased office furniture for her law practice from a company that had just declared bankruptcy. The furniture was worth at least $12,000 but Anita was able to buy it for only $8,000.
8. On March 23, she purchased $6,500 of computer and other equipment for her law practice for $2,000 plus a $4,500 note payable due in six months.
9. On March 24, she purchased $500 of office supplies on account.
10. On March 31, she performed $3,000 of legal services on account.
11. On March 31, she paid her receptionist $500 for the week.

Instructions

(a) Prepare a tabular analysis of the effects of the above transactions on the accounting equation.
(b) Calculate net income and owner's equity for the month ended March 31.
(c) Prepare a balance sheet at March 31.

P1–9B Tony Tiberio opens a law office under the name Tony Tiberio, Barrister & Solicitor, on July 1, 2008. On July 31, the balance sheet showed Cash $4,000; Accounts Receivable $1,500; Supplies $500; Office Equipment $5,000; Accounts Payable $5,100; and T. Tiberio, Capital $5,900. During August, the following transactions occurred:

Analyze transactions and prepare financial statements.
(SO 4, 5) AP

Aug. 4 Collected $1,200 of accounts receivable.
      7 Paid $2,700 on accounts payable.

Aug. 8 Earned fees of $6,500, of which $3,000 was collected from clients and the remainder is on account.
   12 Purchased additional office equipment for $1,200, paying $400 cash and leaving the balance on account.
   15 Paid salaries, $3,500; rent for August, $900; and advertising expenses, $275.
   18 Collected the unpaid fees from August 8.
   20 Withdrew $500 for personal use.
   26 Borrowed $2,000 from the Bank of Montreal on a note payable.
   28 Signed a contract to provide legal services to a client in September for $4,500. The client will pay the amount owing after the work has been completed.
   29 Received utility bill for the month, $275.
   30 Billed a client $1,000 for services provided.

Instructions

(a) Beginning with the July 31 balances, prepare a tabular analysis of the effects of the August transactions on the accounting equation.
(b) Prepare an income statement and statement of owner's equity for August, and a balance sheet at August 31.

Prepare financial statements.
(SO 5) AP

P1–10B Bennett's Home Renovations was started in 2005 by Jim Bennett. Jim operates the business from an office in his home and uses his truck for business purposes only. Listed below, in alphabetical order, are the assets and liabilities of the company as at December 31, 2008, and the revenues, expenses, and drawings for the year ended December 31, 2008:

Accounts payable	$ 6,600	Note payable	$ 22,000
Accounts receivable	7,200	Office supplies	425
Cash	5,500	Office supplies expense	2,125
Equipment	21,000	Renovation fee revenue	110,500
Interest expense	850	Truck	30,000
J. Bennett, drawings	32,000	Truck operating expenses	13,960
Liability insurance expense	2,410	Wages expense	62,450

Jim's capital at the beginning of 2008 was $38,820. He made no investments during the year.

Instructions

Prepare an income statement and statement of owner's equity for the year, and a balance sheet at December 31.

Determine missing amounts, and comment.
(SO 5) AN

P1–11B Here are incomplete financial statements for Wu Company:

WU COMPANY
Balance Sheet
January 31, 2008

Assets		Liabilities and Owner's Equity	
Cash	$ (i)	Liabilities	
Accounts receivable	20,000	Notes payable	$29,600
Land	15,000	Accounts payable	(iii)
Building and equipment	40,000	Total liabilities	45,000
Total assets	$ (ii)	Owner's equity	
		W. Wu, capital	(iv)
		Total liabilities and owner's equity	$85,000

```
                        WU COMPANY
                      Income Statement
                 Year Ended January 31, 2008


   Revenues
      Fees earned                                   $75,000
   Expenses
      Salaries expense              $29,000
      Other expenses                    (v)
      Supplies expense               7,000
          Total expenses                             54,000
   Net income                                     $     (vi)
```

```
                        WU COMPANY
                 Statement of Owner's Equity
                 Year Ended January 31, 2008


   W. Wu, capital, February 1, 2007                $10,000
   Add:  Investments                                  (vii)
           Net income                               (viii)
                                                     51,000
   Less: W. Wu, drawings                               (ix)
   W. Wu, capital, January 31, 2008               $     (x)
```

Instructions

(a) Calculate the missing amounts (i) to (x).
(b) Write a memo explaining (1) the sequence for preparing the financial statements, and (2) the inter-relationships between the income statement, statement of owner's equity, and balance sheet.

Continuing Cookie Chronicle

The **Continuing Cookie Chronicle** starts in this chapter and continues in every chapter.

Natalie Koebel spent much of her childhood learning the art of cookie-making from her grandmother. They passed many happy hours mastering every type of cookie imaginable and later creating new recipes that were both healthy and delicious. Now at the start of her second year in college, Natalie is investigating various possibilities for starting her own business as part of the requirements of the Entrepreneurship program she is taking. A long-time friend insists that Natalie has to somehow include cookies in her business plan and, after a series of brainstorming sessions, Natalie settles on the idea of operating a cookie-making school. She will start on a part-time basis and offer her services in peoples' homes. Now that she has started thinking about it, the possibilities seem endless. During the fall, she will concentrate on Christmas cookies. She will offer group sessions (which will probably be more entertainment than education for the participants) and individual lessons. Natalie also decides to include children in her target market. The first difficult decision is coming up with the perfect name for her business. In the end, she settles on "Cookie Creations" and then moves on to more important issues.

Instructions

(a) What form of business organization—proprietorship, partnership, corporation, or income trust—do you recommend that Natalie use for her business? Discuss the benefits and weaknesses of each form and give the reasons for your choice.
(b) Will Natalie need accounting information? If yes, what information will she need and why? How often will she need this information?
(c) Identify specific asset, liability, and equity accounts that Cookie Creations will likely use to record its business transactions.
(d) Should Natalie open a separate bank account for the business? Why or why not?

BROADENING YOUR PERSPECTIVE

Financial Reporting and Analysis

Financial Reporting Problem

BYP1–1   The Forzani Group Ltd.'s financial statements have been reproduced in Appendix A at the back of the textbook.

Instructions

(a) How many notes to the financial statements are presented for The Forzani Group? How many pages of the financial statement package do these notes use? How many pages do the financial statements themselves use?

(b) Notice that the dates on the financial statements are January 29, 2006, and January 30, 2005. (The company's 2004 financial statements were dated February 1, 2004.) What is The Forzani Group's fiscal year end?

(c) What were The Forzani Group's total assets as at January 29, 2006? January 30, 2005?

(d) What is the amount of change in The Forzani Group's net income (Forzani calls this net earnings) from 2005 to 2006?

(e) What amount of cash did The Forzani Group have on January 29, 2006? January 30, 2005?

Interpreting Financial Statements

BYP1–2   Research in Motion Limited (RIM) is an innovative Canadian company that designs, manufactures, and markets mobile communications solutions. RIM's award-winning products include the BlackBerry wireless platform, software development tools, and software/hardware licensing agreements. In the assets section of its 2005 balance sheet, the following data were presented:

RESEARCH IN MOTION LIMITED Balance Sheet (partial) February 26, 2005 (in U.S. thousands)		
	2005	2004
Assets		
Cash and cash equivalents	$ 610,354	$1,156,419
Receivables	240,875	107,362
Inventory	92,489	42,836
Investments	1,069,363	339,285
Land, buildings, and equipment	210,112	147,709
Intangible assets	83,740	64,269
Goodwill	29,026	30,109
Other assets	285,035	48,788
Total assets	$2,620,994	$1,936,777

Instructions

(a) For a company such as RIM, what do you think its most important economic resources (assets) would be? Where would these be recorded on the balance sheet? At what value (if any) should they be shown?

(b) Does the balance sheet tell you what RIM is worth? What information does the balance sheet give you about the company's value?

(c) Why do you think a Canadian company such as RIM would prepare its financial statements in U.S. dollars?

Critical Thinking

Collaborative Learning Activity

Note to instructors: Additional instructions and material for this group activity can be found on the Instructor Resource Site.

BYP1–3   In this group activity, you will analyze and record the transactions for a service company.

Instructions

(a) Complete the transaction table supplied by your instructor without consulting your classmates.

(b) Your instructor will divide the class into groups. One member of your group will take on the role of recorder as the group completes a new transaction table. You can refer to your individual transaction table for answers during the group activity but you should not change your individual answers. When your answers differ, you must explain your reasoning to the other members of the group.

(c) Each group will hand in the group transaction table along with the individual transaction tables of each member.

Study Aids:
Working in Groups

Communication Activity

BYP1–4   Robert Joote is the owner of Peak Company. Robert has prepared the following balance sheet:

Study Aids:
Writing Handbook

PEAK COMPANY Balance Sheet Month Ended December 31, 2008	
Assets	
Equipment	$20,500
Cash	10,500
Supplies	2,000
Accounts payable	(5,000)
Total assets	$28,000
Liabilities and Owner's Equity	
R. Joote, capital	$21,000
Accounts receivable	(3,000)
R. Joote, drawings	(2,000)
Notes payable	12,000
Total liabilities and owner's equity	$28,000

Robert didn't know how to determine the balance for his capital account so he just plugged the number (he had heard somewhere that assets had to equal liabilities and owner's equity).

Instructions

In a memo, explain to Robert (a) how to determine the balance for his capital account, (b) why his balance sheet is incorrect, and (c) what he should do to correct it.

Ethics Case

**Study Aids:
Ethics in Accounting**

BYP1–5 Chief executive officers (CEOs) and chief financial officers (CFOs) of publicly traded companies must personally certify that their companies' financial statements and other financial information contain no untrue statements and do not leave out any important facts. After many corporate scandals, the certification requirement was introduced as a way to hold top executives personally responsible for the integrity of their company's financial information.

Khan Corporation just hired a new management team, and its members say they are too new to the company to know whether the most recent financial reports are accurate or not. They refuse to sign the certification.

Instructions

(a) Who are the stakeholders in this situation?
(b) Should the CEO and CFO sign the certification? Explain why or why not.
(c) What are the CEO's and CFO's alternatives?

ANSWERS TO CHAPTER QUESTIONS

Answers to Accounting in Action Insight Questions

Ethics Insight, p. 4

Q: How can the "tone at the top" set by management make fraudulent financial reporting less common?

A: Fraudulent financial reporting might happen when individuals see an opportunity for personal gain or when they are pressured to falsify numbers, but it can also happen because there is no clear ethical standard in the company. Misplaced loyalty is often part of the reason for fraudulent financial reporting. This happens when employees are not reporting accounting information accurately but they are not really aware of the consequences of their actions. In other words, they often genuinely believe that they are doing what is best for the company. The best way to communicate acceptable ethical behaviour throughout a company is by example. When employees see management making the right ethical decisions even though the company's operating results may not look as good, they are more likely to do the same thing when they face similar choices.

Across the Organization Insight, p. 5

Q: How is accounting useful for non-accountants?

A: Regardless of your career aspirations, you will need to understand financial reports in any company that you are part of so that you can ask the right questions and understand the answers. As explained in the Across the Organization insight, the company 1-800-GOT-JUNK? uses financial information to manage costs and relationships, build team spirit, and set goals, among other purposes.

International Insight, p. 8

Q: How will the change to international accounting standards benefit the users of financial statements?

A: Having one set of accounting standards, instead of different standards for different countries, will significantly reduce the number of rules that users have to understand and apply. This will make it easier for international companies to prepare their statements and it will also be easier for statement users to compare them.

Answer to Forzani Review It Question 3, p. 24

The net earnings amount of $13,757 thousand (also known as net income) on the statement of operations (also known as the income statement) is included on the statement of retained earnings to determine the ending balance in retained earnings of $135,878 thousand. Note that Forzani presents its income statement and statement of retained earnings as one statement, instead of providing two separate financial statements. A statement of retained earnings is prepared by corporations, and is similar to the statement of owner's equity prepared by proprietorships.

The ending retained earnings balance of $135,878 thousand on Forzani's statement of retained earnings is also reported on the balance sheet. Finally, the $19,266 thousand ending cash balance reported as an asset on the balance sheet is explained on the statement of cash flows (also known as the cash flow statement), which ends with this same ending cash balance.

Answers to Self-Study Questions

1. d   2. d   3. c   4. a   5. b   6. d   7. b   8. b   9. c   10. d

Remember to go back to the Navigator Box at the beginning of the chapter to check off your completed work.

chapter | 2

concepts for review >>

the navigator

Before studying this chapter, you should understand or, if necessary, review:

   a. Why assets equal liabilities plus owner's equity. (Ch. 1, p. 11)

   b. What assets, liabilities, owner's capital, drawings, revenues, and expenses are. (Ch. 1, pp. 11–13)

   c. What transactions are, and how they affect the basic accounting equation. (Ch. 1, pp. 15–20)

Dancing to Her Own Business Tune

CALGARY, Alta.—At the Prestige Dance Academy, tiny pink ballerinas admire themselves before the mirrors. Their energetic teacher, Amanda Hunsley, dances along with them, encouraging them to express themselves through music.

Even when she was a young child taking dance lessons, Ms. Hunsley knew she wanted to run her own business. At just 19, while in her second year of studies at Mount Royal College, she opened her own dance school. Four years later, the Prestige Dance Academy has a part-time staff of eight teaching some 400 students tap, jazz, ballet, musical theatre, and hip-hop.

"I combined my love for kids and for business," she says. "I get to come to work everyday and have this place that is mine and teach the kids what I love."

Ms. Hunsley takes care of hiring and scheduling the staff, registrations, and any other administrative work, as well as advertising and marketing. To ensure that the business's finances don't fall through the cracks, a bookkeeper helps with her record keeping.

While the dance academy offers birthday parties and summer camps, most of the business is weekly dance lessons that run from September to June. Parents register their children in the fall, providing postdated cheques or giving a lump-sum payment for the entire year.

Using QuickBooks accounting software, Ms. Hunsley creates an account for each student and tracks payments. Not surprisingly, September is the busiest time as new accounts are created and the first monthly payments are recorded, as well as the lump sums. At the beginning of each month after that, Ms. Hunsley records payments by post-dated cheques and then deposits the money in the bank.

Expenses, such as lease payments (including heat, light, and water), phone and Internet bills, and staff salaries, are also entered.

When she receives her bank statement at month end, Ms. Hunsley reconciles it with her own records. Her bookkeeper then produces monthly financial statements, which include a balance sheet and income statement so she can see how the business is doing. The bookkeeper also files quarterly sales tax reports and produces the T4s. At year end, Ms. Hunsley saves her QuickBooks file to disk and passes it on to her accountant, who looks for any problems and produces the annual financial statements.

"I don't think you could run a business properly without being so on top of the finances," she stresses. "That's why I have a bookkeeper . . . You can't put some of that stuff off."

Good record keeping also gives Ms. Hunsley more time for what she enjoys most. Despite the tremendous growth of the business, she still teaches 25 hours a week. "Teaching and working with kids is my favourite part," she says.

the navigator

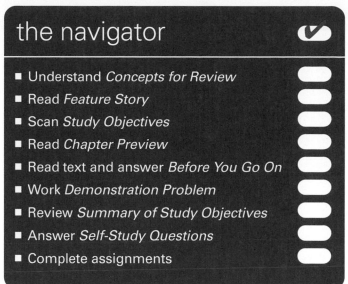

the navigator

- Understand *Concepts for Review*
- Read *Feature Story*
- Scan *Study Objectives*
- Read *Chapter Preview*
- Read text and answer *Before You Go On*
- Work *Demonstration Problem*
- Review *Summary of Study Objectives*
- Answer *Self-Study Questions*
- Complete assignments

chapter 2

The Recording Process

study objectives >>

After studying this chapter, you should be able to:

1. Define debits and credits and illustrate how they are used to record business transactions.
2. Describe the basic steps in the recording process, explain what a journal is, and journalize business transactions.
3. Explain what a ledger is, and post journal entries.
4. Explain the purpose of a trial balance, and prepare one.

In Chapter 1, we used the accounting equation to analyze business transactions. The combined effects of these transactions were presented in a tabular form. This method could work for small companies like Softbyte (the fictitious company discussed in Chapter 1) because they have relatively few transactions. But imagine Prestige Dance in the feature story using the same tabular format as Softbyte. With 400 students, the dance academy has too many transactions to record each one this way. Instead, a set of procedures and records are used to keep track of transaction data more easily.

This chapter introduces and illustrates the basic procedures and records. It is organized as follows:

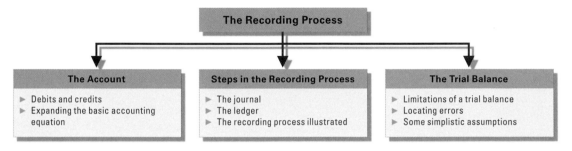

The Account	Steps in the Recording Process	The Trial Balance
▶ Debits and credits ▶ Expanding the basic accounting equation	▶ The journal ▶ The ledger ▶ The recording process illustrated	▶ Limitations of a trial balance ▶ Locating errors ▶ Some simplistic assumptions

The Account

An **account** is an individual accounting record of increases and decreases in a specific asset, liability, or owner's equity item. For example, Softbyte has separate accounts called Cash, Accounts Receivable, Accounts Payable, Service Revenue, Salaries Expense, and so on. In its simplest form, an account has three parts: (1) the title of the account, (2) a debit side on the left, and (3) a credit side on the right. Because these parts of an account are positioned like the letter T, it is called a **T account**. The basic form of an account is shown in Illustration 2-1.

Illustration 2-1 ▶

Basic form of T account

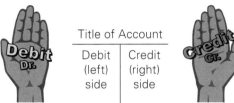

Title of Account

Debit (left) side	Credit (right) side

This form of account will be used throughout the book to explain basic accounting relationships.

Debits and Credits

The term **debit** indicates left. The term **credit** indicates right. They are usually abbreviated Dr. for debit and Cr. for credit. These terms come from the Latin words for debtor and creditor, but today they are used as directional signals. They indicate which side of a T account to record on. Entering an amount on the left side of an account is called debiting the account. Making an entry on the right side is called crediting the account.

Having debits on the left side of an account and credits on the right side is simply an accounting custom or rule (in the same way that driving on the right-hand side of the road is just a custom or rule). This rule is for all accounts. When the totals of the two sides are compared, an account will have a debit balance if the total of the debit amounts exceeds the credits. On the other hand, an account will have a credit balance if the credit amounts are more than the debits.

The recording of debits and credits in an account is shown below for Softbyte's cash transactions. The data are taken from the Cash column of the tabular summary in Illustration 1-7.

Tabular Summary		
Cash		
+$15,000		
−7,000		
+1,200		
+1,500		
−600		
−900		
−200		
−250		
+600		
−1,300		
$ 8,050		

Account Form		
Cash		
(Debits)		(Credits)
15,000		7,000
1,200		600
1,500		900
600		200
		250
		1,300
Balance	8,050	

In the tabular summary, every positive item is a receipt of cash. Every negative amount is a payment of cash. Notice that in the account format the increases in cash are recorded as debits, and the decreases in cash are recorded as credits. Having increases on one side and decreases on the other makes it easier to total each side of the account, as well as the balance in the account. The account balance, a debit of $8,050, indicates that Softbyte had $8,050 more increases than decreases in cash.

Debit and Credit Procedure

In Chapter 1, you learned that each transaction must affect two or more accounts to keep the basic accounting equation in balance. We will also see that, for each transaction, debits must equal credits. The equality of debits and credits is the basis for the double-entry system of recording transactions.

Helpful hint Debits must equal credits for each transaction.

In the **double-entry system**, the dual (two-sided) effect of each transaction is recorded in appropriate accounts. This system is used all over the world and gives a logical method for recording transactions. It also offers a simple way of finding obvious errors when the amounts are first recorded. If every transaction is recorded with equal debits and credits, then the sum of all the debits to the accounts must equal the sum of all the credits. If they don't, a mistake has definitely been made.

Assets and Liabilities. In the Softbyte illustration, increases in Cash—an asset account—were entered on the left side, and decreases in Cash were entered on the right side. Why did we do this instead of the opposite? First, we know that in the basic accounting equation (assets = liabilities + owner's equity), assets are on the left or debit side of the equation. So, to be consistent, when the double-entry system was created, it was decided that the normal balance of asset accounts should also be on the left side. Second, there are usually more increases in asset accounts than decreases. Logically, then, for the balance in an asset account to be on the debit side, increases also need to be recorded on that side. This is why asset accounts normally show debit balances.

So remember this: debits to a specific asset account should be more than the credits to that account. And increases in assets must therefore be entered on the left or debit side, and decreases in assets must be entered on the right or credit side.

Similarly, because liabilities are on the right or credit side of the accounting equation, liability accounts normally show credit balances. Credits to a liability account should be more than the debits to that account. Increases in liabilities must be entered on the right or credit side, and decreases in liabilities must be entered on the left or debit side.

To summarize, because assets are on the opposite side of the accounting equation from liabilities, increases and decreases in assets are recorded opposite from increases and decreases in liabilities. In this way, the total amount of debits always equals the total amount of credits and the equation stays in balance. The effects that debits and credits have on assets and liabilities and the normal balances are as follows:

Helpful hint Increases in accounts are always on the same side as the normal balance for that account.

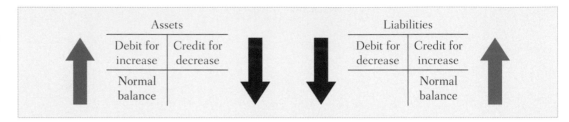

Knowing the normal balance in an account may also help you find errors. In automated systems, the computer is programmed to find these normal balance exceptions and to print out error or exception reports. In manual systems, a careful inspection of the accounts has to be done to find balances that are not normal. For example, a credit balance in an asset account such as Land or a debit balance in a liability account such as Wages Payable probably means there was a recording error. Occasionally, an abnormal balance may be correct. The Cash account, for example, will have a credit balance when a company has overdrawn its bank balance.

Owner's Equity. As explained in Chapter 1, owner's equity is increased by owner's investments and revenues. It is decreased by owner's drawings and expenses. Separate accounts are kept for each of these types of transactions.

Owner's Capital. Investments by owners are credited to the owner's capital account. Like liability accounts, the owner's capital account is increased by credits and decreased by debits. For example, when cash is invested in the business, the Cash account is debited and Owner's Capital is credited.

The rules of debit and credit for the owner's capital account and the normal balance in this account are as follows:

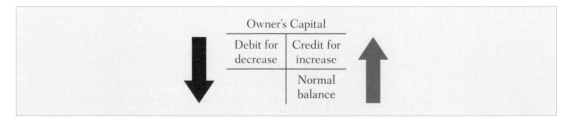

As liabilities and owner's equity are on the same side of the accounting equation, the rules of debit and credit are the same for these two types of accounts.

Owner's Drawings. An owner may withdraw cash or other assets for personal use. Withdrawals could be debited directly to Owner's Capital to indicate a decrease in owner's equity. However, it is better to have a separate account, called Drawings, as we did in Chapter 1. The separate account makes it easier to add up the total withdrawals for the accounting period and to prepare the statement of owner's equity. Because the drawings account decreases owner's equity, its increases and decreases are recorded opposite to how they are recorded in Owner's Capital, which increases owner's equity. Owner's drawings are therefore recorded by debits and the account has a normal debit balance. Credits to an owner's drawings account are unusual, but might be used to correct a withdrawal recorded in error, for example.

The rules of debit and credit for the Drawings account and the normal balance are as follows:

	Drawings	
↑	Debit for increase	Credit for decrease
	Normal balance	↓

Net Income. Net income results when revenues are greater than expenses. Remember that the main reason for earning revenues is to benefit the owner of the business. When revenues are earned, owner's equity is increased. Accordingly, the effect of debits and credits on revenue accounts is the same as their effect on Owner's Capital. Revenue accounts are increased by credits and decreased by debits.

Expenses have the opposite effect: expenses decrease owner's equity. As a result, expenses are recorded as debits because debits decrease owner's equity. Since expenses are the negative factor in calculating net income, and revenues are the positive factor, it is logical that the increase and decrease sides of expense accounts should be the reverse of revenue accounts. Thus, expense accounts are increased by debits and decreased by credits.

Credits to revenue accounts should exceed the debits. Debits to expense accounts should exceed the credits. Thus, revenue accounts normally show credit balances. Expense accounts normally show debit balances.

The effect of debits and credits on revenues and expenses and the normal balances are as follows:

	Revenues				Expenses	
↓	Debit for decrease	Credit for increase	↑	↑	Debit for increase	Credit for decrease	↓
	Normal balance				Normal balance	

Expanding the Basic Accounting Equation

You have already learned the basic accounting equation. Illustration 2-2 expands this equation to show the accounts that form owner's equity. In addition, the debit/credit rules and effects on each type of account are shown. Study this diagram carefully. It will help you to understand the basics of the double-entry system. Like the basic equation, the expanded basic equation must always be in balance (total debits must equal total credits).

Illustration 2-2 ▶

Expanded basic equation and debit/credit rules and effects

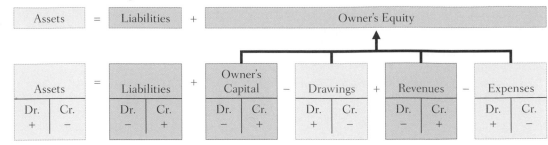

The normal balance of each account is on its increase side. So assets, drawings, and expense accounts have a normal debit balance, while liabilities, owner's capital, and revenue accounts have a normal credit balance.

BEFORE YOU GO ON . . .

▶ Review It

1. What do the terms "debit" and "credit" mean?
2. What are the effects of debits and credits on the asset, liability, and owner's equity accounts?
3. What are the effects of debits and credits on the revenue, expense, and drawings accounts?
4. What are the normal balances for these Forzani accounts: Accounts Receivable; Accounts Payable and Accrued Liabilities; Retail Revenue; and Store Operating Expense? The answer to this question is at the end of this chapter.

▶ Do It

Eszter Schwenke has just rented space in a shopping mall where she will open a beauty salon called Hair It Is. Long before opening day and before purchasing equipment, hiring employees, and remodelling the space, Eszter is advised to set up a double-entry set of accounting records to record all of her business transactions.

Name the balance sheet accounts that Eszter will need to record the transactions that open her business. Indicate whether the normal balance of each account is a debit or a credit.

Action Plan

- Determine the types of accounts needed. Eszter will need asset accounts for each different type of asset she invests in the business. She will need liability accounts for any debts she has.
- Understand the types of owner's equity accounts: only owner's capital will be needed when Eszter begins the business. Other owner's equity accounts will be added later.

Solution

Eszter will probably need the following accounts to record the transactions that prepare her beauty salon for opening day: Cash (debit balance); Supplies (debit balance); Equipment (debit balance); Accounts Payable (credit balance); Notes Payable (credit balance) if she borrows money; and E. Schwenke, Capital (credit balance).

Related exercise material: BE2–1, BE2–2, BE2–3, BE2–4, BE2–5, E2–2, E2–3, and E2–4.

Steps in the Recording Process

study objective 2

Describe the basic steps in the recording process, explain what a journal is, and journalize business transactions.

The basic steps in the recording process are:

1. Analyze each transaction for its effects on the accounts.
2. Enter the transaction information in a journal (book of original entry).
3. Transfer the journal information to the correct accounts in the ledger (book of accounts).

Although transaction information can be entered directly into the accounts without using a journal or ledger, few businesses do that.

The sequence of events in the recording process begins with the transaction. Evidence is provided by a business document such as a sales slip, cheque, bill, or cash register tape. Ms. Hunsley's Prestige Dance Academy in the feature story uses customers' payments, and the company's cheques written for expenses to begin its recording process. This evidence is analyzed to determine the effects of the transaction on specific accounts. The transaction is then entered in the journal. Finally, the journal entry is transferred to the correct accounts in the ledger. The sequence of events in the recording process is shown in Illustration 2-3:

Analyze each transaction   Enter transaction in a journal   Transfer journal information to ledger accounts

Illustration 2-3 ◀

The recording process

The basic steps in the recording process are repeated again and again in every business, whether a computerized or manual accounting system is used. However, the first step—the analysis of each transaction—must be done by people even when a computerized system is used. Deciding what to record is the most critical point in the accounting process. For most businesses, it is also the most expensive step. There are more examples of this step in this and later chapters.

The basic difference between a computerized and a manual accounting system is in the next two steps in the recording process—entering and transferring information. In computerized systems, the information is input and processed through file merging and report generation. These steps occur invisibly. To understand how computerized systems do this, we need to understand the manual way of processing accounting data.

ACCOUNTING IN ACTION ▶ Across the Organization Insight

Sometimes change is good—and profitable—for all involved. In August 2005, professional hockey player Dany Heatley needed a break from the demons associated with his life as a forward for the Atlanta Thrashers. Two years earlier, his friend and teammate Dan Snyder died from injuries suffered in the crash of Heatley's Ferrari, with Heatley at the wheel. After the legal issues had been resolved, Heatley asked to be traded. The Ottawa Senators took up the call, offering to trade goal scorer Marian Hossa and verteran defenceman Greg de Vries. The trade turned out to be a win-win situation for everyone. Heatley became one of the top 10 scorers in the league, and a key contributor to the Senators' run at the playoffs and Stanley Cup contention. While no money exhanged hands in the trade its results definitely had a financial impact on the value of the Senators franchise. As for Heatley, the opportunity to start over in a new place with a new team has no doubt been priceless.

Source: "Senators Sign and Trade Hossa for Heatley," Canadian Press, August 23, 2005, Allen Panzeri, "Hossa, Heatley Delivering after the Deal," *The Ottawa Citizen*, Jan. 2, 2006, "Dany Heatley: Hard Road to Turin," CBC Sports, Feb. 13, 2006.

? The Ottawa Senators and Dany Heatley signed a contract at the time of the trade. Would signing this contract result in a journal entry in the Ottawa Senators' accounting records?

The Journal

Transactions are first recorded in chronological (date) order in a **journal**. Then they are transferred to the accounts. For this reason, the journal is referred to as the book of original entry. For each transaction, the journal shows the debit and credit effects on specific accounts. Companies can use various kinds of journals, but every company has the most basic form of journal, a **general journal**. Whenever we use the term "journal" in this textbook without an adjective, we mean the general journal.

The journal makes some important contributions to the recording process:

- It discloses, in one place, the complete effect of a transaction.
- It provides a chronological record of transactions.
- It helps to prevent and locate errors, because the debit and credit amounts for each entry can easily be compared.
- It gives an explanation of the transaction and, if there is one, identifies the source document.

In a computerized system, "journals" are kept as files, and "accounts" are recorded in computer databases.

Journalizing

Entering transaction data in the journal is known as **journalizing**. Separate journal entries are made for each transaction. A complete entry consists of the following: (1) the date of the transaction, (2) the accounts and amounts to be debited and credited, and (3) a brief explanation of the transaction.

To illustrate the technique of journalizing, let's look at the first two transactions of Softbyte. These transactions were (1) September 1, Marc Doucet invested $15,000 cash in the business, and (2) computer equipment was purchased for $7,000 cash (we will assume that this transaction also occurred on September 1). In tabular form, these transactions appeared in Chapter 1 as follows:

		Assets		=	Liabilities	+	Owner's Equity
	Cash	+	Equipment				M. Doucet, Capital
(1)	+$15,000						+$15,000
(2)	−7,000		+$7,000				

Typically, a general journal has columns for dates, account titles and explanations, references, and two money columns (debit and credit). Since the illustration shows the first page of Softbyte's general journal, it is numbered J1. In journal form, the entries would appear as follows:

GENERAL JOURNAL				J1
Date	Account Titles and Explanation	Ref.	Debit	Credit
2008 Sept. 1	Cash		15,000	
	M. Doucet, Capital			15,000
	Invested cash in business.			
1	Equipment		7,000	
	Cash			7,000
	Purchased equipment for cash.			

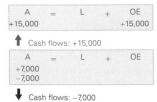

A   =   L   +   OE
+15,000   +15,000

↑ Cash flows: +15,000

A   =   L   +   OE
+7,000
−7,000

↓ Cash flows: −7,000

The standard form and content of journal entries are as follows:

1. The date of the transaction is entered in the Date column. The date recorded should include the year, month, and day of the transaction.
2. The debit account title (the account to debit) is entered first at the left margin of the column headed Account Titles and Explanation. The credit account title (the account to credit) is entered on the next line, indented from the left margin. The indentation separates the debit and credit amounts better so there is less chance of confusing them.
3. The amounts for the debits are recorded in the Debit (left) column and the amounts for the credits are recorded in the Credit (right) column.
4. A brief explanation of the transaction is given on the line below the credit account title. This explanation also gives an important reference to the source document (invoice number, cheque number, etc.), if there is one. To simplify the illustrations in this textbook, journal entry explanations are often left out (after all, you would just be recopying the information you are given). Remember, however, that in real life, explanations are essential for every journal entry.
5. A space is left between journal entries. The blank space separates individual journal entries and makes the entire journal easier to read.
6. The column titled Ref. (which stands for "reference") is left blank when the journal entry is made. This column is used later, when the journal entries are transferred to the ledger accounts. At that time, the ledger account number is placed in the Reference column to indicate where the amount in the journal entry was transferred to.

Computerized journals and manual journals serve the same purpose. The format of the computerized journal may be slightly different from the format described above, but the content is almost always the same. Computerized systems, such as QuickBooks accounting software used by Prestige Dance Academy in the feature story, often use an account number rather than an account name to be entered. The account name is automatically inserted for you by the computer. We will discuss account numbers in more detail later in this chapter. The main criterion is that each title has to accurately describe the content of the account. For example, the account title used for the computer equipment purchased by Softbyte may be Equipment, Computer Equipment, Computers, or Office Equipment. However, once a company chooses the specific title to use, all transactions for the account should be recorded under that account title.

In assignments, when specific account titles are given, they should be used. When account titles are not given, create account titles that identify the nature and content of each account. The account titles used in journalizing should not contain explanations (such as Cash Paid or Cash Received).

If an entry affects only two accounts, one debit and one credit, it is considered a simple journal entry. Some transactions, however, use more than two accounts in journalizing. When three or more accounts are required in one journal entry, the entry is called a **compound entry**. To illustrate, recall from Chapter 1 that Softbyte provided $3,500 of programming services to customers on September 9. It received $1,500 cash from the customers for these services. The balance, $2,000, was owed on account. The compound entry to record this transaction is as follows:

GENERAL JOURNAL					J1
Date	Account Titles and Explanation	Ref.	Debit	Credit	
2008					
Sept. 9	Cash		1,500		
	Accounts Receivable		2,000		
	Service Revenue			3,500	
	Performed services for cash and credit.				

A = L + OE
+1,500   +3,500
+2,000

↑ Cash flows: +1,500

In a compound entry, the total debit and credit amounts must equal. Also, the standard format requires that all debits be listed before the credits are listed.

BEFORE YOU GO ON . . .

▶**Review It**

1. What is the sequence of steps in the recording process?
2. What contribution does the journal make to the recording process?
3. What is the standard form and content of a journal entry in the general journal?
4. How is a manual journal entry different from a computerized journal entry?

▶**Do It**

In starting her beauty salon, Hair It Is, Eszter Schwenke did the following:

May 1   Opened a bank account in the name of Hair It Is and deposited $20,000 of her own money in this account as her initial investment.
     3   Purchased equipment on account (to be paid in 30 days), for a total cost of $4,800.
     7   Hired a stylist and agreed to pay her $500 per week.

(a) In what form (type of record) should Eszter record these three activities?
(b) Prepare the entries to record the transactions.

Action Plan

- Understand which activities need to be recorded and which do not.
- Analyze the effects of the transactions on asset, liability, and owner's equity accounts.
- Record the transactions in the general journal, which creates a chronological record of the transactions.

Solution

(a) Each transaction that is recorded is entered in the general journal.
(b)

May	1	Cash	20,000	
		E. Schwenke, Capital		20,000
		Invested cash in the business.		
	3	Equipment	4,800	
		Accounts Payable		4,800
		Purchased equipment on account.		
	7	No entry because no transaction has occurred.		

Related exercise material: BE2–6, BE2–7, BE2–8, E2–5, and E2–6.

The Ledger

study objective 3

Explain what a ledger is, and post journal entries.

The entire group of accounts maintained by a company is called the ledger. The **ledger** keeps in one place all the information about changes in each account.

Companies can use different kinds of ledgers, but every company has a general ledger. A **general ledger** contains all the asset, liability, and owner's equity accounts. Some of these accounts are shown in Illustration 2-4. A business can use a loose-leaf binder or card file for the ledger. Each account is kept on a separate sheet or card if a manual accounting system is used. In a computerized accounting system, each account is kept in a separate file. Whenever we use the term "ledger" in this textbook without an adjective, we mean the general ledger.

Illustration 2-4 ◀
The general ledger

Assets	Liabilities	Owner's Equity
Cash	Notes Payable	M. Doucet, Capital
Accounts Receivable	Accounts Payable	M. Doucet, Drawings
Supplies	Salaries Payable	Service Revenue
Equipment	Unearned Revenue	Salaries Expense

The ledger should be arranged in the same order that is used to present the accounts in the financial statements, beginning with the balance sheet accounts. The asset accounts come first, followed by liability accounts, owner's capital, drawings, revenues, and expenses. In a computerized system, each account is numbered so that it is easier to identify.

The ledger gives the balance in each account. For example, the Cash account shows the amount of cash that is available for current objectives. Amounts due from customers can be found by examining Accounts Receivable. Amounts owed to creditors can be found by examining Accounts Payable.

Standard Form of Account

The simple T account form used in accounting textbooks is often very useful for illustrations. In reality, however, the account forms that are used in ledgers are designed to include additional information. A very popular form in both manual and electronic systems using data (and assumed dates) from Softbyte's Cash account follows:

GENERAL LEDGER					
CASH					
Date	Explanation	Ref.	Debit	Credit	Balance
2008					
Sept. 1			15,000		15,000
1				7,000	8,000
3			1,200		9,200
9			1,500		10,700
17				600	10,100
17				900	9,200
20				200	9,000
25				250	8,750
30			600		9,350
30				1,300	8,050

This form is often called the three-column form of account because it has three money columns—debit, credit, and balance. The balance in the account is determined after each transaction. Note that the explanation space and reference columns make it possible to give information about the transaction. The explanation space is usually left blank in manual accounting systems because it is too time-consuming to copy explanations from the general journal. In computerized accounting systems, however, it is easy to include in the ledger the explanation that was originally recorded in the journal entry.

Posting

The procedure of transferring journal entries to the ledger accounts is called **posting**. Posting has the following steps:

1. **General Ledger.** In the ledger, enter the following in the correct columns of each affected account: the date, journal page, and debit or credit amount shown in the journal.

2. **General Journal.** In the reference column of the journal, write the account numbers to which the debit and credit amounts were posted in the ledger.

These steps are shown in Illustration 2-5 using Softbyte's first journal entry.

Illustration 2-5 ▶

Posting a journal entry

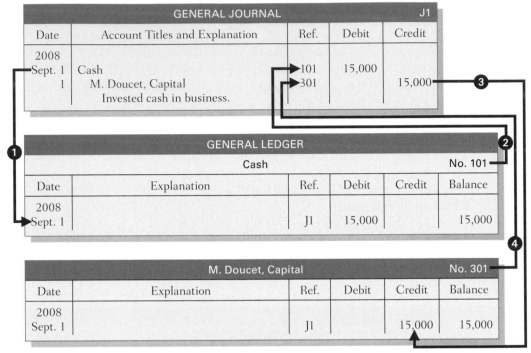

1. Post to debit account: enter date, journal page number, and amount.
2. Enter debit account number in journal reference column.
3. Post to credit account: enter date, journal page number, and amount.
4. Enter credit account number in journal reference column.

The reference column in the journal has several purposes. The numbers in this column indicate the entries that have been posted. After the last entry has been posted, this column should be looked at carefully to see that all postings have been made. The references also show the account numbers to which the amounts have been posted. The reference column of a ledger account indicates the journal page where the transaction was posted from.

Posting should be done in chronological order. That is, all the debits and credits of one journal entry should be posted before going to the next journal entry. Postings should be made on a timely basis—normally monthly—to keep the ledger up to date.

In a computerized accounting system, posting usually occurs automatically right after each journal entry is prepared. The system finds obvious errors in the recording process (e.g., unbalanced entries or the use of non-existent accounts) and does not process them until they are corrected. Because the initial entry is so important, many systems also search for less obvious errors, such as unreasonable dollar amounts or strange account balances for specific accounts (e.g., a debit balance when the account normally has a credit balance).

Chart of Accounts

Because each company is different, the types of accounts they have and how many they have are also different. The number of accounts depends on the amount of detail management wants. The management of one company may want one account for all types of utility expense. Another company may keep separate expense accounts for each type of utility expense, such as gas, electricity, and water. Similarly, a sole proprietorship like Softbyte has fewer accounts than a corporation like The Forzani Group. Softbyte may be able to manage and report its activities in 20 to 30 accounts, while The Forzani Group requires hundreds of accounts to keep track of its activities.

The first step in designing an accounting system—whether computerized or manual—is to create a **chart of accounts**. The chart of accounts is the framework for the entire database of accounting information. It lists the accounts and the account numbers that identify where the accounts are in the ledger. The numbering system that is used to identify the accounts usually starts with the balance sheet accounts. The income statement accounts come next.

ACCOUNTING IN ACTION ▶ Business Insight

The numbering system to identify accounts can be quite sophisticated or pretty simple. For example, at Goodyear Tire & Rubber Company, an eight-digit system is used. The first three digits identify the account classification as follows:

100–199 Assets	300–399 Revenues
200–299 Liabilities and Owner's Equity	400–599 Expenses

Other digits describe the location of a specific plant, product line, region of the country, and so on.

? **Why is it useful for managers to have a sophisticated chart of accounts like the one described above?**

In this and the next two chapters, we will explain the accounting for a proprietorship named Pioneer Advertising Agency (a service company). Accounts 100–199 indicate asset accounts; 200–299 indicate liabilities; 300–399 indicate owner's equity accounts; 400–499, revenues; and 600–999, expenses. The chart of accounts for Pioneer Advertising Agency (Clarence Byrd, owner) is shown in Illustration 2-6. Accounts shown in red are used in this chapter; accounts shown in black are explained in later chapters.

Illustration 2-6 ◀

Chart of accounts

PIONEER ADVERTISING AGENCY
Chart of Accounts

Assets		Owner's Equity	
101.	Cash	301.	C. Byrd, Capital
112.	Accounts Receivable	306.	C. Byrd, Drawings
129.	Advertising Supplies	350.	Income Summary
130.	Prepaid Insurance		
151.	Office Equipment	**Revenues**	
152.	Accumulated Amortization—	400.	Service Revenue
	Office Equipment		
		Expenses	
Liabilities		611.	Advertising Supplies Expense
200.	Notes Payable	711.	Amortization Expense
201.	Accounts Payable	722.	Insurance Expense
209.	Unearned Revenue	726.	Salaries Expense
212.	Salaries Payable	729.	Rent Expense
230.	Interest Payable	905.	Interest Expense

You will notice that there are gaps in the numbering system of the chart of accounts for Pioneer Advertising. Gaps make it possible to insert new accounts whenever they are needed.

A master chart of accounts for a sample company is included in the Study Aids section of the website that goes with this text.

Study Aids:
Chart of Accounts

The Recording Process Illustrated

Illustrations 2-7 through 2-17 show the basic steps in the recording process, using the October 2008 transactions of the Pioneer Advertising Agency. The agency's accounting period is one month. A basic analysis and a debit/credit analysis are done before each transaction is journalized and posted. For simplicity, the T account form is used in the illustrations instead of the standard account form. Study these transaction analyses carefully. The purpose of transaction analysis is first to identify the type of account involved, second whether it is increased or decreased, and third whether it needs to be debited or credited. You should always do this analysis before preparing a journal entry. It will help you understand the journal entries discussed in this chapter, as well as more complex journal entries in later chapters.

Remember that every journal entry affects one or more of the following items: assets, liabilities, owner's capital, revenues, expenses, or drawings. By becoming skilled at transaction analysis, you will be able to quickly recognize the impact of any transaction on these items.

Illustration 2-7 ▶

Investment of cash by owner

Transaction	October 1, Clarence Byrd invests $10,000 cash in an advertising venture to be known as the Pioneer Advertising Agency.
Basic Analysis	The asset Cash is increased by $10,000, and the owner's equity account C. Byrd, Capital, is increased by $10,000.
Debit/Credit Analysis	Debits increase assets: debit Cash $10,000. Credits increase owner's equity: credit C. Byrd, Capital, $10,000.

Journal Entry	Oct. 1	Cash
		    C. Byrd, Capital
		        Invested cash in business.
			101
			301
				10,000	10,000

Posting	Cash	101		C. Byrd, Capital	301
	Oct. 1	10,000			Oct. 1	10,000

Illustration 2-8 ▶

Purchase of office equipment

Transaction	October 2, office equipment costing $5,000 is purchased by signing a $5,000, 6% note payable, due in three months on January 2, 2009.
Basic Analysis	The asset Office Equipment is increased by $5,000, and the liability Notes Payable is increased by $5,000.
Debit/Credit Analysis	Debits increase assets: debit Office Equipment $5,000. Credits increase liabilities: credit Notes Payable $5,000.

Journal Entry	Oct. 2	Office Equipment
		    Notes Payable
		        Issued 6%, 3-month note for office equipment.
			151
			200
				5,000	5,000

Posting	Office Equipment	151		Notes Payable	200
	Oct. 2	5,000			Oct. 2	5,000

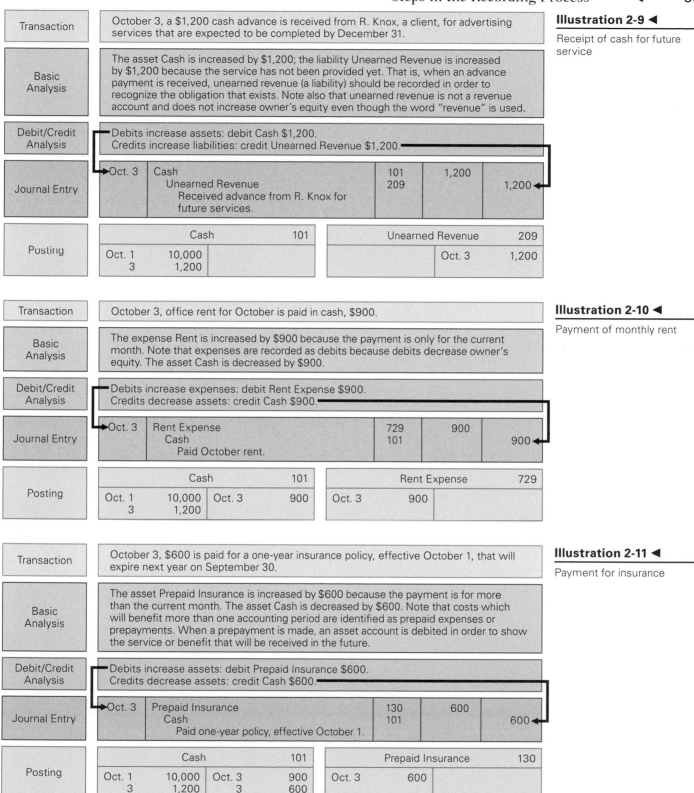

Transaction	October 3, a $1,200 cash advance is received from R. Knox, a client, for advertising services that are expected to be completed by December 31.

Illustration 2-9 ◀

Receipt of cash for future service

Basic Analysis	The asset Cash is increased by $1,200; the liability Unearned Revenue is increased by $1,200 because the service has not been provided yet. That is, when an advance payment is received, unearned revenue (a liability) should be recorded in order to recognize the obligation that exists. Note also that unearned revenue is not a revenue account and does not increase owner's equity even though the word "revenue" is used.

Debit/Credit Analysis	Debits increase assets: debit Cash $1,200. Credits increase liabilities: credit Unearned Revenue $1,200.

Journal Entry	Oct. 3	Cash	101	1,200	
		Unearned Revenue	209		1,200
		Received advance from R. Knox for future services.			

Posting

Cash		101
Oct. 1	10,000	
3	1,200	

Unearned Revenue		209
	Oct. 3	1,200

Transaction	October 3, office rent for October is paid in cash, $900.

Illustration 2-10 ◀

Payment of monthly rent

Basic Analysis	The expense Rent is increased by $900 because the payment is only for the current month. Note that expenses are recorded as debits because debits decrease owner's equity. The asset Cash is decreased by $900.

Debit/Credit Analysis	Debits increase expenses: debit Rent Expense $900. Credits decrease assets: credit Cash $900.

Journal Entry	Oct. 3	Rent Expense	729	900	
		Cash	101		900
		Paid October rent.			

Posting

Cash		101		
Oct. 1	10,000	Oct. 3	900
3	1,200		

Rent Expense		729
Oct. 3	900	

Transaction	October 3, $600 is paid for a one-year insurance policy, effective October 1, that will expire next year on September 30.

Illustration 2-11 ◀

Payment for insurance

Basic Analysis	The asset Prepaid Insurance is increased by $600 because the payment is for more than the current month. The asset Cash is decreased by $600. Note that costs which will benefit more than one accounting period are identified as prepaid expenses or prepayments. When a prepayment is made, an asset account is debited in order to show the service or benefit that will be received in the future.

Debit/Credit Analysis	Debits increase assets: debit Prepaid Insurance $600. Credits decrease assets: credit Cash $600.

Journal Entry	Oct. 3	Prepaid Insurance	130	600	
		Cash	101		600
		Paid one-year policy, effective October 1.			

Posting

Cash		101		
Oct. 1	10,000	Oct. 3	900
3	1,200	3	600

Prepaid Insurance		130
Oct. 3	600	

Illustration 2-12 ►

Purchase of supplies on credit

Transaction	October 4, an estimated three-month supply of advertising materials is purchased on account from Aero Supply for $2,500.
Basic Analysis	The asset Advertising Supplies is increased by $2,500. The liability Accounts Payable is increased by $2,500.
Debit/Credit Analysis	Debits increase assets: debit Advertising Supplies $2,500. Credits increase liabilities: credit Accounts Payable $2,500.

Journal Entry	Oct. 4	Advertising Supplies	129	2,500	
		Accounts Payable	201		2,500
		Purchased supplies on account from Aero Supply.			

Posting

Advertising Supplies		129		Accounts Payable		201
Oct. 4	2,500				Oct. 4	2,500

Illustration 2-13 ►

Hiring of employees

Transaction	October 6, four employees are hired to begin work on October 13. Each employee is to receive a weekly salary of $500 for a five-day work week (Monday–Friday), payable every two weeks. The first payment will be on October 24.
Basic Analysis	A business transaction has not occurred. There is only an agreement between the employer and the employees to enter into a business transaction beginning on October 13. Thus, a debit/credit analysis is not needed because there is no accounting entry. (See October 24 transaction for first entry.)

Illustration 2-14 ►

Withdrawal of cash by owner

Transaction	October 20, Clarence Byrd withdraws $500 cash for personal use.
Basic Analysis	The owner's equity account, C. Byrd, Drawings, is increased by $500. Note that drawings are recorded as debits because debits reduce owner's equity. The asset Cash is decreased by $500.
Debit/Credit Analysis	Debits increase drawings: debit C. Byrd, Drawings, $500. Credits decrease assets: credit Cash $500.

Journal Entry	Oct. 20	C. Byrd, Drawings	306	500	
		Cash	101		500
		Withdrew cash for personal use.			

Posting

Cash				101	C. Byrd, Drawings		306
Oct. 1	10,000	Oct. 3	900		Oct. 20	500	
3	1,200	3	600				
		20	500				

Illustration 2-15 ►

Service performed on account

Transaction	October 21, Copa Company is billed $10,000 for advertising services performed to date.
Basic Analysis	The asset Accounts Receivable is increased by $10,000. The revenue account Service Revenue is increased by $10,000. Note that revenue is recorded when the service is performed, regardless of when the cash is received. An asset account is created when the work is complete because Pioneer Advertising expects a future benefit—the payment by Copa Company.
Debit/Credit Analysis	Debits increase assets: debit Accounts Receivable $10,000. Credits increase revenues: credit Service Revenue $10,000.

Journal Entry	Oct. 21	Accounts Receivable	112	10,000	
		Service Revenue	400		10,000
		Performed services on account for Copa Company.			

Posting

Accounts Receivable		112		Service Revenue		400
Oct. 21	10,000				Oct. 21	10,000

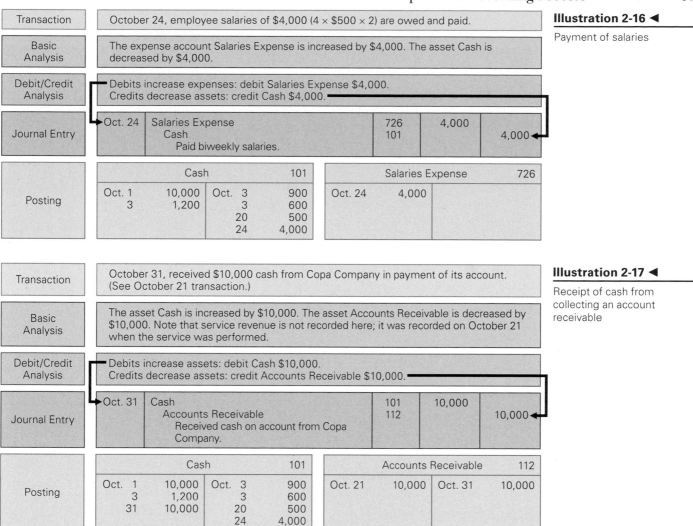

Illustration 2-16 ◀

Payment of salaries

| Transaction | October 24, employee salaries of $4,000 (4 × $500 × 2) are owed and paid. |

| Basic Analysis | The expense account Salaries Expense is increased by $4,000. The asset Cash is decreased by $4,000. |

| Debit/Credit Analysis | Debits increase expenses: debit Salaries Expense $4,000. Credits decrease assets: credit Cash $4,000. |

Journal Entry

Oct. 24	Salaries Expense	726	4,000	
	Cash	101		4,000
	Paid biweekly salaries.			

Posting

Cash				101
Oct. 1	10,000	Oct. 3	900
3	1,200	3	600
		20	500
		24	4,000

| Salaries Expense | | 726 |
| Oct. 24 | 4,000 | |

Illustration 2-17 ◀

Receipt of cash from collecting an account receivable

| Transaction | October 31, received $10,000 cash from Copa Company in payment of its account. (See October 21 transaction.) |

| Basic Analysis | The asset Cash is increased by $10,000. The asset Accounts Receivable is decreased by $10,000. Note that service revenue is not recorded here; it was recorded on October 21 when the service was performed. |

| Debit/Credit Analysis | Debits increase assets: debit Cash $10,000. Credits decrease assets: credit Accounts Receivable $10,000. |

Journal Entry

Oct. 31	Cash	101	10,000	
	Accounts Receivable	112		10,000
	Received cash on account from Copa Company.			

Posting

Cash				101
Oct. 1	10,000	Oct. 3	900
3	1,200	3	600
31	10,000	20	500
		24	4,000

| Accounts Receivable | | | 112 |
| Oct. 21 | 10,000 | Oct. 31 | 10,000 |

Summary Illustration of Journalizing and Posting

The general journal and general ledger for Pioneer Advertising Agency for October follows:

GENERAL JOURNAL				J1
Date	Account Titles and Explanation	Ref.	Debit	Credit
2008 Oct. 1	Cash	101	10,000	
	C. Byrd, Capital	301		10,000
	Invested cash in business.			
2	Office Equipment	151	5,000	
	Notes Payable	200		5,000
	Issued 6%, 3-month note for office equipment.			
3	Cash	101	1,200	
	Unearned Revenue	209		1,200
	Received advance from R. Knox for future services.			
3	Rent Expense	729	900	
	Cash	101		900
	Paid October rent.			
3	Prepaid Insurance	130	600	
	Cash	101		600
	Paid one-year policy, effective October 1.			
4	Advertising Supplies	129	2,500	
	Accounts Payable	201		2,500
	Purchased supplies on account from Aero Supply.			
20	C. Byrd, Drawings	306	500	
	Cash	101		500
	Withdrew cash for personal use.			
21	Accounts Receivable	112	10,000	
	Service Revenue	400		10,000
	Performed services on account for Copa Company.			
24	Salaries Expense	726	4,000	
	Cash	101		4,000
	Paid biweekly salaries.			
31	Cash	101	10,000	
	Accounts Receivable	112		10,000
	Received cash on account from Copa Company.			

GENERAL LEDGER

Cash 101
Oct. 1 10,000 | Oct. 3 900
3 1,200 | 3 600
31 10,000 | 20 500
| 24 4,000
Bal. 15,200

Accounts Receivable 112
Oct. 21 10,000 | Oct. 31 10,000
Bal. 0

Advertising Supplies 129
Oct. 4 2,500
Bal. 2,500

Prepaid Insurance 130
Oct. 3 600
Bal. 600

Accounts payable 201
| Oct. 4 2,500
| Bal. 2,500

Unearned Revenue 209
| Oct. 3 1,200
| Bal. 1,200

C. Byrd, Capital 301
| Oct. 1 10,000
| Bal. 10,000

C. Byrd, Drawings 306
Oct. 20 500
Bal. 500

Service Revenue 400
| Oct. 21 10,000
| Bal. 10,000

Office Equipment		151		Salaries Expense		726
Oct. 2	5,000		Oct. 24	4,000		
Bal.	5,000		Bal.	4,000		

Notes Payable		200		Rent Expense		729
	Oct. 2	5,000	Oct. 3	900		
	Bal.	5,000	Bal.	900		

BEFORE YOU GO ON . . .

▶Review It

1. How is journalizing different from posting in a manual system? In a computerized system?
2. What is the purpose of (a) the ledger, and (b) a chart of accounts?

▶Do It

By May 15, following the successful grand opening of Hair It Is, Eszter Schwenke and her employee had performed $1,280 of hairstyling services ($1,000 was collected in cash and $280 was on account). On May 16, Eszter paid $500 in wages and $92 for utilities. The opening balance in the Cash account was $20,000. Record these transactions in the general journal and post the entries to the general ledger for Eszter.

Action Plan

- Analyze the transactions. Determine the accounts affected and whether the transaction increases or decreases the account.
- Record the transaction in the general journal using debits and credits. Remember that credits are indented slightly and shown to the right.
- Posting involves transferring the journalized debits and credits to specific accounts in the ledger.
- Determine the ending balances by netting (calculating the difference between) the total debits and credits.

Solution

May 15	Cash	1,000	
	Accounts Receivable	280	
	Hairstyling Service Revenue		1,280
	Performed services for cash and on account.		
16	Wages Expense	500	
	Utilities Expense	92	
	Cash		592
	Paid cash for services.		

Cash		Accounts Receivable	Hairstyling Service Revenue	Wages Expense	Utilities Expense
20,000	592	280	1,280	500	92
1,000					
20,408					

Related exercise material: BE2–9 and E2–7.

The Trial Balance

A **trial balance** is a list of accounts and their balances at a specific time. A trial balance is normally prepared monthly, and at least at the end of each accounting period. The accounts are listed in the same order as they are in the ledger, with debit balances in the left column and credit balances in the right column.

The main purpose of a trial balance is to prove (check) that the debits equal the credits after posting. If the debits and credits do not agree, the trial balance can uncover errors in journalizing and posting. In addition, it is useful for preparing the financial statements, as will be explained in the next two chapters.

To prepare a trial balance:

1. List the account titles and their balances in the same order as the chart of accounts. Debit balances are entered in the debit column and credit balances are entered in the credit column.
2. Total the debit and credit columns.
3. Ensure that the two columns are equal.

The trial balance prepared from the ledger of Pioneer Advertising Agency follows:

PIONEER ADVERTISING AGENCY
Trial Balance
October 31, 2008

	Debit	Credit
Cash	$15,200	
Accounts receivable	0	
Advertising supplies	2,500	
Prepaid insurance	600	
Office equipment	5,000	
Notes payable		$ 5,000
Accounts payable		2,500
Unearned revenue		1,200
C. Byrd, capital		10,000
C. Byrd, drawings	500	
Service revenue		10,000
Salaries expense	4,000	
Rent expense	900	
Totals	$28,700	$28,700

Note that the total debits of $28,700 equal the total credits of $28,700. Accounts with zero balances, such as Accounts Receivable, are often omitted from the trial balance. Account numbers are sometimes shown to the left of the account titles in the trial balance.

Limitations of a Trial Balance

Although a trial balance reveals many types of bookkeeping errors, it does not prove that all transactions have been recorded or that the ledger is correct. There can be many errors even when the trial balance columns agree. For example, the trial balance may balance in the following cases: (1) a transaction is not journalized, (2) a correct journal entry is not posted, (3) a journal entry is posted twice, (4) incorrect accounts are used in journalizing or posting, or (5) offsetting errors (errors that hide each other) are made in recording the amount of a transaction. In other words, as long as equal debits and credits are posted, even to the wrong account or in the wrong amount, the total debits will equal the total credits when the trial balance is prepared.

Locating Errors

The procedure for preparing a trial balance is quite simple. However, if the trial balance does not balance, locating an error in a manual accounting system can be time-consuming, tiring, and frustrating. Errors generally result from mathematical mistakes, incorrect postings, or simply re-copying data incorrectly. Errors in a computerized system usually happen in the initial recording rather than because of a software error in posting or the preparation of the trial balance.

What do you do if you have a manual trial balance that does not balance? First determine the amount of the difference between the two columns of the trial balance. After you know this amount, try the following steps:

1. If the error is an amount such as $1, $100, or $1,000, re-add the trial balance columns. Recalculate the account balances.
2. If the error can be evenly divided by two, scan the trial balance to see if a balance equal to half the error has been entered in the wrong column.
3. If the error can be evenly divided by nine, retrace the account balances on the trial balance to see whether they are incorrectly copied from the ledger. For example, if a balance was $12 but was listed as $21, a $9 error has been made. Reversing the order of numbers is called a transposition error.
4. If the error cannot be evenly divided by two or nine, scan the ledger to see whether an account balance in the amount of the error has been omitted from the trial balance. Scan the journal to see whether a posting in the amount of the error has been omitted. Check your additions.

Of course, if there is more than one error, these steps may not work.

Ethics note

Auditors see errors and irregularities as two different things. An error is an unintentional mistake. So it is neither ethical nor unethical. An irregularity, on the other hand, is an intentional misstatement, which is generally viewed as unethical.

ACCOUNTING IN ACTION ▶ Business Insight

If you've ever made an arithmetic error, you may take some comfort from an accountant's mistake at Fidelity Investments, the world's largest mutual fund investment company. The accountant failed to include a minus sign while doing a tax calculation, which made a $1.3-billion loss look like a $1.3-billion gain. No one expects that kind of mistake at a firm like Fidelity, which has sophisticated computer systems and top investment managers.

In explaining the mistake to shareholders, Fidelity manager J. Gary Burkhead wrote: "Some people have asked how, in this age of technology, such a mistake could be made. While many of our processes are computerized, the requirements of the tax code are complex and dictate that some steps must be handled manually by our tax managers and accountants, and people can make mistakes." Evidently so. That's why it pays to do a "reasonableness check." Someone at Fidelity must have had a sense that the year's results shouldn't have been as rosy as the accounting numbers first indicated.

? Is a trial balance useful in finding this type of error?

Some Simplistic Assumptions

To keep things simple, we have made some assumptions in the material in this textbook. These include not using cents and sales taxes in the transaction data.

Use of Dollars and Cents

We have not included cents in the dollar figures we record in journal entries, general ledger accounts, and trial balances. Avoiding cents in entries will save you time and effort and you will still understand the accounting process. In reality, it is important to remember that cents should be, and are, used in the formal accounting records. Cents are important, and quickly add up to dollars!

Dollar signs do not appear in the journals or ledgers. Dollar signs are used only in the trial balance and the financial statements. Generally, a dollar sign is shown only for the first item in the column, and for the total of that column. A single line is placed under the column of figures to be added or subtracted. The total amount is double-underlined to indicate the final sum.

Sales Taxes

Sales taxes in Canada include the Goods and Services Tax (GST) and the Provincial Sales Tax (PST). In the Atlantic Provinces (except for P.E.I.), GST and PST have been combined into one tax, called the Harmonized Sales Tax (HST).

In general, sales taxes are paid by a company on the goods and services it purchases, and are collected on the goods that it sells and the services it provides. However, accounting for sales taxes is complicated and there are many exceptions. For example, not only do provincial sales tax rates vary across the country, but the method of calculating this tax can also vary. In addition, not all companies and their goods are taxable.

Although sales taxes are an important part of business, accounting transactions are presented in this textbook without the added complexity of these taxes. For those students who wish to advance their understanding of this topic, sales taxes are discussed in more detail in Appendix B at the end of this textbook.

BEFORE YOU GO ON . . .

▶ Review It

1. What is a trial balance, and what is its main purpose?
2. How is a trial balance prepared?
3. What are the limitations of a trial balance?

▶ Do It

Koizumi Kollections has the following alphabetical list of accounts and balances at July 31, 2008:

Account	Amount	Account	Amount
Accounts payable	$33,700	Land	$ 51,000
Accounts receivable	71,200	Machinery and equipment	35,700
Building	86,500	Notes payable	49,500
Cash	3,200	Operating expenses	105,100
J. Koizumi, capital	99,400	Service revenue	171,100
J. Koizumi, drawings	4,000	Unearned service revenue	3,000

Each of the above accounts has a normal balance. Prepare a trial balance with the accounts in the same order as they would be in the ledger (in other words, in financial statement order).

Action Plan

- Reorder the accounts as they would normally be in the general ledger—balance sheet accounts are listed first (assets, liabilities, and equity) followed by income statement accounts (revenues and expenses).
- Determine whether each account has a normal debit or credit balance.
- List the amounts in the appropriate debit or credit column.
- Total the trial balance columns. Total debits must equal total credits or a mistake has been made.

Solution

KOIZUMI KOLLECTIONS
Trial Balance
July 31, 2008

	Debit	Credit
Cash	$ 3,200	
Accounts receivable	71,200	
Land	51,000	
Building	86,500	
Machinery and equipment	35,700	
Accounts payable		$ 33,700
Unearned service revenue		3,000
Notes payable		49,500
J. Koizumi, capital		99,400
J. Koizumi, drawings	4,000	
Service revenue		171,100
Operating expenses	105,100	
Totals	$356,700	$356,700

Related exercise material: BE2–10, BE2–11, E2–1, E2–8, E2–9, E2–10, and E2–11.

Demonstration Problem

Nge Aung opened the Campus Laundromat on September 1, 2008. During the first month of operations, the following transactions occurred:

Sept. 1 Invested $20,000 cash in the business.
  2 Paid $1,000 cash for store rent for the month of September.
  3 Purchased washers and dryers for $25,000, paying $10,000 in cash and signing a $15,000, six-month, 5% note payable.
  6 Paid $1,200 for a one-year insurance policy.
  10 Received bill from *The Daily News* for advertising the opening of the laundromat, $200.
  15 Billed a nearby restaurant $500 for laundry services performed on account.
  20 Withdrew $700 cash for personal use.
  25 Received $300 cash from the restaurant billed on September 15. The balance of the account will be collected in October.
  29 A cash advance of $400 is received from the college residence for services to be performed in October.
  30 Cash receipts for laundry services performed for the month were $6,200.
  30 Paid employee salaries of $1,600.

The chart of accounts for the company is the same as the one for Pioneer Advertising Agency in Illustration 2-6 except for the following: No. 153 Laundry Equipment and No. 610 Advertising Expense.

Instructions

(a) Journalize the September transactions.
(b) Open ledger accounts and post the September transactions.
(c) Prepare a trial balance at September 30, 2008.
(d) Prepare an income statement, statement of owner's equity, and balance sheet for Campus Laundromat.

Practice Tools:
Demonstration Problems

Solution to Demonstration Problem

(a)

	GENERAL JOURNAL			J1
Date	Account Titles and Explanation	Ref.	Debit	Credit

2008
Sept. 1
	Cash
	    N. Aung, Capital
	        Invested cash in business.
		101
		301
			20,000	
				20,000

2	Rent Expense
	    Cash
	        Paid September rent.
		729
		101
			1,000	
				1,000

3	Laundry Equipment
	    Cash
	    Notes Payable
	        Purchased laundry equipment for cash and 6-month,
	        5% note payable.
		153
		101
		200
			25,000	
				10,000
				15,000

6	Prepaid Insurance
	    Cash
	        Paid one-year insurance policy.
		130
		101
			1,200	
				1,200

10	Advertising Expense
	    Accounts Payable
	        Received bill from *The Daily News* for advertising.
		610
		201
			200	
				200

15	Accounts Receivable
	    Service Revenue
	        Performed laundry services on account.
		112
		400
			500	
				500

20	N. Aung, Drawings
	    Cash
	        Withdrew cash for personal use.
		306
		101
			700	
				700

25	Cash
	    Accounts Receivable
	        Received cash on account.
		101
		112
			300	
				300

29	Cash
	    Unearned Revenue
	        Received cash in advance from customer.
		101
		209
			400	
				400

30	Cash
	    Service Revenue
	        Received cash for laundry services.
		101
		400
			6,200	
				6,200

30	Salaries expense
	    Cash
	        Paid employee salaries.
		726
		101
			1,600	
				1,600

(b)

GENERAL LEDGER						

Cash				101
Sept. 1	20,000	Sept. 2	1,000
25	300	3	10,000
29	400	6	1,200
30	6,200	20	700
		30	1,600
Bal.	12,400		

Accounts Receivable				112
Sept. 15	500	Sept. 25	300
Bal.	200		

Prepaid Insurance		130
Sept. 6	1,200	
Bal.	1,200	

Laundry Equipment		153
Sept. 3	25,000	
Bal.	25,000	

Notes Payable			200
		Sept. 3	15,000
		Bal.	15,000

Accounts Payable			201
		Sept. 10	200
		Bal.	200

Unearned Revenue			209
		Sept. 29	400
		Bal.	400

N. Aung, Capital			301
		Sept. 1	20,000
		Bal.	20,000

N. Aung, Drawings		306
Sept. 20	700	
Bal.	700	

Service Revenue			400
		Sept. 15	500
		30	6,200
		Bal.	6,700

Advertising Expense		610
Sept. 10	200	
Bal.	200	

Salaries Expense		726
Sept. 30	1,600	
Bal.	1,600	

Rent Expense		729
Sept. 2	1,000	
Bal.	1,000	

(c)

CAMPUS LAUNDROMAT		
Trial Balance		
September 30, 2008		

	Debit	Credit
Cash	$12,400	
Accounts receivable	200	
Prepaid insurance	1,200	
Laundry equipment	25,000	
Notes payable		$15,000
Accounts payable		200
Unearned service revenue		400
N. Aung, capital		20,000
N. Aung, drawings	700	
Service revenue		6,700
Advertising expense	200	
Salaries expense	1,600	
Rent expense	1,000	
Totals	$42,300	$42,300

(d)

CAMPUS LAUNDROMAT		
Income Statement		
Month Ended September 30, 2008		
Revenues		
Service revenue		$6,700
Expenses		
Advertising expense	$ 200	
Salaries expense	1,600	
Rent expense	1,000	2,800
Net income		$3,900

CAMPUS LAUNDROMAT		
Statement of Owner's Equity		
Month Ended September 30, 2008		
N. Aung, capital, September 1		$ 0
Add: Investments	$20,000	
Net income	3,900	23,900
Less: Drawings		700
N. Aung, capital, September 30		$23,200

CAMPUS LAUNDROMAT		
Balance Sheet		
September 30, 2008		
Assets		
Cash		$ 12,400
Accounts receivable		200
Prepaid insurance		1,200
Laundry equipment		25,000
Total assets		$38,800
Liabilities and Owner's Equity		
Liabilities		
Notes payable	$15,000	
Accounts payable	200	
Unearned service revenue	400	$ 15,600
Owner's equity		
N. Aung, capital		23,200
Total liabilities and owner's equity		$38,800

the navigator

Summary of Study Objectives

1. *Define debits and credits and illustrate how they are used to record business transactions.* The term "debit" indicates left and "credit" indicates right. Assets, drawings, and expenses are increased by debits and decreased by credits. Liabilities, owner's capital, and revenues are increased by credits and decreased by debits. The normal balance of an asset is a debit because assets are on the left side of the accounting equation. The normal balance of liabilities and owner's capital is a credit because they are on the right side of the accounting equation. Revenues are recorded as credits because credits increase owner's equity. Expenses and drawings are recorded as debits because debits decrease owner's equity.

2. *Describe the basic steps in the recording process, explain what a journal is, and journalize business transactions.* The basic steps in the recording process are as follows: (a) analyze each transaction for its effect on the accounts, (b) enter the transaction information in a journal, and (c) transfer the journal information to the correct accounts in the ledger. The first accounting record of a transaction is the entry in the journal, and the data are later transferred to the general ledger. A journal (a) discloses in one place the complete effect of a transaction, (b) provides a chronological record of transactions, (c) prevents and helps locate errors because the debit and credit amounts for each entry can be easily compared, and (d) gives an explanation of the transaction and a reference to the source document, if there is one.

3. *Explain what a ledger is, and post journal entries.* The entire group of accounts maintained by a company is called the ledger. The ledger keeps in one place all the information about changes in each of the specific account balances. Posting is the procedure of transferring journal entries to the ledger accounts. This part of the recording process brings together in each account the effects of journalized transactions.

4. *Explain the purpose of a trial balance, and prepare one.* A trial balance is a list of accounts and their balances at a specific time. Its main purpose is to prove that debits and credits are equal after posting. A trial balance also uncovers certain types of errors in journalizing and posting, and is useful in preparing financial statements.

the navigator

Glossary

www.wiley.com/canada/weygandt
Study Aids: Glossary
Practice Tools: Key Term Matching Activity

Account A record of increases and decreases in a specific asset, liability, or owner's equity item. (p. 52)

Chart of accounts A list of accounts and the account numbers that identify where the accounts are in the ledger. (p. 63)

Compound entry An entry that affects three or more accounts. (p. 59)

Credit The right side of an account. (p. 52)

Debit The left side of an account. (p. 52)

Double-entry system A system that records the dual (two-sided) effect of each transaction in appropriate accounts. (p. 53)

General journal The book of original entry that transactions are recorded in when they are not recorded in other specialized journals. (p. 58)

General ledger A ledger that contains accounts for all assets, liabilities, equities, revenues, and expenses. (p. 60)

Journal An accounting record where transactions are recorded in chronological (date) order. (p. 58)

Journalizing The entering of transaction data in the journal. (p. 58)

Ledger A record that contains all of a company's accounts. (p. 60)

Posting The procedure of transferring journal entries to the ledger accounts. (p. 61)

T account A form of account that looks like the letter T. It has the title above the horizontal line. Debits are shown to the left of the vertical line, credits to the right. (p. 52)

Trial balance A list of accounts and their balances at a specific time, usually at the end of the accounting period. (p. 70)

Self-Study Questions

Practice Tools: Self-Assessment Quizzes

Answers are at the end of the chapter.

(SO 1) K   1. Which of the following statements about an account is true?
  (a) The left side of an account is the credit or decrease side.
  (b) An account is an individual accounting record of increases and decreases in specific asset, liability, and owner's equity items.
  (c) There are separate accounts for specific assets and liabilities but only one account for owner's equity items.
  (d) In its simplest form, an account has two parts.

(SO 1) K   2. Debits:
  (a) increase both assets and liabilities.
  (b) decrease both assets and liabilities.
  (c) increase assets and decrease liabilities.
  (d) decrease assets and increase liabilities.

(SO 1) K   3. A revenue account:
  (a) is increased by debits.
  (b) is decreased by credits.
  (c) has a normal balance of a debit.
  (d) is increased by credits.

(SO 1) K   4. Accounts that normally have debit balances are:
  (a) assets, expenses, and revenues.
  (b) assets, expenses, and owner's capital.
  (c) assets, liabilities, and drawings.
  (d) assets, drawings, and expenses.

(SO 2) K   5. Which of the following is not part of the recording process?
  (a) Analyzing transactions
  (b) Preparing a trial balance
  (c) Entering transactions in a journal
  (d) Posting transactions

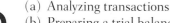

6. Which of these statements about a journal is false?   (SO 2)
  (a) It is not a book of original entry.
  (b) It provides a chronological record of transactions.
  (c) It helps to locate errors because the debit and credit amounts for each entry can be easily compared.
  (d) It shows in one place the complete effect of a transaction.

7. A ledger: (SO 3)
  (a) contains only asset and liability accounts.
  (b) should show accounts in alphabetical order.
  (c) is a collection of the entire group of accounts maintained by a company.
  (d) is a book of original entry.

8. Posting: (SO 3)
  (a) is normally done before journalizing.
  (b) transfers ledger transaction data to the journal.
  (c) is an optional step in the recording process.
  (d) transfers journal entries to ledger accounts.

9. A trial balance: (SO 4)
  (a) is a list of accounts with their balances at a specific time.
  (b) proves that journalized transactions are accurate.
  (c) will not balance if a correct journal entry is posted twice.
  (d) proves that all transactions have been recorded.

10. A trial balance will not balance if: (SO 4)
  (a) a correct journal entry is posted twice.
  (b) the purchase of supplies on account is debited to Supplies and credited to Cash.
  (c) a $100 cash drawing by the owner is debited to Drawings for $1,000 and credited to Cash for $100.
  (d) a $450 payment on account is debited to Accounts Payable for $45 and credited to Cash for $45.

Questions

(SO 1) C   1. Should the balance in total owner's equity equal the balance in the Cash account? Explain why or why not.

(SO 1) C   2. Jos Arcelus, a fellow student, says that the double-entry system means each transaction is recorded in two places: the journal and the ledger. Is Jos correct? Explain.

(SO 1) C   3. Kim Nguyen, a beginning accounting student, believes credit balances are good and debit balances are bad. Is Kim correct? Discuss.

(SO 1) K   4. State the rules of debit and credit, and identify the normal balance for (a) asset accounts, (b) liability accounts, and (c) owner's equity accounts: (1) capital, (2) drawings, (3) revenue, and (4) expense.

(SO 1) K   5. Explain the relationship between the normal balance in each type of account and the basic accounting equation.

(SO 1) K   6. Decide whether each of the following accounts is an asset, liability, or owner's equity account and whether it would have a normal debit or credit balance:
(a) Accounts Receivable   (e) Drawings
(b) Accounts Payable   (f) Supplies
(c) Equipment   (g) Unearned Revenue
(d) Rent Expense   (h) Cash

(SO 1) C   7. For the following transactions, indicate the account debited and the account credited:
(a) Equipment is purchased on account.
(b) Cash is received for services to be provided the next month.
(c) The current month's utility bill is paid in cash.

(SO 1) C   8. Indicate whether the following accounts generally will have (a) debit entries only, (b) credit entries only, or (c) both debit and credit entries:
(a) Accounts Payable   (d) Drawings
(b) Accounts Receivable   (e) Rent Expense
(c) Cash   (f) Service Revenue

(SO 2) C   9. Ben Benoit, a fellow student, is unclear about how the basic steps in the recording process in a computerized system are different from steps in a manual system. Briefly explain the steps and the differences in the two systems.

(SO 2) K   10. Give two examples of business documents that are analyzed when journal entries are being prepared.

(SO 2) C   11. The Cookie Cutter Company has an account with the Princess Printing Company. During the month, Princess Printing performs services for Cookie Cutter, printing flyers and other materials. At the end of the month, Princess Printing sends Cookie Cutter a bill and Cookie Cutter pays cash for the full amount owing. How do each of these three transactions (performing printing services, issuing the monthly bills, and collecting amounts due) affect Princess Printing Company's (a) cash, and (b) owner's equity?

(SO 2) K   12. What is the difference between Accounts Payable and Notes Payable? Between Accounts Payable and Accounts Receivable?

(SO 2) C   13. A company receives cash from a customer. What three accounts could be credited for this transaction? Describe the circumstances for using each of these three accounts.

(SO 2,3) AP   14. Amber Rose believes that accounting would be more efficient if transactions were recorded directly in the ledger accounts. Explain to Amber the advantages of first recording transactions in the journal, and then posting them to the ledger.

(SO 3) AP   15. What are the differences between a ledger and a chart of accounts?

(SO 4) AP   16. What is a trial balance? What are its purposes?

(SO 2,3,4) AP   17. Kap Shin is confused about how accounting information moves through the accounting system. He believes the flow of information is as follows:
(a) Debits and credits are posted to the ledger.
(b) The business transaction occurs.
(c) Information is entered in the journal.
(d) Financial statements are prepared.
(e) A trial balance is prepared.
Show Kap the correct flow of information.

(SO 4) AN   18. Two students are discussing the use of a trial balance. They wonder if the following errors in different companies would prevent a trial balance from balancing. For each error, what would you tell the students?
(a) The bookkeeper debited Supplies for $750 and debited Accounts Payable for $750 for the purchase of supplies on account.
(b) Cash collected on account was debited to Cash for $1,000 and credited to Service Revenue for $1,000.

(SO 4) C   19. A company has a December 31 year end and is wondering if the heading on its trial balance should read "Year Ended December 31" or just "December 31." Which one is correct? Explain why.

Brief Exercises

Calculate account balances.
(SO 1) AP

BE2–1   For the two accounts that follow, calculate the balance and indicate whether it is a debit or credit balance:

Accounts Receivable		Accounts Payable	
8,000	5,210	220	390
6,340	2,750	560	710
	2,390	175	850
		355	

Indicate debit and credit effects and normal balance.
(SO 1) K

BE2–2   For each of the following accounts, indicate (a) the effect of a debit on the account, (b) the effect of a credit on the account, and (c) the normal balance:

1. Accounts Payable
2. Accounts Receivable
3. Cash
4. Computer Equipment
5. J. Takamoto, Capital
6. J. Takamoto, Drawings
7. Notes Payable
8. Prepaid Insurance
9. Rent Expense
10. Salaries Expense
11. Service Revenue
12. Unearned Revenue

Indicate when to use debits and credits.
(SO 1) K

BE2–3   Indicate whether you would use a debit or credit to record the following changes:

1. Increase in Accounts Receivable
2. Decrease in Cash
3. Increase in Notes Payable
4. Increase in Salaries Expense
5. Increase in Drawings
6. Decrease in Equipment
7. Decrease in Accounts Payable
8. Increase in Service Revenue

Identify accounts to be debited and credited.
(SO 1) C

BE2–4   Ing Company had the following transactions for June. Identify the accounts to be debited and credited for each transaction.

June 1 D. Ing invests $5,500 cash in a small welding business.
  2 Buys equipment on account for $3,000.
  3 Pays $500 to a landlord for June rent.
  4 Pays $800 for a one-year insurance policy.
  12 Bills T. Sargeant $350 for welding work done.
  22 Receives $350 cash from T. Sargeant for worked billed on June 12.
  25 Hires an employee to start work on July 2.
  29 Pays for equipment purchased on June 2.

Indicate basic and debit/credit analysis.
(SO 1) C

BE2–5   A. Fisher has the following transactions during August. Indicate (a) the basic analysis, and (b) the debit/credit analysis, as illustrated in the chapter.

Aug. 1 Opens an office as a financial advisor, investing $7,000 in cash.
  4 Pays insurance in advance for six months, $1,900.
  16 Receives $950 from clients for services provided.
  27 Pays secretary $750 salary.
  29 Withdraws $500 cash for personal use.

Identify and explain steps in recording process.
(SO 2) C

BE2–6   M. Therriault, a fellow student, is unclear about the steps in the recording process. Identify and briefly explain the steps in the same order as they are performed.

Journalize transactions.
(SO 2) AP

BE2–7   Using the data in BE2–4 for Ing Company, journalize the transactions.

Journalize transactions.
(SO 2) AP

BE2–8   Using the data in BE2–5 for A. Fisher, journalize the transactions.

Post journal entries.
(SO 3) AP

BE2–9   Post the journal entries from BE2–8 to T accounts.

BE2–10 Use the ledger balances that follow to prepare a trial balance for the Beirsdorf Company at June 30, 2008. All account balances are normal.

Prepare trial balance.
(SO 4) AP

Accounts Payable	$ 3,900	Notes Payable	$5,000
Accounts Receivable	3,000	Rent Expense	800
B. Beirsdorf, Capital	17,000	Salaries Expense	4,000
B. Beirsdorf, Drawings	1,200	Service Revenue	6,600
Cash	8,400	Supplies	650
Equipment	14,600	Unearned Revenue	150

BE2–11 There are two errors in the following trial balance: (1) one account has been placed in the wrong column, and (2) there is a transposition error. Identify the two errors.

Identify errors in trial balance.
(SO 4) AP

BOURQUE COMPANY
Trial Balance
December 31, 2007

	Debit	Credit
Cash	$15,000	
Accounts receivable	1,800	
Prepaid insurance	3,500	
Accounts payable		$ 2,000
Unearned revenue		2,200
L. Bourque, capital		15,400
L. Bourque, drawings	4,900	
Service revenue		27,500
Salaries expense	18,600	
Rent expense		2,400
Totals	$43,800	$49,500

Exercises

E2–1 Here are some of the concepts discussed in the chapter:

Match concepts with descriptions.
(SO 1,2,3,4) K

1. Debit
2. Ledger
3. Posting
4. Chart of accounts
5. Trial balance
6. Journal
7. Account
8. Credit
9. Analyzing transactions
10. Journalizing

Instructions

Match each concept with the best description below. Each concept may be used more than once, or may not be used at all.

(a) ___ The normal balance for liabilities
(b) ___ The first step in the recording process
(c) ___ The procedure of transferring journal entries to the ledger accounts
(d) ___ A record of increases and decreases in a specific asset, liability, or owner's equity item
(e) ___ The left side of an account
(f) ___ The entering of transaction data in the journal
(g) ___ A list of accounts and their balances at a specific time
(h) ___ Used to decrease the balance in an asset account
(i) ___ A list of all of a company's accounts
(j) ___ An accounting record where transactions are recorded in chronological (date) order

Identify increases, decreases, normal balances, and types of accounts.
(SO 1) K

E2–2 Kobayashi Company has the following accounts:

Account	(1) Type of Account	(2) Financial Statement	(3) Normal Balance	(4) Increase	(5) Decrease
1. Cash	Asset	Balance sheet	Debit	Debit	Credit
2. M. Kobayashi, Capital					
3. Accounts Payable					
4. Building					
5. Consulting Fee Revenue					
6. Insurance Expense					
7. Interest Earned					
8. Notes Receivable					
9. Prepaid Insurance					
10. Rent Expense					
11. Unearned Consulting Fees					

Instructions

Complete the table. Identify (1) the type of account (e.g., asset, liability, owner's capital, drawings, revenue, expense); (2) what financial statement it is presented on; (3) the normal balance of the account; (4) whether the account is increased by a debit or credit; and (5) whether the account is decreased by a debit or credit. The first one is done for you as an example.

Identify accounts, debits, credits, and normal balances.
(SO 1) K

E2–3 In her first month of business, L. Visser, an interior decorator, had the following transactions:

Mar. 3 Invested $10,000 cash in the business.
6 Purchased a used car for $6,500 cash, for use in the business.
7 Purchased supplies on account for $500.
12 Billed customers $2,100 for services performed.
21 Paid $225 cash for advertising the launch of the business.
25 Received $700 cash from customers billed on March 12.
28 Paid $500 cash for the supplies purchased on March 7.
31 Withdrew $800 cash for the owner's personal use.
31 Received $750 cash from a customer for services to be performed in April.

Instructions

For each transaction indicate:

(a) The basic type of account debited and credited (asset, liability, owner's equity)
(b) The specific account debited and credited (Cash, Rent Expense, Service Revenue, etc.)
(c) The normal balance of the specific account
(d) Whether the specific account is increased or decreased

Use the following format, in which transaction 1 is given as an example:

	Account Debited				Account Credited			
Transaction	(a) Basic Type	(b) Specific Account	(c) Normal Balance	(d) Effect	(a) Basic Type	(b) Specific Account	(c) Normal Balance	(d) Effect
Mar. 3	Asset	Cash	Debit	Increase	Owner's Equity	L. Visser, Capital	Credit	Increase

Analyze transactions.
(SO 1) AP

E2–4 The information that follows is for Lynn Gardiner of Gardiner Real Estate Agency:

Oct. 1 Begins business as a real estate agent with a cash investment of $15,000.
2 Hires an administrative assistant at an annual salary of $24,000.
3 Buys office equipment for $3,350, paying $850 cash and signing a note payable for the balance.
10 Receives $250 cash as a fee for renting an apartment.

Oct. 16 Sells a house and lot to B. Rollins. The commission due from Rollins is $6,500 (it is not paid by Rollins at this time).
    27 Pays $700 for advertising costs during October.
    30 Pays the administrative assistant $2,000 in salary for October.
    31 Receives $6,500 cash from B. Rollins for the October 16 transaction.

Instructions

Prepare the debit/credit analysis for each transaction, as illustrated in the chapter.

E2–5 Data for L. Visser are presented in E2–3.

Journalize transactions.
(SO 2) AP

Instructions

Journalize the transactions.

E2–6 Transaction data for Gardiner Real Estate Agency are presented in E2–4.

Journalize transactions.
(SO 2) AP

Instructions

Journalize the transactions.

E2–7 Journal entries for Gardiner Real Estate Agency's transaction data were prepared in E2–6.

Post journal entries.
(SO 3) AP

Instructions

Post the journal entries to the general ledger, using T accounts.

E2–8 Fortin Co.'s ledger is as follows:

Journalize transactions and prepare trial balance.
(SO 2, 4) AP

Cash
Oct. 1	1,200	Oct. 3	400
10	650	12	500
15	3,000	30	600
20	800	31	250
25	2,000	31	500

A. Fortin, Capital
| | | Oct. 1 | 1,200 |
| | | 25 | 2,000 |

A. Fortin, Drawings
| Oct. 30 | 600 | |

Accounts Receivable
| Oct. 6 | 1,000 | Oct. 20 | 800 |
| 20 | 940 | |

Service Revenue
		Oct. 6	1,000
		10	650
		15	3,000
		20	940

Supplies
| Oct. 4 | 800 | |

Equipment
| Oct. 3 | 5,400 | |

Advertising Expense
| Oct. 28 | 400 | |

Store Wages Expense
| Oct. 31 | 500 | |

Notes Payable
| | | Oct. 3 | 5,000 |

Rent Expense
| Oct. 31 | 250 | |

Accounts Payable
| Oct. 12 | 500 | Oct. 4 | 800 |
| | | 28 | 400 |

Instructions

(a) Journalize the October transactions, and give explanations for each entry.
(b) Determine the October 31, 2008 balance for each account. Prepare a trial balance at October 31, 2008.

E2–9 On July 31, 2008, Lee Meche, MD, had the following balances in the ledger for his medical practice: Cash $7,500; Accounts Receivable $2,750; Supplies $585; Equipment $14,700; Notes Payable $10,000; L. Meche, Capital $15,000; L. Meche, Drawings $5,125; Medical Fee Revenue $9,410; Rent Expense $1,200; and Salaries Expense $2,550. Selected transactions from the journal follow:

Post journal entries and prepare trial balance.
(SO 3,4) AP

GENERAL JOURNAL				
Date	Account Titles and Explanation	Ref.	Debit	Credit
2008				
Aug. 1	Rent Expense		1,200	
	Cash			1,200
10	Supplies		420	
	Accounts Payable			420
12	Cash		2,400	
	Accounts Receivable			2,400
25	Salaries Expense		2,750	
	Cash			2,750
30	Notes Payable		500	
	Cash			500
31	Cash		5,910	
	Accounts Receivable		2,550	
	Medical Fee Revenue			8,460
31	L. Meche, Drawings		4,770	
	Cash			4,770

Instructions

(a) Create T accounts and enter the July 31 balances.
(b) Post the transactions to the T accounts. Create new T accounts if needed.
(c) Prepare a trial balance at August 31.

Answer questions about trial balance error.
(SO 4) AN

E2–10   As the accountant for Smistad Company, you are disappointed to learn that the column totals of the December 31, 2007, trial balance do not balance. The Machinery account has a debit balance of $31,200. When you analyze the transactions, you notice that a correctly recorded purchase of a machine for $7,500 was posted with a $7,500 credit to the Machinery account and a $7,500 credit to Accounts Payable.

Instructions

(a) Is the balance of the Machinery account overstated, understated, or correct?
(b) Is the balance of the Accounts Payable account overstated, understated, or correct?
(c) Is the debit column total of the trial balance overstated, understated, or correct?
(d) Is the credit column total of the trial balance overstated, understated, or correct?
(e) If the credit column total of the trial balance is $360,000 before correcting the error, what is the total of the debit column before correcting the error?

Prepare trial balance and financial statements.
(SO 4) AP

E2–11   The ledger of Express Delivery Service has the following account balances on July 31, 2008:

Accounts Payable	$ 3,234	Repair Expense	1,582
Accounts Receivable	2,277	Salaries Expense	15,563
Cash	?	Salaries Payable	925
Delivery Equipment	36,620	Service Revenue	37,885
Gas and Oil Expense	12,143	Supplies	265
Insurance Expense	2,020	Supplies Expense	2,650
Interest Expense	975	T. Weld, Capital	39,575
Notes Payable	19,500	T. Weld, Drawings	24,400
Prepaid Insurance	404	Unearned Revenue	675

Instructions

(a) Prepare a trial balance, with the accounts arranged in ledger (financial statement) order as illustrated in the chapter, and determine the missing amount for Cash.
(b) Prepare an income statement and statement of owner's equity for the year, and a balance sheet at the end of the year.

Problems: Set A

P2–1A Brinan Couture Company began operations in 2006. During February 2008, the company had the following transactions:

Perform transaction analysis and journalize transactions. (SO 1, 2) AP

Feb. 1 Paid February rent, $475.
     2 Purchased sewing supplies for $250 on account.
     6 Finished sewing a suit, delivered it to the customer, and billed $750.
     7 Received an order from another customer to design and sew a leather jacket. The customer agreed to pay $385 when the jacket is complete.
   10 Agreed to sew a wedding dress for a customer. Received $250 cash from the customer as a down payment.
   12 The owner of the company, L. Brinan, withdrew $700 cash for personal use.
   15 Finished sewing the leather jacket (see February 7 transaction) and collected $385 cash.
   17 The customer billed on February 6 paid the amount owing.
   25 Paid for the supplies purchased on February 2.
   28 Borrowed $2,000 cash from the bank and signed a note payable for the amount owing.
   28 Purchased a new sewing machine for $2,500 cash.

Instructions

(a) Perform a transaction analysis for each transaction, as illustrated in the chapter. Include the following in your answer:
    1. The basic type of account involved
    2. The specific account names
    3. Whether the accounts are increased or decreased
    4. Whether a debit or credit is needed for each account
(b) Prepare a journal entry for each transaction.

P2–2A The Adventure Biking Park was started on June 1 by Dustin Tanner. The following events and transactions are for June:

Journalize transactions. (SO 2) AP

June 1 Tanner invested $50,000 cash in the business.
     4 Purchased an old ski hill for $320,000, paying $32,000 cash and signing a note payable for the balance. (The price consisted of land, $174,000; building, $101,000; and equipment, $45,000.)
     8 Incurred advertising expenses of $2,800 on account.
   13 Paid $5,500 cash for a one-year insurance policy.
   15 Paid salaries to employees, $1,800.
   17 Withdrew $600 cash for personal use.
   20 Received $2,700 cash for admission fees.
   22 Hired a park manager at a salary of $4,000 per month, effective July 2.
   25 Sold 100 coupon books for $75 each. Each book contains 10 coupons that give the holder one admission to the park.
   30 Received $5,900 cash for admission fees.
   30 Paid $1,650 on account for advertising expenses incurred on June 8.
   30 Paid $1,250 interest expense on the note payable.
   30 Counted the coupons that had been redeemed since June 25. Found that 80 coupons had been used in exchange for admission to the park.

Dustin Tanner uses the following accounts: Cash; Prepaid Insurance; Land; Building; Equipment; Accounts Payable; Unearned Admissions Revenue; Notes Payable; D. Tanner, Capital; D. Tanner, Drawings; Admissions Revenue; Advertising Expense; Salaries Expense; and Interest Expense.

Instructions

Journalize the June transactions.

P2–3A   Carla Liu is a CGA. During the first month of operating her accounting practice, the following events and transactions occurred:

May 1 Invested $18,000 cash and office equipment worth $8,500 in the business.
   1 Paid office rent of $950 cash for the month.
   2 Hired a secretary-receptionist at a salary of $2,400 per month.
   3 Purchased $1,450 of supplies on account from Read Supply Company.
  11 Completed a tax assignment for J. Lau and billed him $1,725 for services rendered.
  12 Received a $3,500 advance on a management consulting engagement with Arch Co.
  17 Completed accounting services and collected $1,350 cash from the client.
  21 J. Lau paid $900 for work completed on May 11.
  23 Paid 60% of the balance due to Read Supply Company.
  31 Received a $215 telephone bill for May, to be paid next month.
  31 Paid the secretary-receptionist $2,400 salary for the month.
  31 Withdrew $925 cash for her personal use.

Carla uses the following chart of accounts: No. 101 Cash; No. 112 Accounts Receivable; No. 126 Supplies; No. 151 Office Equipment; No. 201 Accounts Payable; No. 209 Unearned Revenue; No. 301 C. Liu, Capital; No. 306 C. Liu, Drawings; No. 400 Service Revenue; No. 726 Salaries Expense; No. 729 Rent Expense; and No. 737 Telephone Expense.

Instructions

(a) Journalize the transactions.
(b) Post to the ledger accounts. Use the standard form of account.
(c) Prepare a trial balance at May 31, 2008.

P2–4A   Brisebois Dry Cleaners has a July 31 year end. The company's trial balance on June 30, 2008, is as follows:

BRISEBOIS DRY CLEANERS
Trial Balance
June 30, 2008

	Debit	Credit
Cash	$ 11,659	
Note receivable	5,000	
Accounts receivable	5,845	
Supplies	3,974	
Equipment	31,480	
Accounts payable		$ 13,089
Unearned revenue		1,920
E. Brisebois, capital		55,920
E. Brisebois, drawings	37,050	
Dry cleaning revenue		109,461
Salaries expense	57,750	
Rent expense	11,385	
Repair expense	1,727	
Utilities expense	14,520	
Totals	$180,390	$180,390

The July transactions were as follows:

July 3 Paid July rent, $1,065.
   5 Collected $3,285 cash on the June 30 accounts receivable.
  10 Performed $1,160 of services for customers who paid in advance in June.
  11 Received $4,730 cash from customers for services performed.
  13 Paid $9,742 to creditors on account.
  14 Purchased supplies for $494 on account.

July 24 Billed customers $5,950 for services performed.
25 Collected the $5,000 note receivable plus interest of $250.
26 Signed a contract with a nursing home to provide cleaning services at a rate of $1,650 per month starting in August. The first payment will be collected on August 1.
27 Received $650 cash from a customer for services to be provided in August.
28 Paid utilities of $1,222.
29 Paid employee salaries of $5,550.
30 Purchased a new machine with a suggested manufacturer's price of $4,500. After much negotiating, paid $1,500 cash and signed a note payable for $2,500.
31 Withdrew $3,750 cash for personal use.

Instructions

(a) Journalize the transactions.
(b) Enter the June 30 balances in T accounts.
(c) Post the July journal entries to the T accounts. You may need to add new accounts for some of the transactions.
(d) Prepare a trial balance at July 31, 2008.

P2–5A   The Grand Theatre is owned by Fran Goresht. At March 31, 2008 the ledger showed the following: Cash $6,000; Land $100,000; Buildings (concession stands, projection room, ticket booth, and screen) $80,000; Equipment $25,000; Accounts Payable $5,000; Mortgage Payable $125,000; and F. Goresht, Capital?. During April, the following events and transactions occurred:

Journalize transactions, post, and prepare trial balance.
(SO 2, 3, 4) AP

Apr. 2 Paid film rental of $800 on first movie.
2 Paid advertising expenses, $620.
3 Ordered two additional films at $750 each.
9 Received $1,950 cash from admissions.
10 Made $2,000 payment on mortgage, of which $500 is interest.
10 Paid $2,800 of the accounts payable.
11 Grand Theatre contracted with Seibert Company to operate the concession stand in the future. Seibert is to pay 20% of gross concession receipts (payable monthly) for the right to operate the concession stand.
15 Sold gift certificates totalling $400 cash.
20 Received one of the films ordered on April 3 and was billed $750. The film will be shown in April.
25 Received $5,300 cash from admissions.
28 Customers used $100 of the gift certificates sold on April 15.
29 Paid salaries, $1,900.
30 Received a statement from Seibert: it shows gross concession receipts of $2,600 and a balance due to The Grand Theatre of $520 ($2,600 × 20%) for April. Seibert paid one-half of the balance due and will pay the rest on May 5.
30 Prepaid $700 rental on a special film to be shown in May.

Instructions

(a) Journalize the April transactions.
(b) Enter the beginning balances in the ledger as at April 1. Calculate the correct balance in F. Goresht, Capital as at April 1. Use the standard form of account.
(c) Post the April journal entries to the ledger.
(d) Prepare a trial balance at the end of April 2008.

P2–6A   Rowland Brokerage Services was formed on September 1, 2008. The owner, Rick Rowland, sold all of his personal investments and received $100,000 cash. Rick transferred $90,000 to a bank account in the name of Rowland Brokerage Services. During the month of September, the following events and transactions occurred:

Journalize transactions, post, and prepare trial balance.
(SO 2, 3, 4) AP

Sept. 2 Hired two employees to work in the warehouse. They will each be paid a monthly salary of $3,000.

3 Signed a three-year contract to lease a warehouse for $7,500 per month. Paid the first and last month's rent in cash. (*Hint:* The payment for the final month's rent should be considered an asset and be recorded in Prepaid Rent.)

4 Moved Rick's home office equipment and furniture to the warehouse where it will now be used in the business. The original cost of these items was $25,000 but their current value is $15,000.

5 Purchased warehouse equipment for $88,000 and a forklift for $23,000. Paid $42,000 cash and signed a note payable for the balance.

6 Purchased an annual insurance policy for $8,700 to be paid in monthly instalments on the sixth day of each month. Paid the first month's premium.

7 Purchased supplies for $1,050 cash.

16 Purchased additional supplies for $2,175 on account.

25 Total revenues earned to date were $21,000 ($4,000 cash and $17,000 on account).

26 Paid $1,150 to suppliers on account

27 Collected $1,800 from a customer for services to be provided in October.

28 Collected $4,800 from customers on account.

30 Received $575 of utility bills for September, to be paid in October.

30 Paid employee salaries, $6,000.

30 Paid property taxes of $2,250 for Rick's home.

30 Withdrew $2,500 cash for Rick's personal use.

Instructions

(a) Prepare journal entries to record the transactions.
(b) Post the journal entries to T accounts.
(c) Prepare a trial balance as at September 30, 2008.

Prepare financial statements. (SO 4) AP

P2–7A   Refer to the trial balance prepared for Rowland Brokerage Services in P2–6A part (c).

Instructions

(a) Prepare an income statement for Rowland Brokerage Services for September.
(b) Prepare a statement of owner's equity for Rowland Brokerage Services for September.
(c) Prepare a balance sheet at the end of September 2008.
(d) Discuss how well the company did in its first month of operations.

Journalize transactions, post, and prepare trial balance. (SO 2, 3, 4) AP

P2–8A   Gary Hobson owns and manages Soft-Q Repair Service, which fixes computers. Soft-Q had the following trial balance at March 31, 2008 (its year end):

SOFT-Q REPAIR SERVICE
Trial Balance
March 31, 2008

	Debit	Credit
Cash	$ 2,500	
Accounts receivable	14,000	
Repair parts inventory	15,400	
Prepaid rent	5,100	
Shop equipment	27,000	
Accounts payable		$23,500
G. Hobson, capital		40,500
Totals	$64,000	$64,000

A summary of Soft-Q's transactions for April 2008 follows:

1. Miscellaneous expenses were paid in cash, $2,050.
2. Gary invested $3,000 of his own cash in the business.
3. Repair parts were added to the inventory for $4,200 on account.

4. Borrowed $10,000 from the bank, signing a note payable.
5. Cash was collected from customers on account, $6,000.
6. Cash was paid to creditors on account, $12,000.
7. Advertising costs were paid in cash, $850.
8. A total of $3,075 of repair parts were used in the month. (*Hint:* Debit this to Repair Parts Expense.)
9. Repair services provided in April were for $3,000 cash and $7,000 on account.
10. Wages for April were paid in cash, $4,500.
11. Recorded the rent expense for the month of April. However, no cash was paid. On March 1, 2008, a rent payment of $6,800 had been made in advance for four months.
12. Gary's drawings during April totalled $1,000.
13. Paid $65 interest on the note payable.

Instructions

(a) Explain why the March 31, 2008, balance in the account Prepaid Rent is $5,100. (Refer to the trial balance and item 11 above.)
(b) Prepare journal entries to record each of the April transactions.
(c) Open ledger accounts for each of the accounts listed in the trial balance, and enter the March 31, 2008, balances. Use T accounts.
(d) Post the journal entries to the accounts in the ledger.
(e) Prepare a trial balance as at the end of April.

P2–9A   Refer to the trial balance prepared in part (e) of P2–8A for Soft-Q Repair Service.

Prepare financial statements.
(SO 4) AN

Instructions

Use the trial balance to do the following:

(a) Prepare an income statement for Soft-Q Repair Service for April 2008.
(b) Prepare a statement of owner's equity for April 2008.
(c) Prepare a balance sheet at the end of April 2008.
(d) Gary is considering selling the business. Based on your review of the financial statements, would you be interested in buying the business or do you have concerns? Discuss.

P2–10A   The bookkeeper for Shigeru's Dance Studio did the following in journalizing and posting:

Analyze errors and effects on trial balance.
(SO 4) AN

1. A debit posting to Prepaid Insurance of $3,600 was not done.
2. A debit posting of $500 to Accounts Receivable was debited to Accounts Payable.
3. A purchase of supplies on account of $540 was debited to Supplies for $540 and credited to Accounts Payable for $540.
4. A credit to Wages Payable for $1,200 was credited to Wages Expense.
5. A debit posting of $250 to Cash was posted twice.
6. A debit posting for $1,200 of drawings was posted to Wages Expense.
7. A credit to Service Revenue for $400 was posted as a credit to Unearned Service Revenue.
8. A debit to Accounts Payable of $250 was posted as a credit to Accounts Payable.
9. A purchase of equipment on account for $4,600 was posted as a $6,400 debit to Equipment and a $6,400 credit to Cash.

Instructions

(a) Indicate which of the above transactions are correct and which are incorrect.
(b) For each error identified in (a), answer the following:
    1. Will the trial balance balance?
    2. Which account(s) will be incorrectly stated because of the error?
    3. State whether each of the incorrect account(s) you identified in (2) will be overstated or understated. By how much?
    4. Is the debit column total of the trial balance stated correctly? If not, what is the amount of the overstatement or understatement?
    5. Is the credit column total of the trial balance stated correctly? If not, what is the amount of the overstatement or understatement?

P2–11A   The trial balance that follows for Shawnee Company does not balance:

SHAWNEE COMPANY
Trial Balance
May 31, 2008

	Debit	Credit
Cash	$ 5,875	
Accounts receivable		$ 2,570
Prepaid insurance	500	
Equipment	14,200	
Accounts payable		4,780
Property taxes payable	560	
S. Armstrong, capital		17,900
Service revenue	6,847	
Salaries expense	4,150	
Advertising expense		1,132
Property tax expense	1,100	
Totals	$33,232	$26,382

Your review of the ledger reveals that each account has a normal balance. You also discover the following errors:

1. Prepaid Insurance, Accounts Payable, and Property Tax Expense were each understated by $300.
2. A $410 credit to Service Revenue was incorrectly posted as a $140 credit.
3. A debit posting to Salaries Expense of $350 was not done.
4. A $750 cash withdrawal by the owner was debited to S. Armstrong, Capital, for $750 and credited to Cash for $750.
5. A $650 purchase of supplies on account was debited to Equipment for $650 and credited to Cash for $650.
6. A cash payment of $320 for advertising was debited to Advertising Expense for $230 and credited to Cash for $230.
7. A $160 collection from a customer was debited to Cash for $160 and credited to Accounts Payable for $160.
8. A cash payment on account for $90 was recorded as a $90 credit to Cash and a $90 credit to Accounts Payable.
9. A $2,000 note payable was issued to purchase equipment. The transaction was neither journalized nor posted.

Instructions

Prepare a correct trial balance. (*Note:* You may need to add new accounts.)

Problems: Set B

Perform transaction analysis
and journalize transactions.
(SO 1, 2) AP

P2–1B   CW Paint Designs began operations on March 1, 2008. The company completed the following transactions in its first month:

Mar. 1 The owner, Christie Wong, invested $10,000 cash in the company.
       2 Purchased a one-year insurance policy effective March 1, and paid the first month's premium of $115.
       2 Purchased painting equipment for $3,000 cash.
       3 Purchased supplies for $375 cash.
       7 Finished a painting project for Maya Angelina and billed her $750.
       8 Incurred advertising expenses of $1,325 on account.

Mar. 10 Received a $1,500 contract from a customer, SUB Terrain Inc., to paint its new office space. SUB Terrain will pay when the project is complete.

25 Completed the contract with SUB Terrain Inc. from March 10 and collected the amount owing.

27 Collected the amount owing from March 7.

28 The owner, Christie Wong, withdrew $870 cash for her personal use.

30 Paid $1,000 of the advertising expenses from March 8.

Instructions

(a) Do a transaction analysis for each transaction, as illustrated in the chapter. Include in your answer:
  1. The basic type of account involved
  2. The specific account names
  3. Whether the accounts are increased or decreased
  4. Whether a debit or credit is needed for each account
(b) Prepare a journal entry for each transaction.

P2–2B The Bucket Club Miniature Golf and Driving Range was opened on May 1 by Amin Mawani. The following events and transactions are for May:

Journalize transactions.
(SO 2) AP

May 1 Invested $70,000 cash in the business.

3 Purchased Lee's Golf Land for $210,000. The price consists of land, $95,000; building, $70,000; and equipment, $45,000. Paid $52,000 cash and signed a note payable for the balance.

5 Advertised the opening of the driving range and miniature golf course, $2,300.

6 Paid $2,976 cash for a one-year insurance policy.

10 Purchased golf clubs and other equipment for $6,000 from Woods Company, payable in 20 days.

19 Sold 100 coupon books for $40 each. Each book contains 10 coupons that give the holder one round of miniature golf or one bucket of golf balls to hit.

25 Withdrew $1,750 cash for Mawani's personal use.

30 Paid salaries of $2,445.

30 Paid Woods Company in full.

31 Received $4,200 of fees in cash.

31 Paid $650 of interest on the note payable.

31 Counted the coupons that customers had redeemed since May 19. Found that 85 coupons had been used in exchange for playing mini golf or hitting a bucket of balls.

Amin uses the following accounts: Cash; Prepaid Insurance; Land; Buildings; Equipment; Accounts Payable; Unearned Golf Fees; Notes Payable; A. Mawani, Capital; A. Mawani, Drawings; Golf Fees Earned; Advertising Expense; Salaries Expense; and Interest Expense.

Instructions

Journalize the May transactions.

P2–3B Esther Rojas, a licensed architect, formed a company called Rojas Designs on April 1, 2008. The following events and transactions occurred in the first month:

Journalize transactions, post, and prepare trial balance.
(SO 2, 3, 4) AP

Apr. 1 Esther invested $15,000 cash and $6,000 of office equipment in the company.

1 Hired a secretary-receptionist at a salary of $1,950 monthly.

2 Paid office rent for the month, $950.

3 Purchased architectural supplies on account from Halo Company, $1,750.

10 Completed blueprints on a carport for G. Fellows and billed him $900 for services.

20 Received $1,500 cash for services completed and delivered to P. Donahue.

21 Received $800 cash from G. Fellows for work completed on April 10.

23 Received $500 cash advance from R. Sherstabetoff for the design of a new home.

28 Paid $900 to Halo Company on account.

30 Paid secretary-receptionist for the month, $1,950.

Apr. 30 Esther withdrew $1,500 cash for personal use.
    30 Received April's telephone bill, $135.

Esther uses the following chart of accounts: No. 101 Cash; No. 112 Accounts Receivable; No. 126 Supplies; No. 151 Office Equipment; No. 201 Accounts Payable; No. 209 Unearned Revenue; No. 301 E. Rojas, Capital; No. 306 E. Rojas, Drawings; No. 400 Service Revenue; No. 726 Salaries Expense; No. 729 Rent Expense; and No. 737 Telephone Expense.

Instructions

(a) Journalize the transactions.
(b) Post to the ledger accounts. Use the standard form of account.
(c) Prepare a trial balance as at April 30, 2008.

Journalize transactions, post, and prepare trial balance.
(SO 2, 3, 4) AP

P2–4B Collegiate Laundry has a December 31 year end. The company's trial balance on November 30, 2008, is as follows:

COLLEGIATE LAUNDRY
Trial Balance
November 30, 2008

	Debit	Credit
Cash	$ 2,800	
Accounts receivable	1,800	
Supplies	1,100	
Equipment	21,000	
Accounts payable		$ 5,765
Unearned revenue		1,300
J. Cochrane, capital		19,500
J. Cochrane, drawings	33,000	
Laundry revenue		64,900
Insurance expense	4,015	
Salaries expense	11,525	
Rent expense	9,350	
Utilities expense	6,875	
	$91,465	$91,465

The December transactions were as follows:

Dec. 1 Borrowed $5,000 cash from the First Financial Bank and signed a note payable.
      2 Paid the $365 monthly insurance premium.
      4 Paid $3,200 to creditors on account.
      9 Received $1,050 cash from customers in payment of their accounts.
     10 Performed $600 of services for customers who had paid in advance in November.
     11 Received $1,350 cash from customers for services provided.
     15 Purchased $400 of supplies on account.
     20 Billed customers $5,750 for services provided.
     22 Paid employee salaries of $1,450 (includes an end-of-year bonus of $300).
     24 Owner withdrew $3,000 for personal use.
     29 Received $425 cash from a customer for services to be provided in January.
     30 Purchased a used pressing machine for $2,500 cash from another company. The machine was probably worth $3,000, but the other company was anxious to sell it before the end of the year.
     31 Received the bill for December utilities, $615; will pay it in January.

Instructions

(a) Journalize the December transactions.
(b) Enter the November 30 balances in ledger accounts. Use T accounts.
(c) Post the December journal entries to the T accounts. You may need to add new accounts for some of the transactions.
(d) Prepare a trial balance at December 31, 2008.

P2–5B   The Starlite Theatre, owned by Lee Baroni, is unique as it only shows movies that are part of a theme with two or more sequels. As at February 29, 2008, the ledger of Starlite showed the following: No. 101 Cash, ?; No. 140 Land, $85,000; No. 145, Buildings (concession stand, projection room, ticket booth, and screen) $77,000; No. 157 Equipment, $20,000; No. 201 Accounts Payable, $12,000; No. 275 Mortgage Payable, $118,000; and No. 301 L. Baroni, Capital, $67,000. In March, the following events and transactions occurred:

Journalize transactions, post, and prepare trial balance.
(SO 2, 3, 4) AP

Mar. 2 Acquired the three *Lord of the Rings* movies, to be shown in the first three weeks of March. The film rental was $27,000. Of that amount, $10,000 was paid in cash and the balance will be paid on March 10.

3 Ordered the *Indiana Jones* movies, to be shown the last 10 days of March. The film rental fee will be $300 per night.

9 Received $16,300 cash from admissions.

10 Paid the balance due on the *Lord of the Rings* rental, and $3,000 on accounts payable from February 29.

10 Sold gift certificates totalling $450.

11 Starlite Theatre contracted with Brewer Company to operate the concession stand in the future. Brewer is to pay 18% of gross concession receipts (payable on the last day of each month) for the right to operate the concession stand.

12 Paid advertising expenses, $950.

20 Received $16,600 cash from admissions.

21 Received the *Indiana Jones* movies and paid the rental fee of $3,000 ($300 × 10 nights).

31 Paid salaries of $4,200.

31 Received statement from Brewer showing gross receipts from concessions of $8,500 and the balance due to Starlite Theatre of $1,530 ($8,500 × 18%) for March. Brewer paid one-half the balance due and will pay the rest on April 5.

31 Received $18,400 cash from admissions.

31 Customers used $200 of the gift certificates sold on March 10.

31 Paid a $1,250 mortgage payment, which included $475 of interest.

In addition to the accounts identified above, the chart of accounts shows the following: No. 112 Accounts Receivable; No. 210 Unearned Revenues; No. 405 Admission Revenue; No. 406 Concession Revenue; No. 610 Advertising Expense; No. 632 Film Rental Expense; No. 726 Salaries Expense; and No. 750 Interest Expense.

Instructions

(a) Journalize the March transactions.
(b) Enter the beginning balances in the ledger as at March 1. Calculate the correct balance in Cash as at March 1. Use the standard form of account.
(c) Post the March journal entries to the ledger.
(d) Prepare a trial balance at the end of March.

P2–6B   Bablad Brokerage Services was formed on May 1, 2008. The following events and transactions are from its first month:

Journalize transactions, post, and prepare trial balance.
(SO 2, 3, 4) AP

May 1 Jacob Bablad invested $90,000 cash and $25,000 worth of office equipment in the company.

1 Hired two employees to work in the warehouse. They will each be paid a salary of $2,475 per month.

May 5 Signed a two-year rental agreement on a warehouse and paid $10,500 cash. Half was for the May 2008 rent and the other half was for the final month's rent. (*Hint:* The portion for the final month is considered prepaid rent.)

8 Purchased warehouse equipment costing $70,000. A cash payment of $30,000 was made immediately. Signed a note payable for the balance.

9 Paid $3,600 cash for a one-year insurance policy on the equipment. (*Hint:* The portion of the cost related to May 2008 is an expense for this month.)

12 Purchased supplies for $1,000 cash.

15 Purchased more supplies for $2,000 on account.

20 Total revenues earned to date were $11,500, consisting of $3,000 cash and the balance on account.

22 Paid $800 to suppliers on account.

25 Collected $1,500 from a customer as an advance payment for brokerage services to be provided in June 2008.

26 Withdrew $4,800 cash for personal use.

27 Signed a contract with an advertising agency for a promotion in June. The total cost of $9,000 will be paid in three equal instalments on June 2, 16, and 30.

28 Collected $2,500 from customers on account.

30 Received $500 of utility bills, to be paid next month.

31 Paid the monthly salaries of the two employees, totalling $4,950.

Instructions

(a) Prepare journal entries to record the transactions.
(b) Post the journal entries to ledger accounts. Use T accounts.
(c) Prepare a trial balance as at May 31, 2008.

Prepare financial statements. (SO 4) AP

P2–7B Refer to the trial balance for Bablad Brokerage Services prepared in P2–6B part (c).

Instructions

(a) Prepare an income statement for May.
(b) Prepare a statement of owner's equity for May.
(c) Prepare a balance sheet at the end of May 2008.
(d) Discuss how well the company performed in its first month of operations.

Journalize transactions, post, and prepare trial balance. (SO 2, 3, 4) AP

P2–8B Leo Mataruka owns and manages a computer repair service. It had the following trial balance on December 31, 2007 (its fiscal year end):

CYBERDYNE REPAIR SERVICE
Trial Balance
December 31, 2007

	Debit	Credit
Cash	$ 2,000	
Accounts receivable	15,700	
Repair parts inventory	12,000	
Prepaid rent	4,800	
Shop equipment	28,000	
Accounts payable		$23,000
Unearned revenue		2,000
L. Mataruka, capital		37,500
Totals	$62,500	$62,500

A summary of transactions for January 2008 follows:

1. Leo invested $4,000 of additional cash in the business.
2. Repair parts were added to the inventory for $5,200 on account.
3. Miscellaneous expenses were paid in cash, $1,800.

4. Cash was collected from customers on account, $7,000.
5. Cash was paid to creditors on account, $6,500.
6. A total of $4,500 of repair parts were used in the month. (*Hint:* Debit this to Repair Parts Expense.)
7. Repair services done in January were for $5,000 cash and $15,000 on account.
8. Wages for January were paid in cash, $2,900.
9. Advertising costs were paid in cash, $600.
10. Recorded the rent expense for the month of January. However, no cash was paid. On December 1, 2007, a rent payment of $6,400 had been made in advance for four months.
11. Leo withdrew $750 cash for personal use.
12. Purchased additional equipment for $5,000 cash.

Instructions

(a) Explain why the December 31, 2007, balance in the Prepaid Rent account is $4,800. (Refer to the trial balance and item 10.)
(b) Prepare journal entries to record each of the January transactions.
(c) Open ledger accounts for each of the accounts listed in the trial balance, and enter the December 31, 2007, balances. Use T accounts.
(d) Post the journal entries to the accounts in the ledger.
(e) Prepare a trial balance as at January 31, 2008.

P2–9B   Refer to the trial balance prepared in part (e) of P2–8B for Cyberdyne Repair Service.

Prepare financial statements.
(SO 4) AN

Instructions

Use the trial balance to do the following:

(a) Prepare an income statement for Cyberdyne Repair Service for January 2008.
(b) Prepare a statement of owner's equity for January 2008.
(c) Prepare a balance sheet at the end of January 2008.
(d) Leo does not understand (1) why even though his business is profitable, he still has to invest additional cash, and (2) why he was able to withdraw only $750 cash. Based on your review of the financial statements, what explanations can you give him?

P2–10B   The owner of Insidz Co. asked a first-year accounting student to help him prepare the company's trial balance. The student had a few questions about the following transactions:

Analyze errors and effects on trial balance.
(SO 4) AN

1. Insidz Co. had received $780 cash from a customer on account, which was recorded as a debit to Cash of $870 and a credit to Accounts Receivable of $780.
2. A service provided for cash was posted as a debit to Cash of $2,000 and a credit to Accounts Receivable of $2,000.
3. A credit of $750 for interest earned was neither recorded nor posted. The debit was recorded and posted correctly.
4. The debit to record $1,000 of drawings was posted to the Salary Expense account. The credit was posted correctly.
5. Services of $325 had been provided to a customer on account. Insidz Co. debited Accounts Receivable $325 and credited Service Revenue $325.
6. A purchase of supplies for $2,500 on account was recorded as a debit to Supplies and a debit to Accounts Payable.
7. Insidz Co. received a cash advance of $500 from a customer for work to be performed next month. Cash was debited $500 but there was no credit because no one was sure what to credit.
8. A cash payment of $495 for salaries was recorded as a debit to Salaries Expense and a credit to Salaries Payable.
9. Insidz Co. purchased $1,570 of equipment on account and made a $1,750 debit to Equipment and a $1,750 credit to Accounts Payable.

Instructions

(a) Indicate which transactions are correct and which are incorrect.

(b) For each error identified in (a), answer the following:
1. Will the trial balance balance?
2. Which account(s) will be incorrectly stated because of the error?
3. State whether (each of) the incorrect account(s) you identified in (2) will be overstated or understated. By how much?
4. Is the debit column total of the trial balance stated correctly? If not, what is the amount of the overstatement or understatement?
5. Is the credit column total of the trial balance stated correctly? If not, what is the amount of the overstatement or understatement?

Prepare correct trial balance.
(SO 3, 4) AN

P2–11B   The trial balance of Winau Co. does not balance:

WINAU CO.
Trial Balance
June 30, 2008

	Debit	Credit
Cash		$ 2,635
Accounts receivable	$ 2,729	
Supplies	500	
Equipment	4,200	
Accounts payable		2,200
Unearned fees	1,765	
T. Winau, capital		9,090
T. Winau, drawings	800	
Fees earned		2,380
Salaries expense	3,200	
Office expense	1,010	
	$14,204	$16,305

Your review of the ledger reveals that each account has a normal balance. You also discover the following errors:

1. Cash paid to a creditor on account was credited to Cash for $750 and Accounts Payable was debited for the same amount. The actual payment was for $570.
2. The purchase of supplies on account for $360 was recorded as a debit to Equipment for $360 and a credit to Accounts Payable for $360.
3. Services of $890 were performed on account for a client. Accounts Receivable was debited for $890 and Fees Earned was credited for $89.
4. A debit posting to Salaries Expense of $700 was not done.
5. A collection on account for $205 was credited to Cash for $205 and credited to Accounts Receivable for $502.
6. The withdrawal of $400 cash for Winau's personal use was debited to Salaries Expense for $400 and credited to Cash for $400.
7. A transposition error was made when copying the balance in the capital account to the trial balance. The correct balance recorded in the account was $9,900.
8. The general ledger contained a Prepaid Insurance account with a debit balance of $565.

Instructions

Prepare a correct trial balance. Show calculations for each new amount.

Continuing Cookie Chronicle

(*Note:* The Continuing Cookie began in Chapter 1 and will continue in each chapter.)

After researching the different forms of business organization, Natalie Koebel decides to operate "Cookie Creations" as a proprietorship. She then starts the process of getting the business running. In November 2007, the following activities take place:

Nov. 8 Natalie cashes her Canada Savings Bonds and receives $520, which she deposits in her personal bank account.

8 She opens a bank account under the name "Cookie Creations" and transfers $500 from her personal account to the new account.

11 Natalie pays $165 to have advertising brochures and posters printed. She plans to distribute these as opportunities arise.

13 She buys baking supplies, such as flour, sugar, butter, and chocolate chips, for $125 cash.

14 Natalie starts to gather some baking equipment to take with her when teaching the cookie classes. She has an excellent top-of-the-line food processor and mixer that originally cost her $750. Natalie decides to start using it only in her new business. She estimates that the equipment is currently worth $400.

16 Natalie realizes that her initial cash investment is not enough. Her grandmother lends her $2,000 cash, for which Natalie signs a note payable in the name of the business. Natalie deposits the money in the business bank account.

17 She buys more baking equipment for $900 cash.

20 She teaches her first class and collects $125 cash.

25 Natalie books a second class for December 4 for $125. She receives $25 cash in advance as a down payment.

30 Natalie pays $1,320 for a one-year insurance policy that will expire on December 1, 2008.

Instructions

(a) Prepare journal entries to record the November transactions.
(b) Post the journal entries to general ledger accounts.
(c) Prepare a trial balance at November 30.

BROADENING YOUR PERSPECTIVE

Financial Reporting and Analysis

Financial Reporting Problem

BYP2–1 The financial statements of The Forzani Group for 2006 are shown in Appendix A at the back of this textbook. They contain the following selected accounts (in thousands):

Accounts Payable and Accrued Liabilities	$244,293
Accounts Receivable	68,927
Capital Assets	193,594
Retail Revenue	856,149
Inventory	278,002
Interest Expense	6,145
Prepaid Expenses	2,647

Instructions

(a) Answer the following questions:
  1. What is the increase side (i.e., debit or credit) and decrease side for each of the above accounts?
  2. What is the normal balance for each of these accounts?
(b) Identify the other account that is probably involved in the transaction, and the effect on that account, when:
  1. Accounts Receivable are decreased.   4. Inventory is increased.
  2. Capital Assets are increased.   5. Interest Expense is increased.
  3. Retail Revenue is increased.   6. Prepaid Expenses are increased.

Interpreting Financial Statements

BYP2–2   Agricore United is one of Canada's leading agri-businesses. The following list of accounts and amounts was taken from Agricore United's 2005 financial statements:

AGRICORE UNITED
List of Accounts
October 31, 2005
(in thousands)

Accounts receivable	$ 242,941
Accounts payable and accrued expenses	313,233
Bank and other payables	200,815
Cash and cash equivalents	36,590
Cost of goods sold expense	2,314,698
Depreciation and amortization expense	60,717
Dividends (drawings)	6,288
Dividends payable	2,464
Gain on disposal of assets	1,653
Income tax expense	7,282
Intangible assets	37,779
Interest expense	49,877
Inventories	382,009
Long-term debt	427,613
Operating, general, and administrative expenses	331,844
Other assets	103,700
Other liabilities	42,991
Prepaid expenses	17,106
Property, plant, and equipment	657,074
Sales and revenue from services	2,775,279
Shareholders' (owners') equity, November 1, 2004	483,857

Instructions

(a) Prepare a trial balance for Agricore United, with the accounts in financial statement order.
(b) Present the accounts and balances of Agricore United in the form of the accounting equation: Assets = Liabilities + Shareholders' (Owner's) Equity.

Critical Thinking

Collaborative Learning Activity

Note to instructor: Additional instructions and material for this group activity can be found on the Instructor Resource Site.

BYP2–3 In this group activity, you will write descriptions of five transactions that would occur in the first month of business for a service company, and the corresponding journal entries.

Instructions

(a) Your instructor will divide the class into groups. Members of your group will take on the roles of team recorder, bookkeeper, and presenter(s).

(b) As a group, create five precise transaction descriptions, which the team recorder will write out on an overhead acetate. The bookkeeper will record the corresponding general journal entries (on paper).

(c) Your instructor will select one group's transaction descriptions for use as a class quiz, which all students will answer.

(d) The presenter(s) of the group that prepared the transaction descriptions used in part (c) will review the solution with the class at the end of the quiz.

Study Aids:
Working in Groups

Communication Activity

BYP2–4 White Glove Company offers home cleaning services. Two common transactions for the company are billing customers for services performed and paying employee salaries. For example, on March 15, bills that totalled $6,000 were sent to customers, and $2,000 in salaries was paid to employees.

Instructions

Write a memo to your instructor that explains how these transactions are recorded in the double-entry system. Include in your memo (1) how the debit and credit rules are applied to these transactions, and (2) an explanation of what the normal balances are in the accounts affected by the transactions.

Study Aids:
Writing Handbook

Ethics Case

BYP2–5 Vu Hung is the assistant chief accountant at Lim Company, a manufacturer of computer chips and cellular phones. The company presently has total sales of $20 million. It is the end of the first quarter. Vu is hurriedly trying to prepare a general ledger trial balance so that quarterly financial statements can be prepared and released to management and regulatory agencies. The credits on the trial balance add up to $1,000 more than the debits.

In order to meet the 4 p.m. deadline, Vu decides to force the debits and credits into balance by adding the amount of the difference to the Equipment account. She chose Equipment because it is one of the larger account balances. Proportionally, it will be the least misstated. She believes that the difference will not affect anyone's decisions. She wishes that she had more time to find the error, but realizes that the financial statements are already late.

Study Aids:
Ethics in Accounting

Instructions

(a) Who are the stakeholders in this situation?

(b) What are the ethical issues involved?

(c) What are Vu's alternatives?

ANSWERS TO CHAPTER QUESTIONS

Answers to Accounting in Action Insight Questions

Across the Organization Insight, p. 57

Q: The Ottawa Senators and Dany Heatley signed a contract at the time of the trade. Would signing this contract result in a journal entry in the Ottawa Senators accounting records?

A: The Ottawa Senators would not have recorded a journal entry as a result of signing Dany Heatley because no transaction occurred. The Ottawa Senators would have been committed to paying Heatley a salary in the future. And they were hoping for a positive financial impact in the future. But these future events are not recorded until they occur.

Business Insight, p. 63

Q: Why is it useful for managers to have a sophisticated chart of accounts like the one described above?

A: A sophisticated chart of accounts, like the one they have at Goodyear, gives managers the ability to analyze accounting information in different ways. For example, because Goodyear's chart of accounts identifies each account by product line, a separate income statement can be created for each product line. Management can then compare the different product lines to see which ones are the most profitable, and which ones are the least profitable. If Goodyear did not have a sophisticated chart of accounts it would not be able to do this.

Business Insight, p. 71

Q: Is a trial balance useful in finding this type of error?

A: Not likely. The accountant made a mistake while doing a tax calculation. This error would have resulted in incorrect amounts, and possibly incorrect accounts, in a journal entry, but not an unbalanced journal entry.

Answer to Forzani Review It Question 4

Normal balances: Accounts Receivable (asset)—debit; Accounts Payable and Accrued Liabilities (liability)—credit; Retail Revenue (revenue)—credit; and Store Operating Expense (expense)—debit.

Answers to Self-Study Questions

1. b   2. c   3. d   4. d   5. b   6. a   7. c   8. d   9. a   10. c

Remember to go back to the Navigator Box at the beginning of the chapter to check off your completed work.

concepts for review >>

the navigator

Before studying this chapter, you should understand or, if necessary, review:

  a. The double-entry system. (Ch. 2, p. 53)

  b. How to increase and decrease assets, liabilities, and owner's equity accounts using debit and credit procedures. (Ch. 2, pp. 53–55)

  c. How to journalize transactions. (Ch. 2, pp. 58–60)

  d. How to post transactions to the general ledger. (Ch. 2, pp. 61–62)

  e. How to prepare a trial balance. (Ch. 2, pp. 69–70)

Fiscal Year Ends, but Classes Move On

TORONTO, Ont.—In accounting, as in comedy, timing is everything. An organization's fiscal year end is like a punch line—everything leads up to it. And once it's done, you start all over again.

At Seneca College's 14 locations in the Greater Toronto Area, as at most schools, the majority of students arrive in September and leave in April or May. But the college's fiscal year ends on March 31, rather than at the end of the academic year. "The reason goes back to 1967 and the provincial act establishing community colleges in Ontario," explains Ron Currie, Seneca's Vice-President of Finance and Administration. "That's the government's year end."

If Seneca's fiscal year end were a different date, however, one thing would remain the same. Seneca must apply revenues to the fiscal period when the service is performed. This is the only way to satisfy the revenue recognition and matching principles. For example, Seneca might collect tuition for the summer term in one accounting period, but provide teaching services in the following accounting period. "Typically," says Mr. Currie, "students pay in March for a summer semester course, so those prepayments get deferred on our balance sheet. Same with the student activity fees."

Seneca's main sources of funding for its post-secondary programs are provincial grants and student tuition fees. Private and corporate training, however, is funded on a fee-for-service basis. Still, the principles are the same. "Let's say XYZ Corporation came along and gave us $30,000 to run a program in March, April, and May," Mr. Currie elaborates, "We would defer two-thirds of it to the next [fiscal] year."

Seneca College: www.senecac.on.ca

Expenses, too, must be recorded in the year when they are incurred. "Our utility bills and invoices for legal fees for the last month or two of the fiscal year tend to come in after our year end," Mr. Currie continues. "In order to match the expenses to the proper year, we accrue them based on an estimate."

For things like course study guides, which are usually prepared by staff in one fiscal year but sold to students the following year, it's the other way around. "In that case we take the costs associated with developing the materials and categorize them as a prepaid expense in one fiscal year and match it with the corresponding revenue in the next fiscal year."

Recording revenues and expenses in the correct period is a challenge, but one that must be met to properly reflect the school's activity in each period.

the navigator

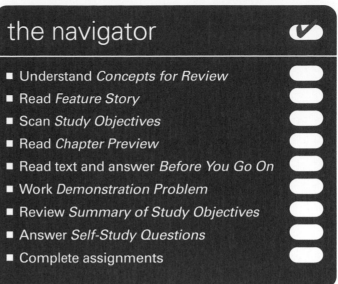

the navigator ✔

- Understand *Concepts for Review*
- Read *Feature Story*
- Scan *Study Objectives*
- Read *Chapter Preview*
- Read text and answer *Before You Go On*
- Work *Demonstration Problem*
- Review *Summary of Study Objectives*
- Answer *Self-Study Questions*
- Complete assignments

chapter 3
Adjusting the Accounts

study objectives >>

After studying this chapter, you should be able to:

1. Explain the time period assumption, revenue recognition principle, matching principle, and accrual basis of accounting.
2. Prepare adjusting entries for prepayments.
3. Prepare adjusting entries for accruals.
4. Describe the nature and purpose of an adjusted trial balance, and prepare one.
5. Prepare adjusting entries for the alternative treatment of prepayments (Appendix 3A).

In Chapter 2, we examined the recording process up to and including the preparation of the trial balance. The next big step is to prepare the financial statements from the trial balance, but before this can be done, additional steps are usually needed. These steps adjust accounts for timing mismatches, like the ones Seneca College has with the tuition it receives for its summer classes and the costs it incurs to offer these classes. More specifically, adjustments make it possible to report revenues and expenses in the appropriate time period. In this chapter, we introduce the accrual accounting concepts that guide the adjustment process.

The chapter is organized as follows:

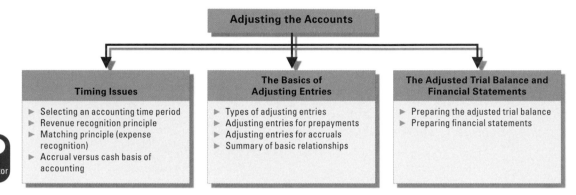

Timing Issues

study objective 1

Explain the time period assumption, revenue recognition principle, matching principle, and accrual basis of accounting.

Accounting would be simple if we could wait until a company ended its operations to prepare its financial statements. As the following anecdote shows, if we waited until then we could easily determine the amount of lifetime income earned:

> A grocery store owner from the old country kept his accounts payable on a spindle, accounts receivable on a notepad, and cash in a shoebox. His daughter, a CGA, chided her father: "I don't understand how you can run your business this way. How do you know what you've earned?"
>
> "Well," her father replied, "when I arrived in Canada 40 years ago, I had nothing but the pants I was wearing. Today, your brother is a doctor, your sister is a teacher, and you are a CGA. Your mother and I have a nice car, a well-furnished house, and a home by the lake. We have a good business and everything is paid for. So, you add all that together, subtract the pants, and there's your net income."

Selecting an Accounting Time Period

Although the grocer may be correct in his evaluation, it is impractical to wait so long for the results of operations. All entities—from the corner grocery, to a company like Forzani, to your college or university—find that it helps them make decisions when they have timely reports on the results of their activities. For example, management usually wants monthly financial statements. Investors want to view the results of publicly traded companies at least quarterly. The Canada Revenue Agency requires financial statements to be filed with annual income tax returns. To meet these needs, accountants have made the assumption that the economic life of a business can be divided into artificial time periods. This is called the **time period assumption**.

Accounting time periods are generally one month, one quarter, or one year. Time periods of less than one year are called **interim periods**. Most large companies are required to report quarterly and annually.

An accounting time period that is one year long is called a **fiscal year**. The accounting period used by many businesses is the same as the calendar year (January 1 to December 31). However, it can be different. Seneca College's fiscal year is April 1 through March 31, which is typical of many colleges, universities, and governments. Some retail companies use a 52-week period for their fiscal year. The Forzani Group does this, and has chosen the last Sunday in January (some years the first Sunday in February) as its fiscal year end.

Regular reporting makes financial statements more useful. But it can also cause accounting problems. Many business transactions affect more than one accounting time period. For example, computer equipment purchased by Seneca College last year and airplanes purchased by Air Canada five years ago are still being used today. We also saw in the feature story that sometimes Seneca College collects tuition fees in one fiscal year and then teaches the course in the next fiscal year. We must therefore determine how relevant each business transaction is to specific accounting periods.

Determining the amount of revenues and expenses to report in a specific accounting period can be difficult. To help in this task, accountants have developed two generally accepted accounting principles: (1) the revenue recognition principle, and (2) the matching principle.

Revenue Recognition Principle

The **revenue recognition principle** states that revenue must be recognized in the accounting period in which it is earned. In a service company, revenue is considered earned at the time the service is performed. For a merchandising company, as we will see in Chapter 5, revenue is considered earned when the merchandise is sold, which is normally at the point of sale. Basically, the general guidelines state that revenue should be recognized when the sales effort is substantially complete and collection is reasonably certain.

To illustrate, assume that a dry-cleaning business cleans clothing on June 30, and customers do not claim and pay for their clothes until the first week of July. Under the revenue recognition principle, revenue is earned in June when the service is performed, rather than in July when the cash is received. So at June 30, the dry cleaner would report a receivable on its balance sheet and revenue on its income statement for the service performed.

While this example is simple, revenue-generating activities have become more and more complex, and the result is that applying the revenue recognition principle might now be the most difficult issue in accounting. In Chapter 11, there is a more detailed discussion of revenue recognition and the issues around it.

Matching Principle (Expense Recognition)

Accountants follow the approach of "let the expenses follow the revenues." That is, expense recognition is tied to revenue recognition. How does this affect the dry-cleaning business in the previous section? It means that the salary expense for the cleaning on June 30 should be reported in the income statement for the same period in which the service revenue is recognized.

The critical issue in expense recognition is to determine when the efforts were made to generate the revenue. This may or may not be the same period in which the expense is paid. If the salary incurred on June 30 is not paid until July, the dry cleaner would still report a salary expense on its June income statement and salaries payable on its June 30 balance sheet. This practice of expense recognition is called the **matching principle** because it matches efforts (expenses) with accomplishments (revenues).

Matching expenses to revenue generation is not complicated when there is a direct relationship, such as in the dry-cleaning example. Sometimes, however, there is no direct relationship between expenses and revenue. In these cases, if it is possible, reasonable assumptions are made to match the expenses to the revenue they help generate. For example, we will see in the next section that long-lived assets generate revenue over many years. Consequently, assumptions are made to allocate the cost of these long-lived assets to expense over the same period that the revenue is generated. In other cases, however, it really is impossible to match costs with the revenues they help earn. In these situations, the costs are reported as expenses in the period they are incurred in.

To summarize, the time period assumption and the revenue recognition and matching principles provide guidelines for when to report revenues and expenses. The relationships between these concepts are shown in Illustration 3-1.

Illustration 3-1 ►

GAAP relationships in revenue and expense recognition

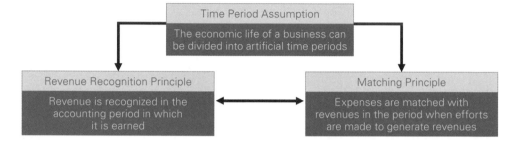

ACCOUNTING IN ACTION ► Business Insight

Canadian-born director Norman Jewison describes the film industry as a terrible business when it comes to accounting. The person behind the lens of the classic *In the Heat of the Night* as well as the more recent *The Hurricane* says, "When I make a film, it has to make three times its negative cost. If a picture costs $20 million, my picture has to earn $60 million before it shows any kind of profit." For a recent Jewison film, the DVD and video cassette distributors pocketed 80% of revenues, leaving 20% to go toward the film's gross revenue. And that $20 million spent on the film has to be expensed over its economic life, which could be less than a year or many years, depending on the film. The filmmaker needs to estimate how much revenue will be earned from box office sales, DVD sales, television, and games and toys (for films like *Star Wars* or the Harry Potter series). Properly matching expenses to revenues is no small task for those focused on big pictures.

Source: Mark Brown, "Live and Learn: Norman Jewison," *Canadian Business*, February 2005.

? **Why is it important for film producers to try to match the cost of producing films with the revenues generated?**

Accrual versus Cash Basis of Accounting

If you follow the revenue recognition and matching principles, you are using the **accrual basis of accounting**. Under the accrual basis, transactions that change a company's financial statements are recorded in the periods in which the events occur. For example, service revenue is recognized when it is earned, rather than when the cash is received. The critical event is the performance of the service, not the collection of cash. Expenses are recognized when services (e.g., salaries) or goods (e.g., supplies) are used or consumed, rather than when the cash is paid. As a result, revenues that have been earned are matched with the expenses incurred to earn these same revenues. Thanks to this practice, financial statements are more meaningful for decision-making.

An alternative to the accrual basis of accounting is the cash basis. Under the **cash basis of accounting**, revenue is recorded when cash is received, and expenses are recorded when cash is paid. The cash basis often leads to misleading financial statements. It fails to record revenue which has been earned if the cash has not been received. This violates the revenue recognition principle. In addition, expenses are not matched with revenues, which violates the matching principle. The cash basis of accounting is not in accordance with generally accepted accounting principles.

Although most companies use the accrual basis of accounting, some small companies use the cash basis. Farmers and fishermen also tend to use the cash basis of accounting, which is justified for these types of businesses because they have few receivables and payables. Accountants are sometimes asked to convert cash-basis records to the accrual basis. As you might expect, many journal entries are needed to do this.

Illustration 3-2 shows the relationship between accrual-based numbers and cash-based numbers for a simple example. Suppose you own a painting company and you paint a large building during year 1. In year 1, you have total expenses of $50,000, which includes the cost of the paint and your employees' salaries. Now assume that you bill your customer $80,000 at the end of year 1, but you are not paid until year 2. On an accrual basis, you report the revenue during the period when it is earned—year 1. The expenses are then recorded (matched) in the period in which the revenues are earned. Thus, your net income for year 1 is $30,000. No revenue or expense from this project is reported in year 2. The $30,000 of income reported for year 1 gives a useful indication of how profitable your efforts were during that period.

If, instead, you were reporting on a cash basis, you would report expenses of $50,000 in year 1 and revenues of $80,000 in year 2. For year 1, you would report a loss of $50,000. For year 2, you would report net income of $80,000. Cash basis measures are not very informative about the results of your efforts during year 1 or year 2.

Note that the total net income for years 1 and 2 is $30,000 for both the accrual and cash bases. However, there is still a significant difference in when the revenue and expense are recognized.

	Year 1	Year 2
Activity	Purchased paint, painted building, paid employees	Received payment for work done in year 1
Accrual basis	Revenue $80,000 Expense 50,000 Net income $30,000	Revenue $ 0 Expense 0 Net income $ 0
Cash basis	Revenue $ 0 Expense 50,000 Net loss $(50,000)	Revenue $80,000 Expense 0 Net income $80,000

Illustration 3-2 ◀

Accrual versus cash basis accounting

BEFORE YOU GO ON . . .

▶ Review It

1. Why do we need the time period assumption?
2. What are the revenue recognition and matching principles?
3. What are the differences between the cash and accrual bases of accounting?

▶Do It

During 2008, Jomerans Co. received $125,000 cash from customers. On January 1, 2008, customers owed Jomerans $30,000 for services provided before December 31, 2007. On December 31, 2008, customers owed Jomerans $19,500 for services provided before December 31, 2008. Calculate revenue using (a) the cash basis of accounting, and (b) the accrual basis of accounting.

Action Plan

- For the cash basis of accounting, revenue is equal to the cash received.
- For the accrual basis of accounting, use the revenue recognition principle. Report revenue in the period in which it is earned, not when it is collected.
- Cash collected in 2008 for revenue earned in 2007 should not be included in the 2008 revenue under the accrual basis of accounting.
- Amounts still owing at the end of 2008 for services provided in 2008 should be included in the 2008 revenue under the accrual basis of accounting.

Solution

(a) Revenue using the cash basis of accounting $125,000

(b) Cash received from customers in 2008 $125,000
    Deduct: Collection of 2007 receivables   (30,000)
    Add: Amounts owing at December 31, 2008   19,500
    Revenue using the accrual basis of accounting $114,500

the navigator

Related exercise material: BE3–1, E3–1 and E3–2.

The Basics of Adjusting Entries

For revenues to be recorded in the period in which they are earned, and for expenses to be matched with the revenues they generate, adjusting entries are made at the end of the accounting period. Under the accrual basis of accounting, because of the time period assumption, **adjusting entries** are needed to ensure that the revenue recognition and matching principles are followed. Adjusting entries also make it possible to report the appropriate assets, liabilities, and owner's equity on the balance sheet.

The unadjusted trial balance—determined the first time transaction data are pulled together—may not contain complete and up-to-date data. This is because of the following reasons:

1. Some events are not journalized daily because it is not efficient to do so. Examples are the consumption of supplies and the earning of wages by employees.
2. Some costs are not journalized during the accounting period, because they expire with the passage of time rather than through daily transactions. Examples are rent, insurance, and amortization.
3. Some items may be unrecorded. An example is a utility service bill that will not be received until the next accounting period. The bill, however, covers services delivered in the current accounting period.

Adjusting entries are needed every time financial statements are prepared. We first analyze each account in the trial balance to see if it is complete and up to date. The analysis requires a full understanding of the company's operations and the interrelationship of accounts. Preparing adjusting entries is often a long process. For example, to accumulate the adjustment data, a company may need to count its remaining supplies. It may also need to prepare supporting schedules of insurance policies, rental agreements, and other contractual commitments.

www.wiley.com/canada/weygandt
Animated Tutorials and Videos:
Accounting Cycle Tutorial

Adjustment data are often not available until after the end of the period. For example, telephone and other bills will not be received until after the month end or year end. In such cases, the data are gathered as soon as possible after the end of the period and adjusting entries are made but they are still dated as at the balance sheet date.

Types of Adjusting Entries

Adjusting entries can be classified as prepayments or accruals, as follows:

Prepayments	Accruals
1. Prepaid Expenses Expenses paid in cash and recorded as assets before they are used or consumed.	1. Accrued Expenses Expenses incurred but not yet paid in cash or recorded.
2. Unearned Revenues Cash received and recorded as a liability before revenue is earned.	2. Accrued Revenues Revenues earned but not yet received in cash or recorded.

Specific examples and explanations of each type of adjustment are given on the following pages. Each example is based on the October 31 trial balance of Pioneer Advertising Agency from Chapter 2, reproduced here in Illustration 3-3. We assume that Pioneer Advertising uses an accounting period of one month. Thus, monthly adjusting entries will be made and they will be dated October 31.

Illustration 3-3 ◄

Trial balance

PIONEER ADVERTISING AGENCY
Trial Balance
October 31, 2008

	Debit	Credit
Cash	$15,200	
Accounts receivable	0	
Advertising supplies	2,500	
Prepaid insurance	600	
Office equipment	5,000	
Notes payable		$ 5,000
Accounts payable		2,500
Unearned revenue		1,200
C. Byrd, capital		10,000
C. Byrd, drawings	500	
Service revenue		10,000
Salaries expense	4,000	
Rent expense	900	
Totals	$28,700	$28,700

Adjusting Entries for Prepayments

Prepayments are either prepaid expenses or unearned revenues. Adjusting entries are used to record the portion of the prepayment that is for the expense incurred or the revenue earned in the current accounting period. This means that for prepaid expenses, the adjusting entry records the expense which applies to the current period and reduces the asset account where the prepaid expense was originally recorded. This type of adjustment is nec-

study objective 2

Prepare adjusting entries for prepayments.

essary because the prepayment no longer has future benefit and so stops being an asset; it has been used. For unearned revenues, the adjusting entry records the revenue earned in the current period and reduces the liability account where the unearned revenue was originally recorded. This type of adjustment is necessary because the unearned revenue is no longer owed and so stops being a liability; the service has been provided and the revenue earned.

Prepaid Expenses

Costs paid in cash and recorded as assets before they are used or consumed are called **prepaid expenses**. When a cost is incurred, an asset account is debited to show the service or benefit that will be received in the future. Prepayments often occur for insurance, supplies, advertising, and rent.

Prepaid expenses expire either with the passage of time (e.g., rent and insurance) or as the asset is used up (e.g., office supplies). It is not practical to record the expiration of these costs on a daily basis. Instead, these expirations are recorded when financial statements are prepared. At each statement date, adjusting entries are made for two purposes: (1) to record the expenses (expired costs) that apply to the current accounting period, and (2) to show the unexpired costs in the asset accounts.

Before the adjustments to prepaid expenses, assets are overstated and expenses are understated. Therefore, as shown below, an adjusting entry for prepaid expenses results in an increase (debit) to an expense account and a decrease (credit) to an asset account.

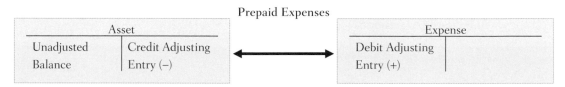

Prepaid Expenses

Asset			Expense		
Unadjusted Balance	Credit Adjusting Entry (−)		Debit Adjusting Entry (+)		

Supplies. Businesses use various types of supplies. For example, an accounting firm will have office supplies such as pens, pencils, paper, and envelopes. An advertising firm will have advertising supplies such as graph paper, video film, and poster paper. Supplies are generally debited to an asset account when they are bought. During daily operations, supplies are used up. However, the amount of supplies used is only recorded during the adjustment process. At that point, a physical inventory of supplies is taken (i.e., the remaining supplies are counted). The difference between the balance in the supplies (asset) account and the cost of supplies actually remaining gives the supplies used (the expense) for the period.

Pioneer Advertising Agency purchased advertising supplies costing $2,500 on October 4. A debit (increase) was made to the asset account Advertising Supplies. This account shows a balance of $2,500 in the October 31 trial balance. An inventory count at the close of business on October 31 reveals that only $1,000 of supplies remains. Thus, the cost of supplies used is $1,500 ($2,500 − $1,000), and the following adjusting entry is made:

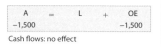

A = L + OE
−1,500   −1,500
Cash flows: no effect

Oct. 31	Advertising Supplies Expense	1,500	
	Advertising Supplies		1,500
	To record supplies used.		

After the adjusting entry is posted, the two advertising supplies accounts show the following:

Advertising Supplies				Advertising Supplies Expense		
Oct. 4	2,500	Oct. 31 Adj.	1,500	Oct. 31 Adj.	1,500	
Oct. 31 Bal.	1,000					

The asset account Advertising Supplies now shows a balance of $1,000, which is the cost of supplies remaining at the statement date. In addition, Advertising Supplies Expense shows a balance of $1,500, which is the cost of supplies used in October. If the adjusting entry is not made, October expenses will be understated and net income overstated by $1,500. Also, both assets and owner's equity will be overstated by $1,500 on the October 31 balance sheet.

Insurance. Most companies have fire and theft insurance for merchandise and equipment, liability insurance for accidents suffered by customers on the company's premises, and automobile insurance for company cars and trucks. The term of coverage is usually one year. Insurance premiums (the cost of the insurance policy) are normally charged to the asset account Prepaid Insurance when they are paid. At the financial statement date, it is necessary to make an adjustment to debit (increase) Insurance Expense and credit (decrease) Prepaid Insurance for the cost that has expired during the period.

On October 3, Pioneer Advertising Agency paid $600 for a one-year fire insurance policy. The starting date for the coverage was October 1. The premium was charged to Prepaid Insurance when it was paid. This account shows a balance of $600 in the October 31 trial balance. An analysis of the policy reveals that $50 ($600 ÷ 12) of insurance expires each month. Thus, the following adjusting entry is made:

Oct. 31	Insurance Expense	50	
	Prepaid Insurance		50
	To record insurance expired.		

A	=	L	+	OE
−50				−50

Cash flows: no effect

After the adjusting entry is posted, the accounts show the following:

Prepaid Insurance				Insurance Expense		
Oct. 3	600	Oct. 31 Adj.	50	Oct. 31 Adj.	50	
Oct. 31 Bal.	550					

The asset Prepaid Insurance shows a balance of $550. This amount represents the unexpired cost for the remaining 11 months of coverage (11 × $50). The $50 balance in Insurance Expense is equal to the insurance cost that has expired in October. If this adjustment is not made, October expenses will be understated by $50 and net income overstated by $50. Also, both assets and owner's equity will be overstated by $50 on the October 31 balance sheet.

Amortization. A business usually owns a variety of long-lived assets such as land, buildings, equipment, and vehicles. Each is recorded as an asset, rather than as an expense, when it is purchased because long-lived assets provide a service for many years. The length of service is called the **useful life**.

From an accounting perspective, the purchase of a long-lived asset is basically a long-term prepayment for services. Similar to other prepaid expenses, it is necessary to recognize the cost that has been used up (the expense) during the period, and report the unused cost (the asset) at the end of the period. **Amortization** is the allocation of the cost of long-lived

Alternative terminology
Amortization is also called *depreciation.*

assets to expense over their useful lives. Only assets with specified useful lives are amortized. When an asset such as land has an unlimited useful life, it is not amortized.

It is important to note that the purpose of amortization is to match expenses with the revenues earned in each period. Amortization is an allocation concept. The portion of the long-lived asset that is used up in each period must be reported as an expense or amortized. Amortization is not a valuation concept: it does not recognize the change in the value of the long-lived asset. Amortization simply allocates the cost of a long-lived asset over its useful life.

Calculation of Amortization. A common procedure for calculating amortization expense is to divide the cost of the asset by its useful life. This is called the **straight-line amortization method**. At the time an asset is acquired, its useful life is not known with certainty. The useful life must be estimated. Thus, it is important to recognize that amortization is an estimate rather than a factual measurement of the cost that has expired.

For example, if the cost of an asset is $5,000 and its useful life is expected to be five years, annual amortization is $1,000 ($5,000 ÷ 5). In its simplest form, the formula to calculate annual amortization is as follows:

Illustration 3-4 ▶

Formula for straight-line amortization

Of course, if you are calculating amortization for partial periods, the annual expense amount must be adjusted for the relevant portion of the year. For example, if we want to determine the amortization for the quarter, we would multiply the annual expense by $\frac{3}{12}$ months. For Pioneer Advertising, amortization on the office equipment is estimated to be $1,000 a year, or $83 per month ($1,000 × $\frac{1}{12}$).

Adjustments of prepayments involve decreasing (or crediting) an asset by the amount of the expired cost. You might expect we should credit Office Equipment when recording amortization. But it is important to keep track of the original cost of long-lived assets as well as to have a record of how much of the original cost has been amortized. We therefore use an account called Accumulated Amortization to show the cumulative sum of the amortization expense since the asset was purchased. Separate accumulated amortization accounts are created for each long-lived asset.

Amortization on the office equipment for the month of October is recognized by the following adjusting entry:

Cash flows: no effect

Oct. 31	Amortization Expense	83	
	Accumulated Amortization—Office Equipment		83
	To record monthly amortization.		

The following shows the accounts after the adjusting entry has been posted:

Office Equipment		Amortization Expense	
Oct. 2	5,000	Oct. 31 Adj.	83

Accumulated Amortization—Office Equipment	
	Oct. 31 Adj.	83

The balance in the Accumulated Amortization account will increase by $83 each month. After journalizing and posting the adjusting entry at November 30, the balance of the accumulated amortization will be $166. At December 31, the balance of the accumulated amortization will be $249, and so on. The balance in the Office Equipment account will remain unchanged until the asset is sold.

Accumulated amortization represents the cumulative total of the amortization expense since the asset was purchased, less any reductions when assets are sold (which we will learn about in Chapter 9). As happens with other adjustments for prepaid expenses, if this adjusting entry is not made, total assets, owner's equity, and net income will be overstated and expenses will be understated.

Statement Presentation. Accumulated Amortization—Office Equipment is deducted from Office Equipment on the balance sheet. Its normal balance is a credit—the opposite of the normal debit balance of Office Equipment. Accumulated amortization accounts are an example of a contra asset account. A **contra account** is an account that is offset against (deducted from) a related account on the income statement or balance sheet. On the balance sheet, it can be a contra asset account (offset against an asset) or a contra liability account (offset against a liability). We will discuss contra income statement accounts in Chapter 5.

Helpful hint Increases, decreases, and normal balances of contra accounts are the opposite of the accounts they relate to.

In the balance sheet, Accumulated Amortization—Office Equipment is deducted from the related asset account, Office Equipment, as follows:

Office equipment	$5,000
Less: Accumulated amortization—office equipment	83
Net book value	$4,917

The difference between the cost of any amortizable asset and its accumulated amortization is called the **net book value** (or simply book value) of that asset. In the above illustration, the book value of the equipment at October 31, 2008, is $4,917. As noted earlier, amortization does not attempt to show what an asset is worth. Thus, the book value of $4,917 does not represent the market value of the office equipment (the price at which it could be sold in the marketplace). It is simply the unallocated cost.

Alternative terminology Net book value is sometimes called *carrying value.*

Unearned Revenues

Revenues received in cash that have not yet been earned are called **unearned revenues**. Such items as rent, magazine subscriptions, and customer deposits for future services may result in unearned revenues. Airlines such as Air Canada treat receipts from the sale of tickets—often paid long before the flight date—as unearned revenue until the flight service is provided. Similarly, tuition fees that are received prior to the start of an academic session, as in the feature story about the summer session at Seneca College, are considered unearned revenue.

Alternative terminology Unearned revenues are sometimes referred to as *deferred revenues* or *future revenues.*

Unearned revenues are the opposite of prepaid expenses. Indeed, unearned revenue on the books of one company is likely to be a prepayment on the books of the company that has made the advance payment. For example, if identical accounting periods are assumed, your landlord will have unearned rent revenue when you (the tenant) have prepaid your rent.

As shown in Chapter 2, when a payment is received for services that will be provided in a future accounting period, Cash should be debited (increased) and an unearned revenue account (a liability) should be credited (increased) to recognize the obligation that exists. Unearned revenues become earned when the service is provided to the customer. It is not practical to make daily journal entries as the revenue is earned. Instead, recognition of earned revenue is normally delayed until the end of the accounting period. Then an adjusting entry is made to record the revenue that has been earned and to show the liability that remains. Before adjustment, liabilities are overstated and revenues are understated. Therefore, as shown below, the adjusting entry for unearned revenues results in a decrease (debit) to a liability account and an increase (credit) to a revenue account.

Unearned Revenue

Pioneer Advertising Agency received $1,200 on October 3 from R. Knox for advertising services that will be completed by December 31. The payment was originally credited (increased) to Unearned Revenue, an account that shows a balance of $1,200 in the October 31 trial balance. Analysis reveals that $400 of those fees was earned in October. So the following adjusting entry is made:

A = L + OE
    −400   +400
Cash flows: no effect

Oct. 31	Unearned Revenue	400	
	Service Revenue		400
	To record revenue for services provided.		

After the adjusting entry is posted, the accounts show:

Unearned Revenue				Service Revenue		
Oct. 31 Adj.	400	Oct. 4	1,200		Oct. 21	10,000
		Oct. 31 Bal.	800		31 Adj.	400
					Oct. 31 Bal.	10,400

The liability Unearned Revenue now shows a balance of $800. This amount represents the remaining advertising services that will be performed in the future. At the same time, Service Revenue shows total revenue of $10,400 earned in October. If this adjustment is not made, revenues and net income will be understated by $400 in the income statement. Also, liabilities will be overstated and owner's equity understated by $400 on the October 31 balance sheet.

BEFORE YOU GO ON . . .

▶**Review It**

1. What are the purposes of adjusting entries?
2. What is the effect on assets, owner's equity, expenses, and net income if a prepaid expense adjusting entry is not made?
3. What is the purpose of amortization?
4. Using Forzani's statement of operations (income statement), find the amount of amortization expense recorded for 2006 and 2005. The answer to this question is at the end of the chapter.
5. What is the effect on liabilities, owner's equity, revenues, and net income if an unearned revenue adjusting entry is not made?

▶**Do It**

The trial balance of Panos Co., on March 31, 2008, includes the following selected accounts before adjusting entries:

	Debit	Credit
Prepaid Insurance	$ 1,200	
Office Supplies	2,800	
Office Equipment	24,000	
Accumulated Amortization—Office Equipment		$2,200
Unearned Revenue		9,300

An analysis of the accounts shows the following:

1. The one-year insurance policy was purchased on March 1, 2008.
2. Office supplies on hand at March 31 total $800.
3. Office equipment was purchased on April 1, 2007, and has an estimated useful life of 10 years.
4. One-third of the unearned revenue was earned in March.

Prepare the adjusting entries for the month of March.

Action Plan

- Make sure you prepare adjustments for the correct time period.
- Adjusting entries for prepaid expenses require a debit to an expense account and a credit to an asset or contra asset account.
- Adjusting entries for unearned revenues require a debit to a liability account and a credit to a revenue account.

Solution

1.	Mar. 31	Insurance Expense	100	
		Prepaid Insurance		100
		To record insurance expired: $1,200 ÷ 12.		
2.	31	Office Supplies Expense	2,000	
		Office Supplies		2,000
		To record supplies used: $2,800 previously on hand − $800 currently on hand = $2,000 used.		
3.	31	Amortization Expense	200	
		Accumulated Amortization—Office Equipment		200
		To record monthly amortization: $24,000 ÷ 10 × $\frac{1}{12}$		
4.	31	Unearned Revenue	3,100	
		Service Revenue		3,100
		To record revenue earned: $9,300 × $\frac{1}{3}$ = $3,100 earned.		

Related exercise material: BE3–2, BE3–3, BE3–4, BE3–5, BE–6, E3–4, and E3–5.

Adjusting Entries for Accruals

The second category of adjusting entries is accruals. Unlike prepayments, which have already been recorded in the accounts, accruals are not recognized through daily entries and thus are not initially recorded in the accounts. Consequently, adjusting entries for accruals are required in order to record revenues that were earned, or expenses that were incurred, in the current accounting period.

    Until an accrual adjustment is made, the revenue account (and the related asset account) is understated for accrued revenues. Similarly, the expense account (and the related liability account) is understated for accrued expenses. Thus, adjusting entries for accruals increase both a balance sheet account and an income statement account. We now look at each type of adjusting entry for accruals—accrued revenues and accrued expenses—in more detail.

> **study objective 3**
> Prepare adjusting entries for accruals.

Accrued Revenues

Revenues earned but not yet received in cash or recorded at the statement date are **accrued revenues**. Accrued revenues may accumulate (accrue) with the passage of time, as happens with interest revenue and rent revenue. Or they may result when services have been performed but the payment has not been billed or collected, as can happen with commissions and fees. The former are unrecorded because the earning of interest and rent does not involve daily transactions. The latter may be unrecorded because only a portion of the total service has been provided or the bill has not been prepared.

An adjusting entry is required for two purposes: (1) to show the receivable that exists at the balance sheet date, and (2) to record the revenue that has been earned during the period. Before adjustment, both assets and revenues are understated. Accordingly, as shown below, an adjusting entry for accrued revenues results in an increase (debit) to an asset account and an increase (credit) to a revenue account.

Accrued Revenues

Asset		Revenue	
Debit Adjusting Entry (+)			Credit Adjusting Entry (+)

In October, Pioneer Advertising Agency earned $200 in fees for advertising services that were not billed to clients until November. Because these services have not been billed, they have not been recorded. The following adjusting entry is made on October 31:

Cash flows: no effect

Oct. 31	Accounts Receivable	200	
	Service Revenue		200
	To accrue revenue earned but not billed or collected.		

After the adjusting entry is posted, the accounts show the following:

Accounts Receivable				Service Revenue		
Oct. 21	10,000	Oct. 31	10,000		Oct. 21	10,000
31 Adj.	200				31 Adj.	400
Oct. 31 Bal.	200				31 Adj.	200
					Oct. 31 Adj.	10,600

The asset Accounts Receivable shows that $200 is owed by clients at the balance sheet date. The balance of $10,600 in Service Revenue represents the total revenue earned during the month. If the adjusting entry is not made, assets and owner's equity on the balance sheet, and revenues and net income on the income statement, will all be understated.

On November 10, Pioneer receives $200 cash for the services performed in October. The following entry is made:

↑ Cash flows: +200

Nov. 10	Cash	200	
	Accounts Receivable		200
	To record cash collected on account.		

Accrued Expenses

Expenses incurred but not yet paid or recorded at the statement date are called **accrued expenses**. Interest, rent, property taxes, and salaries can be accrued expenses. Accrued expenses result from the same causes as accrued revenues. In fact, an accrued expense on the books of one company is an accrued revenue for another company. For example, the $200 accrual of revenue by Pioneer is an accrued expense for the client that received the service.

Adjustments for accrued expenses are needed for two purposes: (1) to record the obligations that exist at the balance sheet date, and (2) to recognize the expenses that apply to the current accounting period. Before adjustment, both liabilities and expenses are understated. Therefore, as shown below, an adjusting entry for accrued expenses results in an increase (debit) to an expense account and an increase (credit) to a liability account.

Alternative terminology
Accrued expenses are also called accrued liabilities.

Accrued Expenses

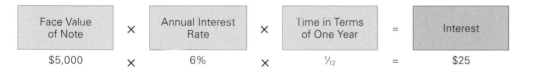

Accrued Interest. On October 2, Pioneer Advertising Agency signed a $5,000, three-month note payable, due January 2, 2009. The note requires interest to be paid at an annual rate of 6 percent. The amount of interest that has accumulated is determined by three factors: (1) the face value, or principal amount, of the note; (2) the interest rate, which is always expressed as an annual rate; and (3) the length of time that the note is outstanding (unpaid).

The formula for calculating interest and its application to Pioneer Advertising Agency for the month of October are shown in Illustration 3-5.

Illustration 3-5 ◄

Formula for interest

Helpful hint The illustration uses a simplified method for calculating interest to make the calculation easier to understand. In reality, interest is calculated using the exact number of days in the interest period and year.

Interest is sometimes due monthly, and sometimes when the principal is due. For Pioneer, the total interest due on the $5,000 note at its due date three months later is $75 ($5,000 × 6% × ³⁄₁₂ months). Interest rates are always expressed as an annual rate. Because the interest rate is for one year, the time period must be adjusted for the fraction of the year that the note is outstanding.

The accrued expense adjusting entry at October 31 is therefore as follows:

Oct. 31	Interest Expense	25	
	Interest Payable		25
	To accrue interest on note payable.		

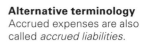

After this adjusting entry is posted, the accounts show:

Interest Expense		Interest Payable	
Oct. 31 Adj. 25			Oct. 31 Adj. 25

Interest Expense shows the interest charges for the month of October. The amount of interest owed at the statement date is shown in Interest Payable. It will not be paid until the note comes due, on January 2, 2009. The Interest Payable account is used instead of crediting Notes Payable in order to show the two types of obligations (interest and principal) in the accounts and statements. If this adjusting entry is not made, liabilities and expenses will be understated, and net income and owner's equity will be overstated.

Since this is a three-month note, Pioneer Advertising will also need to make an identical adjustment at the end of November and at the end of December to accrue for interest expense incurred in each of these months. After the three adjusting entries have been posted, the balance in Interest Payable is $75 ($25 × 3). The following entry is made on January 2, 2009, when the note and interest are paid:

A = L + OE
−5,075   −75
         −5,000

↓ Cash flows: −5,075

Jan. 2	Interest Payable	75	
	Note Payable	5,000	
	Cash		5,075
	To record payment of note and interest.		

This entry does two things: (1) it eliminates the liability for Interest Payable that was recorded in the October 31, November 30, and December 31 adjusting entries; (2) it eliminates the note payable. Notice also that the Interest Expense account is not included in this entry, because the full amount of interest incurred was accrued in previous months.

Accrued Salaries. Some types of expenses, such as employee salaries and commissions, are paid after the work has been performed. At Pioneer Advertising, employees began work on October 13. They were last paid on October 24. The next payment of salaries will not occur until November 7. As shown in the calendar, five working days remain in October.

Helpful hint Recognition of an accrued expense does not mean that a company is slow or bad at paying its debts. The accrued liability may not be payable until after the balance sheet date.

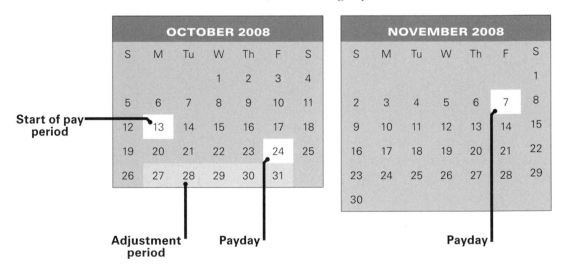

At October 31, the salaries for the last five working days represent an accrued expense and a liability to Pioneer Advertising. The four employees each earn a salary of $500 for a five-day work week, or $100 per day. Thus, accrued salaries for Pioneer Advertising at October 31 are $2,000 ($100 × 5 days × 4 employees). The adjusting entry is as follows:

A = L + OE
    +2,000 −2,000

Cash flows: no effect

Oct. 31	Salaries Expense	2,000	
	Salaries Payable		2,000
	To record accrued salaries.		

After this adjusting entry is posted, the accounts show the following:

Salaries Expense		Salaries Payable	
Oct. 24 4,000			Oct. 31 Adj. 2,000
31 Adj. 2,000			
Oct. 31 Bal. 6,000			

After this adjustment, the balance in Salaries Expense of $6,000 ($100 × 15 days × 4 employees) is the actual salary expense for October (the employees started work on October 13). The balance in Salaries Payable of $2,000 is the amount of the liability for salaries owed as at October 31. If the $2,000 adjustment for salaries is not recorded, Pioneer's expenses and liabilities will be understated by $2,000. Net income and owner's equity will be overstated by $2,000.

At Pioneer Advertising, salaries are payable every two weeks. The next payday is November 7, when total salaries of $4,000 will again be paid. The payment consists of $2,000 of salaries payable at October 31 plus $2,000 of salaries expense for November ($100 × 5 working days [for the period November 1–7] × 4 employees). The following entry is therefore made on November 7:

Nov. 7	Salaries Payable	2,000	
	Salaries Expense	2,000	
	Cash		4,000
	To record November 7 payroll.		

A	=	L	+	OE
−4,000		−2,000		−2,000

Cash flows: −4,000

This entry does two things: (1) it eliminates the liability for salaries payable that was recorded in the October 31 adjusting entry; (2) it records the proper amount of salaries expense for the period between November 1 and November 7.

ACCOUNTING IN ACTION ► Accounting Across the Organization

In ancient Egypt, people were paid with commodities. The average worker would receive a "minimum wage" of loaves of bread and jugs of beer. Wages could also be wheat, fish, vegetables, wood for fuel, pottery, and clothing. A highly paid worker, such as a foreman or a scribe, got 7½ sacks of corn per month. However, a physician earned just 1½ sacks a month. Still, whether money or a commodity, a salary paid after the work is done constitutes an accrued salary

Source: Canadian Payroll Association, http://www.npw-snp.ca/Template.cfm?Section=Quick_Facts

? In what ways is calculating a salary accrual at the end of the month the same today as it would have been in ancient Egypt?

BEFORE YOU GO ON . . .

 Review It

1. If an accrued revenue adjusting entry is not made, what is the effect on assets, owner's equity, revenues, and net income?
2. If an accrued expense adjusting entry is not made, what is the effect on liabilities, owner's equity, expenses, and net income?

► Do It

Calvin Hobbs is the new owner of Micro Computer Services. At the end of August 2008, the first month of business, Calvin is trying to prepare monthly financial statements. The following information is for August:

1. At August 31, Micro Computer Services owed its employees $800 in salaries that will be paid on September 2.
2. On August 1, Micro Computer Services borrowed $30,000 from a local bank on a five-year term loan. The annual interest rate is 5% and interest is paid monthly on the first of each month.
3. Service revenue earned in August but not yet billed or recorded at August 31 totalled $1,100.

Prepare the adjusting entries needed at August 31, 2008.

Action Plan

- Remember that accruals are entries that were not previously recorded; therefore, the adjustment pattern is different from the pattern for prepayments.
- Adjusting entries for accrued revenues require a debit to a receivable account and a credit to a revenue account.
- Adjusting entries for accrued expenses require a debit to an expense account and a credit to a liability account.

Solution

1.	Aug. 31	Salaries Expense	800	
		Salaries Payable		800
		To record accrued salaries.		
2.	31	Interest Expense	125	
		Interest Payable		125
		To record accrued interest: $30,000 \times 5\% \times \frac{1}{12} = \$125$		
3.	31	Accounts Receivable	1,100	
		Service Revenue		1,100
		To accrue revenue earned but not billed or collected.		

Related exercise material: BE3–7, BE3–8, BE3–9, E3–3, E3–6, E3–7, and E3–8.

Summary of Basic Relationships

The two basic types of adjusting entries are summarized below. Take some time to study and analyze the adjusting entries in the summary. Be sure to note that each adjusting entry affects one balance sheet account and one income statement account.

	Type of Adjustment	Reason for Adjustment	Accounts before Adjustment	Adjusting Entry
Prepayments	Prepaid expenses	Prepaid expenses, originally recorded in asset accounts, have been used.	Assets overstated; expenses understated	Dr. Expense Cr. Asset
	Unearned revenues	Unearned revenues, originally recorded in liability accounts, have been earned.	Liabilities overstated; revenues understated	Dr. Liability Cr. Revenue
Accruals	Accrued revenues	Revenues have been earned but not yet received in cash or recorded.	Assets understated; revenues understated	Dr. Asset Cr. Revenue
	Accrued expenses	Expenses have been incurred but not yet paid in cash or recorded.	Expenses understated; liabilities understated	Dr. Expense Cr. Liability

It is important to understand that adjusting entries never involve the Cash account (except for bank reconciliations, which we will study in Chapter 7). In the case of prepayments, cash has already been received or paid, and was already recorded in the original journal entry. The adjusting entry just reallocates or adjusts amounts between a balance sheet account (e.g., prepaid assets or unearned revenues) and an income statement account (e.g., expenses or revenues). In the case of accruals, cash will be received or paid in the future and recorded then. The adjusting entry just records the receivable or payable and the related revenue or expense.

Pioneer Advertising Agency Illustration

The journalizing and posting of adjusting entries for Pioneer Advertising Agency on October 31 are shown below and on the following page. The title "Adjusting Entries" may be inserted in the general journal between the last transaction entry from Chapter 2 and the first adjusting entry so that the adjusting entries are clearly identified. As you review the general ledger, note that the adjustments are highlighted in colour.

GENERAL JOURNAL					J2
Date	Account Titles and Explanation	Ref	Debit		Credit
2008	Adjusting Entries				
Oct. 31	Advertising Supplies Expense	611	1,500		
	Advertising Supplies	129			1,500
	To record supplies used.				
31	Insurance Expense	722	50		
	Prepaid Insurance	130			50
	To record insurance expired.				
31	Amortization Expense	711	83		
	Accumulated Amortization—Office Equipment	152			83
	To record monthly amortization.				
31	Unearned Revenue	209	400		
	Service Revenue	400			400
	To record revenue for services provided.				
31	Accounts Receivable	112	200		
	Service Revenue	400			200
	To accrue revenue earned but not billed or collected.				
31	Interest Expense	905	25		
	Interest Payable	230			25
	To accrue interest on note payable.				
31	Salaries Expense	726	2,000		
	Salaries Payable	212			2,000
	To record accrued salaries.				

GENERAL LEDGER		

Cash   101

Oct.	1	10,000	Oct.	3	900
	3	1,200		3	600
	31	10,000		20	500
				24	4,000
	Bal.	15,200			

Accounts Receivable   112

Oct.	21	10,000	Oct.	31	10,000
	31 Adj.	200			
	Bal.	200			

Advertising Supplies   129

Oct.	4	2,500	Oct. 31 Adj.	1,500
	Bal.	1,000		

Prepaid Insurance   130

Oct.	3	600	Oct. 31 Adj.	50
	Bal.	550		

Office Equipment   151

Oct.	2	5,000	
	Bal.	5,000	

**Acccumulated Amortization—
Office Equipment**   152

		Oct. 31 Adj.	83
		Bal.	83

Notes Payable   200

		Oct.	2	5,000
		Bal.		5,000

Accounts Payable   201

		Oct.	4	2,500
		Bal.		2,500

Unearned Revenue   209

Oct. 31 Adj.	400	Oct.	3	1,200
		Bal.		800

Salaries Payable   212

		Oct. 31 Adj.	2,000
		Bal.	2,000

Interest Payable   230

		Oct. 31 Adj.	25
		Bal.	25

C. Byrd, Capital   301

		Oct.	1	10,000
		Bal.		10,000

C. Byrd, Drawings   306

Oct.	20	500	
	Bal.	500	

Service Revenue   400

		Oct.	21	10,000
			31 Adj.	400
			31 Adj.	200
			Bal.	10,600

Advertising Supplies Expense   611

Oct. 31 Adj.	1,500	
Bal.	1,500	

Amortization Expense   711

Oct. 31 Adj.	83	
Bal.	83	

Insurance Expense   722

Oct. 31 Adj.	50	
Bal.	50	

Salaries Expense   726

Oct.	24	4,000	
	31 Adj.	2,000	
	Bal.	6,000	

Rent Expense   729

Oct.	3	900	
	Bal.	900	

Interest Expense   905

Oct. 31 Adj.	25	
Bal.	25	

Accounting software handles the adjusting process like any other transaction. The accountant simply inputs the adjustment at the right time. The main difference between adjusting entries and regular transactions is that with adjusting entries the accounting software may do the required calculation (for items such as amortization or interest) before sending these figures to the journalizing process.

Such software is also able to display information before and after changes were made. Management may be interested in such information to highlight the impact that adjustments have on the various accounts and financial statements.

ACCOUNTING IN ACTION ▶ Ethics Insight

In the wake of financial scandals that are still making an impression, the Canadian Securities Administrators introduced requirements in 2005 for management to evaluate the reliability of a company's accounting system and controls. This includes a review of year-end procedures, including the procedures that are used to record recurring and nonrecurring adjusting entries.

This review will include asking such questions as the following: How are the adjustments developed, authorized, and checked? What principles does the accounting department use to make adjusting entries? Do the accounting estimates and judgements reflect any biases that would consistently overstate or understate key amounts? Are the proper people involved in the year-end decision making? All of these, and similar questions are designed to improve the quality and reliability of the financial statements.

? How could an adjusting entry be used to overstate net income?

The Adjusted Trial Balance and Financial Statements

After all adjusting entries have been journalized and posted, another trial balance is prepared from the general ledger accounts. This is called an **adjusted trial balance**. The procedures for preparing an adjusted trial balance are the same as those described in Chapter 2 for preparing a trial balance.

> **study objective 4**
> Describe the nature and purpose of an adjusted trial balance, and prepare one.

Preparing the Adjusted Trial Balance

An adjusted trial balance proves that the total debit balances and the total credit balances in the ledger are equal after all adjustments have been made. An adjusted trial balance, like a trial balance, only proves that the ledger is mathematically accurate. As discussed in Chapter 2, it does not prove that there are no mistakes in the ledger. The adjusted trial balance gives all data that are needed for preparing financial statements.

The adjusted trial balance for Pioneer Advertising Agency is presented in Illustration 3-6. It has been prepared from the ledger accounts shown in the previous section. The amounts affected by the adjusting entries are highlighted in colour in the adjusted trial balance columns. Compare these amounts to those in the unadjusted trial balance in Illustration 3-3.

Illustration 3-6 ►

Adjusted trial balance

	Debit	Credit
PIONEER ADVERTISING AGENCY		
Adjusted Trial Balance		
October 31, 2008		
Cash	$15,200	
Accounts receivable	200	
Advertising supplies	1,000	
Prepaid insurance	550	
Office equipment	5,000	
Accumulated amortization—office equipment		$ 83
Notes payable		5,000
Accounts payable		2,500
Unearned revenue		800
Salaries payable		2,000
Interest payable		25
C. Byrd, capital		10,000
C. Byrd, drawings	500	
Service revenue		10,600
Advertising supplies expense	1,500	
Amortization expense	83	
Insurance expense	50	
Salaries expense	6,000	
Rent expense	900	
Interest expense	25	
	$31,008	$31,008

Preparing Financial Statements

Financial statements can be prepared directly from the adjusted trial balance. The preparation of financial statements from the adjusted trial balance of Pioneer Advertising Agency and the interrelationships of the data are shown in Illustrations 3-7 and 3-8.

Illustration 3-7 shows that the income statement is prepared from the revenue and expense accounts. The statement of owner's equity is prepared from the owner's capital and drawings accounts, and from the net income (or net loss) shown in the income statement. As shown in Illustration 3-8, the balance sheet is then prepared from the asset and liability accounts and the ending owner's capital balance that is reported in the statement of owner's equity.

Illustration 3-7 ▼

Preparation of the income statement and statement of owner's equity from the adjusted trial balance

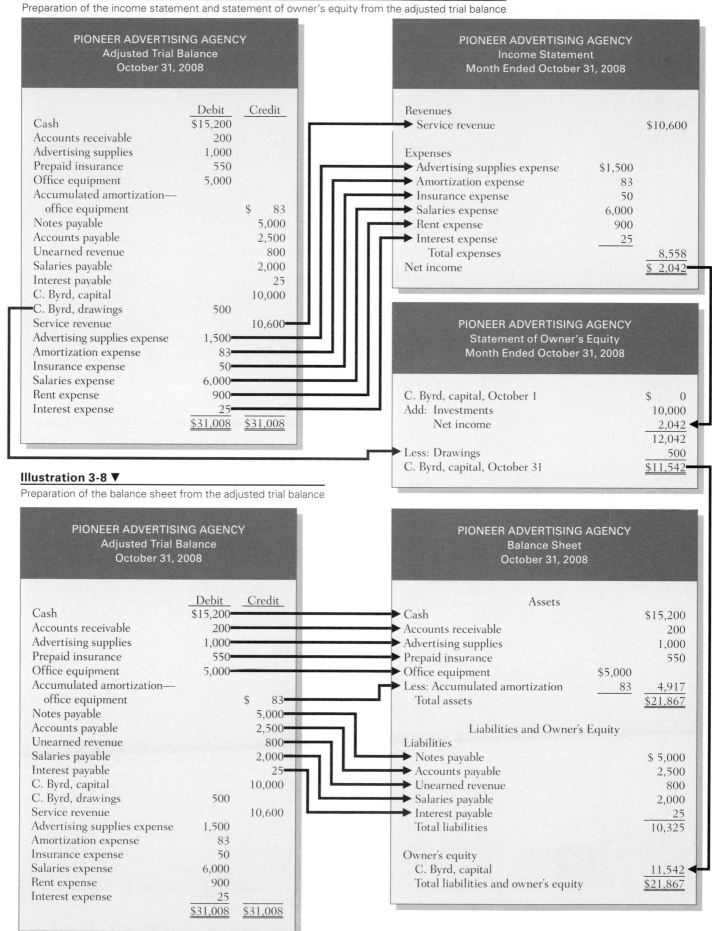

PIONEER ADVERTISING AGENCY
Adjusted Trial Balance
October 31, 2008

	Debit	Credit
Cash	$15,200	
Accounts receivable	200	
Advertising supplies	1,000	
Prepaid insurance	550	
Office equipment	5,000	
Accumulated amortization— office equipment		$ 83
Notes payable		5,000
Accounts payable		2,500
Unearned revenue		800
Salaries payable		2,000
Interest payable		25
C. Byrd, capital		10,000
C. Byrd, drawings	500	
Service revenue		10,600
Advertising supplies expense	1,500	
Amortization expense	83	
Insurance expense	50	
Salaries expense	6,000	
Rent expense	900	
Interest expense	25	
	$31,008	$31,008

PIONEER ADVERTISING AGENCY
Income Statement
Month Ended October 31, 2008

Revenues		
Service revenue		$10,600
Expenses		
Advertising supplies expense	$1,500	
Amortization expense	83	
Insurance expense	50	
Salaries expense	6,000	
Rent expense	900	
Interest expense	25	
Total expenses		8,558
Net income		$ 2,042

PIONEER ADVERTISING AGENCY
Statement of Owner's Equity
Month Ended October 31, 2008

C. Byrd, capital, October 1	$ 0
Add: Investments	10,000
Net income	2,042
	12,042
Less: Drawings	500
C. Byrd, capital, October 31	$11,542

Illustration 3-8 ▼

Preparation of the balance sheet from the adjusted trial balance

PIONEER ADVERTISING AGENCY
Adjusted Trial Balance
October 31, 2008

	Debit	Credit
Cash	$15,200	
Accounts receivable	200	
Advertising supplies	1,000	
Prepaid insurance	550	
Office equipment	5,000	
Accumulated amortization— office equipment		$ 83
Notes payable		5,000
Accounts payable		2,500
Unearned revenue		800
Salaries payable		2,000
Interest payable		25
C. Byrd, capital		10,000
C. Byrd, drawings	500	
Service revenue		10,600
Advertising supplies expense	1,500	
Amortization expense	83	
Insurance expense	50	
Salaries expense	6,000	
Rent expense	900	
Interest expense	25	
	$31,008	$31,008

PIONEER ADVERTISING AGENCY
Balance Sheet
October 31, 2008

Assets		
Cash		$15,200
Accounts receivable		200
Advertising supplies		1,000
Prepaid insurance		550
Office equipment	$5,000	
Less: Accumulated amortization	83	4,917
Total assets		$21,867
Liabilities and Owner's Equity		
Liabilities		
Notes payable		$ 5,000
Accounts payable		2,500
Unearned revenue		800
Salaries payable		2,000
Interest payable		25
Total liabilities		10,325
Owner's equity		
C. Byrd, capital		11,542
Total liabilities and owner's equity		$21,867

BEFORE YOU GO ON . . .

▶Review It

1. What is the purpose of an adjusted trial balance?
2. How is an adjusted trial balance prepared?

▶Do It

Listed below, in alphabetical order, are the account balances (after adjustments) from the general ledger of KS Service Company at December 31, 2008. All accounts have normal balances.

Accounts payable	$ 4,660	K. Samji, drawings	11,700
Accounts receivable	9,584	Note payable	1,000
Accumulated amortization—		Rent expense	20,762
equipment	1,764	Salaries expense	30,714
Amortization expense	588	Salaries payable	310
Cash	1,100	Service revenue	67,200
Equipment	8,820	Supplies	180
Interest expense	524	Supplies expense	672
K. Samji, capital	8,700	Unearned service revenue	1,010

Prepare the adjusted trial balance. Beside each account, identify if it should be included on the income statement (IS), statement of owner's equity (OE), or the balance sheet (BS).

Action Plan

- The title includes the name of the company, the type of trial balance, and the date.
- Accounts are listed in the same order as in a trial balance: assets, liabilities, owner's equity, revenues, and expenses.
- Apply the normal balance rules and list the account balances in the correct columns.
- Ensure the totals of the two columns are equal.

Solution

KS SERVICE COMPANY
Adjusted Trial Balance
December 31, 2008

	Debit	Credit	Statement
Cash	$ 1,100		BS
Accounts receivable	9,584		BS
Supplies	180		BS
Equipment	8,820		BS
Accumulated amortization—equipment		$ 1,764	BS
Note payable		1,000	BS
Accounts payable		4,660	BS
Salaries payable		310	BS
Unearned service revenue		1,010	BS
K. Samji, capital		8,700	OE & BS
K. Samji, drawings	11,700		OE
Service revenue		67,200	IS
Amortization expense	588		IS
Rent expense	20,762		IS
Salaries expense	30,714		IS
Supplies expense	672		IS
Interest expense	524		IS
	$84,644	$84,644	

the navigator

Related exercise material: BE3–10, BE3–11, E3-9, E3-10, and E3–11.

APPENDIX 3A ► ALTERNATIVE TREATMENT OF PREPAID EXPENSES AND UNEARNED REVENUES

In our discussion of adjusting entries for prepaid expenses and unearned revenues, we illustrated transactions which already had entries in balance sheet accounts. In the case of prepaid expenses, the prepayment was debited to an asset account. In the case of unearned revenue, the cash received was credited to a liability account. Recording your first entry in a balance sheet account improves internal control over assets and it imitates the real flow of costs (i.e., from asset to expense).

> **study objective 5**
>
> Prepare adjusting entries for the alternative treatment of prepayments.

Some businesses use an alternative treatment, which is also acceptable. At the time an expense is prepaid, an expense account is debited (increased) and Cash is credited (decreased). At the time of a receipt for future services, Cash is debited (increased) and a revenue account is credited (increased). The following sections describe the circumstances that justify such entries and the different adjusting entries that may be needed.

Prepaid Expenses

Prepaid expenses become expired costs either as time passes, as with insurance, or as they are used up, as with advertising supplies. If, when it makes a purchase, the company expects to consume the supplies before the next financial statement date, it may be more convenient to first debit (increase) an expense account rather than an asset account.

Assume that Pioneer Advertising expects that all of the supplies purchased on October 4 will be used before the end of the month. A debit of $2,500 to Advertising Supplies Expense on October 4, rather than to the asset account Advertising Supplies, will eliminate the need for an adjusting entry on October 31, if all the supplies are used. At October 31, the Advertising Supplies Expense account will show a balance of $2,500, which is the cost of supplies purchased between October 4 and October 31.

But what if the company does not use all the supplies and an inventory of $1,000 of advertising supplies remains on October 31? Obviously, an adjusting entry is needed. The following adjusting entry is then made:

Oct. 31	Advertising Supplies	1,000	
	Advertising Supplies Expense		1,000
	To record supply inventory.		

A	=	L	+	OE
+1,000				+1,000

Cash flows: no effect

After posting of the adjusting entry, the accounts show the following:

Advertising Supplies			Advertising Supplies Expense		
Oct. 31 Adj. 1,000			Oct. 4 2,500	Oct. 31 Adj. 1,000	
			Oct. 31 Bal. 1,500		

After adjustment, the asset account Advertising Supplies shows a balance of $1,000, which is equal to the cost of supplies on hand at October 31. In addition, Advertising Supplies Expense shows a balance of $1,500, which is equal to the cost of supplies used between October 4 and October 31. If the adjusting entry is not made, expenses will be overstated and net income will be understated by $1,000 in the October income statement. Also, both assets and owner's equity will be understated by $1,000 on the October 31 balance sheet.

A comparison of the entries and accounts for advertising supplies in the chapter and here in the appendix follows:

Prepayment Debited to Asset Account (as in chapter)			
Oct. 4	Advertising Supplies	2,500	
	Accounts Payable		2,500
31	Advertising Supplies Expense	1,500	
	Advertising Supplies		1,500

Prepayment Debited to Expense Account (as in appendix)			
Oct. 4	Advertising Supplies Expense	2,500	
	Accounts Payable		2,500
31	Advertising Supplies	1,000	
	Advertising Supplies Expense		1,000

After posting of the entries, the accounts appear as follows:

Prepayment Debited to Asset Account (as in chapter)

Advertising Supplies

Oct. 4	2,500	Oct. 31 Adj.	1,500
Oct. 31 Bal.	1,000		

Advertising Supplies Expense

Oct. 31 Adj.	1,500	

Prepayment Debited to Expense Account (as in appendix)

Advertising Supplies

Oct. 31 Adj.	1,000	

Advertising Supplies Expense

Oct. 4	2,500	Oct. 31 Adj.	1,000
Oct. 31 Bal.	1,500		

Note that the account balances under each alternative are the same at October 31 (Advertising Supplies $1,000; and Advertising Supplies Expense $1,500).

Unearned Revenues

Unearned revenues are earned either as time passes, as with unearned rent, or by providing the service, as with unearned fees. Rather than first crediting (increasing) an unearned revenue (liability) account, a revenue account may be credited (increased) when cash is received for future services. Then a different adjusting entry may be necessary.

To illustrate, assume that when Pioneer Advertising received $1,200 for future services on October 3, the services were expected to be performed before October 31. In such a case, Service Revenue would be credited. If revenue is in fact earned before October 31, no adjustment is needed. However, if at the statement date $800 of the services have not been provided, an adjusting entry is needed. The following adjusting entry is made:

A	=	L	+	OE
		+800		−800

Cash flows: no effect

Oct. 31	Service Revenue		800	
	Unearned Revenue			800
	To record unearned revenue.			

After posting of the adjusting entry, the accounts show:

Unearned Revenue

	Oct. 31 Adj.	800

Service Revenue

Oct. 31 Adj.	800	Oct. 3	1,200	
		Oct. 31 Bal.	400	

The liability account Unearned Revenue shows a balance of $800, which is equal to the services that will be provided in the future. In addition, the balance in Service Revenue equals the services provided in October. If the adjusting entry is not made, both revenues and net income will be overstated by $800 in the October income statement. On the October 31 balance sheet, liabilities will also be understated by $800, and owner's equity will be overstated by $800.

A comparison of the entries and accounts for service revenue and unearned revenue in the chapter and here in the appendix follows:

Unearned Revenue Credited to Liability Account (as in chapter)				Unearned Revenue Credited to Revenue Account (as in appendix)		
Oct. 3	Cash	1,200		Oct. 3	Cash	1,200
	Unearned Revenue		1,200		Service Revenue		1,200
31	Unearned Revenue	400		31	Service Revenue	800
	Service Revenue		400		Unearned Revenue		800

After posting the entries, the accounts will show:

Unearned Revenue Credited to Liability Account (as in chapter)

Unearned Revenue
| Oct. 31 Adj. | 400 | Oct. 3 Adj. | 1,200 |
| | | Oct. 31 Bal. | 800 |

Service Revenue
| | | Oct. 31 Adj. | 400 |

Unearned Revenue Credited to Revenue Account (as in appendix)

Unearned Revenue
| | | Oct. 31 Adj. | 800 |

Service Revenue
| Oct. 31 Adj. | 800 | Oct. 3 | 1,200 |
| | | Oct. 31 Bal. | 400 |

Note that the balances in the accounts are the same under the two alternatives (Unearned Revenue $800; and Service Revenue $400).

There is no method of alternative adjusting entries for accruals or estimates, because no entries occur before these types of adjusting entries are made.

Demonstration Problem

Practice Tools:
Demonstration Problems

Julie Szo opens Green Thumb Lawn Care Company on April 1. At April 30, the trial balance shows the following balances for selected accounts:

Prepaid Insurance	$ 3,600	Note Payable	$20,000
Supplies	850	Unearned Revenue	4,200
Equipment	28,000	Service Revenue	1,800

Analysis reveals the following additional data about these accounts:

1. Prepaid insurance is the cost of a 12-month insurance policy that started April 1.
2. Supplies costing $225 were on hand on April 30.
3. The equipment is expected to have a useful life of four years.
4. The note payable is dated April 1. It is a six-month, 4% note with interest payable on the first of each month.
5. Seven customers paid for the company's six-month lawn-service package of $600, beginning in April. These customers were serviced in April.

6. Lawn services performed for other customers but not billed or recorded at April 30 totalled $1,500.

7. A part-time employee was hired in late April at $10 per hour. He worked 11 hours in April and will be paid for this on May 4.

Instructions

Prepare the adjusting entries for the month of April. Show calculations.

Action Plan

- Note that adjustments are being made for one month.
- Before trying to determine what adjustments are necessary, look at how the amounts are currently recorded in the accounts.
- Select account titles carefully. Use existing titles whenever possible.
- Determine what the balance in the ledger accounts will be after the adjusting entries are posted. Be sure to make the adjustment in the right direction so that the desired balance results.

Solution to Demonstration Problem

	GENERAL JOURNAL				J2
Date	Account Titles and Explanation	Ref.	Debit	Credit	
	Adjusting Entries				
Apr. 30	Insurance Expense		300		
	Prepaid Insurance			300	
	To record insurance expired: $3,600 \div 12 = \$300$ per month.				
30	Supplies Expense		625		
	Supplies			625	
	To record supplies used: $850 - \$225 = \$625$				
30	Amortization Expense		583		
	Accumulated Amortization—Equipment			583	
	To record monthly amortization: $28,000 \div 4 = \$7,000 \div 12 = \$583$ per month.				
30	Interest Expense		67		
	Interest Payable			67	
	To accrue interest on note payable: $\$20,000 \times 4\% \times \frac{1}{12} = \$67$.				
30	Unearned Revenue		700		
	Service Revenue			700	
	To record service revenue: $600 \div 6$ months $= \$100$ per month; 100 per month $\times 7$ customers $= \$700$.				
30	Accounts Receivable		1,500		
	Service Revenue			1,500	
	To accrue revenue earned but not billed or collected.				
30	Wages Expense		110		
	Wages Payable			110	
	To accrue wages earned to April 30: 10 per hour $\times 11$ hours $= \$110$.				

Summary of Study Objectives

1. *Explain the time period assumption, revenue recognition principle, matching principle, and accrual basis of accounting.* The time period assumption divides the economic life of a business into artificial time periods. The revenue recognition principle states that revenue should be recognized (recorded) in the accounting period in which it is earned. The matching principle states that expenses should be recognized (recorded) when they make their contribution to revenues. The accrual basis of accounting means that events that change a company's financial statements are recorded in the periods in which the events occur, rather than in the periods in which the company receives or pays cash.

2. *Prepare adjusting entries for prepayments.* Prepayments are either prepaid expenses or unearned revenues. Ad-

justing entries for prepayments record the portion of the prepayment that applies to the expense or revenue of the current accounting period. The adjusting entry for prepaid expenses debits (increases) an expense account and credits (decreases) an asset account. For a long-lived asset, the contra asset account Accumulated Amortization is used instead of crediting the asset account directly. The adjusting entry for unearned revenues debits (decreases) a liability account and credits (increases) a revenue account.

3. *Prepare adjusting entries for accruals.* Accruals are either accrued revenues or accrued expenses. Adjusting entries for accruals record revenues and expenses that apply to the current accounting period and that have not yet been recognized through daily journal entries. The adjusting entry for accrued revenue debits (increases) a receivable account and credits (increases) a revenue account. The adjusting entry for an accrued expense debits (increases) an expense account and credits (increases) a liability account.

4. *Describe the nature and purpose of an adjusted trial balance, and prepare one.* An adjusted trial balance shows the balances of all accounts, including those that have been adjusted, at the end of an accounting period. Its purpose is to show the effects of all financial events that have occurred during the accounting period. An adjusted trial balance makes it easier to prepare the financial statements.

5. *Prepare adjusting entries for the alternative treatment of prepayments (Appendix 3A).* Prepayments may initially be debited (increased) to an expense account. Unearned revenues may initially be credited (increased) to a revenue account. At the end of the period, these accounts may be overstated. The adjusting entries for prepaid expenses are a debit (increase) to an asset account and a credit (decrease) to an expense account. Adjusting entries for unearned revenues are a debit (decrease) to a revenue account and a credit (increase) to a liability account. It does not matter which alternative is used to record and adjust prepayments, as the ending account balances should be the same with both methods.

Glossary

www.wiley.com/canada/weygandt

Study Aids: Glossary
Practice Tools: Key Term Matching Activity

Accrual basis of accounting A basis for accounting in which revenues are recorded when earned and expenses are recorded in the same period as the revenue they relate to. (p. 106)

Accrued expenses Expenses incurred but not yet paid in cash or recorded. (p. 117)

Accrued revenues Revenues earned but not yet received in cash or recorded. (p. 116)

Adjusted trial balance A list of accounts and their balances after all adjustments have been made. (p. 123)

Adjusting entries Entries made at the end of an accounting period, because of the time period assumption, to ensure that the revenue recognition and matching principles are followed. (p. 108)

Amortization The allocation of the cost of a long-lived asset to expense over its useful life in a rational and systematic manner. (p. 111)

Cash basis of accounting A basis for accounting in which revenue is recorded when cash is received and an expense is recorded when cash is paid. (p. 106)

Contra account An account that is offset against another account on the income statement or balance sheet. (p. 113)

Fiscal year An accounting period that is one year long. It does not need to start and end on the same days as the calendar year. (p. 105)

Interim periods Accounting time periods that are less than one year long. (p. 104)

Matching principle The principle of expense recognition where efforts (expenses) should be matched with accomplishments (revenues). (p. 105)

Net book value The difference between the cost of an amortizable asset and its accumulated amortization; in other words, it is the unallocated or unexpired portion of the amortizable asset's cost. (p. 113)

Prepaid expenses Costs paid in cash and recorded as assets before they are used or consumed. (p. 110)

Revenue recognition principle The principle that revenue should be recognized in the accounting period in which it is earned. (p. 105)

Straight-line amortization method An amortization method in which amortization expense is calculated as the cost divided by the useful life. (p. 112)

Time period assumption An assumption that the economic life of a business can be divided into artificial time periods: normally a month, quarter, or year. (p. 104)

Unearned revenues Revenues received in cash and recorded as liabilities before they are earned. (p. 113)

Useful life The length of service of an amortizable asset. (p. 111)

Note: All questions, exercises, and problems below with an asterisk (*) relate to material in Appendix 3A

Self-Study Questions

Practice Tools: Self-Assessment Quizzes

Answers are at the end of the chapter.

(SO 1) K 1. The time period assumption states that:
  (a) revenue should be recognized in the accounting period in which it is earned.
  (b) expenses should be matched with revenues.
  (c) the economic life of a business can be divided into artificial time periods.
  (d) the fiscal year should match the calendar year.

(SO 1) K 2. The principle which states that efforts (expenses) should be recorded in the same period as the related accomplishments (revenues) is the:
  (a) matching principle.
  (b) cost principle.
  (c) time period assumption.
  (d) revenue recognition principle.

(SO 1) K 3. Adjusting entries are made to ensure that:
  (a) expenses are matched to revenues in the period in which the revenue is generated.
  (b) revenues are recorded in the period in which they are earned.
  (c) balance sheet and income statement accounts have up-to-date balances at the end of an accounting period.
  (d) All of the above

(SO 2) AP 4. The trial balance shows Supplies $1,350 and Supplies Expense $0. If $600 of supplies are on hand at the end of the period, the adjusting entry is:

(a) Supplies	600	
Supplies Expense		600
(b) Supplies	750	
Supplies Expense		750
(c) Supplies Expense	750	
Supplies		750
(d) Supplies Expense	600	
Supplies		600

SO 2) K 5. Accumulated Amortization is:
  (a) an expense account.
  (b) an owner's equity account.
  (c) a liability account.
  (d) a contra asset account.

(SO 2) AP 6. The trial balance shows Unearned Revenue $1,700. Analysis reveals that $700 of that amount was earned by the end of the period. The adjusting entry is:

(a) Unearned Revenue	1,000	
Service Revenue		1,000
(b) Service Revenue	1,000	
Unearned Revenue		1,000
(c) Service Revenue	700	
Unearned Revenue		700
(d) Unearned Revenue	700	
Service Revenue		700

7. In November, Elwood's Electronics earned $550 in service fees that were not billed to customers until December. Elwood's adjusting entry at November 30 is: **(SO 3)**

(a) Cash	550	
Service Revenue		550
(b) Accounts Receivable	550	
Service Revenue		550
(c) Accounts Receivable	550	
Unearned Revenue		550
(d) No entry is required.		

8. Kathy Kiska earned a salary of $400 for the last week of September. She will be paid in October. The adjusting entry for Kathy's employer at September 30 is: **(SO 3)**

(a) Salaries Expense	400	
Salaries Payable		400
(b) Salaries Expense	400	
Cash		400
(c) Salaries Payable	400	
Cash		400
(d) No entry is required.		

9. Which of the following statements about the adjusted trial balance is *incorrect*? **(SO 4)**
  (a) An adjusted trial balance proves that the total debit balances and the total credit balances in the ledger are equal after all adjustments are made.
  (b) The adjusted trial balance is the main basis for preparing financial statements.
  (c) The adjusted trial balance lists the account balances divided into assets and liabilities.
  (d) The adjusted trial balance is prepared after the adjusting entries have been journalized and posted.

*10. The trial balance shows Supplies $0 and Supplies Expense $1,350. If $600 of supplies are on hand at the end of the period, the adjusting entry is: **(SO 5)**

(a) Supplies	600	
Supplies Expense		600
(b) Supplies Expense	750	
Supplies		750
(c) Supplies	750	
Supplies Expense		750
(d) Supplies Expense	600	
Supplies		600

Questions

(SO 1) K 1. (a) How does the time period assumption both increase the usefulness of accounting information and cause accounting problems?
(b) Explain the terms "fiscal year," "calendar year," and "interim period."

(SO 1) C 2. The Higher Education College collects tuition for the fall term from registered students in August. The fall term runs from September to December. In what month(s) should the college recognize the revenue earned from tuition fees? Explain your reasoning.

(SO 1) C 3. Pierce Dussault, a lawyer, accepts a legal engagement in March, does the work in April, and is paid in May. If Dussault's law firm prepares monthly financial statements, when should it recognize revenue from this engagement? Why?

(SO 1) C 4. In completing the engagement in question 3, Dussault incurred $500 of salary expenses in March that are specifically related to this engagement, $2,500 in April, and none in May. How much expense should be deducted from revenue in the month(s) when the revenue is recognized? Why?

(SO 1) C 5. How does the cash basis of accounting differ from the accrual basis of accounting? Which method gives decision-makers more useful information about the company? Why?

(SO 1) C 6. Why are adjusting entries needed? Include in your explanation a description of the assumption and two generally accepted accounting principles that relate to adjusting the accounts.

(SO 2) C 7. The name Prepaid Expense suggests that this account is an expense and belongs on an income statement. Instead the account appears on the balance sheet as an asset. Using the definition of an asset, explain why this is appropriate. What does the balance in a Prepaid Expense account represent?

(SO 2) C 8. "Amortization is a valuation process that results in the reporting of the market value of the asset." Do you agree? Explain.

(SO 2) C 9. Explain the difference between amortization expense and accumulated amortization.

(SO 2) C 10. What is a contra account? Why do we use a contra account to record accumulated amortization instead of directly reducing the long-lived asset?

(SO 2) C 11. The name Unearned Revenue suggests that it is a revenue account and belongs on the income statement. Instead the account appears on the balance sheet as a liability. Using the definition of a liability, explain why this is appropriate. What does the balance in Unearned Revenue represent?

(SO 3) C 12. Waiparous Hotel bills and collects cash from customers at the end of their stay. On March 31, there are customers who have already stayed at the hotel for several days and will not be checking out until later in the week. Is it necessary to make an adjusting entry on March 31? Why or why not? If yes, which accounts are debited and which are credited in the adjusting entry?

(SO 3) C 13. On February 4, ARU Company receives a utility bill for the month of January. Is it necessary to make an adjusting entry for January? Why or why not? If yes, which accounts are debited and credited?

(SO 3) AP 14. A company makes an accrued revenue adjusting entry for $900. Which financial statement items were overstated or understated before this entry? Explain.

(SO 3) AP 15. A company makes an accrued expense adjusting entry for $600. Which financial statement items were overstated or understated before this entry? Explain.

(SO 2, 3) C 16. For each of the following items, indicate the type of adjusting entry (prepaid expense, unearned revenue, accrued revenue, or accrued expense) that is needed to correct the misstatement. If an item could result in more than one type of adjusting entry, indicate each of the types.
(a) Assets are understated.
(b) Liabilities are overstated.
(c) Liabilities are understated.
(d) Expenses are understated.
(e) Assets are overstated.
(f) Revenue is understated.

(SO 2, 3) K 17. One half of the adjusting entry is given below. Indicate the account title for the other half of the entry.
(a) Salaries Payable is credited.
(b) Amortization Expense is debited.
(c) Interest Expense is debited.
(d) Prepaid Insurance is credited.
(e) Accounts Receivable is debited.
(f) Unearned Revenue is debited.

(SO 2, 3) C 18. "An adjusting entry may affect more than one balance sheet or income statement account." Do you agree? Why or why not?

(SO 4) C 19. Identify the similarities and differences between a trial balance and an adjusted trial balance. What is the purpose of each one?

(SO 4) C 20. "The amount included in an adjusted trial balance for a specific account will always be more than the amount that was included in the trial balance for the same account." Do you agree or disagree? Why?

(SO 4) C 21. On Silver Company's trial balance, Accounts Payable is $4,250. After the adjusting entries have been posted, the balance in this account is still $4,250. Since there is no change, it is not necessary to include Accounts Payable on the adjusted trial balance. Do you agree or disagree? Why?

(SO 4) C 22. Net income is shown on the income statement and the statement of owner's equity. It is also indirectly included on the balance sheet. Do you agree or disagree? Why?

*23. Some companies debit an expense account at the time the expense is prepaid instead of debiting an asset account. Will this result in a different net income or different amount of total assets on the balance sheet than if they had instead debited an asset account when the amount was paid? Why or why not? (SO 5)

*24. Jeremiah has been reading about a recent accounting scandal where the company overstated its revenue on purpose. He then argues that it is never appropriate to credit revenue when cash is received in advance of providing a service. Do you agree or disagree? Why? (SO 5)

Brief Exercises

Identify impact of transactions on cash and net income.
(SO 1) AP

BE3–1 Indicate the impact of each of the following transactions on cash and net income. The first transaction has been completed for you as an example.

Transaction	Cash	Net Income
(a) Purchased supplies for cash, $100.	–$100	$0
(b) Recorded the use of $60 of the supplies purchased in (a) in an adjusting journal entry.		
(c) Performed services on account, $1,000.		
(d) Received $800 from customers in payment of their account in (c).		
(e) Purchased office equipment for cash, $5,000.		
(f) Recorded amortization of office equipment for the period, $100.		
(g) Accrued salaries earned but not paid for the month of June, $750.		
(h) On July 3, paid $750 for salaries accrued in (g).		
(i) On May 28, received $500 cash for services to be provided in June.		

Calculate missing data for supplies.
(SO 2) AP

BE3–2 Calculate the missing information in each of the following independent situations:

	A Co.	B Co.
Supplies on hand, May 31, 2007	$ 675	$ 640
Supplies purchased during the year	1,695	2,825
Supplies on hand, May 31, 2008	225	?
Supplies used during the year	?	2,715

Prepare and post transaction and adjusting entries for supplies.
(SO 2) AP

BE3–3 Spahn Cleaning Company had $945 of cleaning supplies on hand on January 1, 2008. On March 2, 2008, it purchased additional cleaning supplies for $3,880 on credit. On December 31, 2008, a count showed $980 of cleaning supplies on hand.

(a) Prepare the journal entry to record the purchase of supplies during the year.
(b) Calculate the amount of cleaning supplies used during the year.
(c) Prepare the adjusting journal entry required at December 31, 2008.
(d) Using T accounts, enter the January 1, 2008, balance in Cleaning Supplies and Cleaning Supplies Expense, post the two journal entries, and indicate the adjusted balance in each account.

Prepare and post transaction and adjusting entries for insurance.
(SO 2) AP

BE3–4 On June 1, 2007, Bere Co. paid $9,900 for a one-year insurance policy. Bere Co. has a December 31 fiscal year end.

(a) Prepare the June 1, 2007, journal entry.

(b) Calculate the amount of insurance that expired during 2007 and the unexpired cost as at December 31, 2007.

(c) Prepare the adjusting entry on December 31, 2007.

(d) Using T accounts, post the above two entries and indicate the adjusted balance in each account.

BE3–5 On January 1, 2007, Creed Co. purchased a delivery truck for $40,000 cash. It estimates the truck will have a five-year useful life. Creed Co. has a December 31 fiscal year end.

> Prepare transaction and adjusting entries for amortization; show statement presentation.
> (SO 2) AP

(a) Prepare the January 1, 2007, journal entry to record the purchase of the delivery truck.

(b) Prepare the adjusting entries that are required on December 31, 2007 and 2008, to record amortization.

(c) Indicate the balance sheet presentation of the delivery truck at December 31, 2007 and 2008, and the amount of amortization expense in the 2007 and 2008 income statements.

BE3–6 On August 1, 2007, Sting Insurance Co. received $1,500 cash from Savita Verma for a one-year insurance policy. Sting Insurance Co. has a December 31 fiscal year end. Complete the following for Sting Insurance Co.:

> Prepare and post transaction and adjusting entries for unearned revenue.
> (SO 2) AP

(a) Prepare the August 1, 2007, journal entry.

(b) Calculate the amount of revenue earned during 2007 and the amount unearned at December 31, 2007.

(c) Prepare the adjusting entry on December 31, 2007.

(d) Using T accounts, post the entries for (a) and (c) above and indicate the adjusted balance in each account.

BE3–7 Zieborg Maintenance Co. has a $375 monthly contract with Crispy Treat Co. for general maintenance services. Zieborg invoices Crispy on the first of the month for the previous month's services provided. Crispy must then pay for the previous month's services by the 10th of the month.

> Prepare transaction and adjusting entries for accrued revenue.
> (SO 3) AP

(a) Zieborg has a November 30 fiscal year end. Why will it need to prepare an adjusting entry on November 30?

(b) Prepare Zieborg's adjusting entry.

(c) Will Zieborg need to record a journal entry on December 1 when it invoices Crispy? Why or why not?

(d) Zieborg receives $375 from Crispy on December 9 for services provided in November. Prepare Zieborg's journal entry.

BE3–8 The total payroll for Classic Autos Co. is $5,000 every Friday ($1,000 per day) for employee salaries earned during a five-day week (Monday through Friday, inclusive). Salaries were last paid on Friday, December 26. This year, the company's fiscal year end, December 31, falls on a Wednesday. Salaries will be paid next on Friday, January 2, at which time employees will receive pay for the five-day work week (including the New Year's holiday). Prepare the journal entries to record the following:

> Prepare transaction and adjusting entries for salaries.
> (SO 3) AP

(a) The payment of salaries on December 26

(b) The adjusting journal entry to accrue salaries at year end

(c) The payment of salaries on January 2

BE3–9 On July 1, 2007, a company purchased a truck for use in the business for $40,000, paying $18,000 cash and signing a 6% note payable for the remainder. The interest and principal of the note are due on December 31, 2008. Prepare the journal entry to record the following:

> Prepare transaction and adjusting entries for interest.
> (SO 3) AP

(a) The purchase of the truck on July 1, 2007

(b) The accrual of the interest at the company's December 31, 2007, fiscal year end

(c) The repayment of the interest and note on December 31, 2008

BE3–10 The account balances (after adjustments) from the general ledger of Winterholt Company at September 30, 2008, follow in alphabetical order. All accounts have normal balances.

> Prepare adjusted trial balance and identify financial statement.
> (SO 4) AP

Accounts payable	$ 2,570	Insurance expense	$ 1,560
Accounts receivable	7,230	Interest expense	500
Accumulated amortization—		Interest payable	125
equipment	6,200	Note payable	10,000
Amortization expense	3,100	Prepaid insurance	780
C. Winterholt, capital	15,450	Rent expense	20,965
C. Winterholt, drawings	21,000	Service revenue	48,950
Cash	1,100	Unearned service revenue	840
Equipment	27,900		

(a) Prepare the adjusted trial balance.
(b) Beside each account, identify if it should be included on the income statement (IS), statement of owner's equity (OE), or balance sheet (BS).

Prepare financial statements.
(SO 4) AP

BE3–11 Refer to BE3–10. Prepare financial statements for the year ended September 30, 2008.

Prepare and post adjusting
entry for supplies.
(SO 5) AP

***BE3–12** Refer to BE3–3. Assume that instead of debiting purchases of cleaning supplies to the Cleaning Supplies account, Spahn Cleaning debits purchases of supplies to the Cleaning Supplies Expense account. Spahn's trial balance at December 31 shows Cleaning Supplies $945 and Cleaning Supplies Expense $3,880. On December 31, there is $980 of supplies on hand.

(a) Prepare the adjusting entry at December 31. Using T accounts, enter the balances in the accounts, post the adjusting entry, and indicate the adjusted balance in each account.
(b) Compare the adjusted balances in BE3–3, where an asset account was originally debited, with the adjusted balances you determined here in (a), where an expense account was originally debited. Does it matter whether an original entry is recorded to an asset account or an expense account? Explain.

Prepare and post adjusting
entry for unearned revenue.
(SO 5) AP

***BE3–13** Refer to BE3–6. Assume that instead of crediting Unearned Revenue for the $1,500 one-year insurance policy, Sting Insurance Co. credits Insurance Revenue on August 1, 2007.

(a) Prepare the adjusting entry at December 31, 2007. Using T accounts, enter the balances in the accounts, post the adjusting entry, and indicate the adjusted balance in each account.
(b) Compare the adjusted balances in BE3–6, where a liability account was originally credited, with the adjusted balances you determined here in (a), where a revenue account was originally credited. Does it matter whether an original entry is recorded to a liability account or a revenue account? Explain.

Exercises

Identify point of revenue
recognition.
(SO 1) AP

E3–1 The following independent situations require professional judgement to determine when to recognize revenue from the transactions:

(a) **Air Canada** sells you an advance purchase airline ticket in September for your flight home at Christmas.
(b) **Leon's Furniture** sells you a home theatre in January on a "no money down, no interest, and no payments for one year" promotional deal.
(c) The **Toronto Blue Jays** sell season tickets to games in the Rogers Centre on-line. Fans can purchase the tickets at any time, although the season does not officially begin until April. It runs from April through October.
(d) The **RBC Financial Group** loans you money at the beginning of August. The loan and the interest are repayable in full at the end of November.
(e) In August, you order a sweater from **Sears** using its on-line catalogue. Sears ships the sweater to you in September and you charge it to your Sears credit card. You receive and pay the Sears bill in October.

(f) You pay for a one-year subscription for **Maclean's** magazine in May.

Instructions

Identify when revenue should be recognized in each of the above situations.

E3–2   In its first year of operations, Brisson Company earned $26,000 in service revenue. Of this amount, $4,000 was on account and the remainder, $22,000, was received in cash.

   The company incurred operating expenses of $15,500. Of these expenses, $13,750 was paid in cash. At year end, $1,750 was still owing on account. In addition, Brisson prepaid $2,000 for insurance that covered the last half of the first year and the first half of the second year.

Determine income using cash and accrual bases. Comment on usefulness.
(SO 1) AP

Instructions

(a) Calculate the first year's net income under the cash basis of accounting.
(b) Calculate the first year's net income under the accrual basis of accounting.
(c) Which basis of accounting (cash or accrual) gives the most useful information for decision-makers?

E3–3   Adjusting entries can be classified into the following types:

1. Prepaid expenses
2. Unearned revenues
3. Accrued expenses
4. Accrued revenues

Match adjusting entry type.
(SO 2, 3) K

Instructions

Match each type of adjusting entry with the adjusting journal entry described below. If an adjusting entry is not required, leave the space blank.

(a) ___ Record interest on a note payable.
(b) ___ Record interest on a note receivable.
(c) ___ Allocate the cost of an amortizable asset over its useful life.
(d) ___ Record revenue that has been earned but not billed or collected.
(e) ___ Record revenue that has been earned that was previously received in advance.
(f) ___ Record the hiring of employees.
(g) ___ Record insurance that has expired.
(h) ___ Record salaries owed.
(i) ___ Record supplies used.

E3–4   Action Quest Games initially records all prepaid costs as assets and all revenue collected in advance as liabilities. The following information is available for the year ended December 31, 2008:

Prepare and post transaction and adjusting entries for prepayments.
(SO 2) AP

1. Purchased a one-year insurance policy on June 1, 2008, for $4,740 cash.
2. On September 15, 2008, received $3,600 cash from a corporation that sponsors a game each month for the most improved students attending a nearby school. The $3,600 was for nine sessions of playing the game on the first Friday of each month. The first month was October. (Use the account Unearned Revenue.)
3. On November 1, 2008, paid $6,875 for five months of rent in advance.
4. Signed a contract for cleaning services starting December 1, 2008, for $1,050 per month. Paid for the first three months on December 1.
5. During the year, sold $1,250 of gift certificates. Determined that on December 31, 2008, $475 of these gift certificates had not yet been redeemed. (Use the account Unearned Gift Certificate Sales.)

Instructions

(a) For each transaction, prepare a journal entry to record the initial transaction.
(b) For each transaction, prepare the adjusting journal entry required on December 31, 2008.
(c) Post each of these entries to T accounts and calculate the final balance in each account. (*Note:* Posting to the Cash account is not necessary).

Prepare adjusting entries
for amortization; calculate
accumulated amortization and
net book value.
(SO 2) AP

E3–5 Action Quest Games owns the following long-lived assets:

Asset	Date Purchased	Estimated Useful Life	Cost
Furniture	January 1, 2008	3 years	$ 9,900
Lighting equipment	December 31, 2005	7 years	28,000
Computer equipment	July 1, 2006	4 years	11,600

Instructions

(a) Prepare amortization adjusting entries for Action Quest Games for the year ended December 31, 2008.

(b) For each asset, calculate its accumulated amortization and net book value at December 31, 2008.

Prepare adjusting and related
transaction entries for
accruals.
(SO 3) AP

E3–6 Action Quest Games has the following information available on accruals that must be recorded for the year ended December 31, 2008:

1. The December utility bill for $425 was unrecorded on December 31. Action Quest paid the bill on January 17, 2009.
2. Action Quest is open seven days a week and employees are paid a total of $3,325 every Friday. December 31, 2008, is a Wednesday, so employees will have worked five days since their last pay day. (The weekly amount can be divided by seven to calculate the daily rate.) Employees will be paid next on January 2, 2009.
3. Action Quest has a 5% note payable with its bank for $45,000. Interest is payable on a monthly basis on the first of the month.
4. Action Quest receives an 8% commission from Pizza Shop next door for all pizzas sold to customers using Action Quest's facility. The amount owing for December is $920, which Pizza Shop will pay on January 5, 2009.
5. Action Quest sold some equipment on November 1, 2008, in exchange for a $6,000, 6% note receivable. The principal and interest are due on February 1, 2009.

Instructions

(a) For each of the above, prepare the adjusting entry required at December 31, 2008.

(b) For each of the above, prepare the journal entry to record the related cash transaction in 2009. Assume all payments and receipts are made as indicated.

Prepare transaction and
adjusting entries.
(SO 2, 3) AP

E3–7 Selected accounts of Nile Company are shown below:

Accounts Receivable				Service Revenue		
July 31	500				July 14	1,200
					31	900
Supplies					31	500
July 1 Bal.	1,100	July 31	500			
10	200			**Rent Expense**		
				July 31	200	
Prepaid Rent						
July 2	600	July 31	200	**Salaries Expense**		
				July 15	1,200	
Salaries Payable				31	1,200	
		July 31	1,200			
				Supplies Expense		
Unearned Service Revenue				July 31	500	
July 31	900	July 1 Bal.	1,500			
		20	700			

Instructions

After analyzing the accounts, journalize (a) the July transactions, and (b) the adjusting entries that were made on July 31. July transactions were all for cash.

E3–8 The ledger of Bourque Rental Agency on March 31, 2008, includes the following selected accounts before preparing quarterly adjusting entries:

Prepare adjusting entries.
(SO 2, 3) AP

	Debit	Credit
Prepaid insurance	$ 3,600	
Supplies	2,800	
Equipment	21,600	
Accumulated amortization—equipment		$ 5,400
Unearned rent revenue		9,300
Notes payable		20,000
Rent revenue		60,000
Wages expense	14,000	

An analysis of the accounts shows the following:

1. The equipment has a six-year useful life.
2. One-third of the unearned rent is still unearned at the end of the quarter.
3. The note payable has an interest rate of 6%. Interest is paid every June 30 and December 31.
4. Supplies on hand total $850.
5. The one-year insurance policy was purchased on October 31, 2007. [*Hint:* The correct adjusting entry was recorded on December 31, 2007.]
6. As of March 31, a tenant owed Bourque $700 for the month of March.

Instructions

Prepare the adjusting entries at March 31, assuming that adjusting entries are made quarterly.

E3–9 Thietke Company's fiscal year end is December 31. On January 31, 2008, the company's partial trial balance shows the following:

Analyze adjusted data.
(SO 2, 3, 4) AN

THIETKE COMPANY
Adjusted Trial Balance (Partial)
January 31, 2008

	Debit	Credit
Supplies	$ 700	
Prepaid insurance	2,400	
Equipment	7,680	
Accumulated amortization—equipment		$4,880
Salaries payable		800
Unearned revenue		750
Service revenue		2,000
Amortization expense	80	
Supplies expense	950	
Insurance expense	400	
Salaries expense	1,900	

Instructions

(a) If the amount in Supplies Expense is the January 31 adjusting entry, and $850 of supplies was purchased in January, what was the balance in Supplies on January 1?
(b) If the amount in Insurance Expense is the January 31 adjusting entry, and the original insurance premium was for one year, what was the total premium, and when was the policy purchased?
(c) If the amount in Amortization Expense is the amortization for one month, when was the equipment purchased?
(d) If $2,500 of salaries was paid in January, what was the balance in Salaries Payable at December 31, 2007?
(e) If $1,700 was received in January for services performed in January, what was the balance in Unearned Revenue at December 31, 2007?

Prepare adjusting entries
from analysis of trial
balances.
(SO 2, 3, 4) AP

E3–10 The trial balances before and after adjustment for Lim Company at the end of its fiscal year are as follows:

LIM COMPANY
Trial Balance
August 31, 2008

	Before Adjustment		After Adjustment	
	Dr.	Cr.	Dr.	Cr.
Cash	$10,500		$10,500	
Accounts receivable	8,700		9,230	
Office supplies	2,445		700	
Prepaid insurance	3,780		2,520	
Office equipment	14,100		14,100	
Accumulated amortization—office equipment		$ 3,525		$ 4,700
Accounts payable		5,800		5,800
Salaries payable		0		1,125
Unearned service revenue		1,600		900
E. Lim, capital		25,600		25,600
E. Lim, drawings	10,000		10,000	
Service revenue		45,000		46,230
Salaries expense	17,000		18,125	
Office supplies expense	0		1,745	
Rent expense	15,000		15,000	
Insurance expense	0		1,260	
Amortization expense	0		1,175	
Totals	$81,525	$81,525	$84,355	$84,355

Instructions

Prepare the adjusting entries that were made.

Prepare financial statements
from adjusted trial balance.
(SO 4) AP

E3–11 The adjusted trial balance for Lim Company is given in E3–10.

Instructions

Prepare Lim Company's income statement, statement of owner's equity, and balance sheet.

Prepare and post transaction
and adjusting entries for
prepayments.
(SO 5) AP

*E3–12 At Devereaux Company, prepaid costs are debited to expenses when paid, and unearned revenues are credited to revenue when received. On January 1 Devereaux had $5,000 cash. During January the following transactions occurred:

Jan. 2 Paid $2,460 for fire insurance for the year.
10 Paid $1,700 for supplies.
15 Received $4,200 for services to be performed in the future.

On January 31, it is determined that $1,500 of the service revenue has been earned and that there is $550 of supplies on hand.

Instructions

(a) Journalize and post the January transactions. Use T accounts.
(b) Journalize and post the adjusting entries at January 31.
(c) Determine the ending balance in each of the accounts.

Prepare and post transaction
and adjusting entries for
prepayments.
(SO 5) AP

*E3–13 Refer to the information provided in E3–4 for Action Quest Games.

Instructions

(a) For each transaction in E3–4, prepare a journal entry, assuming that Action Quest records all prepaid costs as expenses and all revenue collected in advance as revenues.
(b) For each transaction, prepare the adjusting journal entry on December 31, 2008, assuming prepaid costs are recorded as expenses and revenues collected in advance are recorded as revenues.

(c) Post each of the entries in (a) and (b) to T accounts and calculate the final balance in each account. (*Note:* Posting to the Cash account is not necessary).

(d) Compare your balances in (c) above to those obtained in E3–4 part (c). Comment on your findings.

Problems: Set A

P3–1A Your examination of the 2007 records of Northland Co. shows the company collected $156,200 cash from customers and paid $107,800 cash for operating costs. If Northland followed the accrual basis of accounting, it would report the following year-end balances:

Determine income on cash and accrual bases; recommend method.
(SO 1) AP

	2007	2006
Accounts payable	$ 1,810	$ 1,640
Accounts receivable	2,900	3,200
Accumulated amortization	17,250	15,000
Prepaid insurance	1,620	1,330
Unearned revenues	1,400	1,560

Instructions

(a) Determine Northland's net income on a cash basis for 2007.
(b) Determine Northland's net income on an accrual basis for 2007.
(c) Which method do you recommend Northland use? Why?

P3–2A Burke Bros. began operations on January 1, 2008. Its fiscal year end is December 31. It prepares financial statements and adjusts its accounts annually. Selected transactions from 2008 follow:

Prepare transaction and adjusting entries for prepayments.
(SO 2) AP

1. On January 1, 2008, bought office supplies for $3,100 cash. A physical count on December 31, 2008, revealed $770 of supplies still on hand.
2. Bought a $5,040 one-year insurance policy for cash on May 1, 2008. The policy came into effect on this date.
3. On November 15, received a $1,275 advance cash payment from three clients for services to be provided in the future. As at December 31, services had been done for two of the clients ($425 each).
4. On December 15, the company paid $4,500 rent in advance for the month of January 2009.
5. On May 1, purchased equipment for $30,800 cash. The equipment has an estimated seven-year useful life.

Instructions

Prepare the journal entry for the original transaction and any adjusting journal entry required at December 31, 2008, for each of the transactions.

P3–3A Théâtre Dupuis had the following transactions during the year ended November 30, 2007:

Prepare transaction and adjusting entries.
(SO 2, 3) AP

1. Office supplies on hand amounted to $500 on November 30, 2006. On February 17, 2007, additional office supplies were purchased for $1,750 cash. On November 30, 2007, a physical count showed that supplies on hand amounted to $300.
2. Owned a truck during the year that had originally been purchased on December 1, 2005, for $39,000. The estimated useful life of the truck is four years.
3. Théâtre Dupuis has eight plays each season. Season tickets sell for $176 each and 150 were sold in September for the upcoming 2007–2008 season, which starts in October 2007 and ends in May 2008 (one play per month). Théâtre Dupuis credited Unearned Season Ticket Revenue for the full amount received.
4. The total payroll for the theatre is $3,500 every week for employee wages earned during a five-day week (Wednesday through Sunday). Wages were last paid (and recorded) on Sunday, November 25. This year, November 30 falls on a Friday.
5. Théâtre Dupuis rents the theatre to a local seniors' choir which uses the space for rehearsals twice a week at a rate of $400 per month. The new treasurer of the choir accidentally sent a

cheque for $100 at the beginning of November. The treasurer promised to send a cheque in December for the balance when she returns from her vacation. On December 4, Théâtre Dupuis received a cheque for the balance owing from November plus all of December's rent.

6. Upon reviewing the books on November 30, 2007, it was noted that the utility bill for the month of November had not yet been received. A call to Hydro-Québec determined that the utility bill was for $935. The bill was paid on December 10.

7. On August 1, 2007, borrowed $5,000 from La Caisse Populaire Desjardins at an annual interest rate of 6.5%. The principal and interest are to be repaid on June 1, 2008.

Instructions

(a) Prepare the journal entries to record the original transactions for items 1, 3, 4, 5, and 7.
(b) Prepare the year-end adjusting entry for each of the above.
(c) Prepare the journal entry to record:
    1. the payment of wages on Sunday, December 2 (item 4).
    2. the receipt of the cheque from the senior's choir on December 4 (item 5)
    3. the payment of the utility bill on December 10 (item 6)
    4. the payment of the note and interest on June 1, 2008 (item 7)

Prepare adjusting entries.
(SO 2, 3) AP

P3–4A A review of the ledger of Hashmi Company at December 31, 2007, produces the following data for the preparation of annual adjusting entries:

1. Prepaid Insurance has an unadjusted balance of $13,440. The company has separate insurance policies on its buildings and its motor vehicles. Policy B4564 on the building was purchased on July 1, 2006, for $10,320. The policy has a term of two years. Policy A2958 on the vehicles was purchased on January 1, 2007, for $5,700. This policy also has a term of two years.

2. Unearned Subscription Revenue has a balance of $64,800. The company began selling magazine subscriptions in 2007. The selling price of a subscription is $48 for 12 monthly issues. A review of subscription contracts reveals the following:

Subscription Date	Number of Subscriptions
October 1	350
November 1	440
December 1	560
	1,350

3. Salaries Payable has a balance of $0. There are nine salaried employees, each of whom is paid every Monday for the previous week (Monday to Friday). Six employees receive a salary of $625 each per week, and three employees earn $750 each per week. December 31 is a Monday.

4. The company has a note receivable issued on October 1, 2007, for $8,000. The annual interest rate is 7.75% and the note matures on June 1, 2008. Interest and principal are to be paid in full on the maturity date.

5. The company owns two buildings. The first, purchased for $128,250 on September 1, 1993, has an estimated 30-year useful life. The second, purchased for $165,000 on May 1, 2001, has an estimated 40-year useful life.

Instructions

(a) Prepare calculations to show why the balance (before adjustments) in the Prepaid Insurance account is $13,440 and why the balance (before adjustments) in the Unearned Subscription Revenue account is $64,800.
(b) Prepare the adjusting entries at December 31, 2007. Show all your calculations.

Prepare accrual-based financial statements from cash-based information.
(SO 1, 2, 3, 4) AP

P3–5A During the first week of November 2007, Danielle Charron opened a ski and snowboard repair shop, The Radical Edge, on a busy ski hill. She did not do any bookkeeping, but she kept careful track of all her cash receipts and cash payments. She gives you the following information at the end of the ski season, April 30, 2008:

	Cash Receipts	Cash Payments
Investment by owner	$30,000	
Ski and snowboard repair services	33,250	
Repair equipment		23,520
Insurance		1,380
Rent		2,275
Newspaper advertising		460
Utility bills		950
Drawings by owner		6,000
Part-time employee wages		3,600
Totals	$63,250	$38,185

Additional information:

1. The repair equipment was purchased at the beginning of November and has an estimated useful life of eight years.
2. The one-year insurance policy expires on October 31, 2008.
3. On November 1, 2007, the company began renting space at a cost of $325 per month on a one-year lease. As required by the lease contract, Danielle has paid the last month's rent in advance.
4. The part-time employee is owed $120 at April 30, 2008, for unpaid wages.
5. At April 30, 2008, customers owe The Radical Edge $720 for services they have received but have not paid for.

Instructions

(a) Calculate the cash balance at April 30, 2008.
(b) Prepare an accrual-based income statement, statement of owner's equity, and balance sheet for the six months ended April 30, 2008.

P3–6A Orosco Security Service has prepared the following trial balance before preparing its year-end adjusting entries:

Prepare and post adjusting entries, and prepare adjusted trial balance.
(SO 2, 3, 4) AP

OROSCO SECURITY SERVICE
Trial Balance
December 31, 2008

	Debit	Credit
Cash	$ 12,165	
Accounts receivable	3,200	
Prepaid insurance	3,840	
Prepaid rent	1,150	
Supplies	2,535	
Automobiles	62,000	
Accumulated amortization—automobiles		$ 15,500
Office furniture	16,000	
Accumulated amortization—office furniture		5,600
Notes payable		46,000
Unearned revenue		3,600
C. Orosco, capital		56,000
C. Orosco, drawings	38,400	
Service revenue		101,605
Salaries expense	57,500	
Interest expense	2,415	
Rent expense	13,800	
Repair expense	6,000	
Gas and oil expense	9,300	
	$228,305	$228,305

Other data:

1. Service revenue earned but not billed or recorded at December 31, 2008, was $1,750.
2. The one-year insurance policy of $3,840 was paid on March 1, 2008.
3. A physical count of supplies at December 31, 2008, shows $570 of supplies on hand.
4. The automobiles were purchased on January 2, 2007, and have an estimated useful life of four years.
5. The office furniture was purchased on July 2, 2004, and has an estimated useful life of 10 years.
6. Interest on the 7% note payable is paid on the first day of each quarter (January 1, April 1, July 1, and October 1).
7. Employees' salaries total $230 per day. At December 31, three days of salaries are unpaid.
8. One of Orosco's customers paid for a six-month contract at a rate of $600 per month in advance. The contract began on November 1, 2008, and Orosco credited Unearned Revenue at the time.
9. On December 28, 2008, Orosco paid $1,150 for January 2009 rent.

Instructions

(a) Journalize the annual adjusting entries at December 31, 2008.
(b) Prepare a ledger. Enter the trial balance amounts and post the adjusting entries.
(c) Prepare an adjusted trial balance at December 31, 2008.

Prepare and post adjusting entries, and prepare adjusted trial balance and financial statements.
(SO 2, 3, 4) AP

P3–7A Super Motel has a May 31 fiscal year end and prepares adjusting entries on a monthly basis. The following trial balance was prepared before recording the May 31 month-end adjustments:

SUPER MOTEL Trial Balance May 31, 2008		
	Debit	Credit
Cash	$ 2,365	
Prepaid insurance	2,275	
Supplies	975	
Land	80,000	
Lodge	184,000	
Accumulated amortization—lodge		$ 50,217
Furniture	17,200	
Accumulated amortization—furniture		10,033
Accounts payable		4,700
Unearned rent revenue		8,750
Mortgage payable		146,400
S. Sutton, capital		80,500
S. Sutton, drawings	28,055	
Rent revenue		102,100
Advertising expense	500	
Amortization expense	7,370	
Salaries expense	49,350	
Supplies expense	2,240	
Interest expense	10,065	
Insurance expense	5,005	
Utilities expense	13,300	
	$402,700	$402,700

Other data:

1. The company pays $5,460 for its annual insurance policy on September 30 of each year.
2. A count of supplies on May 31 shows $760 of supplies on hand.
3. The lodge was purchased on May 31, 1997, and has an estimated useful life of 40 years.
4. The furniture was purchased on June 1, 2005, and has an estimated useful life of five years.

5. Customers must pay a $50 deposit if they want to book a room in advance during peak times. An analysis of these bookings indicates that 175 deposits were received (all credited to Unearned Rent Revenue) and 60 of the deposits have been earned by May 31, 2008.

6. The mortgage interest rate is 7.5% per year. Interest has been paid to May 1, 2008. The next payment is due on June 1.

7. Salaries accrued to the end of May were $975.

8. The May utility bill of $1,215 is unrecorded and unpaid.

9. On May 28, a local business contracted with Super Motel to rent one of the rooms for four months starting June 1 at a rate of $1,400 per month. An advance payment equal to two months of rent is to be paid on June 1.

10. On May 31, Super Motel has earned $950 of rent revenue from customers who are currently using the rooms but will not pay the amount owing until they check out in June. This amount is in addition to any deposits earned in item (5) above.

Instructions

(a) Journalize the monthly adjusting entries on May 31.
(b) Prepare a ledger. Enter the trial balance amounts and post the adjusting entries.
(c) Prepare an adjusted trial balance at May 31.
(d) Prepare an income statement and statement of owner's equity for the year ended May 31, and a balance sheet at May 31.

P3–8A   The unadjusted and adjusted trial balances of Irabu Co. as at September 30, 2008, follow:

Prepare adjusting entries and financial statements and comment.
(SO 2, 3, 4) AP

IRABU CO.
Trial Balance
September 30, 2008

	Unadjusted Dr.	Unadjusted Cr.	Adjusted Dr.	Adjusted Cr.
Cash	$ 3,250		$ 3,250	
Accounts receivable	6,335		7,435	
Supplies	1,750		1,265	
Prepaid rent	1,500		1,050	
Equipment	15,040		15,040	
Accumulated amortization		$ 5,640		$ 6,110
Notes payable		6,000		6,000
Accounts payable		4,350		4,460
Interest payable		0		60
Salaries payable		0		840
Unearned revenue		875		550
Y. Irabu, capital		14,000		14,000
Y. Irabu, drawings	2,700		2,700	
Commission revenue		14,420		15,845
Salaries expense	13,100		13,940	
Interest expense	0		60	
Amortization expense	0		470	
Supplies expense	0		485	
Utilities expense	710		820	
Rent expense	900		1,350	
	$45,285	$45,285	$47,865	$47,865

Instructions

(a) Journalize the quarterly adjusting entries that were made.
(b) Prepare an income statement and a statement of owner's equity for the three months ending September 30 and a balance sheet at September 30.
(c) If the note bears interest at 6%, how many months has it been outstanding?
(d) A friend of yours is considering purchasing the company from Yosuke Irabu and asks you to comment on the company's results of operations and its financial position. Is the company performing well or not? Does the financial position appear healthy or weak? Use specific information from the financial statements to support your answer.

Prepare and post adjusting entries; prepare adjusted trial balance and financial statements; and comment.
(SO 2, 3, 4) AP

P3–9A Here is an alphabetical list of Mahadeo Consulting Co.'s accounts at its fiscal year end of May 31, 2008, before adjustments. All accounts have normal balances.

Accounts payable	$ 1,476	M. Mahadeo, capital	$18,752
Accounts receivable	2,485	M. Mahadeo, drawings	66,850
Accumulated amortization—		Note receivable	7,500
computer equipment	2,545	Prepaid insurance	1,872
Accumulated amortization—		Rent expense	10,120
furniture	964	Salaries expense	32,950
Cash	2,825	Supplies	2,930
Computer equipment	7,635	Telephone expense	1,560
Consulting fees earned	117,350	Unearned consulting fees	5,280
Furniture	9,640		

Other data:

1. A one-year insurance policy was purchased on September 1, 2007.
2. On May 31, 2007, there was $525 of supplies on hand. During the year, $2,405 of additional supplies was purchased. A count of supplies on May 31, 2008, shows $475 of supplies on hand.
3. The computer equipment has an estimated useful life of three years.
4. The furniture has an estimated useful life of 10 years.
5. An analysis shows that $3,650 of the unearned consulting fees was earned by May 31, 2008.
6. The note receivable, issued on April 1, 2008, bears an annual interest rate of 5.5%. Interest and principal are receivable in full on the December 1, 2008, maturity date.
7. Salaries accrued to May 31 were $890.
8. On May 21, the company signed a contract to provide consulting services to Mawani Inc., starting June 1, 2008. The contract is for three months at a rate of $3,600 per month. Payment is due at the start of each month.
9. On May 31, 2008, the company had earned but not billed or received consulting revenue of $2,925.
10. The telephone bill for May 2008 was for $145. It has not been recorded or paid.

Instructions

(a) Prepare adjusting journal entries for the year ended May 31, 2008, as required.
(b) Prepare an adjusted trial balance in proper account order.
(c) Prepare an income statement, statement of owner's equity, and a balance sheet for the year ended May 31, 2008.
(d) Comment on the company's results of operations and financial position. In your analysis, refer to specific items in the financial statements.

Prepare and post transaction and adjusting entries for prepayments.
(SO 2, 5) AP

*P3–10A Garrett Bass Co. began operations on January 1, 2008. Its fiscal year end is December 31. It prepares financial statements and adjusts its accounts annually. Selected transactions for 2008 follow:

1. On January 1, 2008, bought supplies for $1,250 cash. A physical count at December 31, 2008, revealed $375 of supplies still on hand.
2. Bought a $2,820 one-year insurance policy for cash on March 1, 2008. The policy came into effect on this date.

3. On December 1, Garrett received a $1,200 advance cash payment from three clients ($400 each) for services expected to be provided in the future. As at December 31, services had been performed for only one of the clients.

Instructions

(a) Assume that Garrett Bass Co. records all prepaid costs as assets and all revenues collected in advance as liabilities.
   1. Prepare the journal entries for the original transactions.
   2. Prepare the adjusting journal entries at December 31, 2008.
   3. Post these journal entries to T accounts and calculate the balance in each account after adjustments. You do not need to post to the cash account.
(b) Assume instead that Garrett Bass Co. records all prepaid costs as expenses and all revenues collected in advance as revenues.
   1. Prepare the journal entries for the original transactions.
   2. Prepare the adjusting journal entries at December 31, 2008.
   3. Post these journal entries to T accounts and calculate the balance in each account after adjustments. You do not need to post to the cash account.
(c) Compare the balances in each account calculated under (a) above with those calculated in (b). Comment on your findings.

*P3–11A   Royal Graphics Company was organized on July 1, 2008, by Jan Bejar. Royal Graphics records all prepayments in income statement accounts. At the end of the first six months of operations, the trial balance had the following accounts:

Prepare adjusting entries, adjusted trial balance, and financial statements.
(SO 3, 4, 5) AP

ROYAL GRAPHICS COMPANY
Trial Balance
December 31, 2008

	Debit	Credit
Cash	$ 7,250	
Accounts receivable	7,450	
Equipment	46,500	
Accounts payable		$ 11,000
Note payable		20,000
J. Bejar, capital		34,625
J. Bejar, drawings	17,400	
Graphics fees earned		62,400
Insurance expense	2,220	
Rent expense	3,955	
Salaries expense	38,280	
Supplies expense	3,230	
Utilities expense	1,740	
	$128,025	$128,025

Analysis reveals the following additional data:

1. At December 31, $585 of supplies were on hand.
2. The three-month 6% note payable was issued November 1. Interest and principal are payable at maturity.
3. On August 1, 2008, the company purchased a one-year insurance policy for $2,220.
4. During the first six months of operations, Royal Graphics collected $6,500 cash from customers before providing services to them. At December 31, $1,600 of this amount is still unearned.
5. Equipment was purchased on July 1, 2008 and has an estimated useful life of 15 years.
6. Utilities of $225 are owed at December 31.
7. January 2009 rent of $565 was paid on December 31, 2008, and is included in Rent Expense.

Instructions

(a) Journalize the adjusting entries at December 31. (Adjustments are recorded every six months.)

(b) Prepare an adjusted trial balance.

(c) Prepare an income statement and statement of owner's equity for the six months ended December 31, and a balance sheet at December 31, 2008.

Problems: Set B

Determine income on cash and accrual bases; recommend method.
(SO 1) AP

P3–1B Your examination of the records of Southlake Co. shows the company collected $93,900 cash from customers and paid $54,700 cash for operating costs. If Southlake followed the accrual basis of accounting, it would report the following year-end balances:

	2007	2006
Accounts receivable	$ 4,200	$ 2,700
Prepaid insurance	1,500	1,300
Accumulated amortization	12,300	10,000
Accounts payable	1,500	2,250
Unearned revenues	1,400	1,500

Instructions

(a) Determine Southlake's net income on a cash basis for 2007.

(b) Determine Southlake's net income on an accrual basis for 2007.

(c) Which method do you recommend Southlake use? Why?

Prepare transaction and adjusting entries for prepayments.
(SO 2) AP

P3–2B Ouellette & Associates began operations on January 1, 2008. Its fiscal year end is December 31. It only prepares financial statements and adjusts its accounts annually. Selected transactions for 2008 follow:

1. On January 1, 2008, bought office supplies for $4,100 cash. A physical count at December 31, 2008, revealed $925 of supplies still on hand.

2. Bought a $3,780 one-year insurance policy for cash on August 1, 2008. The policy came into effect on this date.

3. On November 15, received a $1,600 advance cash payment from a client for accounting services expected to be provided in the future. As at December 31, one-quarter of these services had not been performed.

4. On December 15, rented out unneeded office space for a six-month period starting on this date, and received a $540 cheque for the first month's rent.

5. On March 31 purchased equipment for $21,000 cash. The equipment has an estimated seven-year useful life.

Instructions

For each of the transactions, prepare the journal entry for the original transaction and any adjusting journal entry required at December 31, 2008.

Prepare transaction and adjusting entries.
(SO 2, 3) AP

P3–3B Theatre Brunswick had the following transactions related to the year ended December 31, 2007:

1. Office supplies on hand amounted to $810 on December 31, 2006. On July 1, 2007, additional office supplies were purchased for $1,720 cash. On December 31, 2007, a physical count showed that supplies on hand amounted to $990.

2. Owned a truck during the year that had originally been purchased on January 1, 2006 for $23,500. The truck was estimated to have a useful life of five years.

3. Theatre Brunswick has nine plays each season. Season tickets sell for $153 each and there were 200 sold in August for the upcoming 2007–2008 season, which begins in September 2007 and

ends in May 2008 (one play per month). Theatre Brunswick credited Unearned Season Ticket Revenue for the full amount received.

4. Every Saturday, the total payroll is $3,600 for wages earned during a six-day work week (Monday to Saturday). Wages were last paid on Saturday, December 29. This year, December 31 falls on a Monday.

5. Theatre Brunswick rents the theatre to a local children's choir which uses the space for rehearsals twice a week at a rate of $500 per month. The choir was short of cash at the beginning of December and sent Theatre Brunswick a cheque for $375 and a promise to pay the balance in January. On January 4, 2008, Theatre Brunswick received a cheque for the balance owing from December plus all of January's rent.

6. Upon reviewing its books on December 31, 2007, the theatre noted that the telephone bill for the month of December had not yet been received. A call to Aliant determined that the telephone bill was for $375. The bill was paid on January 12.

7. On March 1, 2007, the theatre borrowed $10,000 from the Bank of Montreal at an annual interest rate of 6.25%. The principal and interest are to be repaid on March 1, 2008.

Instructions

(a) Prepare the journal entries to record the original transactions for items 1, 2, 3, 4, 5, and 7.
(b) Prepare the year-end adjusting entry for each of the above.
(c) Prepare the journal entry to record:
    1. the payment of wages on Saturday, January 5 (item 4).
    2. the receipt of the cheque from the children's choir on January 4 (item 5)
    3. the payment of the utility bill on January 12 (item 6)
    4. the payment of the note and interest on March 1, 2008 (item 7)

P3–4B A review of the ledger of Greenberg Company at December 31, 2007, produces the following important data for the preparation of annual adjusting entries:

Prepare adjusting entries. (SO 2, 3) AP

1. Prepaid Advertising has a balance of $14,160. This consists of payments on two advertising contracts for monthly advertising in two trade magazines. The terms of the contracts are as follows:

Contract	Signing Date	Amount	Number of Magazine Issues
A650	Apr. 1	$ 6,240	12
B974	Aug. 1	7,920	24
		$14,160	

The first advertisement runs in the month in which the contract is signed.

2. Unearned Rent Revenue has a balance of $303,000. The company began subleasing office space in its new building on November 1. At December 31, the company had the following rental contracts that were paid in full for the entire term of the lease:

Date	Term (in months)	Monthly Rent	Number of Leases	Total Rent Paid
Nov. 1	6	$4,500	5	$135,000
Dec. 1	6	7,000	4	168,000
				$303,000

3. Notes Payable has a balance of $85,000. This consists of a note for 10 months at an annual interest rate of 7.25%, dated June 1. Interest is payable at maturity.

4. Salaries Payable has a balance of $0. There are nine salaried employees. Salaries are paid every Saturday for a six-day work week (Monday–Saturday). Six employees receive a salary of $750 per week, and three employees earn $600 per week. December 31 is a Monday.

5. The company has two delivery trucks. The first, purchased for $32,000 on January 2, 2005, has an estimated six-year useful life. The second, purchased for $39,000 on June 1, 2006, has an estimated five-year useful life.

Instructions

(a) Prepare the adjusting entries at December 31, 2007. Show all your calculations.
(b) For item 5, calculate the accumulated amortization and net book value on December 31, 2007.

Prepare accrual-based
financial statements from
cash-based information.
(SO 1, 2, 3, 4) AP

P3–5B During the first week of January 2008, Chisata Moritaka began an interior design business, Exotic Designs. She kept no formal accounting records; however, she did keep a list of cash receipts and payments. At the end of 2008, she approached her bank for a loan, and was asked to submit financial statements prepared on an accrual basis.

The following information is available for the year ended December 31, 2008:

	Cash Receipts	Cash Payments
Investment by owner	$28,500	
Equipment		$17,775
Supplies		8,400
Rent payments		9,800
Insurance premium		1,980
Advertising		3,400
Salaries		19,850
Telephone		1,020
Drawings by owner		24,000
Design service revenue	60,350	
Total	$88,850	$86,225

Additional information:

1. The equipment has an estimated five-year useful life and was purchased on January 2, 2008.
2. There were $1,040 of supplies on hand on December 31, 2008.
3. Rent payments included $750 per month of rent and an $800 deposit that is refundable at the end of the two-year lease.
4. The insurance premium was for a one-year period and expires on January 31, 2009.
5. The advertising costs were for newspaper ads during 2008.
6. Salaries earned the last week in December and to be paid in January 2009 amounted to $525.
7. Design revenue earned but not yet collected by December 31, 2008, amounted to $3,900.
8. Chisata used her personal automobile for business purposes, travelling 9,000 kilometres at 40 cents per kilometre. She was not paid for the use of her car, but would like to be paid for it.

Instructions

(a) Calculate the cash balance at December 31, 2008.
(b) Prepare an accrual-based income statement, statement of owner's equity, and balance sheet for the year ended December 31, 2008.

Prepare and post adjusting
entries, and prepare adjusted
trial balance.
(SO 2, 3, 4) AP

P3–6B Atlantic Tours has a December 31 fiscal year end and prepares adjustments on a monthly basis. The following trial balance was prepared before recording the June 30 month-end adjustments:

ATLANTIC TOURS
Trial Balance
June 30, 2008

	Debit	Credit
Cash	$ 3,000	
Prepaid insurance	3,050	
Supplies	340	
Office equipment	13,440	
Accumulated amortization—office equipment		$ 4,060
Buses	140,400	
Accumulated amortization—buses		56,550
Accounts payable		1,985
Notes payable		54,000
Unearned fees		14,000
E. Kaplan, capital		45,000
E. Kaplan, drawings	12,000	
Fees earned		70,600
Salaries expense	46,875	
Advertising expense	825	
Amortization expense	10,450	
Insurance expense	4,270	
Interest expense	1,575	
Rent expense	2,175	
Supplies expense	625	
Gas and oil expense	7,170	
	$246,195	$246,195

Other data:

1. The insurance policy has a one-year term that began November 1, 2007.
2. The office equipment has an estimated useful life of eight years. The buses have an estimated useful life of six years.
3. A physical count shows $210 of supplies on hand at June 30.
4. The note payable has an annual interest rate of 7%. Interest is paid at the start of each month.
5. Deposits of $1,400 each were received for advance tour reservations from 10 school groups. At June 30, three of these deposits have been earned.
6. Bus drivers are paid a combined total of $425 per day. At June 30, three days of salaries are unpaid.
7. A senior citizens' organization that had not made an advance deposit took a Coastal Tour on June 30 for $1,150. This group was not billed for the tour until July 3.
8. Additional advertising costs of $620 have been incurred but not recorded. (Use the Accounts Payable account.)

Instructions

(a) Journalize the monthly adjusting entries at June 30, 2008.
(b) Prepare a ledger. Enter the trial balance amounts and post the adjusting entries.
(c) Prepare an adjusted trial balance at June 30, 2008.

Prepare and post adjusting
entries, and prepare adjusted
trial balance and financial
statements.
(SO 2, 3, 4) AP

P3–7B The Highland Cove Resort has a fiscal year end of August 31. The company's trial balance before adjustments is as follows:

HIGHLAND COVE RESORT
Trial Balance
August 31, 2008

	Debit	Credit
Cash	$ 19,410	
Prepaid insurance	6,360	
Supplies	3,495	
Land	35,000	
Cottages	145,000	
Accumulated amortization—cottages		$ 43,500
Furniture	28,600	
Accumulated amortization—furniture		11,440
Accounts payable		6,500
Unearned rent revenue		35,500
Mortgage payable		60,000
K. Yhap, capital		85,000
K. Yhap, drawings	44,000	
Rent revenue		248,500
Salaries expense	153,000	
Interest expense	3,575	
Utilities expense	37,600	
Repair expense	14,400	
	$490,440	$490,440

Other data:

1. The one-year insurance policy was purchased on May 31, 2008.
2. A count shows $690 of supplies on hand on August 31, 2008.
3. The cottages have an estimated useful life of 50 years.
4. The furniture has an estimated useful life of 10 years.
5. Customers must pay a $100 deposit if they want to book a cottage during peak times. An analysis of these bookings indicates that 355 deposits were received (all credited to Unearned Rent Revenue) and only 45 of the deposits have not yet been earned by August 31, 2008.
6. The mortgage interest rate is 6.5% per year. Interest has been paid to July 31, 2008.
7. Salaries accrued to the end of August were $840.
8. The August utility bill of $1,560 is unrecorded and unpaid.
9. On August 25, a local business contracted with Highland Cove to rent one of the cottages for six months starting October 1 at a rate of $1,500 per month. An advance payment equal to two months of rent is to be paid on September 5.
10. On August 31, Highland Cove has earned $1,350 of rent revenue from customers who are currently using the cottages but will not pay the amount owing until they check out in September. This amount is in addition to any deposits earned in item (5) above.

Instructions

(a) Journalize the adjusting entries on August 31.
(b) Prepare a ledger, enter the trial balance amounts, and post the adjusting entries.
(c) Prepare an adjusted trial balance at August 31.
(d) Prepare an income statement and a statement of owner's equity for the year ended August 31, and a balance sheet as at August 31, 2008.

P3–8B The adjusted and unadjusted trial balances of the Yount Advertising Agency as at December 31, 2008, follow:

YOUNT ADVERTISING AGENCY
Trial Balance
December 31, 2008

	Unadjusted Dr.	Unadjusted Cr.	Adjusted Dr.	Adjusted Cr.
Cash	$ 9,000		$ 9,000	
Accounts receivable	18,650		19,750	
Art supplies	7,200		1,265	
Prepaid insurance	2,352		980	
Printing equipment	66,000		66,000	
Accumulated amortization		$ 28,500		$ 34,000
Accounts payable		4,202		4,852
Interest payable		0		350
Salaries payable		0		1,475
Unearned advertising revenue		7,100		6,200
Note payable		10,000		10,000
T. Yount, capital		37,800		37,800
T. Yount, drawings	23,000		23,000	
Advertising revenue		58,750		60,750
Salaries expense	13,000		14,475	
Insurance expense	0		1,372	
Interest expense	0		350	
Amortization expense	0		5,500	
Art supplies expense	0		5,935	
Rent expense	7,150		7,800	
	$146,352	$146,352	$155,427	$155,427

Instructions

(a) Journalize the annual adjusting entries that were made.

(b) Prepare an income statement and a statement of owner's equity for the year ended December 31, 2008, and a balance sheet at December 31.

(c) Calculate the annual interest rate on the note. The note payable has been outstanding for eight months.

(d) Determine the balance in Salaries Payable on December 31, 2007. The company paid $15,250 in salaries in 2008.

P3–9B Here is an alphabetical list of Scholz Consulting Co.'s accounts at its fiscal year end of March 31, 2008, before adjustments. All accounts have normal balances.

Prepare and post adjusting entries; prepare adjusted trial balance and financial statements; and comment.
(SO 2, 3, 4) AP

Accounts payable	$ 3,495	Furniture	$ 8,780
Accounts receivable	7,270	Note payable	5,500
Accumulated amortization—		Prepaid insurance	1,980
computer equipment	2,465	R. Scholz, capital	11,794
Accumulated amortization—		R. Scholz, drawings	59,500
furniture	1,756	Rent expense	9,625
Cash	2,485	Salaries expense	33,475
Computer equipment	7,395	Supplies	3,290
Consulting fees earned	106,750	Telephone expense	1,700
		Unearned consulting fees	3,740

Other data:

1. A one-year insurance policy was purchased on June 30, 2007.
2. On March 31, 2007, there was $845 of supplies on hand. During the year, $2,445 of additional supplies was purchased. A count of supplies on March 31, 2008, shows $710 of supplies on hand.
3. The computer equipment has an estimated useful life of three years.
4. The furniture has an estimated useful life of 10 years.

5. As at March 31, 2008, an analysis shows $1,825 of the unearned consulting fees were still unearned.
6. The nine-month 6% note was issued on November 1, 2007. Interest and principal are due on the maturity date.
7. Salaries accrued to March 31 were $655.
8. On March 15, the company signed a contract to provide consulting services to Xendor Inc., starting April 1, 2008. The contract is for three months at a rate of $4,100 per month. Payment is due at the start of each month.
9. On March 31, 2008, the company had earned but not billed or recorded consulting revenue of $2,675.
10. The telephone bill for March 2008 was $155. It has not been recorded or paid.

Instructions

(a) Prepare adjusting journal entries for the year ended March 31, 2008, as required.
(b) Prepare an adjusted trial balance in proper account order.
(c) Prepare an income statement and statement of owner's equity for the year ended March 31, 2008, and a balance sheet at March 31, 2008.
(d) Comment on the company's results of operations and its financial position. In your analysis, refer to specific items in the financial statements.

Prepare and post transaction and adjusting entries for prepayments.
(SO 2, 5) AP

*P3–10B Wong Piano Co. began operations on January 1, 2008. Its fiscal year end is December 31. It prepares financial statements and adjusts its accounts annually. Selected transactions for 2008 follow:

1. On January 15, 2008, bought supplies for $960 cash. A physical count on December 31, 2008, revealed $245 of supplies still on hand.
2. Bought a $3,060 one-year insurance policy for cash on May 1, 2008. The policy came into effect on this date.
3. On November 1, received a $1,840 advance cash payment from four clients ($460 each) for services expected to be provided in the future. As at December 31, services had still not been performed for one of the clients.

Instructions

(a) Assume that Wong Piano Co. records all prepaid costs as assets and all revenues collected in advance as liabilities.
    1. Prepare the journal entries for the original transactions.
    2. Prepare the adjusting journal entries at December 31, 2008.
    3. Post these journal entries to T accounts and calculate the balance in each account after adjustments. You do not need to post to the cash account.
(b) Assume instead that Wong Piano Co. records all prepaid costs as expenses and all revenues collected in advance as revenues.
    1. Prepare the journal entries for the original transactions.
    2. Prepare the adjusting journal entries at December 31, 2008.
    3. Post these journal entries to T accounts and calculate the balance in each account after adjustments. You do not need to post to the cash account.
(c) Compare the balance in each account calculated under (a) above with the balances calculated in (b). Comment on your findings.

Prepare adjusting entries, adjusted trial balance, and financial statements.
(SO 3, 4, 5) AP

*P3–11B The Global Graphics Company was organized on January 1, 2008, by Betty Batke. Global Graphics records all prepayments in income statement accounts. At the end of the first six months of operations, the trial balance had the following accounts:

GLOBAL GRAPHICS COMPANY
Trial Balance
June 30, 2008

	Debit	Credit
Cash	$ 8,300	
Accounts receivable	13,000	
Equipment	42,800	
Accounts payable		$ 7,360
Note payable		22,000
B. Batke, capital		35,000
B. Batke, drawings	20,000	
Graphic design revenue		60,700
Insurance expense	2,760	
Rent expense	3,500	
Salaries expense	29,950	
Supplies expense	2,950	
Utilities expense	1,800	
	$125,060	$125,060

Analysis reveals the following additional data:

1. At June 30, there were $930 of supplies on hand.
2. The six-month 7% note payable was issued on March 1. Interest and principal are payable on the maturity date.
3. On February 1, 2008, the company purchased a one-year insurance policy for $2,760.
4. At June 30, graphic design revenue of $1,250 was unearned.
5. Graphic design revenue earned but unbilled and unrecorded at June 30 totalled $1,975.
6. The equipment has an estimated useful life of eight years.
7. July rent of $500 was paid on June 30 and is included in Rent Expense.

Instructions

(a) Journalize the adjusting entries at June 30. (Adjustments are recorded every six months.)
(b) Prepare an adjusted trial balance.
(c) Prepare an income statement and statement of owner's equity for the six months ended June 30, and a balance sheet at June 30, 2008.

Continuing Cookie Chronicle

(*Note:* This is a continuation of the Cookie Chronicle from Chapters 1 and 2. Use the information from the previous chapters and follow the instructions below using the general ledger accounts you have already prepared.)

It is the end of November and Natalie has been in touch with her grandmother. Her grandmother asked Natalie how well things went in her first month of business. Just like her grandmother, Natalie too would like to know if she has been profitable or not during November. Natalie realizes that in order to determine Cookie Creations' income she must first make adjustments. Natalie puts together the following additional information:

1. A count reveals that $75 of brochures and posters remain at the end of November.
2. A count reveals that $35 of baking supplies were used during November.
3. Natalie estimates that all of her baking equipment will have a useful life of five years or 60 months. (Assume Natalie decides to record a full month's worth of amortization, regardless of when the equipment was obtained by the business.)

4. Natalie's grandmother has decided to charge interest of 6% on the note payable extended on November 16. The loan plus interest is to be repaid in 24 months. (Assume that half a month of interest accrued during November.)

5. On November 30, a friend of Natalie's asks her to teach a class at the neighbourhood school. Natalie agrees and teaches a group of 35 grade 1 students how to make Santa Claus cookies. The next day, Natalie prepares an invoice for $250 and leaves it with the school principal. The principal says that he will pass the invoice along to the school board and it will be paid sometime in December.

6. Natalie receives a cellphone bill for $45. She only uses her cellphone for business. The bill is for services provided during November and is due December 15.

Instructions

Using the information that you have gathered through Chapter 2, and based on the new information above, do the following:

(a) Prepare and post the adjusting journal entries.
(b) Prepare an adjusted trial balance.
(c) Prepare an income statement. Was Cookie Creations profitable in November?

Cumulative Coverage—Chapters 1 to 3

On August 31, 2007, the account balances of Pitre Equipment Repair were as follows:

PITRE EQUIPMENT REPAIR
Trial Balance
August 31, 2007

	Debit	Credit
Cash	$ 4,880	
Accounts receivable	3,720	
Supplies	800	
Store equipment	16,500	
Accumulated amortization—store equipment		$ 4,950
Accounts payable		3,100
Unearned service revenue		200
Salaries payable		700
R. Pitre, capital		16,950
	$25,900	$25,900

During September, the following transactions were completed:

Sept. 1 Purchased additional store equipment on account, $3,000.
8 Paid $1,100 for employees' salaries, of which $400 is for September and $700 for August.
10 Received $1,200 cash from customers on account.
12 Received $3,400 cash for services performed in September.
17 Purchased additional supplies on account, $1,500.
20 Paid creditors $4,500 on account.
22 Paid September rent, $500.
25 Paid salaries, $1,200.
27 Performed services on account and billed customers for services provided, $900.
29 Received $700 from customers for future services.

Adjustment data consist of the following:

1. Supplies on hand cost $1,280.
2. Accrued salaries payable total $775.
3. Store equipment has an expected useful life of five years.
4. Unearned service revenue of $550 is earned.

Instructions

(a) Enter the August 31 balances in general ledger accounts.
(b) Journalize the September transactions.
(c) Post to the ledger accounts.
(d) Prepare a trial balance at September 30.
(e) Journalize and post adjusting entries.
(f) Prepare an adjusted trial balance.
(g) Prepare an income statement and a statement of owner's equity for September, and a balance sheet at September 30, 2007.

BROADENING YOUR PERSPECTIVE

Financial Reporting and Analysis

Financial Reporting Problem

BYP3–1 The financial statements of **The Forzani Group** are presented in Appendix A at the end of this textbook.

Instructions

(a) What title does Forzani use for its income statement?
(b) What different types of revenues were reported by Forzani (see note 2 (h))?
(c) Does Forzani report any prepayments on its balance sheet? If yes, identify each item that is a prepaid expense or unearned (deferred) revenue. Indicate the other account title that Forzani would likely use when it prepares adjusting entries for these accounts.
(d) Does Forzani report any accruals on its balance sheet? If yes, identify each item that is an accrued revenue or accrued expense. Indicate the other account title that Forzani would likely use when it prepares adjusting entries for these accounts.

Interpreting Financial Statements

BYP3–2 **Rogers Communications Inc.** is a diversified Canadian communications and media company. Rogers' balance sheet included a current liability of $176,266,000 at December 31, 2005, called Unearned Revenue. The following comes from Rogers' revenue recognition policy note in its financial statements:

> **ROGERS COMMUNICATIONS INC.**
> Notes to the Financial Statements
> December 31, 2005
>
> *Note 2 (n):* **Significant accounting policies—Revenue recognition**
>
> The Company's principal sources of revenue and recognition of these revenues for financial statement purposes are as follows:
>
> - Monthly subscriber fees in connection with wireless and wireline services, cable, telephony, Internet services, rental of equipment, network services, and media subscriptions are recorded as revenue on a pro rata basis over the month as the service is provided;
> - Installation fees and activation fees charged to subscribers do not meet the criteria as a separate unit of accounting. As a result, these fees are deferred and amortized over the related service period, as appropriate. The related service period for Cable is determined to be approximately four years while that of Telecom ranges from 26 to 33 months, based on subscriber disconnects, transfers of service and moves. Incremental direct installation costs related to reconnects are deferred to the extent of deferred installation fees and amortized over the same period as these related installation fees. New connect installation costs are capitalized [added] to PP&E [long-term assets] and amortized over the useful life of the related assets;
> - The Blue Jays' revenue, which is composed primarily of home game admission and concession revenue, is recognized as the related games are played during the baseball season. Revenue from radio and television agreements is recorded at the time the related games are aired.

Unearned revenue includes subscriber deposits, installation fees and amounts received from subscribers related to services and subscriptions to be provided in future periods.

Instructions

(a) When does Rogers recognize its revenue from monthly subscriber fees?
(b) When should Rogers record unearned revenue from its subscription services? When should it record unearned revenue for its Blue Jays home game admission revenue?
(c) If Rogers recorded these unearned revenues as revenue, what would be the effect on the company's financial position (use the basic accounting equation and explain what elements would be overstated or understated)?
(d) Does Rogers follow the matching principle for its installation costs? Explain.

Critical Thinking

Collaborative Learning Activity

Note to instructors: Additional instructions and material for this group activity can be found on the Instructor Resource Site.

BYP3–3 In this group activity, you will review the following types of adjusting entries:
1. Prepayments
   (a) Current assets
   (b) Long-lived assets
2. Unearned revenues
3. Accrued revenues
4. Accrued expenses

Instructions

(a) Your instructor will divide the class into "home" groups. Each member of your group will choose one type of adjusting entry and then move to the "expert" group for that type.

Study Aids:
Working in Groups

(b) In the "expert" group, you will be given a handout explaining your type of adjusting entry. As a group, discuss the handout and ensure that each group member thoroughly understands how to prepare that entry.

(c) Return to your "home" group and explain how to prepare your type of adjusting entry to the other students in the group.

(d) Go back to your "expert" group, where you will work together to create one transaction description and the associated adjusting entry. One person will act as recorder for the group and write the transaction description on the blackboard.

(e) Everyone in the class will write a quiz based on the transaction descriptions that appear on the board.

(f) One member from each "expert" group will then act as presenter and explain the correct adjusting entry for the group's transaction to the class.

(g) As an alternative to (d), (e) and (f) above, you may be asked by your instructor to write a short quiz on this topic.

Communication Activity

BYP3–4 There are many people today who believe that cash-based income is a better indicator of a company's future success than net income. This idea became more popular after many reports of corporate financial scandals where management was easily able to manipulate prepayments and accruals to influence net income.

Study Aids:
Writing Handbook

Instructions

Write a memo discussing whether you believe cash-based income is more reliable for measuring performance than accrual-based net income. Include in your memo the answers to the following questions:

(a) What is the difference between accrual-based and cash-based net income?

(b) Do you believe that it is possible for management to manipulate net income? If yes, identify one way that management might be able to increase net income by manipulating estimates or accruals.

(c) Do you believe that it is possible for management to manipulate cash-based income? If yes, identify one way that management might be able to increase cash flow.

Ethics Case

BYP3–5 Die Hard Company is a pesticide manufacturer. Its sales dropped a lot this year because of new legislation that outlawed the sale of many of Die Hard's chemical pesticides. In the coming year, Die Hard will have new, environmentally safe chemicals to replace these discontinued products. Sales in the next year are expected to be much higher than sales of any previous year. The drop in sales and profits appears to be a one-year aberration. Still, the company president is afraid that a large drop in the current year's profits could cause a significant drop in the market price of Die Hard's shares, and could make the company a takeover target.

Study Aids:
Ethics in Accounting

To protect the company from a takeover, the company president urges Carole Chiasson, the controller, to accrue every possible revenue and to defer as many expenses as possible when preparing this period's December 31 year-end adjusting entries. He says to Carole, "We need the revenues this year, and next year we can easily absorb expenses deferred from this year." Carole did not record the adjusting entries until January 17, but she dated the entries December 31 as if they were recorded then. Carole also did everything possible to follow the president's request.

Instructions

(a) Who are the stakeholders in this situation?

(b) What are the ethical considerations of (1) the president's request, and (2) Carole's decision to date the adjusting entries December 31?

(c) Can Carole aggressively accrue revenues and defer expenses and still be ethical?

ANSWERS TO CHAPTER QUESTIONS

Answers to Accounting in Action Insight Questions

Business Insight, p. 106

Q: Why is it important for film producers to try to match the cost of producing films with the revenues generated?

A: The matching principle states that efforts (expenses) must be matched with accomplishments (revenues). It would be difficult to decide if *The Hurricane* made money if the expenses were reported in one accounting period and the revenues were reported in another accounting period.

Across the Organization, p. 119

Q: In what ways is calculating a salary accrual at the end of the month the same today as it would have been in ancient Egypt?

A: Both in ancient Egypt and today it would be necessary to know how long each employee had worked between the last time they were paid and the end of the month, and how much each employee is paid. The longer the time since the employee was last paid, and the higher the employee's wages, the larger the accrual.

Ethics Insight, p. 123

Q: How could an adjusting entry be used to overstate net income?

A: If the adjusting entry reduces or eliminates an expense that should be recorded, income will be overstated. For example, if the company uses unrealistically long useful lives in its amortization calculations, the amortization expense will be too low, and income too high. Or, if for example, revenues are recognized before they have been earned, then income may be overstated.

Answer to Forzani Review It Question 4, p. 114

Forzani reported amortization expense of $41,343 thousand and $35,885 thousand in fiscal 2006 and 2005, respectively.

Answers to Self-Study Questions

1. c   2. a   3. d   4. c   5. d   6. d   7. b   8. a   9. c   *10. a

Remember to go back to the Navigator Box at the beginning of the chapter to check off your completed work.

chapter 4

concepts for review >>

Before studying this chapter, you should understand or, if necessary, review:

a. How to apply the revenue recognition and matching principles. (Ch. 3, p. 105)

b. How to make adjusting entries. (Ch. 3, pp. 108–119)

c. How to prepare an adjusted trial balance. (Ch. 3, pp. 123–124)

d. How the balance sheet, income statement, and statement of owner's equity are connected. (Ch. 3, pp. 124–125)

Breezing through the Month End with Style

WINNIPEG, Man.—Owned and operated by the Gorenstein family of Winnipeg, Moulé has four gallery-style retail stores in Vancouver and Winnipeg. Each one features gifts, jewellery, and other treasures from around the world. The items have been crafted by talented artists working in glass, ceramics, metal, and other media. Founded in 1987, Moulé also designs and manufactures a signature line of soft, feminine, and sophisticated women's apparel. The clothing is sold in Moulé stores and distributed across North America and as far away as Japan.

Month end finds Moulé's chief operations officer, Laurie Gorenstein, running off extra reports for things like sales, GST and PST, commissions, and inventory on the Smart Vendor computer software he uses for most of the company's accounting. (He tracks payables with an Excel spreadsheet.) "Basically, I receive all the invoices from the stores at month end and check them against the figures in the computer. Then I run the general ledger and the trial balance."

"My accountant checks them, and we make any updates or corrections necessary—such as a cheque posted to the wrong account—with an adjusting or correcting entry," he continues. By checking things monthly, "it usually comes out pretty smoothly." Monthly financial statements then follow.

"So it really is pretty easy," says Mr. Gorenstein. Once a year, the load gets a little heavier when the books are closed—as with many businesses, Moulé's fiscal year ends December 31—and the year's financial statements are prepared. At this point, he's very glad of the care taken to find discrepancies and to make adjustments at month end. If errors are left undetected, "then they come back to haunt you months later and you can spend forever trying to sort them out."

Moulé recently set up an "open-to-buy" system, which allows the store to use past sales data to predict future sales. By inputting merchandise sales daily and analyzing this information monthly, Mr. Gorenstein can track what sells best when, which leads to better planning and purchasing decisions. "The 'open-to-buy system' is specific to 20 different categories of merchandise, so we know what month is best for each," he explains. And tracking the merchandise so closely also significantly reduces the potential for error on the financial side.

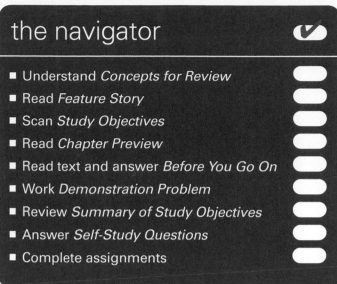

the navigator ✔

- Understand *Concepts for Review*
- Read *Feature Story*
- Scan *Study Objectives*
- Read *Chapter Preview*
- Read text and answer *Before You Go On*
- Work *Demonstration Problem*
- Review *Summary of Study Objectives*
- Answer *Self-Study Questions*
- Complete assignments

chapter | 4

chapter 4

Completion of the Accounting Cycle

study objectives >>

✔ the navigator

After studying this chapter, you should be able to:

1. Prepare closing entries and a post-closing trial balance.
2. List the steps in the accounting cycle.
3. Prepare correcting entries.
4. Prepare a classified balance sheet.
5. Illustrate measures used to evaluate liquidity.
6. Prepare a work sheet (Appendix 4A).
7. Prepare reversing entries (Appendix 4B).

In Chapter 3, we prepared financial statements directly from the adjusted trial balance. In this chapter, we will explain what the remaining steps in the accounting cycle are for—especially the closing process. Once again, we will use the Pioneer Advertising Agency as an example.

After that we will look at correcting entries. As Laurie Gorenstein of Moulé notes in the feature story, locating and correcting errors on a regular basis is very important. We end by discussing the classification and use of balance sheets. The chapter is organized as follows:

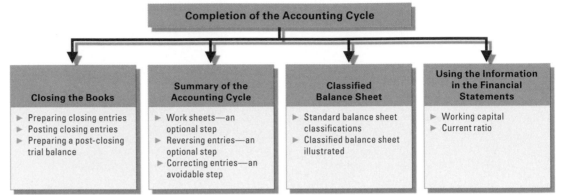

Completion of the Accounting Cycle

Closing the Books	Summary of the Accounting Cycle	Classified Balance Sheet	Using the Information in the Financial Statements
► Preparing closing entries ► Posting closing entries ► Preparing a post-closing trial balance	► Work sheets—an optional step ► Reversing entries—an optional step ► Correcting entries—an avoidable step	► Standard balance sheet classifications ► Classified balance sheet illustrated	► Working capital ► Current ratio

the navigator

Closing the Books

study objective 1

Prepare closing entries and a post-closing trial balance.

At the end of the accounting period, the accounts are made ready for the next period. This is called **closing the books**. When closing the books, it is important to know the difference between temporary and permanent accounts. **Temporary accounts** only collect data for a single accounting period. They include all income statement (revenue and expense) accounts and the owner's drawings account. In previous chapters, you learned that these accounts are subdivisions of the owner's capital account. Revenues, expenses, and drawings are called temporary accounts because they give temporary (for a single accounting period) detail about the changes in the owner's capital account. All temporary accounts are closed at the end of the period.

In contrast, all balance sheet accounts are considered **permanent accounts** because their balances are carried forward into the next accounting period. This means that permanent accounts are not closed. Illustration 4-1 identifies the accounts in each category.

Illustration 4-1 ▶

Temporary versus permanent accounts

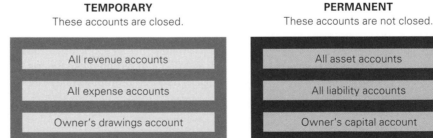

TEMPORARY These accounts are closed.	PERMANENT These accounts are not closed.
All revenue accounts	All asset accounts
All expense accounts	All liability accounts
Owner's drawings account	Owner's capital account

Preparing Closing Entries

At the end of the accounting period, **closing entries** are used to transfer the temporary account balances (revenues, expenses, and drawings) to the permanent owner's capital account. Closing entries formally record in the ledger the transfer of net income (or net loss) and the owner's drawings to the owner's capital account. This updates the owner's capital balance to its balance at the end of the period, as shown on the statement of owner's equity and the balance sheet. These entries also result in a zero balance in each temporary account. The temporary accounts are then ready to collect data in the next accounting period.

Animated Tutorials and Videos: Accounting Cycle Tutorial

Journalizing and posting closing entries is a required step in the accounting cycle. This step is done after financial statements have been prepared. Closing entries are generally journalized and posted only at the end of a company's annual accounting period. Moulé, introduced in the feature story, closes its books once a year.

When closing entries are prepared monthly, annual financial statements are more complicated to prepare. For example, to calculate the owner's drawings for the year, each month's owner's drawings have to be added together. This step would have to be done for each temporary account. As a result, most companies prepare and record closing entries only at their year end.

In preparing closing entries, each income statement account could be closed directly to the owner's capital account. This is often done in computerized accounting systems where the closing process occurs automatically when it is time to start a new accounting period. In manual accounting systems, however, closing directly to the owner's capital account can make it harder to find errors that may have happened when the revenue and expense accounts were being closed. Instead, it is helpful to first close the revenue and expense accounts to another temporary account, **Income Summary**. After the revenue and expense accounts have been closed, the balance in the Income Summary account is then checked to make sure it is equal to the net income or net loss for the period. Once that is done, the net income or net loss can then be transferred from the Income Summary account to owner's capital.

We will therefore use four steps in preparing closing entries:

1. Close revenue accounts: Debit each individual revenue account for its balance, and credit Income Summary for total revenues.
2. Close expense accounts: Debit Income Summary for total expenses, and credit each individual expense account for its balance.
3. Close Income Summary: Debit Income Summary for its balance, and credit the owner's capital account (if there is a net loss, credit Income Summary for the amount of the loss, and debit the owner's capital account).
4. Close drawings: Debit the owner's capital account and credit the owner's drawings account for the balance in drawings.

Separate closing entries could be prepared for each individual revenue and expense account. However, the compound entries described in the first two steps above are more efficient. Closing entries are journalized in the general journal after adjusting entries. To identify these entries, a centre caption titled "Closing Entries" can be inserted in the journal between the last adjusting entry and the first closing entry. Then the closing entries are posted to the ledger accounts.

Illustration 4-2 is a diagram of the four-step closing process for a proprietorship, using T accounts.

Illustration 4-2 ▶

Diagram of closing process

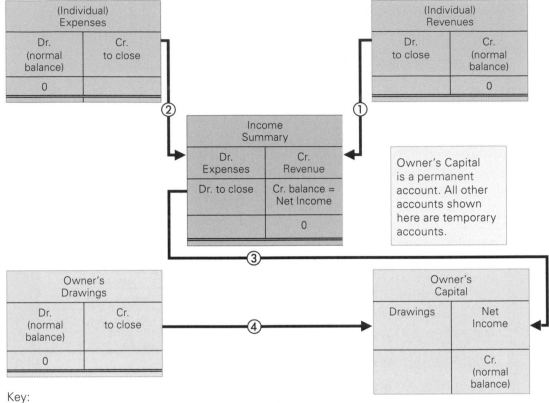

Key:
① Close revenues to Income Summary ③ Close Income Summary to Owner's Capital
② Close expenses to Income Summary ④ Close Owner's Drawings to Owner's Capital

Closing Entries Illustrated

To illustrate the journalizing and posting of closing entries, we will continue using the example of Pioneer Advertising Agency introduced in Chapters 2 and 3. For the illustrations, we have assumed that the company uses October 31 as its fiscal year end. Pioneer Advertising's adjusted trial balance on October 31, first shown in Chapter 3 (Illustration 3-6), is shown again here in Illustration 4-3.

Closing entries can be prepared directly from (1) the adjusted balances in the general ledger or adjusted trial balance, or (2) the income statement and statement of owner's equity. We will use the adjusted trial balance shown here to prepare the four required closing entries.

The temporary accounts have been highlighted in red. C. Byrd, Capital is not a temporary account, but it has also been highlighted because it is used in the closing process. Remember that the capital account balance in the trial balance is the opening balance (plus any investments made by the owner during the period)—it is not the ending balance that appears in the statement of owner's equity and balance sheet. This permanent account is updated to its ending balance by transferring the net income (loss) and drawings for the period from the temporary accounts.

The closing entries at October 31 follow Illustration 4-3:

PIONEER ADVERTISING AGENCY
Adjusted Trial Balance
October 31, 2008

	Debit	Credit
Cash	$15,200	
Accounts receivable	200	
Advertising supplies	1,000	
Prepaid insurance	550	
Office equipment	5,000	
Accumulated amortization—office equipment		$ 83
Notes payable		5,000
Accounts payable		2,500
Unearned revenue		800
Salaries payable		2,000
Interest payable		25
C. Byrd, capital		10,000
C. Byrd, drawings	500	
Service revenue		10,600
Advertising supplies expense	1,500	
Amortization expense	83	
Insurance expense	50	
Salaries expense	6,000	
Rent expense	900	
Interest expense	25	
	$31,008	$31,008

GENERAL JOURNAL J3

Date	Account Titles and Explanation	Ref.	Debit	Credit
	Closing Entries			
2008	(1)			
Oct. 31	Service Revenue	400	10,600	
	Income Summary	350		10,600
	To close revenue account.			
	(2)			
31	Income Summary	350	8,558	
	Advertising Supplies Expense	611		1,500
	Amortization Expense	711		83
	Insurance Expense	722		50
	Salaries Expense	726		6,000
	Rent Expense	729		900
	Interest Expense	905		25
	To close expense accounts.			
	(3)			
31	Income Summary	350	2,042	
	C. Byrd, Capital	301		2,042
	To close net income.			
	(4)			
31	C. Byrd, Capital	301	500	
	C. Byrd, Drawings	306		500
	To close drawings account.			

Be careful when you prepare closing entries: (1) Remember that the reason for making closing entries is to bring the temporary accounts to zero balances. Avoid unintentionally doubling the revenue, expense, drawings, and income summary account balances, rather than bringing them to zero. (2) Do not close owner's drawings with the expenses. The drawings that an owner makes are not an expense, so they are not a factor in determining net income.

Posting Closing Entries

The posting of the closing entries is as follows:

GENERAL LEDGER							

Cash   101

Oct. 1	10,000	Oct. 3	900
3	1,200	3	600
31	10,000	20	500
		24	4,000
Oct. 31 Bal.	15,200		

Accounts Receivable   112

Oct. 21	10,000	Oct. 31	10,000
31 Adj.	200		
Oct. 31 Bal.	200		

Advertising Supplies   129

Oct. 4	2,500	Oct. 31 Adj.	1,500
Oct. 31 Bal.	1,000		

Prepaid Insurance   130

Oct. 3	600	Oct. 31 Adj.	50
Oct. 31 Bal.	550		

Office Equipment   151

Oct. 2	5,000		
Oct. 31 Bal.	5,000		

Acccumulated Amortization—Office Equipment   152

		Oct. 31 Adj.	83
		Oct. 31 Bal.	83

Notes Payable   200

		Oct. 2	5,000
		Oct. 31 Bal.	5,000

Accounts Payable   201

		Oct. 4	2,500
		Oct. 31 Bal.	2,500

Unearned Revenue   209

Oct. 31 Adj.	400	Oct. 3	1,200
		Oct. 31 Bal.	800

Salaries Payable   212

		Oct. 31 Adj.	2,000
		Oct. 31 Bal.	2,000

Interest Payable   230

		Oct. 31 Adj.	25
		Oct. 31 Bal.	25

C. Byrd, Capital   301

		Oct. 1	10,000
Oct. 31 Clos.	500	31 Clos.	2,042
		Oct. 31 Bal.	11,542

C. Byrd, Drawings   306

Oct. 20	500	Oct. 31 Clos.	500
Oct. 31 Bal.	0		

Income Summary   350

Oct. 31 Clos.	8,558	Oct. 31 Clos.	10,600
31 Clos.	2,042		
		Oct. 31 Bal.	0

Service Revenue   400

		Oct. 21	10,000
		31 Adj.	400
Oct. 31 Clos.	10,600	31 Adj.	200
		Oct. 31 Bal.	0

Advertising Supplies Expense   611

Oct. 31 Adj.	1,500	Oct. 31 Clos.	1,500
Oct. 31 Bal.	0		

Amortization Expense   711

Oct. 31 Adj.	83	Oct. 31 Clos.	83
Oct. 31 Bal.	0		

Insurance Expense   722

Oct. 31 Adj.	50	Oct. 31 Clos.	50
Oct. 31 Bal.	0		

Salaries Expense   726

Oct. 24	4,000		
31 Adj.	2,000	Oct. 31 Clos.	6,000
Oct. 31 Bal.	0		

Rent Expense   729

Oct. 3	900	Oct. 31 Clos.	900
Oct. 31 Bal.	0		

Interest Expense   905

Oct. 31 Adj.	25	Oct. 31 Clos.	25
Oct. 31 Bal.	0		

Stop and check your work after the closing entries are posted: (1) The balance in Income Summary, immediately before the final closing entry to transfer the balance to the owner's capital account, should equal the net income (or net loss) reported in the income statement (see Illustration 3-7 in Chapter 3). (2) All temporary accounts (revenues, expenses, owner's drawings, and Income Summary) should have zero balances. (3) The balance in the capital account should equal the ending balance reported in the statement of owner's equity and balance sheet (see Illustrations 3-7 and 3-8 in Chapter 3).

ACCOUNTING IN ACTION ▶ Across the Organization Insight

Ever since the first finance benchmarking studies in the 1980s, chief financial officers (CFOs) have been very interested in information that allows them to compare their companies to other companies. A recent survey of *CFO Magazine* readers that was done by the American Productivity and Quality Center has given even more data about the tasks done by a company's finance or accounting department.

CFOs should find some of these data reassuring. The average total cost of an accounting department is quite low—only 0.8 percent of revenues—and the average company spends only five days closing the books each month. Cycle times this short are considered respectable, if not spectacular.

Source: Don Durfee, "Flabby or Fit?" *CFO Magazine*, February 1, 2006, 24.

? Why are CFOs interested in knowing how long it takes on average for companies to close their books?

Preparing a Post-Closing Trial Balance

After all closing entries have been journalized and posted, another trial balance is prepared from the ledger. It is called a **post-closing trial balance**. The post- (or after-) closing trial balance is a list of permanent accounts and their balances after closing entries have been journalized and posted. The purpose of this trial balance is to prove the equality of the permanent account balances that are carried forward into the next accounting period. Since all temporary accounts have zero balances after closing, the post-closing trial balance contains only permanent (balance sheet) accounts.

The post-closing trial balance for Pioneer Advertising Agency is shown in Illustration 4-4 on the following page. Note that the balances are the same as the ones in the company's balance sheet (Pioneer Advertising's balance sheet was last seen in Chapter 3, Illustration 3-8, and is shown again in this chapter in Illustration 4-13.)

Illustration 4-4 ▶

Post-closing trial balance

Helpful hint Total debits in a post-closing trial balance will not equal total assets on the balance sheet if contra accounts, such as accumulated amortization, are present. Accumulated amortization is deducted from assets on the balance sheet but added to the credit column in a trial balance.

PIONEER ADVERTISING AGENCY Post-Closing Trial Balance October 31, 2008		
	Debit	Credit
Cash	$15,200	
Accounts receivable	200	
Advertising supplies	1,000	
Prepaid insurance	550	
Office equipment	5,000	
Accumulated amortization—office equipment		$ 83
Notes payable		5,000
Accounts payable		2,500
Unearned revenue		800
Salaries payable		2,000
Interest payable		25
C. Byrd, capital		11,542
	$21,950	$21,950

A post-closing trial balance provides evidence that the journalizing and posting of closing entries has been completed properly. It also shows that the accounting equation is in balance at the end of the accounting period and the beginning of the next accounting period.

As in the case of the trial balance, the post-closing trial balance does not prove that all transactions have been recorded or that the ledger is correct. For example, the post-closing trial balance will still balance if a transaction is not journalized and posted, or if a transaction is journalized and posted twice. This is why it is so important, as Laurie Gorenstein of Moulé says in the feature story, to find and correct all errors before the books are closed.

BEFORE YOU GO ON . . .

▶Review It

1. How do permanent accounts differ from temporary accounts?
2. What four different types of entries are required in closing the books?
3. After closing entries are posted, what amounts on what financial statements should the balance in the owner's capital account agree with?
4. What are the differences between a trial balance, adjusted trial balance, and post-closing trial balance?

▶Do It

The adjusted trial balance for the Nguyen Company shows the following: H. Nguyen, Drawings $5,000; H. Nguyen, Capital $42,000; Service Revenue $18,000; Rent Expense $2,000; Supplies Expense $500; and Wages Expense $7,500. Nguyen Company's statement of owner's equity for the year showed net income of $8,000 and closing owner's capital of $45,000. Prepare the closing entries at December 31. Create T accounts for Income Summary and H. Nguyen, Capital, and post the closing entries to these accounts.

Action Plan

- Debit each individual revenue account for its balance and credit the total to Income Summary.
- Credit each individual expense account for its balance and debit the total to Income Summary.
- Stop and check your work: Does the balance in Income Summary equal the reported net income (loss)?
- If there is net income, debit the balance in Income Summary and credit the amount to the owner's capital account (do the opposite if the result is a net loss).

- Credit the balance in the drawings account and debit the amount to the owner's capital account. Do not close drawings with the expenses.
- Stop and check your work: Do the temporary accounts have zero balances? Is the balance in Income Summary equal to net income after closing revenues and expenses? Does the ending balance in the owner's capital account equal the closing owner's capital reported on the statement of owner's equity?

Solution

Dec. 31	Service Revenue	18,000	
	Income Summary		18,000
	To close revenue account.		
31	Income Summary	10,000	
	Rent Expense		2,000
	Supplies Expense		500
	Wages Expense		7,500
	To close expense accounts.		
31	Income Summary	8,000	
	H. Nguyen, Capital		8,000
	To close Income Summary.		
31	H. Nguyen, Capital	5,000	
	H. Nguyen, Drawings		5,000
	To close drawings.		

Income Summary

Clos.	10,000	Clos.	18,000
		Bal.	8,000 *
Clos.	8,000		
		Bal.	0

H. Nguyen, Capital

		Bal.	42,000
Clos.	5,000		
		Clos.	8,000
		Bal.	45,000 **

* Check if this equals net income.

** Check if this equals closing owner's capital.

Related exercise material: BE4–1, BE4–2, BE4–3, E4–1, E4–2, and E4–3.

Summary of the Accounting Cycle

The steps in the accounting cycle are shown in Illustration 4-5 on the following page. You can see that the cycle begins with the analysis of business transactions and ends with the preparation of a post-closing trial balance. The steps in the cycle are done in sequence and are repeated in each accounting period.

Animated Tutorials
and Videos:
Accounting Cycle Tutorial

Illustration 4-5 ▶

Steps in the accounting cycle

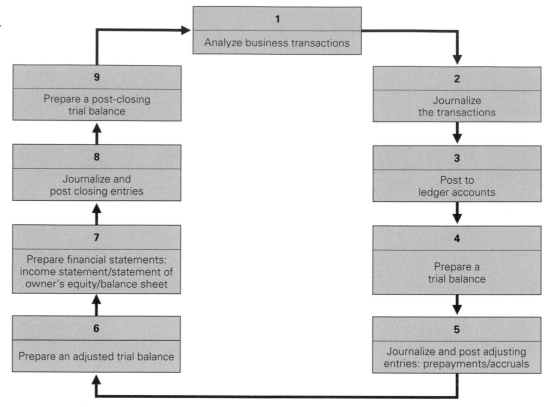

Optional steps: If a work sheet is prepared, steps 4, 5, and 6 are done in the work sheet, and adjusting entries are journalized and posted after step 7. If reversing entries are prepared, they occur between steps 9 and 1.

Steps 1 and 2 can occur every day during the accounting period, as explained in Chapter 2. Steps 3 through 7 are done on a periodic basis, such as monthly, quarterly, or annually. Steps 8 and 9, closing entries and a post-closing trial balance, are usually done only at the end of a company's annual accounting period.

There are also two optional steps in the accounting cycle. As the following two sections explain, a work sheet may be used in the adjustments process and in preparing financial statements; and reversing entries may be used at the beginning of a new accounting period.

Work Sheets—An Optional Step

To help them prepare adjusting entries and the financial statements, some accountants like to use an optional multiple-column form known as a **work sheet**. Work sheets can be prepared by hand, but today most work sheets are created by accounting software or spreadsheet programs.

As its name suggests, the work sheet is a working tool for the accountant. A work sheet is not a permanent accounting record; it is neither a journal nor a part of the general ledger. The work sheet is just something that is used to make it easier to prepare adjusting entries and financial statements. If a work sheet is used, adjusting entries are not formally recorded or posted until after the financial statements are prepared.

Although using a work sheet is optional, it is useful. It can help accountants avoid errors when they are working with a lot of information that involves many accounts and adjustments. A work sheet also makes it easier to prepare interim (e.g., monthly or quarterly) financial information for internal use because adjusting entries can be prepared and entered in the work sheet, and interim financial statements can then be developed easily. In small companies that have relatively few accounts and adjustments, a work sheet may not be needed. In companies with a lot of accounts and adjustments, it is almost indispensable.

As the preparation of a work sheet is optional, its basic form and the procedure for preparing it are explained in Appendix 4A at the end of the chapter.

Reversing Entries—An Optional Step

Some accountants prefer to reverse certain adjusting entries at the beginning of a new accounting period. A **reversing entry** is made at the beginning of the next accounting period. It is the exact opposite of the adjusting entry made in the previous period. The preparation of reversing entries is an optional bookkeeping procedure that is not a required step in the accounting cycle. We have therefore chosen to explain this topic in Appendix 4B at the end of the chapter.

BEFORE YOU GO ON . . .

▶Review It

1. What are the required steps in the accounting cycle?
2. What are the optional steps in the accounting cycle?
3. What are the differences between transaction, adjusting, closing, and reversing journal entries?

Related exercise material: BE4–4.

Correcting Entries—An Avoidable Step

Unfortunately, errors may happen in the recording process. Errors should be corrected as soon as they are discovered by journalizing and posting **correcting entries**. If the accounting records have no errors, no correcting entries are needed.

study objective 3
Prepare correcting entries.

You should understand several differences between correcting entries and adjusting entries. First, adjusting entries are an integral part of the accounting cycle. Correcting entries, on the other hand, are unnecessary if the records have no errors. Second, adjustments are journalized and posted only at the end of an accounting period. In contrast, correcting entries are made whenever an error is discovered. Finally, adjusting entries always affect at least one balance sheet account (not Cash) and one income statement account. In contrast, correcting entries can involve any combination of accounts that need to be corrected. **Adjusting and correcting entries do have one thing in common, however: in both cases, they must be journalized and posted before closing entries.**

To determine the correcting entry, it is useful to compare the incorrect entry with the entry that should have been made. Doing this helps identify the accounts and amounts that should—and should not—be corrected. After comparison, a correcting entry is made to correct the accounts. This approach is shown in the following two cases:

Case 1. On May 10, a $50 cash collection on account from a customer is journalized and posted as a debit to Cash $50 and as a credit to Service Revenue $50. The error is discovered on May 20 when the customer pays the remaining balance in full.

INCORRECT ENTRY (MAY 10)				CORRECT ENTRY (MAY 10)		
Cash	50			Cash	50	
Service Revenue		50		Accounts Receivable		50

A comparison of the incorrect entry with the correct entry that should have been made (but was not) reveals that the debit to Cash of $50 is correct. However, the $50 credit to Service Revenue should have been credited to Accounts Receivable. As a result, both Service Revenue and Accounts Receivable are overstated in the ledger. The following correcting entry is needed:

	Correcting Entry		
May 20	Service Revenue	50	
	Accounts Receivable		50
	To correct entry of May 10.		

Case 2. On May 18, office equipment that costs $450 is purchased on account. The transaction is journalized and posted as a debit to Delivery Equipment $45 and as a credit to Accounts Payable $45. The error is discovered on June 3 when the monthly statement for May is received from the creditor.

INCORRECT ENTRY (MAY 8)		
Delivery Equipment	45	
Accounts Payable		45

CORRECT ENTRY (MAY 8)		
Office Equipment	450	
Accounts Payable		450

A comparison of the two entries shows that three accounts are incorrect. Delivery Equipment is overstated by $45; Office Equipment is understated by $450; and Accounts Payable is understated by $405 ($450 – $45). The correcting entry is as follows:

	Correcting Entry		
June 3	Office Equipment	450	
	Delivery Equipment		45
	Accounts Payable		405
	To correct May 18 entry.		

Instead of preparing a correcting entry, many accountants simply reverse the incorrect entry and then record the correct entry. Even though this approach will result in more entries and postings, it is an easier and often more logical procedure.

Sometimes errors are not found until after the temporary accounts have been closed. A correcting entry that fixes an error from a previous accounting year is called a prior period adjustment. These correcting entries can be very complex, and will be covered in a later chapter.

ACCOUNTING IN ACTION ▶ Business Insight

Canadian telecom equipment maker Nortel Networks' name has become synonymous with accounting woes in recent years. The company had to go over its financial statements for several years, making correcting entries for revenue recognized in the wrong period. "Although the need to restate certain financial statements is unfortunate, it's the right thing to do. This revenue is real—it was recognized in the wrong periods," chief executive Mike Zafirovski said in a press release. In 2006, Nortel expected to correct its revenues by about $120 million for 2005, $220 million for 2004, and $100 million for 2003 (all in U.S. dollars).

? Some of these errors happened several years ago. Why is it still important for Nortel to record entries to correct them?

BEFORE YOU GO ON . . .

▶**Review It**

1. What are the differences between adjusting journal entries and correcting journal entries?
2. What is the advantage of reversing an incorrect journal entry and then preparing the correct journal entry, instead of making one compound correcting journal entry?

▶**Do It**

The Chip 'N' Dough Company made the following adjusting journal entry to record $5,200 of amortization expense on a delivery truck at year end:

Feb. 28	Amortization Expense	520	
	Cash		520
	To record amortization on delivery truck.		

Prepare the required correcting entry.

Action Plan

- Determine the correct entry that should have been made.
- Compare it to the incorrect entry made and make the required corrections.

Solution

Feb. 28	Cash	520	
	Amortization expense	4,680	
	Accumulated Amortization—Truck		5,200
	To correct amortization adjustment.		

Amortization expense is understated by $4,680 ($5,200 − $520).

Related exercise material: BE4–5 and E4–4.

the navigator

Classified Balance Sheet

The financial statements that we have seen so far have all been simplified. We classified items as assets, liabilities, and owner's equity in the balance sheet, and as revenues and expenses in the income statement. In reality, however, financial statements are more useful to management, creditors, and potential investors when the accounts are classified into significant subgroups. In this chapter, we will introduce you to the main balance sheet classifications. The classified income statement will be presented in Chapter 5.

study objective 4
Prepare a classified balance sheet.

Standard Balance Sheet Classifications

A **classified balance sheet** for a proprietorship generally has the following standard classifications:

Assets	Liabilities and Owner's Equity
Current assets	Current liabilities
Long-term investments	Long-term liabilities
Property, plant, and equipment	Owner's equity
Intangible assets	

These sections help the financial statement user determine such matters as (1) the amount of assets available to meet debts as they come due, and (2) the claims of short- and long-term creditors on total assets. A classified balance sheet also makes it easier to compare companies in the same industry, such as Forzani and Foot Locker. Each of the sections of a classified balance sheet is explained next.

Current Assets

Current assets are cash and other resources that will be realized within one year of the balance sheet date. They may be realized in cash or as items sold or consumed in the business. For example, accounts receivable are current assets because they will be realized in cash as the amounts are collected during the year. A prepayment such as supplies is a current asset because the business expects to use or consume the supplies within one year.

In a service company, four types of current assets are usually recognized: (1) cash and cash equivalents (e.g., noncash items such as treasury bills and money-market funds); (2) short-term investments (e.g., debt and equity securities); (3) receivables (e.g., notes receivable, accounts receivable, and interest receivable); and (4) prepaid expenses (e.g., rent, insurance, and supplies). In Chapter 5, we will introduce a fifth category of current assets, inventories (merchandise available for sale), which is used by merchandising companies.

Current assets are listed in the order of their liquidity—that is, in the order in which they are expected to be converted into cash. This arrangement is shown in the presentation used by Canada Post, in Illustration 4-6.

A company's current assets are important in assessing its short-term debt-paying ability, as explained later in the chapter.

Illustration 4-6 ▶

Current assets section

CANADA POST Balance Sheet (partial) December 31, 2005 (in millions)	
Current assets	
Cash and cash equivalents	$ 474
Short-term investments	230
Segregated cash and investments	68
Accounts receivable	555
Income taxes recoverable	21
Prepaid expenses	73
Current portion of future income taxes	45
	1,466

Long-Term Investments

Long-term investments are generally investments in debts (for example, loans, notes, bonds, or mortgages), or shares of other corporations that are expected to be held for many years. They also include investments in long-lived assets such as real estate if the asset is not being used as part of the company's operating activities. These assets are classified as long-term because they are not readily marketable or expected to be converted into cash within one year. Note that these are investments (assets) acquired by the company. They are not the same as investments in the company that are made by the owner (owner's equity).

Power Corporation of Canada's long-term investments are shown in the partial balance sheet in Illustration 4-7.

Illustration 4-7 ◀

Long-term investments
section

POWER CORPORATION OF CANADA
Balance Sheet (partial)
December 31, 2005
(in millions)

Investments	
Shares	$ 4,867
Bonds	59,298
Mortgages and other loans	15,118
Loans to policyholders	6,646
Real estate	1,844
	87,773

Property, Plant, and Equipment

Property, plant, and equipment are long-lived, tangible assets that are used in the business and are not intended for sale. This category includes land, buildings, equipment, and furniture.

Although the order of property, plant, and equipment on the balance sheet can vary among companies, these assets are normally listed in their order of permanency. Land is usually listed first because it has an indefinite life, and is followed by the next asset with the longest useful life (normally buildings), and so on.

Since property, plant, and equipment benefit future periods, their cost is matched to expense over their useful lives through amortization, as we learned in Chapter 3. Assets which are amortized should be reported at their net book value (cost minus accumulated amortization).

As Illustration 4-8 shows, La Senza Corporation reports the net book value (or "net carrying amount" as La Senza calls it) of its property, plant, and equipment on its balance sheet and gives the cost and accumulated amortization in a note to the financial statements. Note that, except for land (which has an unlimited useful life), all other property, plant, and equipment items are amortized. This includes leasehold improvements, which are long-lived additions or renovations made to leased property.

Alternative terminology
Property, plant, and equipment are also known as *capital assets* or *fixed assets*.

Illustration 4-8 ◀

Property, plant, and
equipment section

LA SENZA CORPORATION
Notes to the Financial Statements (partial)
January 28, 2006
(in thousands)

6. Property & equipment

	Cost	Accumulated Amortization	Net Carrying Amount
Land	$ 1,307	$ —	$ 1,307
Building	4,540	1,745	2,795
Furniture and fixtures	28,000	16,623	11,377
Furniture and fixtures under capital lease	12,965	3,011	9,954
Leasehold improvements	47,576	35,291	12,285
Leasehold improvements under capital lease	38,949	9,846	29,103
Computer software and equipment	19,694	11,343	8,351
Computer software and equipment under capital lease	8,429	3,630	4,799
	$161,460	$81,489	$79,971

Intangible Assets

Intangible assets are long-lived assets that do not have physical substance. They give a company rights and privileges and include such things as goodwill, patents, copyrights, trademarks, trade names, and licences. Similar to buildings and equipment, intangible assets with estimated useful lives are amortized. Similar to land, intangible assets with indefinite lives are not amortized.

Illustration 4-9 shows how Shaw Communications reported intangible assets in its balance sheet. All of Shaw Communications' intangible assets have indefinite lives, so they are not amortized.

Illustration 4-9 ▶

Intangible assets section

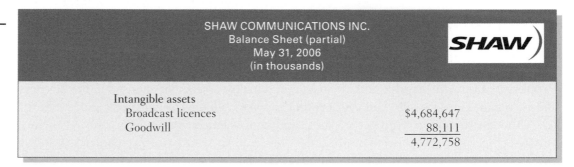

SHAW COMMUNICATIONS INC. Balance Sheet (partial) May 31, 2006 (in thousands)	
Intangible assets	
Broadcast licences	$4,684,647
Goodwill	88,111
	4,772,758

Current Liabilities

Current liabilities are listed first in the liabilities and equity section of the balance sheet. **Current liabilities** are obligations that are expected to be paid in the coming year from current assets or by creating other current liabilities. Current liabilities include notes payable, accounts payable, salaries payable, interest payable, sales taxes payable, unearned revenues, and current maturities of long-term liabilities (payments to be made within the next year on long-term debt). Corporations may also have income taxes payable included in the current liabilities section of the balance sheet.

Current liabilities are often listed in order of currency. That is, the liabilities that will be due first are listed first. Many companies do not use this approach, however. They simply list the items in their current liabilities section according to a company tradition. The current liabilities section from Sears Canada's balance sheet is shown in Illustration 4-10.

Illustration 4-10 ▶

Current liabilities section

SEARS CANADA INC. Balance Sheet (partial) December 31, 2005 (in millions)	
Current liabilities	
Accounts payable	$ 696.6
Accrued liabilities	430.1
Income and other taxes payable	322.5
Principal payments on long-term obligations due within one year	216.1
	1,665.3

Users of financial statements look closely at the relationship between current assets and current liabilities. This relationship is important in evaluating a company's ability to pay its current liabilities. We will talk more about this later in the chapter when we learn how to use the information in the financial statements.

Long-Term Liabilities

Obligations that are expected to be paid after one year or longer are classified as **long-term liabilities**. Liabilities in this category can include future income tax (income taxes payable after more than one year), bonds payable, mortgages payable, notes payable, and lease liabilities, among others. Many companies report long-term debt that matures after one year as a single amount in the balance sheet. Then they show the details of the debt in the notes that accompany the financial statements. As shown in Illustration 4-11, Westjet Airlines Ltd. had total long-term liabilities of $1,166,042 thousand on a recent balance sheet.

Illustration 4-11 ◄

Long-term liabilities section

WESTJET AIRLINES LTD.
Balance Sheet (partial)
December 31, 2005
(in thousands)

Long-term liabilities	
Long-term debt (note 4)	$1,044,719
Obligations under capital lease (note 6)	1,690
Other liabilities (note 5)	16,982
Future income tax (note 8)	102,651
	1,166,042

Equity

As discussed briefly in Chapter 1, the content of the equity section varies with the form of business organization. In a proprietorship, there is one capital account under the heading "Owner's equity." In a partnership, there is a capital account for each partner under the heading "Partners' equity." For a corporation, shareholders' equity is divided into two sections: share capital (sometimes called capital stock) and retained earnings. Amounts that are invested in the business by the shareholders are recorded as share capital. Income that is kept for use in the business is recorded in the retained earnings account. The share capital and retained earnings accounts are combined and reported as shareholders' equity on the balance sheet. You will also recall from chapter one that income trusts are another type of corporation. In an income trust, unitholders' equity is also divided into two sections: unitholders' capital and undistributed income. We will learn more about corporation equity accounts in later chapters.

As noted in Chapter 1, it is difficult to gain access to the financial statements of proprietorships and partnerships. Public corporations and income trusts, on the other hand, issue financial statements for present and potential investors, among others. Illustration 4-12 shows how Andrés Wines Ltd., a corporation, reported its shareholders' equity section in its balance sheet. Subsequent to March 31, 2006, the company has changed its name to Andrew Peller Limited. The company's new name will be used on its March 31, 2007 financial statements.

Illustration 4-12 ◄

Shareholders' equity section

ANDRÉS WINES LTD.
Balance Sheet (partial)
March 31, 2006
(in thousands)

Shareholders' equity	
Capital stock (note 10)	$ 7,375
Retained earnings	82,205
	89,580

Classified Balance Sheet Illustrated

To illustrate the classified balance sheet, we will now return to our example of Pioneer Advertising Agency from earlier in the chapter. Its classified balance sheet can be prepared using either the adjusted trial balance shown in Illustration 4-3 or the post-closing trial balance in Illustration 4-4. The result is the classified balance sheet at October 31, 2008, shown in Illustration 4-13. Note that Pioneer Advertising has only one noncurrent asset, office equipment. Pioneer Advertising rents its premises so it does not report other property, plant, and equipment, such as land or building. As discussed earlier in this chapter, if it did, it would present the longest-lived asset (e.g., land) first. Also note that, for this illustration, we have assumed that $1,000 of the notes payable is currently due and $4,000 is long-term.

Illustration 4-13 ▶

Classified balance sheet

PIONEER ADVERTISING AGENCY Balance Sheet October 31, 2008		
Assets		
Current assets		
Cash		$15,200
Accounts receivable		200
Advertising supplies		1,000
Prepaid insurance		550
Total current assets		16,950
Property, plant, and equipment		
Office equipment	$5,000	
Less: Accumulated amortization	83	4,917
Total assets		$21,867
Liabilities and Owner's Equity		
Current liabilities		
Accounts payable		$ 2,500
Unearned revenue		800
Salaries payable		2,000
Interest payable		25
Current portion of notes payable		1,000
Total current liabilities		6,325
Long-term liabilities		
Notes payable		4,000
Total liabilities		10,325
Owner's equity		
C. Byrd, capital		11,542
Total liabilities and owner's equity		$21,867

The balance sheet is usually presented in report form, as in Illustration 4-13, with the assets shown above the liabilities and owner's equity. The balance sheet may also be presented in account form, with the assets section placed on the left and the liabilities and owner's equity sections on the right. Most Canadian companies use the report form to present their balance sheet.

Now that you are familiar with the components of the classified balance sheet, you should look more closely at The Forzani Group's balance sheet, reproduced in Appendix A at the end of this book. While there are some differences in Forzani's presentation, the format is very similar to the format used by the companies in this chapter.

BEFORE YOU GO ON . . .

▶Review It

1. What are the major sections in a classified balance sheet?
2. How are accounts ordered in the current assets; property, plant, and equipment; and current liabilities sections of the balance sheet? In other words, is the order alphabetical, from smallest to largest, or according to something else?
3. Using Forzani's balance sheet, identify the components of its current assets and current liabilities at January 29, 2006. Can you tell if current assets and current liabilities are listed in order of liquidity, or in some other order? The answers to these questions are at the end of the chapter.

▶Do It

Canadian Tire Corporation, Limited has the following selected accounts listed in a recent balance sheet:

Accounts payable and other	Income taxes payable
Accounts receivable	Long-term debt
Cash and cash equivalents	Merchandise inventories
Credit card receivables	Other long-term liabilities
Current portion of long-term debt	Prepaid expenses and deposits
Goodwill	Property and equipment

Give the balance sheet classification for each of the accounts above.

Action Plan

- Current assets include all assets that will be realized within one year.
- Current liabilities are obligations that are expected to be paid within one year.
- Long-term assets are classified by the type of asset.
- Obligations that are due after more than one year are classified as long-term liabilities.

Solution

Account	Balance Sheet Classification
Accounts payable and other	Current liabilities
Accounts receivable	Current assets
Cash and cash equivalents	Current assets
Credit card receivables	Current assets
Current portion of long-term debt	Current liabilities
Goodwill	Intangible assets
Income taxes payable	Current liabilities
Long-term debt	Long-term liabilities
Merchandise inventories	Current assets
Other long-term liabilities	Long-term liabilities
Prepaid expenses and deposits	Current assets
Property and equipment	Property, plant, and equipment

Related exercise material: BE4–6, BE4–7, E4–5, and E4–6.

the navigator

Using the Information in the Financial Statements

As we explained in Chapter 1, investors use the information in financial statements to decide if they should invest in a business, and creditors use the information to decide if they should grant credit to a business. In this chapter, we will now begin to learn about a tool called ratio analysis, which can help investors and creditors make such decisions. Ratio

study objective 5

Illustrate measures used to evaluate liquidity.

analysis is helpful because it gives additional information about a company by expressing useful relationships between specific items in the financial statements.

As you study the chapters of this book, you will learn about three general types of ratios that are used to analyze financial statements: liquidity, profitability, and solvency ratios. Liquidity ratios measure a company's **liquidity**—the company's ability to pay its obligations as they come due within the next year and to meet unexpected needs for cash. As the name suggests, profitability ratios measure the income or operating success of a company for a specific period of time. Solvency ratios measure the ability of a company to pay its total liabilities and survive over a long period of time. In this chapter, we introduce two liquidity ratios: working capital and the current ratio.

Working Capital

When liquidity is being evaluated, an important relationship is the one between current assets and current liabilities. The difference between current assets and current liabilities is called **working capital**. Working capital is important because it shows a company's ability to pay its short-term debts. When current assets are more than current liabilities at the balance sheet date, the company will likely be able to pay its liabilities. When the reverse is true, short-term creditors may not be paid.

Forzani's working capital is $119,414 thousand, as shown in Illustration 4-14, where amounts are in thousands.

Illustration 4-14 ▶

Working capital

Current Assets	–	Current Liabilities	=	Working Capital
$368,842	–	$249,428	=	$119,414

Current Ratio

A second measure of short-term debt-paying ability is the **current ratio**, which is calculated by dividing current assets by current liabilities. Two companies with the same amount of working capital may have very different current ratios. Of the two liquidity measures, the current ratio is more useful because it is difficult to compare dollar amounts by themselves.

Illustration 4-15 shows the current ratio for Forzani at January 29, 2006 ($ in thousands):

Illustration 4-15 ▶

Current ratio

Current Assets	÷	Current Liabilities	=	Current Ratio
$368,842	÷	$249,428	=	1.48:1

This ratio tells us that on January 29, 2006, Forzani had $1.48 of current assets for every dollar of current liabilities. As a general rule, a higher current ratio indicates better liquidity. As we will learn in later chapters, however, there are also other factors that can affect a company's liquidity. It is also important to be aware that what would be considered a normal working capital ratio depends on the company and the industry the company is in.

Ratios should never be interpreted without considering certain factors: (1) general economic and industry conditions need to be considered; (2) other specific financial information about the company over time needs to be considered, and (3) the ratios should be compared to the ratios for other companies in the same or related industries. We will have more discussion about how to analyze ratios in Chapter 18.

BEFORE YOU GO ON . . .

▶Review It

1. What is working capital? How can it be expressed as a ratio?
2. How can two companies with the same amount of working capital have different current ratios?

Related exercise material: BE4–8, BE4–9, E4–7, and E4–8.

APPENDIX 4A ▶ WORK SHEETS

As discussed in the chapter, a work sheet is a multiple-column form that may be used in the adjustment process and in preparing financial statements. The five steps for preparing a work sheet are described in the next section. They must be done in the order they are presented in.

Steps in Preparing a Work Sheet

We will use the October 31 trial balance and adjustment data for Pioneer Advertising Agency from Chapter 3 to show how to prepare a work sheet. Each step of the process is described below, and is shown in Illustration 4A-1.

study objective 6

Prepare a work sheet.

Animated Tutorials
and Videos:
Work Sheet Walkthrough

Step 1. Prepare a Trial Balance on the Work Sheet. All ledger accounts with balances are entered in the account title space. Debit and credit amounts from the ledger are entered in the trial balance columns.

Step 2. Enter the Adjustments in the Adjustment Columns. When a work sheet is used, all adjustments are entered in the adjustment columns. In entering the adjustments, relevant trial balance accounts should be used. If additional accounts are needed, they should be inserted on the lines immediately below the trial balance totals.

In a manually prepared work sheet, each adjustment is cross-referenced (usually by letter) to make it easier to journalize the adjusting entry in the general journal. This has been done in Illustration 4A-1. It is important to realize that year-end adjustments must still be journalized, but not until after the work sheet is completed and the financial statements have been prepared. The books should not be filled with interim adjustments unless they need to show the adjusted information on a more permanent basis.

The adjustments on Pioneer Advertising Agency's work sheet are the same as the adjustments shown on pages 110 to 119 of Chapter 3. They are recorded in the adjustment columns of the work sheet as follows:

(a) An additional account, Advertising Supplies Expense, is debited $1,500 for the cost of supplies used, and Advertising Supplies is credited $1,500.
(b) An additional account, Insurance Expense, is debited $50 for the insurance that has expired, and Prepaid Insurance is credited $50.
(c) Unearned Revenue is debited $400 for fees, and Service Revenue is credited $400.
(d) Accounts Receivable is debited $200 for fees earned but not billed, and Service Revenue is credited $200.
(e) Two additional accounts relating to interest are needed. Interest Expense is debited $25 for accrued interest, and Interest Payable is credited $25.

(f) Salaries Expense is debited $2,000 for accrued salaries, and an additional account, Salaries Payable, is credited $2,000.

(g) Two additional accounts are needed. Amortization Expense is debited $83 for the month's amortization, and Accumulated Amortization—Office Equipment is credited $83.

Note in the illustration that after all the adjustments have been entered, the adjustment columns are totalled (automatically if the worksheet is computer-generated) and the equality of the column totals is proven.

Step 3. Enter the Adjusted Balances in the Adjusted Trial Balance Columns.

The adjusted balance of an account is obtained by combining the amounts entered in the first four columns of the work sheet for each account. For example, the Prepaid Insurance account in the trial balance columns has a $600 debit balance and a $50 credit in the adjustment columns. These two amounts combine to result in a $550 debit balance in the adjusted trial balance columns. For each account on the work sheet, the amount in the adjusted trial balance columns is equal to the account balance that will appear in the ledger after the adjusting entries have been journalized and posted. The balances in these columns are the same as those in the adjusted trial balance in Illustration 4-3.

After all account balances have been entered in the adjusted trial balance columns, the columns are totalled and their equality is proven. The agreement of the column totals makes it easier to complete the work sheet. If these columns are not in agreement, the error(s) must be found before going to the next step. If the errors are not found, the statement columns will not balance and the financial statements will be incorrect.

Helpful hint Every adjusted trial balance amount must appear in one of the four statement columns.

Step 4. Enter the Adjusted Trial Balance Amounts in the Correct Financial Statement Columns.

The fourth step is to enter adjusted trial balance amounts in the income statement or balance sheet columns of the work sheet. Balance sheet accounts are entered in the correct balance sheet debit and credit columns. For instance, Cash is entered in the balance sheet debit column and Notes Payable is entered in the credit column.

Because the work sheet does not have columns for the statement of owner's equity, the balance in owner's capital is entered in the balance sheet credit column. In addition, the balance in the owner's drawings account is entered in the balance sheet debit column because it is an owner's equity account with a debit balance.

The amounts in revenue and expense accounts such as Service Revenue and Salaries Expense are entered in the correct income statement columns.

Step 5. Total the Statement Columns, Calculate the Net Income (or Net Loss), and Complete the Work Sheet.

Each of the financial statement columns must be totalled. The net income or loss for the period is then found by calculating the difference between the totals of the two income statement columns. If total credits are more than total debits, net income has resulted. In such a case, as shown in Illustration 4A-1, the words "Net income" are inserted in the account title space. The amount is then entered in the income statement debit column and the balance sheet credit column. The debit amount balances the income statement columns, and the credit amount balances the balance sheet columns. In addition, the credit in the balance sheet column indicates the increase in owner's equity that results from net income. Conversely, if total debits in the income statement columns are more than total credits, a net loss has occurred. In such a case, the amount of the net loss is entered in the income statement credit column and the balance sheet debit column.

After the net income or net loss has been entered, new column totals are determined. The totals shown in the debit and credit income statement columns will now match. The totals shown in the debit and credit balance sheet columns will also match. If either the

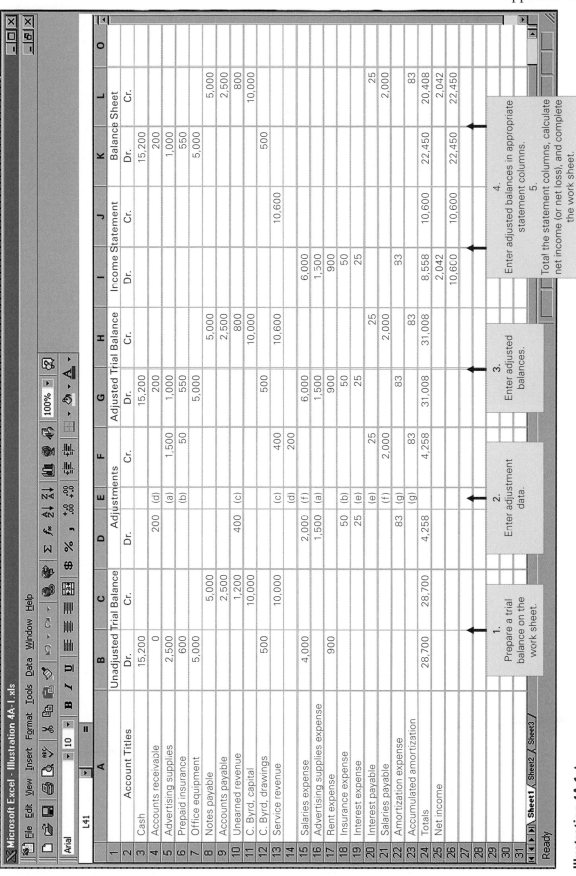

Illustration 4A-1 ▲

Preparing a work sheet—
Steps 1–5

income statement columns or the balance sheet columns are not equal after the net income or net loss has been entered, there is an error in the work sheet.

Preparing Financial Statements from a Work Sheet

After a work sheet has been completed, all the data required to prepare the financial statements are at hand. The income statement is prepared from the income statement columns. The balance sheet and statement of owner's equity are prepared from the balance sheet columns.

Note that the amount shown for owner's capital in the work sheet is the account balance before considering drawings and net income (or loss). When there have been no additional investments of capital by the owner during the period, this amount is the balance at the beginning of the period.

Using a work sheet, accountants can prepare financial statements before adjusting entries have been journalized and posted. However, the completed work sheet is not a substitute for formal financial statements. Data in the financial statement columns of the work sheet are not properly arranged for statement purposes. Also, as noted earlier, the financial statement presentation for some accounts differs from their statement columns on the work sheet. A work sheet is basically an accountant's working tool. It is not given to management or other parties.

APPENDIX 4B ▶ REVERSING ENTRIES

After the financial statements are prepared and the books are closed, it can be helpful to reverse some of the adjusting entries before recording the regular transactions of the next period. Such entries are called reversing entries. A reversing entry is made at the beginning of the next accounting period and is the exact opposite of the adjusting entry that was made in the previous period. The recording of reversing entries is an optional step in the accounting cycle.

The purpose of reversing entries is to simplify the recording of future transactions that are related to an adjusting entry. As you may recall from Chapter 3, the payment of salaries on November 7 after an adjusting entry resulted in two debits: one to Salaries Payable and the other to Salaries Expense. With reversing entries, the entire later payment can be debited to Salaries Expense. You do not have to remember what has gone on before. The use of reversing entries does not change the amounts reported in the financial statements. It simply makes it easier to record future transactions.

Accounting with and without Reversing Entries

study objective 7
Prepare reversing entries.

Reversing entries are used to reverse accruals: accrued revenues and accrued expenses. To illustrate the optional use of reversing entries for accrued expenses, we will use the salaries expense transactions for Pioneer Advertising Agency. The transaction and adjustment data were as follows:

1. October 24 (initial salary entry): Salaries of $4,000 earned between October 13 and October 24 are paid.
2. October 31 (adjusting entry): Salaries earned between October 27 and October 31 (Friday) are $2,000. These will be paid in the November 7 payroll.

3. November 7 (subsequent salary entry): Salaries paid are $4,000. Of this amount, $2,000 applies to accrued salaries payable and $2,000 was earned between November 1 and November 7.

The comparative entries with and without reversing entries are as follows.

* WHEN REVERSING ENTRIES ARE NOT USED (AS IN THE CHAPTER)				WHEN REVERSING ENTRIES ARE USED (AS IN THE APPENDIX)		
Initial Salary Entry				**Initial Salary Entry**		
Oct. 24	Salaries Expense	4,000		Oct. 24	Salaries Expense	4,000	
	Cash		4,000		Cash		4,000
Adjusting Entry				**Adjusting Entry**		
31	Salaries Expense	2,000		31	Salaries Expense	2,000	
	Salaries Payable		2,000		Salaries Payable		2,000
Closing Entry				**Closing Entry**		
31	Income Summary	6,000		31	Income Summary	6,000	
	Salaries Expense		6,000		Salaries Expense		6,000
Reversing Entry				**Reversing Entry**		
Nov. 1	No reversing entry is made.			Nov. 1	Salaries Payable	2,000	
					Salaries Expense		2,000
Subsequent Salary Entry				**Subsequent Salary Entry**		
11	Salaries Payable	2,000		11	Salaries Expense	4,000	
	Salaries Expense	2,000			Cash		4,000
	Cash		4,000				

The first three entries are the same whether or not reversing entries are used. The last two entries are different. The November 1 reversing entry eliminates the $2,000 balance in Salaries Payable that was created by the October 31 adjusting entry. The reversing entry also creates a $2,000 credit balance in the Salaries Expense account. As you know, it is unusual for an expense account to have a credit balance. The balance is correct in this instance, though, because it anticipates that the entire amount of the first salary payment in the new accounting period will be debited to Salaries Expense. This debit will eliminate the credit balance, and the resulting debit balance in the expense account will equal the actual salaries expense in the new accounting period ($2,000 in this example).

When reversing entries are made, all cash payments of expenses can be debited to the expense account. This means that on November 7 (and every payday) Salaries Expense can be debited for the amount paid without regard to any accrued salaries payable. Being able to make the same entry each time simplifies the recording process: future transactions can be recorded as if the related adjusting entry had never been made.

The posting of the entries with reversing entries is as follows, using T accounts.

Salaries Expense				Salaries Payable			
Oct. 24 Paid	4,000			Nov. 1 Rev.	2,000	Oct. 31 Adj.	2,000
31 Adj.	2,000					Nov. 1 Bal.	0
Oct. 31 Bal.	6,000	Oct. 31 Clos.	6,000				
Oct. 31 Bal.	0	Nov. 1 Rev.	2,000				
Nov. 7 Paid	4,000						
Nov. 7 Bal.	2,000						

Practice Tools:
Demonstration Problems

Demonstration Problem

At the end of its first month of operations, Paquet Answering Service has the following unadjusted trial balance, with the accounts presented in alphabetical order rather than in financial statement order:

PAQUET ANSWERING SERVICE
Trial Balance
August 31, 2008

	Debit	Credit
Accounts payable		$ 2,400
Accounts receivable	$ 2,800	
Accumulated amortization—building		500
Accumulated amortization—equipment		1,000
Advertising expense	400	
Amortization expense	1,500	
Building	150,000	
Cash	5,400	
Equipment	60,000	
Insurance expense	200	
Interest expense	350	
Interest payable		1,350
Land	50,000	
Long-term debt investments	15,000	
Long-term equity investments	7,000	
Mortgage payable		140,000
Prepaid insurance	2,200	
R. Paquet, capital		155,000
R. Paquet, drawings	1,000	
Salaries expense	3,200	
Service revenue		5,700
Short-term investments	4,800	
Supplies	1,000	
Supplies expense	300	
Utilities expense	800	
Totals	$305,950	$305,950

Action Plan

• Identify which accounts are balance sheet accounts and which are income statement accounts.
• If revenues are more than expenses, this results in net income; if expenses are more than revenues, this results in a net loss.
• In preparing a classified balance sheet, know the contents of each of the sections.
• In journalizing closing entries, remember that there are four entries. Revenues and expenses are closed to the Income Summary account; the Income Summary account and the drawings account are closed to owner's capital.
• Always check your work. Make sure the balance in Income Summary equals net income before closing the Income Summary account. Make sure that the balance in the owner's capital account after posting the closing entries equals the amount reported on the balance sheet.

Instructions

(a) Calculate the net income or loss for the month.
(b) Calculate owner's equity at August 31, 2008.
(c) Prepare a classified balance sheet for Paquet Answering Service at August 31, 2008. Assume that $5,000 of the mortgage payable is due over the next year.
(d) Journalize the closing entries.
(e) Create T accounts for Income Summary and R. Paquet, Capital, and post closing entries.

Solution to Demonstration Problem

(a) Net income (loss) = Revenue − expenses
 = $5,700 − $400 − $1,500 − $200 − $350 − $3,200 − $300 − $800
 = ($1,050)

(b) Owner's equity August 31, 2008 = Opening capital − net loss − drawings
 = $155,000 − $1,050 − $1,000
 = $152,950

(c)

PAQUET ANSWERING SERVICE
Balance Sheet
August 31, 2008

Assets

Current assets			
Cash			$ 5,400
Short-term investments			4,800
Accounts receivable			2,800
Prepaid insurance			2,200
Supplies			1,000
Total current assets			16,200
Long-term investments			
Equity investments		$ 7,000	
Debt investments		15,000	
Total long-term investments			22,000
Property, plant, and equipment			
Land		$ 50,000	
Building	$150,000		
Less: Accumulated amortization	500	149,500	
Equipment	$ 60,000		
Less: Accumulated amortization	1,000	59,000	258,500
Total assets			$296,700

Liabilities and Owner's Equity

Current liabilities		
Accounts payable		$ 2,400
Interest payable		1,350
Current portion of mortgage payable		5,000
Total current liabilities		8,750
Long-term liabilities		
Mortgage payable		135,000
Total liabilities		143,750
Owner's equity		
R. Paquet, capital		152,950
Total liabilities and owner's equity		$296,700

(d)

Aug. 31	Service Revenue		5,700	
	Income Summary			5,700
	To close revenue account.			
31	Income Summary		6,750	
	Advertising Expense			400
	Amortization Expense			1,500
	Insurance Expense			200
	Interest Expense			350
	Salaries Expense			3,200
	Supplies Expense			300
	Utilities Expense			800
	To close expense accounts.			
31	R. Paquet, Capital		1,050	
	Income Summary			1,050
	To close Income Summary.			
31	R. Paquet, Capital		1,000	
	R. Paquet, Drawings			1,000
	To close drawings.			

(e)

Income Summary					R. Paquet, Capital			
Clos.	6,750	Clos.	5,700				Bal.	155,000
Bal.	1,050				Clos.	1,050		
		Clos.	1,050		Clos.	1,000		
		Bal.	0				Bal.	152,950

Summary of Study Objectives

1. **Prepare closing entries and a post-closing trial balance.** At the end of an accounting period, the temporary account balances (revenue, expense, income summary, and owner's drawings) are transferred to the owner's capital account by journalizing and posting closing entries. Separate entries are made to close revenues and expenses to Income Summary; then Income Summary to owner's capital; and, finally, owner's drawings to owner's capital. The temporary accounts begin the new period with a zero balance and the owner's capital account is updated to show its end of period balance. A post-closing trial balance has the balances in permanent accounts (i.e., balance sheet accounts) that are carried forward to the next accounting period. The purpose of this balance, as with other trial balances, is to prove the equality of these account balances.

2. **List the steps in the accounting cycle.** The steps in the accounting cycle are (1) analyze business transactions, (2) journalize the transactions, (3) post to ledger accounts, (4) prepare a trial balance, (5) journalize and post adjusting entries, (6) prepare an adjusted trial balance, (7) prepare financial statements, (8) journalize and post closing entries, and (9) prepare a post-closing trial balance.

3. **Prepare correcting entries.** One approach for determining the correcting entry is to compare the incorrect entry with the correct entry. After comparison, a correcting entry is made to correct the accounts. An equally acceptable alternative is to reverse the incorrect entry and then record the correct entry.

4. **Prepare a classified balance sheet.** In a classified balance sheet, assets are classified as current assets; long-term investments; property, plant, and equipment; and intangible assets. Liabilities are classified as either current or long-term. There is also an equity section, which varies with the form of business organization.

5. **Illustrate measures used to evaluate liquidity.** One of the measures that is used to evaluate a company's short-term liquidity is its working capital, which is the excess of current assets over current liabilities. This can also be expressed as the current ratio (current assets ÷ current liabilities).

6. **Prepare a work sheet (Appendix 4A).** The steps in preparing a work sheet are (1) prepare a trial balance on the work sheet, (2) enter the adjustments in the adjustment columns, (3) enter adjusted balances in the adjusted trial balance columns, (4) enter adjusted trial balance amounts in correct financial statement columns, and (5) total the statement columns, calculate net income (or net loss), and complete the work sheet.

7. **Prepare reversing entries (Appendix 4B).** Reversing entries are optional entries used to simplify bookkeeping. They are made at the beginning of the new accounting period and are the direct opposite of the adjusting entry made in the preceding period. Only accrual adjusting entries are reversed.

Glossary

Study Aids: Glossary
Practice Tools: Key Term Matching Activity

Classified balance sheet   A balance sheet that has several classifications or sections. (p. 175)

Closing entries   Entries made at the end of an accounting period to transfer the balances of temporary accounts (revenues, expenses, income summary and drawings) to the permanent owner's equity account, owner's capital. (p. 165)

Closing the books   The process of journalizing and posting closing entries to update the capital account and prepare the temporary accounts for the next period's postings. (p. 164)

Correcting entries   Entries to correct errors that were made when transactions were recorded. (p. 173)

Current assets   Cash and other resources that are expected to be realized in cash or sold or consumed in the business within one year. (p. 176)

Current liabilities   Obligations that are expected to be paid from current assets or through the creation of other current liabilities within the next year. (p. 178)

Current ratio   A measure of short-term debt-paying ability that is determined by dividing current assets by current liabilities. (p. 182)

Income summary   A temporary account that is used in closing revenue and expense accounts. (p. 165)

Intangible assets   Long-lived assets that do not have physical substance and are rights and privileges that result from ownership. They include goodwill, patents, copyrights, trademarks, trade names, and licences. (p. 178)

Liquidity   The ability of a company to pay obligations as they come due within the next year and to meet unexpected needs for cash. (p. 182)

Long-term investments   Investments in shares and debts of other companies that are not readily marketable and are expected to be held for more than one year. (p. 176)

Long-term liabilities   Obligations that are expected to be paid after one year or longer. (p. 179)

Permanent accounts   Balance sheet accounts whose balances are carried forward to the next accounting period. (p. 164)

Post-closing trial balance   A list of debit and credit balances of the permanent (balance sheet) accounts after closing entries have been journalized and posted. (p. 169)

Property, plant, and equipment   Tangible assets of a long-lived nature that are used in the operations of the business and are not intended for sale. They include land, buildings, equipment, and furniture. (p. 177)

Reversing entry   An entry made at the beginning of the next accounting period that is the exact opposite of the adjusting entry made in the previous period. (p. 173)

Temporary accounts   Revenue, expense, income summary, and drawings accounts whose balances are transferred to owner's capital at the end of an accounting period. (p. 164)

Working capital   The difference between current assets and current liabilities. (p. 182)

Work sheet   A multiple-column form that may be used in the adjustment process and in preparing financial statements. (p. 172)

Note: All questions, exercises, and problems below with an asterisk (*) relate to material in Appendices 4A and 4B.

Self-Study Questions

Practice Tools: Self-Assessment Quizzes

Answers are at the end of the chapter.

(SO 1) K   1. To close an expense account, the expense account is:
   (a) debited, and Income Summary is credited.
   (b) credited, and Income Summary is debited.
   (c) debited, and owner's capital is credited.
   (d) credited, and owner's drawings is debited.

(SO 1) K   2. After the closing entries have been posted, the balance in the owner's capital account should equal:
   (a) the net income reported on the income statement.
   (b) the opening capital balance reported on the statement of owner's equity.

   (c) the ending capital balance reported on the statement of owner's equity and balance sheet.
   (d) the opening capital balance plus any investments made by the owner during the period.

   3. Which types of accounts will appear in the post-closing trial balance?   **(SO 1) K**
   (a) Permanent (balance sheet) accounts
   (b) Temporary (revenue, expense, and drawings) accounts
   (c) Contra accounts
   (d) All accounts

(SO 2) K 4. Which of the following is an optional step in the accounting cycle?
(a) Journalizing and posting closing entries
(b) Preparing an adjusted trial balance
(c) Preparing a post-closing trial balance
(d) Preparing reversing entries

(SO 2) K 5. Which of the following statements about the work sheet is *incorrect*?
(a) The work sheet is essentially a working tool of the accountant.
(b) The work sheet is an optional step in the accounting cycle.
(c) If a work sheet is used at the year end, it is not necessary to post adjusting entries to the general ledger.
(d) Financial statements can be prepared directly from the work sheet before journalizing and posting the adjusting entries.

(SO 3) AP 6. Cash of $250 is received at the time a service is provided. The transaction is journalized and posted as a debit to Cash of $250 and a credit to Accounts Receivable of $250. The correcting entry is:

(a) Service Revenue	250	
Accounts Receivable		250
(b) Accounts Receivable	250	
Service Revenue		250
(c) Cash	250	
Service Revenue		250
(d) Accounts Receivable	250	
Cash		250

7. Current assets are listed: (SO 4)
(a) by liquidity.
(b) by importance.
(c) by longevity.
(d) alphabetically.

8. A company reports current assets of $10,000 and current liabilities of $8,000. Its current ratio is: (SO 5)
(a) $2,000.
(b) 80%.
(c) 1.25:1.
(d) More information is needed to calculate the ratio.

*9. In a work sheet, net income is entered in the following columns: (SO 6)
(a) income statement (Dr.) and balance sheet (Dr.).
(b) income statement (Cr.) and balance sheet (Dr.).
(c) income statement (Dr.) and balance sheet (Cr.).
(d) income statement (Cr.) and balance sheet (Cr.).

*10. On December 31, Mott Company correctly made an adjusting entry to recognize $2,000 of accrued salaries payable. On January 8 of the next year, total salaries of $3,400 were paid. Assuming the correct reversing entry was made on January 1, the entry on January 8 will result in a credit to Cash of $3,400, and the following debit(s): (SO 7)
(b) Salaries Payable $1,400, and Salaries Expense $2,000.
(c) Salaries Payable $2,000, and Salaries Expense $1,400.
(d) Salaries Expense $3,400.
(e) Salaries Payable $3,400.

Questions

(SO 1) C 1. What are the two reasons for recording closing entries?

(SO 1) K 2. Identify the account(s) debited and credited in each of the four closing entries.

(SO 1) C 3. What is the purpose of using an income summary account? If an income summary account was not used, how would the closing entries change?

(SO 1) C 4. Why is the owner's drawings account not closed with the expense accounts? Why is a separate entry required for this account?

(SO 1) C 5. Brenda has been told that after the closing entries have been posted, she should stop and check her work. Explain to Brenda what she should be checking for.

(SO 1) K 6. What are the content and purpose of a post-closing trial balance?

(SO 2) K 7. Which steps in the accounting cycle may be done daily, which steps are done on a periodic basis (monthly, quarterly, or annually), and which steps are usually done only at the company's fiscal year end?

8. Although using a work sheet is optional, it is useful. Do you agree? Explain. (SO 2)

9. How are correcting entries different from adjusting entries? (SO 3)

10. What is the purpose of classifying assets and liabilities into categories on the balance sheet? (SO 4)

11. Define "current assets." What basis is used for the order of the individual items in the current assets section? (SO 4)

12. What are the differences between the three categories of noncurrent assets: long-term investments; property, plant, and equipment; and intangible assets? (SO 4)

13. How are current liabilities different from long-term liabilities? (SO 4)

(SO 4) K 14. (a) What terms are used to describe the equity section of (1) a proprietorship, (2) a partnership, (3) a corporation, and (4) an income trust? (b) Identify the two equity accounts in a corporation and state the purpose of each.

(SO 5) C 15. What is liquidity? Identify one measure of liquidity.

(SO 5) C 16. What factors need to be considered when interpreting ratios?

(SO 6) C *17. How is net income or loss calculated on a work sheet? How is this number entered on the work sheet if the company has net income? How is it entered if the company has a net loss?

*18. Why is it necessary to journalize and post adjusting (SO 6) C entries if they have already been entered on the work sheet?

*19. What are the differences between a reversing entry and (SO 7) C an adjusting entry? Are reversing entries required?

*20. When and how is it helpful to use reversing entries? (SO 7) C When should reversing entries not be used?

Brief Exercises

BE4–1 The following selected accounts and balances (in U.S. thousands) appear in the financial statements of The Jean Coutu Group (PJC) Inc.:

Identify temporary and permanent accounts. (SO 1) C

Accounts payable	$1,109,902	Long-term debt	$2,495,801
Accounts receivable	544,810	Other revenues	169,020
Amortization expense	195,308	Prepaid expenses	40,981
General and operating expenses	1,878,296	Property, plant, and equipment	1,492,499
Income taxes payable	32,870	Short-term investments	78,489
Interest on long-term debt expense	152,731		

Which accounts are temporary and which ones are permanent?

BE4–2 The adjusted trial balance for Mosquera Golf Club at its October 31, 2008, year end included the following:

Prepare and post closing entries. (SO 1) AP

	Debit	Credit
Cash	$ 8,500	
Prepaid expenses	3,000	
Equipment	85,000	
Accumulated amortization—equipment		$ 17,000
Accounts payable		12,000
Unearned golf fees		1,500
N. Mosquera, capital		75,000
N. Mosquera, drawings	48,000	
Golf fees earned		160,000
Maintenance expense	25,000	
Rent expense	12,000	
Salaries expense	84,000	

Instructions

(a) Prepare closing entries.
(b) Using T accounts, post the closing entries and calculate the balance in each account.

BE4–3 Refer to the information in BE4–2 for Mosquera Golf Club. Prepare a post-closing trial balance.

Prepare post-closing trial balance. (SO 1) AP

BE4–4 The required steps in the accounting cycle are listed below in random order. List the steps in the correct order by writing the numbers 1 to 9 in the blank spaces.

List steps in accounting cycle. (SO 2) K

(a) ___ Prepare a post-closing trial balance.   (f) ___ Journalize and post the closing entries.
(b) ___ Prepare an adjusted trial balance.   (g) ___ Prepare the financial statements.

(c) ___ Analyze business transactions.   (h) ___ Journalize and post the adjusting entries.
(d) ___ Prepare a trial balance.   (i) ___ Post to the ledger accounts.
(e) ___ Journalize the transactions.

Identify impact of error and prepare correcting entries.
(SO 3) AP

BE4–5 At Hébert Company, the following errors were discovered after the transactions had been journalized and posted:

1. A collection of cash on account from a customer for $880 was recorded as a debit to Service Revenue of $880 and a credit to Accounts Receivable of $880.
2. The purchase of office supplies on account for $1,850 was recorded as a debit to Equipment of $1,580 and a credit to Accounts Payable of $1,580.

(a) Indicate the impact of each error on the balance sheet and income statement by stating whether assets, liabilities, owner's equity, revenues, expenses, and net income are understated (U), overstated (O), or not affected (NA).
(b) Prepare the correcting entries.

Classify balance sheet accounts.
(SO 4) K

BE4–6 The standard balance sheet classifications for assets and liabilities are as follows:

1. Current assets   4. Intangible assets
2. Long-term investments   5. Current liabilities
3. Property, plant, and equipment 6. Long-term liabilities

Match the classifications above with the accounts below by writing the correct number in the blank spaces:

(a) ___ Supplies   (g) ___ Unearned Revenue
(b) ___ Accounts Payable   (h) ___ Accounts Receivable
(c) ___ Building   (i) ___ Accumulated Amortization—Building
(d) ___ Prepaid Insurance   (j) ___ Patents
(e) ___ Note Payable (due in 5 years) (k) ___ Land Held for Resale
(f) ___ Goodwill   (l) ___ Note Receivable (due in 3 years)

Prepare current assets section of balance sheet.
(SO 4) AP

BE4–7 The adjusted trial balance of Reuben Company includes the following accounts: Accounts Receivable $12,500; Prepaid Insurance $3,900; Cash $18,400; Supplies $5,200; and Short-term Investments $8,200. Prepare the current assets section of the balance sheet as at December 31, 2008, with the accounts in the right order.

Calculate working capital and current ratio; compare liquidity.
(SO 5) AP

BE4–8 Cool Delight Company specializes in creating novelty ice cream desserts. It reported current assets of $165,211 and $190,548 at August 31, 2008 and 2007, respectively. It reported current liabilities of $136,742 and $72,410 at August 31, 2008 and 2007, respectively. Calculate Cool Delight's working capital and current ratio for 2008 and 2007. Was Cool Delight's liquidity stronger or weaker in 2008 than it was in 2007?

Calculate working capital and current ratio and compare liquidity ratios measures.
(SO 5) K

BE4–9 On December 31, 2008, Big Company had $1,000,000 of current assets and $900,000 of current liabilities. On the same day, Small Company had $200,000 of current assets and $100,000 of current liabilities. Calculate the working capital and current ratio for both companies and compare the results. Which liquidity measure is more relevant?

Identify work sheet columns for selected accounts.
(SO 6) C

*BE4–10 The following accounts appear in the adjusted trial balance columns of the work sheet for Khanna Company: Accounts Payable; Accounts Receivable; Accumulated Amortization; Amortization Expense; H. Khanna, Capital; H. Khanna, Drawings; Prepaid Expenses; Rent Expense; Service Revenue; and Unearned Service Revenue. Indicate the financial statement column (income statement Dr., balance sheet Cr., etc.) each balance should be extended to (recorded in).

Complete work sheet.
(SO 6) AP

*BE4–11 The accountant for Coulombe Company is almost finished preparing the work sheet for the year ended July 31, 2008. The totals of the accounts in the income statement and balance sheet columns are presented below. Calculate the net income or loss, write this number in the proper columns, and calculate the final totals for these columns. Clearly indicate whether the company had net income or a net loss.

	Income Statement		Balance Sheet	
	Dr.	Cr.	Dr.	Cr.
Totals	17,450	21,600	29,700	25,550
Net income or loss				
Totals				

*BE4–12 The accountant for Orange Line Company is almost finished preparing the work sheet for the year ended August 31, 2008. The totals of the accounts in the income statement and balance sheet columns are presented below. Calculate the net income or loss, write this in the proper columns, and calculate the final totals for these columns. Clearly indicate whether the company had a net income or net loss.

Complete work sheet. (SO 6) AP

	Income Statement		Balance Sheet	
	Dr.	Cr.	Dr.	Cr.
Totals	35,800	29,750	56,150	62,200
Net income or loss				
Totals				

*BE4–13 At October 31, Orlaida Company made an accrued expense adjusting entry of $1,200 for salaries. On November 4, it paid salaries of $2,000; $1,200 for October salaries and $800 for November salaries. (a) Prepare the November 1 reversing entry and the November 4 journal entry to record the payment of salaries. (b) Indicate the balances in Salaries Payable and Salaries Expense after posting the two entries.

Prepare and post reversing entry. (SO 7) AP

*BE4–14 At December 31, interest receivable totalled $4,500. On January 10, interest of $5,000 was received. (a) Assuming that reversing entries are made at January 1, prepare the January 1 and January 10 entries. (b) Repeat part (a), assuming reversing entries are not made. (c) Compare the balances of the Interest Receivable and Interest Revenue accounts after all entries are made and posted in (a) and (b).

Prepare entries with and without reversing entries. (SO 7) AP

Exercises

E4–1 Selected T accounts for Roth Beauty Salon follow. All June 30 postings are from closing entries.

Prepare closing entries. (SO 1) AP

Salaries Expense

June 10	4,200	June 30	9,800
28	5,600		
June 30 Bal.	0		

J. Roth, Capital

		June 1 Bal.	12,000
June 30	2,500	30	2,000
		June 30 Bal.	11,500

Supplies Expense

June 12	600	June 30	1,300
24	700		
June 30 Bal.	0		

J. Roth, Drawings

June 13	1,000	June 30	2,500
25	1,500		
June 30 Bal.	0		

Service Revenue

June 30	16,100	June 15	7,700
		24	8,400
		June 30 Bal.	0

Income Summary

June 30	14,100	June 30	16,100
30	2,000		
		June 30 Bal.	0

Rent Expense

| June 1 | 3,000 | June 30 | 3,000 |
| June 30 Bal. | 0 | | |

Instructions

(a) Prepare the closing entries that were made.
(b) What should the ending balance of the account J. Roth, Capital, agree with and in which financial statement(s)?

Prepare and post closing entries and prepare post-closing trial balance.
(SO 1) AP

E4–2 At the end of its fiscal year, the adjusted trial balance of Rafael Company is as follows:

RAFAEL COMPANY
Adjusted Trial Balance
July 31, 2008

	Debit	Credit
Cash	$ 5,840	
Accounts receivable	15,540	
Prepaid expenses	1,620	
Supplies	470	
Equipment	17,600	
Accumulated amortization—equipment		$ 5,400
Accounts payable		4,245
Interest payable		525
Unearned service revenue		2,750
Notes payable (due on July 1, 2010)		15,000
D. Rafael, capital		31,200
D. Rafael, drawings	14,000	
Service revenue		73,800
Amortization expense	2,700	
Salaries expense	56,050	
Interest expense	1,350	
Rent expense	15,900	
Supplies expense	1,850	
	$132,920	$132,920

Instructions

(a) Prepare the closing entries, and post them to the correct accounts.
(b) Prepare a post-closing trial balance at July 31, 2008.

Prepare and post closing entries and prepare post closing trial balance.
(SO 1) AP

E4–3 An alphabetical list of the adjusted account balances (all accounts have normal balances) at December 31, 2008, for Summit's Bowl-A-Drome Alley is as follows:

Accounts payable	$ 12,300	Insurance expense	$ 870
Accounts receivable	13,880	Interest expense	2,600
Accumulated amortization—		Interest payable	2,600
building	50,600	Land	64,000
Accumulated amortization—		Mortgage payable	99,780
equipment	17,770	Prepaid insurance	4,590
Amortization expense	7,360	Supplies	740
Bowling revenues	14,180	T. Bolgos, capital	115,000
Building	128,800	T. Bolgos, drawings	10,000
Cash	17,940	Unearned bowling revenue	950
Equipment	62,400		

Instructions

(a) Prepare the closing entries at December 31.
(b) Prepare T accounts for the accounts affected by the closing entries. Post the closing entries.
(c) Prepare a post-closing trial balance at December 31, 2008.

E4-4 Choi Company has an inexperienced accountant. During the first two weeks on the job, the accountant made the following errors in journalizing transactions. All incorrect entries were posted.

Prepare correcting entries.
(SO 3) AP

1. A payment on account of $920 to a creditor was debited $290 to Accounts Payable and credited $290 to Cash.
2. The purchase of supplies on account for $560 was debited $56 to Equipment and credited $56 to Accounts Payable.
3. A $400 withdrawal of cash for L. Choi's personal use was debited $400 to Salaries Expense and credited $400 to Cash.
4. The purchase of $1,200 of office equipment with a three-year useful life was debited to Office Supplies.
5. A customer was billed $175 for services provided. Accounts Receivable was debited $175 and Unearned Service Revenue was credited $175.

Instructions

Prepare the correcting entries.

E4-5 Sobeys Inc. has the following selected accounts listed in a recent balance sheet:

Identify balance sheet classifications.
(SO 4) K

Accounts payable and accrued liabilities	Long-term debt due within one year
Cash and cash equivalents	Long-term lease obligation
Employee future benefit obligation	Mortgages and loans receivable
Goodwill	Prepaid expenses
Income taxes payable	Property and equipment
Income taxes recoverable	Receivables
Inventories	Retained earnings
Long-term debt	

Instructions

Identify the classification on the balance sheet for each of the accounts.

E4-6 The adjusted trial balance for Rafael Company is presented in E4-2.

Prepare financial statements.
(SO 4) AP

Instructions

(a) Prepare an income statement and statement of owner's equity for the year. Mr. Rafael invested $5,000 cash in the business during the year.
(b) Prepare a classified balance sheet at July 31, 2008.

E4-7 Refer to the list of adjusted account balances presented in E4-3 for Summit's Bowl-A-Drome Alley at December 31, 2008.

Prepare financial statements and comment on liquidity.
(SO 4, 5) AN

Instructions

(a) Prepare an income statement and statement of owner's equity for the year ended December 31, 2008, and a classified balance sheet at December 31, 2008. Assume that $12,750 of the mortgage payable will be paid in 2009.
(b) Calculate working capital and the current ratio, and comment on the company's liquidity.

E4-8 Theratechnologies, located in Quebec, is a leader in the Canadian biopharmaceutical industry. The following data (in thousands) were taken from Theratechnologies' financial statements:

Calculate working capital and current ratio; comment on liquidity.
(SO 5) AN

	Nov. 30, 2005	Nov. 30, 2004	Nov. 30, 2003
Current assets	$17,192	$20,842	$42,523
Current liabilities	4,639	4,996	7,132

Instructions

(a) Calculate the working capital and current ratio for each year.
(b) Discuss Theratechnologies' liquidity in 2005 compared to the two previous years.

*E4–9   The unadjusted trial balance for Kwok Yuen Ho Company at its month end, April 30, 2008, is as follows:

KWOK YUEN HO COMPANY
Trial Balance
April 30, 2008

	Debit	Credit
Cash	$14,770	
Accounts receivable	8,230	
Prepaid rent	3,050	
Equipment	23,040	
Accumulated amortization—equipment		$ 4,480
Accounts payable		5,670
Notes payable		11,600
K. Ho, capital		28,960
K. Ho, drawings	3,650	
Service revenue		11,870
Salaries expense	9,840	
	$62,580	$62,580

Other data:

1. Revenue of $720 was earned but unrecorded as at April 30, 2008.
2. On April 1, the company paid $3,050 rent in advance for April 1 to August 31.
3. The equipment has an estimated useful life of three years.
4. Interest on the note payable is due on the first day of each month for the previous month's interest. The note payable has a 6% annual interest rate.

Instructions

Prepare the work sheet for the month ended April 30, 2008.

*E4–10   Selected work sheet data for Blanchard Company follow:

	Trial Balance		Adjusted Trial Balance	
	Dr.	Cr.	Dr.	Cr.
Accounts receivable	(1)		34,000	
Prepaid insurance	25,000		18,000	
Supplies	7,000		(3)	
Accumulated amortization		12,000		(5)
Salaries payable				5,000
Service revenue		88,000		95,000
Insurance expense			(4)	
Amortization expense			10,000	
Supplies expense			4,000	
Salaries expense	(2)		49,000	

Instructions

(a) Fill in the missing amounts.
(b) Prepare the adjusting entries that were made.

*E4–11   On December 31, the unadjusted trial balance of Masterson Employment Agency shows the following selected data:

Accounts receivable	$24,000	Commission revenue	$92,000
Interest expense	7,750	Interest payable	0
I. Masterson, capital	48,000		

Analysis shows that adjusting entries were made to (1) accrue $4,400 of commission revenue, and (2) accrue $1,550 of interest expense.

Instructions

(a) Prepare and post (1) the adjusting entries, and (2) the closing entries for the temporary accounts at December 31.
(b) Prepare and post reversing entries on January 1.
(c) Prepare and post the entries to record (1) the collection of $6,000 of commissions (including the accrued commission from December 31) on January 10, and (2) the payment of $2,235 interest on January 31 (consisting of the accrued interest from December 31 plus January's interest).

*E4–12   Rosborough Company provides property management services to a variety of companies. At its fiscal year end on April 30, 2008, adjustments were required for the following items:

Prepare adjusting, reversing, and subsequent entries.
(SO 7) AP

1. Property management revenue of $600 was earned but not recorded.
2. Of the balance in the Unearned Property Management Revenue account, $250 had been earned.
3. Amortization expense for the year ended April 30, 2008, was $4,850.
4. Interest of $545 on a note payable had accrued.
5. Prepaid insurance of $385 had expired.
6. Property taxes are payable every year on June 30. The company estimated property taxes for 2008 to be $3,912.

Instructions

(a) Identify the adjustments for which it could be useful to prepare reversing entries.
(b) Prepare these reversing entries on May 1, 2008.
(c) Explain why and how the reversing entries are useful for these adjustments but not for the other adjustments.

Problems: Set A

P4–1A   The following T accounts show the balances before the accounts were closed, and the closing entries which were posted to them:

Analyze account data and prepare and post closing entries.
(SO 1) AN

Other Revenue	
35,000	35,000

Repair Service Expense	
125,000	125,000

Repair Service Revenue	
180,000	180,000

R. Laporte, Drawings	
50,000	50,000

R. Laporte, Capital	
50,000	800,000
	60,000

Other Expenses	
30,000	30,000

Income Summary	
?	?

Instructions

(a) Identify the normal account balance (debit or credit) for each of the above accounts.
(b) Reconstruct, in general journal format, the closing entries that were journalized and posted to the above T accounts. (*Hint:* Notice that some of the amounts in the T accounts are repeated several times. Think about which ones are related to each other in terms of the closing entries.)
(c) Post the closing entries to the Income Summary account.

Prepare adjusting entries, adjusted trial balance, financial statements, and closing entries.

(SO 1, 4) AP

P4–2A The following is Edge Sports Repair Shop's trial balance at September 30, 2008, the company's fiscal year end:

EDGE SPORTS REPAIR SHOP
Trial Balance
September 30, 2008

	Debit	Credit
Cash	$ 10,470	
Accounts receivable	1,450	
Prepaid insurance	4,140	
Supplies	3,780	
Land	55,000	
Building	98,000	
Accumulated amortization—building		$ 17,150
Equipment	38,000	
Accumulated amortization—equipment		9,500
Accounts payable		4,300
Unearned revenue		2,280
Mortgage payable		105,000
L. Bachchan, capital		60,000
L. Bachchan, drawings	93,525	
Service revenue		198,450
Salaries expense	75,900	
Utilities expense	11,100	
Interest expense	5,315	
	$396,680	$396,680

Other data:

1. Service revenue earned but not recorded at September 30, 2008, was $1,150.
2. The 12-month insurance policy was purchased on February 1, 2008.
3. A physical count of supplies shows $960 on hand on September 30, 2008.
4. The building has an estimated useful life of 40 years. The equipment has an estimated useful life of 8 years.
5. Salaries of $1,075 are accrued and unpaid at September 30, 2008.
6. The mortgage payable has a 6% interest rate. Interest is paid on the first day of each month for the previous month's interest.
7. On September 30, 2008, one quarter of the unearned revenue was still unearned.
8. During the next fiscal year, $5,400 of the mortgage payable is to be paid.

Instructions

(a) Prepare the adjusting entries.
(b) Prepare an adjusted trial balance.
(c) Prepare an income statement, statement of owner's equity, and classified balance sheet. L. Bachchan invested $4,000 cash in the business on November 21, 2007.
(d) Prepare the closing entries.

P4–3A The adjusted trial balance for Zazu Pits Raisin Company is as follows:

Prepare financial statements, closing entries, and post-closing trial balance.
(SO 1, 4) AP

ZAZU PITS RAISIN COMPANY
Adjusted Trial Balance
December 31, 2008

	Debit	Credit
Cash	$ 8,400	
Accounts receivable	7,500	
Prepaid insurance	1,800	
Supplies	570	
Land	102,500	
Building	150,000	
Accumulated amortization—building		$ 24,000
Equipment	28,000	
Accumulated amortization—equipment		8,400
Accounts payable		12,740
Salaries payable		2,850
Interest payable		1,400
Unearned revenue		2,190
Mortgage payable ($3,000 is payable in 2009)		198,000
P. Zazu, capital		58,500
P. Zazu, drawings	7,200	
Service revenue		73,500
Salaries expense	47,040	
Amortization expense	5,800	
Utilities expense	5,280	
Interest expense	12,870	
Insurance expense	1,200	
Supplies expense	3,420	
	$381,580	$381,580

Instructions

(a) Prepare an income statement, statement of owner's equity, and classified balance sheet. The owner, Patrice Zazu, invested $4,500 cash in the business during 2008.

(b) Prepare the closing entries.

(c) Using T accounts, post the closing entries and calculate the balance in each account. (Ignore the accounts that are not affected by the closing entries.)

(d) Prepare a post-closing trial balance.

P4–4A Eric Mayers, CA, was hired by Interactive Computer Repair to prepare its financial statements for March 2008. Using all the ledger balances in the owner's records, Mayers put together the following trial balance:

INTERACTIVE COMPUTER REPAIR
Trial Balance
March 31, 2008

	Debit	Credit
Cash	$ 7,400	
Accounts receivable	3,600	
Supplies	1,100	
Equipment	11,400	
Accumulated amortization		$ 5,795
Accounts payable		3,000
Salaries payable		750
Unearned revenue		935
H. Maurice, capital		12,725
Service revenue		6,450
Salaries expense	5,100	
Advertising expense	600	
Miscellaneous expense	210	
Amortization expense	95	
Repair expense	150	
Totals	$29,655	$29,655

Mayers then reviewed the records and found the following errors:

1. Cash received from a customer on account was recorded as $670 instead of $760.
2. The purchase on account of a computer monitor that cost $900 was recorded as a debit to Supplies and a credit to Accounts Receivable for $900.
3. The computer monitor purchased in item 2 was purchased on March 1 and has an estimated useful life of five years. Amortization for March has not yet been recorded.
4. A payment of $75 for advertising expense was entered as a debit to Miscellaneous Expense of $50 and a credit to Cash of $50.
5. The first salary payment made in March was for $2,000, which included $750 of salaries payable on February 28. The payment was recorded as a debit to Salaries Expense of $2,000 and a credit to Cash of $2,000. (No reversing entries were made on March 1.)
6. A $110 cash payment for a repair expense on equipment was recorded as a debit to Equipment of $101 and a credit to Cash of $101.
7. The owner, Hubert Maurice, paid himself $1,800 and recorded this as salary expense.
8. March rent of $1,150 was paid on March 26. The company has not recorded this transaction.

Instructions

(a) Prepare an analysis of each error that shows (1) the incorrect entry, (2) the correct entry, and (3) the correcting entry.
(b) Prepare a correct trial balance.

Determine impact of errors
on financial statements.
(SO 3) AP

P4–5A The following accounting errors were made in the records of Fu Company and were not found. If nothing is said about it, assume that the other side of the entry was correctly recorded and posted.

1. A $700 debit to Supplies was debited to Supplies Expense.
2. A $600 debit to Accounts Payable was debited to Cash.
3. A $350 cash sale was posted to the Cash and Service Revenue accounts twice.
4. The amortization adjusting entry was recorded and posted as $850, rather than $580.
5. A $680 posting to Accounts Receivable and Service Revenue was posted by mistake as $600.
6. A $750 debit to Interest Expense was posted to Interest Revenue as a debit.
7. A $500 collection in advance was not posted to the Cash and Unearned Service Revenue accounts.

8. A $300 collection in advance was credited to Service Revenue instead of Unearned Service Revenue.
9. A $950 payment for rent for the owner's apartment was debited to Rent Expense.

Instructions

(a) For each item, indicate the effect and amount of the error—understatement (U), overstatement (O), or no effect (NE)—on the income statement and balance sheet components. Use the following format, where the first one has been done for you as an example.

	Income Statement			Balance Sheet		
Item	Revenue	Expenses	Net Income	Assets	Liabilities	Owner's Equity
1.	NE	O $700	U $700	U $700	NE	U $700

(b) Determine the total amount of the understatement or overstatement that results from the errors.

P4–6A Below is an alphabetical list of the adjusted accounts of Matrix Consulting Services at its year end, March 31, 2008. All accounts have normal balances.

Prepare financial statements and liquidity ratios.
(SO 4, 5) AP

Accounts payable	$ 8,000	N. Anderson, capital	$41,000
Accounts receivable	7,400	N. Anderson, drawings	12,000
Accumulated amortization—		Note payable	26,000
computer equipment	18,000	Note receivable	10,000
Advertising expense	12,000	Patent	16,000
Amortization expense	6,000	Prepaid insurance	4,400
Cash	4,600	Salaries expense	45,000
Computer equipment	44,000	Salaries payable	2,600
Insurance expense	4,000	Service revenue	79,800
Interest expense	2,000	Short-term investments	4,000
Interest payable	1,000	Supplies	2,300
Interest receivable	800	Supplies expense	3,700
Interest revenue	600	Unearned revenue	1,200

Other data:

1. Of the notes payable, $10,000 becomes due on July 1, 2008, and the rest on July 1, 2009.
2. The note receivable is due on June 1, 2008.
3. On September 20, 2007, Nco Anderson invested $3,600 cash in the business.

Instructions

(a) Prepare an income statement and statement of owner's equity for the year ended March 31, 2008, and a classified balance sheet as at March 31, 2008.
(b) On March 31, 2007, Matrix Consulting Services had current assets of $30,700 and current liabilities of $15,950. Calculate the company's working capital and current ratio on March 31, 2007, and March 31, 2008. Has the company's ability to pay its debts improved or weakened over the year?

P4–7A Big Rock Brewery creates and sells premium natural unpasteurized beer. Its 2005 balance sheet showed current assets of $12,770,157 and current liabilities of $3,895,903. The 2004 balance sheet reported current assets of $9,947,060 and current liabilities of $4,014,186. The 2003 balance sheet had current assets of $10,006,747 and current liabilities of $4,958,338.

Calculate working capital and current ratio, and comment on liquidity.
(SO 5) AN

Instructions

(a) Calculate Big Rock's working capital and current ratio for each year.
(b) What do each of the measures calculated in (a) show? Comment on Big Rock's liquidity.

*P4–8A The unadjusted trial balance and adjustment data for Edge Sports Repair Shop are presented in P4–2A.

Prepare work sheet.
(SO 6) AP

Instructions

Prepare a work sheet for the year ended September 30, 2008.

Prepare work sheet,
classified balance sheet,
adjusting and closing entries,
and post-closing trial balance.
(SO 1, 4, 6) AP

*P4–9A Kumar Management Services manages condominiums for owners (service revenue) and rents space in its own office building (rent revenue). The trial balance and adjusted trial balance columns of the work sheet at the end of the fiscal year are as follows:

KUMAR MANAGEMENT SERVICES
Work Sheet (partial)
Year Ended December 31, 2008

	Trial Balance		Adjusted Trial Balance	
	Dr.	Cr.	Dr.	Cr.
Cash	$ 12,550		$ 12,550	
Accounts receivable	23,600		25,100	
Supplies	3,150		690	
Prepaid insurance	3,100		1,400	
Land	58,000		58,000	
Building	112,500		112,500	
Accumulated amortization— building		$ 22,500		$ 25,000
Equipment	51,000		51,000	
Accumulated amortization— equipment		17,000		21,250
Accounts payable		10,640		11,340
Salaries payable		0		845
Interest payable		0		1,250
Unearned rent revenue		5,000		3,100
Mortgage payable		100,000		100,000
M. Kumar, capital		113,150		113,150
M. Kumar, drawings	28,500		28,500	
Service revenue		66,100		67,600
Rent revenue		24,000		25,900
Salaries expense	38,675		39,520	
Utilities expense	15,800		16,500	
Property tax expense	5,265		5,265	
Insurance expense	0		1,700	
Interest expense	6,250		7,500	
Amortization expense	0		6,750	
Supplies expense	0		2,460	
	$358,390	$358,390	$369,435	$369,435

Instructions

(a) Complete the work sheet, using the partial information provided above.
(b) Prepare a classified balance sheet. (*Note:* In the next year, $10,000 of the mortgage payable is due for payment.)
(c) Journalize the adjusting entries.
(d) Journalize the closing entries.
(e) Prepare a post-closing trial balance.

Use work sheet relationships
to determine missing
amounts.
(SO 6) AN

*P4–10A A work sheet for Nohe's Carpet Cleaners follows, with certain amounts replaced by letters:

NOHE'S CARPET CLEANERS
Work Sheet
Month Ended April 30, 2008

	Trial Balance Dr.	Trial Balance Cr.	Adjustments Dr.	Adjustments Cr.	Adjusted Trial Balance Dr.	Adjusted Trial Balance Cr.	Income Statement Dr.	Income Statement Cr.	Balance Sheet Dr.	Balance Sheet Cr.
Cash	(a)				950				950	
Accounts receivable	1,350		(e)		1,500				1,500	
Cleaning supplies	1,400			(i)	(m)				500	
Prepaid insurance	(b)			(j)	1,650				1,650	
Equipment	7,510				7,510				7,510	
Accumulated amortization		1,200		(k)		1,500				1,500
Accounts payable		2,115				2,115				(z)
Unearned revenue		800	550			250				250
J. Nohe, capital		9,400				9,400				9,400
J. Nohe, drawings	(c)				1,280				1,280	
Service revenue		4,000		(l)		(q)		(u)		
Rent expense	975				975		975			
Salaries expense	(d)		(f)		(n)		2,790			
Totals	17,515	17,515								
Amortization expense			(g)		(o)		(s)			
Insurance expense			210		210		210			
Cleaning supplies expense			(h)		(p)		(t)			
Salaries payable				600		(r)				600
Totals			2,710	2,710	18,565	18,565	5,175	(v)	(x)	13,865
Net income							0	475	(y)	
Totals							5,175	(w)	13,865	13,865

Instructions

Determine the amounts that should appear in the work sheet where there is currently a letter. (*Hint:* You will not be able to determine the missing items in alphabetical order.)

*P4–11A The Friendly Food Company had the following balances on its December 31, 2007, balance sheet:

Prepare and post transaction entries, with and without reversing entries.
(SO 7) AP

Rent receivable	$3,700	Property taxes payable	$ 3,150
Prepaid insurance	5,250	Unearned service revenue	25,000

During 2008, the following transactions occurred:

1. On January 5, rent for November 2007, December 2007, and January 2008 totalling $5,550 cash was collected.
2. On April 15, property tax of $8,400 was paid.
3. On July 31, 2008, the company's insurance policy expired and a new one-year policy was purchased for $9,000.
4. Services provided of $415,000 in 2008 included $390,000 of services for cash and $25,000 of services to customers who had made advance payments in 2007.

Instructions

(a) Assuming that the company does not use reversing entries:
  1. Prepare journal entries to record the transactions above for 2008.
  2. Post your entries to T accounts and calculate the balance in each account.
(b) Assuming that the company uses reversing entries:
  1. Prepare reversing entries where appropriate for January 1, 2008.
  2. Prepare journal entries to record the transactions above for 2008.
  3. Post your entries to T accounts and calculate the balance in each account.
(c) Compare the account balances in (a) to those in (b). Comment on the usefulness of reversing entries.

Prepare adjusting, reversing, and subsequent cash entries. (SO 7) AP

*P4–12A The unadjusted trial balance for Larry's Laser Games at its fiscal year end of April 30, 2008, is as follows:

LARRY'S LASER GAMES
Trial Balance
April 30, 2008

	Debit	Credit
Cash	$ 3,525	
Accounts receivable	0	
Supplies	3,370	
Equipment	135,000	
Accumulated amortization—equipment		$ 40,500
Wages payable		0
Interest payable		0
Note payable		85,000
Unearned game fee revenue		1,875
L. Ng, capital		32,800
L. Ng, drawings	28,500	
Game fee revenue		82,545
Rent expense	14,400	
Wages expense	53,250	
Supplies expense	0	
Amortization expense	0	
Interest expense	4,675	
	$242,720	$242,720

Other data:

1. On April 30, 2008, Larry's Laser Games had earned but not collected or recorded $775 of game fee revenue. On May 17, 2008, Larry's Laser Games collected this amount plus an additional $1,150 for game fee revenue earned in May.
2. There was $540 of supplies on hand on April 30, 2008.
3. The equipment has an estimated useful life of 10 years.
4. On April 30, salaries earned but not paid or recorded were $720. The next pay day is May 10 and the employees will be paid a total of $2,785 that day.
5. The note payable has a 6% annual interest rate. Interest is paid quarterly. Interest was last paid on March 31, 2008. The next payment is due on June 30, 2008.
6. On April 30, $1,475 of the unearned game fee revenue had been earned.

Instructions

(a) Prepare adjusting journal entries for the year ended April 30, 2008, as required.
(b) Prepare reversing entries where appropriate.
(c) Prepare journal entries to record the May and June 2008 cash transactions.
(d) Now assume reversing entries were not prepared as in (b) above. Prepare journal entries to record the May and June 2008 cash transactions.

Problems: Set B

P4–1B   The following T accounts show the balances before the accounts were closed and the closing entries which were posted to them:

Analyze account data and prepare and post closing entries.
(SO 1) AN

Professional Fees Earned	
	275,000	275,000

Other Expenses	
20,000	20,000

J. Lecoure, Drawings	
125,000	125,000

Operating Expenses	
145,000	145,000

J. Lecoure, Capital	
125,000	70,000
	130,000

Other Revenue	
20,000	20,000

Income Summary	
?	?

Instructions

(a) Reconstruct, in general journal format, the closing entries that were journalized and posted to the above T accounts. (*Hint:* Notice that some of the amounts in the T accounts are repeated several times. Think about which ones are related to each other in terms of the closing entries.)

(b) Post the closing entries to the Income Summary account.

P4–2B   The following is Campus Cycle Shop's trial balance at January 31, 2008, the company's fiscal year end:

Prepare adjusting entries, adjusted trial balance, financial statements, and closing entries.
(SO 1, 4) AP

CAMPUS CYCLE SHOP
Trial Balance
January 31, 2008

	Debit	Credit
Cash	$ 8,200	
Accounts receivable	1,630	
Prepaid insurance	4,020	
Supplies	5,240	
Land	50,000	
Building	90,000	
Accumulated amortization—building		$ 11,000
Equipment	27,000	
Accumulated amortization—equipment		4,500
Accounts payable		4,000
Unearned revenue		1,950
Mortgage payable		102,000
K. Dude, capital		66,000
K. Dude, drawings	101,100	
Service revenue		231,065
Salaries expense	115,200	
Utilities expense	12,000	
Interest expense	6,125	
	$420,515	$420,515

Other data:

1. Service revenue earned but not recorded at January 31, 2008, was $1,550.
2. The 12-month insurance policy was purchased on April 1, 2007.
3. A physical count of supplies shows $670 on hand on January 31, 2008.

4. The building has an estimated useful life of 45 years. The equipment has an estimated useful life of 15 years.
5. Salaries of $1,325 are accrued and unpaid at January 31, 2008.
6. The mortgage payable has a 7% interest rate. Interest is paid on the first day of each month for the previous month's interest.
7. By January 31, 2008, $1,700 of the unearned revenue has been earned.
8. During the next fiscal year, $4,500 of the mortgage payable is to be paid.

Instructions

(a) Prepare the adjusting entries.
(b) Prepare an adjusted trial balance.
(c) Prepare an income statement, statement of owner's equity, and classified balance sheet. K. Dude invested $3,000 cash in the business on November 17, 2007.
(d) Prepare the closing entries.

Prepare financial statements, closing entries, and post-closing trial balance.
(SO 1, 4) AP

P4–3B The adjusted trial balance for Raisin Oatmeal Company is as follows:

RAISIN OATMEAL COMPANY
Adjusted Trial Balance
December 31, 2008

	Debit	Credit
Cash	$ 6,185	
Accounts receivable	13,500	
Prepaid insurance	3,500	
Supplies	1,140	
Land	46,800	
Building	187,580	
Accumulated amortization—building		$ 37,520
Equipment	26,000	
Accumulated amortization—equipment		5,600
Accounts payable		13,220
Salaries payable		3,000
Interest payable		350
Unearned revenue		2,190
Notes payable ($7,500 must be paid in 2009)		63,925
R. Ospina, capital		140,000
R. Ospina, drawings	59,200	
Service revenue		139,800
Advertising expense	2,400	
Amortization expense	10,300	
Utilities expense	2,175	
Interest expense	4,155	
Insurance expense	8,400	
Salaries expense	32,100	
Supplies expense	2,170	
	$405,605	$405,605

Instructions

(a) Prepare an income statement, statement of owner's equity, and classified balance sheet. The owner, Ricardo Ospina, invested $2,500 cash in the business during the year.
(b) Prepare the closing entries.
(c) Use T accounts post the closing entries and calculate the balance in each account. (Ignore the accounts not affected by the closing entries.).
(d) Prepare a post-closing trial balance.

P4–4B Bob Thebeau, CA, was hired by Campus DVD Repair to prepare its financial statements for April 2008. Using all the ledger balances in the owner's records, Thebeau put together the following trial balance: Analyze errors and prepare corrections.
(SO 3) AP

CAMPUS DVD REPAIR Trial Balance April 30, 2008		
	Debit	Credit
Cash	$ 4,960	
Accounts receivable	3,200	
Supplies	3,800	
Equipment	10,926	
Accumulated amortization—equipment		$ 2,925
Accounts payable		2,100
Salaries payable		500
Unearned revenue		590
S. Morris, capital		16,900
Service revenue		6,886
Salaries expense	6,000	
Advertising expense	400	
Miscellaneous expense	290	
Amortization expense	225	
Repair expense	100	
Totals	$29,901	$29,901

Thebeau reviewed the records and found the following errors:

1. Cash received from a customer on account was recorded as $690 instead of $580.
2. The purchase on account of a computer that cost $3,240 was recorded as a debit to supplies and a credit to accounts payable for $3,240.
3. The computer in error 2 was purchased February 1, 2008, and is expected to have a three-year useful life. Amortization for the month of April has not been recorded.
4. A payment of $145 for a miscellaneous expense was entered as a debit to Advertising Expense of $45 and a credit to Cash of $45.
5. The first salary payment made in April was for $1,900, which included $500 of salaries payable on March 31. The payment was recorded as a debit to Salaries Expense of $1,900 and a credit to Cash of $1,900. (No reversing entries were made on April 1.)
6. A cash payment for a repair expense on equipment of $126 was recorded as a debit to Equipment of $126 and a credit to Cash of $126.
7. The owner, Stuart Morris, paid himself $2,200 and recorded this as salary expense.
8. April rent of $950 was paid on April 26. The company has not recorded this transaction.

Instructions

(a) Prepare an analysis of each error that shows (1) the incorrect entry, (2) the correct entry, and (3) the correcting entry.
(b) Prepare a correct trial balance.

P4–5B The following accounting errors were made in the records of Mróz Company and were not found. If nothing is said about it, assume that the other side of each entry was correctly recorded and posted. Determine impact of errors on financial statements.
(SO 3) AP

1. A $500 debit to Rent Expense was debited to Rent Payable.
2. A $300 debit to Supplies was debited to Rent Expense.
3. A $450 credit to Cash was posted to the Cash account twice.
4. A debit to Utilities Expense of $91 was posted as a debit of $19.

5. A collection of $580 on account from a customer was debited to Service Revenue and credited to Accounts Receivable.
6. A $600 accrual of Interest Expense was posted as a debit to Interest Payable and a credit to Interest Expense.
7. A $250 debit to Accounts Receivable was not posted.
8. A $300 advance from a customer was credited to Service Revenue.

Instructions

(a) For each item, indicate the effect and amount of the error—understatement (U), overstatement (O), or no effect (NE)—on the income statement and balance sheet components. Use the following format, where the first one has been done for you as an example.

Item	Income Statement			Balance Sheet		
	Revenue	Expenses	Net Income	Assets	Liabilities	Owner's Equity
1.	NE	U $500	O $500	NE	U $500	O $500

(b) Determine the total amount of the understatement or overstatement that results from the errors.

Prepare financial statements and liquidity ratios.
(SO 4, 5) AP

P4–6B   Below is an alphabetical list of the adjusted accounts of Cormier Company at its year end, December 31, 2008. All accounts have normal balances.

Accounts payable	$ 6,000	Office equipment	$34,000
Accounts receivable	7,200	P. Cormier, capital	32,800
Accumulated amortization—		P. Cormier, drawings	10,000
office equipment	8,000	Patent	22,000
Amortization expense	8,000	Prepaid insurance	2,800
Cash	6,200	Rent expense	14,000
Insurance expense	5,000	Salaries expense	38,100
Interest expense	1,800	Salaries payable	3,500
Interest payable	800	Service revenue	92,000
Interest receivable	600	Short-term investments	4,500
Interest revenue	600	Supplies	2,000
Note payable	18,000	Unearned revenue	2,000
Note receivable	7,500		

Other data:

1. In 2009, $4,000 of the notes payable becomes due.
2. The note receivable is due in 2010.
3. On July 18, 2008, Pierre Cormier invested $3,200 cash in the business.

Instructions

(a) Prepare an income statement, statement of owner's equity, and classified balance sheet.
(b) On December 31, 2007, Cormier Company had current assets of $17,400 and current liabilities of $22,300. Calculate the company's working capital and current ratio on December 31, 2007, and December 31, 2008. Has the company's ability to pay its debts improved or weakened over the year?

Calculate working capital and current ratio, and comment on liquidity.
(SO 5) AN

P4–7B   Sleeman Breweries Ltd. is the largest craft brewer in Canada and the country's leading maker of premium beers. Its 2005 balance sheet showed current assets of $97,998 thousand and current liabilities of $71,887 thousand, including a bank overdraft (negative cash balance) of $9,744 thousand. The 2004 balance sheet reported current assets of $90,574 thousand and current liabilities of $60,823 thousand, including bank indebtedness of $9,634 thousand. The 2003 balance sheet reported current assets of $73,118 thousand and current liabilities of $55,512 thousand, including bank indebtedness of $555 thousand.

Instructions

(a) Calculate Sleeman's working capital and current ratio for each year.
(b) What do each of the measures calculated in (a) show? Comment on Sleeman's liquidity.

*P4–8B The unadjusted trial balance and adjustment data for Campus Cycle Shop are presented in P4–2B.

Prepare work sheet.
(SO 6) AP

Instructions

Prepare a work sheet for the year ended January 31, 2008.

*P4–9B Water World Park's year end is September 30. Selected data from the September 30 work sheet follow:

Prepare work sheet,
classified balance sheet,
adjusting and closing entries,
and post-closing trial balance.
(SO 1, 4, 6) AP

WATER WORLD PARK
Work Sheet (partial)
Year Ended September 30, 2008

	Trial Balance		Adjusted Trial Balance	
	Dr.	Cr.	Dr.	Cr.
Cash	$ 11,770		$ 11,770	
Accounts receivable	0		1,250	
Supplies	18,600		1,200	
Prepaid insurance	31,900		3,900	
Land	80,000		80,000	
Building	480,000		480,000	
Accumulated amortization—building		$120,000		$136,000
Equipment	120,000		120,000	
Accumulated amortization—equipment		44,000		52,000
Accounts payable		14,600		15,850
Wages payable		0		2,960
Interest payable		0		2,040
Unearned admission revenue		3,700		700
Mortgage payable		350,000		350,000
M. Berge, capital		159,700		159,700
M. Berge, drawings	14,000		14,000	
Admission revenue		250,070		253,070
Concession revenue		16,720		17,970
Wages expense	123,000		125,960	
Repairs expense	30,500		31,750	
Advertising expense	9,660		9,660	
Utilities expense	16,900		16,900	
Insurance expense	0		28,000	
Interest expense	22,460		24,500	
Amortization expense	0		24,000	
Supplies expense	0		17,400	
	$958,790	$958,790	$990,290	$990,290

Instructions

(a) Complete the work sheet, using the partial information provided above.
(b) Prepare a classified balance sheet. (*Note:* In the next fiscal year, $50,000 of the mortgage payable is due for payment.)
(c) Journalize the adjusting entries.
(d) Journalize the closing entries.
(e) Prepare a post-closing trial balance.

*P4–10B A work sheet for Steam Carpet Cleaners follows, with certain amounts replaced by letters:

Use work sheet relationships
to determine missing
amounts.
(SO 6) AN

STEAM CARPET CLEANERS
Work Sheet
Month Ended January 31, 2008

	Trial Balance Dr.	Trial Balance Cr.	Adjustments Dr.	Adjustments Cr.	Adjusted Trial Balance Dr.	Adjusted Trial Balance Cr.	Income Statement Dr.	Income Statement Cr.	Balance Sheet Dr.	Balance Sheet Cr.
Cash	(a)				1,200				1,200	
Accounts receivable	4,400		(e)		5,000				5,000	
Cleaning supplies	1,950			(i)	(m)				900	
Prepaid insurance	(b)			(j)	1,650				1,650	
Equipment	7,000				7,000				7,000	
Accumulated amortization		1,000		(k)		1,250				1,250
Accounts payable		1,200				1,200				(x)
Unearned service revenue		750	450			300				300
H. Kohl, capital		10,000				10,000				10,000
H. Kohl, drawings	(c)				900				900	
Service revenue		6,000		(l)		(q)		(u)		
Rent expense	200				200		200			
Salaries expense	(d)		(f)		(n)		2,000			
Totals	18,950	18,950								
Amortization expense			(g)		(o)		(s)			
Insurance expense			150		150		150			
Cleaning supplies expense			(h)		(p)		(t)			
Salaries payable				500		(r)				500
Totals			3,000	3,000	20,300	20,300	3,650	(v)	16,650	(y)
Net income							3,400			(z)
Totals							7,050	(w)	16,650	16,650

Instructions

Determine the amounts that should appear in the work sheet where there is currently a letter. (*Hint:* You will not be able to determine the missing items in alphabetical order.)

Prepare and post transaction entries, with and without reversing entries.
(SO 7) AP

P4–11B Farid Company had the following balances on its December 31, 2007, balance sheet:

Interest receivable	$1,500	Wages payable	$28,000
Prepaid insurance	5,000	Unearned service revenue	15,000

During 2008, the following transactions occurred:

1. On January 10, $85,000 was paid to employees for wages earned between December 11, 2007, and January 10, 2008.
2. On January 31, $2,000 cash was collected for interest on a note receivable for the period October 1, 2007, to January 31, 2008.
3. On May 1, the company's insurance policy expired and the company paid $15,000 for a one-year policy.
4. Services of $190,000 provided in 2008 included $175,000 of services for cash and $15,000 of services to customers who had made advance payments during 2007.

Instructions

(a) Assuming that the company does not use reversing entries:
    1. Prepare journal entries to record the transactions above for 2008.
    2. Post your entries to T accounts, and calculate the balance in each account.
(b) Assuming that Farid uses reversing entries:
    1. Prepare reversing entries as appropriate on January 1, 2008.
    2. Prepare journal entries to record the transactions above for 2008.
    3. Post your entries to T accounts and calculate the balance in each account.
(c) Compare the account balances in (a) to those in (b). Comment on the usefulness of reversing entries.

*P4–12B The unadjusted trial balance for Veda's Video Arcade at its fiscal year end of May 31, 2008, is as follows:

VEDA'S VIDEO ARCADE
Trial Balance
May 31, 2008

	Debit	Credit
Cash	$ 4,485	
Accounts receivable	0	
Supplies	2,810	
Equipment	128,000	
Accumulated amortization—equipment		$ 38,400
Wages payable		0
Interest payable		0
Note payable		60,000
Unearned game fee revenue		1,500
V. Gupta, capital		35,000
V. Gupta, drawings	22,500	
Game fee revenue		82,545
Rent expense	13,800	
Wages expense	42,600	
Supplies expense	0	
Amortization expense	0	
Interest expense	3,250	
	$217,445	$217,445

Other data:

1. On May 31, 2008, Veda's Video Games had earned but not collected or recorded $1,050 of game fee revenue. On June 19, it collected this amount plus an additional $770 for game fee revenue earned in June.
2. There was $950 of supplies on hand on May 31, 2008.
3. The equipment has an estimated useful life of 10 years.
4. Accrued salaries to May 31 were $910. The next payday is June 10 and the employees will be paid a total of $1,980 that day.
5. The note payable has a 6.5% annual interest rate. Interest is paid quarterly. Interest was last paid on March 31, 2008. The next payment is due on June 30, 2008.
6. On May 28, $950 of the unearned game fee revenue had been earned.

Instructions

(a) Prepare adjusting journal entries for the year ended May 31, 2008, as required.
(b) Prepare reversing entries where appropriate.
(c) Prepare journal entries to record the June 2008 cash transactions.
(d) Now assume reversing entries were not prepared as in (b) above. Prepare journal entries to record the June 2008 cash transactions.

Continuing Cookie Chronicle

(*Note*: This is a continuation of the Cookie Chronicle from Chapters 1 through 3.)

Natalie had a very busy December. At the end of the month, after Natalie has journalized and posted her December transactions and adjusting entries, her company has the following adjusted trial balance:

COOKIE CREATIONS
Adjusted Trial Balance
December 31, 2007

	Debit	Credit
Cash	$1,130	
Accounts receivable	875	
Baking supplies	350	
Prepaid insurance	1,210	
Baking equipment	1,300	
Accumulated amortization—baking equipment		$ 43
Accounts payable		75
Salaries payable		56
Unearned revenue		300
Interest payable		15
Note payable, 6%, principal and interest due November 16, 2009		2,000
N. Koebel, capital		900
N. Koebel, drawings	500	
Teaching revenue		4,315
Salaries expense	856	
Telephone expense	125	
Advertising supplies expense	165	
Baking supplies expense	1,025	
Amortization expense	43	
Insurance expense	110	
Interest expense	15	
	$7,704	$7,704

Instructions

Using the information in the adjusted trial balance, do the following:

(a) Prepare an income statement and a statement of owner's equity for the two months ended December 31, 2007, and a classified balance sheet as at December 31, 2007.
(b) Natalie has decided that her year end will be December 31, 2007. Prepare closing entries as at December 31, 2007.
(c) Prepare a post-closing trial balance.

Cumulative Coverage—Chapters 2 to 4

Lee Chan opened Lee's Window Washing on July 1, 2008. In July, the following transactions were completed:

July 1 Invested $14,000 cash in the business.
1 Purchased a used truck for $26,400, paying $6,400 cash and signing a note payable for the balance.
3 Purchased cleaning supplies for $850 on account.
5 Paid $1,800 on a one-year insurance policy, effective July 1.
12 Billed customers $3,800 for cleaning services.

July 18 Paid $400 of amount owed on cleaning supplies.
   20 Paid $1,600 for employee salaries.
   21 Collected $1,400 from customers billed on July 12.
   25 Billed customers $3,000 for cleaning services.
   31 Paid gas and oil for the month on the truck, $350.
   31 Withdrew $1,600 cash for personal use.

Instructions

(a) Journalize and post the July transactions.
(b) Prepare a trial balance at July 31.
(c) Journalize and post the following adjustments:
   1. Earned but unbilled fees at July 31 were $1,500.
   2. The truck has an estimated useful life of four years.
   3. One-twelfth of the insurance expired.
   4. An inventory count shows $375 of cleaning supplies on hand at July 31.
   5. Accrued but unpaid employee salaries were $400.
   6. The note payable has a 6% annual interest rate.
(d) Prepare an adjusted trial balance.
(e) Prepare the income statement and statement of owner's equity for July, and a classified balance sheet at July 31, 2008. Of the note payable, $5,000 must be paid by July 1, 2009.
(f) Journalize and post the closing entries, and complete the closing process.
(g) Prepare a post-closing trial balance at July 31.

BROADENING YOUR PERSPECTIVE

Financial Reporting and Analysis

Financial Reporting Problem

BYP4–1 The financial statements and accompanying notes of **The Forzani Group** are presented in Appendix A at the end of this book.

Instructions

(a) How is Forzani's balance sheet classified? What classifications does it use?
(b) How are Forzani's assets and liabilities ordered (e.g., in order of liquidity, permanency, etc.)?
(c) Forzani's working capital and current ratio for the fiscal year 2006 are calculated in the chapter. Calculate its working capital and current ratio for the fiscal year 2005. Compare them to the 2006 results and comment on the differences.

Interpreting Financial Statements

BYP4–2 The following information was reported by **The Gap, Inc.** in its 2005 annual report:

	2005	2004	2003	2002	2001
Total assets (in U.S. millions)	$10,048	$10,713	$10,283	$8,096	$7,387
Working capital (in U.S. millions)	$4,062	$4,156	$2,972	$1,018	$(153)
Current ratio	2.81:1	2.63:1	2.08:1	1.48:1	0.95:1

Instructions

(a) By what percentage did The Gap's total assets increase overall from 2001 to 2005? What was the average increase for each year?

(b) Comment on the change in The Gap's liquidity. Which measure seems to give a better indication of The Gap's liquidity: working capital or the current ratio? What could the reason be for the change in The Gap's liquidity during the period?

(c) Do you believe that The Gap's creditors should be concerned about its liquidity?

(d) If you were a creditor of The Gap and noted that it did not have enough current assets to cover its current liabilities in 2001, what additional information could you ask for to help you assess its liquidity?

Critical Thinking

Collaborative Learning Activity

Note to instructor: Additional instructions and material for this group activity can be found on the Instructor Resource Site.

BYP4–3   In this group activity, you will classify and define accounts.

Instructions

(a) Your instructor will divide the class into groups and provide each with an envelope filled with account names. As a group, place each account in the proper financial statement classification on the handout provided.

(b) Using the second handout provided, identify each account's normal balance and whether it is permanent or temporary.

(c) You may be asked by your instructor to write a short quiz on this topic.

**Study Aids:
Working in Groups**

Communication Activity

BYP4–4   Your best friend is thinking about opening a business. He has never studied accounting and has no idea about the steps that must be followed in order to produce financial statements for his business.

Instructions

Write a memo to your friend that lists and explains each of the steps in the accounting cycle in the order in which they should be completed. Include information on when each of these steps should be done and explain the purpose of the different types of journal entries and trial balances. Your memo should also discuss the optional steps in the accounting cycle.

**Study Aids:
Writing Handbook**

Ethics Case

BYP4–5   As the controller of Breathless Perfume Company, you discover a significant misstatement that overstated net income in the previous year's financial statements. The misleading financial statements are in the company's annual report, which was issued to banks and other creditors less than a month ago.

    After much thought about the consequences of telling the president, Eddy Lieman, about this misstatement, you gather your courage to inform him. Eddy says, "Hey! What they don't know won't hurt them. But, just so we set the record straight, we'll adjust this year's financial statements for last

**Study Aids:
Ethics in Accounting**

year's misstatement. We can absorb that misstatement better this year than last year anyway! Just don't make that kind of mistake again."

Instructions

(a) Who are the stakeholders in this situation?
(b) What are the ethical issues in this situation?
(c) As a controller, what would you do in this situation?

ANSWERS TO CHAPTER QUESTIONS

Across the Organization Insight, p. 169

Q: Why are CFOs interested in knowing how long it takes on average for companies to close their books?

A: There are two basic reasons: (1) the more time a company needs to close its books, the more it costs the company; and (2) accounting information must be timely to be useful.

Business Insight, p. 174

Q: Some of these errors happened several years ago. Why is it still important for Nortel to record entries to correct them?

A: Investors and creditors often use several years of a company's financial statements to determine if the company's performance is getting better or worse. If statements from previous years are incorrect, investors and creditors would not be able to make useful comparisons.

Answer to Forzani Review It Question 3, p. 181

Forzani's current assets include Cash, $19,266; Accounts Receivable, $68,927; Inventory, $278,002; and Prepaid Expenses, $2,647. Its current liabilities include Accounts Payable and Accrued Liabilities, $244,293; and the Current Portion of Long-Term Debt, $5,135. All amounts are listed in thousands. Forzani's current assets and current liabilities appear to be listed in order of liquidity, with the most current or liquid account listed first.

Answers to Self-Study Questions

1. b   2. c   3. a   4. d   5. c   6. b   7. a   8. c   *9. c   *10. d

 Remember to go back to the Navigator Box at the beginning of the chapter to check off your completed work.

concepts for review >>

Before studying this chapter, you should understand or, if necessary, review:

a. How to close revenue, expense, and drawings accounts. (Ch. 4, pp. 165–169)

b. The steps in the accounting cycle. (Ch. 4, p. 172)

c. How to prepare an income statement (Ch. 3, pp. 124–125)

d. How to prepare a classified balance sheet (Ch. 4, pp. 175-180)

Minding the Books on Campus

ST. JOHN'S, N.L.—Like campus bookstores across Canada, the bookstore at the College of the North Atlantic's Prince Philip Drive campus does most of its business in the fall term. In fact, 60 percent of the $1.1 million in projected sales for 2005–2006 were recorded in the first three weeks of September. But with four terms each year, the bookstore—the largest of the college's 17 campus bookstores—buys books year-round for the 3,000 students it serves.

As general manager Ed Pinto explains, the number of copies to be ordered for each title depends on the age of the book and the likelihood of used sales. "A few months before the start of a semester, we send a request to the Department Heads' Office for itemized enrolment," he says. "If a textbook is new, 100 percent of an order is processed. For books that are one to two years old or more, we cut the order based on past performance."

To keep track of the 650 items in its inventory—which include stationery and novelty items bearing the school's logo—the Prince Philip Drive Campus Bookstore uses a computerized perpetual inventory system running on Master Merchant point-of-sale software. With terminals in each of the college's 17 bookstores, the purchasing or procurement process is centralized, which keeps prices the same throughout the province. "All bookstore inventories can be viewed by other campus bookstores to allow for stock transfers between branches," explains Dean Batten, the Prince Philip Drive campus financial officer. This reduces the carrying costs of aging unused inventory and freight costs of ordering and returning stock to publishers.

A monthly valuation report gives itemized figures for quantities in stock, latest cost, average cost, total inventory

The College of the North Atlantic's Prince Philip Drive Campus Bookstore: www.cna.nl.ca

value, list price, and gross margin percentage. The bookstore finds it easier to use the average cost flow assumption to track inventory because of price fluctuations with its purchases. "If we have to reorder a title in the same semester, we do not change the price to students even if our cost has gone up," says Mr. Pinto.

To confirm that the report matches actual quantities on hand, the Prince Philip Drive bookstore, along with all bookstores provincially, does a physical count of the entire inventory each quarter—June 30, September 30, December 31, and March 31.

Sometimes there is more merchandise on hand than required. "We normally return any surplus books to the publisher for credit," says Mr. Pinto. "When that's not possible, we reduce the price to clear the inventory and document the markdown in our records."

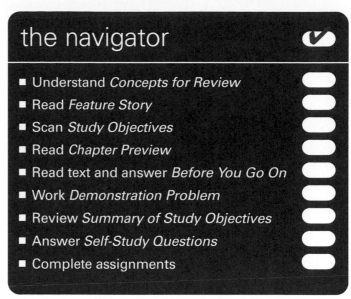

the navigator ☑

- Understand *Concepts for Review*
- Read *Feature Story*
- Scan *Study Objectives*
- Read *Chapter Preview*
- Read text and answer *Before You Go On*
- Work *Demonstration Problem*
- Review *Summary of Study Objectives*
- Answer *Self-Study Questions*
- Complete assignments

c h a p t e r   5

Accounting for Merchandising Operations

study objectives >>

☑ the navigator

After studying this chapter, you should be able to:

1. Describe the differences between service and merchandising companies.
2. Prepare entries for purchases under a perpetual inventory system.
3. Prepare entries for sales under a perpetual inventory system.
4. Perform the steps in the accounting cycle for a merchandising company.
5. Prepare multiple-step and single-step income statements.
6. Calculate the gross profit margin and profit margin.
7. Prepare the entries for purchases and sales under a periodic inventory system and calculate cost of goods sold (Appendix 5A).

The first four chapters of this text focused mostly on service companies, like the fictional Pioneer Advertising. Other examples of service companies include Air Canada, Canada Post, College Pro Painters, and Bank of Montreal. The Prince Phillip Drive Campus Bookstore, as indicated in the feature story, buys and sells goods instead of performing services to earn a profit. Merchandising companies that purchase and sell directly to consumers—such as the Prince Phillip Drive Campus Bookstore, Forzani, Canadian Tire, Mountain Equipment Co-op, and Toys "R" Us—are called retailers.

The steps in the accounting cycle for a merchandising company are the same as the steps for a service company. However, merchandising companies need additional accounts and entries in order to record merchandising transactions.

The chapter is organized as follows:

Merchandising Operations

study objective 1

Describe the differences between service and merchandising companies.

Measuring net income for a merchandising company is basically the same as for a service company. That is, net income (or loss) results when expenses are matched with revenues. In a merchandising company, the main source of revenues is the sale of merchandise. These revenues are called **sales revenue**, or simply sales. Unlike expenses for a service company, expenses for a merchandising company are divided into two categories: (1) cost of goods sold, and (2) operating expenses.

The **cost of goods sold** is the total cost of merchandise sold during the period. This expense is directly related to the revenue earned from the sale of the goods. Sales revenue less cost of goods sold is called **gross profit**. For example, when a pocket calculator that costs $15 is sold for $25, the gross profit is $10. Merchandisers report gross profit earned on sales in the income statement.

After gross profit is calculated, operating expenses are deducted to determine net income (or net loss). **Operating expenses** are expenses that are incurred in the process of earning sales revenue. The operating expenses of a merchandising company include many of the same expenses found in a service company, such as salaries, advertising, insurance, rent, and amortization.

The calculation of income for a merchandising company is shown in Illustration 5-1. The items in the two blue boxes are used only by a merchandising company. They are not used by a service company.

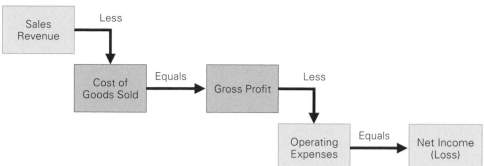

Illustration 5-1 ◀

Income measurement process for a merchandising company

Operating Cycles

A company's **operating cycle** is the average time it takes to go from cash to cash in producing revenues. The normal operating cycle of a merchandising company is longer than the cycle of a service company. The purchase of merchandise inventory and its eventual sale lengthen the cycle. The operating cycles of service and merchandising companies can be contrasted as shown in Illustration 5-2. Note that the added asset account for a merchandising company is an inventory account. It is usually titled Merchandise Inventory. Merchandise inventory is reported as a current asset on the balance sheet.

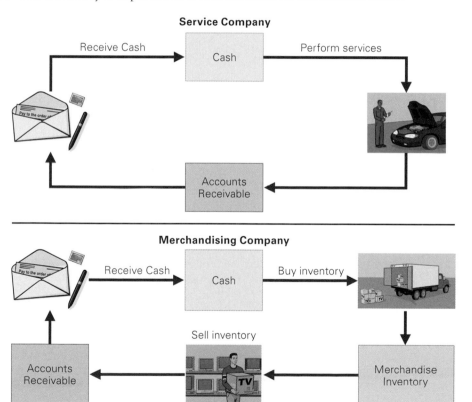

Inventory Systems

A merchandising company keeps track of its inventory to determine what is available for sale (inventory) and what has been sold (cost of goods sold). One of two systems is used to account for inventory and cost of goods sold: a perpetual inventory system or a periodic inventory system.

Perpetual Inventory System

In a **perpetual inventory system**, detailed records of each inventory purchase and sale are maintained. This system continuously—perpetually—shows the quantity and cost of the inventory purchased, sold, and on hand. The Prince Philip Drive Campus Bookstore in our feature story uses its perpetual inventory system to prepare monthly reports of items in stock and total inventory value. With the use of bar codes, optical scanners, and point-of-sale software, a store can keep a running record of every item that it buys and sells.

When inventory items are sold under a perpetual inventory system, the cost of the goods sold (the original purchase cost of the merchandise) is obtained from the inventory records. This cost is transferred from the Merchandise Inventory account (an asset) to the Cost of Goods Sold account (an expense). Under a perpetual inventory system, the cost of goods sold and reduction in inventory are recorded each time a sale occurs.

Inventory is usually the largest current asset for a merchandiser. Effective control over inventory is critical for success. A perpetual inventory system gives strong internal control over inventories. Since the inventory records show the quantities that should be on hand, the goods can be counted at any time to see whether the amount of goods actually on hand agrees with the inventory records. Any shortages that are uncovered can be investigated. In our feature story, the College of the North Atlantic's campus bookstores do a physical count of their entire inventory at the end of each quarter. The quantities in stock for each item in the inventory reports are then matched with the actual quantities on hand. For control purposes, a physical inventory count is always taken at least once a year under the perpetual inventory system. We will learn more about how to determine the quantity and cost of inventory later in this chapter and in the next chapter.

Another benefit of a perpetual inventory system is that it makes it possible to answer questions from customers about merchandise availability. Management can also maintain optimum inventory levels and avoid running out of stock. As discussed in the feature story, the College of the North Atlantic's campus bookstores use their perpetual inventory system to decide when to transfer inventory between campuses. This helps reduce the costs of aging inventory and the freight costs of ordering and returning stock to publishers.

 ACCOUNTING IN ACTION ▶ Business Insight

No question: Wal-Mart is the largest retailer in the world. And it achieved this status largely because of its inventory control with rarely a product out of stock. In 2004, Wal-Mart further improved on its perpetual inventory system with the introduction of electronic product codes (EPCs). EPCs help distinguish one box of a specific product from another, allowing retailers to better monitor their product inventory as it travels from supplier to distribution centre to store. Suppliers put EPC tags, which use radio frequency identification (RFID) technology -- on cases and pallets they ship to Wal-Mart. The tags are passed by a special RFID reader, which receives and transmits their unique product identifier codes to the inventory control system. RFID readers installed at distribution centres automatically let Wal-Mart's operations people, merchandising teams, and suppliers know that the shipment has arrived. The readers at stores automatically confirm the shipment is in the back room. Individual products are then stocked as needed.

Source: Kimmel et al. "Financial Accounting: Tools for Decision-Making," Wiley, p. 208.

> **?** How could RFID technology help Wal-Mart avoid being out of stock?

Periodic Inventory System

In a **periodic inventory system**, detailed inventory records of the goods on hand are not kept throughout the period. The cost of goods sold is determined only at the end of the accounting period—that is, periodically—when a physical inventory count is taken to determine the quantity and cost of the goods on hand.

In a periodic inventory system, after the cost of the goods on hand at the end of the period has been determined, the cost of the goods sold is then calculated as follows:

1. Start with the cost of goods on hand at the beginning of the accounting period (beginning inventory).
2. Add the cost of goods purchased.
3. Subtract the cost of goods on hand at the end of the accounting period (ending inventory).

Illustration 5-3 presents the formula to calculate cost of goods sold.

Illustration 5-3 ◄

Formula for cost of goods sold

This calculation is, in fact, also used in a perpetual inventory system. However, the cost of goods sold is calculated and recorded at the point of each sale in a perpetual inventory system, and totalled at the end of the accounting period. In a periodic inventory system, one calculation to find the total cost of goods sold for that period is instead done at the end of the accounting period.

Illustration 5-4 compares when each activity is done and the timing of the cost of goods sold calculation under the two inventory systems.

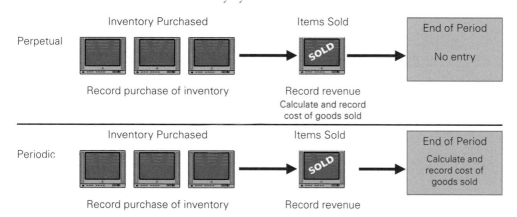

Illustration 5-4 ◄

Comparing perpetual and periodic inventory systems

How do companies decide which inventory system to use? They compare the cost of the detailed record keeping that is required for a perpetual inventory system to the benefits of having the additional information about, and control over, their inventory. Traditionally, only companies that sold merchandise with high unit values—such as automobiles or major home appliances—used the perpetual inventory system. However, over time computerized perpetual inventory software and electronic scanners have become much less expensive, to the point where many companies, selling nearly any product, are now using it.

Although using a perpetual inventory system is now less costly than in the past, there are still some companies that use a periodic inventory system. They can adequately control merchandise and manage day-to-day operations without perpetual inventory records. Periodically, they count their merchandise to determine quantities on hand and establish costs for accounting purposes.

Because the perpetual inventory system is widely used, we illustrate it in this chapter. The periodic system is described in Appendix 5A.

BEFORE YOU GO ON . . .

▶Review It

1. How is the measurement of net income in a merchandising company different from measuring net income in a service company?
2. What are the steps in the operating cycle of a merchandising company?
3. Describe the differences between a perpetual inventory system and a periodic inventory system.

Related exercise material: BE5–1.

Recording Purchases of Merchandise

study objective 2

Prepare entries for purchases under a perpetual inventory system.

Purchases of inventory may be made for cash or on account (on credit). The purchase is normally recorded by the buyer when the goods are received from the seller. Every purchase should be supported (proven) by business documents that give written evidence of the transaction. In larger companies, when an order is placed it is documented with a **purchase order**.

Cash purchases should be supported by a cash register receipt indicating the items purchased and the amount paid. Credit purchases should be supported by a **purchase invoice** showing the total purchase price and other relevant information. Note that the buyer does not prepare a separate purchase invoice. Instead, the copy of the sales invoice sent by the seller becomes the purchase invoice for the buyer. In Illustration 5-5, the sales invoice prepared by Highpoint Electronic serves as both a sales invoice for the seller (Highpoint Electronic) and a purchase invoice for the buyer (Chelsea Video).

Illustration 5-5 ▶

Sales/purchase invoice

INVOICE NO. 731

Highpoint Electronic
277 Wellington Street, West
Toronto, Ontario, M5V 3H2

SOLD TO

Firm name:	Chelsea Video	
Attention of:	James Hoover, Purchasing Agent	
Address:	21 King Street, West	
	Hamilton	Ontario	L8P 4W7
	City	Province	Postal Code

Date: May 4, 2008	Salesperson: Malone	Terms 2/10, n/30	FOB shipping point		
Catalogue No.	Description		Quantity	Price	Amount
X572Y9820	50″ Widescreen Plasma HDTV		1	2,300	$2,300
A2547Z45	High Definition Video Recorder Cable Box		5	300	1,500
IMPORTANT: ALL RETURNS MUST BE MADE WITHIN 10 DAYS			TOTAL		$3,800

The buyer, Chelsea Video, would make the following entry to record the purchase of merchandise from Highpoint Electronic:

May 4	Merchandise Inventory	3,800	
	Accounts Payable		3,800
	To record goods purchased on account per invoice #731, terms 2/10, n/30.		

A = L + OE
+3,800   +3,800
Cash flows: no effect

Under a perpetual inventory system, when merchandise is purchased for resale to customers, the current asset account Merchandise Inventory is debited for the cost of the goods. Only purchases of merchandise for resale are debited to Merchandise Inventory. Purchases of assets to use in the business—such as supplies, equipment, and similar items—should be debited to specific asset accounts rather than to Merchandise Inventory. For example, the College of the North Atlantic's Campus Bookstores would debit the supplies account for the supplies it purchases and uses to make shelf signs and labels. On the other hand, the stationery it purchases for resale to students would be debited to Merchandise Inventory.

Subsidiary Inventory Records

Imagine an organization like the College of the North Atlantic's bookstores recording purchases and sales of its 650 inventory items in only one general ledger account—Merchandise Inventory. It would be almost impossible to determine the balance remaining of any particular inventory item at any specific time.

Instead, a subsidiary ledger is used to organize and track individual inventory items. A **subsidiary ledger** is a group of accounts that share a common characteristic (for example, all inventory accounts). The subsidiary ledger frees the general ledger from the details of individual balances. In addition to having one for inventory, it is common to have subsidiary ledgers for accounts receivable (to track individual customer balances), accounts payable (to track individual creditor balances), and payroll (to track individual employee pay records).

A subsidiary ledger is an addition to, and an expansion of, the general ledger, as Illustration 5-6 shows.

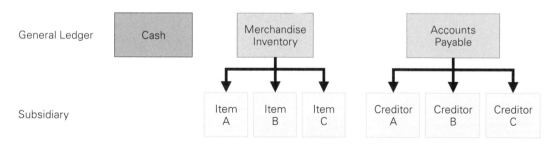

Illustration 5-6 ◀

Relationship of general ledger and subsidiary ledgers

The general ledger account that summarizes the subsidiary ledger data is called a **control account**. In this illustration, the general ledger accounts Merchandise Inventory and Accounts Payable are control accounts with subsidiary ledgers. Cash is not a control account because there is no subsidiary ledger for this account.

Purchases and sales of each item of merchandise are recorded and posted to the individual inventory subsidiary ledger account. At any point in time, the inventory subsidiary ledger shows detailed information about the quantity and cost of each inventory item.

The detailed individual data from the inventory subsidiary ledger are summarized in the Merchandise Inventory control account in the general ledger. At all times, the control account balance must equal the total of all the individual inventory account balances.

Additional information about how to record and balance subsidiary and control account transactions can be found in Appendix C at the end of this textbook.

Sales Taxes

Sales taxes include the federal Goods and Services Tax (GST), the Provincial Sales Tax (PST), and in the Atlantic Provinces, except for P.E.I., the Harmonized Sales Tax (HST), which is a combination of GST and PST. GST is paid by merchandising companies on the goods they purchase for resale. However, this cost is not part of the cost of the merchandise, because companies can get back any GST they pay on purchases by offsetting it against the GST they collect from customers.

PST is not paid by a merchandiser—it is paid only by the final consumer. Therefore, retail businesses do not have to pay PST on any merchandise purchased for resale.

As mentioned in Chapter 2, the accounting transactions described in this textbook are presented without the added complexity of sales taxes. That is why Invoice No. 731 shown in Illustration 5-5 did not include GST, which would normally be added to the invoice price. Sales taxes are discussed in more detail in Appendix B at the end of this textbook.

Freight Costs

Alternative terminology
Other common shipping terms include FCA (free carrier), CIF (cost, insurance, freight), and CPT (carriage paid to).

The sales/purchase invoice should indicate when ownership of the goods transfers from the seller to the buyer. The company that owns the goods while they are being transported to the buyer's place of business pays the transportation charges and is responsible for any damage to the merchandise during transit. The point where ownership is transferred is called the FOB point and may be expressed as either FOB shipping point or FOB destination. The letters FOB mean "free on board."

FOB shipping point means that the buyer accepts ownership when the goods are placed on the carrier by the seller, and the buyer pays the freight costs and is responsible for damages. Conversely, **FOB destination** means that the buyer accepts ownership when the goods are delivered to the buyer's place of business—thus the seller pays the freight and is responsible for damages. For example, the purchase invoice in Illustration 5-5 indicates that freight is FOB shipping point. The buyer (Chelsea Video) therefore pays the freight charges. Illustration 5-7 illustrates these shipping terms.

Illustration 5-7 ▶

Terms of shipping

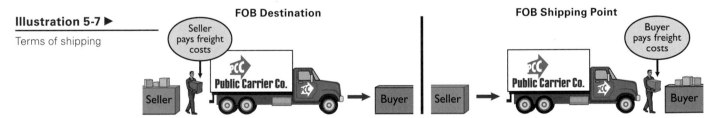

When the buyer pays for the freight costs, Merchandise Inventory is debited for the cost of the transportation. Why? Recall from Chapter 1 that the cost principle dictates that assets should be stated at their cost. Any freight paid by the buyer is part of the cost of the merchandise purchased. Freight costs paid by the College of the North Atlantic Campus Bookstore on its textbooks, for example, form part of the cost of these products.

To illustrate the buyer's journal entry to record the cost of shipping, assume that when the goods are delivered to Chelsea Video on May 4 Chelsea pays Public Carrier Co. $150 for freight charges. The entry on Chelsea Video's books is:

A	=	L	+	OE
+150				
−150				

↓ Cash flows: −150

May 4	Merchandise Inventory	150	
	Cash		150
	To record payment of freight on goods purchased.		

Purchase Returns and Allowances

A buyer may be dissatisfied with the merchandise purchased if the goods are damaged or defective, of inferior quality, or if the goods do not meet the buyer's specifications. In such cases, the buyer may return the goods to the seller. Alternatively, the buyer may choose to keep the merchandise if the seller is willing to grant an allowance (deduction) from the purchase price. The buyer calls these transactions **purchase returns** and **purchase allowances**, respectively. In both cases, the result is a decrease in the cost of the goods purchased.

The buyer will receive a cash refund from the seller if the purchase was made for cash. If the purchase was made on account, the seller will issue a **credit memorandum** (also called a credit memo) which allows the buyer to reduce its liability to the seller.

Assume that Chelsea Video returned goods costing $300 to Highpoint Electronic on May 9. The entry by Chelsea Video for the returned merchandise is as follows:

May 9	Accounts Payable	300	
	Merchandise Inventory		300
	To record return of goods to Highpoint Electronic.		

A	=	L	+	OE
−300		−300		

Cash flows: no effect

Chelsea Video increased Merchandise Inventory and Accounts Payable when the goods were originally purchased. So Chelsea Video decreases Merchandise Inventory and Accounts Payable when it returns the goods, or when it is granted an allowance. Merchandise Inventory is credited to show the reduction in the cost of the inventory. Accounts Payable is debited to show the reduction in the amount owed to Highpoint Electronic.

Discounts

The terms of a credit purchase may include an offer of a **quantity discount** for a bulk purchase. A quantity discount gives a reduction in price according to the volume of the purchase—in other words, the larger the number of items purchased, the better the discount. Quantity discounts are not recorded or accounted for separately. For example, Highpoint may offer a 10-percent price discount on orders of 25 or more items. Then, if 25 50" wide-screen plasma HDTVs were ordered, the price per HDTV would be $2,070 ($2,300 × 90%) rather than $2,300. Only the $2,070 amount would be recorded by Chelsea Video.

Quantity discounts are not the same as **purchase discounts**, which are offered to customers for early payment of the balance due. Purchase discounts are noted on the invoice by the use of credit terms that specify the amount and time period for the purchase discount. They also indicate the length of time the buyer has to pay the full invoice price. In the sales invoice in Illustration 5-5, credit terms are 2/10, n/30 (read "two ten, net thirty"). This means that a 2-percent cash discount may be taken on the invoice price (less any returns or allowances) if payment is made within 10 days of the invoice date (the discount period). Otherwise, the invoice price, less any returns or allowances, is due 30 days from the invoice date.

Not every seller offers purchase discounts, although they are common in certain industries. When the seller chooses not to offer a discount for early payment, credit terms will specify only the maximum time period for paying the balance due. For example, the time period may be stated as n/30 meaning that the net amount must be paid in 30 days.

In contrast to quantity discounts, purchase discounts are recorded separately. When an invoice is paid within the discount period, the Merchandise Inventory account will be reduced by the amount of the discount because inventory is recorded at cost. By paying within the discount period, a company reduces the cost of its inventory.

To illustrate, assume that Chelsea Video pays the balance owing to Highpoint Electronic of $3,500 (gross invoice price of $3,800 less purchase returns and allowances of $300) on May 14, the last day of the discount period. The discount is $70 ($3,500 × 2%), and the amount of cash paid by Chelsea Video to Highpoint Electronic is $3,430 ($3,500 − $70). Chelsea Video's entry to record its May 14 payment to Highpoint Electronic is:

May 14	Accounts Payable	3,500	
	Merchandise Inventory		70
	Cash		3,430
	To record payment of invoice #731 within discount period.		

It makes sense to take advantage of any available purchase discount. Not taking a discount is viewed as paying interest for use of the money not yet paid to the seller. For example, if Chelsea Video passed up the discount, it would have paid 2 percent for the use of $3,500 for 20 days. This equals an annual interest rate of 36.5 percent (2% × 365 ÷ 20). Obviously, it would be better for Chelsea Video to borrow at bank interest rates than to lose the purchase discount.

So that purchase discounts are not missed, unpaid invoices should be filed by due dates. This procedure helps the purchaser remember the discount date, prevents early payment of bills, and maximizes the time that cash can be used for other purposes.

If, contrary to best practices, Chelsea Video did not take advantage of the purchase discount and instead made full payment of $3,500 on June 3, the journal entry to record this payment would be:

June 3	Accounts Payable	3,500	
	Cash		3,500
	To record payment of invoice #731 with no discount taken.		

Summary of Purchase Transactions

The following T account (with transaction descriptions in parentheses) gives a summary of the effects of the transactions on Merchandise Inventory. Chelsea Video originally purchased $3,800 worth of inventory for resale. It paid $150 in freight charges. It then returned $300 worth of goods. And Chelsea Video received a discount of $70 by paying Highpoint Electronic in the discount period. This results in a balance in Merchandise Inventory of $3,580.

	Merchandise Inventory			
(Purchase) May 4	3,800	May 9	300	(Purchase return)
(Freight) 4	150	14	70	(Purchase discount)
Bal.	3,580			

BEFORE YOU GO ON . . .

▶ Review It

1. What do the terms "FOB shipping point" and "FOB destination" mean?
2. Under the perpetual inventory system, what entries are made to record purchases, freight costs, purchase returns and allowances, quantity discounts, and purchase discounts?
3. Why is the merchandise inventory account reduced if the company receives a purchase allowance or a purchase discount?

▶Do It

On September 4, New Idea Company buys merchandise on account from Junot Company for $1,500, terms 2/10, n/30, FOB shipping point. The correct company pays freight charges of $75 on September 5. On September 8, New Idea Company returns $200 of the merchandise to Junot Company. On September 14, New Idea Company pays the total amount owing. Record the transactions on New Idea Company's books.

Action Plan

- Purchases of goods for resale are recorded in the asset account Merchandise Inventory.
- Examine freight terms to determine which company pays the freight charges.
- Freight charges paid by the purchaser increase the cost of the merchandise inventory.
- The Merchandise Inventory account is reduced by the cost of merchandise returned.
- Calculate purchase discounts using the net amount owing.
- Reduce the Merchandise Inventory account by the amount of the purchase discount.

Solution

New Idea Company (buyer)

Sept. 4	Merchandise Inventory	1,500	
	Accounts Payable		1,500
	To record goods purchased on account.		
5	Merchandise Inventory	75	
	Cash		75
	To record freight paid on goods purchased.		
8	Accounts Payable	200	
	Merchandise Inventory		200
	To record return of goods.		
14	Accounts Payable ($1,500 − $200)	1,300	
	Merchandise Inventory ($1,300 × 2%)		26
	Cash ($1,300 − $26)		1,274
	To record cash payment within the discount period.		

Related exercise material: BE5–2, BE5–3, BE5–4, BE5–5, and E5–2.

the navigator

Recording Sales of Merchandise

study objective 3

Prepare entries for sales under a perpetual inventory system.

Sales revenue, like service revenue, is recorded when it is earned. This is in accordance with the revenue recognition principle. Typically, sales revenue is earned when the goods are transferred from the seller to the buyer. At this point, the sales transaction is completed and the sale price has been established.

Sales may be made on credit or for cash. Every sales transaction should be supported by a business document that gives written evidence of the sale. Cash register tapes provide evidence of cash sales. A sales invoice, like the one shown in Illustration 5-5, provides support for a credit or cash sale. The buyer and the seller both need a copy of the invoice.

Two entries are made for each sale in a perpetual inventory system. The first entry records the sales revenue: Cash (or Accounts Receivable, if it is a credit sale) is increased by a debit, and the revenue account Sales is increased by a credit for the selling (invoice) price of the goods. The second entry records the cost of the merchandise sold: the expense account Cost of Goods Sold is increased by a debit, and the asset account Merchandise Inventory is decreased by a credit for the cost of the goods. As a result, the Merchandise Inventory account will always show the amount of inventory that should be on hand.

To illustrate a credit sales transaction, we will use the sales invoice shown earlier in Illustration 5-5. Assuming that the merchandise cost Highpoint Electronic $2,400 when

Highpoint purchased the merchandise, Highpoint Electronic's $3,800 sale to Chelsea Video on May 4 is recorded as follows:

A = L + OE			
+3,800			+3,800

Cash flows: no effect

A = L + OE			
−2,400			−2,400

Cash flows: no effect

May 4	Accounts Receivable	3,800	
	Sales		3,800
	To record credit sale to Chelsea Video per invoice #731.		
4	Cost of Goods Sold	2,400	
	Merchandise Inventory		2,400
	To record cost of merchandise sold to Chelsea Video per invoice #731.		

For internal purposes, merchandisers may use more than one sales account, just as they use more than one inventory account. For example, Highpoint Electronic may keep separate sales accounts for its televisions, DVD players, home theatre systems, and camcorders. By using separate sales accounts for major product lines, company management can monitor sales trends more closely and respond more strategically to changes in sales patterns. For example, if home theatre system sales are increasing while DVD player sales are decreasing, the company can re-evaluate its advertising and pricing policies on each of these items.

However, on the income statement that it shows to outside investors, a merchandiser would normally give only a single sales figure—the sum of all of its individual sales accounts. This is done for two reasons. First, giving detail on individual sales accounts would add too much length to the income statement. Second, companies do not want their competitors to know the details of their operating results.

Sales Taxes

Sales taxes are collected by merchandising companies on the goods that they sell. When a company collects sales taxes from selling a good or service, these sales taxes are not recorded as revenue. The sales taxes are collected for the federal and provincial governments, and must be periodically given to these collecting authorities. Sales taxes that are collected from selling a good or service are recorded as a liability until they are paid to the governments. As stated earlier, accounting for sales taxes is complicated and is explained in Appendix B at the end of this textbook.

Freight Costs

As discussed earlier in the chapter, freight terms—FOB destination and FOB shipping point— on the sales invoice indicate when ownership is transferred, and they therefore indicate who is responsible for shipping costs. If the term is FOB destination, the seller is responsible for getting the goods to their intended destination. Freight costs paid by the seller on merchandise sold are an operating expense to the seller. These costs are debited to a Freight Out or Delivery Expense account. When the freight charges are paid by the seller, the seller will usually set a higher invoice price for the goods in order to cover the cost of shipping.

In Highpoint Electronic's sale of electronic equipment to Chelsea Video, the freight terms (FOB shipping point) indicate that the purchaser, Chelsea Video, must pay the cost of shipping the goods from Highpoint Electronic's location in Toronto to Chelsea Video's location in Hamilton. Highpoint Electronic, the seller, makes no journal entry to record the cost of shipping, since this is Chelsea's cost. If the freight terms had been FOB destination, Highpoint Electronic would have paid the freight costs and prepared a journal entry to record the cost as an expense, as described above.

Sales Returns and Allowances

As discussed earlier in the chapter, sometimes the buyer is unhappy with the merchandise purchased and will return the goods, or request a price reduction. When customers return goods, or are given price reductions, the seller refers to these transactions as **sales returns and allowances.** The seller will either return cash to the buyer, or reduce the buyer's account receivable if the goods were originally purchased on credit.

The seller will also need to reduce sales when a sales return or allowance is given to a customer. But it is important for management to know about the amount of sales returns and allowances. A large amount of returns and allowances suggests that there is inferior merchandise, inefficiencies in filling orders, errors in billing customers, and/or mistakes in the delivery or shipment of goods. Instead of debiting Sales, however, the seller debits a **contra revenue account** to Sales called Sales Returns and Allowances. By using a contra account, management can keep track of both the original sales and the amount of sales returns and allowances in the accounts. The normal balance of Sales Returns and Allowances is a debit.

Helpful hint Remember that the increases, decreases, and normal balances of contra accounts are the opposite of the accounts they correspond to.

To illustrate, recall that earlier in the chapter we assumed that on May 9 Chelsea Video returned $300 of the goods it had purchased on account from Highpoint Electronic. The seller, Highpoint Electronic, records the following entry:

May 9	Sales Returns and Allowances	300	
	Accounts Receivable		300
	To record credit granted to Chelsea Video for returned goods.		

A	=	L	+	OE
−300				−300

Cash flows: no effect

Note that if the sales return or allowance had been on a cash sale, a cash refund would normally be made and Cash would be credited instead of Accounts Receivable.

The seller will also need to record a second entry when goods are returned. If the merchandise is not damaged and can be sold again, the seller will need to record an entry to decrease or credit the Cost of Goods Sold account and increase or debit the Merchandise Inventory account by the original cost of the merchandise. If the goods are returned because they are damaged or defective and they can no longer be sold, the second entry still credits Cost of Goods Sold (since the goods have not been sold), but the debit is to a loss (expense) account, Loss from Damaged Goods, rather than to the asset account Merchandise Inventory. If the inventory can be repaired and resold, it is debited to Merchandise Inventory.

We will assume the goods returned to Highpoint Electronic were not damaged and can be sold again. We will also assume that they originally cost $140. Highpoint Electronic therefore records a second entry as follows:

May 9	Merchandise Inventory	140	
	Cost of Goods Sold		140
	To record cost of returned goods.		

A	=	L	+	OE
+140				+140

Cash flows: no effect

A second entry is not required when the seller gives the buyer an allowance. Since the goods have not been returned, the seller cannot increase its Merchandise Inventory and the original cost of goods sold recorded is still the correct amount. Giving a customer a sales allowance does not change the cost of the goods sold; it only changes the amount of revenue earned on the sale.

ACCOUNTING IN ACTION ▶ Across the Organization Insight

Returned goods can put a dent in a business' profits. When a customer returns a product, the business has to decide whether to scrap, liquidate, refurbish, return to vendor, or return to stock. Calgary-based Liquidation World has made a successful business out of offering businesses an opportunity to get some value out of unwanted products by liquidating them. The first retail outlet opened in 1986, and now Liquidation World is the largest liquidator in Canada, with more than 1,800 employees in outlets and offices across Canada and the United States. It's essentially a win-win situation for businesses and consumers: consumers get good value on a variety of quality goods, while manufacturers, wholesalers, and retailers have a place to dispose of unwanted merchandise.

? **What accounting information would help a manager decide what to do with returned goods?**

Discounts

Quantity discounts and sales discounts given on sales prices affect the seller, as well as the buyer. No separate entry is made to record a quantity discount. Sales are recorded at invoice price—whether it is the full retail price, a sale price, or a volume discount price.

A seller may offer the customer a cash discount for the early payment of the balance due. From the seller's point of view, this is called a **sales discount**. Like a purchase discount, a sales discount is based on the invoice price less returns and allowances, if any. Although no new account is added to record purchase discounts in a perpetual inventory system—the discount is recorded as a reduction in the Merchandise Inventory account—a new account called Sales Discounts is added to record sales discounts.

Sales Discounts is a contra revenue account, with a normal debit balance. This account is used, instead of debiting Sales, to show the amount of cash discounts taken by customers. To determine net sales, the balances in Sales Discounts and in Sales Returns and Allowances are both subtracted from the balance in Sales.

The entry by Highpoint Electronic to record the cash receipt from Chelsea Video on May 14 (within the discount period) is:

A   =   L   +   OE
+3,430   −70
−3,500

↑ Cash flows: +3,430

May 14	Cash	3,430	
	Sales Discounts	70	
	Accounts Receivable		3,500
	To record collection of invoice #731 within discount period.		

If the discount is not taken, Highpoint Electronic increases Cash and decreases Accounts Receivable by $3,500 at the date of collection.

Summary of Sales Transactions

The following T accounts summarize the effects of the previous transactions on Sales and its contra accounts. Highpoint Electronic sold merchandise for $3,800, with $300 of it later returned. A sales discount of $70 was given because the invoice was paid within the discount period. In contrast to the purchase transactions shown on page 230, which affected only one account, Merchandise Inventory, sales transactions are recorded in different accounts. In addition, cost of goods sold is also calculated and recorded at the time of each sale transaction in a perpetual inventory system.

Sales			Sales Returns and Allowances		
	May 4	3,800	May 9	300	

Sales Discounts			Cost of Goods Sold		
May 14	70		May 4	2,400	May 9	140
			Bal.	2,260	

BEFORE YOU GO ON . . .

▶**Review It**

1. Under a perpetual inventory system, what are the two entries that must be recorded at the time of each sale?
2. What journal entries (if any) are recorded by the seller when the shipping terms are FOB destination? FOB shipping point?
3. When goods are returned or payment is received within a discount payment period, why is it important to use the contra revenue accounts Sales Returns and Allowances and Sales Discounts, rather than simply reduce the Sales account?

▶**Do It**

On September 4, Junot Company sells merchandise for $1,500 on account to New Idea Company, terms 2/10, n/30, FOB shipping point. The original cost of the merchandise to Junot Company was $800. The correct company pays freight charges of $75 on September 5. On September 8, goods with a selling price of $200 and a cost of $80 are returned and restored to inventory. On September 14, Junot Company receives the correct payment from New Idea Company. Record the transaction on the books of Junot Company.

Action Plan

- Record both the sale and the cost of goods sold at the time of the sale.
- Freight costs are paid by the seller only when the freight terms are FOB destination.
- Record sales returns in the contra account Sales Returns and Allowances and reduce Cost of Goods Sold when merchandise is returned to inventory.
- Calculate sales discounts using the net amount owing.
- Record sales discounts in the contra account Sales Discounts.

Solution

Junot Company (seller)

Sept. 4	Accounts Receivable	1,500	
	Sales		1,500
	To record credit sale.		
4	Cost of Goods Sold	800	
	Merchandise Inventory		800
	To record cost of goods sold.		
8	Sales Returns and Allowances	200	
	Accounts Receivable		200
	To record credit given for receipt of returned goods.		
8	Merchandise Inventory	80	
	Cost of Goods Sold		80
	To record cost of goods returned.		
14	Cash ($1,300 − $26)	1,274	
	Sales Discounts ($1,300 × 2%)	26	
	Accounts Receivable ($1,500 − $200)		1,300
	To record cash receipt within the discount period.		

Related exercise material: **BE5–6, BE5–7, and E5–3.**

the navigator

Completing the Accounting Cycle

Up to this point, we have shown the basic entries for recording transactions for purchases and sales in a perpetual inventory system. Now, it is time to consider the remaining steps in the accounting cycle for a merchandising company. Each of the required steps described in Chapter 4 for a service company is also used for a merchandising company.

Adjusting Entries

A merchandising company generally has the same types of adjusting entries as a service company. But a merchandiser that uses a perpetual inventory system may need one additional adjustment to make the accounting inventory records the same as the actual inventory on hand.

In a perpetual inventory system, the Merchandise Inventory account balance should equal the cost of the merchandise on hand (ending inventory) at all times. As mentioned earlier in the chapter, a physical inventory count adds an important control feature to the perpetual inventory system. Even though the Merchandise Inventory account gives a record of the inventory on hand, it only indicates what *should* be there, not what actually is there. If inventory errors have occurred, or if inventory has been stolen or damaged, it is important that management be aware of this at an early stage so that preventive controls can be put in place.

Taking a physical inventory involves the following:

1. Counting the units on hand for each item of inventory.
2. Applying unit costs to the total units on hand for each item of inventory.
3. Totalling the costs for each item of inventory to determine the total cost of goods on hand.

If Highpoint Electronic's accounting records show an ending inventory balance of $40,500 at the end of May and a physical inventory count indicates only $40,000 on hand, the following adjusting journal entry should be prepared. The inventory shortage increases the Cost of Goods Sold account. Although this inventory has not been *sold*, inventory losses are part of the cost of the goods.

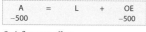

A	=	L	+	OE
−500				−500

Cash flows: no effect

May 31	Cost of Goods Sold	500	
	Merchandise Inventory		500
	To record difference between inventory records and physical units on hand.		

The non-existent inventory is removed from the Merchandise Inventory account so that the balance stays accurate and performance measures that are based on inventory are not distorted.

ACCOUNTING IN ACTION ▶ Ethics Insight

Inventory losses can be substantial. Shop theft is a big crime in Canada. Canadian retailers lose merchandise worth tens of millions of dollars every day to customer and employee theft, according to Retail Council of Canada (RCC). Store losses can range between 1 and 5 percent of a store's gross sales.

"The total losses suffered by Canadian retailers due to theft remain unacceptably high," commented Diane Brisebois, RCC's president and CEO. "As consumers, we all pay the price when customers and store employees steal. The good news is that more retailers are taking action." Many retailers have set up a loss-prevention department. They have also adopted procedures to stem their losses, including strong inventory management controls through computerized point-of-sale systems, better product return policies and practices, and sophisticated exception reports that expose unusual results that need to be examined more carefully.

? How can a computerized point-of-sale system help reduce inventory losses?

Closing Entries

Using assumed data, an adjusted trial balance follows for Highpoint Electronic at May 31, the company's year end. The accounts that are only used by a merchandising company are highlighted in red.

Illustration 5-8 ◄

Adjusted trial balance

HIGHPOINT ELECTRONIC Adjusted Trial Balance May 31, 2008	Debit	Credit
Cash	$ 9,500	
Accounts receivable	16,100	
Merchandise inventory	40,000	
Prepaid insurance	1,800	
Store equipment	80,000	
Accumulated amortization		$ 24,000
Accounts payable		20,400
Salaries payable		5,000
R. Lamb, capital		83,000
R. Lamb, drawings	15,000	
Sales		480,000
Sales returns and allowances	16,700	
Sales discounts	4,300	
Cost of goods sold	315,000	
Salaries expense	45,000	
Rent expense	19,000	
Utilities expense	17,000	
Advertising expense	16,000	
Amortization expense	8,000	
Freight out	7,000	
Insurance expense	2,000	
Totals	$612,400	$612,400

For a merchandising company, just as for a service company, all temporary accounts (revenues, expenses, and drawings) must be closed at the end of the year. In journalizing, the steps are as follows:

1. All temporary accounts with credit balances are debited for their individual balances. The total is credited to Income Summary. Note that Sales is a new account that must be closed to the Income Summary account.
2. All temporary accounts with debit balances are credited for their individual balances. The total is debited to Income Summary. Four new accounts are included in this entry: Sales Returns and Allowances, Sales Discounts, Cost of Goods Sold, and Freight Out.
3. The Income Summary account is closed to the owner's capital account. If there is net income, Income Summary would be debited and owner's capital credited. If there is a net loss, the reverse would happen.
4. Drawings, a temporary account with a debit balance, is credited separately to the owner's capital account.

These steps are shown in the closing entries on the following page:

A	=	L	+	OE
				−480,000
				+480,000

Cash flows: no effect

A	=	L	+	OE
				−450,000
				+16,700
				+4,300
				+315,000
				+45,000
				+19,000
				+17,000
				+16,000
				+8,000
				+7,000
				+2,000

Cash flows: no effect

A	=	L	+	OE
				−30,000
				+30,000

Cash flows: no effect

A	=	L	+	OE
				−15,000
				+15,000

Cash flows: no effect

Date	Account	Debit	Credit
May 31	Sales	480,000	
	Income Summary		480,000
	To close income statement accounts with credit balances.		
31	Income Summary	450,000	
	Sales Returns and Allowances		16,700
	Sales Discounts		4,300
	Cost of Goods Sold		315,000
	Salaries Expense		45,000
	Rent Expense		19,000
	Utilities Expense		17,000
	Advertising Expense		16,000
	Amortization Expense		8,000
	Freight Out		7,000
	Insurance Expense		2,000
	To close income statement accounts with debit balances.		
31	Income Summary	30,000	
	R. Lamb, Capital		30,000
	To close income summary to capital.		
31	R. Lamb, Capital	15,000	
	R. Lamb, Drawings		15,000
	To close drawings to capital.		

After the closing entries are posted, all temporary accounts have zero balances. In addition, the R. Lamb, Capital account should have an ending balance of $98,000 (beginning balance of $83,000 + net income of $30,000 − drawings of $15,000), which is the same as what is reported on the statement of owner's equity and balance sheet.

Post-Closing Trial Balance

After the closing entries are posted, a post-closing trial balance should be prepared. You will recall that the purpose of this trial balance is to ensure that debits equal credits in the permanent (balance sheet) accounts after all temporary accounts have been closed. The only new account in the post-closing trial balance is the current asset account Merchandise Inventory.

The post-closing trial balance is prepared in the same way as described in Chapter 4 and is not shown again here.

Summary of Merchandising Entries

A summary of the entries for the merchandising accounts using a perpetual inventory system follows:

	Transactions	Recurring Journal Entries	Debit	Credit
Sales	Selling merchandise to customers.	Cash or Accounts Receivable Sales	XX	 XX
		Cost of Goods Sold Merchandise Inventory	XX	 XX
	Giving sales returns or allowances to customers.	Sales Returns and Allowances Cash or Accounts Receivable	XX	 XX
		Merchandise Inventory Cost of Goods Sold	XX	 XX
	Paying freight costs on sales, FOB destination.	Freight Out Cash	XX	 XX
	Receiving payment on account from customers within discount period.	Cash Sales Discounts Accounts Receivable	XX XX	 XX
	Receiving payment on account from customers after discount period.	Cash Accounts Receivable	XX	 XX
Purchases	Purchasing merchandise for resale.	Merchandise Inventory Cash or Accounts Payable	XX	 XX
	Paying freight costs on merchandise purchased, FOB shipping point.	Merchandise Inventory Cash	XX	 XX
	Receiving purchase returns or allowances from suppliers.	Cash or Accounts Payable Merchandise Inventory	XX	 XX

	Paying creditors on account within discount period.	Accounts Payable
		   Merchandise Inventory
		   Cash
			XX	
				XX
				XX

	Paying creditors on account after the discount period.	Accounts Payable Cash	XX	 XX

	Transactions	Recurring Journal Entries	Debit	Credit
Adjusting Entries	Determining, after a physical count, that inventory in general ledger is higher than inventory actually on hand.	Cost of Goods Sold Merchandise Inventory	XX	 XX
Closing Entries	Closing temporary accounts with credit balances.	Sales Income Summary	XX	 XX

	Closing temporary accounts with debit balances (drawings closed separately).	Income Summary
		   Sales Returns and Allowances
		   Sales Discounts
		   Cost of Goods Sold
		   Freight Out
		   Other expenses
			XX	
				XX
				XX
				XX
				XX
				XX

	Closing Income Summary account (assuming net income).	Income Summary Capital	XX	 XX
	Closing drawings account.	Capital Drawings	XX	 XX

BEFORE YOU GO ON . . .

▶Review It

1. Why is an adjustment to the Merchandise Inventory account sometimes necessary?
2. How are closing entries for a merchandising company different from closing entries for a service company?
3. What merchandising account(s) will appear in the post-closing trial balance?

▶Do It

The trial balance of Yee Clothing Company at December 31 shows Merchandise Inventory $25,000; J. Yee, Capital $12,000; Sales $162,400; Sales Returns and Allowances $4,800; Sales Discounts $950; Cost of Goods Sold $110,000; Rental Revenue $6,000; Freight Out $1,800; Rent Expense $8,800; Salaries Expense $22,000; and J. Yee, Drawings $3,600. Yee Clothing Company's statement of owner's equity for the year showed net income of $20,050 and closing owner's capital of $28,450. Prepare the closing entries for the above accounts. Create T accounts for Income Summary and J. Yee, Capital, and post the closing entries to these accounts.

Action Plan

- Debit each temporary account with a credit balance and credit the total to the Income Summary account.
- Credit each temporary account with a debit balance and debit the total to the Income Summary account.
- Stop and check your work: Does the balance in the Income Summary account equal the reported net income?
- Debit the balance in the Income Summary account and credit the amount to the owner's capital account. (Do the opposite if the company had a net loss.)
- Credit the balance in the drawings account and debit the amount to the owner's capital account. Do not close drawings with the expenses.
- Stop and check your work: Does the balance in the owner's capital account equal the ending balance reported in the statement of owner's equity?

Solution

Dec. 31	Sales	162,400	
	Rental Revenue	6,000	
	Income Summary		168,400
	To close income statement accounts with credit balances.		
31	Income Summary	148,350	
	Sales Returns and Allowances		4,800
	Sales Discounts		950
	Cost of Goods Sold		110,000
	Freight Out		1,800
	Rent Expense		8,800
	Salaries Expense		22,000
	To close income statement accounts with debit balances.		
31	Income Summary	20,050	
	J. Yee, Capital		20,050
	To close Income Summary account.		
31	J. Yee, Capital	3,600	
	J. Yee, Drawings		3,600
	To close drawings account.		

Income Summary				J. Yee, Capital			
Clos.	148,350	Clos.	168,400			Bal.	12,000
Clos.	20,050	Bal.	20,050 *	Clos.	3,600	Clos.	20,050
		Bal.	0			Bal.	28,450 **

* Check = Net Income   ** Check = Closing Owner's capital

the navigator

Related exercise material: BE5–8, BE5–9, E5–4, and E5–5.

Merchandising Financial Statements

Merchandisers use the classified balance sheet introduced in Chapter 4. In addition, two forms of income statements are widely used by merchandising companies. One is the **multiple-step income statement**, which gets its name because it shows multiple steps in determining net income. A second form is the **single-step income statement**—called this because only one step, subtracting total expenses from total revenues, is required to calculate net income. We will look at each of these statement forms in the following sections.

study objective 5

Prepare multiple-step and single-step income statements.

Multiple-Step Income Statement

The **multiple-step income statement** shows several steps in determining net income (or net loss). This form is often considered more useful than a single-step income statement because the steps give additional information about a company's profitability.

The multiple-step income statement shows five main steps:

1. Net Sales: Sales returns and allowances and sales discounts are subtracted from sales to calculate net sales.
2. Gross Profit: Cost of goods sold is subtracted from net sales to calculate gross profit.
3. Income from Operations: Operating expenses are deducted from gross profit to calculate income from operations.
4. Non-Operating Activities: The results of activities that are not related to operations are added (as other revenue) or subtracted (as other expenses) to calculate total non-operating activities.
5. Net Income: Total non-operating activities are added to, or subtracted from, income from operations to calculate net income.

The first three steps involve the company's main operating activities. The last two steps are only needed if a company has non-operating activities. These steps give information about the difference between a company's results from operating activities and its overall profitability.

Net Sales

The multiple-step income statement for a merchandising company begins by presenting sales revenues. The contra revenue accounts Sales Returns and Allowances and Sales Discounts are deducted from Sales in the income statement to arrive at **net sales**. The sales revenue section for Highpoint Electronic (using data from the adjusted trial balance in Illustration 5-8) is as follows:

Sales revenue		
Sales		$480,000
Less: Sales returns and allowances	$16,700	
Sales discounts	4,300	21,000
Net sales		459,000

This presentation shows the key aspects of the company's main revenue-producing activities. Many companies condense this information and report only the net sales figure in their income statement.

Gross Profit

From Illustration 5-1, you learned that cost of goods sold is deducted from sales revenue to determine **gross profit**. Based on the sales data above and a cost of goods sold of $315,000, the gross profit for Highpoint Electronic is $144,000, calculated as follows:

Net sales	$459,000
Cost of goods sold	315,000
Gross profit	144,000

Income from Operations

Operating expenses are the next component in measuring net income for a merchandising company. As indicated earlier, these expenses are similar in merchandising and service companies. At Highpoint Electronic, operating expenses total $114,000 (from Illustration 5-8, $45,000 + $19,000 + $17,000 + $16,000 + $8,000 + $7,000 + $2,000). **Income from operations**, or the results of the company's normal operating activities, is determined by subtracting operating expenses from gross profit:

Gross profit	$144,000
Operating expenses	114,000
Income from operations	$ 30,000

Sometimes operating expenses are subdivided into selling expenses and administrative expenses. **Selling expenses** are associated with making sales. They include expenses for sales promotion, as well as the expenses of completing the sale (e.g., freight costs). **Administrative expenses** relate to general operating activities such as management, accounting, and legal costs.

Non-Operating Activities

Non-operating activities consist of other revenues and expenses that are unrelated to the company's main operations. When a company has non-operating activities, they are shown in the income statement after "income from operations." It is important to distinguish between operating and non-operating activities because income from operations is viewed as normal or long-term, but non-operating activities are viewed as non-recurring or short-term. Interest expense is considered an non-operating expense because it is incurred as a result of a decision to borrow. The decision to either borrow cash or have the owner invest more cash in the business is a financing decision, not an operating decision.

The results of non-operating activities are often shown in two sections: **other revenues** and **other expenses**. Examples of each are shown in Illustration 5-9.

Non-Operating Activities	
Other Revenues	Other Expenses
Interest from notes receivable and short-term investments	Interest expense on notes and loans payable
Dividend revenue from equity investments	Casualty losses from vandalism and accidents
Rent revenue from subleasing a portion of the store	Losses from the sale of property, plant, and equipment
Gains from the sale of property, plant, and equipment	Losses from strikes by employees and suppliers

In the non-operating activities sections, items are generally reported at their net amount. For example, if a company received a $2,500 insurance settlement on vandalism losses of $2,700, only the $200 loss is reported. Note, too, that the results of the two non-operating sections are netted to show the total income or loss from non-operating activities. It is also common for companies to combine these two non-operating sections into a single "Other Revenues and Expenses" section.

Illustration 5-9 ▲

Items reported in non-operating sections

If there are no non-operating activities, the company's income from operations becomes its net income—or "bottom line." Highpoint Electronic had no activities other than those from main operations. However, most companies have some non-operating activities.

To show an example of non-operating activities in a multiple-step income statement, we have assumed the following data for Highpoint Electronic:

Other revenues	
Interest revenue	$3,000
Gain on sale of equipment	600
Total non-operating revenues	3,600
Other expenses	
Interest expense	$1,800
Casualty loss from vandalism	200
Total non-operating expenses	2,000
Net non-operating revenues	1,600

Net Income

Net income is the final outcome of all the company's operating and non-operating activities. Highpoint's net income is $31,600 after adding its assumed net non-operating revenue of $1,600 to income from operations as follows:

Income from operations	$30,000
Net non-operating revenues	1,600
Net income	$31,600

In Illustration 5-10 on the following page, we bring together all the above steps in a comprehensive multiple-step income statement for Highpoint Electronic.

Illustration 5-10 ▶

Multiple-step income
statement

HIGHPOINT ELECTRONIC
Income Statement
Year Ended May 31, 2008

Calculation of net sales and gross profit	Sales revenue		
	Sales		$480,000
	Less: Sales returns and allowances	$16,700	
	Sales discounts	4,300	21,000
	Net sales		459,000
	Cost of goods sold		315,000
	Gross profit		144,000
Calculation of income from operations	Operating expenses		
	Salaries expense	$45,000	
	Rent expense	19,000	
	Utilities expense	17,000	
	Advertising expense	16,000	
	Amortization expense	8,000	
	Freight out	7,000	
	Insurance expense	2,000	
	Total operating expenses		114,000
	Income from operations		30,000
Calculation of non-operating activities and net income	Other revenues		
	Interest revenue	$ 3,000	
	Gain on sale of equipment	600	
	Total non-operating revenues	3,600	
	Other expenses		
	Interest expense	$ 1,800	
	Casualty loss from vandalism	200	
	Total non-operating expenses	2,000	
	Net non-operating revenues		1,600
	Net income		$ 31,600

Single-Step Income Statement

In a **single-step income statement**, all data are classified under two categories: (1) revenues, and (2) expenses. The **revenues** category includes both operating revenues and other revenues. The **expenses** category includes cost of goods sold, operating expenses, and other expenses. No distinction is made between operating and non-operating items. In addition, the contra revenue accounts Sales Returns and Allowances and Sales Discounts are never shown separately from gross sales. A single-step income statement only shows net sales.

The single-step income statement is the form we have used in the text so far. There are two main reasons for using the single-step form: (1) a company does not realize any type of profit or income until total revenues exceed total expenses, so it makes sense to divide the statement into these two categories; and (2) the single-step form is simple and easy to read.

A single-step income statement for Highpoint Electronic, using the same assumed data, is shown in Illustration 5-11. Note that the net income amounts in Illustrations 5-10 (multiple-step) and 5-11 (single-step) are the same. The only differences between the two forms of income statements are the amount of detail shown and the order of presentation.

Illustration 5-11 ◄

Single-step income statement

HIGHPOINT ELECTRONIC
Income Statement
Year Ended May 31, 2008

Revenues		
Net sales		$459,000
Interest revenue		3,000
Gain on sale of equipment		600
Total revenues		462,600
Expenses		
Cost of goods sold	$315,000	
Operating expenses	114,000	
Interest expense	1,800	
Casualty loss from vandalism	200	
Total expenses		431,000
Net income		$ 31,600

Classified Balance Sheet

In the balance sheet, merchandise inventory is reported as a current asset immediately following accounts receivable. Recall from Chapter 4 that items are listed under current assets in their order of liquidity. Merchandise inventory is less liquid than accounts receivable because the goods must first be sold before revenue can be collected from the customer. Illustration 5-12 presents the assets section of a classified balance sheet for Highpoint Electronic.

Illustration 5-12 ◄

Assets section of a classified balance sheet

Helpful hint The $40,000 is the cost of the inventory on hand, not its expected selling price.

HIGHPOINT ELECTRONIC
Balance Sheet (partial)
May 31, 2008

Assets		
Current assets		
Cash		$ 9,500
Accounts receivable		16,100
Merchandise inventory		40,000
Prepaid insurance		1,800
Total current assets		67,400
Property, plant, and equipment		
Store equipment	$80,000	
Less: Accumulated amortization	24,000	56,000
Total assets		$123,400

The remaining two financial statements, the statement of owner's equity and cash flow statement (to be discussed in Chapter 17), are the same as those of a service company. They are not shown in this chapter.

BEFORE YOU GO ON . . .

►Review It

1. How is a multiple-step income statement different from a single-step income statement?
2. What are non-operating activities and how are they reported in a single-step income statement and in a multiple-step income statement?

▶Do It

Silver Store reported the following information: Sales $620,000; Sales Returns and Allowances $32,000; Sales Discounts $10,200; Cost of Goods Sold $422,000; Rent Expense $15,000; Salaries Expense $80,000; Insurance Expense $5,000; Amortization Expense $10,000; and Interest Expense $1,700. Calculate the following amounts: (a) net sales, (b) gross profit, (c) total operating expenses, (d) income from operations, and (e) net income.

Action Plan

- Deduct Sales Returns and Allowances and Sales Discounts from Sales to arrive at net sales.
- Deduct Cost of Goods Sold from net sales to arrive at gross profit.
- Identify which expenses are operating expenses and which are non-operating expenses.
- Deduct operating expenses from gross profit to arrive at income from operations.
- Deduct any non-operating expenses from (and add any non-operating revenues to) income from operations to arrive at net income.

Solution

(a) Net sales: $620,000 − $32,000 − $10,200 = $577,800
(b) Gross profit: $577,800 − $422,000 = $155,800
(c) Total operating expenses: $15,000 + $80,000 + $5,000 + $10,000 = $110,000
(d) Income from operations: $155,800 − $110,000 = $45,800
(e) Net income: $45,800 − $1,700 = $44,100

the navigator

Related exercise material: BE5–10, BE5–11, E5–6, E5–7, and E5–8.

Using the Information in the Financial Statements

study objective 6

Calculate the gross profit margin and profit margin.

In Chapter 4, we introduced a tool called ratio analysis that investors and creditors use to determine additional information about how a company is performing. In this chapter we introduce two profitability ratios. **Profitability ratios measure a company's income or operating success for a specific period of time.** Inventory has a significant effect on a company's profitability because cost of goods sold is usually the largest expense on the income statement. The two ratios we will examine are the gross profit margin and profit margin. Both help evaluate a company's profitability.

Gross Profit Margin

A company's gross profit may be expressed as a percentage, called the **gross profit margin**. This is done by dividing the amount of gross profit by net sales. For Highpoint Electronic, the gross profit margin is 31.4 percent, as calculated in Illustration 5-13.

Illustration 5-13 ▶

Gross profit margin

Gross Profit	÷	Net Sales	=	Gross Profit Margin
$144,000	÷	$459,000	=	31.4%

The gross profit margin is generally considered to be more useful than the gross profit amount. The margin expresses a more meaningful (relative) relationship between net sales and gross profit. For example, a gross profit amount of $1 million may sound impressive. But, if it is the result of a gross profit margin of only 7 percent, it is not so impressive.

Gross profit represents the merchandising profit of a company. It is not a measure of the overall profitability, because operating expenses have not been deducted. The amount and trend of gross profit are closely watched by management and other interested parties. They compare current gross profit to amounts reported in past periods. They also compare the company's gross profit margin to the margin of competitors and to industry averages. Such comparisons give information about the effectiveness of a company's purchasing and the soundness of its pricing policies. In general, a higher gross profit margin is seen as being more favourable than a lower gross profit margin.

Profit Margin

Net income is often expressed as a percentage of sales, similar to the gross profit margin. The **profit margin** measures the percentage of each dollar of sales that results in net income. It is calculated by dividing net income by net sales. Highpoint Electronic's profit margin of 6.9 percent is calculated in Illustration 5-14.

Net Income	÷	Net Sales	=	Profit Margin
$31,600	÷	$459,000	=	6.9%

Illustration 5-14 ◀

Profit margin

How do the gross profit margin and profit margin differ? The gross profit margin measures how much more the selling price is than the cost of goods sold. The profit margin measures by how much the selling price covers all expenses (including the cost of goods sold). A company can improve its profit margin by increasing its gross profit margin, or by controlling its operating expenses (and non-operating activities), or by doing both.

BEFORE YOU GO ON . . .

▶Review It

1. Explain the difference between the gross profit margin and profit margin.
2. Calculate The Forzani Group Ltd.'s gross profit margin and profit margin for fiscal 2006 and 2005. Indicate whether these ratios improved or weakened in 2006. The answers to these questions are at the end of the chapter.

Related exercise material: BE5–12, E5–1, and E5–9.

the navigator

APPENDIX 5A ▶ PERIODIC INVENTORY SYSTEM

As described in this chapter, there are two basic systems of accounting for inventories: (1) the perpetual inventory system, and (2) the periodic inventory system. In the chapter, we focused on the characteristics of the perpetual inventory system. In this appendix, we discuss and illustrate the periodic inventory system.

One key difference between the two inventory systems is when the cost of goods sold is calculated. In a periodic inventory system, revenues from the sale of merchandise are recorded when sales are made, in the same way as in a perpetual inventory system, but on the date of sale the cost of the merchandise sold is not recorded. Instead, the cost of goods sold during the period is calculated by taking a physical inventory count at the end of the period, and deducting the cost of this inventory from the cost of the merchandise available for sale during the period.

There are other differences between the perpetual and periodic inventory systems. Under a periodic inventory system, purchases of merchandise are recorded in the Purchases expense

study objective 7

Prepare the entries for purchases and sales under a periodic inventory system and calculate cost of goods sold.

account, rather than the Merchandise Inventory asset account. Also, under a periodic system, it is customary to record purchase returns and allowances, purchase discounts, and freight in separate accounts. That way, accumulated amounts are known for each.

To illustrate the recording of merchandise transactions under a periodic inventory system, we will use the purchase and sale transactions between Highpoint Electronic (the seller) and Chelsea Video (the buyer) from earlier in this chapter.

Recording Purchases of Merchandise

Based on the sales invoice (Illustration 5-5) and receipt of the merchandise ordered from Highpoint Electronic, Chelsea Video records the $3,800 purchase as follows:

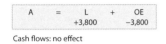

A = L + OE
+3,800 −3,800
Cash flows: no effect

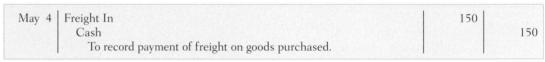

May 4	Purchases	3,800	
	Accounts Payable		3,800
	To record goods purchased on account per invoice #731, terms 2/10, n/30.		

Purchases is a temporary expense account reported on the income statement. Its normal balance is a debit.

Freight Costs

When the buyer pays for the freight costs, the account Freight In is debited. For example, when the goods are delivered, Chelsea pays Public Carrier Co. $150 for freight charges on its purchase from Highpoint Electronic. The entry on Chelsea's books is as follows:

A = L + OE
−150 −150
⬇ Cash flows: −150

May 4	Freight In	150	
	Cash		150
	To record payment of freight on goods purchased.		

Like Purchases, Freight In is a temporary expense account whose normal balance is a debit. Just as freight was a part of the cost of the merchandise inventory in a perpetual inventory system, freight in is part of the cost of goods purchased in a periodic inventory system. Freight in is added to net purchases to determine the cost of goods purchased. In accordance with the cost principle, the cost of goods purchased should include any freight charges for bringing the goods to the buyer.

Purchase Returns and Allowances

Chelsea Video returns $300 worth of goods. The following entry recognizes the purchase return:

A = L + OE
−300 +300
Cash flows: no effect

May 9	Accounts Payable	300	
	Purchase Returns and Allowances		300
	To record return of goods to Highpoint Electronic.		

Purchase Returns and Allowances is a temporary account whose normal balance is a credit. It is a contra account whose balance is deducted from the balance in Purchases.

Purchase Discounts

Recall the invoice terms were 2/10, n/30. If Chelsea Video pays the balance owing to Highpoint Electronic of $3,500 (gross invoice price of $3,800 less purchase returns and allowances

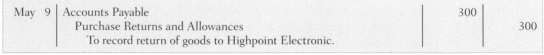
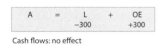

of $300) on May 14, Chelsea will be able to reduce the amount paid by 2 percent of $3,500. Chelsea Video would record the following entry on May 14:

May 14	Accounts Payable	3,500	
	Purchase Discounts ($3,500 × 2%)		70
	Cash ($3,500 − $70)		3,430
	To record payment of invoice #731 within discount period.		

Purchase Discounts is a temporary account whose normal balance is a credit. Like Purchase Returns and Allowances, it is a contra expense account subtracted from the Purchases account to calculate net purchases. If Chelsea pays after the discount period, the entry is the same as it is in a perpetual inventory system.

In each of the above cases, a temporary expense account was used to record purchases of merchandise rather than the Merchandise Inventory account used in a perpetual inventory system. The Purchases and Freight In accounts were debited rather than Merchandise Inventory in the first two entries, and Purchase Returns and Allowances and Purchase Discounts were credited in the last two entries rather than the Merchandise Inventory account. As we will see later in this appendix, these temporary accounts are needed to calculate the cost of goods sold.

Recording Sales of Merchandise

The sale of $3,800 of merchandise to Chelsea Video on May 4 shown in the sales invoice in Illustration 5-5 is recorded by the seller, Highpoint Electronic, as follows:

May 4	Accounts Receivable	3,800	
	Sales		3,800
	To record credit sale to Chelsea Video per invoice #731.		

Freight Costs

There is no difference between the accounting for freight costs by the seller in a perpetual and a periodic inventory system. In both systems, freight costs paid by the seller are debited to Freight Out or Delivery Expense, which are both operating expense accounts. In this example, the freight costs are paid by Chelsea, the purchaser, so Highpoint does not record a journal entry for this cost.

Sales Returns and Allowances

The $300 return of goods on May 9 is recorded by Highpoint Electronic as follows:

May 9	Sales Returns and Allowances	300	
	Accounts Receivable		300
	To record credit given to Chelsea Video for returned goods.		

Sales Discounts

On May 14, Highpoint Electronic receives a payment of $3,430 on account from Chelsea Video. Highpoint records this payment as follows:

A	=	L	+	OE
+3,430				−70
−3,500				

↑ Cash flows: +3,430

May 14	Cash	3,430	
	Sales Discounts ($3,500 × 2%)	70	
	Accounts Receivable		3,500
	To record collection of invoice #731 within discount period.		

The sales entries shown in this section are exactly the same as those shown earlier in the chapter for a perpetual inventory system, with one exception. In a perpetual inventory system, two journal entries are made for the sale and for the return of merchandise. The first entry records the accounts receivable and sales revenue (or return), as shown above. The second journal entry records the cost of the sale by transferring the inventory to the cost of goods sold account (or the opposite in the case of a return).

In a periodic inventory system, there is only one journal entry made at the time of the sale (the entry to record the sales revenue) and at the time of the return (the entry to record the sales return). The cost of the sale is not recorded. Instead, the cost of goods sold is determined by calculation at the end of the period.

Comparison of Entries—Perpetual vs. Periodic

Illustration 5A-1 ▼

Comparison of journal entries under perpetual and periodic inventory systems

The periodic inventory system entries for sales and purchases are shown in Illustration 5A-1 next to the perpetual inventory system entries that were shown earlier in the chapter. Having these entries side by side should help you compare the differences. The entries that are different in the two inventory systems are highlighted.

ENTRIES ON CHELSEA VIDEO'S BOOKS (BUYER)

Transaction	Perpetual Inventory System			Periodic Inventory System		

May 4 Purchase of merchandise on credit.	Merchandise Inventory
	  Accounts Payable
		3,800	3,800	Purchases
				  Accounts Payable
					3,800	3,800

4 Freight cost on purchases.	Merchandise Inventory
	  Cash
		150	150	Freight In
				  Cash
					150	150

9 Purchase returns and allowances.	Accounts Payable
	  Merchandise Inventory
		300	300	Accounts Payable
				  Purchase Returns
				    and Allowances
					300	300

14 Payment on account with a discount.	Accounts Payable
	  Merchandise Inventory
	  Cash
		3,500	70
			3,430
				Accounts Payable
				  Purchase Discounts
				  Cash
					3,500	70
						3,430

ENTRIES ON HIGHPOINT ELECTRONIC'S BOOKS (SELLER)

Transaction	Perpetual Inventory System			Periodic Inventory System		

May 4 Sale of merchandise on credit.	Accounts Receivable
	  Sales
		3,800	3,800	Accounts Receivable
				  Sales
					3,800	3,800

	Cost of Goods Sold Merchandise Inventory	2,400	2,400	No entry		

9 Return of merchandise sold.	Sales Returns
	  and Allowances
	    Accounts Receivable
		300	300	Sales Returns
				  and Allowances
				    Accounts Receivable
					300	300

	Merchandise Inventory Cost of Goods Sold	140	140	No entry		

14 Collection within discount period.	Cash
	Sales Discounts
	  Accounts Receivable
		3,430
		70
			3,500	Cash
				Sales Discounts
				  Accounts Receivable
					3,430
					70
						3,500

Calculating Cost of Goods Sold

As shown earlier in the chapter, in a perpetual inventory system the cost of goods sold is calculated for each sale, and the Merchandise Inventory account is updated each time for purchases, freight costs on a purchase, purchase returns and allowances, purchase discounts received, and sales. In a periodic inventory system, the Merchandise Inventory account is not continuously updated for each purchase and sale. As we saw in the entries above, temporary accounts are used instead to accumulate the increases and decreases in purchases and sales throughout the period. The dollar amount of merchandise on hand is not known, and neither is the cost of goods sold.

To determine the cost of goods sold in a periodic inventory system, three steps are needed:

1. Calculate the cost of goods purchased.
2. Determine the cost of goods on hand at the beginning and end of the accounting period.
3. Calculate the cost of goods sold.

We will discuss each of these steps in the following sections.

Cost of Goods Purchased

Earlier in this appendix, we used four accounts—Purchases, Purchase Returns and Allowances, Purchase Discounts, and Freight In—to record the purchase of inventory using a periodic inventory system. These four accounts are combined as follows to calculate the cost of goods purchased:

1. The balances in Purchase Returns and Allowances and Purchase Discounts are subtracted from the balance in Purchases. The result is **net purchases**.
2. The balance in Freight In is added to net purchases. The result is **cost of goods purchased**.

To illustrate, assume that Highpoint Electronic shows the following balances for the accounts above: Purchases $325,000; Purchase Returns and Allowances $10,400; Purchase Discounts $6,800; and Freight In $12,200. Net purchases is $307,800, and cost of goods purchased is $320,000, calculated as follows:

Purchases		$325,000
Less: Purchase returns and allowances	$10,400	
Purchase discounts	6,800	17,200
Net purchases		307,800
Add: Freight in		12,200
Cost of goods purchased		$320,000

Cost of Goods on Hand

To determine the cost of the inventory on hand, Highpoint Electronic must take a physical inventory. As described earlier in this chapter, we use these steps to take a physical inventory:

1. Count the units on hand for each item of inventory.
2. Apply unit costs to the total units on hand for each item of inventory.
3. Total the costs for each item of inventory to determine the total cost of goods on hand.

The total cost of goods on hand is known as the ending inventory. Highpoint's physical inventory count on May 31, 2008, determines that the cost of its goods on hand, or ending inventory, is $40,000. This ending inventory amount will be used to calculate the cost of goods sold (as shown in the next section) and will be recorded as part of the closing process in the Merchandise Inventory account, as you will learn later in this appendix.

Cost of Goods Sold

There are two steps in calculating the cost of goods sold:

1. Add the cost of goods purchased to the cost of goods on hand at the beginning of the period (beginning inventory). The result is the **cost of goods available for sale**.
2. Subtract the cost of goods on hand at the end of the period (ending inventory) from the cost of goods available for sale. The result is the cost of goods sold.

For Highpoint Electronic, the cost of goods available for sale is $355,000 and the cost of goods sold is $315,000, as follows:

Inventory, June 1, 2007		$ 35,000
Purchases	$325,000	
Less: Purchase returns and allowances		
and discounts	17,200	
Net purchases	307,800	
Add: Freight in	12,200	
Cost of goods purchased		320,000
Cost of goods available for sale		355,000
Inventory, May 31, 2008		40,000
Cost of goods sold		$315,000

Once cost of goods sold is calculated, gross profit, operating expenses, and net income are reported in a multiple-step or single-step income statement in a periodic inventory system in the same way as they are in a perpetual inventory system. The only reporting difference in a multiple-step income statement is that the cost of goods sold section has more detail in a periodic inventory system—the same detail shown above—than in a perpetual inventory system where only one line is reported for the cost of goods sold.

Using the periodic inventory system does not affect the content of the balance sheet. As in the perpetual system, merchandise inventory is reported in the current assets section, and at the same amount.

Completing the Accounting Cycle

After preparing the financial statements, closing entries and a post-closing trial balance complete the accounting cycle. It is now time to look at these two remaining steps.

For a merchandising company, as for a service company, all accounts that affect the determination of net income are closed to the owner's capital account, whether a perpetual or periodic inventory system is used.

In a periodic inventory system, the closing entries are the same as those we previously learned about, with one exception: the treatment of Merchandise Inventory. In the adjusted trial balance, the balance reported for inventory is its beginning balance, not the ending balance reported in a perpetual inventory system. During the year (or period), **no entries are made to the Merchandise Inventory account** since the temporary Purchases account and other related accounts are used instead. The beginning inventory remains unchanged in the account all year. At year end, entries must be made to eliminate the beginning inventory ($35,000 at June 1, 2007, for Highpoint) and to record the current year's new ending inventory ($40,000 at May 31, 2008, for Highpoint).

Two journal entries close the Merchandise Inventory account in a periodic inventory system:

1. The beginning inventory balance is debited to the Income Summary account and credited to Merchandise Inventory to bring the account balance to zero.
2. The ending inventory balance is debited to Merchandise Inventory and credited to the Income Summary account to record the current end-of-period balance in the account.

The two entries for Highpoint Electronic are as follows:

May 31	Income Summary	35,000	
	Merchandise Inventory		35,000
	To close beginning inventory.		
31	Merchandise Inventory	40,000	
	Income Summary		40,000
	To close ending inventory.		

A	=	L	+	OE
−35,000				−35,000

Cash flows: no effect

A	=	L	+	OE
+40,000				+40,000

Cash flows: no effect

After the closing entries are posted, the Merchandise Inventory account will show the following:

Merchandise Inventory			
June 1, 2007 Bal.	35,000	May 31, 2008 Clos.	35,000
May 31, 2008 Clos.	40,000		
May 31, 2008 Bal.	40,000		

As a permanent balance sheet account, Merchandise Inventory is not actually closed through this process as temporary accounts are. Instead, the closing process updates the inventory account for the change in inventory during the period. This is similar to the effect that the closing process has on the owner's capital account. The ending inventory and capital balances must be updated to agree with the balance sheet at the end of the period. It is these ending balances that are reported on the balance sheet, not the opening balances found in the adjusted trial balance.

The remaining closing entries are as we saw in prior chapters and are not shown here. To summarize:

1. The Merchandise Inventory account is credited for its beginning inventory balance, and debited to the Income Summary account.
2. The Merchandise Inventory account is debited for its ending inventory balance, and credited to the Income Summary account.
3. Temporary accounts with credit balances (including the Sales, Purchase Returns and Allowances, and Purchases Discount accounts) are debited for their individual account balances and the total is credited to the Income Summary account.
4. Temporary accounts with debit balances (including the Sales Returns and Allowances, Sales Discounts, Purchases, and Freight In accounts) are credited for their individual account balances and the total is debited to the Income Summary account.
5. The Income Summary account is debited for its balance (if there is net income) and credited to the owner's capital account. The reverse happens if there is a net loss.
6. The drawings account is credited and its balance is debited to owner's capital.

Closing entries for accounts with credit balances (items 2 and 3), and accounts with debit balances (items 1 and 4) are often combined for convenience. After the closing entries are posted, a post-closing trial balance is prepared. Note that in the post-closing trial balance, the balance after closing in the current asset account Merchandise Inventory equals ending inventory. This amount now becomes the beginning inventory amount for the new period.

The post-closing trial balance is prepared in the same way as described in earlier chapters and is not explained again here.

**Practice Tools:
Demonstration Problems**

Demonstration Problem

The adjusted trial balance data for the year ended December 31, 2008, for Dykstra Company are as follows:

**DYKSTRA COMPANY
Adjusted Trial Balance
December 31, 2008**

	Debit	Credit
Cash	$ 14,500	
Accounts receivable	15,100	
Merchandise inventory	29,000	
Prepaid insurance	2,500	
Land	150,000	
Building	500,000	
Accumulated amortization—building		$ 40,000
Equipment	95,000	
Accumulated amortization—equipment		18,000
Accounts payable		10,600
Property taxes payable		4,000
Mortgage payable—currently due		25,000
Mortgage payable—long-term		530,000
G. Dykstra, capital		81,000
G. Dykstra, drawings	12,000	
Sales		627,200
Sales returns and allowances	5,700	
Sales discounts	1,000	
Cost of goods sold	353,800	
Salaries expense	61,000	
Property tax expense	24,000	
Utilities expense	18,000	
Advertising expense	12,000	
Amortization expense	29,000	
Freight out	7,600	
Insurance expense	4,500	
Interest revenue		2,500
Interest expense	3,600	
Totals	$1,338,300	$1,338,300

Instructions

(a) Prepare a multiple-step income statement for the year ended December 31, 2008.
(b) Prepare a statement of owner's equity for Dykstra Company for the year ended December 31, 2008. No additional investments were made by Mr. Dykstra during the year.
(c) Prepare a classified balance sheet as at December 31, 2008.

Solution to Demonstration Problem

(a)

DYKSTRA COMPANY
Income Statement
Year Ended December 31, 2008

Sales revenues		
Sales		$627,200
Less: Sales returns and allowances	$ 5,700	
Sales discounts	1,000	6,700
Net sales		620,500
Cost of goods sold		353,800
Gross profit		266,700
Operating expenses		
Salaries expense	$61,000	
Property tax expense	24,000	
Utilities expense	18,000	
Advertising expense	12,000	
Amortization expense	29,000	
Freight out	7,600	
Insurance expense	4,500	
Total operating expenses		156,100
Income from operations		110,600
Other revenues		
Interest revenue	$ 2,500	
Other expenses		
Interest expense	3,600	(1,100)
Net income		$109,500

(b)

DYKSTRA COMPANY
Statement of Owner's Equity
Year Ended December 31, 2008

G. Dykstra, capital, January 1, 2008	$ 81,000
Add: Net income	109,500
	190,500
Deduct: Drawings	12,000
G. Dykstra, capital, December 31, 2008	$178,500

(c)

DYKSTRA COMPANY
Balance Sheet
December 31, 2008

Assets

Current assets		
Cash		$ 14,500
Accounts receivable		15,100
Merchandise inventory		29,000
Prepaid insurance		2,500
		61,100
Property, plant, and equipment		
Land		150,000
Building	$500,000	
Less: Accumulated amortization	40,000	460,000
Equipment	$ 95,000	
Less: Accumulated amortization	18,000	77,000
		687,000
Total assets		$748,100

Liabilities and Owner's Equity

Current liabilities		
Accounts payable		$ 10,600
Property taxes payable		4,000
Current portion of mortgage payable		25,000
		39,600
Long-term liabilities		
Mortgage payable		530,000
Total liabilities		569,600
Owner's Equity		
G. Dykstra, capital		178,500
Total liabilities and owner's equity		$748,100

the navigator

Summary of Study Objectives

1. **Describe the differences between service and merchandising companies.** A service company performs services. It has service or fee revenue and operating expenses. A merchandising company sells goods. It has sales revenue, cost of goods sold, gross profit, and operating expenses.

2. **Prepare entries for purchases under a perpetual inventory system.** The Merchandise Inventory account is debited for all purchases of merchandise and freight, if freight is paid by the buyer. It is credited for purchase returns and allowances and purchase discounts. Purchase discounts are cash reductions to the net invoice price for early payment.

3. **Prepare entries for sales under a perpetual inventory system.** When inventory is sold, two entries are required: (1) Accounts Receivable (or Cash) is debited and Sales is credited for the selling price of the merchandise. (2) Cost of Goods Sold is debited and Merchandise Inventory is credited for the

cost of the inventory items sold. Contra revenue accounts are used to record sales returns and allowances and sales discounts. Two entries are also required to record sales returns when the returned merchandise can be sold again in the future. Freight costs on sales are recorded as an operating expense.

4. **Perform the steps in the accounting cycle for a merchandising company.** Each of the required steps in the accounting cycle for a service company is also done for a merchandising company. An additional adjusting journal entry may be required under a perpetual inventory system. The Merchandise Inventory account must be adjusted to agree with the physical inventory count if there is a difference in the amounts. Merchandising companies have additional temporary accounts that must also be closed at the end of the accounting year.

5. **Prepare multiple-step and single-step income statements.** A multiple-step income statement shows several steps

in determining net income. Step 1 deducts sales returns and allowances and sales discounts from sales to determine net sales. Step 2 deducts the cost of goods sold from net sales to determine gross profit. Step 3 deducts operating expenses from gross profit to determine income from operations. Step 4 deducts other expenses from other revenues to calculate total non-operating activities. Step 5 adds or deducts any non-operating activities to determine net income. In a single-step income statement, all data are classified under two categories (revenues or expenses), and net income is determined by one step.

6. *Calculate the gross profit margin and profit margin.* The gross profit margin, calculated by dividing gross profit by net sales, measures the gross profit earned for each dollar of sales. The profit margin, calculated by dividing net income by net sales, measures the net income (total profit) earned for each dollar of sales. Both are measures of profitability that are closely watched by management and other interested parties.

7. *Prepare the entries for purchases and sales under a periodic inventory system and calculate cost of goods sold (Appendix 5A).* In a periodic inventory system, separate temporary accounts are used to record (a) purchases, (b) purchase returns and allowances, (c) purchase discounts, and (d) freight costs paid by the buyer. Purchases – purchase returns and allowances – purchase discounts = net purchases. Net purchases + freight in = cost of goods purchased.

In a periodic inventory system, only one journal entry is made to record a sale of merchandise. Cost of goods sold is not recorded at the time of the sale. Instead it is calculated as follows at the end of the period: Beginning inventory + cost of goods purchased = cost of goods available for sale. Cost of goods available for sale – ending inventory = cost of goods sold.

Glossary

Study Aids: Glossary
Practice Tools: Key Term Matching Activity

Contra revenue account An account that is offset against (deducted from) a revenue account on the income statement. (p. 231)

Control account An account in the general ledger that summarizes the detail for a subsidiary ledger and controls it. (p. 225)

Cost of goods available for sale A term used in a periodic inventory system. It is calculated by adding the cost of goods purchased to beginning inventory. (p. 250)

Cost of goods purchased A term used in a periodic inventory system. It is calculated by adding freight in to net purchases. (p. 249)

Cost of goods sold The total cost of merchandise sold during the period. In a perpetual inventory system, it is calculated and recorded for each sale. In a periodic inventory system, it is calculated at the end of the accounting period by deducting ending inventory from the cost of goods available for sale. (p. 220)

Credit memorandum A document prepared by the seller and given to the buyer as recognition of a reduction in the amount owed because of a return or allowance on goods previously purchased. It is also called a credit memo. (p. 227)

FOB destination A freight term indicating that the buyer accepts ownership when the goods are delivered to the buyer's place of business. The seller pays the shipping costs and is responsible for damages to the goods during transit. (p. 226).

FOB shipping point A freight term indicating that the buyer accepts ownership when the goods are placed on the carrier by the seller. The buyer pays freight costs from the shipping point to the destination and is responsible for damages. (p. 226)

Gross profit Sales revenue less cost of goods sold. (p. 220)

Gross profit margin Gross profit expressed as a percentage of net sales. It is calculated by dividing gross profit by net sales. (p. 244)

Income from operations Income from a company's main operating activity, determined by subtracting operating expenses from gross profit. (p. 240)

Multiple-step income statement An income statement that shows several steps to determine net income or net loss. (p. 239)

Net purchases A term used in a periodic inventory system. It is calculated by deducting purchase returns and allowances and purchase discounts from purchases. (p. 249)

Net sales Sales less sales returns and allowances and sales discounts. (p. 239)

Non-operating activities Other revenues and expenses that are unrelated to the company's main operations. (p. 240)

Operating cycle The time required to go from cash to cash in producing revenues. (p. 221)

Operating expenses Expenses incurred in the process of earning sales revenues. They are deducted from gross profit in the income statement. (p. 220)

Other expenses A non-operating activities section of the income statement that shows expenses and losses that are unrelated to the company's main operations. (p. 240)

Other revenues A non-operating activities section of the income statement that shows revenues and gains that are unrelated to the company's main operations. (p. 240)

Periodic inventory system An inventory system where detailed records are not maintained. The cost of goods sold is determined only at the end of the accounting period. (p. 222)

Perpetual inventory system A detailed inventory system where the quantity and cost of each inventory item are maintained. The records continuously show the inventory that should be on hand. (p. 222)

Profit margin Net income expressed as a percentage of net sales. It is calculated by dividing net income by net sales. (p. 245)

Profitability ratios Measures of a company's income or operating success for a specific period of time. (p. 244)

Purchase discount A discount, based on the invoice price less any returns and allowances, given to a buyer for early payment of a balance due. (p. 227)

Purchase returns (allowances) The return (or reduction in price) of unsatisfactory merchandise that was purchased. It results in a debit to Cash or Accounts Payable. (p. 227)

Quantity discount A cash discount that reduces the invoice price and is given to the buyer for volume purchases. (p. 227)

Sales discount A reduction, based on the invoice price less any returns and allowances, given by a seller for early payment of a credit sale. (p. 232)

Sales returns (allowances) The return, or reduction in price, of unsatisfactory merchandise that was sold. It results in a credit to Cash or Accounts Receivable. (p. 231)

Sales revenue The main source of revenue in a merchandising company. (p. 220)

Single-step income statement An income statement that shows only one step (revenues less expenses) in determining net income (or net loss). (p. 242)

Subsidiary ledger A group of accounts that give details for a control account in the general ledger. (p. 225)

Note: All questions, exercises, and problems below with an asterisk (*) relate to material in Appendix 5A.

Self-Study Questions

Practice Tools: Self-Assessment Quizzes

Answers are at the end of the chapter.

(SO 1) K 1. Which of the following statements about the perpetual inventory system is false?
  (a) The cost of goods sold is calculated and recorded with each sale.
  (b) The perpetual inventory system continuously shows the quantity and cost of inventory on hand.
  (c) It is not necessary to do a physical count of the inventory if the perpetual inventory system is used.
  (d) A perpetual inventory system results in more clerical work and additional costs compared to the periodic inventory system.

(SO 2) K 2. When goods are shipped with the freight terms FOB shipping point:
  (a) the buyer pays the freight costs and debits Merchandise Inventory.
  (b) the buyer pays the freight costs and debits Freight Expense.
  (c) the seller pays the freight costs and debits Delivery Expense.
  (d) the seller pays the freight costs and debits Cost of Goods Sold.

(SO 2) AP 3. A $750 purchase of merchandise inventory is made on June 13, terms 2/10, n/30. On June 16, merchandise costing $50 is returned. What amount will be paid as payment in full on June 22?
  (a) $686   (c) $735
  (b) $700   (d) $750

(SO 4. To record the sale of goods for cash in a perpetual inventory system:
  (a) only one journal entry is necessary to record the cost of goods sold and reduction of inventory.
  (b) only one journal entry is necessary to record the receipt of cash and the sales revenue.
  (c) two journal entries are necessary: one to record the receipt of cash and sales revenue, and one to record the cost of the goods sold and reduction of inventory.
  (d) two journal entries are necessary: one to record the receipt of cash and reduction of inventory, and one to record the cost of the goods sold and sales revenue.

(SO   5. Which of the following is a contra sales account that normally has a debit balance?
  (a) Sales Returns and Allowances
  (b) Sales
  (c) Freight Out
  (d) Cost of Goods Sold

(SO   6. The steps in the accounting cycle for a merchandising company using the perpetual inventory system are the same as those for a service company *except*:
  (a) an additional adjusting journal entry for inventory may be needed in a merchandising company.
  (b) closing journal entries are not required for a merchandising company.
  (c) a post-closing trial balance is not required for a merchandising company.
  (d) a multiple-step income statement is required for a merchandising company.

(SO 5) K 7. Which of the following appears on both a single-step and a multiple-step income statement?
(a) Merchandise inventory
(b) Gross profit
(c) Income from operations
(d) Cost of goods sold

(SO 6) AP 8. Net sales are $400,000, cost of goods sold is $310,000, operating expenses are $60,000, and other revenues are $5,000. What are the gross profit margin and profit margin?
(a) 7.5% and 8.8%   (c) 22.5% and 8.8%
(b) 22.5% and 7.4%   (d) 77.5% and 8.8%

(SO 7) K *9. When goods are purchased for resale by a company using a periodic inventory system:
(a) purchases are debited to Merchandise Inventory.
(b) purchases are debited to Purchases.
(c) purchase returns are debited to Purchase Returns and Allowances.
(d) freight costs are debited to Purchases.

(SO 7) AP *10. If beginning inventory is $60,000, purchases are $400,000, purchase returns and allowances are $25,000, freight in is $5,000, and ending inventory is $50,000, what is the cost of goods sold?
(a) $385,000   (c) $410,000
(b) $390,000   (d) $430,000

Questions

(SO 1) C 1. What components in revenues and expenses are different for a merchandising company and a service company?

(SO 1) C 2. What is meant by the term "operating cycle"? Why is the normal operating cycle for a merchandising company likely to be longer than the operating cycle for a service company?

(SO 1) C 3. Song Yee wonders why a physical inventory count is necessary in a perpetual inventory system. After all, the accounting records show how much inventory is on hand. Explain why a physical inventory count is required in a perpetual inventory system.

(SO 1) C 4. Describe the benefits and costs of using a perpetual inventory system.

(SO 2) C 5. What is the purpose of an inventory subsidiary ledger? What are the advantages of using one?

(SO 2) C 6. What is the relationship between the inventory subsidiary ledger and the Merchandise Inventory account in the general ledger?

(SO 2) C 7. Fukushima Company received an invoice for $16,000, terms 1/10, n/30. It will have to borrow from its bank in order to pay the invoice in 10 days. The interest rate Fukushima pays on its bank loans is 7.25%. Should it take advantage of the cash discount offered or not? Support your answer with calculations.

(SO 2, 3) C 8. Explain the difference between a quantity discount and a purchase/sales discount, and include the differences in how they are recorded.

(SO 2, 3) C 9. What are the differences between FOB shipping point and FOB destination? Explain the differences between how freight costs are recorded for inventory purchases as opposed to inventory sales.

(SO 2, 3) C 10. Inventory was purchased on credit in April and paid for in May. It was sold in June. In which month should the company record this cost as an expense? Why?

(SO 2, 3) C 11. Explain why purchase returns are credited directly to the Merchandise Inventory account but sales returns are not debited directly to the Sales account.

(SO 4) C 12. "The steps in the accounting cycle for a merchandising company are different from those in the accounting cycle for a service company." Do you agree or disagree? Explain.

(SO 4) C 13. Snow Co. uses a perpetual inventory system. The company's accounting records show $65,500 in the Merchandise Inventory account. A physical count of inventory indicates there is $62,750 of inventory on hand. What may have caused the difference?

(SO 4) K 14. Compared to a service company, what additional accounts must be closed for a merchandising company using a perpetual inventory system ?

(SO 5) C 15. Explain the terms "net sales," "gross profit," and "income from operations." Are these terms used only by merchandising companies or are they used by service companies also?

(SO 5) K 16. Explain the differences between a multiple-step and a single-step income statement.

(SO 5) C 17. Why is interest expense reported as a non-operating expense instead of as an operating expense on a multiple-step income statement?

(SO 6) C 18. What factors affect a company's gross profit margin? In other words, what can cause the gross profit margin to increase and what can cause it to decrease?

(SO 6) C 19. How is the gross profit margin different from the profit margin?

(SO 7) K *20. Renata purchases merchandise at garage sales and later sells these goods at a flea market. Assuming Renata uses a periodic inventory system, how would she calculate her cost of goods sold and gross profit?

(SO 7) C *21. In a periodic system, purchases of inventory are recorded in the Purchases account. Why are purchases of supplies or equipment not also recorded in the Purchases account?

*22. In a periodic inventory system, closing entries are posted to the Merchandise Inventory account. What is the purpose of these entries? (SO 7)

Brief Exercises

Calculate missing amounts in determining net income.
(SO 1) AP

BE5–1   The components in the income statements of companies A, B, C, and D follow. Determine the missing amounts.

	Sales	Cost of Goods Sold	Gross Profit	Operating Expenses	Net Income
Company A	$250,000	$150,000	$ (a)	$40,000	$ (b)
Company B	108,000	70,000	(c)	(d)	29,500
Company C	75,000	(e)	31,500	(f)	10,800
Company D	(g)	71,900	(h)	39,500	70,500

Calculate balance in inventory control account.
(SO 2) AP

BE5–2   The Big C Company sells three types of cookies. The company uses a perpetual inventory system and a subsidiary ledger to keep track of its inventory. Determine the balance in the inventory control account in the general ledger if the company had the following items on hand on March 31:

Inventory Item	Packages on Hand	Cost per Package
Oatmeal	200	$1.75
Chocolate Chip	600	2.10
Ginger Snaps	450	1.50

Calculate inventory balances.
(SO 2) AP

BE5–3   The Big C Company (see BE5–2) has decided to expand its sales to include Double Chocolate Chip cookies. It purchases 1,000 packages from its supplier at a cost of $2.50 per package, terms 2/10, n/30, FOB shipping point. The freight charges are $120. Big C pays for the merchandise within the discount period. What are the total cost and cost per package of this inventory item, and the balance in the Merchandise Inventory control account in the general ledger after these transactions?

Record purchase transactions—perpetual system.
(SO 2) AP

BE5–4   Prepare the journal entries to record the following purchase transactions in Xiaoyan Company's books. Xiaoyan uses a perpetual inventory system.

Jan. 3 Xiaoyan purchased $9,000 of merchandise from Feng Company, terms n/30, FOB shipping point.
   4 The correct company paid freight costs of $135.
   6 Xiaoyan returned $1,000 of the merchandise purchased on January 3 because it was not needed.
  12 Xiaoyan paid the balance owing to Feng.

Record purchase transactions with a purchase discount—perpetual system.
(SO 2) AP

BE5–5   Prepare the journal entries to record the following purchase transactions in Jarek Company's books. Jarek uses a perpetual inventory system.

Mar. 12 Jarek purchased $12,000 of merchandise from Dalibor Company, terms 2/10, n/30, FOB destination.
  13 The correct company paid freight costs of $155.
  14 Jarek returned $2,000 of the merchandise purchased on March 12 because it was damaged.
  22 Jarek paid the balance owing to Dalibor.

Record sales transactions—perpetual system.
(SO 3) AP

BE5–6   Prepare journal entries to record the following sales transactions in Feng Company's books. Feng uses a perpetual inventory system.

Jan. 3 Feng sold $9,000 of merchandise to Xiaoyan Company, terms n/30, FOB shipping point. The cost of the merchandise sold was $6,000.

Jan. 4 The correct company paid freight costs of $135.
6 Xiaoyan returned $1,000 of the merchandise purchased on January 3 because it was not needed. The cost of the merchandise returned was $800, and it was restored to inventory.
12 Feng received the balance due from Xiaoyan.

BE5–7 Prepare journal entries to record the following sales transactions in Dalibor Company's books. Dalibor uses a perpetual inventory system.

Mar. 12 Dalibor sold $12,000 of merchandise to Jarek Company, terms 2/10, n/30, FOB destination. The cost of the merchandise sold was $7,500.
13 The correct company paid freight costs of $155.
14 Jarek returned $2,000 of the merchandise purchased on March 12 because it was damaged. The cost of the merchandise returned was $1,250. Dalibor examined the merchandise, decided it was not longer saleable, and discarded it.
22 Dalibor received the balance due from Jarek.

Record sales transactions—perpetual system. (SO 3) AP

BE5–8 At its August 31 year end, the inventory records of Dren Company showed merchandise inventory of $98,000. Through a physical count, the company determined that its actual inventory on hand was $97,100. Record the necessary adjusting entry.

Prepare adjusting entry. (SO 4) AP

BE5–9 Prasad Company has the following merchandise account balances at its July 31 year end: Sales $180,000; Sales Returns and Allowances $2,000; Sales Discounts $750; Cost of Goods Sold $100,000; Merchandise Inventory $40,000; Freight Out $2,500; and S. Prasad, Capital $150,000. Prepare the closing entries.

Prepare closing entries. (SO 4) AP

BE5–10 Crisp Company has the following account balances: Sales $500,000; Interest Revenue $8,000; Sales Returns and Allowances $15,000; Sales Discounts $5,000; Cost of Goods Sold $350,000; Amortization Expense $12,000; Insurance Expense $3,000; Interest Expense $10,000; Rent Expense $40,000; Salaries Expense $50,000; Supplies Expense $4,000 and Gain on Sale of Equipment $2,000. Assuming Crisp Company uses a multiple-step income statement, calculate the following: (a) net sales, (b) gross profit, (c) income from operations, and (d) net income.

Calculate net sales, gross profit, income from operations, and net income. (SO 5) AP

BE5–11 Refer to the information given in BE5–10 for Crisp Company. Assuming Crisp Company uses a single-step income statement, calculate the following: (a) total revenues, (b) total expenses, and (c) net income.

Calculate total revenues, total expenses, and net income. (SO 5) AP

BE5–12 In 2007, Ry Company reported net sales of $550,000; cost of goods sold of $300,000; and operating expenses of $200,000. In 2008, Ry reported net sales of $600,000; cost of goods sold of $350,000; and operating expenses of $225,000. Calculate the gross profit margin and profit margin for each of 2007 and 2008. Has Ry's profitability improved or weakened?

Calculate profitability ratios and comment. (SO 6) AP

*BE5–13 From the information in BE5–5, prepare the journal entries to record the purchase transactions on Jarek Company's books, assuming a periodic inventory system is used instead of a perpetual inventory system.

Record purchase transactions—periodic system. (SO 7) AP

*BE5–14 From the information in BE5–7, prepare the journal entries to record the sales transactions on Dalibor Company's books, assuming a periodic inventory system is used instead of a perpetual inventory system.

Record sales transactions—periodic system. (SO 7) AP

*BE5–15 Bassing Company uses a periodic inventory system and reports the following information: net sales $630,000; purchases $400,000; purchase returns and allowances $11,000; purchase discounts $3,500; freight in $16,000; beginning inventory $60,000; ending inventory $90,000; and freight out $12,500. Calculate (a) net purchases, (b) cost of goods purchased, (c) cost of goods sold, and (d) gross profit.

Calculate net purchases, cost of goods purchased, cost of goods sold, and gross profit. (SO 6) AP

Exercises

Match concepts with descriptions.
(SO 1, 2, 3, 4, 5, 6) K

E5–1 Here are some of the concepts discussed in the chapter:

1. Gross profit
2. Perpetual inventory system
3. Cost of goods sold
4. Purchase discounts
5. Freight out
6. FOB shipping point
7. Periodic inventory system

8. Subsidiary ledger
9. FOB destination
10. Sales allowance
11. Non-operating activities
12. Profit margin
13. Contra revenue account
14. Merchandise inventory

Instructions

Match each concept with the best description below. Each concept may be used more than once, or may not be used at all.

(a) ___ An expense account that shows the cost of merchandise sold

(b) ___ A group of accounts that share a common characteristic, such as all inventory accounts

(c) ___ An account, such as Sales Discounts, that is deducted from a revenue account on the income statement

(d) ___ A reduction in the amount owing that is given to a buyer for early payment of a balance due

(e) ___ Freight terms where the seller will pay for the cost of shipping the goods

(f) ___ An inventory system where the inventory records need to be updated at year end to show the inventory on hand

(g) ___ A reduction in price given for unsatisfactory inventory

(h) ___ Sales revenue less cost of goods sold

(i) ___ Revenues, expenses, gains, and losses that are not part of the company's main operations

(j) ___ Freight terms where the buyer will pay for the cost of shipping the goods

(k) ___ An inventory system where the cost of goods sold is calculated and recorded with every sales transaction

(l) ___ An asset that shows goods purchased for resale

(m) ___ Net income divided by net sales

E5–2 Information for Olaf Co. follows:

Apr. 5 Purchased merchandise from DeVito Company for $15,000, terms, 2/10, n/30, FOB shipping point.
   6 The correct company paid freight costs of $900.
   7 Purchased supplies for $2,600 cash.
   8 Returned damaged merchandise to DeVito Company and was given a $3,000 purchase allowance.
May 2 Paid the amount due to DeVito Company in full.

Instructions

(a) Prepare the journal entries to record these transactions on the books of Olaf Co., assuming a perpetual inventory system is used.

(b) What is the balance in the Merchandise Inventory account after recording these transactions?

(c) Assume that Olaf Co. paid DeVito in full on April 15 instead of May 2. Record this journal entry. What would the balance in the Merchandise Inventory account be using this assumption?

E5–3 The following merchandise transactions occurred in December. Pippen uses a perpetual inventory system.

Dec. 3 Pippen Company sold merchandise to Thomas Co. for $48,000, terms 2/10, n/30, FOB destination. This merchandise cost Pippen Company $32,000.
   4 The correct company paid freight of $750.

Dec. 8 Pippen Company gave Thomas Co. a sales allowance of $2,400 for defective merchandise purchased on December 3. No merchandise was returned.

31 Pippen Company received the balance due from Thomas Co.

Instructions

(a) Prepare the journal entries to record these transactions on the books of Pippen Company.

(b) Calculate the gross profit earned by Pippen in December on the above transactions.

(c) Assume that Thomas Co. paid Pippen Company in full on December 13 instead of December 31. Record this journal entry. Calculate the gross profit earned by Pippen using this assumption.

E5–4 Collegiate Office Supply sells various office furniture items and uses a perpetual inventory system. At the beginning of October, it had no office chairs in stock. The following events occurred during October and November:

Record and post inventory transactions and adjusting entry—perpetual system.
(SO 2, 3, 4) AP

Oct. 6 Purchased 100 office chairs from Katts Ltd. for $68 each, terms n/30, FOB shipping point.

7 Paid $200 cash to Freight Company for the delivery of the chairs.

9 Sold 30 chairs to Butler Inc. for $135 each on credit, terms n/30, FOB destination. (*Hint:* Note that the freight charges from the October 7 transaction will increase the cost per chair.)

10 Paid $30 cash to Freight Company for the delivery of the chairs to Butler Inc.

11 Gave Butler Inc. credit for five returned chairs. The chairs were returned to inventory.

31 Counted the inventory and determined there were 74 chairs on hand.

Nov. 5 Paid Katts Ltd. for the chairs purchased on October 6.

8 Received payment from Butler Inc. for the amount owing.

Instructions

(a) Record the above transactions and events.

(b) Post the appropriate entries to the Merchandise Inventory and Cost of Goods Sold accounts and determine their ending balances.

E5–5 On June 10, Pele Company purchased $5,000 of merchandise from Duvall Company, terms 2/10, n/30, FOB shipping point. Pele paid $300 of freight costs to Hoyt Movers on June 11. Damaged goods totalling $500 were returned to Duvall for credit on June 12. On June 20, Pele paid Duvall Company in full. On July 15, Pele sold all of the remaining merchandise purchased from Duvall for $8,500 cash. On that same date, Pele paid $250 of freight costs to AAA Transit to deliver the goods to the customer. On July 17, Pele gave its customer a $300 cash sales allowance for damaged goods. Pele uses a perpetual inventory system.

Record inventory transactions and closing entries—perpetual system.
(SO 2, 3, 4) AP

Instructions

(a) Record each of the above transactions on the books of Pele Company.

(b) Prepare closing entries on July 31 for the temporary accounts.

E5–6 Financial information follows for three different companies:

Calculate missing amounts.
(SO 5) AP

	Natural Cosmetics	Mattar Grocery	Allied Wholesalers
Sales	$95,000	$ (e)	$148,000
Sales returns and allowances	(a)	5,000	12,000
Net sales	84,000	95,000	(i)
Cost of goods sold	56,000	(f)	(j)
Gross profit	(b)	38,000	24,000
Operating expenses	15,000	(g)	18,000
Income from operations	(c)	(h)	(k)
Other expenses	4,000	7,000	(l)
Net income	(d)	10,000	5,000

Instructions

Determine the missing amounts.

Prepare multiple-step and single-step income statements and closing entries—perpetual system. (SO 4, 5) AP

E5–7   The following information from Chevalier Company's general ledger is presented below for the year ended December 31, 2008:

Advertising expense	$ 45,000	Interest revenue	$ 30,000
Amortization expense	125,000	Loss on sale of equipment	10,000
Cost of goods sold	985,000	Merchandise inventory	92,000
Delivery expense	25,000	Salaries expense	875,000
G. Chevalier, capital	535,000	Sales	2,400,000
G. Chevalier, drawings	150,000	Sales discounts	8,500
Insurance expense	15,000	Sales returns and allowances	41,000
Interest expense	70,000	Unearned sales revenue	8,000

Instructions

(a) Prepare a multiple-step income statement.
(b) Prepare a single-step income statement.
(c) Prepare closing entries.

Classify accounts of merchandising company. (SO 5) K

E5–8   You are given the following list of accounts from the adjusted trial balance of Swirsky Company:

Accounts payable	Land
Accounts receivable	Merchandise inventory
Accumulated amortization—office building	Mortgage payable
Accumulated amortization—store equipment	Office building
Advertising expense	Prepaid insurance
Amortization expense	Property tax payable
B. Swirsky, capital	Salaries expense
B. Swirsky, drawings	Salaries payable
Cash	Sales
Freight out	Sales discounts
Insurance expense	Sales returns and allowances
Interest expense	Store equipment
Interest payable	Unearned sales revenue
Interest revenue	Utilities expense

Instructions

For each account, identify whether it should be reported on the balance sheet, statement of owner's equity, or income statement. Assuming Swirsky Company prepares a classified balance sheet and a multiple-step income statement, specify how the account should be classified. For example, Accounts Payable would be classified under current liabilities on the balance sheet.

Calculate profitability ratios. (SO 6) AN

E5–9   Best Buy Co., Inc. reported the following information for three recent fiscal years (in U.S. millions):

	2005	2004	2003
Sales	$27,433	$24,548	$20,943
Cost of goods sold	20,938	18,677	15,998
Operating income	1,442	1,304	1,010
Net income	984	705	99

Instructions

Calculate the gross profit margin and profit margin for Best Buy for each of the three years. Also calculate profit margin using operating income as opposed to net income. Comment on whether the ratios improved or weakened over the three years.

*E5–10 The Furano Company had the following merchandise transactions in May:

Record purchase and sales transaction entries— perpetual and periodic systems.
(SO 2, 3, 7) AP

May 2 Purchased $1,200 of merchandise from Digital Suppliers, terms 2/10, n/30, FOB shipping point.

    2 The correct company paid $100 freight costs.

    3 Returned $200 of the merchandise to Digital as it did not meet specifications.

    9 Paid Digital the balance owing.

  12 Sold three-quarters of the remaining merchandise to SunDial Company for $1,500, terms 2/10, n/30.

  14 SunDial complained that some of the merchandise was slightly damaged. Furano gave SunDial a sales allowance of $100.

  22 Received the correct balance owing from SunDial.

Instructions

(a) Prepare journal entries for Furano Company assuming it uses a perpetual inventory system.
(b) Prepare journal entries for Furano Company assuming it uses a periodic inventory system.

*E5–11 Here are the cost of goods sold sections for four companies:

Determine missing amounts for cost of goods sold section.
(SO 7) AP

	Co. 1	Co. 2	Co. 3	Co. 4
Beginning inventory	$ 250	$ 120	$1,000	$ (l)
Purchases	1,500	1,080	(i)	43,590
Purchase returns and allowances	65	40	290	(m)
Purchase discounts	25	(e)	160	400
Net purchases	(a)	1,030	7,210	42,090
Freight in	110	(f)	(j)	2,240
Cost of goods purchased	(b)	1,230	7,940	(n)
Cost of goods available for sale	(c)	(g)	(k)	49,530
Ending inventory	310	(h)	1,450	(o)
Cost of goods sold	(d)	1,230	7,490	43,300

Instructions

Fill in the missing amounts to complete the cost of goods sold sections.

*E5–12 The following selected information is for Okanagan Company for the year ended January 31, 2008:

Prepare multiple-step income statement and closing entries.
(SO 7) AP

Accounts receivable	25,000	Purchase discounts	1,000
Freight in	10,000	Purchase returns and allowances	6,000
Freight out	7,000	Rent expense	20,000
Insurance expense	12,000	Salaries expense	61,000
Interest expense	6,000	Salaries payable	2,500
Merchandise inventory, beginning	42,000	Sales	315,000
Merchandise inventory, ending	61,000	Sales discounts	4,000
O. Pogo, capital	105,000	Sales returns and allowances	13,000
O. Pogo, drawings	42,000	Unearned sales revenue	4,500
Purchases	200,000		

Instructions

(a) Prepare a multiple-step income statement.
(b) Prepare closing entries.

Problems: Set A

Identify problems and recommend inventory system.

(SO 1) C

P5–1A Home Décor Company sells a variety of home decorating merchandise, including pictures, small furniture items, dishes, candles, and area rugs. The company uses a periodic inventory system and counts inventory once a year. Most customers use the option to purchase on account and many take more than a month to pay. The owner of Home Décor, Rebecca Sherstabetoff, has decided that the company needs a bank loan because the accounts payable need to be paid long before the accounts receivable are collected. The bank manager is willing to give Home Décor a loan but wants monthly financial statements.

Rebecca has also noticed that while some of her merchandise sells very quickly, other items do not. Sometimes she wonders just how long she has had some of those older items. She has also noticed that she seems to run out of some merchandise items on a regular basis. And she is wondering how she is going to find time to count the inventory every month so she can prepare the monthly financial statements for the bank. She has come to you for help.

Instructions

(a) Explain to Rebecca what an operating cycle is and why she is having problems paying her bills.
(b) Explain to Rebecca how her inventory system is contributing to her problems.
(c) Make a recommendation about what inventory system she should use and why.

Record inventory transactions and post to inventory account—perpetual system.

(SO 2, 3) AP

P5–2A Phantom Book Warehouse distributes hardcover books to retail stores and extends credit terms of n/30 to all of its customers. Phantom uses a perpetual inventory system and at the end of May had an inventory of 230 books purchased at $6 each. During the month of June, the following merchandise transactions occurred:

June 1 Purchased 160 books on account for $6 each from Reader's World Publishers, terms n/30.
   3 Sold 150 books on account to Book Nook for $10 each.
   6 Received $60 credit for 10 books returned to Reader's World Publishers.
   18 Issued a $50 credit memorandum to Book Nook for the return of five damaged books. The books were determined to be no longer saleable and were destroyed.
   20 Purchased 110 books on account for $6 each from Read More Publishers, terms n/30, FOB destination.
   27 Sold 100 books on account to Readers Bookstore for $10 each.
   28 Granted Readers Bookstore $150 credit for 15 returned books. These books were restored to inventory.
   30 Paid Reader's World Publishers in full.
   30 Received the balance owing from Book Nook.

Instructions

(a) Record the transactions for the month of June for Phantom Book Warehouse.
(b) Create a T account for merchandise inventory. Post the opening balance and June's transactions, and calculate the June 30 balance.
(c) How many books does Phantom have on hand on June 30? What is the relationship between the number of books on hand and the balance in the merchandise inventory account?

Record inventory transactions—perpetual system.

(SO 2, 3) AP

P5–3A Transactions follow for Leeland Company during October and November of the current year. Leeland uses a perpetual inventory system.

Oct. 2 Purchased merchandise on account from Gregory Company at a cost of $70,000, terms 2/10, n/30, FOB shipping point.
   4 The correct company paid freight charges of $1,800 to Rail Company for shipping the merchandise purchased on October 2.
   5 Returned damaged goods having a gross invoice cost of $6,000 to Gregory Company. Received a credit for this.
   11 Paid Gregory Company the balance owing for the October 2 purchase.

Oct. 17 Sold all of the remaining merchandise purchased from Gregory Company to Kurji Company for $92,500, terms 2/10, n/30, FOB shipping point.

18 The correct company paid Intermodal Co. $1,500 freight costs for the October 17 sale.

19 Issued Kurji Company a sales allowance of $2,500 because some of the goods did not meet Kurji's exact specifications.

27 Received the balance owing from Kurji Company for the October 17 sale.

Nov. 1 Purchased merchandise on account from Romeo Company at a cost of $85,000, terms 1/15, n/30, FOB destination.

2 The correct company paid freight charges of $2,200.

3 Obtained a purchase allowance of $3,000 from Romeo Company to compensate for some minor damage to the goods purchased on November 1.

5 Sold all of the merchandise purchased from Romeo Company to Barlow Company for $109,300, terms 2/10, n/30, FOB destination.

6 The correct company paid freight charges of $2,600.

7 Issued Barlow a credit of $7,000 for returned goods. These goods had cost Leeland $5,250 and were returned to inventory.

29 Received a cheque from Barlow Company for the balance owing on the November 5 sale.

30 Paid Romeo Company the amount owing on the November 1 purchase.

Instructions

Prepare journal entries to record the above transactions for Leeland Company.

P5–4A Copple Hardware Store had the following merchandising transactions in the month of May. At the beginning of May, Copple's ledger showed Cash $15,000 and B. Copple, Capital, $15,000.

Record and post inventory transactions—perpetual system. Prepare partial income statement and balance sheet.
(SO 2, 3, 5) AP

May 1 Purchased 120 tool sets for resale from Lathrop Wholesale Supply Co. for $5,800, terms 2/10, n/30, FOB shipping point.

3 The correct company paid $200 cash for freight charges on the May 1 merchandise purchase.

4 Sold 30 of the tool sets on account for $2,250, terms 2/10, n/30, FOB destination.

5 The correct company paid $100 freight on the May 4 sale.

6 Issued a credit memorandum for the return of three tool sets sold on May 4. The tool sets were returned to inventory.

8 Purchased supplies for $900 cash.

9 Purchased merchandise from Harlow Distributors for $2,000, terms 2/10, n/30, FOB shipping point.

10 The correct company paid $300 freight on the May 9 purchase.

12 Received $200 credit from Harlow Distributors for returned merchandise.

19 Paid Harlow Distributors for the balance owing.

24 Sold one-half of the remaining merchandise purchased from Harlow for $2,600 cash. The merchandise sold had a cost of $1,032.

25 Purchased merchandise from Horicon Inc. for $1,000, terms n/30, FOB destination.

27 Received collections in full from customers billed on May 4.

28 Made cash refunds to customers for returned merchandise, $100. The returned merchandise had a cost of $70 and was restored to inventory.

28 Purchased merchandise for $2,400 cash.

29 Received a $230 refund from a supplier for poor-quality merchandise purchased with cash.

31 Paid Lathrop Wholesale Supply for the balance owing.

31 Sold merchandise on account for $1,600, FOB shipping point, terms n/30. The cost of the merchandise sold was $1,000.

Instructions

(a) Record the transactions assuming Copple uses a perpetual inventory system.

(b) Set up general ledger accounts, enter the beginning cash and capital balances, and post the transactions.

(c) Prepare a partial multiple-step income statement, up to gross profit, for the month of May 2008.

(d) Prepare the current assets section of the balance sheet at May 31, 2008.

Prepare adjusting and closing
entries—perpetual system.
Prepare financial statements.

(SO 4, 5) AP

P5–5A The unadjusted trial balance of Global Enterprises for the year ending December 31, 2008, follows:

GLOBAL ENTERPRISES
Trial Balance
December 31, 2008

	Debit	Credit
Cash	$ 10,360	
Accounts receivable	31,500	
Merchandise inventory	28,955	
Supplies	2,940	
Prepaid insurance	1,980	
Land	30,000	
Building	150,000	
Accumulated amortization—building		$ 18,750
Office equipment	45,000	
Accumulated amortization—office equipment		9,000
Accounts payable		30,250
Unearned sales revenue		4,000
Mortgage payable		161,250
I. Rochefort, capital		74,275
I. Rochefort, drawings	35,500	
Sales		263,870
Sales returns and allowances	5,275	
Sales discounts	2,635	
Cost of goods sold	171,225	
Salaries expense	30,950	
Utilities expense	5,100	
Interest expense	9,975	
	$561,395	$561,395

Other data:

1. The 12-month insurance policy was purchased on February 1, 2008.
2. There was $650 of supplies on hand on December 31, 2008.
3. The building has a 40-year useful life and the equipment has a 10-year useful life.
4. Accrued interest expense at December 31, 2008, is $895.
5. Unearned sales revenue of $975 is still unearned at December 31, 2008. On the sales that were earned, the cost of goods sold was $2,000.
6. A physical count of merchandise inventory indicates $26,200 on hand on December 31, 2008.
7. Of the mortgage payable, $9,000 is to be paid in 2009.
8. Ingrid Rochefort invested $7,500 cash in the business on May 21, 2008.

Instructions

(a) Prepare the adjusting journal entries assuming they are prepared annually.
(b) Prepare a multiple-step income statement, statement of owner's equity, and classified balance sheet.
(c) Prepare the closing entries.

Prepare adjusting and closing
entries, and multiple-step
and single-step income
statements—perpetual
system. Calculate ratios.

(SO 4, 5, 6) AP

P5–6A The trial balance of Poorten Wholesale Centre contained the following accounts at November 30, the company's fiscal year end:

```
                           POORTEN WHOLESALE CENTRE
                                 Trial Balance
                              November 30, 2008

                                                      Debit           Credit

    Cash                                          $    12,100
    Accounts receivable                                15,700
    Merchandise inventory                              45,200
    Supplies                                            1,500
    Notes receivable                                   25,000
    Land                                               60,000
    Building                                           85,000
    Accumulated amortization—building                              $   17,000
    Delivery equipment                                 48,000
    Accumulated amortization—delivery equipment                        24,000
    Accounts payable                                                   48,500
    Unearned sales revenue                                              3,000
    Mortgage payable                                                   51,000
    K. Poorten, capital                                               132,000
    K. Poorten, drawings                               12,000
    Sales                                                             750,300
    Interest revenue                                                    1,620
    Sales returns and allowances                        4,200
    Sales discounts                                     3,750
    Cost of goods sold                                497,500
    Advertising expense                                26,400
    Amortization expense                               10,125
    Freight out                                        16,700
    Insurance expense                                   3,420
    Interest expense                                    3,700
    Salaries expense                                  136,625
    Supplies expense                                    6,500
    Utilities expense                                  14,000
                                                  $1,027,420       $1,027,420
```

Other data:

1. All adjustments have been recorded and posted except for the inventory adjustment. Merchandise inventory actually on hand at November 30, 2008, is $42,600.
2. Last year, Poorten Wholesale had a gross profit margin of 35% and a profit margin of 5%.

Instructions

(a) Prepare the adjusting entry.
(b) Prepare a multiple-step income statement.
(c) Prepare a single-step income statement.
(d) Compare the two income statements and comment on the usefulness of each one.
(e) Calculate the gross profit margin and profit margin for 2008. Compare these results to the previous year's results and comment on any trends.
(f) Prepare the closing entries. Post to the Income Summary account. Check that the balance in Income Summary before closing it is equal to net income.

Prepare financial statements
and closing entries, and
calculate ratios—perpetual
system.

(SO 4, 5, 6) AP

P5–7A An alphabetical list of Betty's Boutique's adjusted account balances at its fiscal year end, March 31, 2008, follows. All accounts have normal balances.

Accounts payable	$ 24,200	Merchandise inventory	$ 78,200
Accounts receivable	4,870	Note payable	21,500
Accumulated amortization—		Office furniture	16,700
office furniture	6,680	Prepaid insurance	1,280
Accumulated amortization—		Rent expense	61,000
store equipment	12,320	Salaries expense	91,545
Amortization expense	4,750	Salaries payable	2,100
B. Tainch, capital	65,780	Sales	550,545
B. Tainch, drawings	90,800	Sales discounts	2,725
Cash	9,975	Sales returns and allowances	5,445
Cost of goods sold	277,750	Store equipment	30,800
Insurance expense	1,280	Supplies	840
Interest expense	1,615	Supplies expense	5,040
Interest payable	360	Unearned sales revenue	1,640
Loss on sale of equipment	510		

Other data:

1. Of the notes payable, $5,000 becomes due on January 31, 2009. The balance is due in 2010.
2. On August 7, 2007, Betty invested $1,000 cash in the business.
3. The average gross profit margin for this industry is 45%.

Instructions

(a) Prepare a multiple-step income statement, statement of owner's equity, and classified balance sheet.
(b) Prepare closing entries.
(c) Calculate the gross profit margin and profit margin.
(d) Compare Betty's Boutique's gross profit margin to the industry average, and comment.

Calculate ratios and
comment.

(SO 6) AN

P5–8A The following information (in thousands) is for Danier Leather Inc.:

	2005	2004	2003
Current assets	$ 52,455	$ 54,579	$ 46,223
Current liabilities	8,170	10,377	9,350
Sales revenue	166,350	175,270	175,487
Cost of goods sold	82,863	88,742	88,788
Net income	(185)	(7,097)	5,394

Instructions

(a) Calculate the gross profit margin, profit margin, and current ratio for Danier Leather for 2005, 2004, and 2003. Comment on whether the ratios have improved or weakened over the three years.
(b) Compare the profit margins and current ratios to the following industry averages: 2005 profit margin, 3.9%; 2004 profit margin, 3.6%; 2003 profit margin, 1.5%; and 2005 current ratio, 2.1 to 1. State whether Danier Leather's ratios are better or worse than those of its industry.

Record inventory
transactions—periodic
system.

(SO 7) AP

*P5–9A Data for Phantom Book Warehouse are presented in P5–2A.

Instructions

Record the July transactions for Phantom Book Warehouse assuming a periodic inventory system is used instead of a perpetual inventory system.

Record inventory
transactions—periodic
system.

(SO 7) AP

*P5–10A Data for Leeland Company are presented in P5–3A.

Instructions

Record the October and November transactions for Leeland Company assuming a periodic inventory system is used instead of a perpetual inventory system.

*P5–11A Data for Copple Hardware Store are presented in P5–4A. A physical inventory count shows the company has $7,922 of inventory on hand at May 31, 2008.

Record and post inventory transactions—periodic system. Prepare partial income statement.
(SO 7) AP

Instructions

(a) Record the transactions assuming Copple uses a periodic inventory system.
(b) Set up general ledger accounts, enter the beginning cash and capital balances, and post the transactions.
(c) Prepare a partial multiple-step income statement, up to gross profit, for the month of May 2008.

*P5–12A The following is an alphabetical list of Tse's Tater Tots' adjusted account balances at the end of the company's fiscal year on December 31, 2008:

Prepare financial statements and closing entries—periodic system.
(SO 7) AP

Accounts payable	$ 56,200	Inventory, Jan. 1, 2008	$ 40,500
Accounts receivable	19,400	Mortgage payable	80,000
Accumulated amortization—		Property tax expense	4,800
building	51,800	Property tax payable	4,800
Accumulated amortization—		Purchase discounts	4,450
equipment	42,900	Purchase returns and allowances	6,400
Amortization expense	23,400	Purchases	441,600
Building	190,000	Salaries expense	122,500
Cash	22,000	Salaries payable	3,500
Equipment	110,000	Sales	623,000
Freight in	5,600	Sales discounts	6,200
H. Tse, capital	178,600	Sales returns and allowances	8,000
H. Tse, drawings	28,000	Supplies	400
Insurance expense	7,200	Supplies expense	2,000
Interest expense	5,400	Unearned sales revenue	2,300
Interest revenue	1,050	Utilities expense	18,000

Additional facts:

1. Merchandise inventory on December 31, 2008, is $72,600.
2. Of the mortgage payable, $7,300 is to be paid during the next year.

Instructions

(a) How do you know from the list of accounts that Tse uses a periodic inventory system?
(b) Prepare a multiple-step income statement, a statement of owner's equity, and a classified balance sheet.
(c) Prepare the closing journal entries.
(d) Post the closing entries to the inventory and capital accounts. Check that the balances in these accounts are the same as the amounts on the balance sheet.

Problems: Set B

P5–1B AAA Dog n' Cat Shop sells a variety of merchandise for the pet owner, including pet food, grooming supplies, toys, and kennels. Most customers use the option to purchase on account and take 60 days, on average, to pay their accounts. The owner of AAA Dog n' Cat Shop, Adam Fleming, has decided the company needs a bank loan because the accounts payable need to be paid in 30 days. Adam estimates that it takes 45 days, on average, to sell merchandise from the time it arrives at his store. Since the company earns a good profit every year, the bank manager is willing to give AAA Dog n' Cat Shop a loan but wants monthly financial statements.

Identify problems and recommend inventory system.
(SO 1) C

Adam has also noticed that while some of the merchandise sells very quickly, other items do not. Sometimes he wonders just how long he has had some of those older items. He has also noticed that he seems to run out of some merchandise items on a regular basis. Adam is also concerned about preparing monthly financial statements. The company uses a periodic inventory system and Adam counts inventory once a year. He is wondering how he is going to calculate the cost of goods sold for the month without counting the inventory at the end of every month. He has come to you for help.

Instructions

(a) Explain to Adam what an operating cycle is and why he is having problems paying the bills.
(b) Explain to Adam how the periodic inventory system is contributing to his problems.
(c) Make a recommendation about what inventory system the company should use and why.

Record inventory transactions and post to inventory account—perpetual system. (SO 2, 3) AP

P5–2B Travel Warehouse distributes suitcases to retail stores and extends credit terms of n/30 to all of its customers. Travel Warehouse uses a perpetual inventory system and at the end of June its inventory consisted of 40 suitcases purchased at $30 each. During the month of July, the following merchandising transactions occurred:

July 1 Purchased 50 suitcases on account for $30 each from Trunk Manufacturers, FOB destination, terms n/30.
2 Received $150 credit for five suitcases returned to Trunk Manufacturers because they were the wrong colour.
3 Sold 35 suitcases on account to Satchel World for $55 each.
4 Issued a $55 credit memorandum to Satchel World for the return of a damaged suitcase. The suitcase was determined to be no longer saleable and was destroyed.
18 Purchased 60 suitcases on account for $1,700 from Holiday Manufacturers, FOB shipping point, terms n/30.
18 Paid $100 freight to AA Trucking Company for merchandise purchased from Holiday Manufacturers.
21 Sold 54 suitcases on account to Fly-By-Night for $55 each.
23 Gave Fly-By-Night $220 credit for four returned suitcases. The suitcases were in good condition and were restored to inventory.
30 Paid Trunk Manufacturers in full.
31 Received balance owing from Satchel World.

Instructions

(a) Record the transactions for the month of July for Travel Warehouse.
(b) Create a T account for merchandise inventory. Post the opening balance and July's transactions, and calculate the July 31 balance.
(c) How many suitcases does Travel Warehouse have on hand on July 31? What is the relationship between the number of suitcases on hand and the balance in the merchandise inventory account?

Record inventory transactions—perpetual system. (SO 2, 3) AP

P5–3B Presented below are selected transactions for Norlan Company during September and October of the current year. Norlan uses a perpetual inventory system.

Sept. 1 Purchased merchandise on account from Hillary Company at a cost of $65,000, FOB shipping point, terms 1/15, n/30.
2 The correct company paid $2,000 of freight charges to Trucking Company on the September 1 merchandise purchase.
5 Returned damaged goods having a gross invoice cost of $7,000 to Hillary Company. Received a credit for this.
15 Sold all of the remaining merchandise purchased from Hillary Company to Irvine Company for $90,000, FOB shipping point, terms 2/10, n/30.
17 Issued Irvine Company a credit of $4,000 for returned goods. These goods had cost Norlan Company $2,400 and were returned to inventory.
25 Received the balance owing from Irvine Company for the September 15 sale.
30 Paid Hillary Company the balance owing for the September 1 purchase.
Oct. 1 Purchased merchandise on account from Kimmel Company at a cost of $50,000, FOB destination, terms 2/10, n/30.
2 The correct company paid freight costs of $1,200 on the October 1 purchase.

Oct. 3 Obtained a purchase allowance of $2,000 from Kimmel Company to compensate for some minor damage to goods purchased on October 1.

10 Paid Kimmel Company the amount owing on the October 1 purchase.

11 Sold all of the merchandise purchased from Kimmel Company to Kieso Company for $80,000, FOB destination, terms 2/10, n/30.

12 The correct company paid $800 freight costs on the October 11 sale.

17 Issued Kieso Company a sales allowance of $1,500 because some of the goods did not meet Kieso's exact specifications.

31 Received a cheque from Kieso Company for the balance owing on the October 11 sale.

Instructions

Prepare journal entries to record the above transactions for Norlan Company.

P5–4B Nisson Distributing Company had the following merchandising transactions in the month of April 2008. At the beginning of April, Nisson's ledger showed Cash $9,000 and M. Nisson, Capital, $9,000.

Record and post inventory transactions—perpetual system. Prepare partial income statement and balance sheet.
(SO 2, 3, 5) AP

Apr. 2 Purchased 100 tables for resale from Kananaskis Supply Co. for $8,900, terms 1/15, n/30, FOB shipping point.

3 The correct company paid $100 cash for freight charges on the April 2 purchase.

4 Sold 80 of these tables on account for $145 each, terms 2/10, n/30, FOB destination.

5 The correct company paid $75 freight on the April 4 sale.

6 Issued a credit memorandum for the return of four tables sold on April 4. The tables were returned to inventory.

8 Purchased merchandise from Testa Distributors for $4,200, terms 2/10, n/30, FOB destination.

9 The correct company paid $110 freight costs on the April 8 purchase.

10 Received a $300 credit from Testa for returned merchandise.

18 Paid Testa the balance owing from the April 8 purchase.

23 Sold merchandise for $6,400 cash. The cost of this merchandise was $5,200.

24 Purchased merchandise for $3,800 cash.

25 Made refunds to cash customers for merchandise, $90. The returned merchandise had a cost of $60. The merchandise was returned to inventory for future resale.

26 Received a $500 refund from a supplier for returned goods on the cash purchase of April 24.

26 Purchased merchandise for $2,300 cash.

28 Collected the balance owing from customer billed on April 4.

30 Sold merchandise on account for $3,800, terms n/30, FOB shipping point. Nisson's cost for this merchandise was $2,700.

30 Paid Kananaskis Supply Co. the amount due.

Instructions

(a) Record the transactions assuming Nisson uses a perpetual inventory system.

(b) Set up general ledger accounts, enter the beginning cash and capital balances, and post the transactions.

(c) Prepare a partial multiple-step income statement, up to gross profit, for the month of April 2008.

(d) Prepare the current assets section of the balance sheet at the end of April.

Prepare adjusting and closing
entries—perpetual system.
Prepare financial statements.
(SO 4, 5) AP

P5–5B The unadjusted trial balance of World Enterprises for the year ending December 31, 2008, follows:

WORLD ENTERPRISES
Trial Balance
December 31, 2008

	Debit	Credit
Cash	$ 12,550	
Accounts receivable	30,600	
Merchandise inventory	27,850	
Supplies	1,650	
Prepaid insurance	1,800	
Office furniture	26,800	
Accumulated amortization—office furniture		$ 10,720
Store equipment	42,000	
Accumulated amortization—store equipment		8,400
Accounts payable		34,400
Unearned sales revenue		3,000
Note payable		36,000
S. Kim, capital		59,700
S. Kim, drawings	45,850	
Sales		238,500
Sales returns and allowances	4,600	
Sales discounts	1,450	
Cost of goods sold	157,870	
Salaries expense	31,600	
Rent expense	6,100	
	$390,720	$390,720

Other data:

1. The 12-month insurance policy was purchased on August 1, 2008.
2. There is $750 of supplies on hand on December 31, 2008.
3. Both the store equipment and office furniture have an estimated 10-year useful life.
4. Accrued interest expense at December 31, 2008, is $2,520.
5. Of the unearned sales revenue, $1,950 has been earned by December 31, 2008. The cost of goods sold to earn this revenue is $1,275.
6. A physical count of merchandise inventory indicates $25,600 on hand on December 31, 2008.
7. Of the note payable, $6,000 is to be paid in 2009.
8. Seok Kim invested $5,000 cash in the business on July 18, 2008.

Instructions

(a) Prepare the adjusting journal entries assuming they are prepared annually.
(b) Prepare a multiple-step income statement, statement of owner's equity, and classified balance sheet.
(c) Prepare the closing entries.

Prepare adjusting and closing
entries, and multiple-step
and single-step income
statements—perpetual
system. Calculate ratios.
(SO 4, 5, 6) AP

P5–6B The trial balance of Club Canada Wholesale Company contained the following accounts at December 31, the company's fiscal year end:

CLUB CANADA WHOLESALE COMPANY
Trial Balance
December 31, 2008

	Debit	Credit
Cash	$ 18,875	
Accounts receivable	7,600	
Merchandise inventory	72,400	
Supplies	3,780	
Notes receivable	30,000	
Land	72,000	
Building	197,000	
Accumulated amortization—building		$ 93,575
Equipment	83,500	
Accumulated amortization—equipment		33,400
Accounts payable		37,500
Unearned revenue		7,550
Mortgage payable		186,000
E. Martel, capital		120,265
E. Martel, drawings	72,500	
Sales		923,470
Interest revenue		1,200
Sales returns and allowances	18,050	
Sales discounts	4,615	
Cost of goods sold	712,100	
Amortization expense	13,275	
Insurance expense	3,640	
Interest expense	8,525	
Freight out	5,900	
Salaries expense	69,800	
Utilities expense	9,400	
	$1,402,960	$1,402,960

Other data:

1. All adjustments have been recorded and posted except for the inventory adjustment. Merchandise inventory actually on hand at December 31, 2008, is $70,600.
2. Last year, Canada Club Wholesale had a gross profit margin of 25% and a profit margin of 5%.

Instructions

(a) Prepare the adjusting entry.
(b) Prepare a multiple-step income statement.
(c) Prepare a single-step income statement.
(d) Compare the two income statements and comment on the usefulness of each one.
(e) Calculate the gross profit margin and profit margin for 2008. Compare the results to the previous year's results and comment on any trends.
(f) Prepare the closing entries. Post to the Income Summary account. Check that the balance in the Income Summary account before closing it is equal to net income.

Prepare financial statements
and closing entries, and
calculate ratios—perpetual
system.

(SO 4, 5, 6) AP

P5–7B An alphabetical list of Rikard's adjusted accounts at its fiscal year end, August 31, 2008, follows. All accounts have normal balances.

Accounts payable	$ 29,100	Office furniture	$ 18,500
Accounts receivable	2,570	Prepaid insurance	2,205
Accumulated amortization—		R. Martinson, capital	52,950
office furniture	7,400	R. Martinson, drawings	76,000
Accumulated amortization—		Rent expense	14,000
store equipment	13,040	Salaries expense	55,000
Amortization expense	5,110	Salaries payable	2,250
Cash	5,640	Sales	457,680
Cost of goods sold	273,360	Sales discounts	2,275
Gain on sale of equipment	625	Sales returns and allowances	4,555
Insurance expense	1,575	Store equipment	32,600
Interest expense	1,995	Supplies	1,680
Interest payable	450	Supplies expense	5,040
Merchandise inventory	91,350	Unearned sales revenue	1,460
Note payable	28,500		

Other data:

1. Of the notes payable, $5,000 becomes due on February 28, 2009. The balance is due in 2010.
2. On July 6, 2008, Rikard invested $1,500 cash in the business.
3. The average gross profit margin for this industry is 45%.

Instructions

(a) Prepare a multiple-step income statement, statement of owner's equity, and classified balance sheet.
(b) Prepare closing entries.
(c) Calculate the gross profit margin and profit margin.
(d) Compare Rikard's gross profit margin to the industry average, and comment.

P5–8B Selected financial information (in U.S. thousands) follows for IPSCO Inc., which is head-quartered in Regina, Saskatchewan:

	2005	2004	2003
Sales	$3,032,727	$2,531,390	$1,358,811
Cost of goods sold	2,051,491	1,807,339	1,243,151
Net income	585,816	454,942	4,672
Current assets	1,517,086	1,182,455	649,302
Current liabilities	348,776	356,044	198,181

Instructions

(a) Calculate the gross profit margin, profit margin, and current ratio for each year.
(b) Evaluate IPSCO's performance over the three-year period.

*P5–9B Data for Travel Warehouse are presented in P5–2B.

Instructions

Record the July transactions for Travel Warehouse, assuming a periodic inventory system is used instead of a perpetual inventory system.

*P5–10B Data for Norlan Company are presented in P5–3B.

Instructions

Record the September and October transactions for Norlan Company, assuming a periodic inventory system is used instead of a perpetual inventory system.

*P5–11B Data for Nisson Distributing Company are presented in P5–4B. A physical inventory count shows $3,742 of inventory on hand on April 30, 2008.

Record and post inventory transactions—periodic system. Prepare partial income statement.
(SO 7) AP

Instructions

(a) Record the transactions assuming Nisson uses a periodic inventory system.
(b) Set up general ledger accounts, enter the beginning cash and capital balances, and post the transactions.
(c) Prepare a partial multiple-step income statement, up to gross profit, for the month of April 2008.

*P5–12B The following is an alphabetical list of Bud's Bakery's adjusted account balances at the end of the company's fiscal year on November 30, 2008:

Prepare financial statements and closing entries—periodic system.
(SO 7) AP

Accounts payable	$ 35,910	Inventory, December 1, 2007	$ 34,360
Accounts receivable	8,470	Land	85,000
Accumulated amortization—		Mortgage payable	142,000
building	96,250	Prepaid insurance	4,500
Accumulated amortization—		Property tax expense	3,500
equipment	35,000	Purchase discounts	6,300
Amortization expense	11,375	Purchase returns and allowances	3,315
Building	175,000	Purchases	630,700
B. Hachey, capital	76,800	Salaries expense	121,500
B. Hachey, drawings	12,000	Salaries payable	8,000
Cash	12,700	Sales	844,000
Delivery expense	8,200	Sales discounts	4,250
Equipment	84,000	Sales returns and allowances	9,845
Freight in	5,060	Unearned sales revenue	3,000
Insurance expense	9,000	Utilities expense	19,800
Interest expense	11,315		

Additional facts:

1. Of the mortgage payable, $15,500 is due in the next year.
2. Merchandise inventory at November 30, 2008, is $38,550.

Instructions

(a) How do you know from the list of accounts that Bud's Bakery uses a periodic inventory system?
(b) Prepare a multiple-step income statement, statement of owner's equity, and classified balance sheet.
(c) Prepare the closing journal entries.
(d) Post closing entries to the inventory and capital accounts. Check that the balances in these accounts are the same as the amounts on the balance sheet.

Continuing Cookie Chronicle

(*Note:* This is a continuation of the Cookie Chronicle from Chapters 1 through 4. From the information gathered in the previous chapters, follow the instructions below using the general ledger accounts you have already prepared.)

Because Natalie has had such a successful first few months, she is considering other opportunities to develop her business. One opportunity is the sale of fine European mixers. The owner of Kzinski Supply Co. has approached Natalie to become the exclusive Canadian distributor of these fine mixers. The current cost of a mixer is approximately $525 Canadian, and Natalie would sell each one for $1,050. Natalie comes to you for advice on how to account for these mixers. Each appliance has a serial number and can be easily identified.

Natalie asks you the following questions:

1. "Would you consider these mixers to be inventory? Or should they be classified as supplies or equipment?"
2. "I've learned a little about keeping track of inventory using both the perpetual and the periodic systems of accounting for inventory. Which system do you think is better? Which one would you recommend for the type of inventory that I want to sell?"
3. "How often do I need to count inventory if I maintain it using the perpetual system? Do I need to count inventory at all?"

In the end, Natalie decides to use the perpetual inventory system. The following transactions happen during the month of January:

Jan. 4 Bought five deluxe mixers on account from Kzinski Supply Co. for $2,625, FOB shipping point, terms n/30.
   6 Paid $100 freight on the January 4 purchase.
   7 Returned one of the mixers to Kzinski because it was damaged during shipping. Kzinski issues Cookie Creations a credit note for the cost of the mixer plus $20 for the cost of freight that was paid on January 6 for one mixer.
   8 Collected $375 of the accounts receivable from December 2007.
   12 Three deluxe mixers are sold on account for $3,150, FOB destination, terms n/30.
   14 Paid the $75 of delivery charges for the three mixers that were sold on January 12.
   14 Bought four deluxe mixers on account from Kzinski Supply Co. for $2,100, FOB shipping point, terms n/30.
   17 Natalie was concerned that there was not enough cash available to pay for all of the mixers purchased. She invested an additional $1,000 cash in Cookie Creations.
   18 Paid $80 freight on the January 14 purchase.
   20 Sold two deluxe mixers for $2,100 cash.
   28 Natalie issued a cheque to her assistant for all the help the assistant has given her during the month. Her assistant worked 20 hours in January and was also paid the $56 owing at December 31, 2007. (Recall that Natalie's assistant earns $8 an hour.)
   28 Collected the amounts due from customers for the January 12 transaction.
   30 Paid a $145 cell phone bill ($75 for the December 2007 account payable and $70 for the month of January). (Recall that the cell phone is only used for business purposes.)
   31 Paid Kzinski all amounts due.
   31 Nathalie withdrew $750 cash for personal use.

As at January 31, the following adjusting entry data are available:

1. A count of baking supplies reveals that none were used in January.
2. Another month's worth of amortization needs to be recorded on the baking equipment bought in November. (Recall that the baking equipment cost $1,300 and has a useful life of five years or 60 months.)
3. An additional month's worth of interest on her grandmother's loan needs to be accrued. (Recall Cookie Creations borrowed $2,000 and the interest rate is 6%.)
4. During the month, $110 of insurance has expired.
5. An analysis of the unearned revenue account reveals that Natalie has not had time to teach any of these lessons this month because she has been so busy selling mixers. As a result, there is no change to the unearned revenue account. Natalie hopes to book the outstanding lessons in February.
6. An inventory count of mixers at the end of January reveals that Natalie has three mixers remaining.

Instructions

Using the information from previous chapters and the new information above, do the following:

(a) Answer Natalie's questions.
(b) Prepare and post the January 2008 transactions.
(c) Prepare a trial balance.
(d) Prepare and post the adjusting journal entries required.
(e) Prepare an adjusted trial balance.
(f) Prepare a multiple-step income statement for the month ended January 31, 2008.

Cumulative Coverage—Chapters 2 to 5

The Board Shop, owned by Andrew John, sells skateboards in the summer and snowboards in the winter. The shop has an August 31 fiscal year end and uses a perpetual inventory system. On August 1, 2008, the company had the following balances in its general ledger:

Cash	$ 17,840	A. John, capital	$ 54,650
Accounts receivable	2,975	A. John, drawings	41,000
Inventory	112,700	Sales	762,300
Store supplies	2,660	Sales returns and allowances	11,420
Prepaid insurance	4,140	Sales discounts	3,805
Store equipment	53,800	Cost of goods sold	517,680
Accumulated amortization—		Salaries expense	92,900
store equipment	13,450	Rent expense	17,050
Accounts payable	18,625	Advertising expense	9,625
Unearned sales revenue	4,820	Interest expense	2,250
Notes payable	36,000		

During August, the last month of the fiscal year, the company had the following transactions:

Aug. 1 Paid $1,550 for August's rent.
    2 Paid $4,500 on account.
    4 Sold merchandise costing $8,500 for $12,250 cash.
    5 Purchased merchandise on account from Orange Line Co., FOB shipping point, for $24,500.
    5 Paid freight charges of $500 on merchandise purchased from Orange Line Co.
    8 Purchased store supplies on account for $345.
    9 Refunded a customer $425 cash for returned merchandise. The merchandise had cost $290 and was returned to inventory.
   10 Sold merchandise on account to Spider Company for $16,750, terms 2/10, n/30, FOB shipping point. The merchandise had a cost of $11,340.
   11 Paid Orange Line Co. for half of the merchandise purchased on August 5.
   12 Spider Company returned $750 of the merchandise it purchased. Board Shop issued Spider a credit memo. The merchandise had a cost of $510 and was returned to inventory.
   15 Paid salaries, $4,200.
   17 Andrew John withdrew $3,800 cash.
   19 Spider Company paid the amount owing.
   21 Purchased $9,900 of merchandise from Rainbow Option Co. on account, terms 2/10, n/30, FOB destination.
   23 Returned $800 of the merchandise to Rainbow Option Co. and received a credit memo.
   24 Received $525 cash in advance from customers for merchandise to be delivered in September.
   26 Purchased merchandise for $4,500 cash.
   29 Paid $1,200 for advertising.
   30 Paid Rainbow Option Co. the amount owing.
   31 Collected $775 of the August 1 accounts receivable.

Instructions

(a) Create a general ledger account for each of the above accounts and enter the August 1 balances.
(b) Record and post the August transactions.
(c) Prepare a trial balance at August 31.
(d) Record and post the following adjustments:
 1. Four months of the 12-month insurance policy have expired.
 2. A count shows $610 of store supplies on hand at August 31.
 3. The store equipment has an estimated eight-year useful life.
 4. The note payable has an annual interest rate of 6.5%. Two months of interest has accrued on August 31.
 5. Of the note payable, $6,000 must be paid on December 1 each year.
 6. An analysis of the Unearned Sales Revenue account shows that $3,570 has been earned by August 31. A corresponding $2,430 for Cost of Goods Sold will also need to be recorded for these sales.
 7. Salaries earned but not paid at August 31 total $3,080.
 8. A count of the merchandise inventory on August 31 shows $127,620 of inventory on hand.
(e) Prepare an adjusted trial balance at August 31.
(f) Prepare a multiple-step income statement, statement of owner's equity, and classified balance sheet.
(g) Record and post closing entries.
(h) Prepare a post-closing trial balance at August 31.

BROADENING YOUR PERSPECTIVE

Financial Reporting and Analysis

Financial Reporting Problem

BYP5–1 The financial statements for **The Forzani Group Ltd.** are reproduced in Appendix A at the end of this text.

Instructions

(a) Is The Forzani Group a service company or a merchandising company?
(b) Significant accounting policies are identified in Note 2 to the consolidated financial statements. In regard to Note 2 (b), does The Forzani Group recognize any volume rebates and/or supplier discounts? If yes, how are they recognized?
(c) Does The Forzani Group show the amount of sales returns? Why do you think it does this?
(d) Are any non-operating revenues and non-operating expenses included in The Forzani Group's income statement (what Forzani calls its "statement of operations")?
(e) Determine the following values:
 1. Percentage change in revenue from 2005 to 2006
 2. Percentage change in "operating earnings before undernoted items" from 2005 to 2006
 3. Gross profit margin for each of the 2005 and 2006 fiscal years
 4. Profit margin for each of the 2005 and 2006 fiscal years
(f) Based on the data in part (e) above, what conclusions can be drawn about Forzani's profitability in 2006 compared to 2005?

Interpreting Financial Statements

BYP5–2 Selected information from **Sleeman Breweries Ltd.'s** income statement (statement of operations) for the past three years follows (in thousands):

	2005	2004	2003
Net revenue	$206,674	$213,354	$185,036
Cost of goods sold	100,565	106,207	96,703
Operating expense	85,478	78,376	61,824
Interest expense	7,837	6,643	5,506
Income tax expense	4,697	7,702	8,750

Instructions

(a) Calculate gross profit and net income for each of the three years.
(b) Calculate the percentage change in net revenue and net income from 2003 to 2005.
(c) Calculate the gross profit margin for each of the three years. Comment on any trend in this percentage.
(d) Calculate the profit margin for each of the three years. Comment on any trend in this percentage.
(e) How well has Sleeman Breweries managed its operating expenses over the three-year period?

Critical Thinking

Collaborative Learning Activity

Note to instructor: Additional instructions and material for this group activity can be found on the Instructor Resource Site.

BYP5–3 In this group activity, you will journalize merchandising transactions.

The Academic Bookstore (the buyer) started its business on the first day of this month and purchased books from Evergreen Publishing (the sellers). Each transaction between the two companies generates a journal entry in the books of each company.

Instructions

(a) Your instructor will divide the class into groups. Each group will split into two sub-groups: buyers and sellers.
(b) In your smaller groups, journalize the transactions given to you by your instructor. Record the entries once everyone is in agreement.
(c) Form a pair with a student from the other sub-group. Review the entries of the buyer and the seller with your partner and identify and understand the differences from the two points of view.
(d) You may be asked by your instructor to write a short quiz on this topic.

Study Aids:
Working in Groups

Communication Activity

BYP5–4 Consider the following events listed in chronological order:

1. Dexter Maersk decides to buy a custom-made snowboard and calls The Great Canadian Snowboard Company to inquire about its products.
2. Dexter asks The Great Canadian Snowboard Company to manufacture a custom board for him.
3. The company sends Dexter a purchase order to fill out, which he immediately completes, signs, and sends back with the required 25% down payment.

Study Aids:
Writing Handbook

4. The Great Canadian Snowboard Company receives Dexter's purchase order and down payment, and begins working on the board.
5. The Great Canadian Snowboard Company has its fiscal year end. At this time, Dexter's board is 75% completed.
6. The company completes the snowboard for Dexter and notifies him that he can take delivery.
7. Dexter picks up his snowboard from the company and takes it home.
8. Dexter tries the snowboard out and likes it so much that he carves his initials in it.
9. The Great Canadian Snowboard Company bills Dexter for the cost of the snowboard, less the 25% down payment.
10. The company receives partial payment from Dexter.
11. The company receives payment of the balance due from Dexter.

Instructions

In a memo to the president of The Great Canadian Snowboard Company, answer these questions:

(a) When should The Great Canadian Snowboard Company record the revenue and expense related to the snowboard? Refer to the revenue recognition and matching principles in your answer.
(b) Suppose that, with his purchase order, Dexter was not required to make a down payment. Would that change your answer to part (a)?

Ethics Case

**Study Aids:
Ethics in Accounting**

BYP5–5   Rita Pelzer was just hired as the assistant controller of Liu Stores. The company is a specialty chain store with nine retail stores concentrated in one metropolitan area. Among other things, the payment of all invoices is centralized in one of the departments Rita will manage. Her main responsibilities are to maintain the company's high credit rating by paying all bills when they are due and to take advantage of all cash discounts.

Jamie Caterino, the former assistant controller, who has now been promoted to controller, is training Rita in her new duties. He instructs Rita to continue the practice of preparing all cheques "net of discount" and dating the cheques the last day of the discount period. "But," Jamie continues, "we always hold the cheques at least four days beyond the discount period before mailing them. That way we get another four days of interest on our money. Most of our creditors need our business and don't complain. And, if they scream about our missing the discount period, we blame it on the mail room or the post office. Believe me, everybody does it. By the way, welcome to our team!"

Instructions

(a) What are the ethical considerations in this case?
(b) Who are the stakeholders that are harmed or benefited in this situation?
(c) Should Rita continue the practice started by Jamie? Does she have any choice?

ANSWERS TO CHAPTER QUESTIONS

Answers to Accounting in Action Insight Questions

Business Insight, p. 222

Q: How could RFID technology help Wal-Mart avoid being out of stock?
A: By knowing exactly where its inventory is, each Wal-Mart store can better estimate how long it will take to send items to its stores and replace items that have been sold. This information, combined with information from the perpetual inventory system on how quickly an item is sold, can be used to decide the best time to reorder merchandise.

Across the Organization Insight, p. 232

Q: What accounting information would help a manager decide what to do with returned goods?

A: The manager would need to know the potential revenues and expenses for each alternative. For example, returning goods to stock and selling them again may provide the highest revenue but the cost of getting the goods ready for resale may also be high. The revenue earned from liquidating the returned goods may be much lower but the cost of doing this may also be very low. The manager should compare the estimated net income—not just the revenue earned— of each alternative when deciding what to do.

Ethics Insight, p. 234

Q. How can a computerized point-of-sale system help reduce inventory losses?

A. A computerized point-of-sale system will automatically update inventory balances as sales are recorded at the cash register. The merchandiser can regularly check parts of its inventory and determine which inventory items suffer the most from shoplifting. This helps merchandisers decide where they should increase their theft prevention efforts and where current efforts are working well.

Answer to Forzani Review It Question 4, p. 245

Forzani's gross profit margin for 2005 is 33.9% ($333,896 ÷ $985,054). The company's gross profit margin improved slightly in 2006, to 33.92% ($383,091 ÷ $1,129,404). Forzani's profit margin for 2005 is 2.2% ($21,545 ÷ $985,054). The profit margin weakened in 2006, to 1.2% ($13,757 ÷ $1,129,404). All dollar amounts are given in thousands.

Answers to Self-Study Questions

1. c   2. a   3. a   4. c   5. a   6. a   7. d   8. c   *9. b   *10. b

Remember to go back to the Navigator Box at the beginning of the chapter to check off your completed work.

concepts for review >>

Before studying this chapter, you should understand or, if necessary, review:

a. The cost principle (Ch. 1, p. 8) and matching principle of accounting (Ch. 3, p. 105).

b. The difference between calculating cost of goods sold in a perpetual inventory system and in a periodic inventory system. (Ch. 5, pp. 231–234 and 251–252)

c. How to journalize inventory transactions in perpetual and periodic inventory systems. (Ch. 5, pp. 226–234 and 247–250)

d. How to prepare financial statements for a merchandising company. (Ch. 5, pp. 240–245)

Last In, First Out

CALGARY, Alta.—At Petro-Canada, one of Canada's largest integrated oil and gas companies, inventory is recorded at cost and includes the cost of crude oil, plus refining and distribution costs.

The Calgary-based company, which has an inventory of around 13.5 million barrels of crude oil and refined petroleum products, uses the LIFO ("last-in, first-out") method to determine the cost of its crude oil and product inventories. "Under LIFO, the most recent cost of commodity purchases is reflected in the cost of sales," says controller Mike Barkwell. "As a result, LIFO provides a better matching of costs and revenues."

Petro-Canada: www.petro-canada.ca

Before the war in the Persian Gulf in 1991–1992, Petro-Canada and other oil and gas companies used FIFO ("first-in, first-out") as their inventory cost flow assumption, where the costs of the first goods manufactured are the first ones to come out of inventory and be included in sales. "Under FIFO, in times of rising prices, the carrying value of the closing inventory would be increasing and income would be higher," Mr. Barkwell explains. Similarly, if crude oil prices fell, so would the cost of the inventory and the company's income.

With the rising oil prices before the 1991 war in the Persian Gulf and their subsequent fall, Canadian companies found that selling a high-cost inventory into a lower-priced market resulted in significant losses. "Petro-Canada changed from FIFO to LIFO in '92 to match costs and revenues more closely, and we ended up recog-

nizing a reduction in our inventory carrying value of $130 million as a result," Mr. Barkwell says.

Still, the Canada Revenue Agency does not permit companies to use LIFO for their inventory costing. "For income taxes, we maintain our costs on a FIFO basis," Mr. Barkwell confirms. "So in effect we have two costing measures for inventory."

One criticism of LIFO is that if a company's opening inventory was purchased when oil prices were low, the carrying value of the inventory remains at that low price, which may not be realistic in a current balance sheet. "LIFO provides a better matching in the income statement, but can provide an out-of-date valuation in the balance sheet. FIFO gives a more current valuation in the balance sheet, but a less current matching in the income statement," Mr. Barkwell says. "Both methods have their pros and cons."

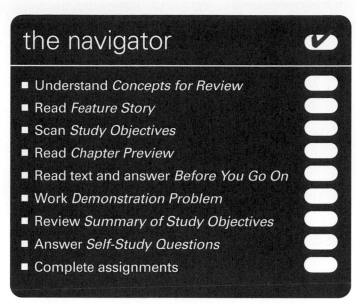

the navigator ✓

- Understand *Concepts for Review*
- Read *Feature Story*
- Scan *Study Objectives*
- Read *Chapter Preview*
- Read text and answer *Before You Go On*
- Work *Demonstration Problem*
- Review *Summary of Study Objectives*
- Answer *Self-Study Questions*
- Complete assignments

chapter 6

Inventory Costing

study objectives >>

✓
the navigator

After studying this chapter, you should be able to:

1. Describe the steps in determining inventory quantities.
2. Calculate ending inventory and cost of goods sold in a periodic inventory system using inventory cost flow assumptions.
3. Determine the effects of inventory cost flow assumptions and inventory errors on the financial statements.
4. Demonstrate the presentation and analysis of inventory.
5. Calculate ending inventory and cost of goods sold in a perpetual inventory system using inventory cost flow assumptions (Appendix 6A).
6. Estimate ending inventory using the gross profit and retail inventory methods (Appendix 6B).

For companies like Petro-Canada, accounting for inventory can be time-consuming and complex. In this chapter, we first explain the procedures for determining inventory quantities. We then discuss the cost flow assumptions for determining the cost of goods sold and the cost of inventory on hand. Next we see the effects of cost flow assumptions and inventory errors on a company's financial statements. We end by illustrating methods to report and analyze inventory.

The chapter is organized as follows:

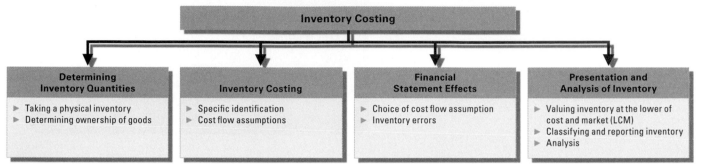

Determining Inventory Quantities

study objective 1

Describe the steps in determining inventory quantities.

All companies need to count their entire inventory at least once a year whether they are using a perpetual or periodic inventory system. This is called taking a physical inventory. Companies using a perpetual inventory system use this information to check the accuracy of their perpetual inventory records. Recall from Chapter 5 that in a perpetual inventory system the accounting records continuously—perpetually—show the amount of inventory that should be on hand, not the amount that actually is on hand. An adjusting entry is required if the physical inventory count does not match what was recorded in the general ledger.

In a periodic inventory system, inventory quantities are not continuously updated. Companies using a periodic inventory system must take a physical inventory to determine the amount on hand at the end of the accounting period. Once the ending inventory amount is known, this amount is then used to calculate the cost of goods sold for the period and to update the Merchandise Inventory account in the general ledger.

Inventory quantities are determined in two steps: (1) by taking a physical inventory of goods on hand, and (2) by determining the ownership of goods.

Taking a Physical Inventory

Taking a physical inventory involves actually counting, weighing, or measuring each kind of inventory on hand. Taking an inventory can be an enormous task for many companies, especially for such a large and complex company as Petro-Canada, which has thousands of inventory items. An inventory count is generally more accurate when goods are not being sold or received during the counting. This is why companies often count their inventory when the business is closed or when business is slow.

To make fewer errors in taking the inventory, a company should ensure that it has a good system of internal control. Internal control is the process designed and implemented by management to help their organization achieve reliable financial reporting, effective and efficient operations, and compliance with relevant laws and regulations. Some of the internal control procedures for counting inventory are as follows:

1. The counting should be done by employees who are not responsible for either custody of the inventory or keeping inventory records.

2. Each counter should establish that each inventory item actually exists, how many there are of it, and what condition each item is in. For example, does each box actually contain what it is supposed to contain?
3. There should be a second count by another employee or auditor. Counting should be done in teams of two.
4. Prenumbered inventory tags should be used to ensure that all inventory items are counted and that no items are counted more than once.

We will learn more about internal controls in Chapter 7.

After the physical inventory is taken, the quantity of each kind of inventory item is listed on inventory summary sheets. To ensure accuracy, the listing should be verified by a second employee, or auditor. Unit costs are then applied to the quantities in order to determine the total cost of the inventory—this will be explained later in the chapter when we discuss inventory costing.

To estimate the cost of inventory when a physical count cannot be taken (if the inventory is destroyed, for example) or when it is inconvenient (during interim periods), estimating methods are used. These methods (the gross profit and retail inventory methods) are discussed in Appendix 6B.

Determining Ownership of Goods

Before we can begin to calculate the cost of inventory, we need to consider the ownership of goods. Specifically, we need to be sure that we have not included in the inventory quantities any goods that do not belong to the company, and have not forgotten any items that do belong to the company.

Goods in Transit

Goods are considered in transit when they are on board a public carrier such as a railway, airline, trucking, or shipping company at the end of the accounting period. The problem is determining who should include the goods in its inventory, the purchaser or the seller. Only one company has legal title to the goods while they are in transit. As we learned in Chapter 5, legal title is determined by the terms of sale as follows:

1. FOB (free on board) shipping point. Legal title (ownership) of the goods passes to the buyer when the public carrier accepts the goods from the seller.
2. FOB destination. Legal title (ownership) of the goods remains with the seller until the goods reach the buyer.

If the shipping terms are FOB shipping point, the buyer is responsible for paying the shipping costs and has legal title to the goods while they are in transit. If the shipping terms are FOB destination, the seller is responsible for paying the shipping costs and has legal title to the goods while they are in transit. These terms are important in determining the exact date for recording a purchase or sale of inventory and what items should be included in inventory.

Inventory quantities may be seriously miscounted if goods in transit at the statement date are ignored. The company may have purchased goods that have not yet been received, or it may have sold goods that have not yet been delivered. Assume that Hill Company has 20,000 units of inventory in its warehouse on December 31. It also has the following goods in transit: (1) sales of 1,500 units shipped December 31, FOB destination, and (2) purchases of 2,500 units shipped FOB shipping point by the seller on December 31. Hill has legal title to both the units sold and the units purchased. If units in transit are ignored, inventory quantities would be understated by 4,000 units (1,500 + 2,500). As we will see later in this chapter, inaccurate inventory quantities affect not only the inventory amount on the balance sheet; they also affect the cost of goods sold reported in the income statement.

The following table summarizes who pays the shipping costs, and who has legal title to (owns) the goods, while they are in transit between the seller's location (the shipping point) and the buyer's location (the destination):

Shipping Terms	Shipping Costs	Legal Title
FOB shipping point	Buyer	Buyer
FOB destination	Seller	Seller

Consigned Goods

In some lines of business, it is customary to hold goods belonging to other parties and to sell them, for a fee, without ever taking ownership of the goods. These are called **consigned goods**. Under a consignment arrangement, the holder of the goods (called the *consignee*) does not own the goods. Ownership remains with the shipper of the goods (called the *consignor*) until the goods are actually sold to a customer. Because consigned goods are not owned by the consignee, they should not be included in the consignee's physical inventory count. The consignor, on the other hand, should include merchandise held by the consignee as part of the consignor's inventory.

For example, artists often display their paintings and other works of art on consignment at galleries. In such cases, the art gallery does not take ownership of the art—it still belongs to the artist. Therefore, if an inventory count is taken, any art on consignment should not be included in the art gallery's inventory. When the art sells, the gallery then takes a commission and pays the artist the remainder. Many craft stores, second-hand clothing stores, sporting goods stores, and antique dealers sell goods on consignment to keep their inventory costs down and to avoid the risk of purchasing an item they will not be able to sell.

Other Situations

Sometimes goods are not physically present at a company because they have been taken home *on approval* by a customer. Goods on approval should be added to the physical inventory count because they still belong to the seller. The customer will either return the item or decide to buy it.

In other cases, goods are sold but the seller is holding them for alteration, or until they are picked up or delivered to the customer. These goods should not be included in the physical count, because legal title to ownership has passed to the customer. Damaged or unsaleable goods should be separated from the physical count and any loss should be recorded. We will discuss losses in the valuation of inventories later in the chapter.

ACCOUNTING IN ACTION ▶ Across the Organization Insight

Liaison Can./U.S. is a Montreal-based courier company that ships a variety of goods and packages across the Canada–United States border. In the past, to track and locate customers' inventory, an employee had to walk around the warehouse to find it, then write down where the product was located and how much stock was available, and manually input the information into the system back at the office. Once the inventory was on a truck, there was no way of knowing where the truck was or the condition of the inventory. The company realized that it needed to reduce its costs associated with inventory tracking and improve its inventory management. That's when it turned to Radio Frequency Identification (RFID) technology. With RFID technology, silicon chips and antennas, which can receive and respond to radio-frequency queries, are attached to products. Using RFID technology, employees can now easily locate goods in the warehouse or even during transit, saving hours each day and greatly improving their management of inventory.

Source: Microsoft Visual Studio.Net, "Shipping Company Boosts Revenue with Help of Microsoft-Based RFID Solution."

 How might a warehouse manager use RFID technology to assist in doing a year-end physical inventory count?

BEFORE YOU GO ON . . .

▶**Review It**

1. What are the steps for determining inventory quantities?
2. How is ownership determined for goods in transit?
3. Who has title to consigned goods?

▶**Do It**

The Too Good To Be Threw Company completed its inventory count. It arrived at a total inventory value of $200,000, counting everything currently on hand in its warehouse. You have been given the information listed below. Discuss how this information affects the reported cost of inventory.

1. Goods costing $15,000 that are being held on consignment were included in the inventory.
2. Goods purchased for $10,000 and in transit (terms FOB shipping point) were not included in the count.
3. Inventory with a cost of $12,000 that was sold and in transit (terms FOB shipping point) was not included in the count.

Action Plan

- Apply the rules of ownership to goods held on consignment:
  - Goods held on consignment for another company are not included in inventory.
  - Goods held on consignment by another company are included in inventory.
- Apply the rules of ownership to goods in transit:
  - FOB shipping point: Goods sold or purchased and shipped FOB shipping point belong to the buyer.
  - FOB destination: Goods sold or purchased and shipped FOB destination belong to the seller until they reach their destination.

Solution

1. The goods held on consignment should be deducted from Too Good To Be Threw's inventory count ($200,000 − $15,000 = $185,000).
2. The goods in transit purchased FOB shipping point should be added to the company's inventory count ($185,000 + $10,000 = $195,000).
3. The goods sold in transit FOB shipping point for $12,000 were correctly excluded from Too Good To Be Threw's ending inventory, since title passed when the goods were handed over to the railway company.

The correct inventory totals $195,000 not $200,000.

Related exercise material: BE6–1, BE6–2, E6–1, and E6–2.

the
navigator

Inventory Costing

After the quantities in units have been determined for each inventory item, unit costs are matched to those quantities to determine the total cost of the ending inventory and the cost of the goods sold. When all inventory items have been purchased at the same unit cost, this calculation is simple. However, when identical items have been purchased at different costs during the period, it is difficult to decide what the unit costs are of the items that remain in inventory and what the unit costs are of the items that have been sold.

study objective 2

Calculate ending inventory and cost of goods sold in a periodic inventory system using inventory cost flow assumptions.

In Chapter 5, you did not have this problem because you were either told the cost of goods sold or, in examples with identical inventory items, these inventory items always had the same unit cost. In Chapter 6, we build on what you learned in Chapter 5. In this chapter, you are not given the cost of the ending inventory or the cost of the goods sold. Instead, you have to calculate it.

For example, assume that throughout the calendar year Fraser Valley Electronics buys at different prices 1,000 Astro Condenser units for resale. Some Astro Condensers cost $10 when they were originally purchased in the previous year. Units purchased in April cost $11, those purchased in August cost $12, and those acquired in November cost $13. Now suppose Fraser Valley Electronics has 450 Astro Condensers remaining in inventory at the end of December. Should these inventory items be assigned a cost of $10, $11, $12, $13, or some combination of all four?

To determine the cost of goods sold, as well as the cost of ending inventory, we need a method of allocating the purchase cost to each item in inventory and each item that has been sold. One allocation method—specific identification—uses the actual physical flow of goods to determine cost. We will look at this method first.

www.wiley.com/canada/weygandt

Animated Tutorials and Videos: Inventory Cost Flow Tutorial

Specific Identification

The **specific identification** method tracks the actual physical flow (movement) of the goods. Each item of inventory is marked, tagged, or coded with its specific unit cost. Items that are still in inventory at the end of the year are specifically costed to determine the total cost of the ending inventory.

Assume, for example, that Fraser Valley Electronics buys three identical LCD TVs at costs of $700, $750, and $800. During the year, two are sold at a selling price of $1,200 each. At December 31, the company determines that the $750 LCD TV is still on hand. The ending inventory is $750 and the cost of goods sold is $1,500 ($700 +$800).

Illustration 6-1 ▶

Specific identification

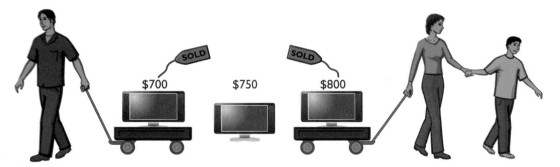

Specific identification is the ideal method for determining cost. This method reports ending inventory at actual cost and matches the cost of goods sold against sales revenue. However, there are also disadvantages to this method. For example, specific identification may allow management to manipulate net income. To see how, assume that Fraser Valley Electronics wants to maximize its net income just before year end. When selling one of the three LCD TVs referred to earlier, management could choose the TV with the lowest cost ($700) to match against revenues ($1,200). Or, it could minimize net income by selecting the TV with the highest cost ($800).

Specific identification is practical when a company sells a limited number of high-unit-cost items that can be clearly identified from purchase through to sale. Automobiles are a good example of a type of inventory that works well with specific identification because they can be individually identified by serial number. On the other hand, many of the parts sold by an automobile dealership are identical low-cost items. It may not be practical to track each item separately.

Today, with bar coding, it is theoretically possible to use specific identification with nearly any type of product. The reality is that this practice is still quite expensive and rare. While bar coding is often used to identify an inventory item—such as a 284 ml can of

Campbell's condensed tomato soup—it is rare to use the bar code to identify whether the specific can of soup was purchased in, say, January at one cost or in February at a different cost. Instead, rather than keep track of the cost of each particular item sold, most companies make assumptions—cost flow assumptions—about which items are sold. There are also companies that simply cannot track each unit of inventory separately, because the inventory physically mixes together, for example Petro-Canada's crude oil. Petro-Canada has no choice but to use a cost flow assumption to determine the cost of each barrel of crude oil it sells.

Cost Flow Assumptions

Cost flow assumptions are different from specific identification as they assume flows of costs that may not be the same as the physical flow of goods. There are three commonly used cost flow assumptions:

1. First-in, first-out (FIFO)
2. Average cost
3. Last-in, first-out (LIFO)

Any of the three cost flow assumptions can be applied in a perpetual inventory system or a periodic inventory system. Recall from Chapter 5 that the difference between the two systems is when the cost of goods sold is calculated and recorded. Under a perpetual inventory system, this allocation is made as each item is sold. Under a periodic inventory system, the allocation is made at the end of the period. We will discuss the periodic inventory system here. Appendix 6A explains the use of these cost flow assumptions under a perpetual inventory system.

We have chosen to use the periodic inventory system to illustrate cost flow assumptions in this chapter for several reasons. First, many companies that use a perpetual inventory system use it only to keep track of *quantities* on hand. When they determine their cost of goods sold at the end of the period, they use one of the three cost flow assumptions under a periodic inventory system. Second, most companies that use the average cost flow assumption use it under a periodic inventory system. Third, the FIFO cost flow assumption gives the same results under the periodic and perpetual inventory systems. Finally, it is simpler to demonstrate the cost flow assumptions under the periodic inventory system, which will make it easier for you to understand them.

To illustrate these three inventory cost flow assumptions in a periodic inventory system, we will assume that Fraser Valley Electronics has the following information for one of its products, a Z202 Astro Condenser:

FRASER VALLEY ELECTRONICS Z202 Astro Condensers				
Date	Explanation	Units	Unit Cost	Total Cost
Jan. 1	Beginning inventory	100	$10	$ 1,000
Apr. 15	Purchase	200	11	2,200
Aug. 24	Purchase	300	12	3,600
Nov. 27	Purchase	400	13	5,200
Total		1,000		$12,000

The company had a total of 1,000 units available for sale during the year. The total cost of the 1,000 units available for sale was $12,000. A physical inventory count at the end of the year determined that 450 units remained on hand. Consequently, it can be calculated that 550 (1,000 − 450) units were sold during the year.

The question to be answered next is this: Which unit costs should be allocated to the 450 units remaining in ending inventory so that we can calculate the cost of the ending inventory? Once we have calculated the cost of the ending inventory, we can then use this information to calculate the cost of the goods sold.

The answer to the question depends on which inventory cost flow assumption is being used by a company. In our example, the total cost (or "pool of costs") of the 1,000 units available for sale is $12,000. We will now demonstrate the allocation of this pool of costs using the three cost flow assumptions—FIFO, average cost, and LIFO—in the next sections.

Note that, throughout these sections, the total cost of goods available for sale will remain the same for each inventory cost flow assumption. The pool of costs does not change with the choice of cost flow assumption—what changes is the allocation of these costs between the ending inventory and the cost of goods sold. Illustration 6-2 shows this allocation.

Illustration 6-2 ▶

Allocation of cost of goods available for sale

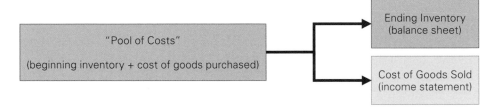

First-In, First-Out (FIFO)

The **first-in, first-out (FIFO)** cost flow assumption assumes that the goods that were purchased the earliest are the first ones to be sold. This does not necessarily mean that the oldest units are actually sold first; it means only that the cost of the oldest units is used first to calculate cost of goods sold. Note that there is no accounting requirement that the cost flow assumption match the actual movement of the goods. Nonetheless, FIFO often matches the actual physical flow of merchandise, because it generally is good business practice to sell the oldest units first.

In the periodic inventory system, we ignore the different dates of each of the sales. Remember in Chapter 5 we learned that in the periodic inventory system we do not determine the cost of goods sold with each sale. Instead, we determine cost of goods sold at the end of a period by deducting the ending inventory from the cost of goods available for sale. Illustration 6-3 shows how the cost of goods available for sale is allocated at Fraser Valley Electronics using FIFO in a periodic inventory system.

Illustration 6-3 ◀

Periodic system—FIFO

COST OF GOODS AVAILABLE FOR SALE				
Date	Explanation	Units	Unit Cost	Total Cost
Jan. 1	Beginning inventory	100	$10	$ 1,000
Apr. 15	Purchase	200	11	2,200
Aug. 24	Purchase	300	12	3,600
Nov. 27	Purchase	400	13	5,200
	Total	1,000		$12,000

Step 1: Ending Inventory				Step 2: Cost of Goods Sold	
Date	Units	Unit Cost	Total Cost		
Nov. 27	400	$13	$5,200	Cost of goods available for sale	$12,000
Aug. 24	50	12	600	Less: Ending inventory	5,800
Total	450		$5,800	Cost of goods sold	$ 6,200

The cost flow assumption—FIFO, in this case—always indicates the order of selling. That is, with FIFO, the order in which the goods are assumed to be sold is first-in, first-out. With FIFO, we are therefore assuming that the most recent purchases are still in inventory. Thus the cost of the ending inventory is determined by taking the unit cost of the most recent purchase and working backward until all units of inventory have been costed. With FIFO, 450 units of ending inventory are costed using the most recent purchase costs. The last purchase was 400 units at $13 on November 27. The remaining 50 units (450 – 400) are costed at the price of the second most recent purchase, $12 on August 24.

Once the cost of the ending inventory is determined, the cost of goods sold is calculated by subtracting the cost of the ending inventory (the cost of the goods not sold) from the cost of the goods available for sale.

The cost of goods sold can also be separately calculated or proven as shown below. To determine the cost of goods sold under the FIFO cost flow assumption, simply start at the first item of beginning inventory and count forward until the total number of units sold (550) is reached. The result is that only 250 units are assumed sold of the 300 units purchased on August 24. Recall that 50 of the units purchased on August 24 are included in our ending inventory.

Date	Units	Unit Cost	Cost of Goods Sold
Jan. 1	100	$10	$1,000
Apr. 15	200	11	2,200
Aug. 24	250	12	3,000
Total	550		$6,200

Because of the potential for calculation errors, we recommend that the cost of goods sold be calculated both ways in your assignments. It is also helpful to check that the total of the cost of goods sold and ending inventory is equal to the cost of goods available for sale (e.g., $6,200 + $5,800 = $12,000).

Average Cost

The **average cost** flow assumption assumes that it is impossible to measure a specific physical flow of inventory and that it is therefore better to cost items using an average price. Under this assumption, the allocation of the cost of goods available for sale is based on the weighted average unit cost. This average cost is not calculated by taking a simple average ([$10 + $11 + $12 + $13] ÷ 4 = $11.50 per unit). Rather, it is calculated by weighting the quantities purchased at each unit cost. The formula and calculation of the **weighted average unit cost** are presented in Illustration 6-4.

Illustration 6-4 ▶

Calculation of weighted average unit cost

Cost of Goods Available for Sale	÷	Total Units Available for Sale	=	Weighted Average Unit Cost
$12,000	÷	1,000	=	$12

The weighted average unit cost is then applied to the units on hand to determine the cost of the ending inventory. Illustration 6-5 shows how the cost of goods available for sale is allocated at Fraser Valley Electronics using the weighted average cost in a periodic inventory system.

Illustration 6-5 ▶

Periodic system—weighted average cost

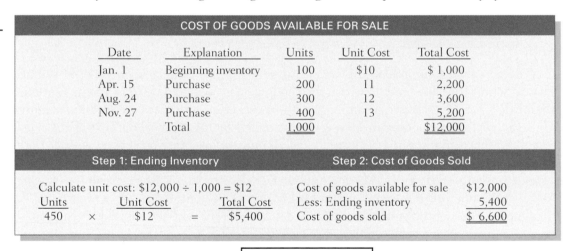

COST OF GOODS AVAILABLE FOR SALE

Date	Explanation	Units	Unit Cost	Total Cost
Jan. 1	Beginning inventory	100	$10	$ 1,000
Apr. 15	Purchase	200	11	2,200
Aug. 24	Purchase	300	12	3,600
Nov. 27	Purchase	400	13	5,200
	Total	1,000		$12,000

Step 1: Ending Inventory	Step 2: Cost of Goods Sold

Calculate unit cost: $12,000 ÷ 1,000 = $12

Units		Unit Cost		Total Cost
450	×	$12	=	$5,400

Cost of goods available for sale	$12,000
Less: Ending inventory	5,400
Cost of goods sold	$ 6,600

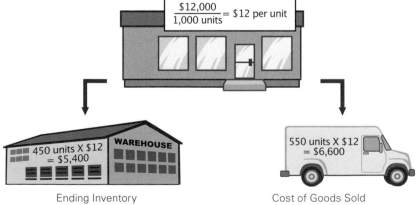

$\dfrac{\$12,000}{1,000\ \text{units}} = \$12$ per unit

450 units X $12 = $5,400 WAREHOUSE

Ending Inventory

550 units X $12 = $6,600

Cost of Goods Sold

We can prove our calculation of the cost of goods sold under the average cost flow assumption by multiplying the units sold by the weighted average unit cost (550 × $12 = $6,600).

And, again, we can prove our calculations by ensuring that the total of the ending inventory and the cost of goods sold equals the cost of goods available for sale ($5,400 + $6,600 = $12,000).

Last-In, First-Out (LIFO)

The **last-in, first-out (LIFO)** cost flow assumption assumes that the goods that were purchased the most recently are the first ones to be sold. For most companies, LIFO almost never matches the actual physical flow of inventory. Only for goods stored in piles, such as sand, hay, or gravel, would LIFO match the physical flow of inventory. But, as explained earlier, this does not mean that the LIFO cost flow assumption cannot be used in other cases. It is the flow of costs that is important, not the physical flow of goods. Petro-Canada in our feature story uses LIFO because it matches costs and revenues better on the income statement, not because it matches the physical flow of the company's crude oil. Illustration 6-6 shows how the cost of goods available for sale is allocated at Fraser Valley Electronics using LIFO in a periodic inventory system.

Illustration 6-6 ◄

Periodic system—LIFO

COST OF GOODS AVAILABLE FOR SALE

Date	Explanation	Units	Unit Cost	Total Cost
Jan. 1	Beginning inventory	100	$10	$ 1,000
Apr. 15	Purchase	200	11	2,200
Aug. 24	Purchase	300	12	3,600
Nov. 27	Purchase	400	13	5,200
	Total	1,000		$12,000

Step 1: Ending Inventory / **Step 2: Cost of Goods Sold**

Date	Units	Unit Cost	Total Cost
Jan. 1	100	$10	$1,000
Apr. 15	200	11	2,200
Aug. 24	150	12	1,800
Total	450		$5,000

Cost of goods available for sale	$12,000
Less: Ending inventory	5,000
Cost of goods sold	$ 7,000

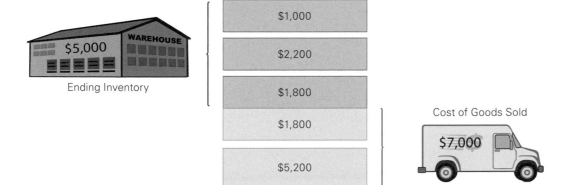

Under LIFO, since it is assumed that the goods that are sold first are the ones that were purchased the most recently, ending inventory is based on the costs of the oldest units purchased. That is, the cost of the ending inventory is determined by taking the unit cost of the earliest goods available for sale and working forward until all units of inventory have been costed.

In our example, therefore, the 450 units of ending inventory must be costed using the earliest purchase prices. The first purchase was 100 units at $10 in the January 1 beginning inventory. Then 200 units were purchased at $11. The remaining 150 units are costed at $12 per unit, the August 24 purchase price.

Under LIFO, the cost of the last goods in is the first to be assigned to cost of goods sold. We can prove the cost of goods sold in our example by starting at the end of the period and counting backwards until we reach the total number of units sold (550). The result is that 400 units from the last purchase (November 27) are assumed to be sold first, and only 150 units from the next purchase (August 24) are needed to reach the total 550 units sold.

Date	Units	Unit Cost	Cost of Goods Sold
Nov. 27	400	$13	$5,200
Aug. 24	150	12	1,800
Total	550		$7,000

As shown for FIFO and average cost, when the ending inventory and cost of goods sold amounts are then added together, they should equal the cost of goods available for sale. This is also true in LIFO: $5,000 + $7,000 = $12,000.

Remember that, under a periodic inventory system, all goods that are bought during the period are assumed to be available for sale, regardless of when they were purchased. Note that because goods that are purchased late in a period are assumed to be available for the first sale in a periodic inventory system, income could be manipulated by a last-minute end-of-period purchase of inventory in the LIFO cost flow assumption.

BEFORE YOU GO ON . . .

▶Review It

1. Why is the specific identification method not always used to determine the cost of ending inventory and the cost of goods sold?
2. What are the differences between the three cost flow assumptions—FIFO, average cost, and LIFO?
3. Why is the cost of the last purchases, not the first purchases, used to calculate the ending inventory under FIFO?

▶Do It

The accounting records of Cookie Cutters Company show the following data:

Beginning inventory   4,000 units at $3
Purchases   6,000 units at $4
Sales   8,000 units at $8

Determine the cost of goods sold and ending inventory under a periodic inventory system using (a) FIFO, (b) average cost, and (c) LIFO.

Action Plan

- Ignore the selling price in allocating cost.
- Calculate the number of units available for sale, cost of goods available for sale, and the ending inventory in units.
- Determine the cost of ending inventory first. Calculate cost of goods sold by subtracting ending inventory from the cost of goods available for sale.
- For FIFO, allocate the latest costs to the goods on hand. (The first costs will be allocated to the cost of goods sold.)
- For average cost, determine the weighted average unit cost (cost of goods available for sale ÷ number of units available for sale). Multiply this cost by the number of units on hand.
- For LIFO, allocate the earliest costs to the goods on hand. (The latest costs will be allocated to the cost of goods sold.)

- Prove your work: Calculate the cost of goods sold separately and then check that ending inventory + cost of goods sold = cost of goods available for sale.

Solution

Total units available for sale = 4,000 + 6,000 = 10,000
Cost of goods available for sale = (4,000 × $3) + (6,000 × $4) = $36,000
Ending inventory = 4,000 + 6,000 − 8,000 = 2,000 units

(a) FIFO ending inventory: 2,000 × $4 = $8,000
   FIFO cost of goods sold: $36,000 − $8,000 = $28,000
   Cost of goods sold (COGS) proof: (4,000 × $3) + (4,000 × $4) = $28,000
   Check: $28,000 + $8,000 = $36,000

(b) Weighted average unit cost: $36,000 ÷ 10,000 = $3.60
   Average ending inventory: 2,000 × $3.60 = $7,200
   Average cost of goods sold: $36,000 − $7,200 = $28,800
   COGS proof: 8,000 × $3.60 = $28,800
   Check: $28,800 + $7,200 = $36,000

(c) LIFO ending inventory: 2,000 × $3 = $6,000
   LIFO cost of goods sold: $36,000 − $6,000 = $30,000
   COGS proof: (6,000 x $4) + (2,000 × $3) = $30,000
   Check: $30,000 + $6,000 = $36,000

Related exercise material: BE6–3, BE6–4, E6–3, E6–4, E6–5, and E6–6.

the navigator

Financial Statement Effects

Inventory affects both the income statement and the balance sheet. The ending inventory is included as a current asset on the balance sheet and it is used to calculate cost of goods sold on the income statement. Cost of goods sold will affect net income, which in turn, will affect owner's equity on the balance sheet. Thus, the choice of cost flow assumption can have a significant impact on the financial statements. Errors can also occur when a physical inventory is being taken or inventory is costed. The effects of these errors on financial statements can be major. We will address both of these topics in the next two sections.

study objective 3

Determine the effects of inventory cost flow assumptions and inventory errors on the financial statements.

Choice of Cost Flow Assumption

About an equal number of companies in Canada use the FIFO and average cost flow assumptions. Only a very few companies, about three percent, use LIFO. The Canadian companies that do use LIFO generally use it to harmonize their reporting practices to the U.S., where LIFO is used more often. Companies can choose specific identification or one of the three cost flow assumptions. However, at the time of writing this text, new Canadian accounting standards disallowing the use of LIFO had been proposed. The main reason for the change is because Canadian accounting standards are being revised to be consistent with international accounting standards. Petro-Canada, in our feature story, is one of a relatively small number of companies that will be affected by this change if it is approved.

Although the FIFO and average cost flow assumptions have been more popular in Canada—and LIFO will likely not be allowed at all in the future—students need to have some understanding of the impact of the LIFO cost flow assumption so that they can understand global financial reporting. LIFO will continue to be used in the United States, which is one of Canada's largest trading partners.

To compare companies that use different cost flow assumptions, it is necessary to understand what impact each cost flow assumption has on the financial statements. Depending on the direction of prices, the choice of cost flow assumption will have very different effects on the financial statements (as will be seen in the next section). Is the financial reporting objective of providing useful information for decision-making achieved if managers can choose a cost flow assumption based on how it will influence the company's financial results? The answer is no.

While the accounting profession does allow companies to choose from among the acceptable cost flow methods, this is allowed because different companies and industries have different circumstances. After a company chooses a cost flow assumption, this assumption should be used from one period to the next. Consistency is what makes it possible to compare financial statements from successive time periods. Using FIFO in one year and average cost in the next year would make it difficult to compare the net incomes for the two years.

Although consistency is preferred, a company can change its cost flow assumption. Petro-Canada in our feature story changed from FIFO to LIFO in 1992 in order to match costs and revenues more closely. As mentioned above, it will also have to change again if LIFO is not allowed for Canadian financial reporting purposes. Such changes and their effect on net income should be disclosed in the financial statements. Where possible, companies must also go back and restate the prior years' financial statements using the new method. This respects the **full disclosure principle**, which requires all relevant information to be disclosed. The full disclosure principle is discussed more in Chapter 11.

On the other hand, companies may also use more than one cost flow assumption at the same time. Finning International, for example, uses specific identification to account for its equipment inventory, FIFO to account for about two-thirds of its inventory of parts and supplies, and average cost to account for the rest. A company must use the same cost flow assumption for all inventories having a similar nature and use to the company. But for inventories with a different nature or use, different cost flow assumptions may be justified.

Income Statement Effects

To help you understand why companies might choose a particular cost flow assumption, we will compare the effects of each assumption on the financial statements of Fraser Valley Electronics. The condensed income statements in Illustration 6-7 assume that Fraser Valley sold its 550 units for $11,500 and that its operating expenses were $2,000.

Illustration 6-7 ▶

Comparative effects of cost flow assumptions

FRASER VALLEY ELECTRONICS Condensed Income Statement					
	FIFO		Average Cost		LIFO
Sales		$11,500		$11,500	$11,500
Beginning inventory	$ 1,000		$ 1,000		$ 1,000
Purchases	11,000		11,000		11,000
Cost of goods available for sale	12,000		12,000		12,000
Ending inventory	5,800		5,400		5,000
Cost of goods sold		6,200		6,600	7,000
Gross profit		5,300		4,900	4,500
Operating expenses		2,000		2,000	2,000
Net income		$ 3,300		$ 2,900	$ 2,500

The cost of goods available for sale ($12,000) is the same under each of the three inventory cost flow assumptions. But both the ending inventories and the cost of goods sold are different. This difference is because of the unit costs that are allocated to each. Each dollar of difference in ending inventory results in a corresponding dollar difference in cost of goods sold and net income. For Fraser Valley, there is an $800 difference between FIFO and LIFO.

In periods of changing prices, the choice of cost flow assumption can have a significant impact on net income. In a period of rising prices, as is the case here, FIFO produces a higher income. This happens because the expenses matched against revenues are the lower unit costs of the first units purchased. As indicated in Illustration 6-7, FIFO reports the highest income ($3,300) and LIFO the lowest ($2,500). Average cost falls somewhere in the middle ($2,900). To management, higher net income is an advantage. It causes external users to view the company more favourably. Also, if management bonuses are based on net income, FIFO will provide the higher income for higher bonuses.

If prices are falling, the results from the use of FIFO and LIFO are reversed. FIFO will report the lowest income and LIFO the highest. If prices are stable, all three cost flow assumptions will report the same results.

LIFO gives the best income statement valuation since it matches current costs with current revenues. This is because, under LIFO, the cost of goods sold is assumed to be the cost of the goods most recently acquired. As described in our feature story, Petro-Canada and other integrated oil and gas companies use LIFO. Because oil prices can change very rapidly, LIFO provides these companies with a better matching of costs and revenues. Even though LIFO does result in the best match of revenues and expenses, it can result in some income statement distortions if the beginning inventory is ever liquidated. It can also be manipulated by the timing of purchases.

As discussed in the previous section, if proposed changes to Canadian accounting standards are approved, LIFO will no longer be allowed for Canadian financial reporting purposes. The use of LIFO has never been permitted for income tax purposes in Canada, and because most firms do not want to keep two sets of inventory records—one for accounting purposes and another for tax purposes—the LIFO cost flow assumption has not been used as often as FIFO and average cost in Canada. Petro-Canada in our feature story is a bit of an exception. If the proposed changes are approved, only the few Canadian companies that have special reporting requirements in the United States will continue to use LIFO in the future.

Balance Sheet Effects

FIFO gives the best balance sheet valuation. A major advantage of FIFO is that, in a period of rising prices, the costs allocated to ending inventory will approximate the inventory's current, or replacement, cost. For example, for Fraser Valley, 400 of the 450 units in the ending inventory are costed at the November 27 unit cost of $13. Since management needs to replace inventory after it is sold, a valuation that is closer to the replacement cost is helpful for decision-making.

A major weakness of LIFO is evident during periods of rising prices, because the costs allocated to ending inventory may be much lower than the current cost of replacing that inventory. This understatement becomes even larger if the inventory includes goods that were purchased in one or more prior accounting periods. This is true for Fraser Valley Electronics. The cost of the ending inventory includes the $10 unit cost of the beginning inventory. The controller of Petro-Canada also states in our feature story that LIFO can give an out-of-date valuation in the balance sheet.

Summary of Effects

The key differences that result from the different cost flow assumptions during a period of rising prices are summarized below. The effects will be reversed if prices are falling. When prices are constant, the ending inventory and cost of goods sold will be the same for all three cost flow assumptions.

	FIFO	Average Cost	LIFO
Cost of goods sold	Lowest	Results will fall in between FIFO and LIFO	Highest
Gross profit/Net income	Highest	Results will fall in between FIFO and LIFO	Lowest
Cash flow	Same	Same	Same
Ending inventory	Highest	Results will fall in between FIFO and LIFO	Lowest

We have seen that both inventory on the balance sheet and net income on the income statement are higher when FIFO is used in a period of rising prices. Do not confuse this with cash flow. All three cost flow assumptions produce exactly the same cash flow. Revenues and purchases are not affected by the choice of cost flow assumption. The only thing that is affected is the allocation between ending inventory and cost of goods sold, which does not involve cash.

It is also worth remembering that all three cost flow assumptions will give exactly the same results over the life cycle of the business or its product. That is, the allocation between cost of goods sold and ending inventory may vary within a period, but over time each assumption will give the same cumulative results. Although much has been written about the impact of the choice of inventory cost flow assumption on a variety of performance measures, in reality there is little real economic distinction among them *over time*.

Inventory Errors

Unfortunately, errors sometimes occur in taking or costing inventory. Some errors are caused by mistakes in counting or pricing the inventory. Other errors are because of mistakes in recognizing the transfer of legal title for goods in transit. When errors happen, they affect both the income statement and the balance sheet.

Income Statement Effects

The cost of goods available for sale (beginning inventory plus cost of goods purchased) is allocated between ending inventory and cost of goods sold. Therefore, an error in any one of these components will affect both the income statement (through cost of goods sold and net income) and the balance sheet (ending inventory and owner's capital).

The dollar effects of errors on cost of goods sold and net income can be determined by entering the incorrect data in the income statement formula (shown in Illustration 6-8), and then substituting the correct data.

Illustration 6-8 ◄
Income formula

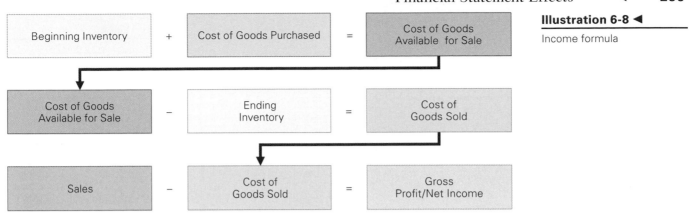

The overall effects of inventory errors on the current year's income statement are summarized below. U stands for understatement, O for overstatement, and NE for no effect.

Nature of Error	Beginning Inventory	+	Cost of Goods Purchased	=	Cost of Goods Available for Sale	–	Ending Inventory	=	Cost of Goods Sold		Sales	–	Cost of Goods Sold	=	Gross Profit/ Net Income
Understate beginning inventory	U	+	NE	=	U	–	NE	=	U		NE	–	U	=	O
Overstate beginning inventory	O	+	NE	=	O	–	NE	=	O		NE	–	O	=	U
Understate cost of goods purchased	NE	+	U	=	U	–	NE	=	U		NE	–	U	=	O
Overstate cost of goods purchased	NE	+	O	=	O	–	NE	=	O		NE	–	O	=	U
Understate ending inventory	NE	+	NE	=	NE	–	U	=	O		NE	–	O	=	U
Overstate ending inventory	NE	+	NE	=	NE	–	O	=	U		NE	–	U	=	O

If beginning inventory is understated, cost of goods sold will be understated (assuming that there are no other offsetting errors). On the other hand, an understatement of ending inventory will overstate cost of goods sold, because ending inventory must be deducted to determine cost of goods sold.

Cost of goods sold is deducted from sales to determine gross profit, and finally net income. An understatement in cost of goods sold will produce an overstatement in net income. An overstatement in cost of goods sold will produce an understatement in net income.

Since the ending inventory of one period becomes the beginning inventory of the next period, an error in ending inventory of the current period will have a reverse effect on the net income of the next period. This is shown in Illustration 6-9. Note that the $3,000 understatement of ending inventory in 2007 will result in an overstatement of cost of goods sold and an understatement of net income. It also results in an understatement of beginning inventory in 2008, an understatement of cost of goods sold, and an overstatement of net income of the same amount.

	2007				2008			
	Incorrect		Correct		Incorrect		Correct	
Sales		$80,000		$80,000		$90,000		$90,000
Beginning inventory	$20,000		$20,000		$12,000		$15,000	
Cost of goods purchased	40,000		40,000		68,000		68,000	
Cost of goods available for sale	60,000		60,000		80,000		83,000	
Ending inventory	12,000		15,000		23,000		23,000	
Cost of goods sold		48,000		45,000		57,000		60,000
Gross profit		32,000		35,000		33,000		30,000
Operating expenses		10,000		10,000		20,000		20,000
Net income		$22,000		$25,000		$13,000		$10,000

($3,000)
Net income understated

$3,000
Net income overstated

The combined net income for two years is correct
because the errors cancel each other out.

Illustration 6-9 ▲

Effects of inventory errors on income statements of two successive years

Over the two years, total net income is correct. The errors offset one another. Notice that total income using incorrect data is $35,000 ($22,000 + $13,000). This is the same as the total income of $35,000 ($25,000 + $10,000) using correct data. Nevertheless, the distortion of the year-by-year results can have a serious impact on financial analysis and management decisions.

Note that an error in the beginning inventory does not result in a corresponding error in the ending inventory. The accuracy of the ending inventory depends entirely on correctly taking and costing the inventory at the balance sheet date.

Balance Sheet Effects

The effects of errors on the balance sheet can be determined by using the basic accounting equation: assets = liabilities + owner's equity. In the following table, U is for understatement, O is for overstatement, and NE is for no effect.

Nature of Error	Assets	=	Liabilities	+	Owner's Equity
Understate ending inventory	U	=	NE	+	U
Overstate ending inventory	O	=	NE	+	O

Errors in beginning inventory have no impact on the balance sheet if ending inventory is correctly calculated in the current period. Understating ending inventory (assuming there are no other offsetting errors) will understate net income. If net income is understated, then owner's equity will be understated, because net income is part of owner's equity.

The effect of an error in ending inventory on the next period was shown in Illustration 6-9. If the error is not corrected, total net income for the two periods would be correct. Thus, total assets and owner's equity reported on the balance sheet at the end of 2008 will also be correct.

Regardless of the nature of the error (and there are many possible combinations of errors), using the income statement and balance sheet equation will help ensure that you catch the total effect of inventory errors.

 **ACCOUNTING IN ACTION ▶ Ethics Insight**

Over the years, inventory has played a role in many fraud cases. A classic one involved salad oil. Management filled storage tanks mostly with water, and since oil rises to the top, the auditors thought the tanks were full of oil. In this instance, management also said the company had more tanks than it really did—numbers were repainted on the tanks to confuse the auditors.

Another involves a building supplies company in Prince George, B.C., where a manager falsified inventory records by altering written records of physical inventory counts to match computerized inventory records. The overstatement increased over time as the manager did not write off damaged or obsolete inventory, inventory lost as a result of theft, or donations of inventory to local charities. In this case, the company's auditors were not responsible since they depended on the information management provided.

Source: Trevor McCann, "Who's at Fault?" *CAmagazine*, June 2005.

> **?** **Why might a manager deliberately overstate inventory? Is it a problem?**

BEFORE YOU GO ON . . .

▶Review It

1. Which inventory cost flow assumption gives the highest net income in a period of rising prices? The highest balance sheet valuation? The highest cash flow?
2. What factors should management consider when it chooses an inventory cost flow assumption?
3. Which inventory cost flow assumption does The Forzani Group Ltd. use? The answer to this question is at the end of the chapter.
4. How do inventory errors affect the income statement? The balance sheet?

▶Do It

On December 31, Silas Company counted and recorded $600,000 of inventory. This count did not include $90,000 of goods in transit, shipped to Silas on December 29, FOB shipping point. Silas recorded the purchase on January 3 when the goods were received. (a) If Silas reports ending inventory of $600,000 on its December 31 balance sheet, what is the correct December 31 inventory. (b) Which financial statement accounts may be in error, and what would be the amount and direction (i.e., overstatement or understatement) of the error?

Action Plan

- Use income statement relationships to determine the impact of an error on the income statement.
- Use the accounting equation to determine the impact of an error on the balance sheet.

Solution

(a) The correct inventory count should have been $690,000 ($600,000 + $90,000).

(b) *Income statement accounts:* Purchases are understated (U) by $90,000. However, since ending inventory is also understated, cost of goods sold and net income will be correct.

Beginning inventory	No effect
Plus: Cost of goods purchased	U $90,000
Cost of goods available for sale	U $90,000
Less: Ending inventory	U $90,000
Cost of goods sold	No effect because the errors cancel each other

Balance sheet accounts: Merchandise Inventory (ending) is understated by $90,000, as is Accounts Payable. [assets (U $90,000) = liabilities (U $90,000) + owner's equity.]

Related exercise material: BE6–5, BE6–6, BE6–7, BE6–8, E6–5, E6–6, E6–7, and E6–8.

the navigator

Presentation and Analysis of Inventory

study objective 4

Demonstrate the presentation and analysis of inventory.

Presenting inventory on the financial statements is important because inventory is usually the largest current asset (ending inventory) on the balance sheet and the largest expense (cost of goods sold) on the income statement. In addition, these reported numbers are critical for analyzing how well a company manages its inventory. In the next sections, we will discuss the presentation and analysis of inventory.

Valuing Inventory at the Lower of Cost and Market (LCM)

Before reporting inventory on the financial statements, we must first ensure that it is properly valued. The value of inventory items sometimes falls due to changes in technology or style. For example, suppose you manage a retail store that sells computers, and at the end of the year the value of the computers has dropped almost 25 percent. Do you think inventory should be stated at cost, in accordance with the cost principle, or at its lower market value?

As you probably reasoned, this situation requires an exception to following the cost basis of accounting. When the value of inventory is lower than its cost, the inventory is written down to its market value. This is done by valuing the inventory at the **lower of cost and market (LCM)** in the period in which the decline occurs. LCM is an example of the accounting characteristic of conservatism. Conservatism means that when choosing among alternatives, the best choice is the one that is least likely to overstate assets and net income.

The term *market* in the "lower of cost and market" phrase has recently been defined in Canada as **net realizable value**. For a merchandising company, net realizable value is the selling price less any costs required to make the goods ready for sale. LCM is applied to the items in inventory after specific identification or one of the cost flow assumptions (FIFO, average cost, or LIFO) has been applied to determine the inventory cost.

Assume that Wacky World has the following lines of merchandise with costs and market values as indicated. LCM produces the following results:

	Cost	Market	Lower of Cost and Market
Television sets			
LCD	$ 60,000	$ 55,000	$ 55,000
Plasma	45,000	52,000	45,000
	105,000	107,000	100,000
Video equipment			
VCRs	48,000	45,000	45,000
DVD recorder/players	15,000	14,000	14,000
	63,000	59,000	59,000
Total inventory	$168,000	$166,000	$159,000

Inventories are usually written down to net realizable value item by item, rather than in total. In some circumstances, similar or related items can be grouped together. For example, inventory in the same product line (e.g., television sets and video equipment) may be grouped together. LCM should be applied consistently from period to period. If Wacky World applied the LCM rule on an item by item basis, it would report its inventory at $159,000 on its balance sheet.

If Wacky World uses a periodic inventory system, no entry is needed to adjust the inventory. Wacky World would instead use $159,000 as the ending inventory amount in the cost of goods sold calculation on the income statement. This will result in cost of goods sold being $9,000 higher than if the cost of goods sold had been calculated using $168,000 as the ending inventory. Wacky World will then use $159,000 for its ending inventory when the accounting cycle is completed and it updates the inventory account in its closing entries at the end of the accounting period.

If Wacky World uses a perpetual inventory system, the entry to adjust inventory from cost to market would be the following:

Cost of Goods Sold	9,000	
Merchandise Inventory		9,000
To record decline in inventory value from original cost of $168,000 to market value of $159,000.		

A	=	L	+	OE
−9,000				−9,000

Cash flows: no effect

The result is the same in both perpetual and periodic inventory systems. Cost of Goods Sold is increased by $9,000, which in turn reduces net income and owner's equity by $9,000. In both systems, ending inventory is reported on the balance sheet at $159,000, which is $9,000 lower than cost.

Historically companies were not allowed to reverse a write-down to market, even if the market price increased in a subsequent period. But the new accounting proposals state that if there is clear evidence of an increase in net realizable value, the amount of the write-down is reversed. This means that in a perpetual inventory system, a company will debit the Merchandise Inventory account and credit the Cost of Goods Sold account. This is a significant change from the previous rules.

ACCOUNTING IN ACTION ▶ Business Insight

Markham, Ontario–based ATI Technologies, the world's No. 2 maker of computer-graphics chips, experienced a 40-percent drop in net income from the same quarter a year earlier despite having record sales in its 2006 second quarter. Still, net income was better than analysts had expected and the company's share price jumped. The share price had taken a hit in 2005, after several disappointing quarters forced a U.S. $67-million inventory write-down in the fourth quarter.

Some analysts said the company's inventory levels were still too high in 2006, but management indicated this was not a concern because the company was moving a lot of volume. "New products are flying off the shelf," according to ATI Chief Executive, David Orton.

Source: Roma Luciw and Omar El Akkad, "ATI Shares Rise," *The Globe and Mail*, March 30, 2006.

?   **Why would analysts be concerned that inventory levels are too high?**

Classifying and Reporting Inventory

How a company classifies its inventory depends on whether the company is a merchandiser or a manufacturer. A merchandiser *buys* its inventory. A manufacturer *produces* its inventory. In a merchandising company, inventory consists of many different items. Textbooks, paper, and pens, for example, are just a few of the inventory items on hand in a bookstore. These items have two common characteristics: (1) they are owned by the company, and (2) they are in a form ready for sale to customers. Only one inventory classification, merchandise inventory, is needed to describe the many different items that make up the total inventory.

In a manufacturing company, some goods may not yet be ready for sale. As a result, inventory is usually classified into three categories: raw materials, work in process, and finished goods. For example, Bombardier classifies the steel, fibreglass, upholstery material, and other components that are on hand waiting to be used in production as raw materials.

Motorized consumer products such as Ski-Doos and Sea-Doos that are on the assembly line in various stages of production are classified as work in process. Ski-Doos and Sea-Doos that are completed and ready for sale are identified as finished goods.

In the notes to a company's financial statements, the following information should be included: (1) the major inventory classifications, (2) the cost flow assumption (specific identification, FIFO, average cost, or LIFO), and (3) the amount of any write-down to net realizable value or reversals of previous write-downs, including the reason why the write-down was reversed.

Forzani reported inventory of $278,002 thousand under current assets in its 2006 balance sheet. It reported cost of sales (another term for cost of goods sold) of $746,313 thousand in its income statement. Note 2(b) to Forzani's financial statements, reproduced in Appendix A at the end of this textbook, discloses that inventory is valued at the lower of cost and net realizable value. Cost is determined using the weighted average cost flow assumption, as you saw when you answered the Review It question about Forzani earlier in the chapter.

Analysis

A delicate balance must be kept between having too little inventory and too much inventory. On one hand, management wants to have a variety and quantity of merchandise available so that customers will find a wide selection of items in stock. But having too much inventory on hand can cost the company money in storage costs, interest costs (on money tied up in inventory), and costs due to technology goods becoming obsolete or changing fashions. On the other hand, low inventory levels can result in stockouts, lost sales, and unhappy customers.

How quickly a company sells its inventory, or turns it over, is one way to determine whether the company has too much or too little inventory. We can also use this information to evaluate a company's liquidity, or its ability to pay obligations that are expected to come due in the next year. In Chapter 4, we introduced the current ratio, which is also a measure of liquidity. Inventory is a significant component of the current ratio and a high level of inventory will result in a high current ratio. But if the inventory is not turning over very quickly, this may be a problem. In this section, we add another liquidity ratio that is commonly used to evaluate inventory levels: the inventory turnover ratio. We also present a related measure: the average days to sell the inventory.

Inventory Turnover

The **inventory turnover** ratio measures the number of times, on average, inventory is sold (turned over) during the period. It is calculated by dividing the cost of goods sold by average inventory.

Whenever a ratio compares a balance sheet figure (e.g., inventory) to an income statement figure (e.g., cost of goods sold), the balance sheet figure must be averaged. Average balance sheet figures are determined by adding beginning and ending balances together and dividing by two. Averages are used to ensure that the balance sheet figures (which represent end-of-period amounts) cover the same period of time as the income statement figures (which represent amounts for the entire period). Illustration 6-10 shows the formula for calculating the inventory turnover ratio for The Forzani Group for fiscal 2006 (dollars in thousands).

Illustration 6-10 ▶

Inventory turnover

Cost of Goods Sold	÷	Average Inventory	=	Inventory Turnover
$746,313	÷	($278,002 + $278,631) / 2	=	2.7 times

Generally, the more times that inventory turns over each year, the more efficiently sales are being made.

Days Sales in Inventory

The inventory turnover ratio is complemented by the **days sales in inventory** ratio. It converts the inventory turnover ratio into a measure of the average age of the inventory on hand. This ratio is calculated by dividing 365 days by the inventory turnover ratio, as in Illustration 6-11.

Days in Year	÷	Inventory Turnover	=	Days Sales in Inventory
365 days	÷	2.7	=	135 days

Illustration 6-11 ◀

Days sales in inventory

This means that Forzani's inventory, on average, is in stock for 135 days. This ratio must be interpreted carefully: it should be compared to the company's ratio in previous years, and to the industry average. However, you must recognize that this average will be different for each type of inventory item (e.g., sneakers vs. bicycles). What we see here is a total average only.

BEFORE YOU GO ON . . .

▶**Review It**

1. When should inventory be reported at an amount different from cost?
2. What inventory information should be disclosed in the financial statements?
3. How can you tell if a company has too much or too little inventory on hand?

▶**Do It**

Westwood Hockey Company uses a perpetual inventory system and has the following items in its inventory at December 31, 2008:

Product	Quantity	Per Unit Cost	Per Unit Market
Jerseys	95	$50	$45
Socks	155	5	6

(a) What amount for inventory should Westwood Hockey Company report on its financial statements, assuming the lower of cost or market is applied on an individual item basis? (b) Record any necessary adjustments.

Action Plan

- Calculate the cost of the inventory.
- Calculate the market value of the inventory.
- For each inventory item determine which number is lower—cost or market.
- Record a journal entry to adjust the inventory account if required.

Solution

(a)

	Cost		Market		Lower of Cost and Market
Jerseys	(95 × $50)	$4,750	(95 × $45)	$4,275	$4,275
Socks	(155 × $5)	775	(155 × $6)	930	775
Total inventory		$5,525		$5,205	$5,050

(b)

Cost of Goods Sold ($5,525 − $5,050)		475	
Merchandise Inventory			475
To record decline in inventory value from original cost of $5,525 to market value of $5,050.			

Related exercise material: BE6–9, BE6–10, BE6–11, E6–9, and E6–10.

APPENDIX 6A ▶ INVENTORY COST FLOW ASSUMPTIONS IN A PERPETUAL INVENTORY SYSTEM

study objective 5

Calculate ending inventory and cost of goods sold in a perpetual inventory system using inventory cost flow assumptions.

Each of the inventory cost flow assumptions described in the chapter for a periodic inventory system can be used in a perpetual inventory system. To show how the three cost flow assumptions (FIFO, average cost, and LIFO) are applied, we will use the data below and shown earlier in this chapter for Fraser Valley Electronics' Astro Condensers. Note that in a perpetual system it is necessary to include information about sales because the cost of goods sold must be calculated and recorded for each sale. We have therefore added information about the number of units sold on May 1 and September 1 to data shown earlier in the chapter. We have not provided information about the sales price, because this is not needed to determine the *cost* of the goods sold or the *cost* of the ending inventory.

	FRASER VALLEY ELECTRONICS Z202 Astro Condensers				
Date	Explanation	Units	Cost	Unit Cost	Total Units in Inventory
Jan. 1	Beginning inventory	100	$10	$ 1,000	100
Apr. 15	Purchases	200	11	2,200	300
May 1	Sales	150			150
Aug. 24	Purchases	300	12	3,600	450
Sept. 1	Sales	400			50
Nov. 27	Purchases	400	13	5,200	450
				$12,000	

First-In, First-Out (FIFO)

Under perpetual FIFO, the cost of the oldest goods on hand before each sale is allocated to the cost of goods sold. For example, as shown in Illustration 6A-1, the cost of goods sold on May 1 is assumed to consist of all the January 1 beginning inventory and 50 units of the items purchased on April 15. Similarly, the cost of goods sold on September 1 is assumed to consist of the remaining 150 units purchased on April 15, plus 250 of the items purchased on August 24.

	PURCHASES			COST OF GOODS SOLD			BALANCE		
Date	Units	Cost	Total	Units	Cost	Total	Units	Cost	Total
Jan. 1							100	$10	$1,000
Apr. 15	200	$11	$ 2,200				100	10	} 3,200
							200	11	
May 1				100	$10	} $1,550	150	11	1,650
				50	11				
Aug. 24	300	12	3,600				150	11	} 5,250
							300	12	
Sept. 1				150	11	} 4,650	50	12	600
				250	12				
Nov. 27	400	13	5,200				50	12	} 5,800
							400	13	
	900		$11,000	550		$6,200			

Proof
$6,200 + $5,800 = $12,000

Note that the total cost of goods available for sale of $12,000 (beginning inventory of $1,000 + purchases of $11,000) is allocated between ending inventory ($5,800) and cost of goods sold ($6,200), as shown in the margin proof. We also saw this in the chapter under the periodic inventory system.

In addition, the ending inventory and cost of goods sold under FIFO in a perpetual system are the same as in a periodic system (see Illustration 6-3 where, similarly, the ending inventory is $5,800 and the cost of goods sold is $6,200). Under both inventory systems, the first costs are the ones assigned to cost of goods sold regardless of when the sales actually happened.

Average Cost

The average cost flow assumption in a perpetual inventory system is often called the moving average cost flow assumption. The average cost is calculated in the same way as we calculated the weighted average unit cost: by dividing the cost of goods available for sale by the units available for sale. The difference is that under the perpetual inventory system, a new average is calculated after each purchase. The average cost is then applied to (1) the units sold, to determine the cost of goods sold, and (2) the remaining units on hand, to determine the ending inventory amount. Illustration 6A-2 shows how the moving average cost flow assumption is applied by Fraser Valley Electronics using the perpetual inventory system.

	PURCHASES			COST OF GOODS SOLD			BALANCE		
Date	Units	Cost	Total	Units	Cost	Total	Units	Cost	Total
Jan. 1							100	$10.00	$1,000.00
Apr. 15	200	$11.00	$ 2,200.00				300	10.67	3,200.00
May 1				150	$10.67	$1,600.00	150	10.67	1,600.00
Aug. 24	300	12.00	3,600.00				450	11.56	5,200.00
Sept. 1				400	11.56	4,622.22	50	11.56	577.78
Nov. 27	400	13.00	5,200.00				450	12.84	5,777.78
	900		$11,000.00	550		$6,222.22			

Proof
$6,222.22 + $5,777.78 = $12,000

As indicated above, a new average is calculated each time a purchase is made. On April 15, after 200 units are purchased for $2,200, a total of 300 units that cost $3,200 ($1,000 + $2,200) is on hand. The average unit cost is $3,200 divided by 300 units, or $10.67. Accordingly, the unit cost of the 150 units sold on May 1 is $10.67, which results in a total cost of goods sold of $1,600. This unit cost is used in costing units on hand and units sold until another purchase is made, when a new unit cost is calculated.

On August 24, following the purchase of 300 units for $3,600, there are 450 units on hand with a total cost of $5,200 ($1,600 + $3,600). The new average unit cost is $11.56 ($5,200 ÷ 450). This new cost is now used to calculate the cost of the September 1 sale and the units still on hand after the sale.

A new unit cost will be calculated again after the November 27 purchase of 400 units for $5,200. After this purchase, there are 450 units on hand with a total cost of $5,777.78 ($577.78 + $5,200). The new average cost is $12.84 ($5,777.78 ÷ 450). This average unit cost will be used until another purchase is made in the following year.

In practice, these average unit costs may be rounded to the nearest cent, or even to the nearest dollar. This illustration used the exact unit cost amounts, as would a computerized schedule, even though the unit costs have been rounded to the nearest digit for presentation in Illustration 6A-2. However, it is important to remember that this is an *assumed* cost flow, and using four digits, or even cents, may suggest a false level of accuracy.

Compare the moving average cost under the perpetual inventory system to Illustration 6-5 (shown earlier in the chapter), which shows the weighted average cost under a periodic inventory system. Notice that under a periodic inventory system, the ending inventory of $5,400 and cost of goods sold of $6,600 are not the same as the values calculated under a perpetual inventory system even though the average cost method was used for both systems. This is because in a perpetual system, a new weighted average is calculated with each purchase; in a periodic system, the same weighted average is used to calculate the cost of goods sold for all the units sold during the period.

Last-In, First-Out (LIFO)

With the LIFO cost flow assumption under a perpetual system, the cost of the most recent purchase before a sale is allocated to the units sold. Therefore, the cost of the goods sold on May 1 is assumed to consist of the units from the latest purchase, on April 15, at the cost of $11 per unit. The cost of the goods sold on September 1 counts backward, first allocating the 300 units purchased on August 24, then the 50 remaining units from the April 15 purchase, and finally the 50 units necessary to equal the 400 units sold from the beginning inventory.

Illustration 6A-3 shows the cost of goods sold and ending inventory for Fraser Valley Electronics under LIFO in a perpetual inventory system.

| Date | PURCHASES | | | COST OF GOODS SOLD | | | BALANCE | | |
	Units	Cost	Total	Units	Cost	Total	Units	Cost	Total
Jan. 1							100	$10	$1,000
Apr. 15	200	$11	$ 2,200				100	10	} 3,200
							200	11	
May 1				150	$11	$1,650	100	10	} 1,550
							50	11	
Aug. 24	300	12	3,600				100	10	} 5,150
							50	11	
							300	12	
Sept. 1				300	12	} 4,650	50	10	500
				50	11				
				50	10				
Nov. 27	400	13	5,200				50	10	} 5,700
							400	13	
	900		$11,000	550		$6,300			

Proof
$6,300 + $5,700 = $12,000

The ending inventory in this illustration of LIFO in a perpetual system is $5,700 and the cost of goods sold is $6,300, as compared to the LIFO example in a periodic system in Illustration 6-6, where the ending inventory is $5,000 and cost of goods sold is $7,000.

The use of LIFO in a perpetual system will usually produce cost allocations that are different from using LIFO in a periodic system. In a perpetual system, the latest units purchased *before each sale* are allocated to the cost of goods sold. In a periodic system, the latest units bought *during the period* are allocated to the cost of goods sold. When a purchase is made after the last sale, the LIFO periodic system will apply this purchase to the previous sale. See Illustration 6-6, where the 400 units at $13 purchased on November 27 are applied to the sale of 550 units. As shown under the LIFO perpetual system, the 400 units at $13 purchased on November 27 are all applied to the ending inventory.

If we compare the cost of goods sold and ending inventory figures for all three cost flow assumptions in a perpetual inventory system, we find the same proportionate outcomes that we saw in a periodic system. That is, in a period of rising prices (prices rose from $10 to $13 in this problem), FIFO will always give the highest ending inventory valuation and LIFO the lowest. LIFO will always give the highest cost of goods sold figure (and lowest gross profit and net income), and FIFO will give the lowest cost of goods sold (and highest gross profit and net income). The following table summarizes these effects under a perpetual inventory system:

	FIFO	Average	LIFO
Cost of goods sold	$ 6,200	$ 6,222	$ 6,300
Ending inventory	5,800	5,778	5,700
Cost of goods available for sale	$12,000	$12,000	$12,000

Of course, if prices are falling, the reverse occurs. If prices are constant, all three cost flow assumptions will give the same results. Finally, remember that the sum of the cost of goods sold and ending inventory always equals the cost of goods available for sale, which is the same with each cost flow assumption under both inventory systems.

study objective 6

Estimate ending inventory using the gross profit and retail inventory methods.

As we have seen in this chapter, when a company uses a periodic inventory system, it must be able to do a physical count of its inventory in order to determine the cost of its ending inventory and the cost of goods sold. But what if a company cannot do a physical count? It may be impractical or impossible to count the inventory. Fortunately, it is possible to do an estimate.

There are two reasons for sometimes needing to estimate inventories. First, management may want monthly or quarterly financial statements but does not have the time for, or want the expense of, doing a physical inventory count every month or quarter. Second, a casualty such as a fire or flood may make it impossible to take a physical inventory. As you may have guessed, companies that use a perpetual inventory system are less likely to need inventory estimates since the perpetual inventory system keeps detailed inventory records continuously. Inventory estimates are usually associated with the periodic system.

There are two widely used methods of estimating inventories: (1) the gross profit method, and (2) the retail inventory method.

Gross Profit Method

The **gross profit method** estimates the cost of ending inventory by applying the gross profit margin to net sales. It is commonly used to prepare interim (e.g., monthly) financial statements in a periodic inventory system. This method is relatively simple but effective.

To use this method, a company needs to know its net sales, cost of goods available for sale (beginning inventory + cost of goods purchased), and gross profit margin. Gross profit for the period is estimated by multiplying net sales by the gross profit margin. The estimated gross profit is then used to calculate the estimated cost of goods sold and the estimated ending inventory.

The formulas for using the gross profit method are given in Illustration 6B-1.

Illustration 6B-1 ▶

Gross profit method formulas

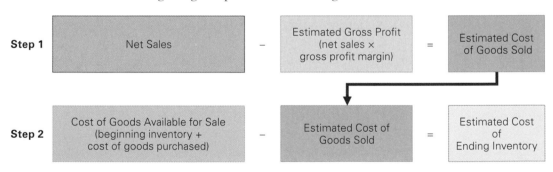

To illustrate, assume that Lalonde Company wants to prepare an income statement for the month of January. Its records show net sales of $200,000, beginning inventory of $40,000, and cost of goods purchased of $120,000. In the preceding year, the company had a 30% gross profit margin. It expects to earn the same margin this year. Given these facts and assumptions, the estimated cost of the ending inventory at January 31 under the gross profit method is $20,000, calculated as follows:

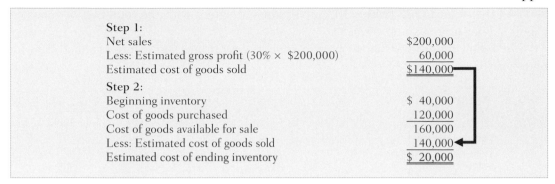

Step 1:
Net sales $200,000
Less: Estimated gross profit (30% × $200,000)   60,000
Estimated cost of goods sold $140,000

Step 2:
Beginning inventory $ 40,000
Cost of goods purchased   120,000
Cost of goods available for sale   160,000
Less: Estimated cost of goods sold   140,000
Estimated cost of ending inventory $ 20,000

The gross profit method is based on the assumption that the gross profit margin will remain constant from one year to the next. It may not remain constant, though, because of a change in merchandising policies or in market conditions. In such cases, the margin should be adjusted to reflect the current operating conditions. In some cases, a better estimate can be had by applying this method to a department or product-line as a whole.

The gross profit method should not be used in preparing a company's financial statements at the end of the year. These statements should be based on a physical inventory count. Accountants and managers often use the gross profit method to test the reasonableness of the ending inventory amount, however.

Retail Inventory Method

A retail store, such as The Forzani Group's Sport Chek, has thousands of types of merchandise. In such cases, determining the cost of each type of merchandise can be difficult and time-consuming if the company has used a periodic inventory system. For these retail companies, it can be easier to calculate the selling price, or retail price of the total inventory, than to look at the purchase invoices to find the cost of each individual inventory item. In most retail businesses, a relationship between cost and selling price—called the cost-to-retail percentage or ratio—can be established. The cost-to-retail percentage is then applied to the ending inventory at retail prices to determine the estimated cost of the inventory. This is called the **retail inventory method** of estimating the cost of inventory.

To use the retail inventory method, a company's records must show both the cost and the retail value of the goods available for sale. The formulas for using the retail inventory method are given in Illustration 6B-2.

Helpful hint In determining inventory at retail, selling prices on the unit are used. Tracing actual unit costs to invoices is unnecessary.

Illustration 6B-2 ◀

Retail inventory method formulas

The logic of the retail method can be demonstrated by using unit cost data. Assume that 10 units purchased at $7 each ($70 in total) are priced to sell for $10 per unit ($100 in total). The cost-to-retail ratio is 70% ($70 ÷ $100). If four units remain unsold, their retail value is

$40 and their cost is $28 ($40 × 70%). This amount agrees with the total cost of goods on hand on a per-unit basis (4 × $7).

The following example shows how to apply the retail method, using assumed data for Zboyovsky Co.:

	At Cost	At Retail
Beginning inventory	$14,000	$ 21,500
Goods purchased	61,000	78,500
Goods available for sale	$75,000	100,000
Net sales		70,000
Step 1: Ending inventory at retail		$ 30,000
Step 2: Cost-to-retail ratio = $75,000 ÷ $100,000 = 75%		
Step 3: Estimated cost of ending inventory ($30,000 × 75%)	$22,500	

Using the retail inventory method also makes it easier to take a physical inventory at the end of the year. The goods on hand can be valued at the prices marked on the merchandise. The cost-to-retail ratio is then applied to the goods on hand at retail to determine the ending inventory at cost. This value can be used for reporting purposes in the year-end financial statements if the results are similar to using cost.

The retail inventory method is also useful for estimating the amount of shrinkage due to breakage, loss, or theft. For example, assume that the retail value of Zboyovsky's physical inventory count is $29,400. When this amount is compared to the estimated retail value of $30,000 that was calculated above, it reveals a $600 estimated inventory shortage at retail. The estimated inventory shortage at cost is $450 ($600 × 75%).

The major disadvantage of the retail method is that it is an averaging technique. It may produce an incorrect inventory valuation if the mix of the ending inventory is not representative of the mix in the goods available for sale. Assume, for example, that the cost-to-retail ratio of 75% in the Zboyovsky Co. illustration consists of equal proportions of inventory items that have cost-to-retail ratios of 70%, 75%, and 80%, respectively. If the ending inventory contains only items with a 70% ratio, an incorrect inventory cost will result. This problem can be lessened by applying the retail method to a department or product-line as a whole.

**Practice Tools:
Demonstration Problems**

Demonstration Problem

Englehart Company has the following inventory, purchases, and sales data for the month of March:

Inventory, March 1		200 units @ $4.00	$ 800
Purchases			
	March 10	500 units @ $4.50	2,250
	20	400 units @ $4.75	1,900
	30	300 units @ $5.00	1,500

Englehart Company uses a periodic inventory system. The physical inventory count on March 31 shows 500 units on hand.

Instructions

Determine the cost of ending inventory at March 31 and cost of goods sold for March, under (a) FIFO, (b) average cost, and (c) LIFO.

Solution to Demonstration Problem

The cost of goods available for sale is $6,450, calculated as follows:

Inventory, March 1	200	units @ $4.00	$ 800
Purchases			
March 10	500	units @ $4.50	2,250
20	400	units @ $4.75	1,900
30	300	units @ $5.00	1,500
Total units and cost of goods available for sale	1,400		$6,450

The number of units sold is 900 (1,400 units available for sale – 500 units on hand).

(a) FIFO

Ending inventory:

Date	Units	Unit Cost	Total Cost
Mar. 30	300	$5.00	$1,500
20	200	4.75	950
	500		$2,450

Cost of goods sold: $6,450 – $2,450 = $4,000

Proof of cost of goods sold:

Date	Units	Unit Cost	Total Cost
Mar. 1	200	$4.00	800
10	500	4.50	2,250
20	200	4.75	950
	900		$4,000

Check: $4,000 + $2,450 = $6,450

(b) Average Cost

Weighted average unit cost: $6,450 ÷ 1,400 units = $4.607 per unit
Ending inventory: 500 units × $4.607 = $2,304
Cost of goods sold: $6,450 – $2,304 = $4,146
Proof of cost of goods sold: 900 units × $4.607 = $4,146
Check: $4,146 + $2,304 = $6,450

(c) LIFO

Ending inventory:

Date	Units	Unit Cost	Total Cost
Mar. 1	200	$4.00	$ 800
10	300	4.50	1,350
	500		$2,150

Cost of goods sold: $6,450 – $2,150 = $4,300

Proof of cost of goods sold:

Date	Units	Unit Cost	Total Cost
Mar. 30	300	$5.00	$1,500
20	400	4.75	1,900
10	200	4.50	900
	900		$4,300

Check: $4,300 + $2,150 = $6,450

Action Plan

- Calculate the total units and cost of goods available for sale.
- Allocate costs to ending inventory. Subtract ending inventory from the cost of goods available for sale to determine the cost of goods sold for each cost flow assumption.
- For FIFO, allocate the latest costs to the goods on hand. (The first costs will be allocated to the cost of goods sold.)
- For average, calculate the weighted average unit cost (cost of goods available for sale divided by the total units available for sale). Multiply this cost by the number of units on hand.
- For LIFO, allocate the earliest costs to the goods on hand. (The latest costs will be allocated to the cost of goods sold.)
- Prove your work: do an independent calculation of cost of goods sold and check that cost of goods sold + ending inventory = cost of goods available for sale.

the navigator

Summary of Study Objectives

1. **Describe the steps in determining inventory quantities.** The steps in determining inventory quantities are (1) taking a physical inventory of goods on hand and (2) determining the ownership of goods in transit, on consignment, and in similar situations.

2. **Calculate ending inventory and cost of goods sold in a periodic inventory system using inventory cost flow assumptions.** The cost of goods available for sale (beginning inventory + cost of goods purchased) may be allocated to cost of goods sold and ending inventory by specific identification or by one of the three cost flow assumptions—FIFO (first-in, first-out), average cost, or LIFO (last-in, first-out).

Specific identification allocates the exact cost of each merchandise item to cost of goods sold and ending inventory. FIFO assumes a first-in, first-out cost flow for sales. Ending inventory is determined by allocating the cost of the most recent purchases to the units on hand. Cost of goods sold includes the cost of the earliest goods purchased. Average cost assumes an average cost flow for both ending inventory and cost of goods sold. Goods available for sale in dollars and units are used to determine the weighted average cost. This unit cost is then applied to the number of units remaining to determine the ending inventory and the number of units sold to prove the cost of goods sold. LIFO assumes a last-in, first-out cost flow for sales. Ending inventory is determined by allocating the cost of the earliest purchases to the units on hand. Cost of goods sold includes the cost of the most recent goods purchased.

3. **Determine the effects of inventory cost flow assumptions and inventory errors on the financial statements.** When prices are rising, FIFO results in a lower cost of goods sold and higher net income than average and LIFO. The reverse is true when prices are falling. LIFO produces the cost of goods sold that best matches current costs with current revenues. FIFO produces the best balance sheet valuation. It results in an ending inventory that is closest to current value or replacement cost. FIFO and average are the most commonly used. LIFO can produce undesirable income effects in certain circumstances and is not permitted for income tax or financial reporting purposes in Canada.

An error in beginning inventory will have a reverse effect on net income in the current year (e.g., an overstatement of beginning inventory results in an overstatement of cost of goods sold and an understatement of net income). An error in the cost of goods purchased will have a reverse effect on net income (e.g., an overstatement of purchases results in an overstatement of cost of goods sold and an understatement of net income). An error in ending inventory will have a similar effect on net income (e.g., an overstatement of ending inventory results in an understatement of cost of goods sold and an overstatement of net income). If ending inventory errors are not corrected in the following period, their effect on net income for the second period is reversed and total net income for the two years will be correct. In the balance sheet, ending inventory errors will have the same effects on total assets and total owner's equity, and no effect on liabilities.

4. **Demonstrate the presentation and analysis of inventory.** Ending inventory is reported as a current asset on the balance sheet. Cost of goods sold is reported on the income statement. Inventory is valued at the lower of cost and market (LCM), which results in a write-down in inventory, and an increase in cost of goods sold, when the market value (net realizable value) is less than cost. Additional disclosures include information about the major inventory classifications, the cost flow assumption, and the amount of write-downs to net realizable value.

The inventory turnover ratio is calculated as cost of goods sold divided by average inventory. It can be converted to days in inventory by dividing 365 days by the inventory turnover.

5. **Calculate ending inventory and cost of goods sold in a perpetual inventory system using inventory cost flow assumptions (Appendix 6A).** Under FIFO, the cost of the earliest goods on hand is allocated to cost of goods sold. The cost of the most recent goods purchased is allocated to ending inventory. Under average cost, a new average (moving average) cost is calculated after each purchase and applied to the number of units sold and the number of units remaining in ending inventory. Under LIFO, the cost of the most recent purchase is allocated to cost of goods sold. The cost of the earliest goods purchased is allocated to ending inventory.

Each of these assumptions is applied in the same cost flow order as in a periodic inventory system. The main difference is that in a perpetual inventory system, the cost flow assumption is applied at the date of each sale to determine the cost of goods sold. In a periodic inventory system, the cost flow assumption is applied at the end of the period.

6. **Estimate ending inventory using the gross profit and retail inventory methods (Appendix 6B).** The two methods of estimating inventories are the gross profit method and the retail inventory method. Under the gross profit method, the gross profit margin is applied to net sales to determine the estimated cost of goods sold. The estimated cost of goods sold is subtracted from the cost of goods available for sale to determine the estimated cost of the ending inventory. Under the retail inventory method, a cost-to-retail ratio is calculated by dividing the cost of goods available for sale by the retail value of the goods available for sale. This ratio is then applied to the ending inventory at retail to determine the estimated cost of the ending inventory.

Glossary

Study Aids: Glossary
Practice Tools: Key Term Matching Activity

Average cost An inventory cost flow assumption which assumes that it is impossible to measure a specific physical flow of inventory and that it is therefore better to cost items using an average price, calculated by dividing the cost of the goods available for sale by the units available for sale. (p. 292)

Consigned goods Goods shipped by a consignor, who retains ownership, to a party called the consignee. (p. 286)

Days sales in inventory A measure of the average number of days that inventory is held. It is calculated as 365 days divided by the inventory turnover ratio. (p. 305)

First-in, first-out (FIFO) An inventory cost flow assumption which assumes that the costs of the earliest goods purchased are the first to be recognized as the cost of goods sold. The costs of the latest goods purchased are assumed to remain in ending inventory. (p. 290)

Full disclosure principle The requirement that all information that is relevant for decision-making be disclosed. (p. 296)

Gross profit method A method for estimating the cost of the ending inventory by applying the gross profit margin to net sales. (p. 310)

Inventory turnover A liquidity measure of the number of times, on average, that inventory is sold during the period. It

is calculated by dividing cost of goods sold by average inventory. (p. 304)

Last-in, first-out (LIFO) An inventory cost flow assumption which assumes that the costs of the latest units purchased are the first to be allocated to the cost of goods sold. The costs of the earliest units purchased are allocated to ending inventory. (p. 293)

Lower of cost and market (LCM) A basis for stating inventory at the lower of the original cost and the current market value (net realizable value). (p. 302)

Net realizable value The estimated amount for which an asset can be sold, less any estimated costs that are necessary to make the sale. (p. 302)

Retail inventory method A method for estimating the cost of the ending inventory by applying a cost-to-retail ratio to the ending inventory at retail prices. (p. 311)

Specific identification An inventory costing method which matches the actual physical flow of goods. Items are specifically costed to arrive at the cost of goods sold and the cost of the ending inventory. (p. 288)

Weighted average unit cost Average cost that is weighted by the number of units purchased at each unit cost. It is calculated by dividing the cost of goods available for sale by the number of units available for sale. (p. 292)

Note: All questions, exercises, and problems below with an asterisk (*) relate to material in Appendices 6A and 6B.

Self-Study Questions

Practice Tools: Self-Assessment Quizzes

Answers are at the end of the chapter.

(SO 1) K 1. Which of the following should not be included in the physical inventory of a company?
  (a) Goods held on consignment from another company
  (b) Goods shipped on consignment to another company
  (c) Goods in transit that were purchased from a supplier and shipped FOB shipping point
  (d) Goods in transit that were sold to a customer and shipped FOB shipping point

(SO 2) AP 2. Kam Company uses a periodic inventory system and has the following:

	Units	Unit Cost	Total Cost
Inventory, Jan. 1	8,000	$11	$ 88,000
Purchase, June 19	13,000	12	156,000
Purchase, Nov. 8	5,000	13	65,000
	26,000		$309,000

If 9,000 units are on hand at December 31, the cost of the ending inventory under FIFO is:
  (a) $100,000.   (c) $196,000.
  (b) $113,000.   (d) $209,000.

3. Using the data in question 2 above, the cost of goods (SO 2) AP sold under average cost is:
  (a) $106,962.   (c) $180,000.
  (b) $108,000.   (d) $202,038.

4. In periods of rising prices, the average cost flow assumption will produce: (SO 3) C
  (a) higher net income than FIFO.
  (b) the same net income as FIFO.
  (c) lower net income than FIFO.
  (d) lower net income than LIFO.

(SO 3) C 5. In Fran Company, ending inventory is understated by $4,000. The effects of this error on the current year's cost of goods sold and net income, respectively, are:
(a) understated, overstated.
(b) overstated, understated.
(c) overstated, overstated.
(d) understated, understated.

(SO 4) K 6. The lower of cost and market rule for inventory is an example of the application of:
(a) the conservatism characteristic.
(b) the cost principle.
(c) the matching principle.
(d) the economic entity assumption.

(SO 4) AP 7. If a company's cost of goods sold is $120,000, its beginning inventory is $15,000, and its ending inventory is $25,000, what are its inventory turnover and days sales in inventory?
(a) 0.2 times and 1,825 days.
(b) 4.8 times and 76 days.
(c) 6 times and 61 days.
(d) 8 times and 46 days.

(SO 5) AP *8. Fine Wine Company uses a perpetual inventory system and has the following opening inventory, purchases, and sales of inventory in March:

	Units	Unit Cost	Total Cost
Inventory, Mar. 1	8,000	$11	$ 88,000
Purchase, Mar. 9	12,000	12	144,000
Sale, Mar. 12	15,000	?	
Purchase, Mar. 18	5,000	13	65,000

What was the moving average cost per unit after the last purchase on March 18?
(a) $11.60
(b) $12.00
(c) $11.88
(d) $12.30

(SO 6) *9. Somers Company has sales of $150,000 and a cost of goods available for sale of $135,000. If the gross profit margin is 30%, the estimated cost of the ending inventory under the gross profit method is:
(a) $15,000.
(b) $30,000.
(c) $40,500.
(d) $105,000.

(SO 6) *10. Retail Home Company reports the following selected information: cost of goods available for sale at cost, $60,000; at retail, $100,000; and net sales at retail, $80,000. What is the estimated cost of Retail Home Company's ending inventory under the retail method?
(a) $12,000
(b) $20,000
(c) $40,000
(d) $60,000

Questions

(SO 1) C 1. Your friend Tom Wetzel has been hired to help take the physical inventory in Kikujiro's Hardware Store. Explain to Tom what this job will involve.

(SO 1) C 2. Explain to Janine Company what errors can occur in determining inventory quantities if goods in transit are ignored.

(SO 1) C 3. What are consigned goods? Which company, the consignee or the consignor, should include consigned goods in its inventory balance? Explain why.

(SO 2) C 4. Dave Wier believes that the allocation of the cost of goods available for sale to ending inventory and cost of goods sold should be based on the actual physical flow of the goods. Explain to Dave why this may be both impractical and inappropriate.

(SO 2) K 5. Which inventory cost flow assumption:
(a) is usually the same as the actual physical flow of merchandise?
(b) assumes that the last units purchased are the first to be sold?
(c) assumes that it is often impossible to measure a specific physical flow of inventory?

(SO 2) 6. Vance is studying for his next accounting quiz. He argues that the earliest costs should be used when calculating ending inventory using FIFO because they are the first costs. Is he correct? Why or why not?

(SO 2) 7. Explain how the cost of goods sold can be manipulated when (a) the specific identification method is used, and (b) the LIFO cost flow assumption is used.

(SO 3) 8. Compare the financial statement effects of using the FIFO and average cost flow assumptions during a period of declining prices on (a) cash, (b) ending inventory, (c) cost of goods sold, and (d) net income.

(SO 3) 9. In a period of rising prices, the inventory reported in Plato Company's balance sheet is close to the replacement cost of the inventory. York Company's inventory is considerably below its current cost. Identify the inventory cost flow assumption being used by each company. Which company is reporting the higher gross profit?

(SO 3) 10. "The selection of an inventory cost flow assumption depends on whether prices are rising or falling." Do you agree? Explain. Once an assumption has been chosen, what accounting characteristic applies?

(SO 3) C 11. Swift Company has been using the FIFO cost flow assumption during a long period of inflation. During the same period, the owner of Swift has been withdrawing a substantial amount of the company's net income. What undesirable effects may result from this policy?

(SO 3) C 12. Mila Company discovers in 2007 that its ending inventory at December 31, 2007, was understated by $5,000. What effect will this error have on (a) 2007 net income, (b) 2008 net income, and (c) the combined net income for the two years?

(SO 3) C 13. If an error in ending inventory in one year will have the reverse effect in the following year, does this error need to be corrected when it is discovered?

(SO 4) C 14. Lucy Ritter is studying for the next accounting exam. What should Lucy know about (a) when not to use the cost basis of accounting for inventories, and (b) the meaning of "market" in the lower of cost and market method?

(SO 4) C 15. "The key to successful business operations is effective inventory management." Do you agree? Explain.

(SO 4) AN 16. What problems may occur if a company's inventory turnover ratio is too high or too low?

(SO 4) C 17. If a company's days sales in inventory ratio increases from one year to the next, would this be viewed as a sign that the company is managing its inventory better or worse? Explain.

(SO 4) K 18. Wabanaki Company's balance sheet shows inventories of $162,800. What additional disclosures should be made?

(SO 5) C *19. When perpetual inventory records are kept, the results under the FIFO cost flow assumption are the same as they would be in a periodic inventory system. If this is the case, why would a company bother using a perpetual inventory system?

(SO 5) K *20. How is the average cost flow assumption different when it is used in a perpetual inventory system and in a periodic inventory system?

(SO 6) K *21. When is it necessary to estimate inventories?

(SO 6) C *22. Both the gross profit method and the retail inventory method are based on averages. For each method, describe the average used, how it is determined, and how it is applied.

Brief Exercises

BE6–1 Helgeson Company has identified the following items to include or exclude when it takes its physical inventory. Indicate whether each item should be included or excluded.

Identify items in inventory. (SO 1) K

1. Goods shipped on consignment by Helgeson to another company
2. Goods in transit to Helgeson from a supplier, shipped FOB shipping point
3. Goods sold to a customer but being held for delivery
4. Goods from another company held on consignment by Helgeson
5. Goods in transit to a customer, shipped FOB shipping point

BE6–2 Mary Ann's Hat Shop counted the entire inventory in the store on August 31 and arrived at a total inventory cost of $65,000. The count included $5,000 of inventory held on consignment for a local designer; $500 of inventory that was being held for customers who were deciding if they actually wanted to purchase the merchandise; and $750 of inventory that had been sold to customers but was being held for alterations. There were two shipments of inventory received on September 1. The first shipment cost $6,000. It had been shipped on August 29, terms FOB destination, and the freight charges were $240. The second shipment cost $3,750. It had been shipped on August 28, terms FOB shipping point, and the freight charges were $150. Neither of these shipments were included in the August 31 count. Calculate the correct cost of the inventory on August 31.

Calculate inventory cost. (SO 1) AP

BE6–3 On January 3, Piano Company purchased three model EBS electronic pianos for $1,000 each. On January 20, it purchased two additional model EBS electronic pianos for $1,200 each. An inventory count on January 31 revealed that three of the pianos were still on hand. Piano Company uses a periodic inventory system. Calculate the ending inventory and cost of goods sold on January 31 under (a) specific identification, (b) FIFO, (c) average cost, and (d) LIFO. Assume for (a) that one of the pianos sold during January was purchased on January 3 and the other was purchased on January 20.

Apply specific identification and periodic cost flow assumptions. (SO 2) AP

BE6–4 In its first month of operations, Quilt Company made three purchases of merchandise in the following sequence: 250 units at $6, 400 units at $7, and 350 units at $8. There are 400 units

Apply periodic cost flow assumptions. (SO 2) AP

on hand at the end of the period. Quilt uses a periodic inventory system. Calculate the cost to be allocated to ending inventory and cost of goods sold under (a) FIFO, (b) average cost, and (c) LIFO.

Identify inventory cost flow assumptions.
(SO 3) C

BE6–5   For each statement which follows, identify the inventory cost flow assumption which best fits the description, assuming a period of rising prices:

(a) It results in a balance sheet inventory amount that is closest to the replacement cost.
(b) It matches recent costs against revenue.
(c) It is the best choice because each product has unique features that affect cost.
(d) It understates the current value of the inventory on the balance sheet.

Compare financial effects of inventory cost flow assumptions.
(SO 3) C

BE6–6   Interactive.com just started business and is trying to decide which inventory cost flow assumption to use. Assuming prices are falling, as they often do in the information technology industry, answer the following questions for Interactive.com:

(a) Which cost flow assumption will give the highest ending inventory? Why?
(b) Which cost flow assumption will give the highest cost of goods sold? Why?
(c) Which cost flow assumption will result in the highest cash flow? Explain.
(d) What factors are important for Interactive.com to consider as it tries to choose the most appropriate cost flow assumption?

Determine effects of inventory error.
(SO 3) AN

BE6–7   Creole Company reports net income of $90,000 in 2007. Ending inventory was overstated by $7,000. What is the correct net income for 2007? What effect, if any, will this error have on total assets and owner's equity reported on the balance sheet at December 31, 2007?

Determine effect of ending inventory error on balance sheet for two years.
(SO 3) AN

BE6–8   Johal Company incorrectly included $25,000 of goods held on consignment for Hajol Company in Johal's ending inventory as at December 31, 2007. Assuming that this error was not later discovered and corrected, what is the impact of this error on assets, liabilities, and owner's equity at the end of 2007? At the end of 2008?

Determine LCM valuation.
(SO 4) AP

BE6–9   Svenska Electronic Centre accumulates the following cost and market data at December 31:

Inventory Categories	Cost	Market
Cameras	$12,000	$11,200
MP3 players	9,000	9,500
DVD players	14,000	11,800

(a) Calculate the lower of cost and market valuation, applying LCM to each inventory category.
(b) What adjustment should Svenska record if it uses a perpetual inventory system?

Apply LCM.
(SO 4) AP

BE6–10   Piper Music uses a periodic inventory system and has just finished the year-end physical inventory count. After determining the cost of the ending inventory, cost of goods sold was calculated as follows:

Beginning inventory	$ 45,600
Purchases	319,200
Cost of goods available for sale	364,800
Ending inventory (at cost)	54,700
Cost of goods sold	$310,100

It was then discovered that the value of the ending inventory using lower of cost and net realizable value was $52,500. (a) What is the correct ending inventory and cost of goods sold that should be reported in the financial statements? (b) What adjustment should Piper Music record?

Calculate inventory ratios.
(SO 4) AP

BE6–11   Ry Company reported net sales of $550,000; cost of goods purchased of $300,000; beginning inventory of $22,250; and ending inventory of $27,750. Calculate the inventory turnover and days sales in inventory ratios.

Apply perpetual cost flow assumptions.
(SO 5) AP

*** BE6–12**   Poirier Department Store uses a perpetual inventory system. Data for a product include the following purchases:

Date	Units	Unit Cost
May 7	50	$10
July 28	27	15

On June 1, Poirier sold 32 units for $20 each, and on August 27 it sold 33 more units for $22 each. What are the cost of goods sold and ending inventory under (a) FIFO, (b) average cost, and (c) LIFO?

*BE6–13 Yip Company uses a perpetual inventory system. The following data are available for its first month of operations:

> May 2 Purchased 250 units for $6 each.
> 3 Purchased 400 units for $7 each.
> 10 Sold 275 units for $10 each.
> 15 Purchased 350 units for $8 each.
> 25 Sold 325 units for $12 each.

Calculate the cost of goods sold and ending inventory under (a) FIFO and (b) average cost.

Apply perpetual FIFO and average cost flow assumptions.
(SO 5) AP

*BE6–14 At the beginning of the year, Seller Company had 700 units with a cost of $3 per unit in its beginning inventory. The following inventory transactions occurred during the month of January:

> Jan. 3 Sold 500 units on account for $5 each.
> 9 Purchased 1,000 units on account for $4 per unit.
> 15 Sold 800 units for cash for $8 each.

Prepare journal entries assuming that Seller Company uses FIFO under (a) the periodic inventory system and (b) the perpetual inventory system.

Record transactions in periodic and perpetual inventory systems.
(SO 2, 5) AP

*BE6–15 Jansen Company had beginning inventory of $60,000; net sales of $350,000; and cost of goods purchased of $250,000. In the previous year, the company had a gross profit margin of 40%. Calculate the estimated cost of the ending inventory using the gross profit method.

Apply gross profit method.
(SO 6) AP

*BE6–16 On June 30, Fabric Villa has the following data related to the retail inventory method: Goods available for sale at cost $35,000; at retail $50,000; and net sales of $40,000. Calculate the estimated cost of the ending inventory, using the retail inventory method.

Apply retail inventory method.
(SO 6) AP

Exercises

E6–1 Shippers Company had the following inventory situations to consider at January 31, its year end:

1. Goods held on consignment for MailBoxes Etc. since December 12
2. Goods held on consignment by Rinehart Holdings for Shippers Company since January 5
3. Goods still in transit and purchased from a supplier, FOB destination, on January 25
4. Goods still in transit and shipped to a customer, FOB destination, on January 26
5. Goods still in transit and shipped to a customer, FOB shipping point, on January 27
6. Goods still in transit and purchased from a supplier, FOB shipping point, on January 29
7. Freight costs paid on inventory purchased and received on January 30
8. Freight costs paid on inventory sold and shipped to a customer on January 31
9. Office supplies on hand at January 31

Identify items in inventory.
(SO 1) K

Instructions

Identify which of the above items should be included in inventory. If the item should not be included in inventory, state where it should be recorded.

E6–2 First Bank is considering giving Moghul Company a loan. First, however, it decides that it would be a good idea to have further discussions with Moghul's accountant. One area of particular

Determine correct inventory amount.
(SO 1) AP

concern is the inventory account, which has a year-end balance of $281,000 based on the results of the physical inventory count on December 31. Discussions with the accountant reveal the following:

1. Moghul sold goods that cost $35,000 to Novotna Company, FOB destination, on December 28. The goods are not expected to arrive at their destination in India until January 12. The goods were not included in the physical inventory because they were not in the warehouse.
2. The physical count of the inventory did not include goods that cost $95,000 that were shipped to Moghul, FOB shipping point, on December 27 and were still in transit at year end.
3. Moghul received goods that cost $28,000 on January 2. The goods were shipped on December 26 by Cellar Co., FOB destination. The goods were not included in the physical count.
4. Moghul sold goods that cost $49,000 to Sterling of Canada, FOB shipping point, on December 30. The goods were received by Sterling on January 8. They were not included in Moghul's physical inventory.
5. Moghul received goods that cost $44,000 on January 2 that were shipped, FOB destination, on December 29. The shipment was a rush order that was supposed to arrive December 31. This purchase was not included in the ending inventory of $281,000.
6. On December 31, Board Company had $30,500 of goods held on consignment for Moghul. The goods were not included in Moghul's ending inventory balance.

Instructions

Determine the correct inventory amount at December 31.

Apply specific identification. (SO 2) AP

E6–3 On December 1, Discount Electronics has three identical LCD TVs in inventory. The purchase dates, serial numbers, and cost of each of the three items are as follows:

Date	Serial Number	Cost
June 1	#1012	$500
September 1	#1045	450
November 30	#1056	400

All three LCD TVs are priced to sell at $750. At December 31, one TV remained in inventory. Discount Electronics uses a periodic inventory system.

Instructions

(a) Explain how Discount Electronics would use specific identification to determine the cost of the ending inventory and cost of goods sold in December.
(b) If Discount Electronics used the specific identification method, how might it manipulate its income? What would Discount's gross profit and ending inventory be if the company wanted to maximize income? What would Discount's gross profit and ending inventory be if the company wanted to minimize income?
(c) What are the benefits of using specific identification?
(d) Should Discount Electronics use specific identification or one of the three cost flow assumptions instead? Explain.

Apply periodic FIFO and average cost flow assumptions. (SO 2) AP

E6–4 Zambia Company uses a periodic inventory system. Its records show the following for the month of May, with 25 units on hand at May 31:

		Units	Unit Cost	Total Cost
May 1	Inventory	30	$ 8	$240
15	Purchases	45	11	495
24	Purchases	15	12	180
	Total	90		$915

Instructions

Calculate the ending inventory and cost of goods sold at May 31 using the FIFO and average cost flow assumptions. Prove the cost of goods sold calculations.

E6–5   Dene Company uses a periodic inventory system and reports the following inventory transactions for the month of June. A physical inventory count showed 180 units were on hand on June 30.

Apply periodic FIFO and average cost flow assumptions. Answer questions about results.

(SO 2, 3) AP

		Units	Unit Cost	Total Cost
June 1	Inventory	150	$5	$ 750
12	Purchases	230	6	1,380
16	Purchases	495	8	3,960
23	Purchases	175	9	1,575

Instructions

(a) Calculate the cost of the ending inventory and the cost of goods sold under (1) FIFO and (2) average cost.

(b) For part 2 of instruction (a), explain why the average unit cost is not $7.

(c) Which cost flow assumption gives the higher ending inventory? Why?

(d) Which cost flow assumption results in the higher cost of goods sold? Why?

(e) Which cost flow assumption results in the higher cash flow? Why?

E6–6   Inventory data for Dene Company are presented in E6–5.

Apply periodic LIFO cost flow assumption. Answer questions about results.

(SO 2, 3) AP

Instructions

(a) Calculate the cost of the ending inventory and the cost of goods sold using the LIFO cost flow assumption.

(b) Should the results in (a) be higher or lower than the results under (1) FIFO and (2) average cost? Explain.

E6–7   Seles Hardware reported its cost of goods sold as follows:

Determine effects of inventory errors.

(SO 3) AN

	2008	2007
Beginning inventory	$ 35,000	$ 30,000
Cost of goods purchased	160,000	175,000
Cost of goods available for sale	195,000	205,000
Ending inventory	25,000	35,000
Cost of goods sold	$170,000	$170,000

Seles made two errors: (1) 2007 ending inventory was overstated by $3,000, and (2) 2008 ending inventory was understated by $4,000.

Instructions

(a) Calculate the correct cost of goods sold for each year.

(b) Describe the impact of the error on the financial statements for each year and in total for the two years.

(c) Explain why it is important that Seles Hardware correct these errors.

E6–8   Aruba Company reported the following income statement data for the years ended December 31:

Correct partial income statements and comment.

(SO 3) AN

	2008	2007
Sales	$265,000	$250,000
Cost of goods sold		
Beginning inventory	42,000	45,000
Cost of goods purchased	212,000	202,000
Cost of goods available for sale	254,000	247,000
Ending inventory	49,000	42,000
Cost of goods sold	205,000	205,000
Gross profit	$ 60,000	$ 45,000

The inventories at January 1, 2007, and December 31, 2008, are correct. However, the ending inventory at December 31, 2007, was understated by $10,000.

Instructions

(a) Prepare the correct income statement up to gross profit for the two years.
(b) What is the combined effect of the inventory error on total gross profit for the two years?
(c) Calculate the gross profit margin for each of the two years, before and after the correction.
(d) In a letter to the president of Aruba Company, explain what has happened: discuss the nature of the error and its effect on the financial statements.

Determine LCM valuation.
(SO 4) AP

E6–9 Cody Camera Shop is determining the lower of cost and market of its inventory. The following data are available at December 31:

		Units	Unit Cost	Market
Cameras:	Minolta	5	$175	$160
	Canon	7	140	142
Light Meters:	Vivitar	12	135	129
	Kodak	10	115	120

Instructions

(a) Determine the total cost of the ending inventory.
(b) Determine the total market value of the ending inventory.
(c) What amount should be reported on Cody Camera Shop's financial statements, assuming the lower of cost and market rule is applied to individual inventory items?
(d) Prepare the journal entry to record the adjustment from cost to market, if required, for Cody Camera Shop assuming (1) Cody uses a periodic inventory system, and (2) Cody uses a perpetual inventory system.

Calculate inventory turnover and days sales in inventory.
(SO 4) AP

E6–10 The following information is available for **Danier Leather Inc.** for three recent years (in thousands):

	2005	2004	2003
Inventory	$ 29,031	$ 29,483	$ 37,029
Sales	166,350	175,270	175,487
Cost of goods sold	82,863	88,742	88,788

Instructions

Calculate the inventory turnover, days sales in inventory, and gross profit margin for Danier Leather Inc. for 2005 and 2004. Comment on any trends.

Apply perpetual cost flow assumptions.
(SO 5) AP

*E6–11 Inventory data for Dene Company are presented in E6–5.

Instructions

(a) Assume there were sales of 250 units on June 14 for $10 each and 620 units on June 26 for $12 each. Calculate the cost of goods sold and the cost of the ending inventory under (1) FIFO, (2) average cost, and (3) LIFO, using a perpetual inventory system.
(b) How are the results in (a) different from the results in E6–5 and E6–6?

Apply periodic and perpetual cost flow assumptions.
(SO 2, 5) AP

*E6–12 Powder Co. sells an Xpert snowboard that is popular with snowboard enthusiasts. Information follows for Powder's purchases and sales of Xpert snowboards during September:

Date	Transaction	Units	Unit Purchase Price	Unit Sales Price
Sept. 1	Beginning inventory	25	$295	
5	Purchase	30	300	
12	Sale	(32)		$449
19	Purchase	35	305	
22	Sale	(50)		454
25	Purchase	15	310	

Instructions

(a) Calculate the cost of goods sold and the ending inventory using FIFO and average cost, assuming Powder Co. uses a perpetual inventory system.

(b) What would the cost of goods sold and ending inventory be if Powder Co. used each of these cost flow assumptions in a periodic inventory system?

*E6–13 Refer to the data for Powder Co. in E6–12. Powder makes all sales for cash and purchases on account.

Record transactions in perpetual and periodic inventory systems. (SO 2, 5) AP

Instructions

(a) Record the purchases and sales for Powder Co. in a perpetual inventory system under each of the following cost flow assumptions: (1) FIFO and (2) average cost.

(b) Record the purchases and sales for Powder Co. in a periodic inventory system under each of the following cost flow assumptions: (1) FIFO and (2) average cost.

*E6–14 The inventory of Farhad Company was destroyed by fire on March 1. From an examination of the accounting records, the following data for the first two months of the year are obtained: Sales $51,000; Sales Returns and Allowances $1,000; Sales Discounts $500; Freight Out $1,500; Purchases $31,200; Freight In $1,200; Purchase Returns and Allowances $1,400; and Purchase Discounts $300.

Estimate inventory loss using gross profit method. (SO 6) AP

Instructions

Determine the inventory lost by fire, assuming a beginning inventory of $25,000 and a gross profit margin of 30%.

*E6–15 Agnew Shoe Store uses the retail inventory method for its two departments: men's shoes and women's shoes. The following information is obtained for each department:

Estimate ending inventory at cost using retail method. (SO 6) AP

Item	Men's Shoes	Women's Shoes
Beginning inventory at cost	$ 36,550	$ 45,000
Goods purchased at cost	152,150	132,750
Net sales	177,000	180,000
Beginning inventory at retail	45,000	60,000
Goods purchased at retail	179,000	177,000

Instructions

Calculate the estimated cost of the ending inventory for each shoe department under the retail inventory method.

*E6–16 Nancy's Running Store has two departments: running shoes and running clothes. The selling price of running clothes is double their cost; the selling price of running shoes is 1.6 times their cost. During the previous year, the company had an overall gross profit margin of 43.75%. The information for the first six months of the current year is as follows:

Estimate ending inventory using gross profit and retail methods. Compare results. (SO 6) AN

	Running Shoes	Running Clothes
Beginning inventory at cost	$ 48,000	$ 35,000
Sales for the six months	249,600	207,000
Purchases at cost	144,000	92,500

Instructions

(a) Estimate the cost of the ending inventory using the gross profit method.

(b) Estimate the cost of the ending inventory using the retail method.

(c) Do the two methods give the same estimate? Why or why not? Which method would you recommend in this situation?

Problems: Set A

Identify items in inventory.
(SO 1) AP

P6–1A Banff Company is trying to determine the value of its ending inventory as at February 29, 2008, the company's year end. The accountant counted everything that was in the warehouse as at February 29, which resulted in an ending inventory cost of $56,000. However, she was not sure how to treat the following transactions, so she did not include them in inventory:

1. On February 26, Banff shipped goods costing $800 to a customer. The goods were shipped FOB shipping point. The receiving report indicates that the customer received the goods on March 1.
2. On February 27, Wah Company shipped goods to Banff, FOB destination. The invoice price was $350 plus $25 for freight. The receiving report indicates that the goods were received by Banff on March 2.
3. Banff had $620 of inventory at a customer's warehouse "on approval." The customer was going to let Banff know whether it wanted the merchandise by the end of the week, March 7.
4. Banff also had $570 of inventory on consignment at a Jasper craft shop.
5. On February 25, Banff ordered goods costing $750. The goods were shipped FOB shipping point on February 27. The receiving report indicates that Banff received the goods on March 1.
6. On February 29, Banff packaged goods and moved them to the shipping department for shipping to a customer, FOB destination. The invoice price was $425 plus $20 for freight. The cost of the items was $360. The receiving report indicates that the goods were received by the customer on March 2.
7. Banff had damaged goods set aside in the warehouse because they were not saleable. These goods originally cost $400. Banff had expected to sell these items for $600 before they were damaged.
8. On February 20, Banff Company had received $875 of inventory on consignment from Kananaskis Company. By February 29, Banff Company had sold $365 of this inventory for Kananaskis.
9. On February 29, Banff was holding merchandise that had been sold to a customer on February 25 but needed some engraving done before the customer would pick it up. The customer has paid for the goods and will pick them up on March 3 after the engraving is finished. This inventory cost $940 and was sold for $1,340.

Instructions

(a) For each of the above transactions, specify whether the item in question should be included in ending inventory, and if so, at what amount. Explain your reasoning.
(b) How much is the revised ending inventory cost?

Apply periodic cost flow assumptions. Prepare income statements and answer questions.
(SO 2, 3) AP

P6–2A Savita Company had a beginning inventory on January 1, 2008, of 100 units of product E2-D2 at a cost of $30 per unit. During the year, purchases were as follows:

	Units	Unit Cost
Feb. 20	600	$32
May 5	300	36
Oct. 12	200	42
Nov. 8	150	44

Savita uses a periodic inventory system. At the end of the year, there were 225 units on hand.

Instructions

(a) Determine the cost of goods available for sale.
(b) Determine the ending inventory and the cost of goods sold under each of the three cost flow assumptions: (1) FIFO, (2) average cost, and (3) LIFO.
(c) During the year, Savita Company sold product E2-D2 for $70 per unit. Prepare a partial income statement up to gross profit for each of the three cost flow assumptions.
(d) What cost flow assumption should Savita use if it needs to give its financial statements to the bank as part of a loan application? Explain.

(e) Will one cost flow assumption always give a higher net income than the other two assumptions? Explain. If not, can Savita Company choose a different cost flow assumption each year in order to always have the highest possible net income? Explain.

P6–3A Tumatoe Company uses a periodic inventory system. Its management asks for your help in determining the different effects of the FIFO and average cost flow assumptions. For 2008, the accounting records show the following data:

Apply periodic FIFO and average cost flow assumptions. Prepare income statements and answer questions.
(SO 2, 3) AP

Inventory, January 1 (15,000 units)	$ 56,250
Net sales	700,000
Operating expenses	120,000

Details of inventory purchases during the year are as follows:

Date	Units	Unit Cost
May 10	40,000	$4.00
August 15	50,000	4.25
November 20	20,000	4.50

A physical count of inventory on December 31 showed 25,000 units on hand.

Instructions

(a) Prepare condensed income statements for 2008 under FIFO and average cost.
(b) Write a business letter which answers the following questions for management:
  1. Which inventory cost flow assumption gives the more meaningful inventory amount for the balance sheet? Why?
  2. Which inventory cost flow assumption gives the more meaningful net income? Why?
  3. Which inventory cost flow assumption is more likely to be close to the actual physical flow of the goods? Why?
  4. How much more cash would be available to management under average cost than under FIFO? Why?
  5. What factors should influence management's choice of cost flow assumption?

P6–4A You are given the following information for transactions by Schwinghamer Co. All transactions are settled in cash. Returns are normally not damaged and are restored immediately to inventory for resale. Schwinghamer uses a periodic inventory system and the FIFO cost flow assumption.

Record transactions using periodic FIFO. Apply lower of cost and market.
(SO 2, 3, 4) AP

Date		Transaction	Units	Unit Price
Oct.	1	Beginning inventory	60	$15
	5	Purchase	120	14
	8	Sale	150	24
	10	Sale return	25	24
	15	Purchase	40	13
	16	Purchase return	5	13
	20	Sale	65	18
	25	Purchase	10	11

Instructions

(a) Prepare the required journal entries for the month of October for Schwinghamer Co.
(b) Determine the ending inventory and cost of goods sold for Schwinghamer, using the FIFO cost flow assumption.
(c) On October 31, Schwinghamer Co. learns that its product has a net realizable value of $10 per unit. What amount should ending inventory be valued at on the October 31 balance sheet? Discuss the accounting characteristic that is relevant to this decision.
(d) What amount should cost of goods sold be valued at on the October income statement? Prepare the journal entry, if required, to recognize the decrease in value of this product.
(e) If Schwinghamer used a perpetual inventory system, what journal entry, if any, would be recorded to recognize the decrease in the value of this product?

P6–5A The records of Leblanc Company show the following amounts in its December 31 financial statements:

	2006	2007	2008
Total assets	$400,000	$450,000	$475,000
Owner's equity	250,000	275,000	290,000
Cost of goods sold	300,000	335,000	315,000
Net income	40,000	60,000	50,000

Leblanc made the following errors in determining its ending inventory:

1. The ending inventory account balance at December 31, 2006, included $15,000 of goods held on consignment for Gillies Company.
2. The ending inventory account balance at December 31, 2007, did not include goods that were purchased for $25,000 and shipped on December 30, 2007, FOB shipping point.

The cost of goods purchased was correctly calculated each year.

Instructions

(a) Calculate the correct amount for each of the following for 2006, 2007, and 2008:
   1. Total assets   3. Cost of goods sold
   2. Owner's equity   4. Net income
(b) Indicate the effect of these errors (overstated, understated, or no effect) on cash at the end of 2006, 2007, and 2008.

Determine effects of
inventory errors. Calculate
inventory turnover.
(SO 3, 4) AN

P6–6A The records of Pelletier Company show the following data:

	2006	2007	2008
Sales	$300,000	$312,000	$324,000
Beginning inventory	25,000	17,000	29,000
Cost of goods purchased	250,000	285,000	245,000
Ending inventory	17,000	29,000	35,000
Operating expenses	50,000	52,000	54,000

After its July 31, 2008, year end, Pelletier discovered two errors:

1. Ending inventory in 2006 was understated by $10,000.
2. The cost of goods purchased for the year ended July 31, 2007, included $25,000 of merchandise that should have been recorded as a purchase in the year ended July 31, 2008. The July 31, 2007 inventory was correctly calculated.

Instructions

(a) Prepare incorrect and corrected income statements for the years ended July 31, 2006, 2007, and 2008.
(b) What is the combined effect of the errors on owner's equity at July 31, 2008, before correction?
(c) Calculate the correct and incorrect inventory turnover ratios for each of the years 2006, 2007, and 2008.

P6–7A The following information is available for Calgary-based **Big Rock Brewery Income Trust** for the years ended December 31:

	2005	2004	2003
Cost of goods sold	$15,255,008	$13,696,549	$10,298,575
Inventory	3,048,610	4,667,950	4,512,097
Current assets	12,770,157	9,947,060	10,006,747
Current liabilities	3,895,903	4,014,186	4,958,338

Instructions

(a) Calculate the inventory turnover, days sales in inventory, and current ratios for 2005 and 2004. Comment on Big Rock's liquidity.

(b) Big Rock uses the average cost flow assumption to determine the cost of its inventory. If prices are rising, how would you expect the inventory turnover, days sales in inventory, and current ratios to change (e.g., increase or decrease) if Big Rock used FIFO instead of average cost?

*P6–8A   You are given the following information for Danielle Company for the month ended June 30, 2008:

Date	Description	Units	Unit Price
June 1	Beginning inventory	30	$60
4	Purchase	85	66
10	Sale	90	90
18	Purchase	35	68
25	Sale	50	95
26	Sale return	5	95
28	Purchase	20	72

Apply perpetual cost flow assumptions. Calculate gross profit.
(SO 5) AP

Danielle Company uses a perpetual inventory system.

Instructions

(a) Calculate the ending inventory and cost of goods sold using FIFO, average cost, and LIFO.

(b) Calculate and compare the gross profit earned by Danielle using each of the three cost flow assumptions.

(c) How would the results change for each cost flow assumption if the cost of new inventory for Danielle was decreasing?

*P6–9A   Grinder Company sells a variety of skateboards and accessories. Information follows for Grinder's purchases and sales during April and May 2008 of GrindKing, one of its top brands of skateboards:

Apply perpetual FIFO and average cost flow assumptions. Answer questions about financial statement effects.
(SO 3, 5) AP

	Purchases		Sales	
Date	Units	Unit Cost	Units	Unit Price
Apr. 8			18	$319
23	50	$202		
26			50	299
May 9	24	198		
21			32	291

Grinder uses a perpetual inventory system. On April 1, Grinder had 36 units on hand at a cost of $210 each. All purchases and sales during April and May were on account.

Instructions

(a) Determine the cost of goods sold and ending inventory under a perpetual inventory system using (1) FIFO and (2) average cost.

(b) Prepare all required journal entries for the April transactions using (1) FIFO and (2) average cost.

(c) Calculate gross profit using (1) FIFO and (2) average cost.

(d) Which cost flow assumption produces the higher cash flow?

(e) What factors should the owner of Grinder consider when choosing a cost flow assumption?

*P6–10A You are given the following information for Armadillo Company for January 2008:

Date	Description	Units	Unit Price
Jan. 1	Beginning inventory	25	$60
5	Purchase	125	64
7	Sale	110	90
14	Purchase	30	68
20	Sale	60	95
21	Sale return	5	95
25	Purchase	20	72

Instructions

(a) Calculate the ending inventory and cost of goods sold using the FIFO cost flow assumption in (1) a perpetual inventory system, and (2) a periodic inventory system.
(b) Compare the ending inventory and cost of goods sold amounts using FIFO in a perpetual system and FIFO in a periodic system. Comment on any differences or similarities between the two inventory systems.

*P6–11A Thierry Company lost 80% of its inventory in a fire on March 23, 2008. The accounting records showed the following gross profit data for February and March:

	February	March (to Mar. 23)
Sales	$325,000	$292,500
Sales returns and allowances	6,500	5,850
Sales discounts	3,000	2,700
Purchases	218,000	196,000
Purchase returns and allowances	4,360	3,920
Purchase discounts	2,000	1,950
Freight in	3,270	2,940
Beginning inventory	17,500	25,200
Ending inventory	25,200	?

Thierry is fully insured for fire losses but must prepare a report for the insurance company.

Instructions

Determine both the estimated total inventory and the inventory lost in the March fire.

*P6–12A Lincoln Department Store uses the retail inventory method to estimate its monthly ending inventories. The following information is available for two of its departments at August 31, 2008:

	Clothing		Jewellery and Cosmetics	
	Cost	Retail	Cost	Retail
Sales		$1,375,000		$895,000
Sales returns and allowances		27,000		5,400
Purchases	$770,000	1,440,000	$560,000	918,000
Purchase returns and allowances	36,000	65,500	12,200	19,700
Purchase discounts	5,000		2,800	
Freight in	7,900		5,700	
Beginning inventory	50,600	92,000	29,000	48,000

On August 31, Lincoln Department Store takes a physical inventory count at retail. The actual retail values of the inventories in each department on August 31, 2008, are as follows: Clothing $112,750 and Jewellery and Cosmetics $53,300.

Instructions

(a) Determine the estimated cost of the ending inventory for each department on August 31, 2008, using the retail inventory method.
(b) Calculate the store's loss on August 31, 2008, from theft and other causes, at retail and at cost.

*P6–13A Outback Clothing Company uses a periodic inventory system and uses the retail method to estimate inventories at cost for financial statements. It does a physical inventory count every January 31, the company's fiscal year end. Data for the year ended January 31, 2008, follow:

	Cost	Retail
Sales		$795,000
Sales returns and allowances		14,200
Purchases	$443,300	790,000
Purchase returns and allowances	7,200	12,900
Purchase discounts	2,300	
Freight in	12,800	
Inventory, January 31, 2007	39,875	73,500

Determine ending inventory using retail method and comment. Prepare partial income statement.
(SO 6) AP

Instructions

(a) Use the retail method to estimate the January 31, 2008, inventory at cost and at retail.

(b) The physical inventory count at retail prices at January 31, 2008, was $60,400. Compare this to the estimated inventory and comment on your findings.

(c) Prepare a partial income statement up to gross profit and calculate the gross profit margin for the year ended January 31, 2008.

(d) The owner of Outback Clothing is considering investing in a perpetual inventory system. Would you recommend this or not? Why?

Problems: Set B

P6–1B Kananaskis Country Company is trying to determine the value of its ending inventory as at February 29, 2008, the company's year end. The accountant counted everything that was in the warehouse as at February 29, which resulted in an ending inventory valuation of $65,000. However, he was not sure how to treat the following transactions, so he did not include them in inventory:

Identify items in inventory.
(SO 1) AP

1. On February 27, Kananaskis shipped goods costing $950 to a customer and charged the customer $1,300. The goods were shipped FOB destination and the receiving report indicates that the customer received the goods on March 3.

2. On February 26, Seller Company shipped goods to Kananaskis, FOB shipping point. The invoice price was $375 plus $30 for freight. The receiving report indicates that the goods were received by Kananaskis on March 2.

3. Kananaskis had $630 of inventory put aside in the warehouse. The inventory is for a customer who has asked that the goods be shipped on March 10.

4. Also in Kananaskis' warehouse is $400 of inventory that Craft Producers shipped to Kananaskis on consignment.

5. On February 26, Kananaskis issued a purchase order to acquire goods costing $750. The goods were shipped FOB destination. The receiving report indicates that Kananaskis received the goods on March 2.

6. On February 26, Kananaskis shipped goods to a customer, FOB shipping point. The invoice price was $350 plus $25 for freight. The cost of the items was $280. The receiving report indicates that the goods were received by the customer on March 2.

7. On February 29, Kananaskis was holding merchandise that had been sold to a customer on February 25 but needed some minor alterations before the customer would take possession. The customer has paid for the goods and will pick them up on March 3 after the alterations are complete. This inventory cost $490 and was sold for $880.

8. Kananaskis shipped $875 of inventory on consignment to Banff Company on February 20. By February 29, Banff Company had sold $365 of this inventory for Kananaskis.

Instructions

(a) For each of the above transactions, specify whether the item should be included in ending inventory, and if so, at what amount. Explain your reasoning.
(b) How much is the revised ending inventory valuation?

Apply periodic cost flow assumptions. Prepare income statements and answer questions.
(SO 2, 3) AP

P6–2B Ng Company had a beginning inventory on January 1 of 250 units of Product SXL at a cost of $16 per unit. During the year, the following purchases were made:

	Units	Unit Cost
Mar. 15	700	$18
July 20	500	20
Sept. 4	450	22
Dec. 2	100	24

At the end of the year, there were 300 units on hand. Ng Company uses a periodic inventory system.

Instructions

(a) Determine the cost of goods available for sale.
(b) Determine (1) the cost of the ending inventory and (2) the cost of goods sold under each of the three cost flow assumptions: (1) FIFO, (2) average cost, and (3) LIFO.
(c) During the year, Ng Company sold product SXL for $33 per unit. Prepare a partial income statement up to gross profit for each of the three cost flow assumptions.
(d) What cost flow assumption should Ng Company use if its main objective is to minimize income taxes? Explain.
(e) Which assumption would have the best impact on the company's cash flow?

Apply periodic FIFO and average cost flow assumptions. Prepare income statements and answer questions.
(SO 2, 3) AP

P6–3B The management of Réal Novelty uses a periodic inventory system and is re-evaluating the appropriateness of its present inventory cost flow assumption, average cost. It asks for your help in determining the results of operations for the year ended December 31, 2008, if the FIFO cost flow assumption had been used. For 2008, the accounting records show the following data:

Inventories		Purchases and Sales	
Beginning (25,000 units)	$56,250	Total net sales	$920,000
Ending (20,000 units)	?	Total cost of goods purchased	574,750

Purchases were made quarterly, as follows:

Quarter	Units	Unit Cost
1	50,000	$2.30
2	50,000	2.50
3	60,000	2.60
4	65,000	2.75

Operating expenses were $151,000.

Instructions

(a) Prepare condensed income statements for 2008 under periodic FIFO and average cost.
(b) Write a business letter which answers the following questions for management:
　1. Which cost flow assumption produces the more meaningful inventory amount for the balance sheet? Why?
　2. Which cost flow assumption produces the more meaningful net income? Why?
　3. Which cost flow assumption produces the more realistic gross profit figure? Why?
　4. How much additional cash will be available for management under average cost than under FIFO? Why?
　5. What factors should management consider in choosing its inventory cost flow assumption?

Record transactions using periodic average cost. Apply lower of cost and market.
(SO 2, 3, 4) AP

P6–4B You are given the following information for Amelia Company. All transactions are settled in cash. Returns are usually not damaged and are restored immediately to inventory for resale. Amelia uses a periodic inventory system and the average cost flow assumption. Increased competition has reduced the price of the product.

Date	Transaction	Units	Unit Price
July 1	Beginning inventory	200	$10
5	Purchase	600	9
8	Sale	650	11
10	Sale return	100	11
15	Purchase	450	8
16	Purchase return	50	8
20	Sale	600	9
25	Purchase	100	7

Instructions

(a) Prepare the required journal entries for the month of July for Amelia Company.
(b) Determine the ending inventory and cost of goods sold for Amelia using the average cost flow assumption.
(c) On July 31, Amelia Company learns that the product has a net realizable value of $6 per unit. What amount should ending inventory be valued at on the July 31 balance sheet? Discuss the accounting characteristic that is relevant to this decision.
(d) What amount should cost of goods sold be valued at on the July income statement? Prepare the journal entry, if required, to recognize the decrease in value of this product.
(e) If Amelia used a perpetual inventory system, what journal entry, if any, would be recorded to recognize the decrease in the value of this product?

P6–5B The records of Gillies Company show the following amounts in its December 31 financial statements:

Determine effects of inventory errors.
(SO 1, 3) AN

	2006	2007	2008
Total assets	$800,000	$900,000	$925,000
Owner's equity	625,000	700,000	750,000
Cost of goods sold	500,000	550,000	515,000
Net income	110,000	125,000	140,000

Gillies made the following errors in determining its ending inventory:

1. The ending inventory account balance at December 31, 2006, did not include $15,000 of goods held on consignment by Leblanc Company.
2. The ending inventory account balance at December 31, 2007, included goods sold and shipped on December 30, 2007, FOB shipping point. The cost of the goods sold was $25,000. The goods arrived at the destination on January 4, 2008.

The cost of goods purchased was correctly calculated each year.

Instructions

(a) Calculate the correct amount for each of the following for 2006, 2007, and 2008:
  1. Total assets   3. Cost of goods sold
  2. Owner's equity   4. Net income
(b) Indicate the effect of these errors (overstated, understated, or no effect) on cash at the end of 2006, 2007, and 2008.

P6–6B The records of Alyssa Company show the following data:

Determine effects of inventory errors. Calculate inventory turnover.
(SO 3, 4) AN

	2006	2007	2008
Sales	$300,000	$320,000	$330,000
Beginning inventory	35,000	20,000	35,000
Cost of goods purchased	200,000	240,000	230,000
Ending inventory	20,000	35,000	45,000
Operating expenses	60,000	64,000	66,000

After its July 31, 2008, year end, Alyssa discovered two errors:

1. Ending inventory for the year ended July 31, 2007, was actually $43,000, not $35,000.
2. The cost of goods purchased for the year ended July 31, 2007, included $30,000 of merchandise that should have been recorded as a purchase in the year ended July 31, 2006.

Instructions

(a) Prepare incorrect and corrected income statements for Alyssa for the years ended July 31, 2006, 2007, and 2008.
(b) What is the impact of these errors on the owner's equity at July 31, 2008?
(c) Calculate the correct and incorrect inventory turnover ratios for each of 2006, 2007, and 2008.

Calculate ratios and comment.
(SO 4) AN

P6–7B The following financial information (in U.S. millions) is for two major corporations for the three years ended December 31:

PepsiCo Inc.	2005	2004	2003
Net sales	$32,562	$29,261	$26,971
Cost of sales	14,176	12,674	11,691
Net income	4,078	4,212	3,568
Inventory	1,693	1,541	1,421
Current assets	10,454	8,639	6,930
Current liabilities	9,406	6,752	6,415

Coca-Cola Company	2005	2004	2003
Net sales	$23,104	$21,742	$20,857
Cost of sales	8,195	7,674	7,776
Net income	4,872	4,847	4,347
Inventory	1,424	1,420	1,252
Current assets	10,250	12,281	8,396
Current liabilities	9,836	11,133	7,886

Instructions

(a) Calculate the inventory turnover, days sales in inventory, current ratio, gross profit margin, and profit margin for each company for 2005 and 2004.
(b) Comment on each company's profitability and liquidity.

Apply perpetual cost flow assumptions. Calculate gross profit.
(SO 5) AP

*P6–8B You are given the following information for Lahti Company for the month ended October 31, 2008:

Date		Description	Units	Unit Price
Oct.	1	Beginning inventory	60	$50
	9	Purchase	195	46
	10	Purchase return	5	46
	15	Sale	200	65
	22	Purchase	150	44
	29	Sale	85	60
	30	Sale return	5	60
	31	Purchase	45	42

Lahti Company uses a perpetual inventory system.

Instructions

(a) Calculate the ending inventory and cost of goods sold using FIFO, average cost, and LIFO.
(b) Calculate and compare the gross profit earned by Lahti using each of the three cost flow assumptions.
(c) How would the results change for each cost flow assumption if the cost of new inventory for Lahti was increasing?

*P6–9B Reliable Camera Mart sells a wide variety of special digital cameras and uses a perpetual inventory system. On May 1, 2008, Reliable had five Model 25 digital cameras on hand at a unit cost of $95. During May and June, the company had the following purchases and sales for this camera (all for cash):

Apply perpetual FIFO and average cost flow assumptions. Answer questions about financial statement effects.
(SO 3, 5) AP

Date	Purchases		Sales	
	Units	Unit Cost	Units	Unit Price
May 4			2	$209
18	7	$104		
31			6	219
June 5	6	110		
12			3	229
25			3	229

Instructions

(a) Determine the cost of goods sold and ending inventory under a perpetual inventory system using (1) FIFO and (2) average cost.
(b) Prepare all required journal entries for May using (1) FIFO and (2) average cost.
(c) Calculate gross profit using (1) FIFO and (2) average cost.
(d) Which cost flow assumption produces the higher cash flow?
(e) What factors should the owner of Reliable Camera Mart consider when choosing a cost flow assumption?

*P6–10B You are given the following information for Yuan Company for January 2008:

Apply average cost flow assumption in perpetual and periodic inventory systems.
(SO 2, 3, 5) AP

Date	Description	Units	Unit Price
Jan. 1	Beginning inventory	250	$30
8	Purchase	110	32
10	Sale	175	60
15	Purchase	100	35
25	Sale	120	65
26	Purchase	110	39
27	Purchase return	6	39

Instructions

(a) Calculate the ending inventory and cost of goods sold using the average cost flow assumption in (1) a periodic inventory system and (2) a perpetual inventory system.
(b) Compare the ending inventory and cost of goods sold using the average cost flow assumption in a perpetual system and in a periodic system. Comment on any differences or similarities between the two systems.

*P6–11B Chung Company lost all of its inventory in a fire on December 28, 2008. The accounting records showed the following gross profit data for November and December:

Determine inventory loss using gross profit method.
(SO 6) AP

	November	December (to Dec. 28)
Sales	$500,000	$600,000
Sales returns and allowances	10,000	12,000
Sales discounts	4,500	5,400
Purchases	325,745	390,235
Purchase returns and allowances	11,700	12,900
Purchase discounts	2,950	3,500
Freight in	4,573	4,100
Beginning inventory	22,700	26,270
Ending inventory	26,270	?

Chung is fully insured for fire losses but must prepare a report for the insurance company.

Determine ending inventory
using retail method.
(SO 6) AP

Instructions

Determine the amount of inventory lost by Chung as a result of the fire.

*P6–12B Varocher's Sound Barn uses the retail inventory method to estimate its monthly ending inventories. The following information is available at October 31, 2008:

	CDs		DVDs	
	Cost	Retail	Cost	Retail
Beginning inventory	$ 275,000	$ 423,000	$ 190,000	$ 322,000
Purchases	1,180,000	1,800,000	1,045,000	1,771,000
Purchase returns and allowances	23,600	36,000	20,900	35,400
Purchase discounts	5,900		5,100	
Freight in	5,000		6,200	
Sales		1,825,000		1,650,000
Sales returns and allowances		27,000		24,000

At October 31, Varocher's Sound Barn takes a physical inventory count at retail. The actual retail values of the inventories in each department on October 31, 2008, are as follows: CDs $381,250 and DVDs $426,100.

Instructions

(a) Determine the estimated cost of the ending inventory at October 31, 2008, using the retail inventory method.

(b) Calculate the store's loss on October 31, 2008, from theft and other causes, at retail and at cost.

Determine ending inventory
using gross profit method
and comment. Prepare partial
income statement.
(SO 6) AP

*P6–13B Country Lace Clothing Company has a periodic inventory system and uses the gross profit method to estimate inventories for monthly financial statements. The business has had an average gross profit margin of 35% for the last five years. It does a physical count of inventory every March 31, the company's fiscal year end. Data for the year ended March 31, 2008, follow:

Inventory, March 31, 2007	$ 63,000	Sales	$330,000
Purchases	200,000	Sales returns and allowances	13,000
Purchase returns and allowances	6,000	Inventory, March 31, 2008	56,000
Purchase discounts	2,500	Freight in	10,000

Instructions

(a) Prepare a partial income statement up to gross profit and calculate the actual gross profit margin for the year ended March 31, 2008.

(b) Use the gross profit method to estimate the March 31, 2008, inventory. Compare this amount to the actual inventory and comment on your findings.

(c) The owner of Country Lace is considering investing in a perpetual inventory system. Would you recommend this or not? Why?

Continuing Cookie Chronicle

(*Note:* This is a continuation of the Cookie Chronicle from Chapters 1 through 5.)

Natalie is busy establishing both divisions of her business (cookie classes and mixer sales) and completing her business diploma. Her goals for the next 11 months are to sell one mixer per month and to give two to three classes per week.

The cost of the fine European mixers is expected to increase. Natalie has just negotiated new terms with Kzinski that include shipping costs in the negotiated purchase price (mixers will be shipped FOB destination). Natalie has chosen to use the average cost flow assumption for her mixer inventory.

The following transactions occur in February to May, 2008:

Feb. 2 Natalie buys two deluxe mixers on account from Kzinski Supply Co. for $1,100 ($550 each), FOB destination, terms n/30.

16 She sells one deluxe mixer for $1,050 cash.

25 She pays the amount owing to Kzinski.

Mar. 2 She buys one deluxe mixer on account from Kzinski Supply Co. for $567, FOB destination, terms n/30.

30 Natalie sells two deluxe mixers for a total of $2,100 cash.

31 She pays the amount owing to Kzinski.

Apr. 1 She buys two deluxe mixers on account from Kzinski Supply Co. for $1,122 ($561 each), FOB destination, terms n/30.

13 She sells three deluxe mixers for a total of $3,150 cash.

30 Natalie pays the amounts owing to Kzinski.

May 4 She buys three deluxe mixers on account from Kzinski Supply Co. for $1,720 ($573.33 each), FOB destination, terms n/30.

27 She sells one deluxe mixer for $1,050 cash.

Natalie is finding it tedious to track the inventory information using average cost in a perpetual inventory system. She wonders if using average cost in a periodic inventory system would save her both time and effort.

Instructions

(a) Using the average cost flow assumption in a perpetual inventory system, prepare a schedule to track the purchases and sales, and the balance of the mixers inventory account. Use the format from Illustration 6A-2. Recall from Chapter 5 that at the end of January Cookie Creations had three mixers on hand at a cost of $525 each.

(b) Using the average cost flow assumption in a periodic inventory system, calculate the cost of goods available for sale, the cost of the ending inventory, and the cost of goods sold for the mixer inventory. Use the format from Illustration 6-5. Recall from Chapter 5 that at the end of January Cookie Creations had three mixers on hand at a cost of $525 each.

(c) Answer Natalie's concerns. What are the differences in results using each of these two inventory systems? What are the differences in information provided by each of these systems? Which inventory system—perpetual or periodic—would you recommend that Cookie Creations use for its mixer inventory? Why?

BROADENING YOUR PERSPECTIVE

Financial Reporting and Analysis

Financial Reporting Problem

BYP6–1 Refer to the financial statements and Notes to Consolidated Financial Statements for **The Forzani Group Ltd.** in Appendix A.

Instructions

(a) How does Forzani value its inventory?

(b) Which inventory cost flow assumption does Forzani use? Is this cost flow assumption applied in a perpetual or periodic inventory system?

(c) Do you think that using a different cost flow assumption than the one identified in (b) above would have a material effect on Forzani's results? Explain.

(d) For 2006 and 2005, calculate Forzani's inventory as a percentage of current assets and its cost of sales as a percentage of total revenue. Comment on the results.

(e) Forzani's inventory turnover and days sales in inventory were calculated for fiscal 2006 in Illustrations 6-10 and 6-11. Calculate these same two ratios for fiscal 2005. Forzani's inventory at the end of fiscal 2004 was $258,816 thousand. Comment on whether Forzani's management of its inventory improved or weakened in 2006.

Interpreting Financial Statements

BYP6–2 The following information was taken from the April 2, 2005, financial statements of **Indigo Books & Music Inc.** (in thousands):

	2005	2004	2003
Cost of product, purchasing, selling, and administration	$743,327	$760,554	$737,228
Inventories	207,643	199,421	202,455

Additional information from the company's financial statements:

1. Indigo uses the moving average cost flow assumption to determine the cost of its inventories. The average cost of an article is continuously updated based on the cost of each new purchase that is recorded.
2. When the company permanently reduces the retail price of an item, a corresponding reduction in inventory is recognized in the period if the markdown brings the retail price below the cost of the item.
3. Before fiscal 2005, the retail inventory method was used. Under this method, inventory was separated into similar merchandise categories. All receipts were added into an inventory pool using actual costs, and all sales were removed from the inventory pool using an average margin for the pool. The average margin was continuously updated based on the flow of goods into and out of the pool.

Instructions

(a) Calculate the company's inventory turnover and days sales in inventory ratios for 2005 and 2004. Use "cost of product, purchasing, selling, and administration" in place of cost of goods sold. Comment on whether Indigo's management of its inventory improved or weakened in 2005.
(b) Does Indigo use a periodic or perpetual inventory system? Explain.
(c) Does Indigo follow the lower of cost or market rule? Explain.
(d) In fiscal 2005, Indigo changed from using the retail inventory method to using the moving average cost basis of valuing inventories. Why might Indigo have decided to make this change? Include in your answer a discussion of the costs and benefits of both methods.
(e) Indigo uses the moving average cost basis to account for its inventories. Indigo's main competitor, Amazon.com, Inc., uses the FIFO cost flow assumption to account for its inventories. What difficulties would this create in comparing Indigo's financial results to those of Amazon.com? Explain.

Critical Thinking

Collaborative Learning Activity

Note to instructor: Additional instructions and material for this group activity can be found on the Instructor Resource Site.

BYP6-3 In this group activity, you will review the following three inventory cost flow assumptions using a periodic inventory system:

1. First-In, First-Out (FIFO)

2. Average Cost
3. Last-In, First-Out (LIFO)

Brown & Co. had a beginning inventory on January 1 of 500 cases of Doggie Treats at a cost of $20 per case. During the year, the following purchases were made:

	Units	Unit Cost
Feb. 10	700	$16
Nov. 15	100	22

Instructions

(a) Your instructor will divide the class into "home" groups. Each group member will select one of the above cost flow assumptions and join the "expert" group for that cost flow assumption.

(b) In your "expert" group, you will be given material explaining the inventory cost flow assumption you have chosen. You will work together to 1) calculate ending inventory, cost of goods sold, and gross profit, and 2) illustrate income statement and balance sheet presentation for your cost flow assumption. Ensure that each group member thoroughly understands that cost flow assumption.

(c) Return to your "home" group and explain the cost flow assumption to the other students in the group. Compare the differences between the various assumptions.

(d) You may be asked by your instructor to write a short quiz on this topic.

Communication Activity

BYP6–4 You are the controller of Small Toys. Mutahir Kazmi, the president, recently mentioned to you that he found an error in the 2007 financial statements that he believes has now corrected itself. In discussions with the Purchasing Department, Mutahir determined that the 2007 ending inventory was understated by $1 million. However, the 2008 ending inventory is correct. Mutahir assumes that 2008 income is correct and comments to you, "What happened has happened—there's no point in worrying about it now."

Study Aids:
Writing Handbook

Instructions

You conclude that Mutahir is wrong. Write a brief, tactful memo to him that clarifies the situation.

BYP6–5 Discount Diamonds carries only one brand and size of diamond—all are identical. Each batch of diamonds that is purchased is carefully coded and marked with its purchase cost. You are given the following data from March:

Study Aids:
Ethics in Accounting

Mar. 1 Beginning inventory was 140 diamonds at a cost of $300 per diamond.
     3 Purchased 200 diamonds at a cost of $340 each.
     5 Sold 170 diamonds for $600 each.
    10 Purchased 340 diamonds at a cost of $370 each.
    25 Sold 500 diamonds for $650 each.

Instructions

(a) Assume that Discount Diamonds uses the specific identification cost flow method:
   1. Show how Discount Diamonds could maximize its gross profit for the month by choosing which diamonds to sell on March 5 and March 25.
   2. Show how Discount Diamonds could minimize its gross profit for the month by choosing which diamonds to sell on March 5 and March 25.

(b) Assume that Discount Diamonds uses the average cost flow assumption and a periodic inventory system. How much gross profit would Discount Diamonds report under this cost flow assumption?

(c) Who are the stakeholders in this situation? Is there anything unethical in choosing which diamonds to sell in a month?

(d) Which cost flow assumption should Discount Diamonds choose? Explain.

ANSWERS TO CHAPTER QUESTIONS

Answers to Accounting in Action Insight Questions

Across the Organization Insight, p. 286

Q: How might a warehouse manager use RFID technology to assist in doing a year-end physical inventory count?

A: RFID technology can be used to locate the inventory items being counted instead of having employees search for every item. This reduces the time required to count inventory. It could also be used to easily find out if goods shipped to a customer FOB destination had reached the destination prior to year end so ownership of the inventory could be determined.

Ethics Insight, p. 301

Q: Why might a manager deliberately overstate inventory? Is it a problem?

A: If a company is not doing as well as expected, a manager might try to make the company look better by falsely increasing the value of assets. When inventory is overstated, it also results in net income and owner's equity being overstated. This is a problem because investors and creditors would be misled into thinking the company is doing better than it really is.

Business Insight, p. 303

Q: Why would analysts be concerned that inventory levels are too high?

A: ATI Technologies operates in an industry where its products can become obsolete very quickly, as shown by ATI's inventory write-down to market in 2005. In 2006, even though the company had new products which are selling quickly, there is still a risk that this could quickly change. The higher the inventory level, the greater the risk of having another large write-down of inventory to market value if the products suddenly become obsolete.

Answer to Forzani Review It Question 3, p. 301

In Note 2(b) to its financial statements, Forzani discloses that it uses the weighted average cost flow assumption.

Answers to Self-Study Questions

1. a   2. b   3. d   4. c   5. b   6. a   7. c   *8. d   *9. b   *10. a

Remember to go back to the Navigator Box at the beginning of the chapter to check off your completed work.

concepts for review >>

Before studying this chapter, you should understand or, if necessary, review:

a. The role of ethics in financial reporting. (Ch. 1, p. 3)

b. How cash transactions are recorded. (Ch. 2, pp. 64–67)

c. How cash is classified on a balance sheet. (Ch. 4, p. 176)

d. What internal control is. (Ch. 6, p. 222)

Keeping Track of the Cash

CHARLOTTETOWN, P.E.I.—Located right in the heart of downtown Charlottetown, Beanz Espresso Bar is bustling with activity on weekdays. On average, 1,200 customers stop by each day for its selection of specialty coffees, homemade soups, sandwiches, and baked goods. "Our back door leads into a federal government building, so we get a lot of office workers coming through," says owner Lori Kays, who started the business with her husband and business partner Doug Hurry back in 1995. "But we really cater to every age group since we're open seven days a week."

Lunch is the busiest time for Beanz, which has room for 65 customers on the main floor plus an additional 45 on its deck. The two cash registers are shared by the six staff members working behind the counter on each shift. "In an ideal situation, one or two people would be designated to ring in orders, but when we get swamped, we all have to work together to keep things running smoothly," says Ms. Kays.

The prices of most items are pre-programmed in the machines, which reduces the chances of entry errors. Each register generates a sales report at the end of the day. Ms. Kays checks the day's cash receipts against the report to make sure they match. She also verifies the closing balances for the two floats—$250 for each till. "I tend to allow a few dollars' leeway since we round down amounts here and there when customers are short a few cents."

If the difference is larger, she goes through the register's internal tape to find the source. "I will backtrack and try to make sure there weren't any payouts for which a receipt should have been turned in—we often make a run to the grocery store for something we need using cash from the till," she explains. "A lot of times it's just an item that's been rung in improperly."

Ms. Kays does all of her bookkeeping herself using Simply Accounting software. "I post my sales totals each day and reconcile everything with my bank statements once a month," she says. "At the end of every year, I do everything except the last few adjusting entries before sending things off to the accountants." Careful cash control throughout the year helps ensure everything adds up every time!

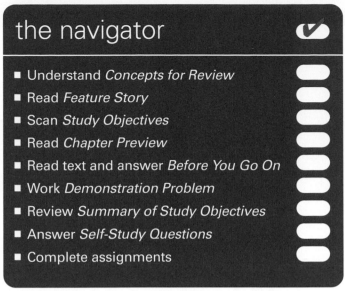

the navigator

- Understand *Concepts for Review*
- Read *Feature Story*
- Scan *Study Objectives*
- Read *Chapter Preview*
- Read text and answer *Before You Go On*
- Work *Demonstration Problem*
- Review *Summary of Study Objectives*
- Answer *Self-Study Questions*
- Complete assignments

chapter 7

Internal Control and Cash

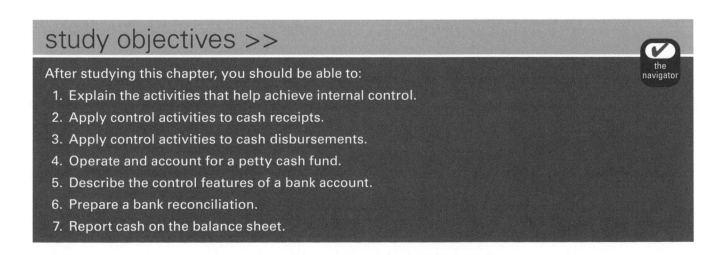

study objectives >>

After studying this chapter, you should be able to:

1. Explain the activities that help achieve internal control.
2. Apply control activities to cash receipts.
3. Apply control activities to cash disbursements.
4. Operate and account for a petty cash fund.
5. Describe the control features of a bank account.
6. Prepare a bank reconciliation.
7. Report cash on the balance sheet.

the navigator

As the feature story about Beanz Espresso Bar shows, control of cash is important. Business owners and managers are responsible for safeguarding cash and other assets and for making sure that financial information is reliable. In this chapter, we explain the important features of an internal control system and describe how these controls apply to cash receipts and disbursements, including the use of a petty cash fund. Then we describe the use of a bank and explain how cash is reported on the balance sheet.

The chapter is organized as follows:

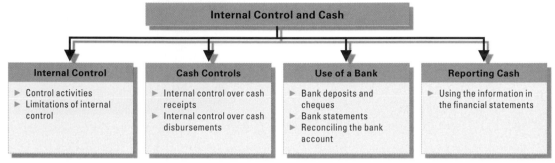

the navigator

Internal Control

study objective 1

Explain the activities that help achieve internal control.

Could there be dishonest employees where you work? Unfortunately, the answer sometimes is "Yes." The following real occurrences show this well:

- The general accountant of a Canadian charity embezzled $2 million over a four-year period by putting contributions to the charity into her personal bank account.
- The controller of a Canadian manufacturing company paid himself $2 million more than his normal pay level by writing unauthorized cheques on the company's payroll account. He got rid of the cancelled cheques when they were returned from the bank and then he altered the books.
- An assistant bank manager stole more than $10 million from a Toronto bank by making loans to fictitious companies.
- A Public Works official and two individuals running advertising companies were convicted on criminal charges for defrauding the federal government of millions of dollars in what became known as the Federal Sponsorship Scandal.

Helpful hint Errors are unintentional mistakes. Irregularities are intentional mistakes and misrepresentations.

These situations, as well as the possibility of honest errors, emphasize that a good system of internal control is necessary.

Internal control is the process that management designs and implements to help an organization achieve:

1. Reliable financial reporting
2. Effective and efficient operations
3. Compliance with relevant laws and regulations

Internal control is the responsibility of management. Effective internal control depends on how important internal control is for management and what actions it takes as a result. Management must determine the business risks that threaten the achievement of any of these objectives; it must create and implement the control activities; and it must ensure that the controls are monitored. The accounting system—the procedures and records created to record, process, and report the organization's transactions—is part of internal control.

Control Activities

Control activities are the policies and procedures that help ensure that management's directions are followed. They are the actions that must be taken to respond to risks that threaten the achievement of reliable financial reporting, effective and efficient operations, and compliance with relevant laws and regulations. Of course, the specific control activities that are used depend on the size and type of business, and on management's control philosophy. The activities listed in Illustration 7-1 apply to most companies and are explained in the following sections.

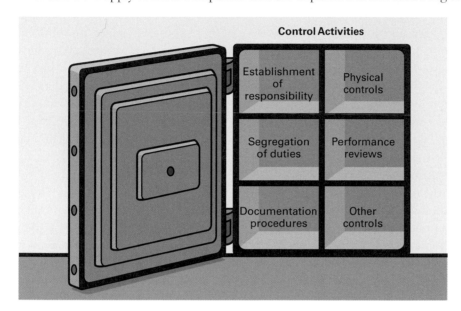

Control Activities

- Establishment of responsibility
- Physical controls
- Segregation of duties
- Performance reviews
- Documentation procedures
- Other controls

Illustration 7-1 ◀

Control activities

Establishment of Responsibility

An essential control activity is to make specific employees responsible for specific tasks. Control is most effective when only one person is responsible for a task. To illustrate, assume that the cash in the cash register at the end of the day at Beanz Espresso Bar in the feature story is $50 less than it should be according to the tape in the cash register. If only one person at the restaurant has operated the register, that person is probably responsible for the shortage. If two or more individuals have worked the register, however, as happens at Beanz Espresso Bar when the restaurant is busy, it may be impossible to determine who is responsible for the error. Internal control would be strengthened at Beanz Espresso Bar if each staff member had their own cash drawer. On the other hand, the owner, Lori Kays, has a procedure to reduce the problems that may result from having more than one person using the same cash drawer. Lori is able to quickly identify any shortages at Beanz Espresso Bar by checking the cash receipts against the cash register sales report at the end of each day.

Responsibility for authorizing and approving transactions must also be given to the correct person. For example, the vice-president of finance should establish policies for making credit sales, not the vice-president of sales.

Segregation of Duties

Segregation of duties is essential in a system of internal control. As long as it does not double how much effort is needed, the work of one employee should be a reliable basis for monitoring the work of another employee. In other words, duties should be divided up so that one person cannot both commit a fraud and cover it up. There are two common ways of applying this control activity:

1. The responsibility for related activities should be assigned to different individuals.
2. The responsibility for accounting for an asset should be separate from the responsibility for physical custody of that asset.

Related Activities. When one person is responsible for all related activities, the potential for errors and irregularities increases. To show how this can be a problem, we will look at the related activities in purchasing and selling merchandise.

Related purchasing activities include ordering merchandise, receiving the goods, and paying (or authorizing payment) for the merchandise. How could someone commit a fraud if he or she is responsible for all—or even two—of these activities? Here are some examples. If the same person is responsible for ordering and for receiving, he can arrange to have an order sent to his home and pretend the goods were received by the company. Or if the same person is responsible for ordering and paying for the merchandise, she can place orders with friends or with suppliers who give kickbacks. When a second person is not needed to authorize the payment, it can happen that no one notices that the company is perhaps paying too much for its purchases of merchandise. Or, even worse, fictitious invoices might be approved for payment. When the responsibility for ordering, receiving, and paying is given to different individuals, there is less risk of such abuses.

Similarly, related sales activities should be done by different individuals. Related selling activities include making a sale, shipping (or delivering) the goods to the customer, and billing the customer. When one person handles related sales transactions, he or she can make sales at unauthorized prices to increase sales commissions, ship goods to him- or herself, or understate the amount that is billed in sales to friends and relatives. These abuses are reduced by dividing the sales tasks: salespersons make the sale, shipping department employees ship the goods based on the sales order, and billing department employees prepare the sales invoice after comparing the sales order with the report of goods shipped.

It is also important to segregate selling duties in small businesses such as Beanz Espresso Bar in our feature story. For the reasons mentioned above, the same person should not take and fill an order, and then collect payment from the customer. Since segregation of selling duties in a small business can be difficult, because there are fewer people, it is useful to have the sales price of items pre-programmed into the cash registers—as they are at Beanz Espresso Bar. This decreases the risk of an employee undercharging a friend on purpose.

Custody of Assets. If the same person has physical custody of an asset and keeps the accounting records for that asset, then errors or theft could be hidden by altering the accounting records. When the employee who keeps the records of an asset is a different person than the employee who keeps the asset itself (the custodian), the employee who keeps the asset is unlikely to use it dishonestly. The separation of accounting responsibility from the custody of assets is especially important for cash and inventories because these assets are vulnerable to unauthorized use or theft.

Documentation Procedures

Documents give evidence that transactions and events have happened. At Beanz Espresso Bar, the cash register sales report and internal tape is the restaurant's documentation for a sale and the amount of cash received. Similarly, a shipping document indicates that goods have been shipped, and a sales invoice indicates that the customer has been billed for the goods. Adding signatures (or initials) to the document(s) also helps because this makes it possible to identify the individual(s) responsible for the transaction or event.

Procedures should be established for documents. First, whenever possible, documents should be prenumbered and all documents should be accounted for. Prenumbering helps to prevent a transaction from being recorded more than once, or not at all. Second, documents should be prepared when the transaction happens. Third, source documents (the original receipts, etc.) for accounting entries should be promptly sent to the accounting department to help ensure a timely recording of the transaction. These control activities increase the accuracy and reliability of the accounting records.

Physical Controls

Physical controls include mechanical and electronic controls to safeguard (protect) assets and improve the accuracy and reliability of the accounting records. Examples of these controls are shown in Illustration 7-2.

Illustration 7-2 ◀

Physical controls

Safes, vaults, and safety deposit boxes for cash and business papers

Locked warehouses and storage cabinets for inventories and records

Computer facilities with password or biometric access

Alarms to prevent break-ins

Television monitors and garment sensors to discourage theft

Time clocks to record time worked

Performance Reviews

Most internal control systems include independent internal and/or external reviews of performance and records. This means having someone else review, compare, and reconcile data. To get the most from a performance review:

1. The review should be done periodically or on a surprise basis.
2. The review should be done by someone who is independent of the employee who is responsible for the information.
3. Discrepancies and exceptions should be reported to a management level that can do whatever is necessary to correct the situation.

Internal Review. Segregating the physical custody of assets from accounting record keeping is not enough to ensure that nothing has been stolen. An independent review still needs to be done. In such a review, the accounting records are compared with existing assets or with external sources of information. The reconciliation of the cash register sales report with the cash in the register, by Beanz Espresso Bar owner Lori Kays in the feature story, is an example of comparing records with assets. When the person who does the review works for the organization, we call this an internal review.

In large companies, control activities, including independent internal reviews, are often monitored by internal auditors. **Internal auditors** are company employees who evaluate the effectiveness of the company's system of internal control. They periodically review the activities of departments and individuals to determine whether the correct control activities are being followed. But an internal audit is effective only when the results of the audit are reported to senior management and/or the company's owners.

Internal control over financial reporting is so important to users of financial statements today that the Canadian Securities Administrators (CSA) now require the chief executive officer (CEO) and chief financial officer (CFO) to certify that they have evaluated the effectiveness of the company's internal control over financial reporting. Their conclusions must be included in the company's management discussion and analysis section of the annual report and they must describe the evaluation process that they used.

External Review. It is useful to contrast independent *internal* reviews with independent external reviews. **External auditors**, in contrast to internal auditors, are independent of the company. They are professional accountants and are hired by a company to report on whether or not the company's financial statements fairly present the company's financial position and results of operations.

All public companies, including The Forzani Group Ltd., are required to have an external audit. A copy of Forzani's auditors' report is included in Appendix A. As you will see in the report for Forzani, external auditors plan and perform an audit that will allow them to be reasonably sure that the financial statements do not have any significant errors. In the following section on the limitations of internal control, the concept of reasonable assurance is discussed further.

While external auditors need to understand a company's internal controls, they are not required to test how effective the controls are or to give any kind of assurance about a company's internal control. In Canada, this is the responsibility of company management.

Other Controls

Other control measures can include the following:

1. Bonding of employees who handle cash. Bonding means getting insurance protection—called **fidelity insurance**—against the theft of assets by dishonest employees. If an employer has fidelity insurance, the insurance company will compensate the employer for losses incurred as a result of the dishonesty of an employee. This measure also contributes to the safeguarding of cash in two ways: First, the insurance company carefully screens all individuals before adding them to the policy and may reject risky applicants. Second, bonded employees know that the insurance company will prosecute all offenders.
2. Rotating employees' duties and requiring employees to take vacations. These measures discourage employees from attempting any thefts since they will not be able to permanently hide their improper actions. Many bank embezzlements, for example, have been discovered when the guilty employee was on vacation or assigned to a new position.

Limitations of Internal Control

No matter how well it is designed and operated, a company's system of internal control can only give reasonable assurance that assets are properly safeguarded and that accounting records are reliable. The concept of reasonable assurance is based on the belief that the cost of control activities should not be more than their expected benefit.

To illustrate, consider shoplifting losses in retail stores. Such losses could be eliminated by having a security guard stop and search customers as they leave the store. Store managers have concluded, however, that the negative effects of doing this cannot be justified. Instead, stores have tried to control shoplifting losses by using less costly procedures such as (1) posting signs that state "We reserve the right to inspect all packages" and "All shoplifters will be prosecuted," (2) using hidden TV cameras and store detectives to watch customer activity, and (3) using sensor equipment at exits.

The human factor is an important limit in every system of internal control. A good system can become ineffective as a result of employee fatigue, carelessness, indifference, or lack of proper training. For example, a receiving clerk may not bother to count goods received, or may just "fudge" the counts. In a computerized accounting system, breakdowns in internal control can occur because of human errors in designing the system.

Occasionally, two or more individuals may work together to get around controls. Such collusion eliminates the protection offered by segregation of duties. If a supervisor and a cashier collaborate to understate cash receipts, the system of internal control may be beaten (at least in the short run).

The size of the business may also limit internal control. As mentioned earlier, in small companies it may be difficult to segregate duties or have independent performance reviews. As shown in our feature story, in small companies the owner needs to be responsible for performance reviews and may have to oversee functions that should not be done by the same person, such as authorizations over assets and access to the assets, if it is not possible to segregate these duties.

 ACCOUNTING IN ACTION ▶ Ethics Insight

Along with the huge rise in Internet use has come a similar rise in Internet fraud. And much of this fraud occurs through "phishing"—when a fraudster tricks an unsuspecting computer user into revealing personal bank account information or login passwords. Computer users will receive an e-mail that claims that their account information has either expired or needs updating. The e-mail links to a website that is similar to that of eBay, PayPal, or their bank. Scammers use the account information to purchase stock, manipulate auctions, or buy items on-line. The transactions are difficult to trace, and often go unnoticed until the victim has been cheated out of thousands of dollars.

Source: David Chalk, "Being Vigilant about On-Line Security," *The Globe and Mail*, June 22, 2006.

? What internal control activity has been violated in these frauds? What limitation of internal control allowed the control to be violated?

BEFORE YOU GO ON . . .

▶Review It

1. What are the three things that internal control helps an organization achieve?
2. Identify and describe control activities that help achieve internal control.
3. What are the limitations of internal control?

▶Do It

Li Song owns a small retail store. Li wants to establish good internal control procedures but is confused about the difference between segregation of duties and performance reviews. Explain the differences to Li.

Action Plan

- Understand what is meant by (1) segregation of duties and (2) performance reviews.
- Compare the two and determine the differences.

Solution

Segregation of duties involves assigning responsibility so that one employee cannot commit a fraud and cover up his or her actions. One employee's work will give the basis for checking the work of another employee. Segregation of duties is about how the work is organized and done each day. Performance reviews occur after the work is finished.

Li should segregate duties by having one employee handle cash and another employee prepare the accounting records. The performance review would occur after transactions and activities are done and involves having an independent person compare the assets with the accounting records. In a small retail store like the one owned by Li Song, the owner would probably have to do the review and compare and reconcile the data prepared by one or more employees.

Related exercise material: BE7–1 and E7–1.

Cash Controls

study objective 2

Apply control activities to cash receipts.

Just as cash is the beginning of a company's operating cycle, it is also usually the starting point for a company's system of internal control. Cash is easily concealed and transported, lacks owner identification, and is highly desirable. In addition, because of the large volume of cash transactions, errors may easily happen when handling and recording cash.

To safeguard cash and ensure the accuracy of the accounting records, effective internal control over cash is essential. In the following sections, we explain the application of control activities to cash receipts and disbursements.

Internal Control over Cash Receipts

Cash receipts come from a variety of sources: cash sales; collections on account from customers; the receipt of interest, dividends, and rents; investments by owners; bank loans; and proceeds from the sale of property, plant, and equipment. Generally, internal control over cash receipts is more effective when all cash receipts are deposited intact in the bank account on a daily basis. Illustration 7-3 shows how the control activities explained earlier apply to cash receipt transactions.

Illustration 7-3 ▶

Application of control activities over cash receipts

Control Activities over Cash Receipts

Establishment of Responsibility

Only designated personnel (cashiers) are authorized to handle cash receipts.

Physical Controls

Store cash in safes and bank vaults; limit access to storage areas; use cash registers.

Segregation of Duties

Different individuals receive cash, record cash receipts, and hold the cash.

Performance Reviews

Supervisors count cash receipts daily; controller's office compares total receipts to bank deposits daily.

Documentation Procedures

Use remittance advices (mail receipts), cash register tapes, and deposit slips.

Other Controls

Bond personnel who handle cash; require employees to take vacations; deposit all cash in a bank daily.

As might be expected, companies vary considerably in how they apply these principles. To illustrate internal control over cash receipts, we will discuss useful control activities for a retail store with over-the-counter, mail-in, and electronic receipts.

Over-the-Counter Receipts

Control of over-the-counter receipts in retail businesses is centred on cash registers that customers can see. A cash sale should be "rung up" on a cash register with the amount clearly visible to the customer. This measure prevents the cashier from entering a lower amount and keeping the extra cash. The customer is given a cash register receipt and, if paying with cash, is expected to count the change that is received.

Actual cash—coins and paper currency—receipts are becoming rarer. Most customers pay by debit or bank credit card. Although banks charge retailers when these cards are used, there are many advantages for retailers who accept these forms of payment. As they are convenient for customers, the business may get more sales. They also improve internal control because employees handle less cash. There is more information on debit and credit card transactions in the following sections.

Most companies use point-of-sale cash registers that separate daily sales on the cash register tape according to each type of payment—cash, debit card, credit card, or cheque. The cash register tape shows each transaction, totals for each payment type, and an overall total. Cash register tapes should be locked into the register and removed by a supervisor or manager—never by the cashier.

At the end of his or her shift, the cashier should count the cash in the register, record the amount, and turn over the cash and the record of the amount to either a supervisor or the person responsible for making the bank deposit. The procedures will be different in every company, but the basic principles should be the same. The person or persons who handle the cash and make the bank deposit should not have access to the cash register tapes or the accounting records. The cash register tapes should be used in creating the journal entries in the accounting records. An independent person who does not handle the cash should make sure that the amount deposited at the bank agrees with the cash register tapes and the accounting records.

One very basic control over cash receipts is to ensure that all cash receipts are deposited daily into the bank account, instead of using some of the received cash to make cash disbursements. Beanz Espresso Bar in the feature story violates this basic control when it uses cash directly from the cash register to pay for grocery store purchases. This makes it much more difficult to ensure that all revenues and expenses are recorded. In a later section in this chapter, we will learn how a petty cash system improves internal control over small cash expenditures and ensures that cash receipts remain intact for depositing and recording.

Companies with recurring cash transactions often use a special journal, called a **cash receipts journal**, to record all their receipts of cash. A **special journal** is used to record similar types of transactions. The types of special journals that are used depend largely on the types of transactions that happen frequently. Special journals are shown in Appendix C at the end of this textbook.

Debit Card Transactions. Sales using debit cards are considered cash transactions. Debit cards allow customers to spend only what is in their bank account. When a debit card sale occurs, the bank immediately deducts the cost of the purchase from the customer's bank account. The retailer has a choice about how often the proceeds from debit card transactions are electronically transferred into the retailer's bank account. Some retailers ask the bank to make one deposit at the end of each business day; other retailers wait and have several days of transactions deposited together. Banks usually charge the retailer a transaction fee for each debit card transaction and deduct this fee from the amount deposited in the retailer's bank account.

In many ways, accepting a debit card payment is similar to accepting a personal cheque from a customer. Both are ways for customers to spend the money in their bank accounts. But the major advantage of debit cards is that the retailer knows immediately if the customer has enough money in the bank to pay for the purchase. When a cheque is accepted, it takes several days for the retailer to find out whether the customer had sufficient funds. Most businesses are willing to pay a fee to the bank when customers use debit cards because there is no uncertainty about whether the customer has enough money in their bank account to pay for the purchase.

To illustrate, suppose on March 21 ten customers use debit cards to purchase merchandise totalling $800 from Lee Company. Assuming the bank charges Lee Company $0.50 per debit card transaction, the entry made to record these transactions by Lee Company is as follows:

Mar. 21	Cash	795	
	Debit Card Expense (10 × $0.50)	5	
	Sales		800
	To record debit card sales.		

In addition to the service charge for each transaction, Lee Company will also pay a monthly rental charge for the point-of-sale equipment that it uses for debit and credit card transactions.

Bank Credit Card Transactions. Sales using credit cards issued by banks, such as Visa and MasterCard, are considered cash sales by the retailer. A credit card gives customers access to money made available by a bank or other financial institution (essentially a short-term loan which has to be repaid). When a customer uses a bank credit card, the bank transfers the amount of the sale to the retailer's bank, less a service fee. Banks generally charge the retailer a fee that averages 3.5 percent of the credit card sale. Retailers with a high number of transactions usually get a lower rate; those with a small number of transactions often have a higher rate. Similar to debit card transactions, the retailer's bank will wait until the end of the day and make one deposit for the full day's credit card transactions to the retailer's bank account; there is also the option of having one deposit every few days.

The fees for bank credit cards are generally higher than debit card fees. Why? With a debit card, the bank is charging only for transferring the customer's money to the retailer. With a credit card, the bank is taking the risk that the customer may never repay it for the loan. As we will see in Chapter 8, sometimes companies are not able to collect their receivables. Bank credit cards help retailers avoid this problem. Except for the higher bank charges, recording a bank credit card sale is very similar to recording a debit card sale.

To illustrate, suppose on March 21 Lee Company sells $800 of merchandise to customers who use bank credit cards. The banks charge Lee Company a service fee of 3.5 percent for credit card sales. The entry made to record these transactions by Lee Company is:

Mar. 21	Cash	772	
	Credit Card Expense ($800 × 3.5%)	28	
	Sales		800
	To record bank credit card sales.		

American Express charge cards are very similar to Visa and MasterCard, except that it may take up to three days before the funds are deposited into the retail company's bank account.

In addition to accepting bank credit cards, many large department stores and gasoline companies have their own credit cards. Sales using the retailer's own credit cards are credit sales; they result in accounts receivable, not cash at the point of sale.

Mail-In Receipts

As an individual customer, you may be more familiar with over-the-counter receipts than with mail-in receipts. However, many companies receive payment from their customers through the mail. Think, for example, of the number of cheques received through the mail each day by a national retailer such as Canadian Tire.

All mail-in receipts should be opened in the presence of two mail clerks. These receipts are generally in the form of cheques. Each cheque should be promptly stamped "For Deposit Only." This restrictive endorsement reduces the chances that an employee could take the cheque and use it personally. With this type of endorsement, banks will not give cash to an individual.

A list of the cheques that are received each day should be prepared in duplicate. This list shows the name of the issuer of the cheque, the purpose of the payment, and the amount of the cheque. Each mail clerk should sign the list to establish responsibility for the data. The original copy of the list, along with the cheques and remittance advices, is then sent to the cashier's department, where the daily bank deposit is prepared. A copy of the list is sent to the accounting department, where a journal entry to debit Cash and credit Accounts Receivable, or the appropriate account as required, is recorded. The accounting department will also compare the copy of the list to a copy of the bank deposit to make sure that all mail receipts were included in the bank deposit. In a small company, where it is not possible to have the necessary segregation of duties, the owner should be responsible for cash receipts.

> **Helpful hint** When billing customers, many companies state "Pay by cheque; do not send cash through the mail." This is done to reduce the risk of cash receipts being misappropriated when they are received.

Electronic Receipts

Electronic funds transfer (EFT) systems transfer funds between parties without the use of paper (e.g., deposits, cheques, etc.). Debit and bank credit cards, discussed earlier in this chapter, are examples of electronic funds transfers.

Another type of EFT receipt happens when customers use on-line banking to pay their accounts. When a customer pays his or her account, the cash is instantly transferred from the customer's bank account to the company's bank account. These transactions are journalized directly from the company's bank statement. The only evidence of these electronic cash receipts will be a line on the company's bank statement showing the amount, a reference number, and the name or account number of the person paying.

Other customers pay their accounts using EFT and automatic pre-authorized monthly payments. In this case, the company will begin the transaction and electronically request that the funds be transferred from the customer's bank to the company's bank account. Because the company is initiating the transaction, it knows that the transaction is happening and can therefore journalize the transaction before it receives its bank statement.

According to the Canadian Payments Association, the increase in payment options—debit cards, credit cards, on-line banking, telephone banking, automated teller machines (also called automated banking machines), and automatic pre-authorized monthly bill payments—has resulted in a significant decline in customer payments by cheque. Meanwhile, electronic transactions in Canada grew by approximately 1,301 percent between 1990 and 2005.

Electronic funds transfers normally result in better internal control since no cash or cheques are handled by company employees.

 ACCOUNTING IN ACTION ▶ Business Insight

The *Interac* direct payment and cash dispensing services are switching to chip card technology, which will provide more security, as well as several services on one card. A chip card, or "smart card," has a programmable microchip that can give the card more than one function, such as debit, credit, and stored value. The information on the chip is extremely difficult to copy, which increases security. The infrastructure that is needed for chip technology will be ready in 2007. However, the complete change from bank cards to smart cards will take several years, considering the number of bank cards in circulation, as well as the number of Automated Banking Machines (ABMs) and point-of-sale terminals that will need to be converted. New chip cards will also have magnetic stripes that will make the transition period smoother and allow cardholders to use their banking cards in markets that do not use the chip. However, magnetic stripe transactions will no longer work at ABMs after December 31, 2012, and at point-of-sale devices after December 31, 2015.

Source: Interac Website: http://www.interac.ca/

? **What will be the benefits to the customer of replacing debit and credit cards with chip cards? To the business?**

BEFORE YOU GO ON . . .

▶Review It

1. What control activities should be applied to over-the-counter cash receipts?
2. What control activities should be applied to mail-in cash receipts?
3. What is a benefit of using EFT for cash receipts?

▶Do It

Prepare journal entries to record the following selected debit and credit card transactions for Bulk Department Store:

July 18 A customer used her debit card to pay for a $650 purchase. The company was charged a $2 service fee.

22 A customer paid for a $1,200 purchase with her Visa credit card. The bank charges a service fee of 3%.

25 A customer paid for a $500 purchase with his Bulk Department Store credit card.

Action Plan

- Debit cards are recorded as cash sales, less the service charge.
- Bank credit cards are recorded as cash sales, less the service charge.
- Nonbank credit cards are recorded as receivables. There is no bank service charge when a customer uses a company credit card.

Solution

July 18	Cash	648	
	Debit Card Expense	2	
	Sales		650
	To record debit card sale.		
22	Cash	1,164	
	Credit Card Expense ($1,200 × 3%)	36	
	Sales		1,200
	To record Visa credit card sale.		
25	Accounts Receivable	500	
	Sales		500
	To record company credit card sale.		

the navigator

Related exercise material. BE7–2, BE7–3, E7–2, and E7–3.

Internal Control over Cash Disbursements

Cash is disbursed for a variety of reasons, such as to pay expenses and liabilities, or to purchase assets. Generally, internal control over cash disbursements is better when payments are made by cheque or EFT, rather than by cash. Payment by cheque should occur only after specified control procedures have been followed. The paid cheque gives proof of payment. Illustration 7-4 shows how the control activities explained earlier apply to cash disbursements.

study objective 3
Apply control activities to cash disbursements.

Control Activities over Cash Disbursements

Illustration 7-4 ◄

Application of control activities over cash disbursements

Establishment of Responsibility

Only designated personnel are authorized to sign cheques.

Physical Controls

Store blank cheques in safes with limited access; print cheque amounts electronically

Segregation of Duties

Different individuals approve and make payments; cheque signers do not record disbursements.

Performance Reviews

Compare cheques to invoices; reconcile bank statement monthly.

Documentation Procedures

Use prenumbered cheques and account for them in sequence; each cheque must have an approved invoice.

Other Controls

Stamp invoices PAID.

Cheques

As outlined in Illustration 7-4, the internal controls over cheques include having cheques signed by an authorized person or persons—cheques often require two signatures. The cheque signer(s) should carefully review the supporting documentation for the payment before signing the cheque. There should be a clear segregation of duties between the cheque signing function and the accounts payable function. Cheques should be prenumbered, and all cheque numbers must be accounted for in the payment and recording process. Cheques should never be pre-signed, and blank cheques should be guarded.

Many large companies use purchase orders to improve their internal control over cash disbursements. A purchase order is an authorization form prepared for each expenditure, or for expenditures larger than a specified amount. The purchase order is usually prepared by the purchasing department.

When the good or service is received, the receiving report is matched with the purchase order. When the seller's invoice is later received, it is matched to the purchase order and receiving report. An authorized person in the accounts payable department then approves the invoice for payment. A cheque is sent on the due date, and the invoice is stamped "Paid."

The accounting department records the payment of the invoice. Companies that have a lot of cash disbursements often use a special journal, called a **cash payments journal**, to record all disbursements of cash. As mentioned earlier, Appendix C at the end of this textbook illustrates the use of special journals.

Electronic Payments

Many companies use electronic funds transfer systems to make payments to suppliers and employees. For example, when a company pays its employees' salaries using a direct deposit option, the cash is instantly transferred from the company's bank account to each employee's bank account. No cheques are issued.

In addition, pre-authorized payments, for things like loans and interest paid on a recurring basis, are often made electronically. As with electronic cash receipts, the only evidence of this payment will be a line on the bank statement showing the amount, reference, and usually the name of the company that was paid.

Internal controls over electronic payments must ensure that all such payments are properly authorized. A person who is independent of the accounts payable department should check that the payments agree with a list of authorized electronic payments. These payments are then journalized from the supporting accounts payable documentation.

EFT payments reduce the extra costs of making payments by cheque, such as postage and envelope costs. They also reduce the risk of lost, stolen, or forged cheques.

BEFORE YOU GO ON . . .

▶Review It

1. What control activities apply to cash disbursements made by cheque?
2. What control activities apply to electronic cash disbursements?

Related exercise material: BE7–4 and E7–4.

Petty Cash Fund

study objective 4

Operate and account for a petty cash fund.

As you just learned, a company has better internal control over cash disbursements when it makes its payments by cheque or pre-authorized electronic payments. However, using cheques or EFT to pay for small amounts is both impractical and a nuisance. For example, a company may not want to write cheques to pay for postage, couriers, or taxis. A common way to handle such payments is to use a petty cash fund. A **petty cash fund** is used to pay relatively small amounts, while still maintaining satisfactory control. The petty cash fund is usually operated on an imprest system. The word "imprest" means an advance of a specific amount of money for a designated purpose. To account for an imprest petty cash fund, you must understand three steps: (1) how the fund is established, (2) how payments are made from the fund, and (3) how the fund is replenished.

Establishing the Fund. Two essential steps are required to establish a petty cash fund: (1) appoint a petty cash custodian to be responsible for the fund, and (2) determine the size of the fund. Ordinarily, the amount is expected to be enough for likely payments in a three- to four-week period. To establish the fund, a cheque payable to the petty cash custodian is issued for the determined amount. If Lee Company decides to establish a $100 petty cash fund on March 1, the entry recorded in the general journal is as follows:

A = L + OE				
+100	Mar. 1	Petty Cash	100	
−100		Cash		100
		To establish a petty cash fund.		

Cash flows: no effect

There is no effect on cash flows because the company's total cash has not changed. There is $100 less in the bank account but $100 more cash on hand. After the custodian cashes the cheque he or she should place the proceeds in a locked petty cash box or drawer. The only time entries are made to the Petty Cash account is when the size of the fund is increased or decreased. For example, if Lee Company decides on March 15 to increase the size of the fund to $125, it will debit Petty Cash and credit Cash $25 ($125 − $100).

Making Payments from the Fund. The custodian of the petty cash fund has the authority to make payments from the fund in accordance with management policies. Usually, management limits the size of expenditures that may be made. Likewise, it may not allow the fund to be used for certain types of transactions (such as making short-term loans to employees). Each payment from the fund should be documented on a prenumbered petty cash receipt, signed by both the custodian and the person who receives the payment. If other supporting documents such as a freight bill or invoice are available, they should be attached to the petty cash receipt.

Helpful hint For internal control, the receipt satisfies two principles: (1) establishment of responsibility (signature of the custodian), and (2) documentation.

No accounting entry is made to record a payment at the time it is made from petty cash. It is considered both inefficient and unnecessary to do so. Instead, the accounting effects of each payment are recognized when the fund is replenished. The receipts are kept in the petty cash box until the fund runs low and the cash needs to be replenished. The sum of the petty cash receipts and money in the fund should equal the established total at all times. Surprise counts can be made by an independent person, such as a supervisor or internal auditor, to determine whether the fund is being used properly.

Replenishing the Fund. When the money in the petty cash fund reaches a minimum level, the fund is replenished. The request for reimbursement is made by the petty cash custodian. This individual prepares a schedule (or summary) of the payments that have been made and sends the schedule, supported by petty cash receipts and other documentation, to the controller's office. The receipts and supporting documents are examined in the controller's office to verify that they were proper payments from the fund. The request is approved and a cheque is prepared to restore the fund to its established amount. At the same time, all supporting documentation is stamped "Paid" so that it cannot be submitted again for payment.

Helpful hint Replenishing involves three internal control procedures: segregation of duties, documentation, and performance reviews.

To illustrate, assume that on March 15 the petty cash fund has $13 cash and petty cash receipts for postage $44, freight in $38 (assume a perpetual inventory system is used), and miscellaneous expenses $5. The petty cash custodian will request a cheque for $87 ($100 − $13). The entry to record the cheque is as follows:

Mar. 15	Postage Expense	44	
	Merchandise Inventory	38	
	Miscellaneous Expense	5	
	Cash		87
	To replenish petty cash.		

A	=	L	+	OE
+38				−44
−87				−5

↓ Cash flows: −87

Note that the Petty Cash account is not affected by the reimbursement entry. Replenishment changes what's in the fund by replacing the petty cash receipts with cash. It does not change the balance in the fund.

When replenishing a petty cash fund, it is sometimes necessary to recognize a cash shortage or overage. This results when the receipts plus cash in the petty cash box do not equal the established amount of the petty cash fund. To illustrate, assume in the example above that the custodian had only $12 in cash in the fund, plus the receipts as listed. The request for reimbursement would, therefore, have been for $88. The following entry would be made:

A	=	L	+	OE
+38				−44
−88				−5
				−1

↓ Cash flows: −88

Mar. 15	Postage Expense	44	
	Merchandise Inventory	38	
	Miscellaneous Expense	5	
	Cash Over and Short	1	
	Cash		88
	To replenish petty cash.		

Conversely, if the custodian had $14 in cash, the reimbursement request would have been for $86 and Cash Over and Short would have been credited for $1. A debit balance in Cash Over and Short is reported in the income statement as miscellaneous expense. A credit balance in the account is reported as miscellaneous revenue.

If the petty cash fund is not big enough, it is often increased (or decreased if the amount is too large) when the fund is replenished. Assume that Lee Company decides to increase the size of its petty cash fund from $100 to $125 on March 15 when it replenishes the fund. The entry to record the reimbursement and change in fund size is as follows:

A	=	L	+	OE
+25				−44
+38				−5
−113				−1

↓ Cash flows: −113

Mar. 15	Petty Cash	25	
	Postage Expense	44	
	Merchandise Inventory	38	
	Miscellaneous Expense	5	
	Cash Over and Short	1	
	Cash		113
	To replenish petty cash and increase the fund size by $25.		

In this entry, the Petty Cash account is affected, not because of the reimbursement, but because of the change in size of the fund. After this entry, the general ledger account shows a balance of $125 and the custodian must ensure that cash and paid-out receipts now total $125.

A petty cash fund should be replenished at the end of the accounting period regardless of how much cash is in the fund. Replenishment at this time is necessary in order to recognize the effects of the petty cash payments on the financial statements.

Internal control over a petty cash fund is strengthened by (1) having a supervisor make surprise counts of the fund to check whether the paid receipts and fund cash equal the imprest amount, and (2) cancelling the paid receipts so they cannot be resubmitted for reimbursement.

If Beanz Espresso Bar in the feature story used a petty cash fund instead of making small payments directly from cash receipts, its internal control would be strengthened.

BEFORE YOU GO ON . . .

▶Review It

1. How does using a petty cash system strengthen internal control?
2. When are entries required in a petty cash system?
3. What entries are required in a petty cash system to (1) establish the fund and (2) replenish the fund?

▶Do It

Bateer Company established a $50 petty cash fund on July 1. On July 30, the fund had $12 cash remaining and petty cash receipts for postage $14, office supplies $10, and delivery expense $15. Prepare the journal entries to establish the fund on July 1 and replenish the fund on July 30.

Action Plan

- To establish the fund, set up a separate general ledger account.
- Determine how much cash is needed to replenish the fund—subtract the cash remaining from the petty cash fund balance.
- Total the petty cash receipts. Determine any cash over or short—the difference between the cash needed to replenish the fund and the total of the petty cash receipts.
- Record the expenses incurred according to the petty cash receipts when replenishing the fund.

Solution

July 1	Petty Cash	50	
	Cash		50
	To establish a petty cash fund.		
30	Postage Expense	14	
	Office Supplies	10	
	Delivery Expense	15	
	Cash Over and Short		1
	Cash ($50 − $12)		38
	To replenish petty cash.		

Related exercise material: BE7–5, BE7–6, E7–5, and E7–6.

the navigator

Use of a Bank

Using a bank makes internal control over cash much stronger. A company can safeguard its cash by using a bank as a depository and reduce the amount of currency that must be kept on hand. A bank account acts as a clearing house for cheques and EFT payments that are received and written. In addition, using a bank makes it easier to control cash, because it creates a double record of all bank transactions—one by the business and the other by the bank. The asset account Cash, maintained by the depositor, is the opposite of the bank's liability account for each depositor. It should be possible to reconcile (balance) these accounts at any time.

Opening a bank chequing account is a pretty simple procedure. Typically, the bank runs a credit check on the new customer and the depositor is required to sign a signature card. The card has the signature of each person who is authorized to sign cheques on the account. The signature card is used by bank employees to validate the signature on the cheques. As mentioned earlier in the chapter, many companies require two authorized signatures on each cheque to act as a check and balance on each other.

The bank gives the depositor a book of serially numbered cheques and deposit slips imprinted with the depositor's name and address. Each cheque and deposit slip is imprinted with both a bank and a depositor identification number. This number, printed in magnetic ink, makes it possible for computers to process the transaction.

Many companies have more than one bank account. For efficiency of operations and better control, national retailers like Sears may have local bank accounts. Similarly, a company may have a payroll bank account, as well as one or more general bank accounts. A company may also have accounts with different banks in order to have more than one source for short-term loans when needed.

Bank Deposits and Cheques

Bank deposits should be made by an authorized employee, such as the head cashier. Each deposit must be documented by a deposit slip, as shown in Illustration 7-5.

Illustration 7-5 ▶

Deposit slip (reproduced with permission of BMO Bank of Montreal)

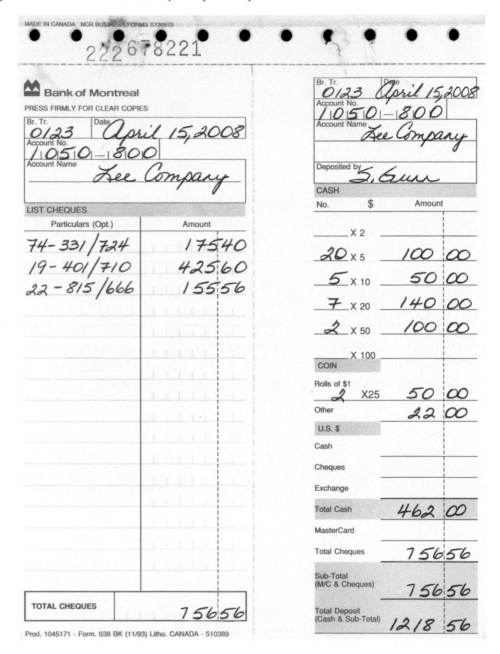

Deposit slips are normally prepared in duplicate. The original is kept by the bank. The duplicate is stamped by the bank to establish its authenticity, and is then kept by the depositor. Deposits are also made by direct deposit, through automated teller machines (ATMs)—also called automated bank machines (ABMs)—or through electronic funds transfers (EFT). In these cases, notification is found on the bank statement.

While bank deposits increase the bank account balance, cheques decrease it. A cheque is a written order signed by the depositor that instructs the bank to pay a specific sum of money to a designated recipient. There are three parties to a cheque: (1) the maker (or drawer) who issues the cheque, (2) the bank (or payer) on which the cheque is drawn, and (3) the payee to whom the cheque is payable. A cheque is a negotiable instrument that can be transferred to another party by endorsement.

Each cheque should clearly explain its purpose. For many businesses, the purpose of a cheque is detailed on the cheque stub, as shown in Illustration 7-6. The purpose of the cheque should also be clear for the payee, either by referencing the invoice directly on the cheque—see the reference to invoice #27622 on the "For" line of the cheque in the illustration—or by attaching a copy of the invoice to the cheque.

Illustration 7-6 ◀

Cheque (reproduced with permission of BMO Bank of Montreal)

ATM or ABM cash withdrawals are not allowed on a business bank account where two signatures are required on cheques. There is no way of knowing if both of the authorized individuals are present when the withdrawal is made. The same principle applies to EFT payments on business bank accounts. If the bank account requires two signatures, the company cannot use on-line banking to pay bills. When two signatures are required, the only way to maintain internal control is to make all payments by cheque or pre-authorized EFT.

For both individuals and businesses, it is important to know the balance in the chequing account at all times. This is easily done in a computerized accounting system, where deposits and cheques are recorded as soon as they are received or issued. In smaller businesses, to keep the balance current, each deposit and cheque must be entered in the cheque book, as shown on the left side of Illustration 7-6.

How does cash actually flow through the banking system? When cheques, debit cards, and pre-authorized or other payments occur, they may result in one financial institution owing money to another. For example, if a company (the maker) writes a cheque to a supplier (the payee), the payee deposits the cheque in its own bank account.

When the cheque is deposited, it is sent to a regional data centre for processing, usually the same day. When the cheque arrives at the regional data centre, it is "presented" to the payee's financial institution, where it is determined whether the cheque will be honoured or returned (for example, for insufficient funds or a stop payment order). This process is automated and happens very quickly. In most cases, the cheque will clear the maker's bank account before the next day. **Clearing** is the term used when a cheque or deposit is accepted by the maker's bank.

In some cases, a cheque cannot be cleared on the day it is deposited. For example, cheques that cannot be processed by automated equipment must be processed manually the next day. As well, cheques deposited at a branch on Saturday will not be cleared until the following Monday, because clearing takes place only on regular business days.

Improvements in technology now allow for images of the front and back of cheques to be taken electronically. The Canadian Payments Association is leading an industry-wide initiative to change to a new clearing process based on transmitting—or clearing—cheque images between financial institutions, rather than transporting the actual paper documents. This new process is expected to be fully implemented across Canada in 2009. The new system will result in faster, more efficient cheque clearing, as well as new services to customers for viewing cheque images.

The clearing process for electronic payments is more direct than for cheques and other paper-based payment items, as there is no requirement to deliver a physical payment item in these cases.

The clearing process nets cash flows in one direction against cash flows in the opposite direction for each bank or financial institution. Then, the financial institutions involved settle the net amounts through central accounts each institution maintains at the Bank of Canada. More than 17 million payments totalling more than $130 billion are cleared on an average business day.

Bank Statements

Each month, the depositor receives a bank statement from the bank. A **bank statement** shows the depositor's bank transactions and balance. A typical statement is presented in Illustration 7-7. It shows (1) cheques paid and other debits that reduce the balance in the depositor's account, (2) deposits and other credits that increase the balance in the depositor's account, and (3) the account balance after each day's transactions.

Bank of Montreal ☒ Banque de Montréal

505 King Street
Fredericton, NB
E3B 1E7

Transit No de dom	Date D/J M/M Y/A	Account Title Désignation de compte	Account Type Type de compte	Account No. No de compte	Page
0123	30 04 08	Operating Account	FBOA	1050-800	58

TRANSACTION CODES*
*CODES DE TRANSACTIONS**

AD Adjustments
    Rectification
CB Cheque Posted By Branch
    Chèque inscrit par la succ.
CC Certified Cheque
    Chèque certifié
CD Customer Deposit
    Dépôt
CK Cheque
    Chèque
CM Credit Memo
    Avis de Crédit
CW Telephone Banking
    Services bancaires par téléphone
DC Other Charges
    Autres frais
DD Direct Deposit/
    Pre-authorized Debit
    Dépôt ou débit direct
DM Debit Memo
    Avis de débit
DN Not Service Chargeable
    Sans frais de gestion
DR Overdraft
    Découvert
DS Service Chargeable
    Avec frais de gestion
EC Error Correction
    Correction d'erreur
FX Foreign Exchange
    Change
GS Tax
    Taxe
IB Instabank
    Instabanque
IN Interest
    Intérêt
LI Loan Interest
    Intérêt sur prêt
LN Loan Payment
    Vesement sur prêt
LP Loan Advance
    Avance sur prêt
LT Large Volume Account
    List Total
    *Liste de chèque - compte
    superactif*
MB Multi-Branch Banking
    Inter-Service
NR Non-Resident Tax
    Impôt de non-résident
NS Cheque returned NSF
    *Chèque retourné - provision
    insuffisante*
NT Nesbitt Burns Entry
    Transaction de Nesbitt Burns
OM Other Machine
    Autre machine
PR Purchase at Merchant
    Achat chez le commerçant
RC NSF Charge
    Frais pour provision insuffisante
RN Merchandise Return
    Retour de marchandise
RT Returned Item
    Article retourné
RV Merchant Reversal
    Correction - Commerçant
SC Service Charge
    Frais de gestion
SO Standing Order
    Ordre de virement
ST Merchant Deposit
    Dépôt du commerçant
TF Transfer of Funds
    Virement
TX Tax
    Taxe
WD Withdrawal
    Retrait
Please see the reverse side
for the Account Types
*Les types de compte
figurent au verso.*

Lee Company
500 Queen Street
Fredericton, NB   E3B 5C2

	Date	
BALANCE FORWARD SOLDE REPORTÉ	03 31	13,256.90

CODE	Description/Message justificatif	Debits/Débits	Credits/Crédits	Mo.	Day Jour	Balance/Solde
CK	NO. 435	644.95		04	01	12,611.95
CD			4,276.85	04	01	16,888.80
CD			2,137.50	04	04	19,026.30
CK	NO. 438	776.65		04	04	18,249.65
CK	NO. 437	1,185.79		04	05	17,063.86
CK	NO. 436	3,260.00		04	05	13,803.86
CD			1,350.47	04	06	15,154.33
CD			982.46	04	07	16,136.79
CK	NO. 440	1,487.90		04	07	14,648.89
CK	NO. 439	1,781.70		04	08	12,867.19
CK	NO. 442	2,420.00		04	08	10,447.19
CD			2,355.28	04	11	12,802.47
CK	NO. 441	1,585.60		04	11	11,216.87
CD			2,720.00	04	12	13,936.87
CK	NO. 443	1,226.00		04	12	12,710.87
CD			757.41	04	14	13,468.28
CD			1,218.56	04	15	14,686.84
CD			715.42	04	15	15,402.26
RT		425.60		04	18	14,976.66
DC		10.00		04	18	14,966.66
CK	NO. 444	3,467.11		04	22	11,499.55
CD			1,578.90	04	25	13,078.45
DD			1,350.55	04	27	14,429.00
SC		30.00		04	28	14,399.00
CD			2,128.60	04	29	16,527.60
CK	NO. 447	659.91		04	29	15,867.69
IN			39.76	04	29	15,907.45

Prompt notification of any change of address would be appreciated. / *Prière de signaler à la Banque tout changement d'adresse.*

Please check this statement and report any errors or omissions within 30 days of its delivery
Prière de vérifier ce relevé de compte et de signaler toute erreur ou omission dans les 30 jours suivant sa réception.

Helpful hint Every deposit received by the bank is credited to the customer's account. The reverse happens when the bank "pays" a cheque issued by a company on the company's chequing account balance. Because payment reduces the bank's liability, the amount is debited to the customer's account with the bank.

At first glance, it may appear that the debits and credits reported on the bank statement are backward. How can a cheque be a debit? And how can a deposit be a credit? Debits and credits are not really backward. To the company, Cash is an asset account. Assets are increased by debits (e.g., for cash receipts) and decreased by credits (e.g., for cash payments). To the bank, on the other hand, the cash in your bank account is a liability account—an amount it must repay to you upon request. Liabilities are increased by credits and decreased by debits. When you deposit money in your bank account, the bank's liability to you increases. That is why the bank shows deposits as credits. When you write a cheque on your account, the bank pays out this amount and decreases (debits) its liability to you.

Although not all the supporting documentation has been shown for the bank statement shown in Illustration 7-7, you can find the cheque for $2,420 shown in Illustration 7-6 on the bank statement's April 8 transaction. Note that although the cheque was written on April 7, it did not clear the bank until April 8. You can also find the deposit slip for $1,218.56 shown in Illustration 7-5 on the bank statement's April 15 transaction. Other deposits and cheques could be found in the same way by examining the supporting documentation kept on file by the company.

All paid cheques are listed in chronological order on the bank statement, with the date the cheque was paid and its amount indicated. A paid cheque is sometimes referred to as a cleared or cancelled cheque. The shift to image-based cheque processing is allowing banks to offer depositors new services that give faster and more convenient access to cancelled cheque images than the common practice of enclosing these cheques with their bank statements once a month. For example, customers can view cancelled cheque images on-line.

Debit Memorandum

Banks charge a monthly fee for using their services, called a **bank service charge**. A **debit memorandum** that explains the charge is usually included with the bank statement and noted on the statement. The symbol DM (debit memo) is often used for such charges. Separate debit memoranda may also be issued for other bank services such as the cost of printing cheques, issuing traveller's cheques, certifying cheques, and transferring funds to other locations.

A debit memorandum is also used by the bank when a deposited cheque from a customer bounces because of insufficient funds. In such a case, the cheque is marked **NSF (not sufficient funds)** or RT (returned item) by the customer's bank, and is returned to the depositor's bank. The bank then debits the depositor's account, as shown by the symbol RT on the bank statement in Illustration 7-7. Note that this cheque for $425.60 was originally included in the deposit made on April 15, detailed in Illustration 7-5. Because the deposit was credited (added) to the bank account on April 15 and the cheque was not honoured, it must be debited (deducted) by the bank on April 18.

The company's bank may also charge the company a service charge of $10 or more for processing the returned cheque. In Illustration 7-7 we can see that BMO uses the symbol DC on the customer's statement for these charges. The company (depositor) then advises the customer who wrote the NSF cheque that the customer's cheque was returned NSF and that a payment is still owed on the account. The company also usually passes the bank charges on to the customer by adding them to the customer's account balance. In summary, the overall effect of an NSF cheque to the depositor is to create an account receivable, and to reduce cash in the bank account. The customer's own bank will also charge the customer a $35 NSF fee for writing an NSF cheque.

Recording an account receivable assumes that the customer will honour the account due by replacing the bounced cheque with a valid cheque, or with cash. This happens in most cases. In the next chapter, we will discuss how to account for uncollectible accounts receivable when customers are unable to pay their accounts.

Credit Memorandum

Credit memoranda (CM) identify interest earned on the bank account, electronic funds transfers into the depositor's account, and other amounts added to the depositor's account. For example, as explained earlier in the chapter, some retailers accept electronic payments for merchandise sold on account. Funds are electronically transferred from the customer's account to the retailer's account in payment of the bill. For example, in Illustration 7-7 Lee Company collected an electronic payment from a customer for $1,350.55 on April 27 as indicated by the symbol DD.

Also note that in Illustration 7-7, interest of $39.76, as indicated by the symbol IN, has been added to Lee Company's bank balance. A bank does not pay interest by sending a cheque to a company. Rather it deposits the interest earned directly into the company's bank account.

BEFORE YOU GO ON . . .

▶**Review It**

1. How does using a bank account contribute to internal control over cash?
2. What is a cleared or cancelled cheque?
3. What are debit memoranda and why do they result in a decrease to the depositor's bank account?
4. What are credit memoranda and why do they result in an increase to the depositor's bank account?

Related exercise material: BE7–8.

Reconciling the Bank Account

The bank and the depositor keep independent records of the depositor's chequing account. If you have never had a chequing account, you might assume that the balances you and the bank have for your account will always agree. In fact, the two balances are almost never the same at any specific time. It is necessary to make the balance per books (the balance recorded in a company's general ledger cash account) agree with the balance per bank (the balance recorded on the bank statement)—a process called reconciling the bank account.

study objective 6

Prepare a bank reconciliation.

The lack of agreement between the two balances is due to the following:

1. Time lags that prevent one of the parties from recording a transaction in the same period as the other
2. Errors by either party in recording transactions

Except in electronic banking applications, time lags happen often. For example, several days pass between the time a cheque is mailed to a payee and the date the cheque is presented to, and cleared (paid) by, the bank. Cheques recorded by a company that have not yet cleared the bank are called **outstanding cheques**.

Similarly, when the depositor uses the bank's night depository to make deposits, there will be a difference of one day (or more if it's the weekend) between the time the receipts are recorded by the depositor and the time they are recorded by the bank. Deposits recorded by the company that have not yet been recorded by the bank are called **deposits in transit**.

Errors also occur. How often errors happen depends on the effectiveness of the internal controls of the depositor and the bank. Bank errors are rare. However, either party could unintentionally record a $450 cheque as $45 or $540. In addition, the bank might mistakenly charge a cheque to the wrong account if the code is missing or if the cheque cannot be scanned.

Reconciliation Procedure

To get the most benefit from a bank reconciliation, the reconciliation should be prepared by an employee who has no other responsibilities related to cash, or by the owner of the company. In the feature story about Beanz Espresso Bar, the owner prepares the bank reconciliation. If the internal control principles of segregation of duties and performance reviews are not followed when the reconciliation is prepared, cash embezzlements may go unnoticed. For example, a cashier who prepares the reconciliation can steal cash and conceal the theft by misstating the reconciliation. Thus, the bank accounts would appear to reconcile and the theft would not be discovered.

In reconciling the bank account, it is customary to reconcile the balance per books (found in the Cash account in the general ledger) and balance per bank (found on the bank statement provided by the bank) to their adjusted (correct) cash balances. The starting point when preparing the reconciliation is to enter the balance per bank statement and balance per books on the schedule. Adjustments are then made to each section, as shown in Illustration 7-8.

Illustration 7-8 ►

Bank reconciliation procedures

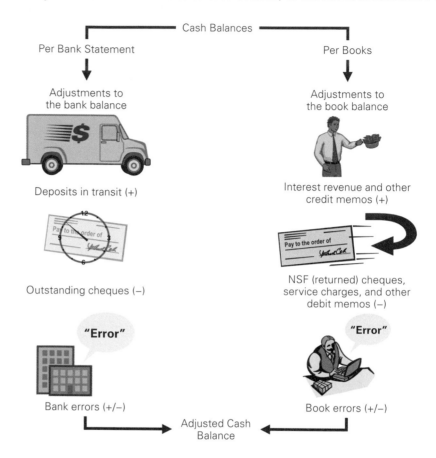

Cash Balances

Per Bank Statement → Adjustments to the bank balance

Deposits in transit (+)

Outstanding cheques (−)

"Error" Bank errors (+/−)

Per Books → Adjustments to the book balance

Interest revenue and other credit memos (+)

NSF (returned) cheques, service charges, and other debit memos (−)

"Error" Book errors (+/−)

Adjusted Cash Balance

Reconciling Items per Bank. On the bank side of the reconciliation, the items to include are deposits in transit, outstanding cheques, and bank errors.

1. **Deposits in transit.** Compare the individual deposits on the bank statement with (1) the deposits in transit from the preceding bank reconciliation, and (2) the deposits recorded in the company's books. Deposits in transit have been recorded on the company's books but have not yet been recorded by the bank. They are added to the balance per bank on the bank reconciliation.

   Before determining deposits in transit for the current period, you must check whether all deposits in transit that are outstanding from a previous period have cleared. For example, Lee Company used a night deposit slot to deposit $2,201.40 on April 30. The bank did not receive or record this deposit until the next day, May 1. This amount would be treated as a deposit in transit at the end of April and would be added to the balance per bank on the bank reconciliation. However, this outstanding deposit would clear the bank in May and would no longer be a deposit in transit at the end of May. As at the end of May, this amount has been recorded by both the company and the bank.

2. **Outstanding cheques.** Compare the paid cheques shown on the bank statement or returned with the bank statement to (1) cheques that are outstanding from the preceding

bank reconciliation, and (2) cheques that have been issued by the company. Outstanding cheques have been recorded on the company's books but have not cleared the bank account yet. They are deducted from the balance per bank on the bank reconciliation.

Note that an outstanding cheque from a previous period means that the cheque was deducted from the books in the previous period but not paid by the bank by the end of that period. If the cheque was paid by the bank in the current month, both sides (book and bank) are now reconciled, the cheque is no longer outstanding, and no further reconciling item is required. If the cheque has still not been presented to the bank for payment, it will continue to be outstanding and needs to be included with the outstanding cheques and deducted from the bank balance on the current month's bank reconciliation.

3. **Bank errors.** Note any errors that are discovered in the previous steps. Errors can be made by either the bank or the company and can be in both directions (increases or decreases). Make sure you include only errors made by the bank as reconciling items when calculating the adjusted cash balance per bank. For example, if the bank processed a deposit of $1,693 as $1,639 in error, the difference of $54 is added to the balance per bank on the bank reconciliation.

Reconciling Items per Books. Reconciling items on the book side include adjustments from any unrecorded credit memoranda (amounts added) and debit memoranda (amounts deducted), and company errors.

1. **Credit memoranda.** Compare the credit memoranda on the bank statement with the company records. Any unrecorded credit memoranda should be added to the balance per books. For example, if the bank statement shows a credit memorandum for interest earned, this amount will be added to the balance per books on the bank reconciliation to make the company's records agree with the bank's records.

2. **Debit memoranda.** Similarly, any unrecorded debit memoranda should be deducted from the balance per books. If the bank statement shows a debit memorandum for bank service charges, this amount is deducted from the balance per books on the bank reconciliation to make the company's records agree with the bank's records.

3. **Company errors.** Make sure you include only errors made by the company as reconciling items when calculating the adjusted cash balance per books. For example, we will see below that Lee Company wrote a cheque for $1,226 and mistakenly recorded it as $1,262. The error of $36 is added to the balance per books because Lee Company reduced the balance per books by $36 too much when it recorded the cheque as $1,262 instead of $1,226.

Bank Reconciliation Illustrated

The bank statement for Lee Company was shown in Illustration 7-7. It shows a balance per bank of $15,907.45 on April 30, 2008. On this date, the balance of cash per books is $11,244.14. Using the above steps, the following reconciling items are determined:
Reconciling items per bank:

1. **Deposits in transit:** After comparing the deposits recorded in the books with the deposits listed in the bank statement, it was determined that the April 30 deposit was not recorded by the bank until May 1. $2,201.40

2. **Outstanding cheques:** After comparing the cheques recorded in the books with the cheques listed on the bank statement, it was determined that three cheques were outstanding:

No. 445	$3,000.00	
No. 446	1,401.30	
No. 448	1,502.70	5,904.00

3. **Bank errors:** None

Reconciling items per books:

1. **Credit memoranda**

Electronic payment by customer on account	$1,350.55
Interest earned	39.76

2. **Debit memoranda**

NSF cheque from J.R. Baron	425.60
Bank service charge for NSF cheque	10.00
Bank service charge	30.00

3. **Company errors:** Cheque No. 443 was correctly written by Lee for $1,226.00 and was correctly paid by the bank. However, it was recorded as $1,262.00 by Lee.   36.00

The bank reconciliation is as follows:

LEE COMPANY
Bank Reconciliation
April 30, 2008

Cash balance per bank statement		$15,907.45
Add: Deposit in transit		2,201.40
		18,108.85
Less: Outstanding cheques		
No. 445	$3,000.00	
No. 446	1,401.30	
No. 448	1,502.70	5,904.00
Adjusted cash balance per bank		$12,204.85
Cash balance per books		$11,244.14
Add: Electronic payment by customer on account	$1,350.55	
Interest earned	39.76	
Error in recording cheque No. 443 ($1,262.00 − $1,226.00)	36.00	1,426.31
		12,670.45
Less: NSF cheque and bank charge ($425.60 + $10.00)	$ 435.60	
Bank service charge	30.00	465.60
Adjusted cash balance per books		$12,204.85

Entries from Bank Reconciliation

When determining the adjusted cash balance per books, each reconciling item should be recorded by the depositor. If these items are not journalized and posted, the Cash account will not show the correct balance. The entries for Lee Company on April 30 are as follows:

Apr. 30	Cash	1,350.55	
	Accounts Receivable		1,350.55
	To record electronic collection of account.		
30	Cash	39.76	
	Interest Revenue		39.76
	To record interest earned.		
30	Cash	36.00	
	Accounts Payable		36.00
	To correct error in recording cheque No. 443.		
30	Accounts Receivable ($425.60 + $10.00)	435.60	
	Cash		435.60
	To record NSF cheque plus bank charge from J.R. Baron.		
30	Bank Charges Expense	30.00	
	Cash		30.00
	To record bank service charge expense for April.		

A	=	L	+	OE
+1,350.55				
−1,350.55				

⬆ Cash flows: +1,350.55

A	=	L	+	OE
+39.76				+39.76

⬆ Cash flows: +39.76

A	=	L	+	OE
+36		+36		

⬆ Cash flows: +36

A	=	L	+	OE
+435.60				
−435.60				

⬇ Cash flows: −435.60

A	=	L	+	OE
−30				−30

⬇ Cash flows: −30

Bank service charges are normally debited to Bank Charges Expense. Some companies use the account Interest Expense; others use Miscellaneous Expense because the charges are often very small in amount. If the bank service charge relates to processing a customer NSF cheque—as in the case of J.R. Baron's NSF cheque—this charge is passed on to the customer and added to their account.

The five journal entries shown above could also be combined into one compound entry. Our presentation assumes that all adjustments are made at the end of the month. In practice, many companies make journal entries throughout the month as they receive information from the bank about their account, or as they check their on-line bank account balances.

Note that in previous chapters Cash was treated as an account that did not require adjustment. This was done to make learning easier, because the bank reconciliation process had not been explained.

After the entries above are posted, the Cash account will show the following:

Cash			
Apr. 30 Bal.	11,244.14	Apr. 30	435.60
30	1,350.55	30	30.00
30	36.00		
30	39.76		
Apr. 30 Bal.	12,204.85		

The adjusted cash balance in the general ledger should agree with the adjusted cash balance per books in the bank reconciliation shown on page 366.

What entries does the bank make? The bank does not make any entries for deposits in transit or outstanding cheques. The bank will record these items when they reach the bank. If any bank errors are discovered in preparing the reconciliation, the bank should be notified. The bank can then make the necessary corrections on its records. The bank does not correct your errors on its books, and you do not correct the bank's errors on your books.

ACCOUNTING IN ACTION ▶ Across the Organization Insight

More than 1,000 mistakes in pre-authorized bank debits are made each day across Canada, according to an Environics survey commissioned in March 2006. Based on this finding, the Canadian Consumer Initiative, a coalition of consumer groups, wants the federal government to legislate electronic payments in its review of the *Bank Act*. The most common problems were debits in the wrong amount (23 percent), on the wrong date (19 percent), and double debits (17 percent). When people noticed a problem, 44 percent of them first reported it to their financial institution. In almost one-fourth of these cases, the banker sent the customer to the merchant, contrary to the rule adopted by the Canadian Payments Association, which requires financial institutions to reimburse their customer immediately in most cases.

Source: "Groups Want Law to Govern Electronic Payments," *Canadian Press*, April 27, 2006.

> **?** How would you know if an error like the ones described above has occurred in your bank account?

BEFORE YOU GO ON . . .

▶Review It

1. What is the purpose of reconciling a bank account?
2. Give some examples of reconciling items per bank and per book.
3. How are errors treated in the reconciliation process?
4. How are deposits in transit and outstanding cheques from the previous period treated in the reconciling process?

▶Do It

The Cash account of Zhizhi Company showed a balance of $16,333 on December 31, 2008. The bank statement as of that date showed a balance of $18,084. After comparing the bank statement with the cash records, the following information was determined:

1. The bank returned an NSF cheque in the amount of $239 that Zhizhi had deposited on December 20. The cheque was a payment on a customer's account.
2. Electronic receipts received from customers on the last day of the month to pay their accounts totalled $2,300. These receipts have not yet been recorded by the company.
3. The bank issued a credit memo for $9 of interest earned on Zhizhi's account.
4. The bank issued a debit memo for bank service charges of $37. This amount included $10 for processing the NSF cheque (see #1 above).
5. The company made an error in recording a customer's deposit. The company recorded the payment on account as $209 when it should have been $290. The bank correctly recorded the deposit at $290.
6. Deposits in transit as at December 31 amounted to $3,643.
7. Outstanding cheques written in the month of December amounted to $3,000. Cheques still outstanding from the month of November totalled $280.

Prepare a bank reconciliation and any required journal entries for Zhizhi Company at December 31, 2008.

Action Plan

- Prepare the bank reconciliation in two sections: one for the bank and one for the company.
- Determine which reconciling items each side has already recorded and adjust the other side accordingly.
- Be careful when you determine the direction of an error correction; think about how the error has affected the bank balance or the cash account balance.
- Prepare journal entries only for reconciling items to the book side; not the bank side.
- The adjusted cash balances must agree with each other when complete, and with the general ledger account after the journal entries are posted.

Solution

ZHIZHI COMPANY
Bank Reconciliation
December 31, 2008

Cash balance per bank statement		$18,084
Add: Deposits in transit		3,643
		21,727
Less: Outstanding cheques ($3,000 + $280)		3,280
Adjusted cash balance per bank		$18,447
Cash balance per books		$16,333
Add: Electronic receipts from customers on account	$2,300	
Interest earned	9	
Deposit error correction ($290 − $209)	81	2,390
		18,723
Less: NSF cheque	$ 239	
Bank service charges	37	276
Adjusted cash balance per books		$18,447

Dec. 31	Cash	2,300	
	Accounts Receivable		2,300
	To record electronic receipts on account.		
31	Cash	9	
	Interest Revenue		9
	To record interest earned on bank account.		
31	Cash	81	
	Accounts Receivable ($290 − $209)		81
	To correct deposit error.		
31	Accounts Receivable ($239 + $10)	249	
	Cash		249
	To re-establish accounts receivable for NSF cheque and related service charge.		
31	Bank Charges Expense ($37 − $10)	27	
	Cash		27
	To record bank service charges.		

		Cash		
Dec. 31	Bal.	16,333	Dec. 31	249
31		2,300	31	27
31		9		
31		81		
Dec. 31	Bal.	18,447		

Related exercise material: BE7–8, BE7–9, BE7–10, BE7–11, BE7–12, E7–7, E7–8, E7–9, E7–10, E7–11, and E7–12.

the
navigator

Reporting Cash

Cash consists of coins, currency (paper money), cheques, money orders, travellers' cheques, and money on deposit in a bank or similar depository. The general rule is that if the bank will accept it for deposit, it is cash. Debit card and bank credit card transactions—such as Visa and MasterCard—are cash, but nonbank credit card transactions are not.

study objective 7

Report cash on the balance sheet.

Cash does not include postdated (payable in the future) cheques, staledated (more than six months old) cheques, or returned (NSF—not sufficient funds) cheques. Postage stamps and IOUs from employees are not cash either, because they cannot be deposited in a bank account. Postage stamps are office supplies and IOUs from employees are receivables.

Cash on hand, cash in banks, and petty cash are normally combined and reported simply as Cash in the balance sheet. Because it is the most liquid asset owned by a company, cash is listed first in the current assets section of the balance sheet. Many companies combine cash with cash equivalents. **Cash equivalents** are short-term, highly liquid (easily sold) investments. They typically have maturities of three months or less from the date they are purchased. These investments include short-term deposits and short-term investments such as treasury bills and money-market funds.

More than 75 percent of Canadian public companies present cash in this manner. The illustration that follows shows how Sears combines cash and cash equivalents (called short-term investments by Sears) on its balance sheet:

SEARS CANADA INC. Balance Sheet (partial) December 31, 2005 (in millions)	
Assets	
Current assets	
Cash and short-term investments	$775.1

In the notes to its financial statements, Sears reports that its cash and short-term investments include all highly liquid investments with maturities of three months or less at the date of purchase.

Some companies may be in a cash deficit or negative position at year end. This can happen when the company is in an overdraft position at the bank. A **bank overdraft** occurs when withdrawals or payments are more than the amount in the bank account. This becomes a short-term loan from the bank, assuming that the bank does not reject the withdrawal or payment. Most companies have overdraft protection up to a certain amount with their banks. In an overdraft situation, the Cash account shows a credit balance in the general ledger and is reported as a current liability called bank indebtedness.

A company may have cash that is not available for general use because it is restricted for a special purpose. An example is funds held on deposit until completion of an offer to buy real estate. Cash that has a restricted use—and is a significant amount—should be reported separately on the balance sheet as **restricted cash**. If the restricted cash is expected to be used within the next year, the amount should be reported as a current asset. When restricted funds will not be used in that time, they should be reported as a noncurrent asset.

In making loans to depositors, banks may require borrowers to keep minimum cash balances. These minimum balances, called **compensating balances**, give the bank support for the loans. They are a form of restriction on the use of cash. Similar to other restricted cash, a compensating balance should be reported as a noncurrent asset.

Using the Information in the Financial Statements

Management must perform a difficult balancing act to properly manage cash. On one hand, it is critical to ensure that enough cash is available to pay bills as they come due, to buy goods, and to take advantage of opportunities as they present themselves. On the other hand, cash itself is an unproductive asset unless it is invested in other assets (e.g., investments, inventory, and property, plant, and equipment). Too much cash on hand may indicate that management is not maximizing its return on assets.

The cash flow statement and the management report are two useful pieces of information to help readers assess management's effectiveness in managing and controlling cash. The cash flow statement, which will be discussed in Chapter 17, gives information about where cash came from and what it was used for.

A management report is included in all publicly distributed financial statements. The purpose of this report is to acknowledge management's responsibility for—among other items—the development of internal controls over the financial reporting process. In Appendix A at the end of this textbook, The Forzani Group Ltd. attaches a statement of Management's Responsibilities for Financial Reporting. This report includes the following statements to assure the reader that management takes its responsibility to produce reliable information seriously: "Management is responsible for the development and maintenance of systems of internal accounting and administrative controls. Such systems are designed to give reasonable assurance that the financial information is accurate, relevant and reliable, and that the Company's assets are correctly accounted for and adequately safeguarded."

BEFORE YOU GO ON . . .

▶Review It

1. What is included as cash on a company's balance sheet?
2. What is the difference between restricted cash and compensating balances?
3. Does Forzani report cash or cash and cash equivalents in its 2006 balance sheet? At what amount? The answer to this question is at the end of the chapter.
4. How should a company report its responsibilities for internal control?

Related exercise material: BE7–13, BE7–14 and E7–13.

Demonstration Problem

Trillo Company reports the following condensed information from its general ledger Cash account and bank statement at June 30, 2008:

Cash			
June 1 Bal.	17,540		
June deposits	17,000	June cheques written	19,760
June 30 Bal.	14,780		

TRILLO COMPANY
Bank Statement
June 30, 2008

	Cheques and Other Debits	Deposits and Other Credits	Balance
Balance, June 1			17,690
Deposits		15,248	32,938
Cheques cleared	18,100		14,838
EFT insurance payment	500		14,338
NSF cheque ($165 + $10 service charge)	175		14,163
Service charge	12		14,151
Interest earned		35	14,186

Additional information:

1. There was a deposit in transit of $600 at May 31, the preceding month, which cleared the bank in June.
2. There were $750 of outstanding cheques at the end of May.
3. The EFT payment for insurance has not been recorded by the company yet.
4. The NSF cheque was for $165 from Massif Co., a customer, in payment of its account. The bank added a $10 processing fee.

Instructions

(a) Prepare a bank reconciliation at June 30.
(b) Journalize the entries required by the reconciliation.

Action Plan

- Compare the deposits in transit at the end of May plus the deposits recorded in the books with the deposits on the bank statement to determine the deposits in transit at the end of June.
- Compare the outstanding cheques at the end of May plus the cheques recorded in the books with the cheques that cleared the bank statement to determine the outstanding cheques at the end of June.
- Identify any items recorded by the bank but not by the company as reconciling items per books.
- All the journal entries should be based on the reconciling items per books.
- Make sure the Cash ledger account balance, after posting the reconciling items, agrees with the adjusted cash balance per books.

Solution to Demonstration Problem

(a)

TRILLO COMPANY
Bank Reconciliation
June 30, 2008

Cash balance per bank statement		$14,186
Add: Deposits in transit [($17,000 + $600) – $15,248]		2,352
		16,538
Less: Outstanding cheques [($19,760 + $750) – $18,100]		2,410
Adjusted cash balance per bank		$14,128
Cash balance per books		$14,780
Add: Interest earned		35
		14,815
Less: EFT insurance payment	$500	
NSF cheque ($165 + $10)	175	
Bank service charge	12	687
Adjusted cash balance per books		$14,128

(b)

June 30	Cash	35	
	Interest Revenue		35
	To record bank interest earned.		
30	Insurance Expense	500	
	Cash		500
	To record monthly insurance payment.		
30	Accounts Receivable	175	
	Cash		175
	To re-establish accounts receivable for Massif Co. for $165 NSF cheque and related $10 service charge.		
30	Bank Charges Expense	12	
	Cash		12
	To record bank service charges.		

Check:

	Cash		
June 30 Bal.	14,780	June 30	500
30	35	30	175
		30	12
June 30 Bal.	14,128		

the navigator

Summary of Study Objectives

1. **Explain the activities that help achieve internal control.** Control activities are the policies and procedures that management implements in order to control the risks that threaten the company's ability to achieve reliable financial reporting, effective and efficient operations, and compliance with relevant laws and regulations. They include establishment of responsibility, segregation of duties, documentation, physical controls, performance reviews, and other controls.

2. **Apply control activities to cash receipts.** Internal controls over cash receipts include (a) designating only personnel such as cashiers to handle cash; (b) assigning the duties of receiving cash, recording cash; and maintaining custody of cash to different individuals; (c) using remittance advices for mail receipts, cash register tapes for over-the-counter receipts, and deposit slips for bank deposits; (d) using company safes and bank vaults to store cash with only authorized personnel having access, and using cash registers to issue over-the-counter receipts; (e) depositing all cash intact daily; (f) making independent daily counts of register receipts and daily comparisons of total receipts with total deposits; and (g) bonding personnel who handle cash.

3. **Apply control activities to cash disbursements.** Internal controls over cash disbursements include (a) authorizing only specified individuals such as the controller to sign cheques; (b) assigning the duties of approving items for payment, paying for the items, and recording the payment to different individuals; (c) using prenumbered cheques and accounting for all cheques, with each cheque supported by an approved invoice; (d) storing blank cheques in a safe or vault, with access restricted to authorized personnel, and using a cheque writer to imprint amounts on cheques; (e) comparing each cheque to the approved invoice before issuing the cheque, and making monthly reconciliations of bank and book balances; and (f) after payment, stamping each approved invoice "Paid."

4. **Operate and account for a petty cash fund.** To operate a petty cash fund, it is necessary to establish the fund, make payments from the fund, and replenish the fund. Journal entries are only made when the fund is established and replenished.

5. **Describe the control features of a bank account.** A bank account contributes to good internal control by giving physical controls for the storage of cash, reducing the amount of currency that must be kept on hand, and creating a double record of a depositor's bank transactions.

6. **Prepare a bank reconciliation.** In reconciling the bank account, the balance per books and balance per bank are reconciled to their adjusted balances. Reconciling items include deposits in transit, outstanding cheques, errors by the bank, unrecorded bank memoranda, and errors by the company. Adjusting entries must be made for any errors made by the company and unrecorded bank memoranda (e.g., interest).

7. ***Report cash on the balance sheet.*** Cash is listed first in the current assets section of the balance sheet. In many cases, cash is reported together with highly liquid, short-term investments (cash equivalents). Cash that is restricted for a special purpose is reported separately as a current asset or a noncurrent asset, depending on when the cash is expected to be used. The cash flow statement and the management report on the financial statements are useful tools to assess management's effectiveness in managing and controlling cash.

Glossary

Study Aids: Glossary
Practice Tools: Key Term Matching Activity

Bank overdraft   The situation when withdrawals are more than the amount available in the bank account. (p. 370)

Bank service charge   A fee charged by a bank for using its services. (p. 362)

Bank statement   A statement received monthly from the bank that shows the depositor's bank transactions and balances. (p. 360)

Cash   Resources such as coins, currency, cheques, and money orders that are accepted at face value when they are deposited in a bank or similar depository. (p. 369)

Cash equivalents   Highly liquid, short-term investments with maturities of three months or less. (p. 370)

Cash payments journal   A special journal used to record all cash paid. (p. 353)

Cash receipts journal   A special journal used to record all cash received. (p. 349)

Clearing   The process of exchanging and settling payment items that results in a transfer of funds from one financial institution to another. (p. 359)

Compensating balances   Minimum cash balances required by a bank as support for bank loans. (p. 370)

Credit memoranda (CM)   Supporting documentation for increases to a bank account that appear on a bank statement. (p. 362)

Debit memoranda (DM)   Supporting documentation for decreases to a bank account that appear on a bank statement. (p. 362)

Deposits in transit   Deposits recorded by the depositor that have not been recorded by the bank. (p. 363)

Electronic funds transfer (EFT)   A disbursement system that uses telephone, computer, or wireless means to transfer cash from one location to another. (p. 351)

External auditors   Auditors who are independent of the organization. They examine internal control and report how reasonable the financial statements or other financial information is. (p. 346)

Fidelity insurance   An insurance policy where the insurance company will compensate the employer for losses incurred as a result of the dishonesty of an employee. (p. 346)

Internal auditors   Company employees who evaluate the effectiveness of the company's system of internal control. (p. 345)

Internal control   The processes designed and implemented by management that helps an organization to achieve reliable financial reporting, effective and efficient operations, and compliance with relevant laws and regulations. (p. 342)

NSF (not sufficient funds) cheque   A cheque that is not paid by the customer's bank and is returned to the depositor's bank because of insufficient funds in the customer's account. (p. 362)

Outstanding cheques   Cheques issued and recorded by a company that have not been paid by the bank. (p. 363)

Petty cash fund   A cash fund that is used for paying relatively small amounts. (p. 354)

Restricted cash   Cash that is not available for general use, but instead is restricted for a particular purpose. (p. 370)

Special journal   A journal that is used to record similar types of transactions, such as all cash receipts or all cash payments. (p. 349)

Self-Study Questions

Practice Tools: Self-Assessment Quizzes

Answers are at the end of the chapter.

(SO 1) K 1. Control activities do not include:
   (a) establishing responsibility.
   (b) documentation procedures.
   (c) cost-benefit constraints.
   (d) performance reviews.

(SO 1) K 2. Which of the following factors could limit a company's system of internal control?
   (a) Collusion by two or more employees
   (b) The cost of internal control being greater than the benefit
   (c) Difficulty in segregating duties in small businesses
   (d) All of the above

(SO 2) C 3. Permitting only designated personnel to handle cash receipts is an application of the concept of:
   (a) segregation of duties.
   (b) establishment of responsibility.
   (c) performance reviews.
   (d) other controls.

(SO 2) AP 4. Morgan Retailers accepted $50,000 of TD Bank Visa credit card charges for merchandise sold on July 1. TD Bank charges Morgan 4% for its credit card use. The entry to record this transaction by Morgan Retailers will include: a credit to Sales of $50,000 and:
   (a) a debit to Cash of $48,000 and a debit to Credit Card Expense of $2,000.
   (b) a debit to Cash of $50,000.
   (c) a debit to Accounts Receivable of $50,000.
   (d) a debit to Accounts Receivable of $48,000 and a debit to Credit Card Expense of $2,000.

(SO 3) C 5. The use of prenumbered cheques in disbursing cash is an application of the principle of:
   (a) establishment of responsibility.
   (b) segregation of duties.
   (c) physical controls.
   (d) documentation procedures.

6. A cheque is written to replenish a $100 petty cash fund (SO 4) AP when the fund has receipts of $92 and $5 in cash. In recording the cheque:
   (a) Cash Over and Short should be debited for $3.
   (b) Cash Over and Short should be credited for $3.
   (c) Petty Cash should be debited for $92.
   (d) Cash should be credited for $92.

7. The control features of a bank account do not include: (SO 5) C
   (a) having bank auditors verify the correctness of the balance per books.
   (b) minimizing the amount of cash that must be kept on hand.
   (c) giving a double record of all bank transactions.
   (d) safeguarding cash by using a bank as a depository.

8. Suzanne Terriault reports an ending cash balance of (SO 6) AP $410 in her cheque book at the end of the month and $500 in her bank statement. Reconciling items include deposits in transit of $250, outstanding cheques of $350, and service charges of $10. What is Suzanne's adjusted cash balance?
   (a) $390   (c) $410
   (b) $400   (d) $500

9. A company mistakenly recorded a $459 cheque written (SO 6) AP in payment of an account as $495. The journal entry required to correct this would be:
   (a) debit Accounts Payable $36; credit Cash $36.
   (b) debit Cash $36; credit Accounts Payable $36.
   (c) debit Cash $36; credit Accounts Receivable $36.
   (d) No journal entry is required.

10. Which of the following correctly describes the reporting (SO 7) K of cash?
   (a) Cash cannot be combined with cash equivalents.
   (b) Restricted cash funds are always reported as a current asset.
   (c) Compensating balances are reported as a current asset.
   (d) Cash and cash equivalents are listed first in the current assets section.

the navigator

Questions

(SO 1) C 1. "The only purpose of internal control is to improve the accuracy of the accounting records." Do you agree? Explain.

(SO 1) K 2. In the corner convenience store, all clerks make change out of the same cash register drawer. Is this a violation of internal control? Why?

(SO 1) C 3. What are two common applications of the concept of segregation of duties?

(SO 1) C 4. How do documentation procedures contribute to good internal control?

(SO 1, 3) K 5. Which internal control objectives do physical controls help achieve? Give an example of how physical controls apply to cash disbursements.

(SO 1) C 6. Matt To is questioning the need for independent performance reviews if the company also segregates duties. Answer Matt's question.

(SO 1) C 7. Viki Kim is trying to design internal control activities so that there is no possibility of errors or theft. Explain to Viki why this may be impractical, and maybe even impossible.

(SO 2) C 8. Creaghan's Department Stores has just installed electronic cash registers with scanners in its stores. How do cash registers such as these improve internal control over cash receipts?

(SO 2) C 9. Explain the procedures that should be followed at the end of the day (or shift) to ensure proper internal control of over-the-counter cash receipts.

(SO 2) C 10. What are the differences to the customer between a debit card sale and a bank credit card sale? To the retailer?

(SO 2) C 11. At Vink Wholesale Company, two mail clerks open all mail receipts. How does this strengthen internal control?

(SO 2) C 12. From a company's point of view, what are the similarities and differences between a customer making a payment using EFT and on-line banking or using EFT and automatic pre-authorized monthly payments?

(SO 3) C 13. "To have maximum effective internal control over cash disbursements, all payments should be made by cheque or by an electronic funds transfer." Is this true? Explain.

(SO 3) C 14. Ouellette Company's internal controls over cash disbursements require the controller to sign cheques imprinted by a computer after she compares the cheque to the approved invoice. Identify the internal control activities that are being followed.

15. Walter's Watches is a small retail store. Walter, the (SO 3) owner of the company, has recently hired a new employee, Wanda, who will be responsible for ordering merchandise, receiving the goods, and authorizing the merchandise invoices for payment. Describe the various ways Wanda could potentially commit a fraud with this arrangement.

16. Koberstein Company has a petty cash fund that is used (SO 4) to pay for a variety of minor items. Olga, the petty cash custodian, regularly borrows cash from the fund to pay for personal expenses. Olga has always repaid these amounts. Is this a problem for Koberstein Company? If it is, explain what the company could do to strengthen internal control.

17. Explain the control features of a bank account, in- (SO 5) cluding the control benefits of (a) signature cards, (b) cheques, and (c) bank statements.

18. Who should be responsible for preparing a bank recon- (SO 6) ciliation? Why?

19. Paul Reimer does not keep a personal record of his (SO 6) bank account and does not see the need to do a bank reconciliation. He says he can always use on-line banking to look up the balance in his bank account before writing a cheque. Explain why Paul should keep his own records and do regular bank reconciliations.

20. Diablo Company wrote cheque #2375 for $1,325 on (SO 6) March 16. As at March 31, the cheque had not cleared the company's bank account and was correctly listed as an outstanding cheque on the March 31 bank reconciliation. The cheque has still not cleared the bank account on April 30. Anah is doing the bank reconciliation for Diablo and thinks it is not necessary to include the cheque in the April bank reconciliation, because it was already listed as an outstanding cheque on March 31. Is she correct? Explain.

21. Omar Basabe asks for your help with an NSF cheque. (SO 6) Explain to Omar (a) what an NSF cheque is, (b) how it is treated in a bank reconciliation, and (c) whether or not it will require an adjusting entry.

22. "Cash equivalents are the same as cash." Do you agree? (SO 7) Explain.

23. What is restricted cash? What are compensating bal- (SO 7) ances? How should these be reported on the balance sheet?

Brief Exercises

BE7–1 Natalie McPhail is the new owner of Liberty Parking—a parking garage. She has heard about internal control but is not clear about its importance for her business. Explain to Natalie the three things that internal control processes are designed to help an organization achieve and who is responsible for implementing internal control. Give her one application of each of these three things for Liberty Parking.

Explain purpose of internal control.
(SO 1) C

BE7–2 Miramichi Company has the following internal controls over cash receipts. Identify the control activity that is applicable to each of the following:

Identify control activities applicable to cash receipts.
(SO 2) K

1. All over-the-counter receipts are recorded on cash registers.
2. All cashiers are bonded.
3. Daily cash counts are made by cashier department supervisors.
4. The duties of receiving cash, recording cash, and maintaining custody of cash are assigned to different individuals.
5. Only cashiers may operate cash registers.
6. All cash is deposited intact in the bank account daily.

BE7–3 St. Mary's Petro Stop accepted a Visa card in payment of a $100 fuel purchase on July 27. The bank charges a 4% fee. What entry should St. Mary's Petro Stop make? How would this entry change if the payment had been made with a St. Mary's Petro Shop credit card instead of a Visa card? A debit card instead of a Visa card? The bank charges $1 for each debit card transaction.

Record credit and debit card transactions.
(SO 2) AP

BE7–4 Bujold Company has the following internal controls over cash disbursements. Identify the control activity that is applicable to each of the following:

Identify control activities applicable to cash disbursements.
(SO 3) K

1. Company cheques are prenumbered.
2. The bank statement is reconciled monthly by an internal auditor.
3. Blank cheques are stored in a safe in the controller's office.
4. Only the controller or assistant controller may sign cheques.
5. Cheque signers are not allowed to record cash disbursement transactions.
6. All payments, except for petty cash transactions, are made by cheque.

BE7–5 On March 2, Pugh Company established a petty cash fund of $100. On March 20, the fund was replenished when it had $8 in cash and receipts for postage $52, freight out $28, and supplies $12. Prepare the journal entries to establish the petty cash fund on March 2 and to replenish it on March 20.

Record petty cash transactions.
(SO 4) AP

BE7–6 Clara's Snack Shop has a petty cash fund of $150. On November 17, the fund contained $10 in cash and receipts for printing $34, supplies $58, postage $19, and delivery expense $26. A cheque was written to replenish the fund and increase the fund balance to $200. Prepare the journal entry(ies) required.

Record petty cash transactions.
(SO 4) AP

BE7–7 Here are some statements about bank accounts. Next to each statement, record the letter T if the statement is true, and F if the statement is false.

Identify bank account operating features.
(SO 5) C

1. ___ A cheque is a negotiable instrument that can be transferred to another party.
2. ___ Banks issue debit memoranda to record decreases to customers' bank accounts.
3. ___ Banks do not require signature cards for business bank accounts, because the company employees who have signing authority may change.
4. ___ From a bank's point of view, a customer's bank account is a liability.
5. ___ Clearing is the term used for when a cheque is accepted by the payee's bank.

BE7–8 For each of the items in the following list, identify where it is included on a bank reconciliation. Next to each item, record the correct letter from this list: (a) increase to bank balance, (b) decrease to bank balance, (c) increase to company cash balance, (d) decrease to company cash balance, or (e) not included in the bank reconciliation.

Indicate location of items in bank reconciliation.
(SO 6) AP

1. ___ Bank debit memorandum for service charges
2. ___ EFT payment made by a customer
3. ___ Outstanding cheques from the current month
4. ___ Outstanding cheques from the previous month that are still outstanding
5. ___ Outstanding cheques from the previous month that are no longer outstanding
6. ___ Bank error in recording a company cheque made out for $200 as $290
7. ___ Bank credit memorandum for interest revenue
8. ___ Company error in recording a deposit of $1,280 as $1,680
9. ___ Bank debit memorandum for an NSF cheque
10. ___ Deposit in transit from the current month
11. ___ Company error in recording a cheque made out for $360 as $630
12. ___ Bank error in recording a $2,575 deposit as $2,755

Identify reconciling items that require journal entries.
(SO 6) C

BE7–9 Referring to BE7–8, indicate (a) the items that will result in an adjustment to the company's records, and (b) why the other items do not require an adjustment.

Analyze outstanding cheques.
(SO 6) AP

BE7–10 In the month of November, Johal Company wrote and recorded cheques in the amount of $9,520. In December, it wrote and recorded cheques in the amount of $12,617. Of these cheques, $8,677 of them were paid by the bank in November, and $10,949 in December. What is the amount for outstanding cheques at the end of November? At the end of December?

Prepare bank reconciliation.
(SO 6) AP

BE7–11 On July 31, Manuliak Company had an unadjusted cash balance of $9,100. An examination of the July bank statement shows a balance of $7,920 on July 31; bank service charges $35; deposits in transit $2,152; interest earned $25; outstanding cheques $1,144; and an NSF cheque of $162. Prepare a bank reconciliation at July 31.

Prepare entries from bank reconciliation.
(SO 6) AP

BE7–12 Refer to the bank reconciliation prepared in BE7–11. Prepare the adjusting journal entries for Manuliak Company on July 31.

Calculate cash and cash equivalents.
(SO 7) AP

BE7–13 Sirois Company owns the following assets at the balance sheet date:

Cash in bank—savings account	$ 6,000
Cash on hand	850
Cash refund due from the Canada Revenue Agency	1,000
Cash in bank—chequing account	12,000
Postage stamps	250
Postdated cheques from customers	500
Treasury bill	2,500

What amount should be reported as cash and cash equivalents in the balance sheet?

Explain statement presentation of cash balances.
(SO 7) C

BE7–14 Dupré Company has the following items: cash in bank $17,500; payroll bank account $6,000; store cash floats $1,500; short-term, highly liquid investments with maturity dates of less than 90 days $15,000; and Plant Expansion Fund Cash $25,000. Dupré maintains a $5,000 compensating bank balance in a separate account. Explain how each balance should be reported on the balance sheet.

Exercises

Identify internal control strengths and weaknesses.
(SO 1) C

E7–1 The following situations suggest either a strength or a weakness in internal control:

1. At McGuigan's, Jill and John work alternate lunch hours. Normally Jill works the cash register at the checkout counter, but during her lunch hour John takes her place. They both use the same cash drawer and count cash together at the end of the day.
2. Guiller is a very hard-working employee at Ivo's. Guiller does such a good job that he is responsible for most of the company's office and accounting tasks. The only thing the owner has to do is sign cheques.

3. At Stangland's, they are very concerned about running an efficient, low-cost business. Consequently, the manager has eliminated the need to prepare purchase orders and receiving reports.

4. At Lemur Lumber Yard, most of the lumber is stored in a fenced outdoor storage area. One of the employees noticed a place where the fence needed to be repaired and reported this to the manager. The fence was fixed before the close of business that night.

5. The internal auditors at Koszegi Co. regularly report their findings to senior management, who get the accounting department to investigate and resolve any problems.

6. All employees at St. Barnabas' Music take vacation every year, and during that time their duties are assigned to another individual.

Instructions

(a) State whether each situation above is a strength or a weakness in internal control.

(b) For each weakness, suggest an improvement.

E7–2 The following control procedures are used in Sheridan Company for over-the-counter cash receipts:

> Identify weaknesses in internal control over cash receipts, and suggest improvements.
> (SO 2) C

1. Cashiers are experienced, so they are not bonded.

2. All over-the-counter receipts are received by one of three clerks who share a cash register with a single cash drawer.

3. To minimize the risk of robbery, when there is more than $100 in cash it is stored in an unlocked desk drawer in a back room until it is deposited in the bank.

4. At the end of each day, the total receipts are counted by the cashier on duty and reconciled to the cash register total.

5. The company accountant makes the bank deposit and then records the day's receipts.

6. If a customer has exact change and does not want a receipt, the sale is not rung through the cash register.

Instructions

(a) For each procedure, explain the weakness in internal control and identify the control principle that is violated.

(b) For each weakness, suggest a change in procedure that will result in better internal control.

E7–3 Presented below are three independent situations:

> Prepare entries for debit and credit card sales.
> (SO 2) AP

(a) On December 20, 40 customers used debit cards to purchase merchandise for a total of $2,550 from Metal Works. Metal Works pays a $0.75 debit card fee for each transaction. Prepare Metal Works' journal entries for these transactions.

(b) On November 15, Guy Benicoeur uses his Visa Desjardins bank credit card to purchase artwork for $1,300 from Galerie d'art Bégin located in the Marché Bonsecours. Le Mouvement Desjardins charges the gallery a 3% credit card transaction fee. On December 10, Benicoeur receives his Visa bill and pays for this purchase. Prepare Galerie d'art Bégin's journal entries for these transactions.

(c) On April 2, P. Zachos uses her Hudson's Bay credit card to purchase merchandise from The Bay for $1,450. On May 1, Zachos receives her Hudson's Bay credit card bill and pays for this purchase. Prepare Hudson's Bay's journal entries for these transactions.

E7–4 In Abekah Company, cheques are not prenumbered. Cheques can be signed by either the purchasing agent or the controller. Each signer has access to unissued cheques kept in an unlocked file cabinet. The purchasing agent pays all bills for goods purchased for resale. Before making a payment, the purchasing agent determines that the goods have been received and verifies the mathematical accuracy of the vendor's invoice. After payment, the invoice is filed by the vendor, and the purchasing agent records the payment in the cash payments journal. The controller pays all other bills after receiving approval from authorized employees. After payment, the controller stamps all bills PAID, files them by payment date, and records the cheques in the cash payments journal. Abekah Company maintains one chequing account that is reconciled by the controller.

> Identify weaknesses in internal control over cash disbursements, and suggest improvements.
> (SO 3) S
>

Instructions

(a) List the weaknesses in internal control over cash disbursements.

(b) Write a memo that recommends improvements to the company controller.

Record petty cash
transactions.
(SO 4) AP

E7–5 Lang Company uses an imprest petty cash system. The fund was established on March 10 with a balance of $100. On March 25, there were $4 cash and the following petty cash receipts in the petty cash box:

Date	Receipt No.	For	Amount
Mar. 15	1	Miscellaneous expense	$14
17	2	Freight in (assume perpetual inventory system)	29
19	3	Miscellaneous expense	12
21	4	Delivery charges on outgoing freight	38
24	5	Miscellaneous expense	5

Instructions

(a) Record the journal entry on March 10 to establish the petty cash fund.

(b) Record the journal entry on March 25 to reimburse the fund and increase the balance to $125.

(c) Assume that instead of increasing the petty cash fund balance to $125 on March 25, the company decided to decrease it to $75. Record the March 25 journal entry using this assumption.

Record petty cash
transactions.
(SO 4) AP

E7–6 Deschênes Company established a $250 petty cash fund on May 1. On May 31, the fund contained receipts for the following: newspaper advertising $62, coffee supplies $46, drawings by the owner $50, and postage $10. A cheque was prepared to reimburse the fund and reduce the balance in the fund to $200.

Instructions

(a) Record the journal entry on May 1 to establish the fund on May 1.

(b) Record the journal entry on May 31 assuming there was $78 cash in the petty cash box.

(c) Assume instead there was $83 cash in the petty cash box on May 31. Record the May 31 journal entry using this assumption.

Prepare bank reconciliation
and related entries.
(SO 6) AP

E7–7 The following information is for Verwey Company in November:

1. Cash balance per bank, November 30: $8,509
2. Cash balance per books, November 30: $7,005
3. Outstanding cheques, $2,449
4. Bank service charge, $24
5. NSF cheque from customer, $319.
6. Deposits in transit, $1,575
7. EFT receipts from customers in payment of their accounts, $883
8. Cheque #373 was correctly written and posted by the bank as $672. Verwey Company had recorded the cheque as $762 in error. The cheque was written for the purchase of office supplies.

Instructions

(a) Prepare a bank reconciliation at November 30, 2008.

(b) Journalize the adjusting entries at November 30, 2008, on Verwey Company's books.

Determine deposits in transit
and other reconciling items.
(SO 6) AP

E7–8 On April 30, the bank reconciliation of Hidden Valley Company shows a deposit in transit of $1,437. The May bank statement and the general ledger Cash account in May show the following:

HIDDEN VALLEY COMPANY Bank Statement (partial) Deposits/Credits		
Date	Description	Amount
May 2	Deposit	$1,437
10	Deposit	2,255
16	Deposit	3,218
20	Deposit	945
24	Deposit	1,298
30	EFT	849
31	Interest Earned	32

HIDDEN VALLEY COMPANY Cash Account (partial) Deposits Made	
Date	Amount
May 6	$2,255
13	3,218
20	954
23	1,298
31	1,353

Additional information:

1. The bank did not make any errors in May.
2. EFT is an electronic on-line payment from a customer.

Instructions

(a) List the deposits in transit at May 31.
(b) List any other items that must be included in the bank reconciliation. Describe the impact of each item on the bank reconciliation.

E7–9   On April 30, the bank reconciliation of Hidden Valley Company shows three outstanding cheques: No. 254 for $560; No. 255 for $262; and No. 257 for $410. The May bank statement and the general ledger Cash account in May show the following:

Determine outstanding cheques and other reconciling items.
(SO 6) AP

HIDDEN VALLEY COMPANY Bank Statement (partial) Cheques Paid/Debits		
Date	Cheque No.	Amount
May 2	254	$560
4	258	159
12	257	410
17	259	275
20	260	50
26	NSF	395
29	263	440
30	262	750
31	SC	54

HIDDEN VALLEY COMPANY Cash Account (partial) Cheques Written		
Date	Cheque No.	Amount
May 2	258	$159
5	259	275
10	260	500
15	261	867
22	262	750
24	263	440
29	264	650

Additional information:

1. The bank did not make any errors in May.
2. NSF is a customer's cheque that is returned because the customer did not have sufficient funds.
3. SC stands for service charge.

Instructions

(a) List the outstanding cheques at May 31.
(b) List any other items that must be included in the bank reconciliation. Describe the impact of each item on the bank reconciliation.

E7–10   Refer to the data presented in E7–8 and E7–9. On May 31, Hidden Valley Company had an unadjusted Cash balance of $6,365 in the general ledger. The bank statement showed a balance of $7,664 on May 31.

Prepare bank reconciliation and related entries.
(SO 6) AP

Instructions

(a) Prepare a bank reconciliation for Hidden Valley Company on May 31.
(b) Prepare the necessary journal entries to bring the Cash account to its adjusted balance on May 31. Assume that all deposits were for recording the collection of accounts receivable, and any cheques that were written were for paying accounts payable.

Calculate deposits in transit and outstanding cheques for two months.
(SO 6) AP

E7–11 The cash records of Shigahiro Company show the following:

Deposits in transit

1. The June 30 bank reconciliation indicated that deposits in transit totalled $1,050. In July, the general ledger Cash account showed deposits of $15,750, but the bank statement indicated that $15,820 of deposits were received in the month.
2. In August, deposits per bank statement totalled $23,500 and deposits per books totalled $22,900.

Outstanding cheques

1. The June 30 bank reconciliation reported outstanding cheques of $970. In the month of July, Shigahiro Company's books showed that cheques worth $17,200 were issued. The bank statement also showed that $16,660 of cheques cleared the bank in July.
2. In August, cash disbursements per books were $21,700 and cheques clearing the bank totalled $22,250.

Instructions

(a) What was the amount of deposits in transit at July 31? At August 31?
(b) What was the amount of outstanding cheques at July 31? At August 31?

Prepare bank reconciliation and related entries.
(SO 6) AP

E7–12 The following information relates to Sharaf Company:

SHARAF COMPANY
Bank Reconciliation
August 31, 2008

Cash balance per bank	$20,860
Add: Deposits in transit	3,370
	24,230
Less: Outstanding cheques	6,880
Adjusted cash balance per bank	$17,350

Additional information:

1. The September bank statement shows the following memoranda:

Debit Memoranda		Credit Memoranda	
NSF cheque: J. Hower	$410	EFT collections	$1,825
Bank service charge	30	Interest earned	45

2. In September, $65,787 of cheques cleared the bank.
3. In September, the company wrote and recorded cheques totalling $63,746.
4. In September, deposits per bank statement (excluding credit memoranda) were $62,789.
5. In September, the company recorded deposits totalling $64,329.

Instructions

(a) Calculate the unadjusted balance in the Cash account on September 30.
(b) Calculate the unadjusted balance in the bank account on September 30.
(c) Calculate the deposits in transit at September 30.
(d) Calculate the outstanding cheques at September 30.
(e) Calculate the adjusted bank balance at September 30.
(f) Calculate the adjusted cash balance at September 30.

E7–13 A new accountant at La Maison is trying to identify which of the following amounts should be reported as the current asset "Cash and Cash Equivalents" in the year-end balance sheet, as at April 30, 2008:

Calculate cash and cash equivalents and report other items.
(SO 7) AP

1. Currency and coin totalling $87 in a locked box used for petty cash transactions
2. A $10,000 guaranteed investment certificate, due May 31, 2008
3. April-dated cheques worth $300 that La Maison has received from customers but not yet deposited
4. An $85 cheque received from a customer in payment of her April account, but postdated May 1
5. A balance of $2,575 in the Royal Bank chequing account
6. A balance of $4,000 in the Royal Bank savings account
7. Prepaid postage of $75 in the postage meter
8. A $100 IOU from the company receptionist
9. Cash register floats of $250.
10. Over-the-counter cash receipts for April 30 consisting of $550 of currency and coin, $185 of cheques from customers, $685 of debit card slips, and $755 of bank credit card slips. These amounts were processed by the bank and posted to the bank account on May 1.

Instructions

(a) What amount should La Maison report as its "Cash and Cash Equivalents" balance at April 30, 2008?
(b) In which financial statement and in which account should the items not included as "Cash and Cash Equivalents" be reported?

Problems: Set A

P7–1A The board of trustees of a local church is concerned about the internal controls of its offering collections made at weekly services and has asked for your help. At a meeting of the board of trustees, you learn the following:

Identify internal control weaknesses over cash receipts.
(SO1, 2) C

1. The church's board of trustees has made the finance committee responsible for the financial management and audit of the financial records. This group prepares the annual budget and approves major disbursements but is not involved in collections or record keeping. No audit has been done in recent years, because the same trusted employee has kept church records and served as financial secretary for 15 years. The church does not carry any fidelity insurance.
2. The collection at the weekly service is taken by a team of ushers who volunteer to serve for one month. The ushers take the collection plates to a basement office at the rear of the church. They hand their plates to the head usher and return to the church service. After all plates have been turned in, the head usher counts the cash collected in them. The head usher then places the cash in the unlocked church safe and includes a note that states the amount counted. The head usher volunteers to serve for three months.
3. The next morning, the financial secretary opens the safe and recounts the collection. The secretary withholds from $150 to $200 in cash, depending on the cash expenditures expected for the week, and deposits the remainder of the collections in the bank. To make the deposit easier, church members who contribute by cheque are asked to make their cheques payable to Cash.
4. Each month, the financial secretary reconciles the bank statement and submits a copy of the reconciliation to the board of trustees. The reconciliations have rarely contained any bank errors and have never shown any errors per books.

Instructions

(a) Indicate the weaknesses in internal control in the handling of collections.
(b) List the improvements in internal control procedures that you plan to recommend at the next meeting of the audit team for (1) the ushers, (2) the head usher, (3) the financial secretary, and (4) the finance committee.

Identify internal controls over cash disbursements.
(SO 1, 3) C

P7–2A Segal Office Supply Company recently changed its system of internal control over cash disbursements. The system includes the following features:

1. All cheques are prenumbered and written with an electronic cheque-writing system.
2. Before a cheque can be issued, each invoice must have the approval of Cindy Moonti, the purchasing agent, and Ian Methven, the receiving department supervisor.
3. Cheques must be signed by either Frank Kepros, the controller, or Mary Arno, the assistant controller. Before signing a cheque, the signer is expected to compare the amount of the cheque with the amount on the invoice.
4. After signing a cheque, the signer stamps the invoice PAID and writes, in the stamp, the date, cheque number, and amount of the cheque. The paid invoice is then sent to the accounting department for recording.
5. Blank cheques are stored in a safe in the controller's office. The combination to the safe is known only by the controller and the assistant controller.
6. Each month, the bank statement is reconciled by the assistant chief accountant.

Instructions

Identify the control activities and how they apply to the cash disbursements for Segal Office Supply Company.

Identify internal controls for cash receipts and cash disbursements.
(SO 1, 2, 3) C

P7–3A Each of the following independent situations has an internal control weakness:

1. Rowena's Cleaning Service provides home cleaning services for a large number of clients who all pay cash. Rowena collects the cash and keeps it in the glove compartment of her car until the end of the week when she has time to count it and prepare a bank deposit.
2. Hornet's Convenience Store sells a variety of items including cigarettes, non-alcoholic beverages, and snack foods. A long-term employee is responsible for ordering all merchandise, checking all deliveries, and approving invoices for payment.
3. At Good 4 U Ice Cream Shoppe, there are three sales clerks on duty during busy times. All three of them use the same cash drawer.
4. Most customers at Never Better Used Car dealership use the option to pay for their vehicles in 24 equal payments over two years. These customers send the company cheques or cash each month. The office manager opens the mail each day, makes a bank deposit with the cheques received in the mail that day, and prepares and posts an entry in the accounting records.
5. Laser Labels manufactures blank labels for use in laser printers. Larry Lemur is the custodian of the company's $500 petty cash fund. The fund is replenished every week. Frequently people do not have a receipt for their expenses—because of things like parking meter expenses. In this case, Larry just creates a receipt for that person and gives them their cash. Larry has been with the company for 15 years and is good friends with many of the employees. Larry is very hard-working and never takes a vacation.

Instructions

(a) Identify the internal control weakness or weaknesses in each situation.
(b) Explain the problems that could occur as a result of these weaknesses.
(c) Make recommendations for correcting each situation.

Record debit and bank credit card and petty cash transactions and identify internal controls.
(SO 2, 3, 4) AP

P7–4A Gamba & Company recently made some changes to its operating procedures. As of June 1, 2008, the company started allowing customers to use debit and bank credit cards for purchases of merchandise. Previously it had accepted only cash or personal cheques from customers. Gamba's bank charges $0.50 for every debit card transaction and 2.75% for credit card transactions.

On June 1, the company also established a petty cash fund. Before creating the petty cash fund, cash was taken from the cash register whenever someone needed cash to pay for a small expense.

The following transactions happened in the first two weeks of June:

June 1 Established the petty cash fund by cashing a cheque for $150.
     8 Total sales for the week were $15,750. Customers paid for these purchases as follows: $5,075 in cash and personal cheques; $4,275 on debit cards (52 transactions); and the balance using bank credit cards.

June 8 Replenished the petty cash fund. On this date, the fund consisted of $9
         in cash and the following petty cash receipts:

Delivery of merchandise to a customer	$42
Postage	28
Advertising in local paper	57
Miscellaneous expense	10

  15 Total sales for the week were $18,200. Customers paid for these pur-
      chases as follows: $4,267 in cash and personal cheques; $5,933 on debit
      cards (78 transactions); and the balance using bank credit cards.
  15 Replenished the petty cash fund and increased the balance to $250. On
      this date, the fund consisted of $4 in cash and the following petty cash receipts:

B. Gamba's personal withdrawal	$50
Office supplies	77
Coffee supplies	20

Instructions

(a) Record the transactions.
(b) What are the advantages and disadvantages of accepting debit and bank credit card transactions
    as opposed to accepting only cash and personal cheques from customers? Consider both the
    internal control and business reasons.
(c) What are the benefits of having a petty cash fund instead of paying small expenses from the
    cash register receipts? What policies and procedures should Gamba follow to ensure there is
    good internal control over its petty cash fund?

P7–5A Vickers Company maintains a petty cash fund for small expenditures. The following transactions happened over a two-month period:

Record and post petty cash transactions and identify internal controls.
(SO 3, 4) AP

Jan. 2 Established the petty cash fund by writing a cheque on First Bank for $200.
     15 Replenished the petty cash fund. On this date, the fund consisted of $13 in cash and the
         following petty cash receipts: freight out $84, postage expense $42, office supplies expense
         $47, and miscellaneous expense $12.
     31 Replenished the petty cash fund. On this date, the fund consisted of $5 in cash and the
         following petty cash receipts: freight out $86, charitable contributions expense $40, post-
         age expense $28, and miscellaneous expense $44.
Feb. 1 Increased the amount of the petty cash fund to $300.
     15 Replenished the petty cash fund. On this date, the fund consisted of $58 in cash and the
         following petty cash receipts: freight out $36, entertainment expense $53, postage expense
         $33, freight in $60 (assume perpetual inventory system), and miscellaneous expense $54.
     28 Replenished the petty cash fund and reduced the balance to $250. On this date, the fund
         consisted of $63 in cash and the following petty cash receipts: postage expense $95, travel
         expense $46, freight out $44, and office supplies expense $57.

Instructions

(a) Journalize the petty cash transactions.
(b) Post to the Petty Cash account.
(c) It was stated in the chapter that "internal control over cash disbursements is better when payments
    are made by cheque." Why, then, are some payments made from petty cash rather than by cheque?
    Does this mean that there is no internal control over payments from petty cash? Explain.

P7–6A The Agricultural Genetics Company's Cash account in its general ledger reported a balance of $9,448 on May 31, 2008. The company's bank statement from Western Bank reported a
balance of $11,689 on the same date.

Prepare bank reconciliation and related entries.
(SO 6) AP

   A comparison of the details in the bank statement to the details in the Cash account revealed
the following facts:

1. The bank statement included a debit memo of $50 for bank service charges.
2. Cash sales of $638 on May 12 were deposited in the bank. The journal entry to record the cash sales and the deposit slip to deposit the cash were correctly made out for $638. The bank credited Agricultural Genetics Company for $386.
3. The April 30 deposit of $2,190 was included on the May bank statement. The deposit had been placed in the bank's night deposit vault on April 30.
4. The May 31 deposit of $1,141 was not included on the May bank statement. The deposit had been placed in the bank's night deposit vault on May 31.
5. Cheques #928 for $233 and #1014 for $689 were outstanding on April 30. Of these, #1014 cleared the bank in May. All of the cheques written in May except for #1127 for $732, #1195 for $813, and #1196 for $401 had cleared the bank by May 31.
6. On May 18, the company issued cheque #1151 for $585 to L. Kingston, on account. The cheque, which cleared the bank in May, was incorrectly journalized and posted by Agricultural Genetics Company for $855.
7. On May 28, the company issued cheque #1192 for $1,738 to Bow Graphics for computer equipment. The cheque was incorrectly recorded by Agricultural Genetics as $1,387. The cheque cleared the bank on May 30.
8. A review of the bank statement revealed that Agricultural Genetics Company received $2,382 of electronic payments from customers on account in May. The bank had also credited the company's account with $24 of interest revenue on May 31. Agricultural Genetics Company had no previous notice of these amounts.
9. On May 31, the bank statement showed an NSF charge of $820 for a cheque issued by Pete Dell, a customer, to Agricultural Genetics Company on account. This amount included a $15 service charge by the bank.

Instructions

(a) Prepare the bank reconciliation at May 31.
(b) Prepare the necessary adjusting entries at May 31.

Prepare bank reconciliation and related entries.
(SO 6) AP

P7–7A The bank portion of the bank reconciliation for Huang Company at November 30, 2008, was as follows:

HUANG COMPANY Bank Reconciliation November 30, 2008		
Cash balance per bank		$14,368
Add: Deposits in transit		2,530
		16,898
Less: Outstanding cheques		
#3451	$2,260	
#3470	1,100	
#3471	845	
#3472	1,427	
#3474	1,050	6,682
Adjusted cash balance per bank		$10,216

The adjusted cash balance per bank agreed with the cash balance per books at November 30. The December bank statement showed the following:

	Cheques and Other Debits		Deposits	
Date	Number	Amount	Amount	Balance
Nov. 30				$14,368
Dec. 1	3451	$2,260	$2,530	14,638
2	3471	845		13,793
4	3475	1,641	1,212	13,364
7	3472	1,427		11,937
8	3476	1,300	2,365	13,002
10	3477	2,130		10,872
15	3479	3,080	3,145	10,937
16			2,673	13,610
21			2,945	16,555
26	NSF	1,027	2,567	18,095
27	3480	600		17,495
29	3483	1,140	2,836	19,191
30	3482	475	1,025	19,741
31	3485	541		19,200
31	SC	45		19,155

HUANG COMPANY
Bank Statement
December 31, 2008

Additional information:

1. The deposit of $3,145 on December 15 is an electronic transfer from a customer in payment of its account. The amount includes $65 of interest, which Huang Company had not previously accrued.
2. The NSF for $1,027 is for a $1,012 cheque from a customer, Hilo Holdings, in payment of its account, plus a $15 processing fee.
3. SC represents bank service charges for the month.

The bank did not make any errors, but errors were made by Huang Company. The cash records per the company's books for December showed the following:

Cash Payments							Cash Receipts	
Date	Number	Amount	Date	Number	Amount		Date	Amount
Dec. 1	3475	$1,641	23	3484	1,274		Dec. 3	$ 1,212
2	3476	1,300	24	3485	441		7	2,365
2	3477	2,130	30	3486	1,390		15	2,673
3	3478	538	Total		$14,816		20	2,954
8	3479	3,080					25	2,567
10	3480	600					28	2,836
17	3481	807					30	1,025
20	3482	475					31	1,198
22	3483	1,140					Total	$16,830

Instructions

(a) Determine the unadjusted cash balance per books as at December 31 before reconciliation.
(b) Prepare a bank reconciliation at December 31.
(c) Prepare the necessary adjusting entries at December 31. (*Note:* The correction of any errors in the recording of cheques should be made to Accounts Payable. The correction of any errors in the recording of cash receipts should be made to Accounts Receivable.)

P7–8A   You are given the following information for River Adventures Company:

RIVER ADVENTURES COMPANY
Bank Reconciliation
April 30, 2008

Cash balance per bank		$9,009
Add: Deposits in transit		846
		9,855
Less: Outstanding cheques		
#526	$1,358	
#533	279	
#541	363	
#555	79	2,079
Adjusted cash balance per bank		$7,776

The adjusted cash balance per bank agreed with the cash balance per books at April 30, 2008. The May bank statement showed the following:

RIVER ADVENTURES COMPANY
Bank Statement
May 31, 2008

| Date | Cheques and Other Debits | | Deposits | |
	Number	Amount	Amount	Balance
Apr. 30				$9,009
May 3	526	$1,358	$ 846	8,497
4	541	363		8,134
6	556	223		7,911
6	557	1,800	1,250	7,361
10			980	8,341
10	559	1,650		6,691
13			426	7,117
13			1,650	8,767
14	561	799		7,968
18	562	2,045		5,923
18			222	6,145
19	563	2,487		3,658
21	564	603		3,055
25	565	1,033		2,022
26			980	3,002
28	NSF	440	1,771	4,333
31	SC	25		4,308

Additional information from the bank statement:

1. The deposit of $1,650 on May 13 is an electronic transfer from a customer in payment of its account. The amount includes $35 of interest, which River Adventures Company had not previously accrued.
2. The NSF for $440 is for a $425 cheque from a customer, Ralph King, in payment of his account, plus a $15 processing fee.
3. SC represents bank service charges for the month.

4. The bank made an error when processing cheque #564. The company also made two errors in the month. All cheques were written to pay accounts payable; all cash receipts were collections of accounts receivable.

The company's cash payments and cash receipts for the month were as follows:

Cash Receipts	
Date	Amount
May 5	$1,250
8	980
12	426
18	222
25	890
28	1,771
31	1,286
Total	$6,825

Cash Payments		
Date	Cheque No.	Amount
May 4	556	$ 223
5	557	1,800
7	558	943
7	559	1,650
8	560	890
10	561	799
15	562	2,045
18	563	2,887
20	564	306
25	565	1,033
31	566	950
Total		$13,526

Instructions

(a) Calculate the unadjusted cash balance in River Adventures' general ledger at May 31.
(b) Prepare a bank reconciliation and the necessary adjusting journal entries at May 31.

P7–9A   When the accountant of Haworth's Marine Centre prepared the bank reconciliation on September 30, 2008, there were three outstanding cheques: #387 for $628, #390 for $553, and #391 for $159. There was a $1,084 deposit in transit as at September 30, 2008. The bank balance at September 30 was $6,469. The following is selected information from the October bank statement:

Prepare bank reconciliation and related entries.
(SO 6) AP

Cheques Cleared				Other Bank Account Transactions		
Date	Cheque No.	Amount		Date	Amount	Transaction
Oct. 1	387	$ 628		Oct. 1	$1,084 +	Deposit
8	406	642		8	2,267 +	Deposit
20	407	150		12	3,818 +	Deposit
22	409	1,848		24	4,410 +	Deposit
22	390	553		25	790 −	NSF cheque
23	405	3,115		31	43 −	Service charge
31	410	317		31	27 +	Interest

The NSF cheque was originally received from a customer, Y. Fujii, in payment of her account of $760. The bank included a $30 service charge for a total of $790.
    Information from the company's accounting records follows:

Cash Receipts			Cash Payments			
Date	Amount		Date	Cheque No.	Amount	
Oct. 5	$2,267		Oct. 5	405	$3,115	
12	3,118		5	406	642	
23	4,410		19	407	150	
31	1,941		19	408	3,266	
			19	409	1,448	
			31	410	317	
			31	411	1,984	

Investigation reveals that cheque #409 was issued to buy office equipment. All deposits are for collections of accounts receivable. The bank made no errors.

Instructions

(a) Calculate the balance per bank statement at October 31 and the unadjusted cash balance per company records at October 31.

(b) Prepare a bank reconciliation for Haworth's Marine Centre at October 31.

(c) Prepare the necessary adjusting entries at October 31.

(d) What balance would Haworth's Marine Centre report as cash in the current assets section of its balance sheet on October 31, 2008?

Prepare bank reconciliation and identify internal controls.
(SO 2, 3, 6) AN

P7–10A Your newly hired assistant prepared the following bank reconciliation:

CAREFREE COMPANY
Bank Reconciliation[1]
March 31, 2008

Book Balance		$3,125	Bank Balance			$7,350
Add: Deposit in transit	$ 750		Add: Error re: cheque #173			45[4]
EFT receipt from customer	2,645					7,395
Interest earned	15	3,410	Deduct: Pre-authorized payments			
		6,535	Hydro[5]	$ 120		
Deduct: Error re: Careless Company's			Telephone[5]	85		
deposit to our account	$1,100[2]		NSF cheque	220		
Bank service charge	55[3]	1,155	Outstanding cheques	1,650	2,075	
Adjusted book balance		$5,380	Adjusted bank balance			$5,320

Notes:

[1] Your assistant did not know why there is a $60 difference between the adjusted book balance and the adjusted bank balance.

[2] The bank credited Carefree's account for a deposit made by Careless Company. Carefree and Careless are unrelated parties.

[3] Of the bank service charge, $15 was due to the NSF cheque.

[4] Carefree's cheque #173 was made for the proper amount of $249 in payment of an account payable; however, it was entered in the cash payments journal as $294.

[5] Carefree authorized the bank to automatically pay its hydro and telephone bills as they are directly submitted to the bank by the hydro and telephone companies. These amounts have not yet been recorded by Carefree.

Instructions

(a) Prepare a correct bank reconciliation at March 31.

(b) Prepare the necessary adjusting entries at March 31.

(c) Explain how the bank reconciliation process can strengthen internal control.

Calculate cash balance.
(SO 7) AP

P7–11A A new CGA student has been asked to determine the balance that should be reported as cash and cash equivalents as at December 31, 2008, for one of the firm's clients. The following information is available:

1. Cash on hand in the cash registers on December 31 totals $1,600. Of this amount, $500 is kept on hand as a cash float.
2. The petty cash fund has an imprest amount of $200. Actual petty cash on hand at December 31 is $43. Paid-out receipts total $155. Of these receipts, $100 is in IOUs from company employees.
3. The balance in the bank chequing account at December 31 is $7,460.
4. Short-term investments include $5,000 in a BMO money-market fund and an investment of $2,500 in a six-month term deposit.
5. The company sold $250 of merchandise to a customer late in the day on December 31. The customer had forgotten her wallet and promised to pay the amount on January 1.
6. The company had a U.S. dollar bank account. At December 31, its U.S. funds were worth the equivalent of $2,241 Canadian.
7. At December 31, the company has American Express credit card slips totalling $500. American Express charges the company a credit card fee of 4%. It normally takes two days for American Express charges to clear the banking system and be deposited in the company's bank account.
8. The company received $500 of cash on December 31 as an advance deposit in trust on a property sale.
9. In order to hook up utilities, the company is required to deposit $1,000 in trust with Ontario Hydro. This amount must remain on deposit until a satisfactory credit history has been established. The company expects to have this deposit back within the year.

Instructions

(a) Calculate the balance for cash and cash equivalents that should be reported on the year-end balance sheet as a current asset.
(b) Identify where any items that were not reported in the balance for cash and cash equivalents in (a) should be reported.

Problems: Set B

P7–1B Red River Theatre's cashier's booth is located near the entrance to the theatre. Two cashiers are employed. One works from 1:00 p.m. to 5:00 p.m., the other from 5:00 p.m. to 9:00 p.m. Each cashier is bonded. The cashiers receive cash from customers and operate a machine that ejects serially numbered tickets. The rolls of tickets are inserted and locked into the machine by the theatre manager at the beginning of each cashier's shift.

Identify internal control activities related to cash receipts.
(SO 1, 2) C

After purchasing a ticket, which may be at different prices depending on the age group, the customer takes the ticket to an usher stationed at the entrance of the theatre lobby, about 10 metres from the cashier's booth. The usher tears the ticket in half, admits the customer, and returns the ticket stub to the customer. The other half of the ticket is dropped into a locked box by the usher.

At the end of each cashier's shift, the theatre manager removes the ticket rolls from the machine and makes a cash count. The cash count sheet is initialled by the cashier. At the end of the day, the manager deposits the receipts in total in a bank night deposit vault located in the mall. The manager also sends copies of the deposit slip and the initialled cash count sheets to the theatre company controller for verification, and to the company's accounting department. Receipts from the first shift are stored in a safe located in the manager's office.

Instructions

(a) Identify the internal control activities and how they apply to the cash receipts transactions of Red River Theatre.
(b) If the usher and the cashier decide to collaborate to steal cash, how might they do this?

P7–2B Cedar Grove Middle School wants to raise money for a new sound system for its auditorium. The main fundraising event is a dance at which the famous disc jockey Obnoxious Al will play hip-hop, R&B, old school, slow jam, and techno music. Roger DeMaster, the music teacher, has been

Identify internal control weaknesses over cash receipts and cash disbursements.
(SO 1, 2, 3) C

given the responsibility for coordinating the fundraising efforts. This is Roger's first experience with fundraising. He asks the Student Representative Council (SRC) to help him with the event.

Roger had 500 unnumbered tickets printed for the dance. He left the tickets in a box on his desk and told the SRC students to take as many tickets as they thought they could sell for $5 each. In order to ensure that no extra tickets would be floating around, he told them to get rid of any unsold tickets. He also told the students to bring him any cash that they received in payment for the tickets. He would then put it in a locked box in his desk drawer.

Some of the students were responsible for decorating the gymnasium for the dance. Roger gave each of them a key to the cash box. He told them that if they took money out to buy materials, they should put a note in the box saying how much they took and what it was used for. After two weeks, the cash box appeared to be getting full so Roger asked Freda Stevens to count the money, prepare a deposit slip, and deposit the money in a bank account Roger had opened.

The day of the dance, Roger wrote a cheque from the account to pay Obnoxious Al. Al said that he accepted only cash and did not give receipts. So Roger took $200 out of the cash box and gave it to Al. At the dance, Roger had Sara Billings working at the entrance to the gymnasium. She collected tickets from students and sold tickets to those who had not prepurchased them. Roger estimated 400 students attended the dance.

The following day Roger closed out the bank account, which had $250 in it. He gave that amount plus the $180 in the cash box to Principal Skinner. Principal Skinner seemed surprised that, after generating roughly $2,000 in sales, the dance netted only $430 in cash. Roger did not know how to respond.

Instructions

Identify as many internal control weaknesses as you can in this scenario. Suggest how each weakness could be corrected.

Identify internal controls for cash receipts and cash disbursements.
(SO 1, 2, 3) C

P7–3B Each of the following independent situations has one or more internal control weaknesses:

1. Board Riders is a small snowboarding club that offers specialized coaching for teenagers who want to improve their skills. Group lessons are offered every day. Members who want a lesson pay a $15 fee directly to the teacher at the start of the lesson that day. Most members pay cash. At the end of the lesson, the teacher reports the number of students and turns over the cash to the office manager.

2. Coloroso Agency offers parenting advice to young single mothers. Most of the agency's revenues are from government grants. The general manager is responsible for all of the accounting work, including approving invoices for payment, preparing and posting all entries into the accounting system, and preparing bank reconciliations.

3. At Nexus Company, each sales person is responsible for deciding on the correct credit policies for his or her customers. For example, the salesperson decides if Nexus should sell to the customer on credit and how high the credit limit should be. Salespeople receive a commission based on their sales.

4. Algorithm Company is a software company that employs many computer programmers. The company uses accounting software that was created by one of the employees. In order to be more flexible and share the workload, all of the programmers have access to the accounting software program in case changes are needed.

5. The warehouse manager at Orange Wing distributors is well known for running an efficient cost-saving operation. He has eliminated the requirement for staff to create receiving reports and purchase orders because it was taking staff too long to prepare them.

Instructions

(a) Identify the internal control weakness or weaknesses in each situation.
(b) Explain the problems that could occur as a result of these weaknesses.
(c) Make recommendations for correcting each situation.

P7–4B   Rossi & Company recently made some changes to its operating procedures. As of April 1, 2008, the company started allowing customers to use debit and bank credit cards for purchases of merchandise. Previously, it accepted only cash or personal cheques from customers. Rossi's bank charges $0.75 for every debit card transaction and 3.25% for bank credit card transactions.

Record debit and bank credit card and petty cash transactions and identify internal controls.
(SO 2, 3, 4) AP

   On April 1, the company also established a petty cash fund. Before creating the petty cash fund, cash was taken from the cash register whenever someone needed cash to pay for a small expense.

   The following transactions happened in the first two weeks of April:

Apr. 1 Established the petty cash fund by cashing a cheque for $200.

   8 Total sales for the week were $31,500. Customers paid for these purchases as follows: $10,150 in cash and personal cheques; $8,550 on debit cards (116 transactions); and the balance using bank credit cards.

   8 Replenished the petty cash fund. On this date, the fund consisted of $56 in cash and the following petty cash receipts:

Freight out	$44
Office supplies	34
Advertising in local paper	50
Personal withdrawal by owner	20

   15 Total sales for the week were $36,400. Customers paid for these purchases as follows: $8,534 in cash and personal cheques; $11,866 on debit cards (160 transactions); and the balance using bank credit cards.

   15 Replenished the petty cash fund and decreased the balance to $175. On this date, the fund consisted of $55 in cash and the following petty cash receipts:

Postage	$53
Advertising in local newspaper	39
Cleaning supplies	48

Instructions

(a) Record the transactions.

(b) What are the advantages and disadvantages of accepting debit and bank credit card transactions as opposed to accepting only cash and personal cheques from customers? Consider both the internal control and business reasons.

(c) What are the benefits of having a petty cash fund instead of paying small expenses from the cash register receipts? What policies and procedures should Rossi follow to ensure there is good internal control over its petty cash fund?

P7–5B   MTR Company maintains a petty cash fund for small expenditures. The following transactions happened over a two-month period:

Record and post petty cash transactions and identify internal controls.
(SO 3, 4) AP

July 1 Established a petty cash fund by writing a cheque on its bank account for $250.

   15 Replenished the petty cash fund. On this date, the fund had $12 in cash and the following petty cash receipts: freight out $94, postage expense $42, entertainment expense $47, and miscellaneous expense $51.

   31 Replenished the petty cash fund. On this date, the fund had $10 in cash and the following petty cash receipts: freight out $82, charitable contributions expense $50, postage expense $68, and miscellaneous expense $42.

Aug. 1 Increased the amount of the petty cash fund to $350.

   15 Replenished the petty cash fund. On this date, the fund had $57 in cash and the following petty cash receipts: freight out $90, entertainment expense $77, postage expense $63, and supplies expense $59.

   31 Replenished the petty cash fund and reduced the balance to $300. On this date, the fund had $65 in cash and the following petty cash receipts: postage expense $122, entertainment expense $91, and freight out $73.

Instructions

(a) Journalize the petty cash transactions.

(b) Post to the Petty Cash account.

(c) Assume MTR has an August 31 year end. What would have been the impact on the financial statements if the petty cash fund had not been reimbursed on August 31?

Prepare bank reconciliation and related entries.

(SO 6) AP

P7–6B On October 31, 2008, Lisik Company had a cash balance per books of $9,693. The bank statement on that date showed a balance of $10,973. A comparison of the statement with the Cash account revealed the following:

1. The statement included debit memos of $40 for the printing of additional company cheques and $35 for bank service charges.

2. Cash sales of $836 on October 12 were deposited in the bank. The cash receipts journal entry and the deposit slip were incorrectly made out and recorded by Lisik as $856. The bank detected the error on the deposit slip and credited Lisik Company for the correct amount.

3. The September 30 deposit of $990 was included on the October bank statement. The deposit had been placed in the bank's night deposit vault on September 30.

4. The October 31 deposit of $963 was not included on the October bank statement. The deposit had been placed in the bank's night deposit vault on October 31.

5. Cheques #1006 for $330 and #1072 for $1,120 were outstanding on September 30. Of these, #1072 cleared the bank in October. All the cheques written in October except for #1278 for $466, #1284 for $587, and #1285 for $293 had cleared the bank by October 31.

6. On October 18, the company issued cheque #1181 for $685 to Helms & Co., on account. The cheque, which cleared the bank in October, was incorrectly journalized and posted by Lisik Company for $568.

7. A review of the bank statement revealed that Lisik Company received electronic payments from customers on account of $2,055 in October. The bank had also credited the account with $39 of interest revenue on October 31. Lisik had no previous notice of these amounts.

8. Included with the cancelled cheques was a cheque issued by Lasik Company for $600 that was incorrectly charged to Lisik Company by the bank.

9. On October 31, the bank statement showed an NSF charge of $715 for a cheque issued by W. Hoad, a customer, to Lisik Company on account. This amount included a $15 service charge by the bank.

Instructions

(a) Prepare the bank reconciliation at October 31.

(b) Prepare the necessary adjusting entries at October 31.

P7–7B The March bank statement showed the following for Yap Co.:

Prepare bank reconciliation
and related entries.
(SO 6) AP

	YAP CO. Bank Statement March 31, 2008			
	Cheques and Other Debits		Deposits	
Date	Number	Amount	Amount	Balance
Feb. 29				$14,368
Mar. 3	3451	$2,260	$2,530	14,638
4	3471	845		13,793
6	3472	1,427	1,221	13,587
7	3473	1,461		12,126
10	NSF	550		11,576
11	3475	487	1,745	12,834
15	3477	915		11,919
17	3476	838	2,283	13,364
20			1,823	15,187
21	3474	2,130		13,057
26	3478	357	2,567	15,267
31	LN	1,062		14,205
31	3480	1,679		12,526
31	SC	49	IN 23	12,500

Additional information:

1. The bank statement contained three debit memoranda:
   - An NSF cheque of $550 that Yap had deposited was returned due to insufficient funds in the maker's bank account. This cheque was originally given to Yap by Mr. Jordan, a customer, in payment of his account. Yap believes it will be able to collect this amount from Mr. Jordan.
   - A bank loan payment (LN) which included $62 of interest and a $1,000 payment on the principal.
   - A service charge (SC) of $49 for bank services provided throughout the month
2. The bank statement contained one credit memorandum for $23 of interest (IN) earned on the account for the month.
3. The bank made an error processing cheque #3474. No other errors were made by the bank.

Yap's list of cash receipts and cash payments showed the following for March:

Cash Receipts	
Date	Amount
Mar. 5	$ 1,221
10	1,745
14	2,283
20	1,832
25	2,567
31	1,025
Total	$10,673

Cash Payments		
Date	Cheque No.	Amount
Mar. 3	3472	$ 1,427
4	3473	1,641
6	3474	2,330
7	3475	487
13	3476	838
14	3477	915
19	3478	357
21	3479	159
28	3480	1,679
31	3481	862
31	3482	1,126
Total		$11,821

The bank portion of the previous month's bank reconciliation for Yap Co., at February 29, 2008, was as follows:

YAP CO.
Bank Reconciliation
February 29, 2008

Cash balance per bank		$14,368
Add: Deposits in transit		2,530
		16,898
Less: Outstanding cheques		
#3451	$2,260	
#3470	1,535	
#3471	845	4,640
Adjusted cash balance per bank		$12,258

Instructions

(a) What is Yap Co.'s unadjusted cash balance in its general ledger on March 31?

(b) Prepare a bank reconciliation at March 31.

(c) Prepare the necessary adjusting entries at March 31. (*Note:* The correction of any errors in the recording of cheques should be made to Accounts Payable. The correction of any errors in the recording of cash receipts should be made to Accounts Receivable.)

Prepare bank reconciliation and related entries.
(SO 6) AP

P7–8B The bank portion of the bank reconciliation for Maloney Company at October 31, 2008, was as follows:

MALONEY COMPANY
Bank Reconciliation
October 31, 2008

Cash balance per bank		$11,545
Add: Deposits in transit		1,530
		13,075
Less: Outstanding cheques		
#2451	$1,260	
#2470	920	
#2471	845	
#2472	504	
#2474	1,050	4,579
Adjusted cash balance per bank		$ 8,496

The adjusted cash balance per bank agreed with the cash balance per books at October 31. The November bank statement showed the following:

	Cheques and Other Debits		Deposits	
Date	Number	Amount	Amount	Balance
Oct. 31				$11,545
Nov. 1	2470	$ 920	$1,530	12,155
2	2471	845		11,310
4	2475	1,641	1,212	10,881
5	2474	1,050		9,831
8	2476	2,830	990	7,991
10	2477	600		7,391
13			2,575	9,966
15	2479	1,750		8,216
18	2480	1,330	1,473	8,359
21			2,966	11,325
25	NSF	260	2,567	13,632
27	2481	695		12,937
28			1,650	14,587
29	2486	900	EFT 2,479	16,166
30	2483	575	1,186	16,777
30	LN	2,250		14,527

MALONEY COMPANY
Bank Statement
November 30, 2008

Additional information from the bank statement:

1. The EFT of $2,479 is an electronic transfer from a customer in payment of its account. The amount includes $49 of interest which Maloney Company had not previously accrued.
2. The NSF for $260 is a $245 cheque from a customer, Pendray Holdings, in payment of its account, plus a $15 processing fee.
3. The LN is a payment of a note payable with the bank and consists of $250 interest and $2,000 principal.
4. The bank did not make any errors.

The cash records per books for November follow. Two errors were made by Maloney Company.

Cash Payments							Cash Receipts	
Date	Number	Amount	Date	Number	Amount		Date	Amount
Nov. 1	2475	$1,641	Nov. 18	2482	$ 612		Nov. 3	$ 1,212
2	2476	2,380	20	2483	575		7	990
2	2477	600	22	2484	830		12	2,575
4	2478	538	23	2485	975		17	1,473
8	2479	1,750	24	2486	900		20	2,699
10	2480	1,330	30	2487	1,200		24	2,567
15	2481	695	Total		$14,026		27	1,650
							29	1,186
							30	1,338
							Total	$15,690

Instructions

(a) Determine the unadjusted cash balance per books as at November 30, before reconciliation.
(b) Prepare a bank reconciliation at November 30.
(c) Prepare the necessary adjusting entries at November 30. (*Note:* The correction of any errors in the recording of cheques should be made to Accounts Payable. The correction of any errors in the recording of cash receipts should be made to Accounts Receivable.)

Prepare bank reconciliation
and related entries.
(SO 6) AP

P7–9B When the accountant of Kurji's Appliances prepared the bank reconciliation on April 30, 2008, there were three outstanding cheques: #286 for $217, #289 for $326, and #290 for $105. There were no deposits in transit as at April 30, 2008. The bank balance at April 30 was $4,261. The following is selected information from the May bank statement:

Cheques Cleared				Other Bank Account Transactions		
Date	Cheque No.	Amount		Date	Amount	Transaction
May 1	286	$ 217		May 8	$2,620 +	Deposit
8	305	402		12	4,718 +	Deposit
20	306	105		24	3,190 +	Deposit
22	308	1,648		25	280 –	NSF cheque
22	289	326		28	28 –	Service charge
23	304	2,735		31	12 +	Interest
31	309	175				

The NSF cheque was originally received from a customer, M. Rafique, in payment of his account of $265. The bank included a $15 service charge for a total of $280. Information from the company's accounting records follows:

Cash Receipts			Cash Payments		
Date	Amount		Date	Cheque No.	Amount
May 5	$2,260		May 5	304	$2,735
12	4,718		5	305	402
23	3,190		19	306	150
31	1,004		19	307	3,266
			19	308	1,648
			31	309	175
			31	310	2,400

Investigation reveals that cheque #306 was issued to pay the telephone bill. All deposits are for collections of accounts receivable. The bank made no errors.

Instructions

(a) Calculate the balance per bank statement at May 31 and the unadjusted Cash balance per company records at May 31.
(b) Prepare a bank reconciliation at May 31.
(c) Prepare the necessary adjusting entries at May 31.
(d) What balance would Kurji's Appliances report as cash in the current assets section of its balance sheet on May 31, 2008?

Prepare bank reconciliation
and identify internal control
weakness.
(SO 2, 3, 6) AN

P7–10B Aura Whole Foods is a very profitable small business. It has not, however, thought much about internal control. For example, in an attempt to keep clerical and office expenses to a minimum, the company has combined the jobs of cashier and bookkeeper. As a result, K. Kilgora handles all cash receipts, keeps the accounting records, and prepares the monthly bank reconciliations.

The balance per bank statement on October 31, 2008, was $19,460. Outstanding cheques were #762 for $514, #783 for $160, #784 for $267, #862 for $171, #863 for $325, and #864 for $173. Included with the statement was an EFT deposit for $750 on October 25 in payment of an account receivable. This EFT has not been recorded by the company.

The company's ledger showed one cash account, with a balance of $19,641. The balance included undeposited cash on hand. Because of the lack of internal controls, Kilgora took all of the undeposited receipts for personal use. He then prepared the following bank reconciliation to try to hide his theft of cash:

Cash balance per books, October 31		$19,641
Add: Outstanding cheques		
#862	$171	
#863	325	
#864	173	669
		20,210
Less Bank credit memorandum		750
Cash balance per bank statement, October 31		$19,460

Instructions

(a) Prepare a correct bank reconciliation. (*Hint:* The theft is the difference between the adjusted balance per books and per bank.)
(b) Indicate the three ways that Kilgora tried to hide the theft and the dollar amount for each method.
(c) What internal control activities were violated in this case?

P7–11B A first year co-op student is trying to determine the amount of cash that should be reported on a company's balance sheet. The following information was given to the student at year end:

Calculate cash balance.
(SO 7) AP

1. Cash on hand in the cash registers totals $5,000.
2. The balance in the Petty Cash account is $500. At year end, the fund had $125 cash and receipts totalling $375.
3. The balance in the Commercial Bank savings account is $100,000. In the chequing account, the balance is $25,000. The company also has a U.S. bank account, which contained the equivalent of $48,000 Canadian at year end.
4. A special bank account holds $150,000 that is restricted for capital asset replacement.
5. A line of credit of $50,000 is available at the bank on demand.
6. The amount due from employees (travel advances) totals $14,000.
7. Short-term investments held by the company include $32,000 in a money-market fund, $75,000 in treasury bills, and $40,000 in shares of The Forzani Group Ltd. The money-market fund and treasury bills had maturity dates of less than 90 days.
8. The company has a supply of unused postage stamps totalling $150.
9. The company has NSF cheques from customers totalling $1,750 that were returned by the bank.
10. In a special account, the company has $9,250 of cash deposits (advances) paid by customers.

Instructions

(a) Calculate the Cash balance that should be reported on the year end balance sheet as a current asset.
(b) Would your answer for (a) change if the company combines its cash and cash equivalents?
(c) Identify where any items that were not reported in the Cash balance in (a) should be reported.

Continuing Cookie Chronicle

(*Note:* This is a continuation of the Cookie Chronicle from Chapters 1 through 6.)

Part 1

Natalie is struggling to keep up with the recording of her accounting transactions. She is spending a lot of time marketing and selling mixers and giving her cookie classes. Her friend John is an accounting student who runs his own accounting service. He has asked Natalie if she would like to have him do her accounting.

John and Natalie meet and discuss her business. John suggests that he do the following for Natalie:

1. Hold onto cash until there is enough to be deposited. (He would keep the cash locked up in his vehicle). He would also take all of the deposits to the bank at least twice a month.
2. Write and sign all of the cheques.
3. Record all of the deposits in the accounting records.
4. Record all of the cheques in the accounting records.
5. Prepare the monthly bank reconciliation.
6. Transfer all of Natalie's manual accounting records to his computer accounting program. John maintains all of the accounting information that he keeps for his clients on his laptop computer.
7. Prepare monthly financial statements for Natalie to review.
8. Write himself a cheque every month for the work he has done for Natalie.

Instructions

Identify the weaknesses in internal control that you see in the system which John is recommending. Can you suggest any improvements if John is hired to do Natalie's accounting?

Part 2

Natalie decides that she cannot afford to hire John to do her accounting. One way that she can ensure that her Cash account does not have any errors and is accurate and up to date is to prepare a bank reconciliation at the end of each month.

Natalie would like you to help her. She asks you to prepare a bank reconciliation for June 2008 using the following information:

GENERAL LEDGER—COOKIE CREATIONS Cash						
Date	Explanation	Ref.	Debit	Credit	Balance	
2008						
June 1	Balance				2,657	
1				750	3,407	
3	Cheque #600		625		2,782	
3	Cheque #601		95		2,687	
8	Cheque #602		56		2,631	
9				1,050	3,681	
13	Cheque #603		425		3,256	
20				155	3,411	
28	Cheque #604		247		3,164	
28				110	3,274	

Date	Explanation	Cheques and Other Debits	Deposits	Balance
THE CANADA BANK Statement of Account—Cookie Creations June 30, 2008				
May 31	Balance			3,256
June 1	Deposit		750	4,006
6	Cheque #600	625		3,381
6	Cheque #601	95		3,286
8	Cheque #602	56		3,230
9	Deposit		1,050	4,280
10	NSF cheque	100		
10	NSF—fee	35		4,145
14	Cheque #603	452		3,693
20	Deposit		125	3,818
23	EFT—Telus	85		3,733
28	Cheque #599	361		3,372
30	Bank charges	13		3,359

Additional information:

1. On May 31, there were two outstanding cheques: #595 for $238 and #599 for $361.
2. The Canada Bank made a posting error to the bank statement: cheque #603 was issued for $425, not $452.
3. The deposit made on June 20 was for $125 that Natalie received for teaching a class. Natalie made an error in recording this transaction.
4. The electronic funds transfer (EFT) was for Natalie's cell phone use. Remember that she only uses this phone for business.
5. The NSF cheque was from Ron Black. Natalie received this cheque for teaching a class to Ron's children. Natalie contacted Ron and he assured her that she will receive a cheque in the mail for the outstanding amount of the invoice and the NSF bank charge.

Instructions

(a) Prepare Cookie Creations' bank reconciliation at June 30.
(b) Prepare any necessary adjusting entries at June 30.
(c) If a balance sheet is prepared for Cookie Creations at June 30, what balance will be reported as cash in the current assets section?

BROADENING YOUR PERSPECTIVE

Financial Reporting and Analysis

Financial Reporting Problem

BYP7–1 Two reports are attached to **The Forzani Group Ltd.'s** consolidated financial statements presented in Appendix A of this book: (1) Management's Responsibilities for Financial Reporting and (2) the Auditors' Report.

Instructions

(a) What comments, if any, about the company's system of internal control are included in Management's Responsibilities for Financial Reporting? In the Auditors' Report?
(b) Who is mainly responsible for the financial statements? Explain.
(c) What is the name of Forzani's external auditing firm?
(d) By how much did cash decrease during the current fiscal year?
(e) How large was the balance of cash at the end of the current fiscal year? Express it (1) in dollars, (2) as a percentage of total assets, (3) as a percentage of current assets, and (4) as a percentage of current liabilities.

Interpreting Financial Statements

BYP7–2   Selected information from **Q9 Networks Inc.'s** comparative balance sheet follows:

Q9 NETWORKS INC.
Balance Sheet (partial)
October 31
(in thousands)

	2005	2004
Current assets		
Cash and cash equivalents	$ 7,843	$ 6,135
Short-term investments (note 2)	67,610	64,023
Accounts receivable	3,242	1,846
Unbilled revenue	718	154
Prepaid expenses	676	646
Total current assets	80,089	72,804
Restricted cash (note 3)	410	1,140
Other assets	37,558	38,533
Total assets	$118,057	$112,477
Total current liabilities	$7,688	$7,271

Instructions

(a) What is a cash equivalent? How are cash equivalents different from other types of short-term investments?
(b) Calculate (1) the working capital and (2) the current ratio for each year. The industry averages for the current ratio were 2.85:1 in 2005 and 3.29:1 in 2004. Comment on your results.
(c) Is it possible to have too much cash? Explain why or why not?
(d) What is meant by restricted cash?

Critical Thinking

Collaborative Learning Activity

Note to instructor: Additional instructions and material for this group activity can be found on the Instructor Resource Site.

BYP7–3 In this group activity, you will review internal controls. The Enron Coffee Co. has three restaurants and over 100 employees. The firm has three areas of cash.

Stores The servers sell coffee and muffins. Customers can pay with cash or debit card. The servers make a nightly bank deposit.

Purchases The head office pays the suppliers once a month

Payroll The employees are paid bi-weekly based on their time card.

The firm has instructed its internal audit group to construct an internal control system to minimize error and theft of cash. Since controls are expensive the company has given the internal audit group a budget of $50,000.

Instructions

(a) Your instructor will divide the class into groups. In your group you will take on two roles. For the first ten minutes you will be internal auditors and for the second ten minutes you will be consultants.

(b) As internal auditors, write a set of controls budget that will minimize the loss from theft or error but remain within budget. Each control costs $5,000. Group the controls into the following categories:
- Establishment of responsibility
- Physical controls
- Segregation of duties
- Performance reviews
- Documentation procedures
- Other controls

(c) Exchange lists with another group and switch to the role of consultant. Review the list you have been given and indicate the types of errors or thefts that may occur because a specific control is missing from the list.

Study Aids:
Working in Groups

Communication Activity

BYP7–4 Tenacity Corporation is a medium-sized private company that sells auto parts. Blake Pike has been with the company from the beginning, ordering the auto parts, taking delivery of the parts, and authorizing payments for the auto parts. Blake often signs cheques and prepares the bank reconciliation if the controller is on vacation. The company has grown in size from five employees to 25. Annual sales have increased tenfold. Blake is still completing the same tasks as he was when the company was small and he says that he does not need any help.

Instructions

Write a letter to L.S. Osman, the owner of Tenacity Corporation, that explains the weaknesses in internal control and gives your recommendations for improving the system. In your answer, address the fact that the company has now grown in both size and revenues.

Study Aids:
Writing Handbook

Study Aids:
Ethics in Accounting

BYP7–5 Banks charge customers fees of up to $35 per cheque for writing "bounced" cheques—that is, cheques that exceed the balance in the account. It has been estimated that processing bounced cheques costs a bank roughly $1.50 per cheque. Thus, the profit margin on a bounced cheque is very high. Realizing this, some banks process cheques from largest to smallest. By doing this, they maximize the number of cheques that bounce if a customer overdraws an account.

Instructions

(a) Who are the stakeholders in this situation?

(b) Antonio Freeman had a balance of $1,200 in his chequing account on a day when the bank received the following five cheques for processing against his account:

Cheque Number	Amount	Cheque Number	Amount
3150	$ 35	3165	$550
3158	1,510	3169	180
3162	400		

Assuming a $35 fee per cheque is assessed by the bank, how much fee revenue would the bank generate if it processed cheques (1) from largest to smallest, (2) from smallest to largest, and (3) in the order of the cheque numbers?

(c) Do you think that processing cheques from largest to smallest is an ethical business practice?

(d) Besides ethical issues, what else should a bank consider when it decides if it should process cheques from largest to smallest?

(e) If you were managing a bank, what would be your policy on bounced cheques?

ANSWERS TO CHAPTER QUESTIONS

Answers to Accounting in Action Insight Questions

Ethics Insight, p. 347

Q: What internal control activity has been violated in these frauds? What limitation of internal control allowed the control to be violated?

A: The physical control of private account numbers and passwords is the control activity that should be used to prevent criminals from getting unauthorized access to bank accounts. When people unsuspectingly give this private information to criminals, it shows how the human element—lack of understanding—can cause limitations in internal control.

Business Insight, p. 352

Q: What will be the benefits to the customer of replacing debit and credit cards with chip cards? To the business?

A: Customers will benefit because it will be more difficult for criminals to fraudulently use their card. Customers will also be able to use one card instead of having both a credit and a debit card. Businesses will benefit as there will be less chance of a customer paying for a purchase with a fraudulent card.

Across the Organization Insight, p. 368

Q: How would you know if an error like the ones described above has occurred in your bank account?

A: By doing a bank reconciliation, you could easily determine if the bank has posted a payment twice or recorded the payment in the wrong amount.

Answer to Forzani Review It Question 3, p. 371

Forzani reports only cash in its 2006 balance sheet. It does not have any short-term investments. The reported cash amount at the end of January 29, 2006, is $19,266,000.

Answers to Self-Study Questions

1. c 2. d 3. b 4. a 5. d 6. a 7. a 8. b 9. b 10. d

 Remember to go back to the Navigator Box at the beginning of the chapter to check off your completed work.

appendix A
Specimen Financial Statements:

The Forzani Group Ltd.

In this appendix we illustrate current financial reporting with a comprehensive set of corporate financial statements that are prepared in accordance with generally accepted accounting principles. We are grateful for permission to use the actual financial statements of The Forzani Group Ltd.— Canada's largest sporting goods retailer.

Forzani's financial statement package features a balance sheet, combined statement of operations (or income statement as we know it) and retained earnings, cash flow statement, and notes to the financial statements. The financial statements are preceded by two reports: a statement of management's responsibilities for financial reporting and the auditors' report.

We encourage students to use these financial statements in conjunction with relevant material in the textbook. As well, these statements can be used to solve the Review It questions in the Before You Go On section within the chapter and the Financial Reporting Problem in the Broadening Your Perspective section of the end-of-chapter material.

Annual reports, including the financial statements, are reviewed in detail on the companion website to this textbook.

Annual Report
Walkthrough

THE FORZANI GROUP LTD.

MANAGEMENT'S RESPONSIBILITIES FOR FINANCIAL REPORTING

The Annual Report, including the consolidated financial statements, is the responsibility of the management of the Company. The consolidated financial statements were prepared by management in accordance with generally accepted accounting principles. The significant accounting policies used are described in Note 2 to the consolidated financial statements. The integrity of the information presented in the financial statements, including estimates and judgments relating to matters not concluded by year-end, is the responsibility of management. Financial information presented elsewhere in this Annual Report has been prepared by management and is consistent with the information in the consolidated financial statements.

Management is responsible for the development and maintenance of systems of internal accounting and administrative controls. Such systems are designed to provide reasonable assurance that the financial information is accurate, relevant and reliable, and that the Company's assets are appropriately accounted for and adequately safeguarded. The Board of Directors is responsible for ensuring that management fulfills its responsibilities for final approval of the annual consolidated financial statements. The Board appoints an Audit Committee consisting of three directors, none of whom is an officer or employee of the Company or its subsidiaries. The Audit Committee meets at least four times each year to discharge its responsibilities under a written mandate from the Board of Directors. The Audit Committee meets with management and with the independent auditors to satisfy itself that they are properly discharging their responsibilities, reviews the consolidated financial statements and the Auditors' Report, and examines other auditing, accounting and financial reporting matters. The consolidated financial statements have been reviewed by the Audit Committee and approved by the Board of Directors of The Forzani Group Ltd. The consolidated financial statements have been examined by the shareholders' auditors, Ernst & Young, LLP, Chartered Accountants. The Auditors' Report outlines the nature of their examination and their opinion on the consolidated financial statements of the Company. The independent auditors have full and unrestricted access to the Audit Committee, with and without management present.

Bob Sartor
Chief Executive Officer

Richard Burnet, CA
Vice-President & Chief Financial Officer

AUDITORS' REPORT

To the Shareholders of
The Forzani Group Ltd.

We have audited the consolidated balance sheet of The Forzani Group Ltd. as at January 29, 2006 and the consolidated statements of operations and retained earnings and cash flows for the 52 weeks then ended. These financial statements are the responsibility of the Company's management. Our responsibility is to express an opinion on these financial statements based on our audit.

We conducted our audit in accordance with Canadian generally accepted auditing standards. Those standards require that we plan and perform an audit to obtain reasonable assurance whether the financial statements are free of material misstatement. An audit includes examining, on a test basis, evidence supporting the amounts and disclosures in the financial statements. An audit also includes assessing the accounting principles used and significant estimates made by management, as well as evaluating the overall financial statement presentation.

In our opinion, these consolidated financial statements present fairly, in all material respects, the financial position of the Company as at January 29, 2006 and the results of its operations and its cash flows for the 52 weeks then ended in accordance with Canadian generally accepted accounting principles.

The consolidated balance sheet as at January 30, 2005 and the consolidated statements of operations and retained earnings and cash flows for the 52 weeks then ended were audited by other auditors who expressed an opinion without reservation on those statements in their report dated March 21, 2005.

Calgary, Canada
March 23, 2006

Ernst & Young LLP

Ernst & Young LLP
Chartered Accountants

THE FORZANI GROUP LTD.

THE FORZANI GROUP LTD.
Consolidated Balance Sheets
(in thousands)

As at	January 29, 2006	January 30,2005
ASSETS (note 6)		
Current		
Cash	**$ 19,266**	$ 26,018
Accounts receivable	**68,927**	58,576
Inventory	**278,002**	278,631
Prepaid expenses	**2,647**	3,022
	368,842	366,247
Capital assets (note 3)	**193,594**	179,702
Goodwill and other intangibles (note 4)	**75,805**	52,790
Other assets (note 5)	**10,080**	9,415
Future income tax asset (note 9)	**4,885**	-
	$ 653,206	$ 608,154
LIABILITIES		
Current		
Accounts payable and accrued liabilities	**$ 244,293**	$ 238,239
Current portion of long-term debt (note 6)	**5,135**	1,580
	249,428	239,819
Long-term debt (note 6)	**58,805**	40,278
Deferred lease inducements	**62,883**	62,613
Deferred rent liability	**3,810**	2,213
Future income tax liability (note 9)	**-**	384
	374,926	345,307
SHAREHOLDERS' EQUITY		
Share capital (note 8)	**138,131**	137,811
Contributed surplus	**4,271**	2,915
Retained earnings	**135,878**	122,121
	278,280	262,847
	$ 653,206	$ 608,154

See accompanying notes to the consolidated financial statements.

Approved on behalf of the Board:

Roman Doroniuk, CA

John M. Forzani

THE FORZANI GROUP LTD.
Consolidated Statements of Operations and Retained Earnings
(in thousands, except share data)

	For the 52 weeks ended January 29, 2006	For the 52 weeks ended January 30, 2005
Revenue		
Retail	$ 856,149	$718,820
Wholesale	273,255	266,234
	1,129,404	985,054
Cost of sales	746,313	651,158
Gross margin	383,091	333,896
Operating and administrative expenses		
Store operating	225,218	190,891
General and administrative	88,720	66,536
	313,938	257,427
Operating earnings before undernoted items	69,153	76,469
Amortization	41,343	35,885
Interest	6,145	4,447
Loss on write-down of investment (note 14)	-	2,208
	47,488	42,540
Earnings before income taxes	21,665	33,929
Provision for income taxes (note 9)		
Current	8,784	10,207
Future	(876)	2,177
	7,908	12,384
Net earnings	13,757	21,545
Retained earnings, opening	122,121	101,528
Adjustment arising from normal course issuer bid (note 8(b))	-	(952)
Retained earnings, closing	$ 135,878	$ 122,121
Earnings per share (note 8(c))	$ 0.42	$ 0.66
Diluted earnings per share (note 8(c))	$ 0.42	$ 0.66

See accompanying notes to the consolidated financial statements.

THE FORZANI GROUP LTD.

THE FORZANI GROUP LTD.
Consolidated Statements of Cash Flows
(in thousands)

	For the 52 weeks ended January 29, 2006	For the 52 weeks ended January 30, 2005
Cash provided by (used in) operating activities		
Net earnings	**$ 13,757**	$ 21,545
Items not involving cash		
Amortization	**41,343**	35,885
Amortization of deferred finance charges	**637**	828
Amortization of deferred lease inducements	**(10,661)**	(10,459)
Rent expense (note 7)	**2,281**	4,565
Stock-based compensation (note 8(d))	**1,356**	27
Write-down of investment and other assets	**-**	2,213
Future income tax expense	**(876)**	2,177
	47,837	56,781
Changes in non-cash elements of working capital (note 7)	**(1,979)**	(6,545)
	45,858	50,236
Cash provided by (used in) financing activities		
Net proceeds from issuance of share capital	**320**	967
Increase in long-term debt	**23,573**	3,563
Decrease in revolving credit facility	**-**	-
Debt assumed on acquisition (note 15(c))	**(17,922)**	-
Proceeds from deferred lease inducements	**9,368**	13,402
	15,339	17,932
Changes in non-cash elements of financing activities (note 7)	**(2,450)**	(4,375)
	12,889	13,557
Cash provided by (used in) investing activities		
Net addition of capital assets	**(50,837)**	(45,726)
Net addition of other assets	**(3,751)**	(7,112)
Acquisition of wholly-owned subsidiary (note 15)	**(12,428)**	(9,589)
	(67,016)	(62,427)
Changes in non-cash elements of investing activities (note 7)	**1,517**	1,337
	(65,499)	(61,090)
Increase (decrease) in cash	**(6,752)**	2,703
Net cash position, opening	**26,018**	23,315
Net cash position, closing	**$ 19,266**	$ 26,018

See accompanying notes to the consolidated financial statements.

The Forzani Group Ltd.
Notes to Consolidated Financial Statements
(Tabular amounts in thousands)

1. Nature of Operations

The Forzani Group Ltd. "FGL" or "the Company" is Canada's largest sporting goods retailer. FGL currently operates 260 corporate stores under the banners: Sport Chek, Sport Mart, Coast Mountain Sports and National Sports. The Company is also the franchisor/licensor of 204 stores under the banners: Sports Experts, Intersport, RnR, Econosports, Atmosphere, Tech Shop/Pegasus, Nevada Bob's Golf, and Hockey Experts. FGL operates four websites, dedicated to the Canadian online sporting goods market, www.sportchek.ca, www.sportmart.ca, www.sportsexperts.ca and www.nationalsports.com.

2. Significant Accounting Policies

The consolidated financial statements have been prepared by management in accordance with Canadian generally accepted accounting principles ("GAAP"). The financial statements have, in management's opinion, been prepared within reasonable limits of materiality and within the framework of the accounting policies summarized below:

(a) Organization

The consolidated financial statements include the accounts of The Forzani Group Ltd. and its subsidiaries, all of which are wholly owned.

(b) Inventory

Inventory is valued at the lower of laid-down cost and net realizable value. Laid-down cost is determined using the weighted average cost method and includes invoice cost, duties, freight, and distribution costs. Net realizable value is defined as the expected selling price.

Volume rebates and other supplier discounts are included in income when earned. Volume rebates are accounted for as a reduction of the cost of the related inventory and are "earned" when the inventory is sold. All other rebates and discounts are "earned" when the related expense is incurred.

(c) Capital assets

Capital assets are recorded at cost and are amortized using the following methods and rates:

Building	- 4% declining-balance basis
Building on leased land	- straight-line basis over the lesser of the length of the lease and estimated useful life of the building, not exceeding 20 years
Furniture, fixtures, equipment and automotive	- straight-line basis over 3-5 years
Leasehold improvements	- straight-line basis over the lesser of the length of the lease and estimated useful life of the improvements, not exceeding 10 years

The carrying value of long-lived assets are reviewed at least annually or whenever events indicate a potential impairment has occurred. An impairment loss is recorded when a long lived asset's carrying value exceeds the sum of the undiscounted cash flows expected from its use and eventual disposition. The impairment loss is measured as the amount by which the carrying value exceeds its fair value.

(d) Variable Interest Entities

Variable interest entities ("VIE") are consolidated by the Company if and when the Company is the primary beneficiary of the VIE, as described in CICA Accounting Guideline 15 "Consolidation of Variable Interest Entities".

(e) Goodwill and other intangibles

Goodwill represents the excess of the purchase price of entities acquired over the fair market value of the identifiable net assets acquired.

Goodwill and other intangible assets with indefinite lives are not amortized, but tested for impairment at year end and, if required, asset values reduced accordingly. The method used to assess impairment is a review of the fair value of the asset based on its earnings and a market earnings multiple.

Non-competition agreement costs are amortized, on a straight-line basis, over the life of the agreements, not exceeding five years.

THE FORZANI GROUP LTD.

(f) Other assets

Other assets include deferred financing charges, system and interactive development costs, long-term receivables and a long-term investment in a trademark licensing company.

Financing charges represent fees incurred in establishing and renegotiating the Company's credit facilities. These costs are being amortized over the term of the facilities.

System development costs relate to the implementation of computer software. Upon activation, costs are amortized over the estimated useful lives of the systems (3 – 8 years).

Interactive development costs relate to the development of the sportchek.ca interactive web site, designed as a part of the Company's multi-channel retailing and branding strategy. These costs are being amortized over five years following the commencement of the web site's operations in June, 2001.

Long-term receivables are carried at cost less a valuation allowance, if applicable.

Long-term investments are carried at cost and periodically reviewed for impairment based on the market value of the shares.

(g) Deferred lease inducements and property leases

Deferred lease inducements represent cash and non-cash benefits that the Company has received from landlords pursuant to store lease agreements. These lease inducements are amortized against rent expense over the term of the lease.

The Company capitalizes any rent expense during the fixturing period as a cost of leasehold improvements. Such expense is recognized on a straight-line basis over the life of the lease.

(h) Revenue recognition

Revenue includes sales to customers through corporate stores operated by the Company and sales to, and service fees from, franchise stores and others. Sales to customers through corporate stores operated by the Company are recognized at the point of sale, net of an estimated allowance for sales returns. Sales of merchandise to franchise stores and others are recognized at the time of shipment. Royalties and administration fees are recognized when earned, in accordance with the terms of the franchise/license agreements.

(i) Store opening expenses

Operating costs incurred prior to the opening of new stores, other than rent incurred during the fixturing period, are expensed as incurred.

(j) Fiscal year

The Company's fiscal year follows a retail calendar. The fiscal years for the consolidated financial statements presented are the 52-week periods ended January 29, 2006 and January 30, 2005.

(k) Foreign currency translation

Foreign currency accounts are translated to Canadian dollars. At the transaction date, each asset, liability, revenue or expense is translated into Canadian dollars using the exchange rate in effect at that date. At the year-end date, monetary assets and liabilities are translated into Canadian dollars using the exchange rate in effect at that date, or by rates fixed by forward exchange contracts, and the resulting foreign exchange gains and losses are included in income in the current period, to the extent that the amount is not hedged.

(l) Financial instruments

Accounts receivable, accounts payable and accrued liabilities, long-term debt and derivative transactions, constitute financial instruments. In the normal course of business the Company also enters into leases in respect of real estate and certain point-of-sale equipment.

The Company enters into forward foreign currency contracts and options, with financial institutions, as hedges of other financial transactions and not for speculative purposes. The Company's policies do not allow leveraged transactions and are designed to minimize foreign currency risk. The Company's policies require that all hedges be linked with specific liabilities on the balance sheet and be formally assessed, both at inception, and on an ongoing basis, as to their effectiveness in offsetting changes in the fair values of the hedged liabilities.

(m) Measurement uncertainty

The preparation of the financial statements, in conformity with GAAP, requires management to make estimates and assumptions that affect the reported amounts of assets and liabilities and disclosures of contingent assets and liabilities at the date of the consolidated financial statements and the reported amounts of revenue and expenses during the reporting period. Actual results could differ from these estimates. Estimates are used when accounting for items such as product warranties, inventory provisions, amortization, uncollectible receivables and the liability for the Company's loyalty program.

[42]

F2006 ANNUAL REPORT

The Forzani Group Ltd.
Notes to Consolidated Financial Statements
(Tabular amounts in thousands)

(n)   Stock-based compensation

The Company accounts for stock-based compensation using the fair value method. The fair value of the options granted are estimated at the date of grant using the Black-Scholes valuation model and recognized as an expense over the option-vesting period.

(o)   Income taxes

The Company follows the liability method under which future income tax assets and obligations are determined based on differences between the financial reporting and tax basis of assets and liabilities, measured using tax rates substantively enacted at the balance sheet date.

Changes in tax rates are reflected in the consolidated statement of operations in the period in which they are substantively enacted.

(p)   Asset retirement obligations

The Company recognizes asset retirement obligations in the period in which a reasonable estimate of the fair value can be determined. The liability is measured at fair value and is adjusted to its present value in subsequent periods through accretion expense. The associated asset retirement costs are capitalized as part of the carrying value of the related asset and amortized over its useful life.

(q)   Comparative figures

Certain 2005 comparative figures have been reclassified to conform with the presentation adopted for the current year ending January 29, 2006.

3.   Capital Assets

| | | 2006 | | | 2005 | |
	Cost	Accumulated Amortization	Net Book Value	Cost	Accumulated Amortization	Net Book Value
Land	$ 3,173	$ -	$ 3,173	$ 3,173	$ -	$ 3,173
Buildings	20,007	3,197	16,810	17,637	2,498	15,139
Building on leased land	4,564	2,330	2,234	3,159	1,898	1,261
Furniture, fixtures, equipment and automotive	176,670	104,254	72,416	145,838	84,042	61,796
Leasehold improvements	205,519	106,595	98,924	187,141	89,177	97,964
Construction in progress	37	-	37	369	-	369
	$ 409,970	$ 216,376	$193,594	$357,317	$177,615	$179,702

4.   Goodwill and Other Intangibles

| | | 2006 | | | 2005 | |
	Cost	Accumulated Amortization	Net Book Value	Cost	Accumulated Amortization	Net Book Value
Goodwill	$ 47,818	$ 1,187	$46,631	$ 25,243	$ 1,187	$ 24,056
Trademarks/Tradenames	28,693	626	28,067	25,715	561	25,154
Non-competition agreements	4,000	2,893	1,107	5,680	2,100	3,580
	$ 80,511	$ 4,706	$75,805	$ 56,638	$ 3,848	$ 52,790

THE FORZANI GROUP LTD.

The Forzani Group Ltd.
Notes to Consolidated Financial Statements
(Tabular amounts in thousands)

5. Other Assets

| | | 2006 | | | 2005 | |
	Cost	Accumulated Amortization	Net Book Value	Cost	Accumulated Amortization	Net Book Value
Interactive development	$2,649	$2,649	$ -	$2,649	$2,133	$ 516
Deferred financing charges	1,660	286	1,374	3,598	2,284	1,314
System development	1,569	1,407	162	1,569	1,277	292
Other deferred charges	3,030	853	2,177	1,808	704	1,104
	$8,908	$5,195	$3,713	$9,624	$6,398	$3,226

	2006	2005
Depreciable other assets net book value (see above)	$ 3,713	$ 3,226
Long-term receivables (at interest rates of prime plus 1% and expiring between September 2009 and July 2010)	3,279	2,973
Investment in a trademark licensing company	3,088	3,088
Other	-	128
	$10,080	$ 9,415

6. Long-term Debt

	2006	2005
G.E. term loan	$ 50,000	$ 25,000
Vendor take-back, unsecured with interest rate of prime plus 1% due August 1, 2006	4,606	4,428
Mortgages, with monthly blended payments of $79,625, including interest at rates from approximately 4.9% to 6.2%, compounded semi-annually, secured by land and buildings, expiring between September 2006 and October 2009 (each with a fifteen year amortization).	9,078	9,658
Amounts due under non-competition agreements, (payment negotiated and retired in 2006)	-	2,680
Asset retirement obligation	97	92
Other	159	-
	63,940	41,858
Less current portion	5,135	1,580
	$ 58,805	$40,278

Principal payments on the above, due in the next five years, are as follows:

2007	$ 3,810
2008	$ 523
2009	$50,519
2010	$ 529
2011	$ 557

Effective June 30, 2005, the Company extended its existing credit agreement to June 30, 2008. The amended and restated agreement with GE Canada Finance Holding Company, National Bank of Canada and Royal Bank of Canada increased the $175 million credit facility to $235 million, comprised of a $185 million revolving loan (2005 - $150 million), and a $50 million term loan (2005 - $25 million) repayable at maturity. Under the terms of the credit agreement, the interest rate payable on both the revolving and term loans is based on the Company's financial performance as determined by its interest coverage ratio. As at January 29, 2006, the average interest rate paid was 4.80% (January 30, 2005 - 4.05%). The facility is collateralized by general security agreements against all existing and future acquired assets of the Company. As at January 29, 2006, the Company is in compliance with all covenants.

The Forzani Group Ltd.
Notes to Consolidated Financial Statements
(Tabular amounts in thousands)

Based on estimated interest rates currently available to the Company for mortgages with similar terms and maturities, the fair value of the mortgages at January 29, 2006 amounted to approximately $8,553,000 (2005 - $9,658,000). Interest costs incurred for the 52-week period ended January 29, 2006 on long-term debt amounted to $2,318,000 (2005 - $1,358,000). The fair value of the other long-term debt components above approximates book value given their short terms to maturity and floating interest rates.

7. **Supplementary Cash Flow Information**

	2006	2005
Rent expense		
Straight-line rent expense	$ 1,484	$ 2,213
Non-cash free rent	797	2,352
	$ 2,281	$ 4,565
Changes in non-cash elements of working capital		
Accounts receivable	$ (10,038)	$(22,257)
Inventory	24,544	(13,607)
Prepaid and other expenses	1,140	8,270
Accounts payable and accrued liabilities	(17,761)	20,363
Non-cash free rent	136	686
	$ (1,979)	$ (6,545)
Changes in non-cash elements of financing activities		
Non-cash lease inducements	$ (2,450)	$ (4,375)
Changes in non-cash elements of investing activities		
Non-cash capital asset additions	$ 1,517	$ 1,337
Cash interest paid	$ 6,183	$ 4,685
Cash taxes paid	$ 7,285	$ 20,613

8. **Share Capital**

(a) Authorized

An unlimited number of Class A shares (no par value)
An unlimited number of Preferred shares, issuable in series

(b) Issued
Class A shares

	Number	Consideration
Balance, February 1, 2004	31,791	$ 128,880
Shares issued upon employees exercising stock options	634	2,477
Shares issued to acquire businesses (note 15)	585	7,012
Shares redeemed pursuant to normal course issuer bid	(135)	(558)
Balance, January 30, 2005	**32,875**	**$ 137,811**
Shares issued upon employees exercising stock options	**47**	**320**
Balance, January 29, 2006	**32,922**	**$ 138,131**

During 2005, 135,100 Class A shares were purchased pursuant to the Company's Normal Course Issuer Bid for a total expenditure of $1,510,000. The price in excess of carrying value was charged to retained earnings.

THE FORZANI GROUP LTD.

The Forzani Group Ltd.
Notes to Consolidated Financial Statements
(Tabular amounts in thousands)

(c) Earnings Per Share

	2006	2005
Basic	$ 0.42	$ 0.66
Diluted	$ 0.42	$ 0.66

The Company uses the treasury stock method to calculate diluted earnings per share. Under the treasury stock method, the numerator remains unchanged from the basic earnings per share calculation, as the assumed exercise of the Company's stock options does not result in an adjustment to earnings. Diluted calculations assume that options under the stock option plan have been exercised at the later of the beginning of the year or date of issuance, and that the funds derived therefrom would have been used to repurchase shares at the average market value of the Company's stock, 2006 - $12.41 (2005 - $12.83). Anti-dilutive options, 2006 - 749,000 (2005 – 1,740,000) are excluded from the effect of dilutive securities. The reconciliation of the denominator in calculating diluted earnings per share is as follows:

	2006	2005
Weighted average number of class A shares outstanding (basic)	32,899	32,572
Effect of dilutive options	248	155
Weighted average number of common shares outstanding (diluted)	33,147	32,727

(d) Stock Option Plan

The Company has granted stock options to directors, officers and employees to purchase Class A shares at prices between $9.39 and $19.19 per share. These options expire on dates between August 22, 2006 and December 2, 2010.

The Company has two stock option plans. The first plan has the following general terms: options vest over a period ranging from 2 to 5 years and the maximum term of the options granted is 5 years. During the year, 250,000 options (2005 – 205,000 options) were issued under this plan. The related stock based compensation was $1,356,000 (2005 - $27,000). The second plan has the following general terms: options vest over a period ranging from 3 to 5 years dependent on the Company achieving certain performance targets, and the maximum term of the options granted is 5 years. During the year, 525,000 options (2005 – 950,000 options) were issued under this plan. There was no related stock based compensation in either 2006 or 2005 as the Company has deemed the targets may not be met. The total number of shares authorized for option grants under both option plans is 3,262,833.

During the 52-weeks ended January 29, 2006, the following options were granted:

Options issued	Weighted average fair value per option	Weighted average risk-free rate	Weighted average expected option life	Weighted average expected volatility	Weighted average expected dividend yield
775,000	$5.52	3.64%	4.08 years	46.55%	0.00%

A summary of the status of the Company's stock option plans as of January 29, 2006 and January 30, 2005, and any changes during the year ending on those dates is presented below:

Stock Options	2006		2005	
	Options	Weighted Average Exercise Price	Options	Weighted Average Exercise Price
Outstanding, beginning of year	2,159	$ 12.13	2,809	$ 13.34
Granted	775	$ 12.15	1,156	$ 10.71
Exercised	47	$ 6.85	634	$ 3.91
Forfeited	100	$ 19.19	1,172	$ 18.12
Outstanding, end of year	2,787	$ 11.88	2,159	$ 12.13
Options exercisable at year end	755		742	

F2006 ANNUAL REPORT

The Forzani Group Ltd.
Notes to Consolidated Financial Statements
(Tabular amounts in thousands)

The following table summarizes information about stock options outstanding at January 29, 2006:

Range of Exercise Prices	Number Outstanding	Options Outstanding Weighted Average Remaining Contractual Life	Weighted Average Exercise Price	Options Exercisable Number of Shares Exercisable	Weighted Average Exercise Price
$9.39 - $10.25	1,160	3.91	$10.24	20	$ 9.39
$11.36 - $12.66	982	2.58	$11.78	497	$11.36
$13.05 - $19.19	645	2.69	$15.01	238	$16.68
	2,787	3.16	$11.88	755	$12.99

9. Income Taxes

The components of the future income tax liability (asset) amounts as at January 29, 2006 and January 30, 2005, are as follows:

	2006	2005
Current assets	$ 3,353	$ 4,342
Capital and other assets	15,842	19,141
Tax benefit of share issuance and financing costs	(166)	(314)
Deferred lease inducements	(22,122)	(22,785)
Non-capital loss carry forward	(1,792)	-
Future income tax liability (asset)	$ (4,885)	$ 384

A reconciliation of income taxes, at the combined statutory federal and provincial tax rate to the actual income tax rate, is as follows:

	2006		2005	
Federal and provincial income taxes	$8,044	37.1%	$11,743	34.6%
Increase (decrease) resulting from:				
Effect of substantively enacted tax rate changes	(68)	(0.3%)	663	2.0%
Other, net	(68)	(0.3%)	(22)	(0.1%)
Provision for income taxes	$7,908	36.5%	$12,384	36.5%

Federal Part I.3 tax and provincial capital tax expense in the amount of $952,000 (2005 - $1,053,000) is included in operating expenses.

The Company has non-capital losses being carried forward of $1,489,000 which expire in 2011 and $2,551,000 which expire in 2015.

10. Commitments

(a) The Company is committed, at January 29, 2006 to minimum payments under long-term real property and data processing hardware and software equipment leases, for the next five years, as follows:

	Gross
2007	$ 75,904
2008	$ 73,146
2009	$ 70,366
2010	$ 63,921
2011	$ 54,517

In addition, the Company may be obligated to pay percentage rent under certain of the leases.

(b) As at January 29, 2006, the Company has open letters of credit for purchases of inventory of approximately $4,579,000 (2005 - $3,108,000).

THE FORZANI GROUP LTD.

11. Employee Benefit Plans

The Company has a defined contribution plan and a deferred profit sharing plan. Deferred profit sharing contributions are paid to a Trustee for the purchase of shares of the Company and are distributed to participating employees on a predetermined basis, upon retirement from the Company. Contributions are subject to board approval and recognized as an expense when incurred. Defined contributions are paid to employee retirement savings plans and are expensed when incurred.

The Company has accrued $100,000 (2005 - $36,000) to the employee deferred profit sharing plan and $807,000 (2005 - $666,000) to the defined contribution plan.

12. Contingencies and Guarantees

In the normal course of business, the Company enters into numerous agreements that may contain features that meet the Accounting Guideline ("AG")14 definition of a guarantee. AG-14 defines a guarantee to be a contract (including an indemnity) that contingently requires the Company to make payments to the guaranteed party based on (i) changes in an underlying interest rate, foreign exchange rate, equity or commodity instrument, index or other variable, that is related to an asset, a liability or an equity security of the counterparty, (ii) failure of another party to perform under an obligating agreement or (iii) failure of a third party to pay its indebtedness when due.

The Company has provided the following guarantees to third parties:

(a) The Company has provided guarantees to certain franchisees' banks pursuant to which it has agreed to buy back inventory from the franchisee in the event that the bank realizes on the related security. The Company has provided securitization guarantees for certain franchisees to repay equity loans in the event of franchisee default. The terms of the guarantees range from less than a year to the lifetime of the particular underlying franchise agreement, with an average guarantee term of 5 years. Should a franchisee default on its bank loan, the Company would be required to purchase between 50% – 100%, with a weighted average of 65%, of the franchisee's inventory up to the value of the franchisee's bank indebtedness. As at January 29, 2006, the Company's maximum exposure is $32,034,000 (2005 - $31,506,000). Should the Company be required to purchase the inventory, it is expected that the full value of the inventory would be recovered. Historically, the Company has not had to repurchase significant inventory from franchisees pursuant to these guarantees. The Company has not recognized the guarantee in its financial statements.

(b) In the ordinary course of business, the Company has agreed to indemnify its lenders under its credit facilities against certain costs or losses resulting from changes in laws and regulations and from any legal action brought against the lenders related to the use, by the Company, of the loan proceeds, or to the lenders having extended credit thereunder. These indemnifications extend for the term of the credit facilities and do not provide any limit on the maximum potential liability. Historically, the Company has not made any indemnification payments under such agreements and no amount has been accrued in the financial statements with respect to these indemnification agreements.

(c) In the ordinary course of business, the Company has provided indemnification commitments to certain counterparties in matters such as real estate leasing transactions, securitization agreements, director and officer indemnification agreements and certain purchases of assets (not inventory in the normal course). These indemnification agreements generally require the Company to compensate the counterparties for costs or losses resulting from any legal action brought against the counterparties related to the actions of the Company or any of the obligors under any of the aforementioned matters or failure of the obligors under any of the aforementioned matters to fulfill contractual obligations thereunder. The terms of these indemnification agreements will vary based on the contract and generally do not provide any limit on the maximum potential liability. Historically, the Company has not made any payments under such indemnifications and no amount has been accrued in the financial statements with respect to these indemnification commitments.

(d) Claims and suits have been brought against the Company in the ordinary course of business. In the opinion of management, all such claims and suits are adequately covered by insurance, or if not so covered, the results are not expected to materially affect the Company's financial position.

13. Financial Instruments

The Company is exposed to credit risk on its accounts receivable from franchisees. The accounts receivable are net of applicable allowance for doubtful accounts, which are established based on the specific credit risks associated with individual franchisees and other relevant information. Concentration of credit risk with respect to receivables is limited, due to the large number of franchisees.

The Forzani Group Ltd.
Notes to Consolidated Financial Statements
(Tabular amounts in thousands)

The Company purchases a portion of its inventory from foreign vendors with payment terms in foreign currencies. To manage the foreign exchange risk associated with these purchases, the Company hedges its exposure to foreign currency by purchasing foreign exchange options and forward contracts to fix exchange rates and protect planned margins. The Company has the following derivative instruments outstanding at January 29, 2006 and January 30, 2005:

	Notional amounts maturing in		2006	2005
	Less than 1 year	Over 1 year	Total	Total
Foreign exchange contracts ($CAD)				
United States dollar contracts	$2,386	-	$2,386	$2,751
EURO contracts	-	-	-	507
Total	$2,386	-	$2,386	$3,258

The Company has included $359,000 (2005 - $320,000) of exchange losses in general and administrative expenses. No other amounts have been recognized in the consolidated financial statements. As at January 29, 2006, these instruments had $37,000 of unrealized losses (2005 - $38,000 unrealized gains).

The Company is exposed to interest rate risk on its credit facility and the term loan. Interest rate risk reflects the sensitivity of the Company's financial condition to movements in interest rates. For fiscal year 2006, a 1% change in interest rates would change interest expense by $1,449,000 (2005 - $1,108,000).

14. Write-down of Investment

During the year ended January 30, 2005, the Company reviewed the carrying value of its investment in a wholesale distribution company. As a result of this review, the Company determined that a decline in the value of this investment that was other than temporary had occurred and recorded a write-down in the amount of $2,207,952 to bring the carrying value of the investment to $26,000, this investment was subsequently disposed of in 2006.

15. Acquisitions

(a) Effective March 19, 2004, the Company acquired 100% of the outstanding shares of Gen-X Sports Inc. The acquisition was accounted for using the purchase method and accordingly the consolidated financial statements include the results of operations since the date of the acquisition.

The consideration for the transaction was $13,513,000 for all the outstanding Class A and Class B common shares. The purchase consideration consisted of $9,589,000 cash and the remainder in the form of a vendor take-back loan, payable over four years. The loan payments are in the form of 300,000 escrowed Company Class A shares distributed over the four-year period.

The assigned fair values of the underlying assets and liabilities acquired by the Company as at March 19, 2004, are summarized as follows:

Inventory	$ 6,208
Trademarks	3,280
Fixed assets	200
Goodwill	3,924
Total assets acquired	**13,612**
Current liabilities	(99)
Total liabilities acquired	**(99)**
Consideration	**$13,513**

(b) Effective December 17, 2004, the Company acquired a 14.29% interest in a trademark licensing company in exchange for 285,160 Class A shares of the Company, with a fair market value of $3,088,283. This acquisition was accounted for using the cost method and the investment is recorded in Other assets.

(c) Effective January 31, 2005, the Company acquired 100% of the outstanding shares of National Gym Clothing Ltd. The acquisition was accounted for using the purchase method and accordingly the consolidated financial statements include the results of operations since the date of the acquisition.

THE FORZANI GROUP LTD.

The consideration for the transaction was $13,026,000 in cash for all the outstanding common shares.

The assigned fair values of the underlying assets and liabilities acquired by the Company as at January 31, 2005, are summarized as follows:

Cash	$ 598
Accounts receivable	313
Inventory	23,915
Prepaid expenses	765
Trademarks	2,535
Fixed assets	2,261
Goodwill	21,848
Future income tax asset	4,393
Total assets acquired	**56,628**
Secured indebtedness	17,922
Accounts payable	23,815
Long-term debt	189
Deferred rent liability	113
Deferred lease inducements	1,563
Total liabilities acquired	**43,602**
Cash consideration	**$13,026**

16. Segmented Financial Information

The Company operates principally in two business segments: corporately-owned and operated retail stores and as a wholesale business selling to franchisees and others. Identifiable assets, depreciation and amortization and interest expense are not disclosed by segment as they are substantially retail in nature, with the exception of accounts receivable of $58.9 million (2005 - $48.1 million), capital assets of $16.8 million (2005 – $13.4 million) and goodwill/other assets of $8.1 million (2005 - $6.9 million) which are wholesale in nature.

In determining the reportable segments, the Company considered the distinct business models of the Retail and Wholesale operations, the division of responsibilities, and the reporting to the Board of Directors.

	2006	2005
Revenues:		
Retail	$ 856,149	$718,820
Wholesale	273,255	266,234
	1,129,404	985,054
Operating Profit:		
Retail	78,236	68,433
Wholesale	23,547	27,583
	101,783	96,016
Non-segment specific administrative expenses	32,630	19,547
Operating activities before under-noted items	69,153	76,469
Amortization	41,343	35,885
Interest expense	6,145	4,447
Loss on write-down of investments	-	2,208
	47,488	42,540
Earnings before income taxes	21,665	33,929
Income tax expense	7,908	12,384
Net earnings	$ 13,757	$ 21,545

The Forzani Group Ltd.
Notes to Consolidated Financial Statements
(Tabular amounts in thousands)

17. Related Party Transactions

(a) An officer of the Company holds an interest in a franchise store operation. During the year, that franchise operation transacted business, in the normal course and at fair market value, with the Company, purchasing product in the amount of $5,608,000 (2005 - $5,492,000). At the end of the year, accounts receivable from the franchise operation were $888,000 (2005 – $993,000). During the year, that franchise operation opened a prototype store in Kirkland Quebec in which, in the normal course of opening prototype stores, the Company owns equipment and fixtures in the amount of $330,000.

(b) The Company has an interest in a trademark licensing company in which an employee, employed by a subsidiary, holds a partial interest. During the year, the Company, in the normal course of operations on similar terms and conditions to transactions entered into with unrelated parties, paid royalties of $346,000 (2005 – $303,000).

(c) During the year the company purchased real estate valued at $215,000 from an officer of the company in the normal course of operations and on similar terms and conditions to transactions entered into with unrelated parties.

(d) During the year the Company entered into a contract to obtain services and paid $44,000 (2005 - $nil) to a company owned by a director of the Company in the normal course of operations and on similar terms and conditions to transactions entered into with unrelated parties.

18. Variable Interest Entities

At January 29, 2006, the Company had a long-term receivable due from an entity which is considered a variable interest entity (VIE) under CICA Accounting Guideline 15. The entity operates several franchise stores. The long-term receivable has been outstanding since July 2003 and the Company has received guarantees for the full amount of the receivable from the shareholders of the entity. The Company has concluded that it is not the primary beneficiary of the VIE and that it is not required to consolidate this VIE in its consolidated financial statements. The Company has no exposure to loss related to the long-term receivable.

19. Subsequent Event

Effective January 31, 2006 the Company has acquired 100% of the outstanding common shares of Fitness Source Inc. for $6.5 million.

appendix B
Sales Taxes

All businesses operating in Canada need to understand how sales taxes apply to their particular business in their particular province or territory. Sales taxes may take the form of the **Goods and Services Tax (GST)**, **Provincial Sales Tax (PST)**, or **Harmonized Sales Tax (HST)**. GST is levied by the federal government. PST is levied by the provinces and territories, with the exception of Alberta, the Northwest Territories, Nunavut, and Yukon, where no provincial sales tax is charged. Nova Scotia, New Brunswick, and Newfoundland and Labrador have combined the GST and PST into one harmonized sales tax, known as the HST.

As an agent of the federal and provincial governments, a business is required to collect sales taxes on the sale of certain goods and services. In addition, businesses pay sales taxes on most disbursements. We will discuss the collection, payment, recording, and remittance of each of these types of sales taxes in the following sections.

Types of Sales Taxes

Goods and Services Tax

The GST is a federal sales tax on most goods and services provided in Canada. A business must register for the GST if it provides taxable goods or services in Canada and if it has revenues of more than $30,000 in any year. Businesses that have to, or decide to, voluntarily register for the GST are called registrants. Registrants can claim a credit—called an **input tax credit (ITC)**—to offset the GST they pay or owe on purchases of goods or services against the GST they collect or are owed. GST returns are submitted quarterly for most registrants (monthly for large registrants) to the Canada Revenue Agency (CRA). The taxes are payable to the Receiver General, who is the collection agent for the federal government.

The GST applies at a rate of 6% on most transactions. Transactions subject to GST are called **taxable supplies**. There are two other categories of goods and services with respect to the GST:

- zero-rated supplies, such as basic groceries and prescription drugs
- exempt supplies, such as educational services, health-care services, and financial services

No GST applies to zero-rated or exempt supplies. However, zero-rated suppliers can claim input tax credits.

Illustration B-1 provides the GST status of some typical goods and services.

Taxable Supplies	Zero-Rated Supplies	Exempt Supplies
Building materials	Prescription drugs	Used house
Ready-to-eat pizza	Uncooked pizza	Dental services
Two doughnuts	Six or more doughnuts	Insurance policy

The reason ready-to-eat pizza and two doughnuts have GST added to the purchase price is because they are considered convenience items and not basic groceries.

Provincial Sales Tax

Provincial sales taxes are charged on retail sales of certain goods and services. In the provinces charging sales tax, except Quebec and Prince Edward Island, this tax is applied to the selling price of the item before GST is applied. Similarly, GST is charged on the selling price of the item before PST is applied, thus avoiding GST being charged on PST. In Quebec and Prince Edward Island, however, the provincial sales tax is cascaded—that is, applied to the total of the selling price plus GST. Quebec's sales tax is also known as the QST (Quebec Sales Tax).

The following example shows the calculation of cascaded sales tax, using a taxable item sold in Quebec for $100:

Selling price	$100.00
GST ($100 × 6%)	6.00
QST [($100 + $6) × 7.5%]	7.95
Total	$113.95

Provincial sales taxes are remitted periodically to the Minister of Finance or Provincial Treasurer in each province.

PST rates vary by province and can change with each provincial budget. It is important to understand that the PST may not be applied at the same rate to all taxable goods and services. For example, in Ontario, the rates vary for insurance premiums and alcoholic beverages. Certain goods are exempt, such as children's clothing, textbooks, and residential rent, and may be purchased with no PST. Examples of exempt services that are not taxable include personal services such as dental and medical services. Because rates and exemptions vary by province, it is important, when starting a business, to check with provincial officials for details on how to calculate the provincial tax that must be applied to sales.

Harmonized Sales Tax

The provinces of Newfoundland and Labrador, Nova Scotia, and New Brunswick charge Harmonized Sales Tax, or HST. Instead of charging GST and PST separately, only the HST is charged at a combined rate of 14%. Similar to GST, HST returns are submitted quarterly for most registrants (monthly for large registrants) to the CRA. The federal government then gives the provincial portion of the tax to the province.

To summarize, four provinces—British Columbia, Manitoba, Ontario, and Saskatchewan—apply PST and GST to the selling price of a taxable good or service. Two provinces—Prince Edward Island and Quebec—apply PST to the total of the purchase price and the GST. Three provinces—New Brunswick, Newfoundland and Labrador, and Nova Scotia—charge a combined GST and PST (harmonized) rate of 14% on the selling price. Four provinces and territories do not charge PST—Alberta, the Northwest Territories, Nunavut, and Yukon. In addition to the different ways of applying sales taxes, the rates of sales tax differ in each province and territory, as shown on the following page:

Province/Territory	GST (HST) Rate	PST Rate	Combined Rate[1]
Alberta	6.0%	0.0%	6.0%
British Columbia	6.0%	7.0%	13.0%
Manitoba	6.0%	7.0%	13.0%
New Brunswick	14.0%	N/A	14.0%
Newfoundland and Labrador	14.0%	N/A	14.0%
Northwest Territories	6.0%	0.0%	6.0%
Nova Scotia	14.0%	N/A	14.0%
Nunavut	6.0%	0.0%	6.0%
Ontario	6.0%	8.0%	14.0%
Prince Edward Island	6.0%	10.0%	16.6%[2]
Quebec	6.0%	7.5%	13.95%[2]
Saskatchewan	6.0%	5.0%	11.0%
Yukon	6.0%	0.0%	6.0%

[1] All of these rates are in effect as of November 30, 2006 and are subject to change.
[2] In Prince Edward Island and Quebec only, the GST is included in the provincial sales tax base.

Illustration B-2 ◄

Sales tax rates

Sales Taxes Collected on Receipts

Sales taxes are collected by businesses from consumers on taxable goods and services. It is important to understand that sales taxes are not a source of revenue for a company. Sales taxes are collected by a company on behalf of the federal and provincial governments. Consequently, collected sales tax is a current liability to the company until remitted to the respective government at regular intervals.

Services

Now let's look at how service companies record sales taxes on the services they provide. Assume that a law firm bills a client for legal services. Some service providers, such as law firms, do not have to charge PST in some provinces. In these provinces, the law firm would only charge 6% GST on the legal services provided.

The following entry would be made to record the billing of a client for $500 of services provided by a law firm in Ontario on May 28. In Ontario, legal services are exempt from PST, so only 6% GST would be charged on these services.

May 28	Accounts Receivable	530	
	Legal Fees Earned		500
	GST Payable ($500 × 6%)		30
	To record revenue earned from legal fees.		

A	=	L	+	OE
+530		+30		+500

Cash flows: no effect

Note that the revenue recorded is $500, and not $530. The legal fees earned are exclusive of the GST amount collected, which is recorded as a current liability.

Assume instead that $250 of cleaning services were provided by a company in Saskatchewan for cash on July 24. These services are subject to both PST (5%) and GST (6%), and would be recorded as follows:

July 24	Cash	277.50	
	Cleaning Service Revenue		250.00
	PST Payable ($250 × 5%)		12.50
	GST Payable ($250 × 6%)		15.00
	To record cleaning service revenue.		

A	=	L	+	OE
+277.50		+12.50		+250
		+15.00		

↑ Cash flows: +277.50

If these same services were provided by a company in New Brunswick, where HST is 14%, the entry would be as follows:

↑ Cash flows: +285

July 24	Cash	285	
	Cleaning Service Revenue		250
	HST Payable ($250 × 14%)		35
	To record cleaning service revenue.		

A	=	L	+	OE
+285		+35		+250

Merchandise

Entries are needed to record the sales taxes owed when merchandise inventory (goods) is sold, or to reduce sales taxes payable when merchandise inventory is returned.

Sales

Assume that Staples sells $1,000 of office furniture, on account, in the province of Ontario, where PST is 8%. GST is 6%. Staples uses a perpetual inventory system and the cost of the furniture to Staples was $800. The following two entries are required to record the sale and the cost of the sale on May 20:

A	=	L	+	OE
+1,140		+60		+1,000
		+80		

Cash flows: no effect

A	=	L	+	OE
−800				−800

Cash flows: no effect

May 20	Accounts Receivable	1,140	
	Sales		1,000
	GST Payable ($1,000 × 6%)		60
	PST Payable ($1,000 × 8%)		80
	To record sale of merchandise on account.		
20	Cost of Goods Sold	800	
	Merchandise Inventory		800
	To record cost of merchandise sold.		

Under the periodic inventory system, the second entry would not be recorded.

Sales Returns and Allowances

If a $300 sales return and allowance were granted by Staples on May 25 for returned merchandise from the above sale, the entry to record the credit memorandum would appear as follows:

A	=	L	+	OE
−342		−18		−300
		−24		

Cash flows: no effect

A	=	L	+	OE
+240				+240

Cash flows: no effect

May 25	Sales Returns and Allowances	300	
	GST Payable ($300 × 6%)	18	
	PST Payable ($300 × 8%)	24	
	Accounts Receivable		342
	To record credit for returned merchandise.		
25	Merchandise Inventory ($300 ÷ $1,000 × $800)	240	
	Cost of Goods Sold		240
	To record cost of merchandise returned.		

Note that the GST and PST payable accounts are debited, rather than debiting a receivable account, to indicate that this is a return of previously collected sales tax. This entry assumes that the merchandise was in good condition and returned to inventory. Note also that the GST and PST did not form part of the original cost of the merchandise, and therefore are not considered in restoring the cost of the merchandise to the inventory account.

Under the periodic inventory system, the second entry would not be recorded.

Sales Taxes Paid on Disbursements

As a consumer of goods and services, a business must pay the applicable PST and GST charged by its suppliers on taxable goods and services.

Purchase of Merchandise for Resale

When purchasing merchandise for resale, the treatment of the PST is different than that of the GST. PST is a single-stage tax collected from the final consumers of taxable goods and services. Consequently, wholesalers do not charge the tax to the retailer who will in turn resell the merchandise, at a higher price, to the final consumer. By presenting a vendor registration number, retailers are able to buy merchandise for resale, exempt of the PST.

Businesses must pay GST on the purchase of merchandise but can then offset the GST paid against any GST collected. Consequently, **when merchandise is purchased, the GST paid by a business is *not* part of the inventory cost.** The GST paid on purchases is debited to an account called GST Recoverable and is called an input tax credit.

In Quebec, the QST works somewhat like the GST. Businesses can offset QST paid against any QST collected. The QST paid on purchases is debited to an account called QST Recoverable and is called an input tax refund. Other differences also exist in the treatment of QST. This appendix will focus on PST and does not discuss the QST in any detail.

Purchases

The following is an entry to record the purchase of merchandise for resale on May 4 at a price of $4,000, on account, using a perpetual inventory system:

May 4	Merchandise Inventory	4,000	
	GST Recoverable ($4,000 × 6%)	240	
	Accounts Payable		4,240
	To record merchandise purchased on account.		

The cost of the merchandise, $4,000, is not affected by the GST, which is recorded as a receivable.

Under a periodic inventory system, the $4,000 debit would have been recorded to the Purchases account.

Purchase Returns and Allowances

The entry to record a $300 return of merchandise on May 8 is as follows:

May 8	Accounts Payable	318	
	GST Recoverable ($300 × 6%)		18
	Merchandise Inventory		300
	To record the return of merchandise.		

Note that the GST Recoverable account is credited instead of the GST Payable account because this is a return of previously recorded GST.

Under the periodic inventory system, the credit of $300 would have been recorded to the Purchase Returns and Allowances account.

To summarize, PST is not paid on purchases of merchandise for resale. GST paid on purchases is normally recoverable and recorded as a current asset in the GST Recoverable account. Purchase returns and allowances require an adjustment of GST only, since PST was not paid on the original purchase.

Operating Expenses

Although PST is not charged on goods purchased for resale, it is charged to businesses that use taxable goods and services in their operations. For example, a business must pay GST and PST when it buys office supplies. As with all purchases made by a registered business, the GST is recoverable (can be offset as an input tax credit against GST collected). Because the PST is not recoverable, the PST forms part of the cost of the asset or expense that is being acquired.

The following is the entry for a cash purchase of office supplies on May 18 in the amount of $200 in the province of Ontario where PST is 8% and GST is 6%:

May 18	Office Supplies ($200 + $16[1] PST)	216	
	GST Recoverable ($200 × 6%)	12	
	Cash		228
	To record purchase of office supplies.		
[1] $200 × 8% = $16			

In this situation, the cost of the supplies includes both the supplies and the PST. Because GST is recoverable, it does not form part of the asset cost.

This same purchase would be recorded as follows if it occurred in the province of Prince Edward Island, where GST is 6% and PST is charged on GST at 10%:

May 18	Office Supplies ($200 + $21.20[2] PST)	221.20	
	GST Recoverable ($200 × 6%)	12.00	
	Cash		233.20
	To record purchase of office supplies.		
[2] $200 + $12 = $212 × 10% = $21.20			

Remember that in Prince Edward Island the provincial sales tax base includes both the cost of the item and the GST. That is, the PST of $21.20 is determined by multiplying 10% by $212 ($200 + $12).

When HST is applied, it is treated in the same manner as GST. HST is recoverable and does not form part of the cost of the item purchased. The purchase of office supplies would be recorded as follows if it had occurred in the province of Newfoundland and Labrador where HST is 14%:

May 18	Office Supplies	200	
	HST Recoverable ($200 × 14%)	28	
	Cash		228
	To record purchase of office supplies.		

Note that the same amount is paid for the supplies in Ontario and Newfoundland and Labrador, $228, but the amount recorded as the cost of the office supplies differs ($216 and $200).

Property, Plant, and Equipment

Businesses incur costs other than those for merchandise and operating expenses, such as for the purchase of property, plant, and equipment. The PST and GST apply to these purchases in the same manner as described in the operating expenses section above. All GST (or HST) paid is recoverable and is not part of the cost of the asset. The PST, however, is part of the cost of the asset being purchased as it is not recoverable.

The following is the entry for the purchase of office furniture on May 20 from Staples, on account, for $1,000 plus applicable sales taxes in Ontario. PST is 8% and GST is 6%.

May 20	Office Furniture ($1,000 + $80[1] PST)	1,080	
	GST Recoverable ($1,000 × 6%)	60	
	Accounts Payable		1,140
	To record purchase of office furniture.		

[1] $1,000 × 8% = $80

A	=	L	+	OE
+1,080		+1,140		
+60				

Cash flows: no effect

Because the PST is not recoverable, the cost of the furniture is $1,080, inclusive of the PST.

Compare this entry made by the buyer to record the purchase, to the entry made by the seller to record the sale on page B4. Both companies record accounts payable and accounts receivable in the same amount, $1,140. However, the seller records both GST and PST payable while the buyer records only GST recoverable. The PST paid by the buyer is not recoverable, so it becomes part of the cost of the office furniture, $1,080.

In Prince Edward Island, where GST is 6% and PST is charged on GST at 10%, the same entry would be recorded as follows:

May 20	Office Furniture ($1,000 + $106[2] PST)	1,106	
	GST Recoverable ($1,000 × 6%)	60	
	Accounts Payable		1,166
	To record purchase of office furniture.		

[2] $1,000 + $60 = $1,060 × 10% = $106

A	=	L	+	OE
+1,106		+1,166		
+60				

Cash flows: no effect

In P.E.I., PST is calculated on a cost base which includes the GST. Therefore, the PST of $106 is calculated on $1,060 ($1,000 + $60).

In Nova Scotia, where HST is 14%, the entry would be recorded as follows:

May 20	Office Furniture	1,000	
	HST Recoverable ($1,000 × 14%)	140	
	Accounts Payable		1,140
	To record purchase of office furniture.		

A	=	L	+	OE
+1,000		+1,140		
+140				

Cash flows: no effect

As we have noted before, the amount paid for the PST changes the amount recorded as the cost of the office furniture in each province: $1,080 in Ontario, $1,106 in Prince Edward Island, and $1,000 in Nova Scotia.

Remittance of Sales Taxes

As mentioned in the introduction, businesses act as agents of the federal and provincial governments in charging and later remitting taxes charged on sales and services. For example, Staples, the seller of office furniture illustrated on page B4, must remit GST to the CRA and PST to the Treasurer of Ontario. Notice that even if Staples has not received payment from a customer buying on account before the due date for the remittance, the tax must still be paid to the government authorities. As a registrant, however, Staples will also benefit from claiming input tax credits and recording a reduction in amounts payable from applying GST on sales.

GST (HST)

When remitting the amount owed to the federal government at the end of a reporting period for GST (or HST), the amount of GST payable is reduced by any amount in the GST Recoverable account. Any difference is remitted, as shown in the following journal entry, using assumed amounts payable and recoverable:

June 30	GST Payable	6,250	
	GST Recoverable		2,500
	Cash		3,750
	To record remittance of GST.		

The GST (HST) remittance form requires the registrant to report at specified dates, depending on the business's volume of sales. The amount of the sales and other revenue as well as the amount of GST charged on these sales, whether collected or not, is reported on the remittance form. The amount of the input tax credits claimed is also entered on the form to reduce the amount owing to CRA. If the GST recoverable exceeds the GST payable, the remittance form should be sent as soon as possible in order to ask for a refund. The entry to record the cash receipt from a GST refund will be similar to the entry shown above, except that there will be a debit to Cash, instead of a credit.

The above discussion of the remittance of GST explains why all registrants need two general ledger accounts. One account, GST Payable, is used to keep track of all GST charged on sales and revenues. The second account, GST Recoverable, is used to keep track of the GST input tax credits that have been paid on all of the business's purchases. Failure by a business to capture the proper amounts of input tax credits has a significant impact on income and on cash flows.

PST

The remittance of PST to the Treasurer or Minister of Finance of the applicable province or territory is similar to that of GST except that, since no credit can be claimed, the amount paid at the end of each reporting period is the amount of the balance in the PST Payable account.

Consequently, the entry to record a remittance of PST, using an assumed amount payable, would appear as follows:

June 30	PST Payable	7,400	
	Cash		7,400
	To record remittance of PST.		

Conclusion

Be careful when you record the amounts of taxes charged or claimed in the business accounts. Numbers must be rounded carefully. If the amount of the tax calculated is less then half a cent, the amount should be rounded down. If the amount of the tax as calculated comes to more than half a cent, the amount should be rounded up. For example, applying 6% GST on an amount of $49.20 would give you $2.952. The tax amount to be recorded can be rounded down to $2.95. Rounding might seem insignificant, but with many transactions the amounts can add up and the registrant is responsible to the government authorities for any shortfall created in error.

Sales tax law is intricate. It has added a lot of complexity to the accounting for most transactions flowing through today's businesses. Fortunately, computers that are programmed to automatically determine and record the correct sales tax rate for each good or service provided have simplified matters somewhat. Before recording sales tax transactions, however, it is important to understand all of the relevant sales tax regulations. Check the federal and provincial laws in your jurisdiction.

Brief Exercises

BEB–1 Record the purchase on account of $7,000 of merchandise for resale in the province of Manitoba. The company uses a perpetual inventory system and the purchase is PST exempt.

Record inventory purchase—perpetual inventory system.

BEB–2 Record the return of $1,000 of the merchandise purchased in BEB–1.

Record purchase return—perpetual inventory system.

BEB–3 Record the cash purchase of $500 of office supplies in the province of Saskatchewan, where PST is 5%.

Record purchase of supplies.

BEB–4 Record the purchase on account of a $15,000 delivery truck in the province of Nova Scotia, where HST is 14%.

Record truck purchase.

BEB–5 Record the purchase on account of $100 of office supplies and $4,000 of merchandise for resale in the province of Ontario. The company uses a perpetual inventory system and the purchase of merchandise is PST exempt. The PST rate is 8%.

Record purchase of supplies and inventory—perpetual inventory system.

BEB–6 Record the sale on account, for $1,800, of merchandise costing $1,200 in the province of Prince Edward Island. Assume the company uses a perpetual inventory system. The PST is 10% and the GST is included in the provincial sales tax base.

Record sales—perpetual inventory system.

BEB–7 Half of the shipment described in BEB–6 is returned as the incorrect sizes have been shipped. Record the return of merchandise on the seller's books.

Record sales return—perpetual inventory system.

BEB–8 Record the sale in BEB–6 and the credit memorandum in BEB–7 assuming the business uses a periodic inventory system.

Record sales and sales return—periodic inventory system.

BEB–9 Record the billing for $250 of services by R. R. Dennis, dentist, in the province of British Columbia. Dental services are exempt from GST and PST.

Record exempt services.

BEB–10 Record the billing of accounting fee revenue of $600 for the preparation of personal income tax returns in the province of Alberta. GST is applicable on this service. Alberta does not charge PST.

Record fees.

BEB–11 Record two payments: one cheque to the Receiver General for GST and one to the Treasurer of Ontario for PST. The balances in the accounts are as follows: GST Payable $4,450, GST Recoverable $1,900, and PST Payable $4,870.

Record the remittance of GST and PST.

BEB–12 Record the deposit of a cheque from the Receiver General for a refund of $690 following the filing of an HST return. The balances in the accounts are as follows: HST Payable $2,920 and HST Recoverable $3,610.

Record HST refund.

Exercises

EB–1 Stratton Company is a merchant operating in the province of Ontario where the PST rate is 8%. Stratton uses a perpetual inventory system. Transactions for the business are shown below:

Record sales transactions—perpetual inventory system.

  Mar. 1 Paid March rent to the landlord for the rental of a warehouse. The lease calls for monthly payments of $5,500 plus 6% GST.

Mar. 3 Sold merchandise on account and shipped merchandise to Marvin Ltd. for $20,000, terms n/30, FOB shipping point. This merchandise cost Stratton $11,000.

5 Granted Marvin a sales allowance of $700 for defective merchandise purchased on March 3. No merchandise was returned.

7 Purchased on account from Tiller Ltd. merchandise for resale at a list price of $14,000, plus applicable tax.

12 Made a cash purchase at Home Depot of a desk for the shipping clerk. The price of the desk was $600 before applicable taxes.

31 Paid the monthly remittance of GST to the Receiver General. The balances in the accounts were as follows: GST Payable $4,280 and GST Recoverable $1,917.

Instructions

(a) Prepare the journal entries to record these transactions on the books of Stratton Company.

(b) Assume instead that Stratton operates in the province of Alberta, where PST is not applicable. Prepare the journal entries to record these transactions on the books of Stratton.

(c) Assume instead that Stratton operates in the province of Prince Edward Island, where PST is charged on GST at 10%. Prepare the journal entries to record these transactions on the books of Stratton.

(d) Assume instead that Stratton operates in the province of New Brunswick, where HST is 14%. Prepare the journal entries to record these transactions on the books of Stratton. Assume that the GST balances on March 31 are the balances in the HST accounts.

Record sales transactions—periodic inventory system.

EB–2 Using the information for the transactions of Stratton Company in EB–1, assume now that Stratton uses a periodic inventory system.

Instructions

(a) Prepare the journal entries to record these transactions on the books of Stratton Company.

(b) Assume now that Stratton operates in the province of Alberta, where PST is not applicable. Prepare the journal entries to record these transactions on the books of Stratton.

(c) Assume now that Stratton operates in the province of Prince Edward Island, where PST is charged on GST at 10%. Prepare the journal entries to record these transactions on the books of Stratton.

(d) Assume now that Stratton operates in the province of New Brunswick, where HST is 14%. Prepare the journal entries to record these transactions on the books of Stratton. Assume that the GST balances on March 31 provided in EB–1 are the balances in the HST accounts.

Record service transactions.

EB–3 Tom LeBrun is a sole practitioner providing accounting services in the province of Manitoba. The provincial sales tax rate in Manitoba is 7%, but accounting services are exempt of provincial sales tax. Transactions for the business are shown below:

June 8 Purchased a printer on account at a cost of $1,500. The appropriate sales taxes were added to this purchase price.

10 Purchased toner for the printer for $50 cash from a local stationery store. The store added the appropriate sales taxes to the purchase price.

12 Billed a client for accounting services provided. The fee charged was $750 and GST was added to the fee billed.

15 Collected $106 on account. The original fee was $100 and the GST charged was $6.

30 Paid the monthly remittance of GST to the Receiver General. The balances in the accounts were as follows: GST Payable $1,520.60 and GST Recoverable $820.45.

Instructions

Prepare the journal entries to record these transactions on the books of Tom LeBrun's accounting business.

Problems

PB–1   Mark's Music is a store that buys and sells musical instruments in Ontario, where the provincial sales tax is charged at a rate of 8%. Mark's Music uses a perpetual inventory system. Transactions for the business are shown below:

Record purchase and sales transactions—perpetual inventory system.

Nov. 2 Purchased two electric guitars from Fender Supply Limited, on account, at a cost of $700 each.

4 Made a cash sale of two keyboards for a total invoice price of $2,200, plus applicable taxes. The cost of each keyboard was $950.

5 Received a credit memorandum from Western Acoustic Inc. for the return of an acoustic guitar which was defective. The original invoice price before taxes was $400 and the guitar had been purchased on account.

7 One of the keyboards from the cash sale of Nov. 4 was returned to the store for a full cash refund because the customer was not satisfied with the instrument.

8 Purchased store supplies from a stationery store. The price of the supplies is $100 before all applicable taxes.

10 Sold one Omega trumpet to the Toronto Regional Band, on account, for an invoice price of $2,700 before applicable taxes. The trumpet had cost Mark's Music $1,420.

13 Purchased two saxophones from Yamaha Canada Inc. on account. The invoice price was $2,100 for each saxophone, excluding applicable taxes.

14 Collected $3,990 on account. The payment included GST of $210 and PST of $280.

16 Returned to Yamaha Canada Inc. one of the saxophones purchased on Nov. 13, as it was the wrong model. Received a credit memorandum from Yamaha for the full purchase price.

20 Made a payment on account for the amount owing to Fender Supply Limited for the purchase of Nov. 2.

30 Paid the monthly remittance of GST to the Receiver General. The balances in the accounts were as follows: GST Payable $5,540 and GST Recoverable $1,860.

30 Paid the monthly remittance of PST to the Treasurer of Ontario. The balance in PST Payable is $5,920.

Instructions

Prepare the journal entries to record the Mark's Music transactions.

PB–2   Transaction data for Mark's Music are available in PB–1. Assume Mark's Music uses a periodic inventory system instead of a perpetual inventory system.

Record purchase and sales transactions—periodic inventory system.

Instructions

Prepare the journal entries to record the Mark's Music transactions.

PB–3   David Simmons, L.L.B., is a lawyer operating as a sole practitioner in Nunavut. Nunavut does not charge provincial sales taxes. Transactions for the business are shown below:

Record service transactions.

May 1 Signed a two-year lease for the office space and immediately paid the first and last months' rent. The lease calls for the monthly rent of $1,700 plus applicable taxes.

4 Purchased an office suite of furniture, on account, from Leon's at a cost of $3,400. The appropriate sales taxes were added to this purchase price.

5 Returned one chair to Leon's due to a defect. The cost of the chair before taxes was 400.

6 Billed a client for the preparation of a will. The client was very pleased with the product and immediately paid David's invoice for fees of $1,000 plus taxes.

10 Purchased paper for the photocopier for $300 cash from a local stationery store. The store added the appropriate sales taxes to the purchase price.

13 Billed Manson Ltd. for legal services rendered connected with the purchase of land. The fee charged is $900 plus applicable taxes.

18 Paid Leon's for the furniture purchase of May 4, net of returned items.

May 19 Paid $8 cash to a local grocery store for coffee for the office coffee machine. Groceries are GST exempt.

21 In accordance with the lease agreement with the landlord, David must pay for water supplied by the municipality. The water invoice was received and the services amounted to $100 plus GST.

25 Collected a full payment from Manson Ltd. for the May 13 bill.

27 Completed the preparation of a purchase and sale agreement for Edwards Inc. and billed fees of $1,200.

June 20 Deposited a cheque from the Receiver General for a refund of $270 following the filing of the May GST return. The balances in the accounts were as follows: GST Payable $990 and GST Recoverable $1,260.

Instructions

Prepare the journal entries to record these transactions on the books of David Simmons' law practice.

appendix C
Subsidiary Ledgers and Special Journals

In the textbook, we learned how to record accounting transactions in a general journal. Each journal entry was then individually posted to its respective general ledger account. However, such a practice is only useful in a company where the volume of transactions is low. In most companies, it is necessary to use additional journals (called special journals) and ledgers (called subsidiary ledgers) to record transaction data.

We will look at subsidiary ledgers and special journals in the next sections. Both subsidiary ledgers and special journals can be used in either a manual accounting system or a computerized accounting system.

Subsidiary Ledgers

Imagine a business that has several thousand customers who purchase merchandise from it on account. It records the transactions with these customers in only one general ledger account—Accounts Receivable. It would be virtually impossible to determine the balance owed by an individual customer at any specific time. Similarly, the amount payable to one creditor would be difficult to locate quickly from a single accounts payable account in the general ledger.

Instead, companies use subsidiary ledgers to keep track of individual balances. A subsidiary ledger is a group of accounts that share a common characteristic (for example, all accounts receivable). The subsidiary ledger frees the general ledger from the details of individual balances. A subsidiary ledger is an addition to, and an expansion of, the general ledger.

Two common subsidiary ledgers are:

1. The accounts receivable (or customers') ledger, which collects transaction data for individual customers
2. The accounts payable (or creditors') ledger, which collects transaction data for individual creditors

Other subsidiary ledgers include an inventory ledger, which collects transaction data for each inventory item purchased and sold, as was described in Chapter 5. Some companies also use a payroll ledger, detailing individual employee pay records. In each of these subsidiary ledgers, individual accounts are arranged in alphabetical, numerical, or alphanumerical order.

The detailed data from a subsidiary ledger are summarized in a general ledger account. For example, the detailed data from the accounts receivable subsidiary ledger are summarized in Accounts

Receivable in the general ledger. The general ledger account that summarizes subsidiary ledger data is called a control account.

Each general ledger control account balance must equal the total balance of the individual accounts in the related subsidiary ledger. This is an important internal control function.

Example

An example of an accounts receivable control account and subsidiary ledger is shown in Illustration C-1 for Mercier Enterprises.

Illustration C-1 ▶

Accounts receivable general ledger control account and subsidiary ledger

> Accounts Receivable is a control account.

GENERAL LEDGER

Accounts Receivable   No. 112

Date	Explanation	Ref.	Debit	Credit	Balance
2008					
Jan. 31			12,000		12,000
31				8,000	4,000

> The subsidiary ledger is separate from the general ledger.

ACCOUNTS RECEIVABLE SUBSIDIARY LEDGER

Aaron Co.   No. 112-172

Date	Explanation	Ref.	Debit	Credit	Balance
2008					
Jan. 11	Invoice 336		6,000		6,000
19	Payment			4,000	2,000

Branden Inc.   No. 112-173

Date	Explanation	Ref.	Debit	Credit	Balance
2008					
Jan. 12	Invoice 337		3,000		3,000
21	Payment			3,000	0

Caron Co.   No. 112-174

Date	Explanation	Ref.	Debit	Credit	Balance
2008					
Jan. 20	Invoice 339		3,000		3,000
29	Payment			1,000	2,000

The example is based on the following transactions:

Credit Sales			Collections on Account		
Jan. 11	Aaron Co.	$ 6,000	Jan. 19	Aaron Co.	$4,000
12	Branden Inc.	3,000	21	Branden Inc.	3,000
20	Caron Co.	3,000	29	Caron Co.	1,000
		$12,000			$8,000

The total debits ($12,000) and credits ($8,000) in Accounts Receivable in the general ledger match the detailed debits and credits in the subsidiary accounts. The balance of $4,000 in the control account agrees with the total of the balances in the individual accounts receivable accounts (Aaron $2,000 + Branden $0 + Caron $2,000) in the subsidiary ledger.

Rather than relying on customer or creditor names in a subsidiary ledger, a computer system expands the account number of the control account. For example, if the general ledger control account Accounts Receivable was numbered 112, the first customer account in the accounts receivable subsidiary ledger might be numbered 112-001, the second 112-002, and so on. Most systems allow inquiries about specific customer accounts in the subsidiary ledger (by account number) or about the control account.

As shown, postings are made monthly to the control account in the general ledger. We will learn, in the next section, how special journals facilitate monthly postings. We will also learn how to fill in the posting references (in the Ref. column) in both the general ledger and subsidiary ledger accounts. Postings to the individual accounts in the subsidiary ledger are made daily. The rationale for posting daily is to ensure that account information is current. This enables Mercier Enterprises to monitor credit limits, send statements to customers, and answer inquiries from customers about their account balances. In a computerized accounting system, transactions are simultaneously recorded in journals and posted to both the general and subsidiary ledgers.

Advantages of Subsidiary Ledgers

Subsidiary ledgers have several advantages:

1. **They show transactions that affect one customer or one creditor in a single account.** They provide up-to-date information on specific account balances.
2. **They free the general ledger of excessive details.** A trial balance of the general ledger does not contain vast numbers of individual customer account balances.
3. **They help locate errors in individual accounts.** The potential for errors is minimized by reducing the number of accounts in one ledger and by using control accounts.
4. **They make possible a division of labour in posting.** One employee can post to the general ledger while different employees post to the subsidiary ledgers. This strengthens internal control, since one employee verifies the work of the other.

In a computerized accounting system, the last two advantages don't apply. Computerized accounting systems do not make errors such as calculation errors and posting errors. Other errors, such as entry errors, can and do still occur. Internal control must be done using different means in computerized systems since account transactions are posted automatically.

Special Journals

As mentioned earlier, journalizing transactions in a two-column (debit and credit) general journal is satisfactory only when there are few transactions. To help with the journalizing and posting of multiple transactions, most companies use special journals in addition to the general journal.

A special journal is used to record similar types of transactions. Examples include all sales of merchandise on account, or all cash receipts. The types of special journals used depend largely on the types of transactions that occur frequently. While the form, type, and number of special journals used will vary among organizations, many merchandising companies use the journals shown in Illustration C-2 to record daily transactions. The letters that appear in parentheses following the journal name represent the posting reference used for each journal.

Illustration C-2 ▶

Use of special journals and
the general journal

Sales Journal (S)	Cash Receipts Journal (CR)	Purchases Journal (P)	Cash Payments Journal (CP)	General Journal (J)
All sales of merchandise on account	All cash received (including cash sales)	All purchases of merchandise on account	All cash paid (including cash purchases of merchandise)	Transactions that cannot be entered in a special journal, including correcting, adjusting, and closing entries

If a transaction cannot be recorded in a special journal, it is recorded in the general journal. For example, if you have four special journals as listed in Illustration C-2, sales returns and allowances are recorded in the general journal. Similarly, correcting, adjusting, and closing entries are recorded in the general journal. Other types of special journals may sometimes be used in certain situations. For example, when sales returns and allowances are frequent, an additional special journal may be used to record these transactions. A payroll journal is another example of a special journal. It organizes and summarizes payroll details for companies with many employees.

The use of special journals reduces the time needed for the recording and posting process. In addition, special journals permit greater division of labour because different employees can record entries in different journals. For example, one employee may journalize all cash receipts. Another may journalize credit sales. The division of responsibilities ensures that one person does not have control over all aspects of a transaction. In this instance, recording the sale has been separated from recording the collection of cash from that sale. This may reduce the opportunity for intentional or unintentional error, and is one aspect of a good internal control system.

For a merchandising company, the same special journals are used whether a company uses the periodic or perpetual system to account for its inventory. The only distinction is the number of, and title for, the columns each journal uses. We will use Karns Wholesale Supply to show the use of special journals in the following sections. Karns uses a perpetual inventory system. The variations between the periodic and perpetual inventory systems are highlighted in helpful hints for your information. In addition, special journals under a periodic inventory system are shown more fully at the end of this appendix.

Sales Journal

The sales journal is used to record sales of merchandise on account. Cash sales of merchandise are entered in the cash receipts journal. Credit sales of assets other than merchandise are entered in the general journal.

Journalizing Credit Sales

Under the perpetual inventory system, each entry in the sales journal results in one entry at selling price and another entry at cost. The entry at selling price is a debit to Accounts Receivable (a control account supported by a subsidiary ledger) and a credit of an equal amount to Sales. The entry at cost is a debit to Cost of Goods Sold and a credit of an equal amount to Merchandise Inventory. Some companies also set up Merchandise Inventory as a control account supported by a subsidiary ledger.

A sales journal with two amount columns can show a sales transaction recognized at both selling price and cost on only one line. The two-column sales journal of Karns Wholesale Supply is shown in Illustration C-3, using assumed credit sales transactions.

| KARNS WHOLESALE SUPPLY | | | | | |
| Sales Journal | | | | | S1 |
Date	Account Debited	Invoice No.	Ref.	Accts. Receivable Dr. Sales Cr.	Cost of Goods Sold Dr. Merchandise Inventory Cr.
2008					
May 3	Abbot Sisters	101		10,600	6,360
7	Babson Co.	102		11,350	7,370
14	Carson Bros.	103		7,800	5,070
19	Deli Co.	104		9,300	6,510
21	Abbot Sisters	105		15,400	10,780
24	Deli Co.	106		21,210	15,900
27	Babson Co.	107		14,570	10,200
				90,230	62,190

Illustration C-3

Sales journal—perpetual inventory system

Helpful hint In a periodic inventory system, the sales journal would have only one column to record the sale at selling price (Accounts Receivable Dr., Sales Cr.). The cost of goods sold is not recorded. It is calculated at the end of the period.

The reference (Ref.) column is not used in journalizing. It is used in posting the sales journal, as explained in the next section. Also, note that, unlike in the general journal, an explanation is not required for each entry in a special journal. Finally, note that each invoice is prenumbered to ensure that all invoices are journalized.

If management wishes to record its sales by department, additional columns may be provided in the sales journal. For example, a department store may have columns for home furnishings, sporting goods, shoes, etc. In addition, the federal government, and practically all provinces, require that sales taxes be charged on items sold. If sales taxes are collected, it is necessary to add more credit columns to the sales journal for GST Payable and PST Payable (or HST Payable).

Posting the Sales Journal

Postings from the sales journal are made **daily to the individual accounts receivable accounts** in the subsidiary ledger. Posting **to the general ledger is done monthly**. Illustration C-4 shows both the daily postings to the accounts receivable subsidiary ledger and the monthly postings to the general ledger accounts. We have assumed that Karns Wholesale Supply does not maintain an inventory subsidiary ledger. However, if it did, the procedure is similar to that illustrated for the accounts receivable subsidiary ledger.

A check mark (√) is inserted in the reference posting column to indicate that the daily posting to the customer's account has been made. A check mark is used when the subsidiary ledger accounts are not individually numbered. If the subsidiary ledger accounts are numbered, the account number is used instead of the check mark in the reference posting column. At the end of the month, the column totals of the sales journal are posted to the general ledger. Here, the column totals are posted as a debit of $90,230 to Accounts Receivable (account no. 112), a credit of $90,230 to Sales (account no. 401), a debit of $62,190 to Cost of Goods Sold (account no. 505), and a credit of $62,190 to Merchandise Inventory (account no. 120). Inserting the account numbers below the column totals indicates that the postings have been made. In both the general ledger and subsidiary ledger accounts, the reference S1 indicates that the posting came from page 1 of the sales journal.

Illustration C-4 ▶

Sales journal—perpetual
inventory system

KARNS WHOLESALE SUPPLY
Sales Journal   S1

Date	Account Debited	Invoice No.	Ref.	Accts. Receivable Dr. Sales Cr.	Cost of Goods Sold Dr. Merchandise Inventory Cr.
2008					
May 3	Abbot Sisters	101	√	10,600	6,360
7	Babson Co.	102	√	11,350	7,370
14	Carson Bros.	103	√	7,800	5,070
19	Deli Co.	104	√	9,300	6,510
21	Abbot Sisters	105	√	15,400	10,780
24	Deli Co.	106	√	21,210	15,900
27	Babson Co.	107	√	14,570	10,200
				90,230	62,190
				(112)/(401)	(505)/(120)

Individual amounts are posted daily to the subsidiary ledger.

Totals are posted at the end of the accounting period to the general ledger.

ACCOUNTS RECEIVABLE SUBSIDIARY LEDGER

Abbot Sisters

Date	Ref.	Debit	Credit	Balance
2008				
May 3	S1	10,600		10,600
21	S1	15,400		26,000

Babson Co.

Date	Ref.	Debit	Credit	Balance
2008				
May 7	S1	11,350		11,350
27	S1	14,570		25,920

Carson Bros.

Date	Ref.	Debit	Credit	Balance
2008				
May 14	S1	7,800		7,800

Deli Co.

Date	Ref.	Debit	Credit	Balance
2008				
May 19	S1	9,300		9,300
24	S1	21,210		30,510

GENERAL LEDGER

Accounts Receivable   No. 112

Date	Ref.	Debit	Credit	Balance
2008				
May 31	S1	90,230		90,230

Merchandise Inventory   No. 120

Date	Ref.	Debit	Credit	Balance
2008				
May 31	S1		62,190	62,190cr[1]

Sales   No. 401

Date	Ref.	Debit	Credit	Balance
2008				
May 31	S1		90,230	90,230

Cost of Goods Sold   No. 505

Date	Ref.	Debit	Credit	Balance
2008				
May 31	S1	62,190		62,190

The subsidiary ledger is separate from the general ledger.

Accounts Receivable is a control account.

[1] The normal balance for Merchandise Inventory is a debit. But, because of the sequence in which we have posted the special journals, with the sales journal first, the credits to Merchandise Inventory are posted before the debits. This posting sequence explains the credit balance in Merchandise Inventory, which exists only until the other journals are posted.

Proving the Ledgers

The next step is to "prove" the ledgers. To do so, we must determine two things: (1) The sum of the subsidiary ledger balances must equal the balance in the control account. (2) The total of the general ledger debit balances must equal the total of the general ledger credit balances. The proof of the postings from the sales journal to the general and subsidiary ledgers follows:

Accounts Receivable Subsidiary Ledger		General Ledger	
		Debits	
Abbot Sisters	$26,000	Accounts Receivable	$ 90,230
Babson Co.	25,920	Cost of Goods Sold	62,190
Carson Bros.	7,800		$152,420
Deli Co.	30,510		
	$90,230	Credits	
		Merchandise Inventory	$ 62,190
		Sales	90,230
			$152,420

Advantages of the Sales Journal

The use of a special journal to record sales on account has a number of advantages. First, the one-line–two-column entry for each sales transaction saves time. In the sales journal, it is not necessary to write out the four account titles for the two transactions. Second, only totals, rather than individual entries, are posted to the general ledger. This saves posting time and reduces the possibility of errors in posting. Third, the prenumbering of sales invoices helps to ensure that all sales are recorded and that no sale is recorded more than once. Finally, a division of labour results, because one individual can take responsibility for the sales journal alone. These last two advantages help internal control.

Cash Receipts Journal

All receipts of cash are recorded in the cash receipts journal. The most common types of cash receipts are cash sales of merchandise and collections of accounts receivable. Many other possibilities exist, such as a receipt of money from a bank loan and cash proceeds from disposals of equipment. A one- or two-column cash receipts journal would not have enough space for all possible cash receipt transactions. A multiple-column cash receipts journal is therefore used.

Generally, a cash receipts journal includes the following columns: a debit column for cash, and credit columns for accounts receivable, sales, and other accounts. The Other Accounts column is used when the cash receipt does not involve a cash sale or a collection of accounts receivable. Under a perpetual inventory system, each sales entry is accompanied by another entry that debits Cost of Goods Sold and credits Merchandise Inventory. A separate column is added for this purpose. A five-column cash receipts journal is shown in Illustration C-5.

Additional credit columns may be used if they significantly reduce postings to a specific account. For example, cash receipts from cash sales normally include the collection of sales taxes, which are later remitted to the federal and provincial governments. Most cash receipts journals have a separate credit column for sales tax collections. Other examples include the cash receipts of a loan company, such as Household Financial Centre, which cover thousands of collections from customers. These collections are credited to Loans Receivable and Interest Revenue. A significant saving in posting time would result from using separate credit columns for Loans Receivable and Interest Revenue, rather than using the Other Accounts credit column. In contrast, a retailer that has only one interest collection a month would not find it useful to have a separate column for Interest Revenue.

Illustration C-5 ►

Cash receipts journal—
perpetual inventory system

Helpful hint In a periodic inventory system, the Cash Receipts journal would have one column fewer. The Cost of Goods Sold Dr. and Merchandise Inventory Cr. would not be recorded.

KARNS WHOLESALE SUPPLY
Cash Receipts Journal — CR1

Date	Account Credited	Ref.	Cash Dr.	Accounts Receivable Cr.	Sales Cr.	Cost of Goods Sold Dr. Mdse. Inv. Cr.	Other Accounts Cr.
2008							
May 1	D. Karns, Capital	301	5,000				5,000
7			1,900		1,900	1,240	
10	Abbot Sisters	√	10,600	10,600			
12			2,600		2,600	1,690	
17	Babson Co.	√	11,350	11,350			
22	Notes Payable	200	6,000				6,000
23	Carson Bros.	√	7,800	7,800			
28	Deli Co.	√	9,300	9,300			
			54,550	39,050	4,500	2,930	11,000
			(101)	(112)	(401)	(505)/(120)	(X)

Individual amounts are posted daily to the subsidiary ledger.

Totals are posted at the end of the accounting period to the general ledger.

ACCOUNTS RECEIVABLE SUBSIDIARY LEDGER

Abbot Sisters

Date	Ref.	Debit	Credit	Balance
2008				
May 3	S1	10,600		10,600
10	CR1		10,600	0
21	S1	15,400		15,400

Babson Co.

Date	Ref.	Debit	Credit	Balance
2008				
May 7	S1	11,350		11,350
17	CR1		11,350	0
27	S1	14,570		14,570

Carson Bros.

Date	Ref.	Debit	Credit	Balance
2008				
May 14	S1	7,800		7,800
23	CR1		7,800	0

Deli Co.

Date	Ref.	Debit	Credit	Balance
2008				
May 19	S1	9,300		9,300
24	S1	21,210		30,510
28	CR1		9,300	21,210

The subsidiary ledger is separate from the general ledger.

Accounts Receivable is a control account.

GENERAL LEDGER

Cash — No. 101

Date	Ref.	Debit	Credit	Balance
2008				
May 31	CR1	54,550		54,550

Accounts Receivable — No. 112

Date	Ref.	Debit	Credit	Balance
2008				
May 31	S1	90,230		90,230
31	CR1		39,050	51,180

Merchandise Inventory — No. 120

Date	Ref.	Debit	Credit	Balance
2008				
May 31	S1		62,190	62,190 Cr.
31	CR1		2,930	65,120 Cr.

Notes Payable — No. 200

Date	Ref.	Debit	Credit	Balance
2008				
May 22	CR1		6,000	6,000

D. Karns, Capital — No. 301

Date	Ref.	Debit	Credit	Balance
2008				
May 1	CR1		5,000	5,000

Sales — No. 401

Date	Ref.	Debit	Credit	Balance
2008				
May 31	S1		90,230	90,230
31	CR1		4,500	94,730

Cost of Goods Sold — No. 505

Date	Ref.	Debit	Credit	Balance
2008				
May 31	S1	62,190		62,190
31	CR1	2,930		65,120

Journalizing Cash Receipt Transactions

To illustrate the journalizing of cash receipts transactions, we will continue with the May transactions of Karns Wholesale Supply. Collections from customers are for the entries recorded in the sales journal in Illustration C-3. The entries in the cash receipts journal are based on the following cash receipts:

May 1 D. Karns makes an investment of $5,000 in the business.
     7 Cash receipts for merchandise sales total $1,900. The cost of goods sold is $1,240.
    10 A cheque for $10,600 is received from Abbot Sisters in full payment of invoice No. 101.
    12 Cash receipts for merchandise sales total $2,600. The cost of goods sold is $1,690.
    17 A cheque for $11,350 is received from Babson Co. in full payment of invoice No. 102.
    22 Cash is received by signing a 4% note for $6,000, payable September 22 to the National Bank.
    23 A cheque for $7,800 is received from Carson Bros. in full payment of invoice No. 103.
    28 A cheque for $9,300 is received from Deli Co. in full payment of invoice No. 104.

Further information about the columns in the cash receipts journal follows:

Debit Columns:

1. **Cash.** The amount of cash actually received in each transaction is entered in this column. The column total indicates the total cash receipts for the month. The total of this column is posted to the cash account in the general ledger.

2. **Cost of Goods Sold.** The Cost of Goods Sold Dr./Merchandise Inventory Cr. column is used to record the cost of the merchandise sold. (The sales column records the selling price of the merchandise.) The cost of goods sold column is similar to the one found in the sales journal. The amount debited to Cost of Goods Sold is the same amount credited to Merchandise Inventory. One column total is posted to both accounts at the end of the month.

Credit Columns:

3. **Accounts Receivable.** The Accounts Receivable column is used to record cash collections on account. The amount entered here is the amount to be credited to the individual customer's account.

4. **Sales.** The Sales column is used to record all cash sales of merchandise. Cash sales of other assets (property, plant, and equipment, for example) are not reported in this column. The total of this column is posted to the account Sales.

5. **Merchandise Inventory.** As noted above, the Cost of Goods Sold Dr./Merchandise Inventory Cr. column is used to record the reduction in the merchandise available for future sale. The amount credited to Merchandise Inventory is the same amount debited to Cost of Goods Sold. One column total is posted to both accounts at the end of the month.

6. **Other Accounts.** The Other Accounts column is used whenever the credit is not to Accounts Receivable, Sales, or Merchandise Inventory. For example, in the first entry, $5,000 is entered as a credit to D. Karns, Capital. This column is often referred to as the sundry accounts column.

In a multi-column journal, only one line is generally needed for each entry. In some cases, it is useful to add explanatory information, such as the details of the note payable, or to reference supporting documentation, such as invoice numbers if cash sales are invoiced. Note also that the Account Credited column is used to identify both general ledger and subsidiary ledger account titles. The former is shown in the May 1 entry for Karns' investment. The latter is shown in the May 10 entry for the collection from Abbot Sisters.

Debit and credit amounts for each line must be equal. When the journalizing has been completed, the amount columns are totalled. The totals are then compared to prove the equality of debits and credits in the cash receipts journal. Don't forget that the Cost of Goods Sold Dr./Merchandise Inventory Cr. column total represents both a debit and a credit amount. Totalling the columns of a journal and proving the equality of the totals is called footing (adding down) and cross-footing (adding across) a journal.

The proof of the equality of Karns' cash receipts journal is on the following page:

Debit		Credits	
Cash	$54,550	Accounts Receivable	$39,050
Cost of Goods Sold	2,930	Merchandise Inventory	2,930
	$57,480	Sales	4,500
		Other Accounts	11,000
			$57,480

Posting the Cash Receipts Journal

Posting a multi-column journal involves the following steps:

1. All column totals, except for the Other Accounts total, are posted once at the end of the month to the account title specified in the column heading, such as Cash, Accounts Receivable, Sales, Cost of Goods Sold, and Merchandise Inventory. Account numbers are entered below the column totals to show that the amounts have been posted.
2. The total of the Other Accounts column is not posted. Individual amounts that make up the Other Accounts total are posted separately to the general ledger accounts specified in the Account Credited column. See, for example, the credit posting to D. Karns, Capital. The symbol X is inserted below the total for this column to indicate that the amount has not been posted.
3. The individual amounts in a column (Accounts Receivable, in this case) are posted daily to the subsidiary ledger account name specified in the Account Credited column. See, for example, the credit posting of $10,600 to Abbot Sisters.

The abbreviation CR is used in both the subsidiary and general ledgers to identify postings from the cash receipts journal.

Proving the Ledgers

After the posting of the cash receipts journal is completed, it is necessary to prove the ledgers. As shown below, the sum of the subsidiary ledger account balances equals the control account balance. The general ledger totals are also in agreement.

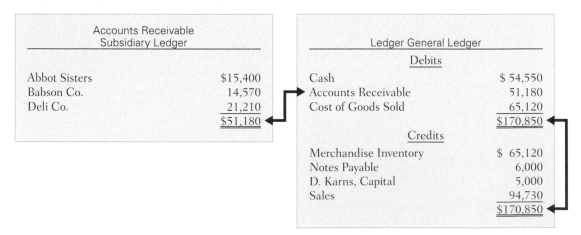

Accounts Receivable Subsidiary Ledger		Ledger General Ledger	
		Debits	
Abbot Sisters	$15,400	Cash	$ 54,550
Babson Co.	14,570	Accounts Receivable	51,180
Deli Co.	21,210	Cost of Goods Sold	65,120
	$51,180		$170,850
		Credits	
		Merchandise Inventory	$ 65,120
		Notes Payable	6,000
		D. Karns, Capital	5,000
		Sales	94,730
			$170,850

Purchases Journal

All purchases of merchandise on account are recorded in the purchases journal. Each entry in this journal results in a debit to Merchandise Inventory and a credit to Accounts Payable. When a one-column purchases journal is used, other types of purchases on account and cash purchases cannot be journalized in it. For example, credit purchases of equipment or supplies must be recorded in the general journal. Likewise, all cash purchases are entered in the cash payments journal. If there are many credit purchases for items other than merchandise, the purchases journal can be expanded to a multi-column format.

The purchases journal for Karns Wholesale Supply is shown in Illustration C-6, with assumed credit purchases.

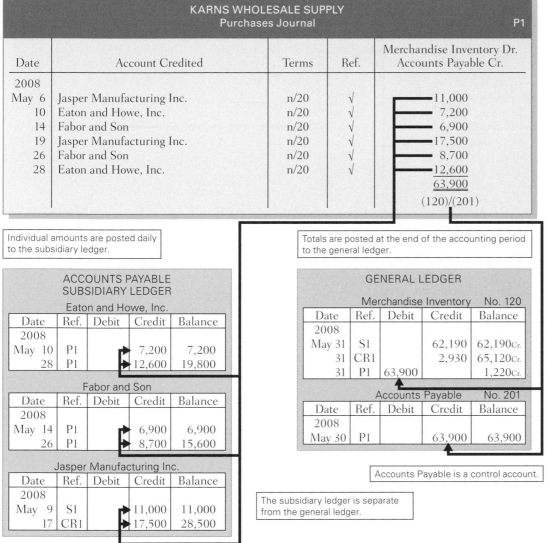

Illustration C-6 ◄

Purchases journal—
perpetual inventory system

Helpful hint When a periodic inventory system is used, this journal is still known as a purchases journal. The debit to the Merchandise Inventory account is replaced by a debit to the Purchases account.

Journalizing Credit Purchases of Merchandise

Entries in the purchases journal are made from purchase invoices. The journalizing procedure for the purchases journal is similar to that for the sales journal. In contrast to the sales journal, the purchases journal may not have an invoice number column, because invoices received from different suppliers would not be in numerical sequence.

Posting the Purchases Journal

The procedures for posting the purchases journal are similar to those for the sales journal. In this case, postings are made daily to the accounts payable subsidiary ledger accounts and monthly to the Merchandise Inventory and Accounts Payable accounts in the general ledger. In both ledgers, P1 is used in the reference column to show that the postings are from page 1 of the purchases journal.

Proof of the equality of the postings from the purchases journal to both ledgers is shown by the following:

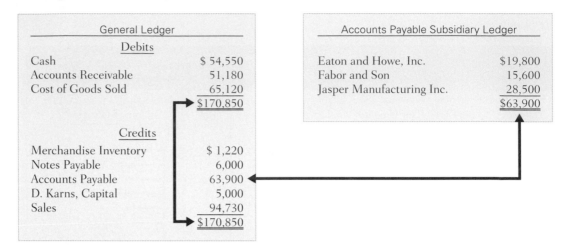

General Ledger		Accounts Payable Subsidiary Ledger	
Debits			
Cash	$ 54,550	Eaton and Howe, Inc.	$19,800
Accounts Receivable	51,180	Fabor and Son	15,600
Cost of Goods Sold	65,120	Jasper Manufacturing Inc.	28,500
	$170,850		$63,900
Credits			
Merchandise Inventory	$ 1,220		
Notes Payable	6,000		
Accounts Payable	63,900		
D. Karns, Capital	5,000		
Sales	94,730		
	$170,850		

Note that not all the general ledger accounts listed above have been included in Illustration C-6. You will have to refer to Illustration C-5 to determine the balances for the accounts Cash, Accounts Receivable, Cost of Goods Sold, Notes Payable, Capital, and Sales.

Cash Payments Journal

Alternative terminology
The cash payments journal is also called the *cash disbursements journal.*

All disbursements of cash are entered in a cash payments journal. Entries are made from prenumbered cheques. Because cash payments are made for various purposes, the cash payments journal has multiple columns. A four-column journal is shown in Illustration C-7.

Journalizing Cash Payments Transactions

The procedures for journalizing transactions in this journal are similar to those described earlier for the cash receipts journal. Each transaction is entered on one line, and for each line there must be equal debit and credit amounts. It is common practice in the cash payments journal to record the name of the company or individual receiving the cheque (the payee), so that later reference to the cheque is possible by name in addition to cheque number. The entries in the cash payments journal shown in Illustration C-7 are based on the following transactions for Karns Wholesale Supply:

May 3	Cheque No. 101 for $1,200 issued for the annual premium on a fire insurance policy from Corporate General Insurance.
3	Cheque No. 102 for $100 issued to CANPAR in payment of freight charges on goods purchased.
7	Cheque No. 103 for $4,400 issued for the cash purchase of merchandise from Zwicker Corp.
10	Cheque No. 104 for $11,000 sent to Jasper Manufacturing Inc. in full payment of the May 6 invoice.
19	Cheque No. 105 for $7,200 mailed to Eaton and Howe, Inc., in full payment of the May 10 invoice.
24	Cheque No. 106 for $6,900 sent to Fabor and Son in full payment of the May 14 invoice.
28	Cheque No. 107 for $17,500 sent to Jasper Manufacturing Inc. in full payment of the May 19 invoice.
31	Cheque No. 108 for $500 issued to D. Karns as a cash withdrawal for personal use.

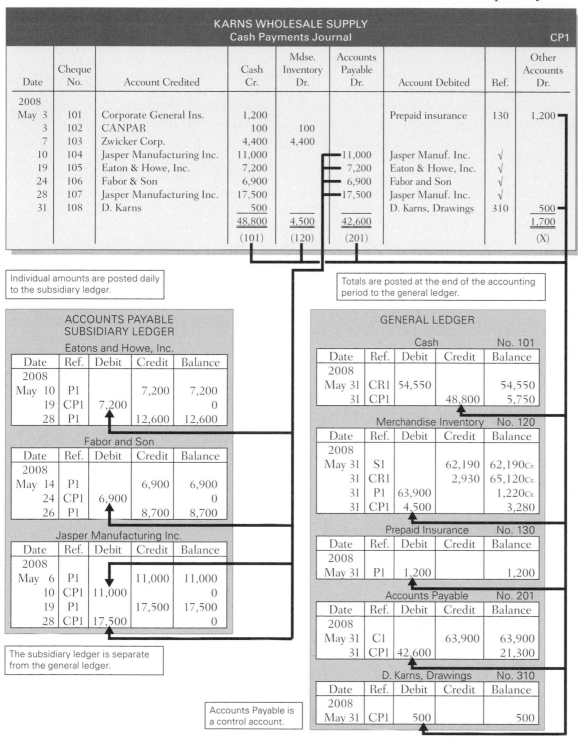

Illustration C-7 ◀

Cash payments journal— perpetual inventory system

Helpful hint In a periodic inventory system, the debits to Merchandise Inventory would be recorded to the accounts Purchases and Freight In.

Note that whenever an amount is entered in the Other Accounts column, a specific general ledger account must be identified in the Account Debited column. The entries for cheque numbers 101 and 108 show this situation. Similarly, a subsidiary account must be identified in the Account Debited column whenever an amount is entered in the Accounts Payable column (as, for example, the entry for cheque no. 104).

After the cash payments journal has been journalized, the columns are totalled. The totals are then balanced to prove the equality of debits and credits. Debits ($4,500 + $42,600 + $1,700 = $48,800) do equal credits ($48,800) in this case.

Posting the Cash Payments Journal

The procedures for posting the cash payments journal are similar to those for the cash receipts journal:

1. Cash and Merchandise Inventory are posted only as a total at the end of the month.
2. The amounts recorded in the Accounts Payable column are posted individually to the subsidiary ledger and in total to the general ledger control account.
3. Transactions in the Other Accounts column are posted individually to the appropriate account(s) noted in the Account Debited column. No totals are posted for the Other Accounts column.

The posting of the cash payments journal is shown in Illustration C-7. Note that the abbreviation CP is used as the posting reference. After postings are completed, the equality of the debit and credit balances in the general ledger should be determined. The control account balance should also agree with the subsidiary ledger total balance. The agreement of these balances is shown below. Note that not all the general ledger accounts have been included in Illustration C-7. You will also have to refer to Illustration C-5 to determine the balances for the Accounts Receivable, Cost of Goods Sold, Notes Payable, Capital, and Sales accounts.

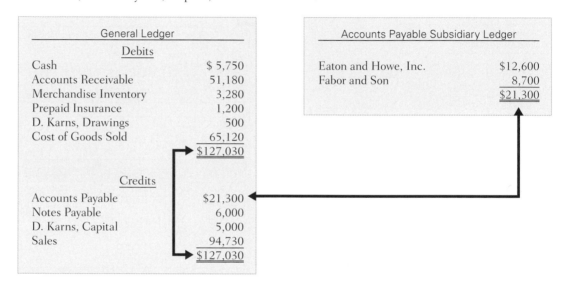

General Ledger		Accounts Payable Subsidiary Ledger	
Debits			
Cash	$ 5,750	Eaton and Howe, Inc.	$12,600
Accounts Receivable	51,180	Fabor and Son	8,700
Merchandise Inventory	3,280		$21,300
Prepaid Insurance	1,200		
D. Karns, Drawings	500		
Cost of Goods Sold	65,120		
	$127,030		
Credits			
Accounts Payable	$21,300		
Notes Payable	6,000		
D. Karns, Capital	5,000		
Sales	94,730		
	$127,030		

Effects of Special Journals on the General Journal

Special journals for sales, purchases, and cash greatly reduce the number of entries that are made in the general journal. **Only transactions that cannot be entered in a special journal are recorded in the general journal.** For example, the general journal may be used to record a transaction granting credit to a customer for a sales return or allowance. It may also be used to record the receipt of a credit from a supplier for purchases returned, the acceptance of a note receivable from a customer, and the purchase of equipment by issuing a note payable. Correcting, adjusting, and closing entries are also made in the general journal.

When control and subsidiary accounts are not used, the procedures for journalizing and posting transactions in the general journal are the same as those described in earlier chapters. When control and subsidiary accounts are used, two modifications of earlier procedures are required:

1. In journalizing, both the control and the subsidiary account must be identified.
2. In posting, there must be a dual posting: once to the control account and once to the subsidiary account.

To illustrate, assume that on May 31 Karns Wholesale Supply returns $500 of merchandise for credit to Fabor and Son. The entry in the general journal and the posting of the entry are shown in Illustration C-8. Note that if cash had been received instead of the credit granted on this return, then the transaction would have been recorded in the cash receipts journal.

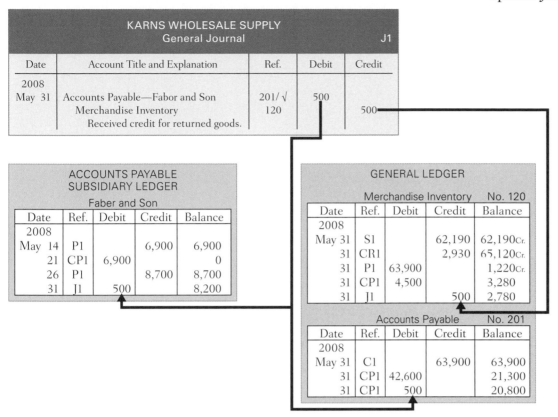

Illustration C-8 ◄

General journal

Helpful hint In a periodic inventory system, the credit would be to the Purchase Returns and Allowances account rather than to Merchandise Inventory.

Notice that in the general journal two accounts are indicated for the debit (the Accounts Payable control account and the Fabor and Son subsidiary account). Two postings (201/√) are indicated in the reference column. One amount is posted to the control account in the general ledger (no. 201) and the other to the creditor's account in the subsidiary ledger (Fabor and Son).

Special Journals in a Periodic Inventory System

Recording and posting transactions in special journals is essentially the same whether a perpetual or a periodic inventory system is used. But there are two differences. The first difference relates to the accounts Merchandise Inventory and Cost of Goods Sold in a perpetual inventory system. In this system, an additional column is required to record the cost of each sale in the sales and cash receipts journals, something which is not required in a periodic inventory system.

The second difference concerns the account titles used. In a perpetual inventory system, Merchandise Inventory and Cost of Goods Sold are used to record purchases and the cost of the merchandise sold. In a periodic inventory system, the accounts Purchases and Freight In accumulate the cost of the merchandise purchased until the end of the period. No cost of goods sold is recorded during the period. Cost of goods sold is calculated at the end of the period in a periodic inventory system.

Each of the special journals illustrated in this appendix is shown again here. Using the same transactions, we assume that Karns Wholesale Supply uses a periodic inventory system instead of a perpetual inventory system.

Illustration C-9 ▶

Sales journal—periodic inventory system

Helpful hint Compare this sales journal to the one presented in Illustration C-4.

	KARNS WHOLESALE SUPPLY			
	Sales Journal			S1
Date	Account Debited	Invoice No.	Ref.	Accts Receivable Dr. Sales Cr.
2008				
May 3	Abbot Sisters	101	√	10,600
7	Babson Co.	102	√	11,350
14	Carson Bros.	103	√	7,800
19	Deli Co.	104	√	9,300
21	Abbot Sisters	105	√	15,400
24	Deli Co.	106	√	21,210
27	Babson Co.	107	√	14,570
				90,230

Illustration C-10 ▶

Cash receipts journal—periodic inventory system

Helpful hint Compare this cash receipts journal to the one presented in Illustration C-5.

	KARNS WHOLESALE SUPPLY					
	Cash Receipts Journal					CR1
Date	Account Credited	Ref.	Cash Dr.	Accounts Receivable Cr.	Sales Cr.	Other Accounts Cr.
2008						
May 1	D. Karns, Capital	301	5,000			5,000
7			1,900		1,900	
10	Abbot Sisters	√	10,600	10,600		
12			2,600		2,600	
17	Babson Co.	√	11,350	11,350		
22	Notes Payable	200	6,000			6,000
23	Carson Bros.	√	7,800	7,800		
28	Deli Co.	√	9,300	9,300		
			54,550	39,050	4,500	11,000

Illustration C-11 ▶

Purchases journal—periodic inventory system

Helpful hint Compare this purchases journal to the one presented in Illustration C-6.

	KARNS WHOLESALE SUPPLY			
	Purchases Journal			P1
Date	Account Credited	Terms	Ref.	Purchases Dr. Accounts Payable Cr.
2008				
May 6	Jasper Manufacturing Inc.	n/20	√	11,000
10	Eaton and Howe, Inc.	n/20	√	7,200
14	Fabor and Son	n/20	√	6,900
19	Jasper Manufacturing Inc.	n/20	√	17,500
26	Fabor and Son	n/20	√	8,700
28	Eaton and Howe, Inc.	n/20	√	12,600
				63,900

Illustration C-12 ▶

Cash payments journal—periodic inventory system

Helpful hint Compare this cash payments journal to the one presented in Illustration C-7.

	KARNS WHOLESALE SUPPLY							
	Cash Payments Journal							CP1
Date	Cheque No.	Payee	Cash Cr.	Accounts Payable Dr.	Account Debited	Ref.	Other Accounts Dr.
2008							
May 3	101	Corporate General Ins.	1,200		Prepaid Insurance	130	1,200
3	102	CANPAR	100		Freight In	516	100
7	103	Zwicker Corp.	4,400		Purchases	510	4,400
10	104	Jasper Manufacturing Inc.	11,000	11,000	Jasper Manuf. Inc.	√	
19	105	Eaton & Howe, Inc.	7,200	7,200	Eaton & Howe, Inc.	√	
24	106	Fabor and Son	6,900	6,900	Fabor and Son	√	
28	107	Jasper Manufacturing Inc.	17,500	17,500	Jasper Manuf. Inc.	√	
31	108	D. Karns	500		D. Karns, Drawings	310	500
			48,800	42,600			6,200

Brief Exercises

BEC–1 Information related to Bryan Company is presented below for its first month of operations. Calculate (a) the balances that appear in the accounts receivable subsidiary ledger for each customer, and (b) the accounts receivable balance that appears in the general ledger at the end of January.

Calculate subsidiary ledger and control account balances.

Credit Sales			Cash Collections		
Jan. 7	Duffy Co.	$8,000	Jan. 17	Duffy Co.	$7,000
15	Hanson Inc.	6,000	24	Hanson Inc.	5,000
23	Lewis Co.	9,000	29	Lewis Co.	9,000

BEC–2 Identify in which ledger (general or subsidiary) each of the following accounts is shown:

Identify general and subsidiary ledger accounts.

1. Rent Expense
2. Accounts Receivable—O'Malley
3. Notes Payable
4. Accounts Payable—Kerns
5. Merchandise Inventory
6. Sales

BEC–3 Chiasson Co. uses special journals and a general journal. Identify the journal in which each of the following transactions is recorded:

Identify special journals.

1. Paid cash for equipment purchased on account.
2. Purchased merchandise on credit.
3. Paid utility expense in cash.
4. Sold merchandise on account.
5. Granted a cash refund for a sales return.
6. Received a credit on account for a purchase return.
7. Sold merchandise for cash.
8. Purchased merchandise for cash.

BEC–4 Swirsky Company uses the cash receipts and cash payments journals illustrated in this appendix for a perpetual inventory system. In April, the following selected cash transactions occurred:

Identify special journals—perpetual inventory system.

1. Made a refund to a customer for the return of damaged goods that had been purchased on credit.
2. Received payment from a customer.
3. Purchased merchandise for cash.
4. Paid a creditor.
5. Paid freight on merchandise purchased.
6. Paid cash for office equipment.
7. Received a cash refund from a supplier for merchandise returned.
8. Withdrew cash for personal use of owner.
9. Made cash sales.

Instructions

Indicate (a) the journal, and (b) the columns in the journal that should be used in recording each transaction.

BEC–5 Identify the journal and the specific column title(s) in which each of the following transactions is recorded. Assume the company uses a periodic inventory system.

Identify special journals—periodic inventory system.

1. Cash sale
2. Credit sale
3. Sales return on account
4. Cash purchase of merchandise
5. Credit purchase of merchandise
6. Payment of freight on merchandise purchased from a supplier
7. Return of merchandise purchased for cash refund
8. Payment of freight on merchandise delivered to a customer

Exercises

Identify special journals.

EC–1 Below are some transactions for Dartmouth Company:

1. Payment of creditors on account
2. Return of merchandise sold for credit
3. Collection on account from customers
4. Sale of land for cash
5. Sale of merchandise on account
6. Sale of merchandise for cash
7. Credit received for merchandise returned to a supplier
8. Payment of employee wages
9. Revenues and expenses closed to income summary
10. Amortization on building
11. Purchase of office supplies for cash
12. Purchase of merchandise on account

Instructions

For each transaction, indicate whether it would normally be recorded in a cash receipts journal, cash payments journal, sales journal, purchases journal, or general journal.

Record transactions in sales and purchases journals—perpetual inventory system.

EC–2 Sing Tao Company uses special journals and a general journal. The company uses a perpetual inventory system and had the following transactions:

Sept. 2 Sold merchandise on account to T. Meto, $520, invoice #101, terms n/30. The cost of the merchandise sold was $360.
  3 Purchased office supplies on account from Berko Co., $350.
  10 Purchased merchandise on account from Miramichi Co., $800, FOB shipping point, terms n/30. Paid freight of $50 to Apex Shippers.
  11 Returned unsatisfactory merchandise to Miramichi Co., $200, for credit on account.
  12 Purchased office equipment on account from Wells Co., $8,000.
  16 Sold merchandise for cash to L. Maille, for $800. The cost of the merchandise sold was $480.
  18 Purchased merchandise for cash from Miramichi Co., $450, FOB destination.
  20 Accepted returned merchandise from customer L. Maille, $800 (see Sept. 16 transaction). Gave full cash refund. Restored the merchandise to inventory.
  24 Paid the correct amount owing for the merchandise purchased from Miramichi earlier in the month.
  25 Received payment from T. Meto for Sept. 2 sale.
  26 Sold merchandise on account to M. Christie, $890, invoice #102, terms n/30, FOB destination. The cost of the merchandise was $520. The appropriate party paid $75 to Freight Co. for shipping charges.
  30 Paid September salaries, $2,800.
  30 Withdrew cash for owner's personal use, $600.
  30 Paid for office supplies purchased on September 3.

Instructions

(a) Draw a sales journal and a purchases journal (see Illustrations C-3 and C-6). Use page 1 for each journal.
(b) Record the transaction(s) for September that should be recorded in the sales journal.
(c) Record the transaction(s) for September that should be recorded in the purchases journal.

EC–3 Refer to the information provided for Sing Tao Company in EC–2.

Instructions

(a) Draw cash receipts and cash payments journals (see Illustrations C-5 and C-7) and a general journal. Use page 1 for each journal.
(b) Record the transaction(s) provided in EC–2 that should be recorded in the cash receipts journal.
(c) Record the transaction(s) provided in EC–2 that should be recorded in the cash payments journal.
(d) Record the transaction(s) provided in EC–2 that should be recorded in the general journal.

EC–4 Argentina Company has the following selected transactions during March:

Mar. 2 Purchased equipment on account, costing $7,400, from Lifetime Inc.
5 Received credit memorandum for $300 from Lyden Company for merchandise returned that had been damaged in shipment to Argentina.
7 Issued a credit memorandum for $400 to Marco Presti for merchandise the customer returned. The returned merchandise has a cost of $275 and was restored to inventory.

Argentina Company uses a purchases journal, a sales journal, two cash journals (receipts and payments), and a general journal. Argentina also uses a perpetual inventory system.

Instructions

(a) Record the appropriate transactions in the general journal.
(b) In a brief memo to the president of Argentina Company, explain the postings to the control and subsidiary accounts.

EC–5 Maureen Company uses both special journals and a general journal. On June 30, after all monthly postings had been completed, the Accounts Receivable controlling account in the general ledger had a debit balance of $320,000, and the Accounts Payable controlling account had a credit balance of $87,000.

The July transactions recorded in the special journals are summarized below. Maureen Company maintains a perpetual inventory system. No entries that affected accounts receivable and accounts payable were recorded in the general journal for July.

Sales journal: total sales, $161,400; cost of goods sold, $112,800
Purchases journal: total purchases, $56,400
Cash receipts journal: accounts receivable column total, $141,000
Cash payments journal: accounts payable column total, $47,500

Instructions

(a) What is the balance of the Accounts Receivable control account after the monthly postings on July 31?
(b) What is the balance of the Accounts Payable control account after the monthly postings on July 31?
(c) To what accounts are the column totals for total sales of $161,400 and cost of goods sold of $112,800 in the sales journal posted?
(d) To what account(s) is the accounts receivable column total of $141,000 in the cash receipts journal posted?

EC–6 On September 1, the balance of the Accounts Receivable control account in the general ledger of Pirie Company was $11,960. The customers' subsidiary ledger contained account balances as follows: Jana, $2,440; Kingston, $2,640; Cavanaugh, $2,060; Bickford, $4,820. At the end of September, the various journals contained the following information:

Sales journal: Sales to Bickford, $800; to Jana, $1,260; to Iman, $1,030; to Cavanaugh, $1,100. The cost of each sale, respectively, was $480, $810, $620, and $660.
Cash receipts journal: Cash received from Cavanaugh, $1,310; from Bickford, $2,300; from Iman, $380; from Kingston, $1,800; from Jana, $1,240.
General journal: A $190 sales allowance is granted to Bickford, on September 30.

Instructions

(a) Set up control and subsidiary accounts, and enter the beginning balances.
(b) Post the various journals to the control and subsidiary accounts. Post the items as individual items or as totals, whichever would be the appropriate procedure. Use page 1 for each journal.
(c) Prepare a list of customers and prove the agreement of the control account with the subsidiary ledger at September 30.

Record transactions in sales and purchases journals—periodic inventory system.

EC–7 Refer to the information provided for Sing Tao Company in EC–2. Complete instructions (a), (b), and (c), assuming that the company uses a periodic inventory system instead of a perpetual inventory system.

Record transactions in cash receipts, cash payments, and general journals—periodic inventory system.

EC–8 Refer to the information provided for Sing Tao Company in EC–3. Complete instructions (a) to (d), assuming that the company uses a periodic inventory system instead of a perpetual inventory system.

Problems

Record transactions in special and general journals—perpetual inventory system.

PC–1 Selected accounts from the chart of accounts of Genstar Company are shown below:

101	Cash	201	Accounts payable
112	Accounts receivable	401	Sales
120	Merchandise inventory	412	Sales returns and allowances
126	Supplies	505	Cost of goods sold
157	Equipment	726	Salaries expense

The company uses a perpetual inventory system. The cost of all merchandise sold is 60% of the sales price. During January, Genstar completed the following transactions:

Jan. 3 Purchased merchandise on account from Sun Distributors, $19,800.
    4 Purchased supplies for cash, $280.
    4 Sold merchandise on account to R. Gilbertson, $6,500, invoice no. 371.
    5 Issued a debit memorandum to Sun Distributors and returned $450 of damaged goods.
    6 Made cash sales for the week totalling $4,650.
    8 Purchased merchandise on account from Irvine Co., $5,400.
    9 Sold merchandise on account to Mays Corp., $5,600, invoice no. 372.
    11 Purchased merchandise on account from Chaparal Co., $4,300.
    13 Paid Sun Distributors account in full.
    13 Made cash sales for the week totalling $2,290.
    15 Received payment from Mays Corp. for invoice no. 372.
    15 Paid semi-monthly salaries of $14,300 to employees.
    17 Received payment from R. Gilbertson for invoice no. 371.
    17 Sold merchandise on account to AMB Co., $1,500, invoice no. 373.
    19 Purchased equipment on account from Johnson Corp., $4,800.
    20 Cash sales for the week totalled $3,400.
    20 Paid Irvine Co. account in full.
    23 Purchased merchandise on account from Sun Distributors, $7,800.
    24 Purchased merchandise on account from Levine Corp., $4,690.
    27 Made cash sales for the week totalling $3,370.
    30 Received payment from AMB Co. for invoice no. 373.
    31 Paid semi-monthly salaries of $13,200 to employees.
    31 Sold merchandise on account to R. Gilbertson, $9,330, invoice no. 374.

Genstar Company uses a sales journal, a purchases journal, a cash receipts journal, a cash payments journal, and a general journal.

Instructions

(a) Record the January transactions in the appropriate journal.
(b) Foot and cross-foot all special journals.
(c) Show how postings would be made by placing ledger account numbers and check marks as needed in the journals. (Actual posting to ledger accounts is not required.)

PC–2 Selected accounts from the chart of accounts of Tigau Company are shown below:

Record transactions in special and general journals—perpetual inventory system.

101	Cash	145	Buildings
112	Accounts receivable	201	Accounts payable
120	Merchandise inventory	401	Sales
126	Supplies	505	Cost of goods sold
140	Land	610	Advertising expense

The company uses a perpetual inventory system. The cost of all merchandise sold was 65% of the sales price. During October, Tigau Company completed the following transactions:

Oct. 2 Purchased merchandise on account from Madison Co., $15,800.
 4 Sold merchandise on account to Petro Corp., $8,600, invoice no. 204.
 5 Purchased supplies for cash, $315.
 7 Made cash sales for the week that totalled $9,610.
 9 Paid the Madison Co. account in full.
 10 Purchased merchandise on account from Quinn Corp., $4,900.
 12 Received payment from Petro Corp. for invoice no. 204.
 13 Issued a debit memorandum to Quinn Corp. and returned $260 of damaged goods.
 14 Made cash sales for the week that totalled $8,810.
 16 Sold a parcel of land for $25,000 cash, the land's book value.
 17 Sold merchandise on account to Callebaut Co., $5,530, invoice no. 205.
 18 Purchased merchandise for cash, $2,215.
 21 Made cash sales for the week that totalled $8,640.
 23 Paid in full the Quinn Corp. account for the goods kept.
 25 Purchased supplies on account from Frey Co., $260.
 25 Sold merchandise on account to Golden Corp., $5,520, invoice no. 206.
 25 Received payment from Callebaut Co. for invoice no. 205.
 26 Purchased for cash a small parcel of land and a building on the land to use as a storage facility. The total cost of $35,000 was allocated $16,000 to the land and $19,000 to the building.
 27 Purchased merchandise on account from Schmid Co., $9,000.
 28 Made cash sales for the week that totalled $9,320.
 30 Purchased merchandise on account from Madison Co., $16,200.
 30 Paid advertising bill for the month from The Gazette, $600.
 30 Sold merchandise on account to Callebaut Co., $5,200, invoice no. 207.

Tigau Company uses a sales journal, purchases journal, cash receipts journal, cash payments journal, and general journal.

Instructions

(a) Record the October transactions in the appropriate journals.
(b) Foot and cross-foot all special journals.
(c) Show how postings would be made by placing ledger account numbers and check marks as needed in the journals. (Actual posting to ledger accounts is not required.)

PC–3 The post-closing trial balance for Gibbs Music Co. follows:

GIBBS MUSIC CO.
Post-Closing Trial Balance
December 31, 2007

		Debit	Credit
101	Cash	$ 49,500	
112	Accounts receivable	15,000	
115	Notes receivable	45,000	
120	Merchandise inventory	22,000	
140	Land	25,000	
145	Building	75,000	
146	Accumulated amortization—building		$ 18,000
157	Equipment	6,450	
158	Accumulated amortization—equipment		1,500
200	Notes payable		–
201	Accounts payable		42,000
275	Mortgage payable		82,000
301	M. Gibbs, capital		94,450
310	M. Gibbs, drawings	–	
401	Sales	–	
410	Sales returns and allowances	–	
505	Cost of goods sold	–	
725	Salaries expense	–	
920	Loss—damaged inventory	–	
		$237,950	$237,950

The subsidiary ledgers contain the following information:

1. Accounts Receivable—R. Christof, $3,000; B. Hibberd, $7,500; S. Armstrong, $4,500
2. Accounts Payable—Fieldstone Corp., $9,000; Watson & Co., $17,000; Harms Distributors, $16,000

Gibbs Music Co. uses a perpetual inventory system. The transactions for January 2008 are as follows:

Jan. 3 Sold merchandise to B. Rohl, $1,000. The cost of goods sold was $550.
  5 Purchased merchandise from Warren Parts, $2,400.
  7 Received a cheque from S. Armstrong, $3,000, in partial payment of its account.
  11 Paid freight on merchandise purchased, $350.
  13 Received payment of account in full from B. Rohl.
  14 Issued a credit memo to acknowledge receipt of $600 of damaged merchandise returned by R. Christof. The cost of the returned merchandise was $250. (*Hint*: Debit Loss—Damaged Inventory instead of Merchandise Inventory.)
  15 Sent Harms Distributors a cheque in full payment of account.
  17 Purchased merchandise from Lapeska Co., $1,900.
  18 Paid salaries of $3,700.
  20 Gave Watson & Co. a 60-day note for $17,000 in full payment of account payable.
  23 Total cash sales amounted to $8,200. The cost of goods sold was $3,840.
  24 Sold merchandise on account to B. Hibberd, $7,800. The cost of goods sold was $3,300.
  27 Sent Warren Parts a cheque for $950 in partial payment of the account.
  29 Received payment on a note of $35,000 from S. Lava.
  30 Returned merchandise costing $600 to Lapeska Co. for credit.
  31 Withdrew $800 cash for personal use.

Instructions

(a) Open general and subsidiary ledger accounts and record December 31, 2007, balances.

(b) Record the January transactions in a sales journal, a purchases journal, a cash receipts journal, a cash payments journal, and a general journal, as illustrated in this appendix.

(c) Post the appropriate amounts to the subsidiary and general ledger accounts.

(d) Prepare a trial balance at January 31, 2008.

(e) Determine whether the subsidiary ledgers agree with control accounts in the general ledger.

PC–4 The post-closing trial balance for Scholz Co. follows:

Record transactions in special and general journals, post, and prepare trial balance—perpetual inventory system.

SCHOLZ CO.
Post-Closing Trial Balance
April 30, 2008

	Debit	Credit
101 Cash	$ 36,700	
112 Accounts receivable	15,400	
115 Notes receivable—Cole Company	48,000	
120 Merchandise inventory	22,000	
157 Equipment	8,200	
158 Accumulated amortization—equipment		$ 1,800
200 Notes payable	–	
201 Accounts payable		43,400
301 C. Scholz, capital		85,100
310 C. Scholz, drawings	–	
401 Sales		–
410 Sales returns and allowances	–	
505 Cost of goods sold	–	
725 Salaries expense	–	
730 Rent expense	–	
	$130,300	$130,300

The subsidiary ledgers contain the following information:

1. Accounts Receivable—W. Karasch, $3,250; L. Cellars, $7,400; G. Parrish, $4,750
2. Accounts Payable—Winterware Corp., $10,500; Elite Sports, $15,500; Buttercup Distributors, $17,400

Scholz uses a perpetual inventory system. The transactions for May 2008 are as follows:

May 3 Sold merchandise to B. Simone, $2,400. The cost of the goods sold was $1,050.
   5 Purchased merchandise from WN Widgit, $2,600, on account.
   7 Received a cheque from G. Parrish, $2,800, in partial payment of account.
  11 Paid freight on merchandise purchased, $318.
  12 Paid rent of $1,500 for May.
  13 Received payment in full from B. Simone.
  14 Issued a credit memo to acknowledge $750 of merchandise returned by W. Karasch. The merchandise (original cost, $325) was restored to inventory.
  15 Sent Buttercup Distributors a cheque in full payment of account.
  17 Purchased merchandise from Lancio Co., $2,100, on account.
  18 Paid salaries of $4,700.
  20 Gave Elite Sports a two-month, 10% note for $15,500 in full payment of account payable.
  20 Returned merchandise costing $510 to Lancio for credit.
  23 Total cash sales amounted to $9,500. The cost of goods sold was $4,450.
  27 Sent WN Widgit a cheque for $1,000, in partial payment of account.
  29 Received payment on a note of $40,000 from Cole Company.
  31 Withdrew $1,000 cash for personal use.

Instructions

(a) Open general and subsidiary ledger accounts and record April 30, 2008, balances.

(b) Record the May transactions in a sales journal, a purchases journal, a cash receipts journal, a cash payments journal, and a general journal, as illustrated in this chapter.

(c) Post the appropriate amounts to the subsidiary and general ledger accounts.

(d) Prepare a trial balance at May 31, 2008.

(e) Determine whether the subsidiary ledgers agree with the control accounts in the general ledger.

Record transactions in special and general journals— periodic inventory system.

PC–5 Selected accounts from the chart of accounts on Weir Company are shown below:

101	Cash	401	Sales
112	Accounts receivable	412	Sales returns and allowances
126	Supplies	510	Purchases
157	Equipment	512	Purchase returns and allowances
201	Accounts payable	726	Salaries expense

During February, Weir completed the following transactions:

Feb. 3 Purchased merchandise on account from Zears Co., $9,200.
    4 Purchased supplies for cash, $290.
    4 Sold merchandise on account to Gilles Co., $7,220, invoice no. 371.
    5 Issued a debit memorandum to Zears Co. and returned $450 worth of goods.
    6 Made cash sales for the week totalling $3,950.
    8 Purchased merchandise on account from Fell Electronics, $5,200,
    9 Sold merchandise on account to Mawani Corp., $7,050, invoice no. 372.
   11 Purchased merchandise on account from Thomas Co., $3,100.
   13 Paid Zears Co. account in full.
   13 Made cash sales for the week totalling $4,850.
   15 Received payment from Mawani Corp. for invoice no. 372.
   15 Paid semi-monthly salaries of $14,700 to employees.
   17 Received payment from Gilles Co. for invoice no. 371.
   17 Sold merchandise on account to Lumber Co., $1,600, invoice no. 373.
   19 Purchased equipment on account from Brown Corp., $6,400.
   20 Cash sales for the week totalled $4,900.
   20 Paid Fell Electronics account in full.
   23 Purchased merchandise on account from Zears Co., $8,800.
   24 Purchased merchandise on account from Lewis Co., $5,130.
   27 Made cash sales for the week totalling $3,560.
   28 Received payment from Lumber Co. for invoice no. 373.
   28 Paid semi-monthly salaries of $14,900 to employees.
   28 Sold merchandise on account to Gilles Co., $9,810, invoice no. 374.

Weir Company uses a sales journal, purchases journal, cash receipts journal, cash payments journal, and general journal. Weir uses a periodic inventory system.

Instructions

(a) Record the February transactions in the appropriate journal.

(b) Foot and cross-foot all special journals.

(c) Show how postings would be made by placing ledger account numbers and check marks as needed in the journals. (Actual posting to ledger accounts is not required.)

Cumulative Coverage—
Chapters 2 to 6 and Appendix C

Kassam Company has the following opening account balances in its general and subsidiary ledgers on January 1. All accounts have normal debit and credit balances. Kassam uses a perpetual inventory system. The cost of all merchandise sold was 40% of the sales price.

GENERAL LEDGER

Account No.	Account Title	January 1 Opening Balance
101	Cash	$ 35,050
112	Accounts receivable	14,000
115	Notes receivable	39,000
120	Merchandise inventory	20,000
125	Office supplies	1,000
130	Prepaid insurance	2,000
140	Land	50,000
145	Building	100,000
146	Accumulated amortization—building	25,000
157	Equipment	6,450
158	Accumulated amortization—equipment	1,500
201	Accounts payable	36,000
275	Mortgage payable	125,000
301	A. Kassam, capital	80,000

Accounts Receivable Subsidiary Ledger			Accounts Payable Subsidiary Ledger	
Customer	January 1 Opening Balance		Creditor	January 1 Opening Balance
R. Draves	$1,500		Liazuk Co.	$10,000
B. Jacovetti	7,500		Mikush Bros.	15,000
S. Kysely	5,000		Nguyen & Son	11,000

Kassam's January transactions follow:

Jan. 3 Sold merchandise on credit to B. Sota $3,100, invoice no. 510, and J. Ebel $1,800, invoice no. 511.

5 Purchased merchandise on account from Welz Wares for $3,000 and Laux Supplies for $2,700.

7 Received cheques for $5,000 from S. Kysely and $2,000 from B. Jacovetti on accounts.

8 Paid freight on merchandise purchased, $180.

9 Sent cheques to Liazuk Co. for $10,000 and Nguyen & Son for $11,000 in full payment of accounts.

9 Issued credit memo for $400 to J. Ebel for merchandise returned. The merchandise was restored to inventory.

10 Summary cash sales totalled $16,500.

11 Sold merchandise on credit to R. Draves for $1,900, invoice no. 512, and to S. Kysely for $900, invoice no. 513.

15 Withdrew $2,000 cash for A. Kassam's personal use.

16 Purchased merchandise on account from Nguyen & Son for $15,000, from Liazuk Co. for $13,900, and from Welz Wares for $1,500.

17 Paid $400 cash for office supplies.

18 Returned $500 of merchandise to Liazuk and received credit.

20 Summary cash sales totalled $17,500.

21 Issued $15,000 note to Mikush Bros. in payment of balance due. The note bears an interest rate of 10% and is due in three months.

21 Received payment in full from S. Kysely.

Jan. 22 Sold merchandise on credit to B. Soto for $1,700, invoice no. 514, and to R. Draves for $800, invoice no. 515.

23 Sent cheques to Nguyen & Son and Liazuk Co. in full payment of accounts.

25 Sold merchandise on credit to B. Jacovetti for $3,500, invoice no. 516, and to J. Ebel for $6,100, invoice no. 517.

27 Purchased merchandise on account from Nguyen & Son for $14,500, from Laux Supplies for $1,200, and from Welz Wares for $2,800.

28 Paid $800 cash for office supplies.

31 Summary cash sales totalled $19,920.

31 Paid sales salaries of $4,300 and office salaries of $2,600.

31 Received payment in full from B. Soto and J. Ebel on account.

In addition to the accounts identified in the trial balance, the chart of accounts shows the following: No. 200 Notes Payable, No. 230 Interest Payable, No. 300 Income Summary, No. 310 A. Kassam, Drawings, No. 401 Sales, No. 410 Sales Returns and Allowances, No. 505 Cost of Goods Sold, No. 711 Amortization Expense, No. 718 Interest Expense, No. 722 Insurance Expense, No. 725 Salaries Expense, and No. 728 Office Supplies Expense.

Instructions

(a) Record the January transactions in the appropriate journal—sales, purchases, cash receipts, cash payments, and general.

(b) Post the journals to the general and subsidiary ledgers. New accounts should be added and numbered in an orderly fashion as needed.

(c) Prepare an unadjusted trial balance at January 31, 2008. Determine whether the subsidiary ledgers agree with the control accounts in the general ledger.

(d) Prepare adjusting journal entries. Prepare an adjusted trial balance, using the following additional information:

1. Office supplies at January 31 total $700.
2. Insurance coverage expires on September 30, 2008.
3. Annual amortization on the building is $6,000 and on the equipment is $1,500.
4. Interest of $45 has accrued on the note payable.
5. A physical count of merchandise inventory has found $44,850 of goods on hand.

(e) Prepare a multiple-step income statement and a statement of owner's equity for January, and a classified balance sheet at the end of January.

(f) Prepare and post the closing entries.

(g) Prepare a post-closing trial balance.

Company Index

A cumulative index appears at the end of each Part.

A&W, 11
Agricore United, 98
Air Canada, 113, 136
American Productivity and Quality Center, 169
Andrés Wines, 179
Andrew Peller Limited, 179
ATI Technologies, 303
Atlanta Thrashers, 57

Beanz Espresso Bar, 340
Best Buy, 262
Big Rock Brewery, 11, 203
Big Rock Brewery Income Trust, 326
Bombardier, 9, 303
Brick Group, 11
Burnaby School Board, 9

Calgary Exhibition and Stampede Limited, 32
Calgary Rotary Club, 9
Canada Post, 176
Canadian Consumer Initiative, 367
Canadian Payments Association, 360, 368
Canadian Tire, 351
Coca-Cola, 332

Danier Leather, 268, 322

Ellen's Boutique, 9
EnCana, 9
Enron, 2

Fidelity Investments, 71
Forzani Group, 1, 6, 29, 46, 97, 105, 157, 215, 278, 304, 335, 346, 371, 401, A1–A17

Gap Inc., 215–216
Goodyear Tire & Rubber Company, 63

Hollinger International, 2

Imperial Oil, 9
Indigo Books & Music, 336
Interac, 352
IPSCO Inc., 274
Irving Group, 9

Jim Pattison Group, 9

Kingsclear Indian Band, 9

La Senza Corporation, 177
Leon's Furniture, 136
Liaison Can./U.S., 286
Liquidation World, 232
Loblaw, 9

Maclean's, 137
Magna, 9
MasterCard, 350
McCain Foods, 9
Moulé, 162

NIKE, 33
Nortel Networks, 2, 174

1-800-GOT-JUNK?, 5
Ottawa Senators, 57

Parmalat, 2
PepsiCo, 332
Petro-Canada, 282, 289
Power Corporation of Canada, 177
Prestige Dance Academy, 50
Prince Philip Drive Campus Bookstore, 218
Province of Alberta, 9

Q9 Networks, 402

RBC Financial Group, 136
Research in Motion Limited (RIM), 46
Rogers Communications, 157
Roots Canada Ltd., 32

Sears, 136, 178, 370
Seneca College, 102, 105
Shaw Communications, 178
Sleeman Breweries, 210, 279

The Gap, 215–216
Toronto Blue Jays, 136

Ville de Montréal, 9
Visa, 350

Wal-Mart, 222
Westjet Airlines, 179
WorldCom, 2

Subject Index

A cumulative index appears at the end of each part.

Account, 52
Accounting
  building blocks, 7–15
  defined, 6
  importance, 2–3
  information system, as, 6
Accounting assumptions
  economic entity assumption, 9
  going concern assumption, 8–9
  monetary unit assumption, 9
Accounting cycle, 172
Accounting equation, 11
Accounting information, users, 4–5
Accounting principles
  cost principle, 8
  full disclosure principle, 8, 296, 315
  matching principle, 105–106
  revenue recognition principle, 105
  time period assumption, 104–105
Accounting Standards Board (AcSB), 7
Accounting Standards Oversight Council (AcSOC), 7
Accounting time period, 104–105
Accounts payable subsidiary ledger, C1
Accounts receivable subsidiary ledger, C1, C2
Accrual adjustment, 115–119
Accrual basis of accounting, 106–107
Accrued expenses, 117–119, 120
Accrued interest, 117–118
Accrued liabilities, 117
Accrued receivables, 116
Accrued revenues, 116, 120
Accrued salaries, 118–119
AcSB, 7
AcSOC, 7
Adjusted trial balance, 123, 124
Adjusting entries, 108–120
  accruals, 115–119
  accrued expenses, 117–119, 120
  accrued interest, 117–118
  accrued revenues, 116, 120
  accrued salaries, 118–119
  insurance, 111
  merchandising company, 234, 237
  prepaid expenses, 110–113, 120, 127–128
  prepayments, 109–114
  summary (table), 120
  supplies, 110–111
  types, 109
  unearned revenues, 113–114, 120, 128–129
Administrative expenses, 240

Amortization
  adjusting entry, 111–113
  allocation concept, as, 112
  defined, 111–112
  straight-line method, 112
Annual report, 24
Assets, 11–12, 53–54
Assumptions. *See Accounting assumptions*
Average cost, 292–293, 307–308

Balance sheet, 23
  accumulated amortization, 113
  classified, 175–180
  current assets, 176
  current liabilities, 178
  intangible assets, 178
  inventory cost flow assumption, 297
  inventory errors, 300
  long-term investments, 176-177
  long-term liabilities, 179
  property, plant, and equipment, 177
  standard classification, 175–179
Bank, 357–369
  cheques/cheque clearing, 359–361
  deposits, 358–359
  reconciling the bank account, 363–367
  statement, 360–363
Bank credit card transactions, 350
Bank deposits, 358–359
Bank embezzlement, 346
Bank errors, 365, 367–368
Bank overdraft, 370
Bank reconciliation, 363–367
Bank service charge, 362
Barkwell, Mike, 282
Batten, Dean, 218
Benchmarking studies, 169
Book of original entry, 58
Brisebois, Diane, 234
Burkhead, J. Gary, 71

Canadian Institute of Chartered Accountants (CICA), 7
Carriage paid to (CPT), 228
Carrying value, 113
Cash, 369–370
Cash basis of accounting, 106–107
Cash controls, 348–357
  cash disbursements, 352–357
  cash receipts, 348–352
  cheques, 354
  credit card transactions, 350–351
  debit card transactions, 350

electronic payments, 354–355
electronic receipts, 352
mail-in receipts, 351
over-the-counter receipts, 349–350
petty cash fund, 355–357
Cash disbursements journal, C12
Cash equivalents, 370
Cash flow statement, 23–24
Cash payments journal, 354, C12–C14
Cash receipts journal, 350, C7–C10
Cash register tapes, 349
Cents, 71
CFO, 169
Chart of accounts, 63
Cheque clearing, 359–360, 362
Cheques, 359–360
Chequing account, 360
Chief financial officer (CFO), 169
Chip card, 352
CICA, 7
CIF, 226
Classified balance sheet. *See Balance sheet*
Clearing, 359–360
Closing entries, 165-167. *See also Closing the books*
Closing the books, 164-170
    benchmarking studies, 169
    defined, 164
    merchandising company, 235–236, 237
    periodic inventory system, 250–251
    post-closing trial balance, 169–170
    posting closing entries, 168–169
    preparing closing entries, 165–168
    steps in process, 165
    temporary/permanent accounts, 164
CM, 363, 365
Compensating balances, 370
Compound entry, 59–60
Conservatism, 302
Consigned goods, 286
Consignee, 286
Consignor, 286
Contra account, 113
Contra asset account, 113
Contra revenue account, 231
Control account, 225, C2
Control activities, 343–346. *See also Internal control*
Corporation, 10
Correcting entries, 173–174
Cost flow assumptions, 289-295
Cost, insurance, freight (CIF), 226
Cost of good purchases, 249
Cost of goods available for sale, 250
Cost of goods on hand, 249
Cost of goods sold, 223, 249–250

Cost principle, 8
CPT, 228
Credit, 52
Credit-debit rules, 52–56
Credit memoranda (CM), 362-363, 365
Credit memorandum, 227
Credit terms, 227
Crediting the account, 52
Current assets, 176
Current liabilities, 178
Current ratio, 182
Currie, Ron, 102

Days sales in inventory, 305
de Vries, Greg, 57
Debit, 52
Debit-credit rules, 52–56
Debit memorandum (DM), 362, 365
Debiting the account, 52
Deferred revenues, 113
Deposit slip, 358, 359
Deposits in transit, 363, 364–365
Depreciation, 111. *See also Amortization*
Discount
    purchase, 227
    purchase transaction, 227–228
    quantity, 227
    sales, 232
    sales transactions, 232
DM, 362, 365
Dollar sign, 72
Double-entry system, 53
Drawings, 12, 54–55

Economic entity assumption, 9
Electronic funds transfer (EFT), 352, 354–355
Employee theft, 234
Ending inventory, 249
Equity, 179
Error, 71
Estimating inventories, 310–312
Ethics, 3
Expanded accounting equation, 55–56
Expense recognition, 105
Expenses, 13
External auditors, 346
External review, 346
External users, 5

FCA, 226
Fidelity insurance, 346
FIFO, 290–292, 306–307
Financial ratios. *See Ratio analysis*
Financial statements, 21–24

balance sheet. *See Balance sheet*
cash flow statement, 23–24
example (Forzani Group), A1–A17
income statement. *See Income statement*
interrelationships, 22
merchandising company, 239–243
preparing, from adjusted trial balance, 124, 125
preparing, from worksheet, 186
reliability, 123
simplifying assumptions, 71–72
statement of owner's equity, 22, 23
First-in, first-out (FIFO), 290–292, 306–307
Fiscal year, 105
FOB destination, 226, 230
FOB shipping point, 226, 230
Forms of business organization
corporation, 10. *See also Corporation*
distinction between different forms, 13–14
income trust, 10–11. *See also Income trust*
partnership, 10. *See also Partnership*
proprietorship, 9–10
Forzani, John, 1
Fraud, 301
Free carrier (FCA), 226
Freight costs, 226, 230, 246, 247
Full disclosure principle, 296
Future revenues, 113

GAAP, 7
Gélinas, Ellen, 9
General journal, 58
General ledger, 60–61
Generally accepted accounting principles (GAAP), 7
Going concern assumption, 8–9
Goods and services tax (GST), B1–B2, B7–B8
Goods in transit, 285–286
Gorenstein, Laurie, 162
Gross profit, 240
Gross profit margin, 244–245
Gross profit method, 310–311
GST, B1–B2, B7–B8

Harmonized sales tax (HST), B2, B7–B8
Heatley, Dany, 57
Hiring of employees, 66
Hossa, Marian, 57
HST, B2, B7–B8
Hunsley, Amanda, 50
Hurry, Doug, 340

IASB, 7
IFRS, 7
Income from operations, 240
Income statement, 23

gross profit, 240
income from operations, 240
inventory cost flow assumption, 296–297
inventory errors, 298–300
multi-step, 239–242
net income, 241
net sales, 239–240
non-operating activities, 240, 241
single-step, 242, 243
Income summary, 165
Income trust, 10–11, 179
Input tax credit (ITC), B1
Insurance, 111
Intangible assets, 178
Interest
accrued, 117–118
adjusting entry, 117–118
Interest expense, 117–118
Interest payable, 117–118
Interim periods, 104
Internal auditors, 346
Internal control, 340–404
bonding of employees, 346
cash controls, 348–357. *See also Cash controls*
custody of assets, 344
defined, 342
documentation procedures, 344–345
establishment of responsibility, 343
limitations, 346–347
management, 342–343
performance review, 345–346
physical controls, 345
rotating employees' duties, 346
segregation of duties, 343–344
Internal review, 345–346
Internal users, 4
International Accounting Standards Board (IASB), 7
International financial reporting standards (IFRS), 7
Internet fraud, 347
Inventory, 282–338
classifying/reporting, 303–304
consigned goods, 286
costing. *See Inventory costing*
determining quantities, 284–286
errors, 298–300
estimating, 310–312
goods in transit, 285–286
LCM, 302
manufacturing company, 303–304
merchandising company, 303
ownership of goods, 285–286
ratio analysis, 304–305
valuation, 302
Inventory costing, 287

average cost, 292–293, 307–308
balance sheet effects, 297
cost flow assumptions, 289
FIFO, 290–292, 306–307
financial statement effects, 295–298
income statement effects, 296–297
LIFO, 293–294, 308–310
perpetual inventory system, 306–310
specific identification, 288–289
Inventory errors, 298–300
Inventory estimation
gross profit method, 310–311
retail inventory method, 311–312
Inventory losses, 234
Inventory systems. *See Periodic inventory system; Perpetual
inventory system*
Inventory turnover, 304
Investment by owner, 16
Investment of cash by owner, 64
Investments by the owner, 12
Irregularity, 71
ITC, B1

Jewison, Norman, 106
Journal, 58
Journalizing, 58–60
cash payments transactions, C12–C13
credit purchases of merchandise, C11
credit sales, C4–C5

Kays, Lori, 340
Kelly, Chris, 4

Last-in, first-out (LIFO), 293–294, 308–310
LCM, 302
Ledger, 60–61
Liabilities, 12, 54
LIFO, 293–294, 308–310
Liquidity, 182
Liquidity ratios, 182, 304
current ratio, 182
days sales in inventory, 305
inventory turnover, 304
working capital, 182
Long-term investments, 176, 177
Long-term liabilities, 179
Lower of cost and market (LCM), 302

Management report, 371
Matching principle, 105–106
Merchandising operations, 218–281
adjusting entries, 234, 237
balance sheet, 243
closing entries, 235–236, 237

financial statements, 239–243
gross profit margin, 244–245
income statement, 239–243
operating cycle, 221
periodic inventory system, 222–223. *See also Periodic
inventory system*
perpetual inventory system, 222, 248. *See also Perpetual
inventory system*
physical inventory count, 234
post-closing trial balance, 236
profit margin, 245
purchases of merchandise, 224–228
sales of merchandise, 229–231
Monetary unit assumption, 9
Multiple-step income statement, 239–242

Net book value, 113
Net income, 12, 55, 241
Net loss, 12
Net purchases, 249
Net realizable value, 302
Net sales, 239–240
Non-financial information, 24
Non-operating activities, 240, 241
Not sufficient funds (NSF), 362
NSF, 362

On-line banking, 352
Operating cycle, 221
Orton, David, 303
Other expenses, 240
Other revenues, 240
Outstanding cheques, 363, 365
Owner's capital, 54
Owner's drawings, 54–55
Owner's equity, 12–13, 179
Ownership of goods, 285–286

Partners' equity, 179
Partnership, 10
Payment for insurance, 65
Payment of accounts payable, 18–19
Payment of expenses, 18
Payment of monthly rent, 65
Payment of salaries, 67
Periodic inventory system, 222–223, 245
closing entries, 250–251
cost of goods sold, 249–250
perpetual inventory system, contrasted, 248
post-closing trial balance, 251–252
purchases of merchandise, 246–247
sales of merchandise, 247–248
special journals, C15
Permanent accounts, 164

Perpetual inventory system, 222-223, 248, 306–310
Phishing, 347
Physical inventory count, 222, 234, 284–285
Pinto, Ed, 218
Post-closing trial balance, 169–170
Posting, 61–62
    cash payments journal, C14
    cash receipts journal, C10
    purchases journal, C11
    sales journal, C5
Pre-authorized monthly payments, 352, 367–368
Prepaid expenses, 110–113, 120, 127–128
Prepaid insurance, 111
Prepayment adjustment, 110–114
Principles. See Accounting principles
Private corporation, 10
Profit margin, 245
Profitability ratios, 182, 244–245
        gross profit margin, 244-245
        profit margin, 245
Property, plant, and equipment, 177
Proprietorship, 9–10
Provincial sales tax (PST), B2, B8
Proving the ledgers
    cash receipts journal, C10
    sales journal, C6
PST, B2, B8
Public corporation, 10
Purchase allowances, 227
Purchase discount, 227, 246–247
Purchase invoice, 224
Purchase of advertising on credit, 17–18
Purchase of equipment for cash, 16
Purchase of office equipment, 64
Purchase of supplies on credit, 16–17, 66
Purchase order, 354
Purchase returns, 227
Purchase returns and allowances, 227, 246
Purchase transactions, 224–228
    discounts, 227–228
    freight costs, 226
    periodic inventory system, 246–247
    purchase returns and allowances, 227
    sales tax, 226
    subsidiary inventory records, 225
Purchases journal, C10–C12

Quantity discount, 227
QuickBooks, 50

Ratio analysis, 181–182
    inventory, 304–305
    liquidity ratios, 182, 304
    profitability ratios, 244–245

types, 182
RC, 362
Reasonable assurance, 346
Receipt of cash for future service, 65
Receipt of cash from collection of A/R, 67
Receipt of cash on account, 19
Reconciling the bank account, 363–367
Recording process, 56–59
    basic steps, 56–57
    chart of accounts, 63
    illustrations, 64–69. See also Recording process illustrated
    journal, 58
    journalizing, 58–60
    ledger, 60–61
    posting, 61–62
Recording process illustrated, 64–67. See also Transactional analysis
    hiring of employees, 66
    investment of cash by owner, 64
    payment for insurance, 65
    payment of monthly rent, 65
    payment of salaries, 67
    purchase of office equipment, 64
    purchase of supplies on credit, 66
    receipt of cash for future service, 65
    receipt of cash from collection of A/R, 67
    services performed on account, 66
Related activities, 344
Related purchasing activities, 344
Related sales activities, 344
Reliability of financial statements, 123
Reporting cash, 369–371
Responsibility, 343. See also Internal control
Restricted cash, 370
Retail inventory method, 311–312
Returned cheque (RC), 362
Returns and allowances
    purchase, 227, 246
    sales, 231, 247
Revenue recognition principle, 105
Revenues, 13
Reversing entry, 173, 186–187

Salary, 118–119
Sales discount, 232, 247–248
Sales journal, C4–C7
Sales/purchase invoice, 224
Sales returns and allowances, 231, 247
Sales tax, 72, B1–B12
    disbursements, B5–B7
    GST, B1–B2, B7–B8
    HST, B2, B7–B8
    operating expenses, B6
    property, plant, and equipment, B6–B7

PST, B2, B8
purchase returns and allowances, B5
purchase transactions, 226
purchases of merchandise for resale, B5
rates, B3
receipts, B3–B4
remittance of, B7–B8
sales of merchandise, B4
sales returns and allowances, B4
sales transactions, 230
service companies, B3–B4
Sales transactions, 229–231
    discounts, 232
    freight costs, 230
    periodic inventory system, 247–248
    sales returns and allowances, 231
    sales tax, 230
Selling expenses, 240
Services performed on account, 66
Services provided for cash, 17
Services provided for cash and credit, 18
Shareholders' equity, 179
Shop theft, 234
Shoplifting losses, 347
Simplifying assumptions, 71–72
Single-step income statement, 242, 243
Smart card, 352
Snyder, Dan, 57
Solvency ratios, 182
Special journals, 350, C3–C15
    cash payments journal, C12–C14
    cash receipts journal, C7–C10
    general journal, and, C14–C15
    periodic inventory system, C15
    purchase journal, C10–C12
    sales journal, C4–C7
Specific identification, 288–289
Standard form of account, 61
Statement of cash flows. *See Cash flow statement*
Statement of earnings. *See Income statement*
Statement of management's responsibilities for financial reporting, 371
Statement of operations. *See Income statement*
Statement of owner's equity, 22, 23
Straight-line amortization method, 112
Subsidiary inventory records, 225
Subsidiary ledger, 225
Subsidiary ledgers, C1–C3
Supplies, 110–111

T account, 52
Taking a physical count, 284–285
Taking a physical inventory, 234
Temporary accounts, 164

Time period assumption, 104–105
Timing issues
    accounting time period, 104–105
    accrual vs. cash basic of accounting, 106–107
    matching principle, 105–106
    revenue recognition principle, 105
Transaction, 15
Transaction analysis. *See also Recording process illustrated*
    investment by owner, 16
    payment of accounts payable, 18–19
    payment of expenses, 18
    purchase of advertising on credit, 17–18
    purchase of equipment for cash, 16
    purchase of supplies on credit, 16–17
    receipt of cash on account, 19
    services provided for cash, 17
    services provided for cash and credit, 18
    summary of transaction, 20
    withdrawal of cash by owner, 19
Transaction identification process, 15
Transposition error, 71
Trial balance
    adjusted, 123, 124
    defined, 70
    financial statements, and, 124, 125
    limitations, 70
    locating errors, 71
    post-closing, 169–170
2/10, n/30, 227

Unearned revenues, 113–114, 120, 128–129
Unitholders' equity, 179
Useful life, 111

Weighted average unit cost, 292
Withdrawal of cash by owner, 19
Work sheet, 172–173, 183–186
Working capital, 182

Zafirovski, Mike, 174